Managerial Paper P2

MANAGEMENT ACCOUNTING – DECISION MANAGEMENT

For exams in 2008

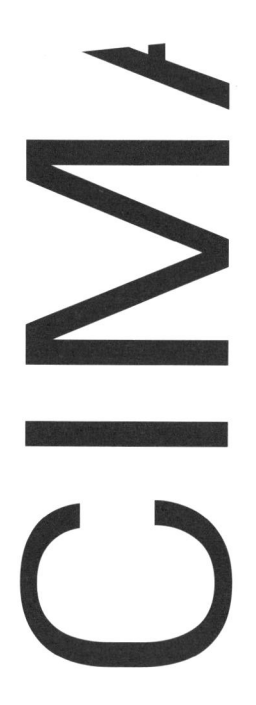

Practice & Revision Kit

CIMA

In this January 2008 new edition

- We discuss the **best strategies** for revising and taking your CIMA exams
- We show you how to be well prepared for the **2008 exams**
- We give you **lots of great guidance** on tackling questions
- We include **genuine student answers** with BPP commentary
- We show you how you can **build your own exams**
- We provide you with **three** mock exams including the **November 2007 exam**

BPP's **i-Pass** product also supports this paper.

BPP
LEARNING MEDIA

First edition 2005
Fourth edition January 2008

ISBN 9780 7517 5186 4 (previous ISBN 9780 7517 4192 6)

British Library Cataloguing-in-Publication Data
A catalogue record for this book is available from the British Library

Published by

BPP Learning Media Ltd
BPP House, Aldine Place
London W12 8AA

www.bpp.com/learningmedia

Printed in Great Britain by
Hobbs the Printers Limited
Brunel Road
Totton, Hampshire
SO40 3WX

Your learning materials, published by BPP Learning Media Ltd, are printed on paper sourced from sustainable, managed forests.

All our rights reserved. No part of this publication may be reproduced, stored in a retrieval system or transmitted, in any form or by any means, electronic, mechanical, photocopying, recording or otherwise, without the prior written permission of BPP Learning Media Ltd.

We are grateful to the Chartered Institute of Management Accountants for permission to reproduce past examination questions. The answers to past examination questions have been prepared by BPP Learning Media Ltd except when otherwise stated.

©
BPP Learning Media Ltd
2008

Contents

	Page
Finding questions	
Question index	iv
Topic index	ix
Using your BPP Practice and Revision Kit	xi
Passing CIMA exams	
Revising and taking CIMA exams	xv
How to revise	xvi
How NOT to revise	xvii
How to PASS your exams	xviii
How to FAIL your exams	xix
Using your BPP products	xx
Passing P2	
Revising P2	xxiii
Passing the P2 exam	xxiv
Formulae to learn	xxx
Recent exams	xxxi
What the examiner means	xxxv
Exam update and useful websites	xxxvi
Planning your question practice	
BPP's question plan	xxxix
Build your own exams	xlvi
Questions and answers	
Questions	1
Answers	125
Exam practice	
Mock exam 1	
• Questions	361
• Plan of attack	371
• Answers	373
Mock exam 2	
• Questions	389
• Plan of attack	401
• Answers	403
Mock exam 3	
• Questions	417
• Plan of attack	431
• Answers	433
Mathematical tables	449
Review form & free prize draw	

FINDING QUESTIONS

Question and Answer checklist/index

The headings in this checklist/index indicate the main topics of questions, but questions often cover several different topics.

Questions set under the old syllabuses *Management Accounting – Performance Management (IMPM)* and *Management Accounting – Decision Making (IDEC)* are included because their style and/or content are similar to those that appear in the Paper P2 exam.

		Marks	Time allocation Mins	Page number Question	Answer
Part B: The treatment of uncertainty in decision making					
1	Section A questions: Uncertainty in decision making	20	36	3	127
2	Ice cream manufacturer	10	18	5	129
3	Sporting simulator	10	18	5	130
4	Homelathe	25	45	6	131
5	Pharmacy	10	18	7	133
6	Purchase options	25	45	8	135
7	Holiday resort	25	45	8	136
8	Concert hall	25	45	10	137
9	MP Organisation (11/05)	25	45	11	139
10	Question with answer plan: Health Clinic (5/06)	25	45	12	142
11	Theatre (11/06)	25	45	13	145
Part C: Financial information for short-term decision making					
Relevant costs and short-term decisions					
12	Section A questions: Relevant costs and short-term decisions	20	36	14	148
13	MOV plc I (IDEC, 5/02, amended)	10	18	16	149
14	MOV plc II (IDEC, 5/02, amended)	10	18	16	149
15	Question with analysis: Z Ltd (5/05)	10	18	17	151
16	Mixit Ltd	25	45	18	152
17	Exe (Pilot paper)	25	45	19	154
18	Question with analysis: CS Group (5/05)	25	45	21	156
19	ML (11/05)	10	18	23	157
20	PK plc (11/05)	10	18	23	158
21	QXY plc (11/06)	10	18	24	160
22	Z (5/07)	10	18	26	162
23	H (5/07)	25	45	27	163
Multi-product breakeven analysis					
24	Section A questions: Multi-product breakeven analysis	20	36	28	165
25	POD and L	10	18	30	167
26	RDF Ltd (IMPM, 5/04)	25	45	30	168

iv

FINDING QUESTIONS

		Marks	Time allocation Mins	Page number Question	Answer
Limiting factor analysis					
27	Section A questions: Limiting factor analysis	20	36	32	170
28	MN Ltd (IMPM, 5/03, amended)	10	18	35	172
29	QP plc (11/05)	25	45	36	173
30	GHK plc (5/06)	25	45	37	176
Linear programming					
31	Section A questions: Linear programming	20	36	38	181
32	Question with answer plan: Fertiliser I	10	18	41	183
33	Fertiliser II	10	18	41	184
34	Staff uniforms (IMPM, 11/03)	25	45	42	185
35	MF plc (IMPM, 5/02, amended)	25	45	43	188
36	Question with helping hand: Venture capital company (IDEC, 5/03)	25	45	44	192
37	HT plc	25	45	45	194
Pricing					
38	Section A questions: Pricing	20	36	46	196
39	Elasticity	10	18	48	197
40	Question with answer plan: Off-the-shelf I (IDEC, 5/03, amended)	10	18	49	198
41	Off-the-shelf II (IDEC, 5/03, amended)	10	18	49	200
42	W (11/06)	10	18	49	202
43	C1, C2, C3 (IDEC, 11/02, amended)	25	45	50	203
44	Mobile telephones (IDEC, 5/01, amended)	25	45	52	207
45	Question with analysis: Q Organisation (5/05)	25	45	53	210
46	TQ (Pilot paper)	25	45	54	213
47	Question with answer plan: AVX plc (5/06)	25	45	55	216

Part D: Financial information for long-term decision making

		Marks	Time allocation Mins	Page number Question	Answer
Investment decision making and DCF techniques					
48	Section A questions: Basic principles of investment decision making	20	36	57	219
49	Intranet I (IDEC, 11/02, amended)	10	18	59	220
50	Intranet II (IDEC, 11/02, amended)	10	18	59	222
51	JLX plc (IDEC, 5/01, amended)	10	18	59	223
52	HPC Ltd	25	45	60	225

FINDING QUESTIONS

		Marks	Time allocation Mins	Page number Question	Answer
Further aspects of investment decision making					
53	Multiple choice questions: Further aspects of investment decision making	20	36	60	227
54	Capital rationing	10	18	62	228
55	Hypermarket (Pilot paper)	10	18	62	229
56	HP	25	45	62	230
57	MN plc (IDEC, 11/01)	25	45	63	232
58	CAF plc (IDEC, 5/02)	25	45	64	235
59	NP plc (IDEC, 5/02, amended)	25	45	65	238
60	Healthcare organisation	25	45	66	241
61	Training courses (IDEC, 5/03)	25	45	67	244
62	CD Ltd	25	45	68	247
63	3-Year project (5/06)	10	18	69	249
64	Canal boats (5/07)	10	18	69	251
Taking account of taxation and inflation					
65	Section A questions: Inflation and taxation	20	36	70	252
66	Compact discs	10	18	71	254
67	AB plc	10	18	72	255
68	Question with analysis: A Company (5/05)	10	18	73	256
69	RAD Enterprises (Pilot paper)	10	18	74	257
70	Question with analysis and student answer: Print Co (5/05)	25	45	75	259
71	CH Ltd (Pilot paper)	25	45	75	263
72	Question with analysis and answer plan: PK Glass plc (IDEC, 11/03, amended)	25	45	76	267
73	Taxi (11/05)	10	18	79	271
74	JK plc (11/06)	25	45	80	272
75	X (5/07)	25	45	81	275

Part E: Cost planning and analysis for competitive advantage

		Marks	Time allocation Mins	Page number Question	Answer
Forecasting and managing future costs					
76	Section A questions: Forecasting and managing future costs	20	36	82	278
77	Experience curve	10	18	83	279
78	ML plc (IMPM, 11/01, amended)	10	18	83	280
79	Wye hotel group (IMPM, 5/01, amended)	10	18	84	281
80	Question with answer plan: Cost management techniques (IDEC, 11/02, amended)	10	18	84	282
81	Telmat (IDEC, 11/01)	25	45	84	283
82	Question with answer plan: SY Ltd (IDEC, 11/03)	25	45	85	286
83	Financial advisors (5/06)	10	18	85	290
84	Learning curve (5/07)	10	18	86	292

FINDING QUESTIONS

		Marks	Time allocation Mins	Page number Question	Page number Answer
Activity based management					
85	Section A questions: Activity based management	20	36	86	293
86	BPR	10	18	88	294
87	LM Hospital (IDEC, 5/01)	25	45	88	295
88	ZP plc (11/05)	25	45	89	299
89	KL (11/06)	25	45	90	301
90	D (5/07)	25	45	91	307
Contemporary techniques					
91	Section A questions: Contemporary techniques	20	36	92	309
92	Question with helping hand: Standard costing, TQM and JIT (IDEC, 5/03, amended)	10	18	94	311
93	Cost management techniques again (IDEC, 11/02, amended)	10	18	94	313
94	Exe plc (IMPM, 5/01, amended)	10	18	95	314
95	Backflush costing	10	18	95	315
96	Question with answer plan: SWAL (Pilot paper)	10	18	95	316
97	Question with analysis: X Group (5/05)	10	18	96	318
98	MN Ltd	25	45	96	319
99	SG plc (IMPM, 11/02)	25	45	97	321
100	Quality costs (5/06)	10	18	98	322
Externally-orientated management accounting techniques					
101	Section A questions: Externally-orientated techniques	20	36	98	323
102	AVN (11/06)	10	18	99	324
103	Offshoring	10	18	99	326
104	Chains	10	18	100	327
105	Preferred suppliers	10	18	100	328
106	Partnering	10	18	100	329
107	Question with analysis: RS plc (IDEC, Pilot paper)	25	45	101	330
108	S&P Products plc (IDEC, 11/01, amended)	25	45	103	332
109	FF plc (IDEC, 11/03, amended)	25	45	104	334
Section A questions					
110	Section A questions: Mixed bank 1	20	36	106	338
111	Section A questions: Mixed bank 2	20	36	108	339
112	Section A questions: Mixed bank 3	20	36	109	341
113	Section A questions: Mixed bank 4 (5/05)	20	36	111	343
114	Section A questions: Mixed bank 5 (Pilot paper)	20	36	113	345
115	Section A questions: Mixed bank 6 (11/05)	20	36	115	347
116	Section A questions: Mixed bank 7 (5/06)	20	36	117	349
117	Section A questions: Mixed bank 8 (11/06)	20	36	119	351
118	Section A questions: Mixed bank 9 (5/07)	20	36	121	354

FINDING QUESTIONS

	Marks	Time allocation Mins	Page number Question	Answer
Mock exam 1			361	369
Questions 119 to 125				
Mock exam 2			389	399
Questions 126 to 132				
Mock exam 3				
Questions 133 to 139			417	429

Planning your question practice

Our guidance from page xxxix shows you how to organise your question practice, either by attempting questions from each syllabus area or by building your own exams – tackling questions as a series of practice exams.

Topic index

Listed below are the key Paper P2 syllabus topics and the numbers of the questions in this Kit covering those topics.

If you need to concentrate your practice and revision on certain topics or if you want to attempt all available questions that refer to a particular subject, you will find this index useful.

Note that Section A questions are not included in this index.

Syllabus topic	Question numbers
Accounting rate of return	49
Activity based cost hierarchy	88
Activity based costing	59, 87, 88, 89, 105, 106, Mock 1, 2 and 3
Activity based management	87, 88, 93, Mock 2
Business process re-engineering	86
Capital rationing	36, 54
Cost of quality	99, 100
Customer profitability analysis	59, 106
Decision trees	5, 10, 59, 60, Mock 1, Mock 3
Direct Product Profitability	107
Discounted payback	49, 58
Distribution channel profitability	105
Expected values and standard deviation	2, 4, 5, 6, 7, 8, 9, 10, 11, 64, 90, Mock 1 and 2
Further processing	15
Gain sharing arrangements, partnering and outsourcing	75, 105, 106
Inflation	66, 67, 73, 75
Internal rate of return	57, 63, 74, Mock 3
Investment decision making, process of	See PCA
Joint cost decisions	16, 22, Mock 2
Just-in-time	43, 92, 93, 94, 99
Kaizen costing	19
Learning curves	44, 45, 77, 84, Mock 3
Life cycle costing	42, 80, 81, 82
Limiting factor	Mock 2
Linear programming – graphical	34, 35, 52, Mock 1, Mock 3
Linear programming – simplex	29, 32, 33, 36, 37
Multi-product breakeven analysis	25, 26, 30
Net present value	49, 52, 56, 57, 58, 59, 61, 62, 63, 64, 66, 67, 68, 69, 70, 71, 72, 73, 74, 75, Mock 1, 2 and 3
Outsourcing	103
Pareto analysis	5
Post completion accounts	51
Pricing decisions and deriving the demand curve	39, 42, 43, 47, 87, Mock 3
Pricing strategies	19, 40, 44, 47, 82, Mock 1
Probabilities in decisions	2, 4, 5, 6, 8, 9, 10
Product mix analysis (with limitations on product/service demand and one other production constraint)	28, 29, 30
Projects with unequal lives	73
Relevant cash flows	13, 14, 23, Mock 2
Relevant costs for pricing	23, 89
Sensitivity analysis	3, 35, 37, 41, 44
Sensitivity analysis (investment appraisal)	57, 58, 60, 62, 63, Mock 1, Mock 3

FINDING QUESTIONS

Syllabus topic	Question numbers
Short-term decisions	14, 20, 21, Mock 3
Standard deviation	Mock 2
Strategic/intangible/non-financial judgements in decision making	3, 4, 44, 58, 62, 72
Supply chain management	104
Target costing	80, 81, 82, Mock 1
Taxation	72
Theory of constraints (and throughput accounting)	29, 87, 98
Total quality management	92, 94, 99
Two-way data table	11, 90
Value analysis	78, 79, 83
Value chain	94, 102, 104
Value of information	6, 8, 11, 60
What if analysis and computers	7

Using your BPP Practice and Revision Kit

Tackling revision and the exam

You can significantly improve your chances of passing by tackling revision and the exam in the right ways. Our advice is based on recent feedback from CIMA examiners.

- We look at the dos and don'ts of revising for, and taking, CIMA exams
- We focus on Paper P2; we discuss revising the syllabus, what to do (and what not to do) in the exam, how to approach different types of question and ways of obtaining easy marks

Selecting questions

We provide signposts to help you plan your revision.

- A full **question index**
- A **topic index** listing all the questions that cover key topics, so that you can locate the questions that provide practice on these topics, and see the different ways in which they might be examined
- A **BPP question plan** highlighting the most important questions and explaining why you should attempt them
- **Build your own exams**, showing you how you can practise questions in a series of exams

Making the most of question practice

At BPP we realise that you need more than just questions and model answers to get the most from your question practice.

- Our **Top tips** provide essential advice on tackling questions, presenting answers and the key points that answers need to include
- We show you how you can pick up **Easy marks** on questions, as we know that picking up all readily available marks often can make the difference between passing and failing
- We summarise **Examiner's comments** to show you how students who sat the exam coped with the questions
- We refer to the 2007 **BPP Study Text** for detailed coverage of the topics covered in each question
- A number of questions include **Analysis** and **Helping hands** attached to show you how to approach them if you are struggling
- We include **annotated student answers** to some questions to highlight how these questions can be tackled and ways answers can be improved.

Attempting mock exams

There are three mock exams that provide practice at coping with the pressures of the exam day. We strongly recommend that you attempt them under exam conditions. **Mock exams 1 and 2** reflect the question styles and syllabus coverage of the exam; **Mock exam 3** is the actual November 2007 exam. To help you get the most out of doing these exams, we not only provide help with each answer, but also guidance on how you should have approached the whole exam.

Passing CIMA exams

Revising and taking CIMA exams

To maximise your chances of passing your CIMA exams, you must make best use of your time, both before the exam during your revision, and when you are actually doing the exam.

- Making the most of your revision time can make a big, big difference to how well-prepared you are for the exam
- Time management is a core skill in the exam hall; all the work you've done can be wasted if you don't make the most of the three hours you have to attempt the exam

In this section we simply show you what to do and what not to do during your revision, and how to increase and decrease your prospects of passing your exams when you take them. Our advice is grounded in feedback we've had from CIMA examiners. You may be surprised to know that much examiner advice is the same whatever the exam, and the reasons why many students fail don't vary much between subjects and exam levels. So if you follow the advice we give you over the next few pages, you will **significantly** enhance your chances of passing **all** your CIMA exams.

PASSING CIMA EXAMS

How to revise

☑ Plan your revision

At the start of your revision period, you should draw up a **timetable** to plan how long you will spend on each subject and how you will revise each area. You need to consider the total time you have available and also the time that will be required to revise for other exams you're taking.

☑ Practise Practise Practise

The **more exam-standard questions** you do, the **more likely you are to pass** the exam. Practising full questions will mean that you'll get used to the time pressure of the exam. When the time is up, you should note where you've got to and then try to complete the question, giving yourself practice everything that the question tests.

☑ Revise enough

Make sure that your revision covers the breadth of the syllabus, as in most papers most topics could be examined in a compulsory question. However it is true that some topics are **key** – they often appear in compulsory questions or are a particular interest of the examiner – and you need to spend sufficient time revising these. Make sure you know the basics – the fundamental calculations, proformas and report layouts.

☑ Deal with your difficulties

Difficult areas are topics you find dull and pointless, or subjects that you found problematic when you were studying them. You mustn't become negative about these topics; instead you should build up your knowledge by reading the **Passcards** and using the **Quick quiz** questions in the Study Text to test yourself. When practising questions in the Kit, go back to the Text if you're struggling.

☑ Learn from your mistakes

Having completed a question you must try to look at your answer critically. Always read the **Top tips** guidance in the answers; it's there to help you. Look at **Easy marks** to see how you could have quickly gained credit on the questions that you've done. As you go through the Kit, it's worth noting any traps you've fallen into, and key points in the **Top tips** or **Examiner's comments** sections, and referring to these notes in the days before the exam. Aim to learn at least one new point from each question you attempt, a technical point perhaps or a point on style or approach.

☑ Read the examiners' guidance

We refer throughout this Kit to **Examiner's comments**; these are available on CIMA's website. As well as highlighting weaknesses, examiners' reports often provide clues to future questions, as many examiners will quickly test again areas where problems have arisen. CIMA's website also contains articles that are relevant to this paper, which you should read.

☑ Complete all three mock exams

You should attempt the **Mock exams** at the end of the Kit under **strict exam conditions** to gain experience of selecting questions, managing your time and producing answers.

How NOT to revise

☒ Revise selectively

Examiners are well aware that some students try to forecast the contents of exams, and only revise those areas that they think will be examined. Examiners try to prevent this by doing the unexpected, for example setting the same topic in successive sittings or setting topics in compulsory questions that have previously only been examined in optional questions.

☒ Spend all the revision period reading

You cannot pass the exam just by learning the contents of Passcards, Course Notes or Study Texts. You have to develop your **application skills** by practising questions.

☒ Audit the answers

This means reading the answers and guidance without having attempted the questions. Auditing the answers gives you **false reassurance** that you would have tackled the questions in the best way and made the points that our answers do. The feedback we give in our answers will mean more to you if you've attempted the questions and thought through the issues.

☒ Practise some types of question, but not others

Although you may find the numerical parts of certain papers challenging, you shouldn't just practise calculations. These papers will also contain written elements, and you therefore need to spend time practising written question parts as well.

☒ Get bogged down

Don't spend a lot of time worrying about all the minute detail of certain topic areas, and leave yourself insufficient time to cover the rest of the syllabus. Remember that a key skill in the exam is the ability to **concentrate on what's important** and this applies to your revision as well.

☒ Overdo studying

Studying for too long without interruption will mean your studying becomes less effective. A five minute break each hour will help. You should also make sure that you are leading a **healthy lifestyle** (proper meals, good sleep and some times when you're not studying).

How to PASS your exams

☑ Prepare for the day

Make sure you set at least one alarm (or get an alarm call), and allow plenty of time to get to the exam hall. You should have your route planned in advance and should listen on the radio for potential travel problems. You should check the night before to see that you have pens, pencils, erasers, watch, calculator with spare batteries, also exam documentation and evidence of identity.

☑ Select the right questions

You should select the optional questions you feel you can answer **best**, basing your selection on the topics covered, the requirements of the question, how easy it will be to apply the requirements and the availability of easy marks.

☑ Plan your three hours

You need to make sure that you will be answering the correct number of questions, and that you spend the right length of time on each question – this will be determined by the number of marks available. Each mark carries with it a **time allocation** of **1.8 minutes**. A 25 mark question therefore should be selected, completed and checked in 45 minutes. With some papers, it's better to do certain types of question first or last.

☑ Read the questions carefully

To score well, you must follow the requirements of the question, understanding what aspects of the subject area are being covered, and the tasks you will have to carry out. The requirements will also determine what information and examples you should provide. Reading the question scenarios carefully will help you decide what **issues** to discuss, what **techniques** to use, **information** and **examples** to include and how to **organise** your answer.

☑ Plan your answers

Five minutes of planning plus twenty-five minutes of writing is certain to earn you more marks than thirty minutes of writing. Consider when you're planning how your answer should be **structured**, what the **format** should be and **how long** each part should take.

Confirm before you start writing that your plan makes **sense**, covers **all relevant points** and does not include **irrelevant material.**

☑ Show evidence of judgement

Remember that examiners aren't just looking for a display of knowledge; they want to see how well you can **apply** the knowledge you have. Evidence of application and judgement will include writing answers that only contain **relevant** material, using the material in scenarios to **support** what you say, **criticising** the **limitations** and **assumptions** of the techniques you've used and making **reasonable recommendations** that follow from your discussion.

☑ Stay until the end of the exam

Use any spare time to **check and recheck** your script. This includes checking you have filled out the candidate details correctly, you have labelled question parts and workings clearly, you have used headers and underlining effectively and spelling, grammar and arithmetic are correct.

How to FAIL your exams

☒ Don't do enough questions

If you don't attempt sufficient questions on the paper, you are making it harder for yourself to pass the questions that you do attempt. If for example you don't do a 20 mark question, then you will have to score 50 marks out of 80 marks on the rest of the paper, and therefore have to obtain 63% of the marks on the questions you do attempt. Failing to attempt all of the paper is symptomatic of poor time management or poor question selection.

☒ Include irrelevant material

Markers are given detailed mark guides and will not give credit for irrelevant content. Therefore you should **NOT** braindump into your answer all you know about a broad subject area; the markers will only give credit for what is **relevant**, and you will also be showing that you lack the ability to **judge what's important.** Similarly forcing irrelevant theory into every answer won't gain you marks, nor will providing uncalled for features such as situation analyses, executive summaries and background information.

☒ Fail to use the details in the scenario

General answers or reproductions of old answers that don't refer to what is in the scenario in **this** question won't score enough marks to pass.

☒ Copy out the scenario details

Examiners see **selective** use of the right information as a key skill. If you copy out chunks of the scenario that aren't relevant to the question, or don't use the information to support your own judgements, you won't achieve good marks.

☒ Don't do what the question asks

Failing to provide all the examiner asks for will limit the marks you score. You will also decrease your chances by not providing an answer with enough **depth** – producing a single line bullet point list when the examiner asks for a discussion.

☒ Present your work poorly

Markers will only be able to give you credit if they can read your writing. There are also plenty of other things as well that will make it more difficult for markers to reward you. Examples include:

- Not using black or blue ink
- Not showing clearly which question you're attempting
- Scattering question parts from the same question throughout your answer booklet
- Not showing clearly workings or the results of your calculations

Paragraphs that are too long or which lack headers also won't help markers and hence won't help you.

Using your BPP products

This Kit gives you the question practice and guidance you need in the exam. Our other products can also help you pass:

> - **Learning to Learn Accountancy** gives further valuable advice on revision
> - **Passcards** provide you with clear topic summaries and exam tips
> - **Success CDs** help you revise on the move
> - **i-Pass CDs** offer tests of knowledge against the clock
> - **Learn Online** is an e-learning resource delivered via the Internet, offering comprehensive tutor support and featuring areas such as study, practice, email service, revision and useful resources

You can purchase these products by visiting www.bpp.com/mybpp.

Visit our website www.bpp.com/cima/learnonline to sample aspects of Learn Online free of charge.

Passing P2

Revising P2

The examiner has stated his intention to examine all of those areas in each exam approximately in their weightings.

The syllabus covers four distinct areas and their syllabus weightings ( ):

- The treatment of uncertainty in decision making (15%)
- Financial information for short-term decision making (30%)
- Financial information for long-term decision making (25%)
- Cost planning and analysis for competitive advantage (30%)

Uncertainty and decision making

The paper looks at techniques for measuring risk and evaluating uncertainty. These include expected values, maximax, maximin and minimax regret, sensitivity analysis and decision trees. You need to be familiar with the techniques and their application across a variety of decision-making tools such as relevant cash flows, DCF and CVP analysis.

Financial information for short-term decision making

This part of the syllabus focuses on the short term so decisions being made cover the near future. You will need to understand and apply relevant cash flows, marginal and full costing, pricing strategies, joint costs, variable and fixed costs and multiple product situations with resource constraints.

Financial information for long-term decision making

You are expected to understand and apply techniques for evaluating long-term proposals. Thus, identifying relevant cash flows, using investment appraisal techniques including DCF and ARR and factoring in inflation and taxation, ranking of projects including those with unequal lives and applying sensitivity analysis.

Cost planning and analysis for competitive advantage

In this section of the syllabus are a range of techniques for measuring cost and looking at the external influences on the organisation. Therefore you will expect to cover JIT, TQM, TOC, ABM, Pareto, target costs, learning curves, continuous improvement, kaizen costing, value and functional costs, lifecycle costing, value chain and gain sharing arrangements.

You should use the Passcards and any brief notes you have to revise these topics, but you mustn't spend all your revision time passively reading. Question practice is vital; doing as many questions as you can in full will help develop your ability to analyse scenarios and produce relevant discussion and recommendations. The revision plan on page xl tells you what questions cover so that you can choose questions covering a variety of organisations and risk situations.

This exam is looking at **application** in addition to knowledge, which is assumed at this level. Eighty percent of the marks available in the exam consist of longer questions looking for application of knowledge to various scenarios. The examiner wants to see how you would apply your knowledge to the scenario he has outlined in the exam questions. The examiner stated recently that common problems with the paper included the following.

- Lack of detail in answering questions. Remember the two questions in Section C are worth 25 marks each so expect to write at least two pages in the exam for each
- Not answering all of the requirements of the question
- Not answering written questions in the context of the scenario provided

Passing the P2 exam

Displaying the right qualities

The examiners will expect you to display the following qualities.

Qualities required	
Business awareness	You are expected to read the business press. This awareness will enable you to apply your knowledge in context when answering questions.
Time management skills	You need to attempt all parts of all questions. So you must work out before you start the exam how much time you will spend on each question. Stick to this!
Flexible thinking	Questions often won't state what technique(s) you should be using. You need to select the appropriate technique yourself.
Evaluation of past and future performance using information provided	You will need to perform calculations that directly evaluate the scenario presented and based on these give advice.
Show strategic awareness	Although this is a Managerial level paper, the examiner is starting to test your wider awareness of the environment and strategic issues that a company faces. For instance, questions on pricing policy or externally-oriented management accounting will require a strategic view.

Avoiding weaknesses

There have been eight sittings of P2 and the examiners have identified weaknesses that occur in many students' answers at every sitting. You will enhance your chances significantly if you ensure you avoid these mistakes:

- Lacking basic management accounting knowledge, for instance, correctly identifying fixed and variable costs
- Syllabus spotting leading to gaps in knowledge
- Not answering requirements stated in questions
- Not using the scenario in written question and not answering the question in the context of that scenario
- For tax and capital allowance calculations, the regime will be clearly explained in the question
- Failing to learn topics in enough detail to answer longer questions
- Brain dumping all that is known about a topic (no credit is given for this)
- Failing to answer sufficient questions because of poor time management
- Not showing clear workings to enable method marks to be awarded

Using the reading time and choosing which questions to answer first

The 20 minutes reading time should be spent reading Section C. You have to choose two out of three questions so use 10 minutes to read the three questions thoroughly. Make sure you concentrate on all requirements. With 10 minutes taken to choose which questions you'll attempt, you can spend the remaining 10 minutes picking out the relevant data from the questions, setting up working layouts and brainstorming ideas for discussion requirements.

Leave the objective questions until the last 40 minutes of answering time. As most of these are three or four marks, little is gained from duplicating workings which cannot go on the answer paper until the actual exam begins.

Tackling questions

Scenario questions

You'll improve your chances by following a step-by-step approach to scenario questions in Sections B and C along the following lines. These are likely to be short scenarios in this paper at this level.

Step 1 **Read the requirement**

You need to identify the knowledge areas being tested and what information will therefore be significant. In particular you need to identify which aspects of risk management you will have to cover in your answer.

Step 2 **Identify the action verbs**

These convey the level of skill you need to exhibit. See the list on page 35.

Step 3 **Identify what each part of the question requires**

When planning, you will need to make sure that you aren't reproducing the same material in more than one part of the question.

Step 4 **Check the mark allocation to each part**

This shows you the depth anticipated and helps allocate time.

Step 5 **Read the scenario through quickly, highlighting key data**

- Size of the organisation
- Factors influencing the decisions (business strategies, financial resources, constraints)
- Changes in circumstances that are about to take place
- Risks/weaknesses
- Procedures/systems/controls that are currently in place

Step 6 **Read the scenario carefully**

Put points under headings related to requirements (e.g. by marginal notes). Consider the techniques you'll need to use.

Step 7 **Consider the consequences of the points you've identified**

Remember that in the answer you will often have to provide recommendations based on the information you've been given. Consider the limitations of any analysis you undertake or other factors that may impact upon your recommendations.

Step 8 **Write a plan**

You may be able to do this on the question paper as often there will be at least one blank page in the question booklet. However any plan you make should be reproduced in the answer booklet when writing time begins.

Step 9 **Write the answer**

Make every effort to present your answer clearly.

Numerical questions

Expect to see a lot of numbers. These can occur anywhere in the exam, particularly in Section A where they are straightforward techniques. Expect them in the longer questions too. Questions may include interpretation of data, frequently in Section C as part of a longer question. Whilst it is not wise to spot questions, if you refer to 'Recent Exams' you will notice that certain techniques turn up frequently in Section A. Ensure that you know these as a minimum.

Discussion questions

Remember that **depth of discussion** is also important. Discussions will often consist of paragraphs containing 2-3 sentences. Each paragraph should:

- **Make a point**
- **Explain the point** (you must demonstrate **why** the point is important)
- **Illustrate the point** (with material or analysis from the scenario, perhaps an example from real-life)

Gaining the easy marks

Examples of suggestions for scoring easy marks are contained in the Answer Section of this kit. They include in Question 36 answering the written part in (d) which is pure knowledge, or shorthand, but correct methods as in Question 28.

It is always a good idea to layout clear formats especially where calculating NPVs and to clearly set out steps taken in a linear programming question. These examples both have clear and consistent approaches so ensure you are familiar with these and use them in the exam.

Tackling multiple choice questions

The MCQs in your exam will contain four possible answers. You have to **choose the option that best answers the question**. The three incorrect options are called distracters. There is a skill in answering MCQs quickly and correctly. By practising MCQs you can develop this skill, giving yourself a better chance of passing the exam.

You may wish to follow the approach outlined below, or you may prefer to adapt it.

Step 1 Skim read all the MCQs and identify which appear to be the easier questions and which questions you will not need a calculator to answer.

Step 2 Remember that the examiner will not expect you to spend an equal amount of time on each MCQ; some can be answered instantly but others will take time to work out.

Step 3 Attempt each question. Starting with the easier questions with Step 1. Read the question thoroughly. You may prefer to work out the answer before looking at the options, or you may prefer to look at the options at the beginning. Adopt the method that works best for you.

You may find that you recognise a question when you sit the exam. Be aware that the detail and/or requirement may be different. If the question seems familiar, read the requirement and options carefully – do not assume that it is identical.

Step 4 Read the options and see if one matches your own answer. Be careful with numerical questions, as the distracters are designed to match answers that incorporate **common errors**. Check that your calculation is correct. Have you followed the requirement exactly? Have you included every stage of the calculation?

Step 5 You may find that none of the options matches your answer.

- Re-read the question to ensure that you understand it and are answering the requirement
- Eliminate any obviously wrong answers
- Consider which of the remaining answers is the most likely to be correct and select that option

Step 6 If you are still unsure, make a note and continue to the next question. Likewise if you are nowhere near working out which option is correct, leave the question and come back to it later.

Step 7 Revisit unanswered questions. When you come back to a question after a break, you often find you can answer it correctly straightaway. If you are still unsure, have a guess. You are not penalised for incorrect answers, so **never leave a question unanswered!**

Step 8 **Rule off answers** to each MCQ in the answer booklet.

Tackling objective test questions

What is an objective test question?

An objective test (**OT**) question is made up of some form of **stimulus**, usually a question, and a **requirement** to do something.

- **MCQs.** Read through the information on page xxvii about MCQs and how to tackle them.
- **True or false.** You will be asked if a statement is true or false.
- **Data entry.** This type of OT requires you to provide figures such as the answer to a calculation, words to fill in a blank, single word answers to questions, or to identify numbers and words to complete a format.
- **Word-limited answers.** You may be asked to state, define or explain things in no more than a certain number of words or within a single line in the answer booklet.
- **Hot spots.** This question format may ask you to identify specific points on a graph or diagram.
- **Interpretation.** You may be asked to interpret or analyse graphical data.
- **Multiple response.** These questions provide you with a number of options and you have to identify those that fulfil certain criteria.
- **Listing.** You may be asked to list items in rank order.
- **Matching.** This OT question format could ask you to classify particular costs into one of a range of cost classifications provided, to match descriptions of variances with one of a number of variances listed, and so on.

OT questions in your exam

Section A of your exam will contain different types of OT questions. It is not certain how many questions in your exam will be MCQs and how many will be other types of OT, nor what types of OT you will encounter in your exam. Practising all the different types of OTs that this Kit provides will prepare you well for whatever questions come up in your exam.

Dealing with OT questions

Again you may wish to follow the approach we suggest, or you may be prepared to adapt it.

Step 1 Work out **how long** you should allocate to each OT, taking into account the marks allocated to it. Remember that you will not be expected to spend an equal amount of time on each one; some can be answered instantly but others will take time to work out.

Step 2 **Attempt each question**. Read the question thoroughly, and note in particular what the question says about the **format** of your answer and whether there are any **restrictions** placed on it (for example the number of words you can use).

You may find that you recognise a question when you sit the exam. Be aware that the detail and/or requirement may be different. If the question seems familiar read the requirement and options carefully – do not assume that it is identical.

Step 3 Read any options you are given and select which ones are appropriate. Check that your calculations are correct. Have you followed the requirement exactly? Have you included every stage of the calculation?

Step 4 You may find that you are unsure of the answer.

- Re-read the question to ensure that you understand it and are answering the requirement
- Eliminate any obviously wrong options if you are given a number of options from which to choose

Step 5 If you are still unsure, **continue to the next question**.

Step 6 Revisit questions you are uncertain about. When you come back to a question after a break you often find you are able to answer it correctly straightaway. If you are still unsure have a guess. You are not penalised for incorrect answers, so **never leave a question unanswered!**

Step 7 Make sure you show your **workings** clearly on calculation OTs, as you may gain some credit for workings even if your final answer is incorrect.

Step 8 Rule off answers to each OT in the answer booklet.

Formulae to learn

You will be provided with certain formulae and mathematical tables in the exam paper but the following formulae are not provided and you may need to use them in the exam.

LEARN THEM.

- The **expected value** of an opportunity is equal to the sum of the probabilities of an outcome occurring multiplied by the return expected if it does occur

    ie $EV = \sum px$

    where p is the probability of an outcome occurring and x is the value (profit or cost) of that outcome

- The **accounting rate of return** (ARR) = $\left(\dfrac{\text{average annual profit from an investment}}{\text{average or initial investment}}\right) \times 100\%$

- The **future value** of an investment (X) plus accumulated interest after n time periods is

    $V = X(1 + r)^n$

    where r is the compound rate of return per time period, expressed as a proportion

- The **present value** of a future sum of money (V) at the end of n time periods is

    $X = V/(1 + r)^n$

    where r is the compound rate of return per time period, expressed as a proportion

- The cumulative **present value** of £1, a **perpetuity,** is £1/r, where r is the compound rate of return per time period, expressed as a proportion

- The internal rate of return (IRR) =

    $A + \left[\dfrac{P}{P+N} \times (B - A)\right]\%$

    where A is the (lower) rate of return with a positive NPV
    B is the (higher) rate of return with a negative NPV
    P is the amount of the positive NPV
    N is the absolute amount of the negative NPV

- (1 + money rate) = (1 + real rate) × (1 + inflation rate) where all rates are expressed as proportions

- Throughput accounting ratio = $\dfrac{\text{throughput contribution or value added per time period}}{\text{conversion cost per time period}}$

    = $\dfrac{(\text{sales} - \text{material costs}) \text{ per time period}}{(\text{labour} + \text{overhead}) \text{ per time period}}$

- Equivalent annual cost

    Take PV of cost over one replacement cycle

    Divide by cumulative PV factor

    Gives annualised equivalent cost

Recent exams

Format of the paper

		Number of marks
Section A:	Up to 10 multiple choice and other objective test questions, 2-4 marks each	20
Section B:	3 compulsory questions, 10 marks each	30
Section C:	2 out of 3 questions, 25 marks each	50
		100

Time allowed: 3 hours

Question weighting will reflect syllabus weighting.

Section A will always contain some multiple choice questions but will not consist solely of multiple choice questions. Section A may contain types of objective test questions that are different from those included in the pilot paper.

Further guidance on objective test questions and multiple choice questions is included on pages xxvii to xxix.

Section B may include a short scenario that could relate to several of the questions.

Section C questions are likely to be scenario-based and include sub questions.

November 2007

Section A

1.1 Pricing
1.2 Bottlenecks
1.3 Quality costs
1.4 Real rate of return
1.5 Sensitivity analysis
1.6 ABC
1.7 Payback period
1.8 Expected value and standard deviation

Section B

2   Learning curves
3   Optimal selling price
4   Decision trees

Section C

5   Investment appraisal
6   Linear programming
7   Decision-making; ABC

These questions make up Mock Exam 3.

May 2007

Section A

		Question in this Kit
1		118
1.1	Profitability index	
1.2	Sensitivity analysis (NPV)	
1.3	Breakeven income	
1.4	Learning rate	
1.5	Accounting rate of return	
1.6	Internal rate of return	
1.7	Optimum product mix	
1.8	Profit maximising selling price	

Section B

2	Learning curves	84
3	Capital replacement decisions	64
4	Joint cost decisions	22

Section C

5	Investment appraisal	75
6	Relevant costs	23
7	Expected values, ABC	90

Examiner's comments. The overall average mark on this paper was above that of previous sittings, with a higher proportion of students gaining good marks. However, many students still struggled with discursive elements of questions, and questions covering fundamental management accounting aspects were poorly answered. General comments included:

- Poorly laid out answers to numerical questions, which made marking difficult.
- Improvement in performance in Question One (objective test questions), although some students continue to fail to follow instructions by not showing workings when required.
- Little evidence of time constraint problems, which suggests that students are making full use of the 20 minutes' reading time.

November 2006

Section A

		Question in this Kit
1		117
1.1	Further processing decision	
1.2	Relevant costing	
1.3	Investment appraisal, profitability index	
1.4	Payback period	
1.5	Perpetuities and NPV	
1.6	Limiting factor	
1.7	Optimum selling price	
1.8	Contribution/Sales ratio	

Section B

2	Value chain analysis	101
3	Lifecycle costing	42
4	Decision-making with price and cost analysis	21

Section C

5	Absorption costing, ABC costing and price setting	89
6	EV, Two-way data tables, VOPI	11
7	NPV, IRR, real and money rates of return	74

Examiner's comments. Candidates performed slightly better on this paper compared with previous sittings. However, some fundamental technical aspects of the paper were poorly answered. General comments included:

- Poorly constructed answers to discursive questions.
- Poor layout of answers to numerical questions, which made marking difficult.
- Failure to respond to question instructions in question one.
- Questions on non-mainstream topics (such as value analysis) were poorly answered.

May 2006

Question in this Kit

Section A

1 116

- 1.1 Relevant costing
- 1.2 Relevant costing
- 1.3 C/S ratio
- 1.4 Make or buy decision
- 1.5 Payback method
- 1.6 Discounted payback
- 1.7 IRR
- 1.8 Learning curves

Section B

2	Sensitivity analysis	63
3	Value analysis	83
4	Quality costs	100

Section C

5	Rates of learning, profit maximising selling price, standard and target costs	47
6	Decision trees, investment decisions, non-financial considerations	10
7	Relevant contributions, limiting factor, C/S ratios, multi-product PV chart	30

Examiner's comments. The May 2006 results showed a slight improvement on November 2005. General comments included:

- Section A performance was better than previous sittings.
- However Sections B and C still revealed candidates with poor application skills especially in scenario questions.
- Candidates must study the whole of the published syllabus.
- Candidates must ensure that they are familiar with lower level management accounting techniques.

Pilot paper

Question in this Kit

Section A

1   114
1.1   Limiting factor analysis (2 marks)
1.2   Linear programming (2 marks)
1.3   Relevant costs (2 marks)
1.4   EV calculation (2 marks)
1.5   Value of perfect information (3 marks)
1.6   Throughput accounting (3 marks)
1.7   Learning curves (3 marks)
1.8   Transfer pricing (3 marks)

Section B

2   JIT   96
3   Investment appraisal and taxation   69
4   Investment appraisal and when-to-replace decision   55

Section C

5   Investment appraisal including taxation and sensitivity analysis   71
6   Relevant costing; use of two-way data tables   17
7   Pricing   46

What the examiner means

The table below has been prepared by CIMA to help you interpret exam questions.

Learning objective	Verbs used	Definition	Examples in the Kit
1 Knowledge What you are expected to know	• List • State • Define	• Make a list of • Express, fully or clearly, the details of/facts of • Give the exact meaning of	 15 54
2 Comprehension What you are expected to understand	• Describe • Distinguish • Explain • Identify • Illustrate	• Communicate the key features of • Highlight the differences between • Make clear or intelligible/state the meaning of • Recognise, establish or select after consideration • Use an example to describe or explain something	16 18 16 77
3 Application How you are expected to apply your knowledge	• Apply • Calculate/compute • Demonstrate • Prepare • Reconcile • Solve • Tabulate	• To put to practical use • To ascertain or reckon mathematically • To prove the certainty or to exhibit by practical means • To make or get ready for use • To make or prove consistent/ compatible • Find an answer to • Arrange in a table	 24 17 18 39
4 Analysis How you are expected to analyse the detail of what you have learned	• Analyse • Categorise • Compare and contrast • Construct • Discuss • Interpret • Produce	• Examine in detail the structure of • Place into a defined class or division • Show the similarities and/or differences between • To build up or complete • To examine in detail by argument • To translate into intelligible or familiar terms • To create or bring into existence	4 46 18 18
5 Evaluation How you are expected to use your learning to evaluate, make decisions or recommendations	• Advise • Evaluate • Recommend	• To counsel, inform or notify • To appraise or assess the value of • To advise on a course of action	11 15

Exam update

The examiner has now specifically included minimax regret, maximin and maximax techniques in CIMA's Official Learning System. He has also included a paragraph on the lowest common multiple method in the System. These have both been examined in recent sittings but not previously specified in the syllabus.

You may want to refer to various articles written on subjects covered in P2. Amongst these is an article by Tim Thompson in June 2006 which covers Gain-sharing deals. This can be found on CIMA's website by going into Studying\Studysupport\Professionalstudyresources\papername\Articlearchive

Useful websites

The websites below provide additional sources of information of relevance to your studies for *Management Accounting – Decision Management*.

- BPP   www.bpp.com

    For details of other BPP material for your CIMA studies

- CIMA   www.cimaglobal.com

    The official CIMA website

- *Financial Times*   www.ft.com
- *The Economist*   www.economist.com
- *Wall Street Journal*   www.wsj.com

Planning your question practice

Planning your question practice

We have already stressed that question practice should be right at the centre of your revision. Whilst you will spend some time looking at your notes and the Paper P2 Passcards, you should spend the majority of your revision time practising questions.

We recommend two ways in which you can practise questions.

- Use **BPP's question plan** to work systematically through the syllabus and attempt key and other questions on a section-by-section basis
- **Build your own exams** – attempt the questions as a series of practice exams

These ways are suggestions and simply following them is no guarantee of success. You or your college may prefer an alternative but equally valid approach.

BPP's question plan

The plan below requires you to devote a **minimum of 45 hours** to revision of Paper P2. Any time you can spend over and above this should only increase your chances of success.

Step 1   **Review your notes** and the chapter summaries in the Paper P2 **Passcards** for each section of the syllabus.

Step 2   **Answer the key questions** for that section. These questions have boxes round the question number in the table below and you should answer them in full. Even if you are short of time you must attempt these questions if you want to pass the exam. You should complete your answers without referring to our solutions.

Step 3   **Attempt the other questions** in that section. For some questions we have suggested that you prepare **answer plans or do the calculations** rather than full solutions. Planning an answer means that you should spend about 40% of the time allowance for the questions brainstorming the question and drawing up a list of points to be included in the answer.

Step 4   **Attempt Mock exams 1, 2 and 3** under strict exam conditions.

PLANNING YOUR QUESTION PRACTICE

Syllabus section	2008 Passcards chapters	Questions in this Kit	Comments	Done ☑
Uncertainty in decision making	14	1	Answer all of these MCQs. Attempting this test under exam conditions will be an excellent way of assessing how much you know about this topic. Rework/review any questions you get wrong. You should aim for at least five correct answers to the nine questions.	☐
		5	Answer in full. This question from November 2006 covers expected values, two way tables and value of perfect information.	☐
		11	Answer this question in full. This question covers the techniques of decision tree analysis and Pareto analysis. If you are short of time, sketch the decision tree, provide brief, bullet-point responses to part (a)(ii) and note the principal points required for the report in (b).	☐
Relevant costs and short-term decisions	2 – 3	12	Answer all of these OT questions. Relevant costing rules can be tested very easily in Section A of the exam so try this test under timed conditions.	☐
		13,14	Do an answer plan. These questions are indicative of the relevant costing skills and techniques you are likely to need. Make sure you attempt both questions, as between them they require calculation and discussion.	☐
		15	Answer this question in full. This was in the May 2005 exam. This is not a difficult question and you should get good marks in part (a) by answering fully. Part (b) needs more calculations and some interpretation.	☐
		17, 18	Answer these questions in full. Question 17 was in the May 2005 exam. They cover some key areas in the syllabus.	☐
		19	This question from the November 2005 exam is a nice short run through of absorption and marginal costing approaches to pricing. Do an answer plan.	☐
		20	Another November 2005 exam question. It covers modern costing approaches for inventory and decision making Try this to practise your report writing. Answer in full.	☐
		21	Answer in full. Asks you to interpret a cost and revenue diagram, which gives you good practice of explaining what issues should be considered when making decisions.	☐
		22	Answer in full. A joint cost question from May 2007, asking for recommendations regarding further processing and viability of the common process.	☐

Syllabus section	2008 Passcards chapters	Questions in this Kit	Comments	Done ☑
		23	Answer in full. A long relevant cost question from May 2007 including 10 marks for the use of relevant costs for pricing.	☐
Multi-product breakeven analysis	4	24	Answer all of these OT questions. Under the previous syllabus, this topic appeared in Section A in every sitting.	☐
		26	Answer this question in full. This was the only 'long' question that was set under the previous syllabus on this topic. At the May 2006 sitting, a longer question included this topic. See question 30 below. Try both questions as they are typical of the sort of question you could encounter on multi-product breakeven analysis.	☐
Limiting factor analysis	5	27	Answer all of these OT questions. OT questions on this topic frequently ask you to rank a number of products in order of production, or to choose those that offer the most and least profitable use of a scarce resource.	☐
		29	Answer this question from the November 2005 exam in full. It links limiting factors to throughput and simplex. Answer in full.	☐
		30	From the May 2006 exam this longer question asked for a range of analyses including limiting factor and multi-product breakeven analysis. Answer in full.	☐
Linear programming	6, 7	31	Answer all of these OT questions. The simplex approach in particular is easy to test with OT questions.	☐
		35	Quite a lot to test you here including graphical analysis and calculating a shadow price. Answer in full.	☐
		36	Answer this question in full. This question gives you the opportunity to practise and revise a typical Paper P2 question in that it covers two seemingly unrelated topics – the simplex approach and capital rationing.	☐
		37	A good question to test simplex programming. If you get stuck, follow our suggested answer step by step. Answer in full.	☐

PLANNING YOUR QUESTION PRACTICE

Syllabus section	2008 Passcards chapters	Questions in this Kit	Comments	Done ☑
Pricing	8 – 9	38	Answer all of these OT questions.	☐
		41	Answer these questions in full.	☐
			Questions on pricing will either ask you to discuss pricing strategies or require you to perform calculations. Working through these two will give you an opportunity to practise both types of requirement.	
		42	Answer in full. A good test of your knowledge of the product life cycle from the November 2006 exam.	☐
		43	Answer the question. It tests a variety of areas in the syllabus. Draft a report plan only.	☐
		44, 45	Answer the questions in full/prepare a plan. Q44 was in the May exam.	☐
			They are ideal for providing you with the chance to practice/revise a wide range of typical Paper P2 pricing techniques and issues.	
		46	A question from the pilot paper. Tests profit maximising price and price strategies. Answer in full.	☐
		47	A good all round test of your syllabus knowledge from the May 2006 exam. Do an answer plan.	☐
Basic principles of investment decision making	10, 11	48	Answer all of these OT questions.	☐
		49	Answer this question in full.	☐
			You must be able to discuss the advantages and disadvantages of various methods of investment appraisal, and this question gives you the opportunity to practise doing just that.	
		50	Answer this question in full.	
			Post-completion appraisal is always a likely exam topic so work through this question carefully.	
		51	A good question covering post-completion appraisal. Answer in full.	☐
Further aspects of investment decision making	13	53	Answer all of these OT questions.	☐
			Investment appraisal is bound to appear very regularly in this section of the paper as it is easy for the examiner to set relatively short calculation questions on the topic.	
		55	A short question from the pilot paper. It takes you through calculating NPVs and annual equivalent costs. Answer in full.	☐
		57	This question asks you to prepare a report using calculations you have made from data provided. Answer in full.	☐

PLANNING YOUR QUESTION PRACTICE

Syllabus section	2008 Passcards chapters	Questions in this Kit	Comments	Done ☑
		59	Answer this question in full.	
			You can use this question to revise decision trees as well as investment decision-making. Of course, any of the techniques covered in Part D of the text could be applied to investment appraisal.	
		61	A lot of calculations are needed here. Look at our answer for a suggested layout and workings. Answer in full.	
		63	A nice question from the May 2006 exam testing your knowledge of sensitivity analysis. Answer in full.	
		64	Answer in full. This question from May 2007 covers optimum replacement cycles and standard deviations of Net Present Value	
Inflation and taxation	12	65	Answer all of these OT questions.	
		67	Answer this question in full.	
			There are two approaches you can adopt to this question involving inflation. The suggested solution illustrates both. We recommend that you use real interest rates to discount the cash flows, however, as you will find this much quicker in the exam.	
		68, 70	These were both from the May 2005 exam.	
			They will give you can idea of the different aspects and level to which this subject can be examined in a 10 and 25 mark question	
		69	Answer in full. A short question from the pilot paper testing a lease or buy decision.	
		71	A tricky question involving inflation, sensitivity analysis and tax. Look at the two methods in part(a).	
		72	Answer this question in full.	☑
			This is the question we recommend you attempt to practise the effect of taxation on investment appraisal. The key in such questions is to make sure that your workings for items such as capital allowances are clearly shown.	
		73	Answer in full. A tricky question from the November 2005 exam. Remember you cannot use annual equivalents if there is inflation.	
		74	Answer in full. A good question from November 2006 on NPV and IRR, which will give you good practice of setting out NPV calculations clearly.	
		75	Answer in full. A long investment appraisal question from May 2007, covering net present value with inflation and tax. There are also 7 marks for a written section on gain sharing arrangements.	

PLANNING YOUR QUESTION PRACTICE

Syllabus section	2008 Passcards chapters	Questions in this Kit	Comments	Done ✓
Forecasting and managing future costs	15	76	Answer all of these OTs.	☐
		80	Answer in full. This question asks you to contrast target costing, lifecycle costing and traditional costing.	☐
		81	Use this question to practise written answers and knowledge of the systems asked for.	☐
		82	Answer this question in full. Questions like this one, which ask for a discussion about how techniques can be applied to a particular scenario, are likely to be a common way of examining topics covered in Part E of the BPP Study Text.	☐
		83	Answer in full. A short question from the May 2006 exam testing value analysis and functional analysis.	☐
		84	Answer in full. Short question from May 2007 on learning curves and their implications for management.	☐
Activity based management	16	85	Answer all of these OT questions. Work through this test under exam conditions. Practice of OT items is an excellent way of testing the depth of your knowledge of a topic.	☐
		87	Answer this question in full. This is probably the best question in the Kit to use for practising and revising ABC as it also covers pricing and throughput accounting.	☐
		88	Answer in full. A longer question from the November 2005 exam testing ABC in detail.	☐
		89	Answer in full. This question from November 2006 provides a good coverage of traditional methods of pricing and the activity based costing approach.	☐
		90	Answer in full. A good question for testing your knowledge on expected values and two way data tables. Ten marks are also available for activity based costing.	☐
Contemporary techniques	17	91	Answer all of these OT questions.	☐
		92	Answer this question in full. Attempt this question as it covers two of the key topics in this section, TQM and JIT.	☐
		96	Answer in full. This question from the pilot paper asks for a report covering JIT.	☐
		97	This is an exam question from May 2005. Although it is only 10 marks you are required to write a report of around one side of A4.	☐
		98	Answer this question in full. Throughput accounting is one of the few topics in this section that could be tested using numbers! This question allows you to practise possible calculations that could be required.	☐

… PLANNING YOUR QUESTION PRACTICE

Syllabus section	2008 Passcards chapters	Questions in this Kit	Comments	Done ☑
		100	Answer in full. A short question from the May 2006 paper asking for a report discussing quality costs.	☐
Externally-orientated techniques	18	101	Answer all of these OT questions.	☐
		102	Answer in full. A short question from November 2006 with scenario on the extended value chain.	☐
		108	Answer this question in full.	☐
			You need to be able to apply activity-based techniques to costing not only products but also customers and distribution channels. Here you need to apply it to various types of sales outlet.	
		103	Do an answer plan. A short question on a specific topic.	☐
		104	Do an answer plan. A short question on a specific topic.	☐
		107	Answer in full. A longer question on a specific topic.	☐
		109	Answer this question in full.	☐
			Another question requiring the application of activity based techniques, this time to analyse customer profitability.	
Section A questions		110-118	Answer all of these OT questions.	☐
			These mixed banks of questions may highlight areas where you are still weak. Do some more work on these areas if necessary.	

Build your own exams

Having revised your notes and the BPP Passcards, you can attempt the questions in the Kit as a series of practice exams. You can organise the questions in the following ways:

- Either you can attempt complete old papers; recent papers are listed below.

	P2			
	Pilot paper	May'06	Nov '06	May '07
Section A				
1	114	116	117	118
Section B				
2	69	63	101	84
3	96	83	42	64
4	55	100	21	22
Section C				
5	17	10	89	75
6	46	30	11	23
7	71	47	74	90

- Or you can make up practice exams, either yourself or using the mock exams that we have listed below.

	Practice exams								
	1	2	3	4	5	6	7	8	9
Section A									
1	110	111	112	*	**	***			
Section B									
2	77	86	80	40	103	2			
3	79	67	95	3	25	78			
4	39	28	105	95	66	106			
Section C									
5	60	44	7	16	98	62			
6	8	61	73	87	34	27			
7	26	109	37	72	52	99			

- Whichever practice exams you use, you must attempt **Mock exams 1, 2 and 3** at the end of your revision.

Notes

*   Do question 1 parts 1, 6 and 7, question 12 part 7, question 53 part 3 and question 76 parts 1 and 2.

**   Do question 1 parts 2, 4 and 5, question 24 parts 5 and 6, question 53 part 4, question 76 part 3, question 85 part 2 and question 91 part 2.

*** Do question 1 parts 8 and 9, question 53 part 6, question 65 part 5 and question 91 parts 4 and 5.

Questions

QUESTIONS

THE TREATMENT OF UNCERTAINTY IN DECISION MAKING

Questions 1 to 11 cover the treatment of uncertainty in decision making, the subject of Part B of the BPP Study Text for Paper P2.

1 Section A questions: Uncertainty in decision making

36 mins

1. Daily sales of product X by Y Ltd are likely to be 400 units, 500 units or 600 units. The probability of sales of 500 units is 0.5, while the probability of sales of 600 units is 0.1.

   Required

   Calculate the expected value of the daily sales volume. (2 marks)

2. Explain (in less than fifty words) how the value of perfect information is calculated.

   ....

   ....

   (2 marks)

3. Indicate whether the following are drawbacks of the decision rule to choose the option with the highest expected value.

   A   The method is too concerned with the need to avoid losses.
   B   The method is concerned only with making the greatest possible profit.
   C   The method ignores less likely outcomes.
   D   The method takes no account of risk aversion. (3 marks)

4. The probability of an expected profit of £2,000 is 0.34, the probability of an expected profit of £1,850 is 0.15, the probability of an expected profit of £1,000 is 0.3 and the probability of an expected loss of £3,000 is 0.21. What is the probability of a profit of £1,000 or less?

   A   0.3
   B   0.49
   C   0.51
   D   0.21 (2 marks)

5. The decision tree below relates to the cost of sales options for a company.

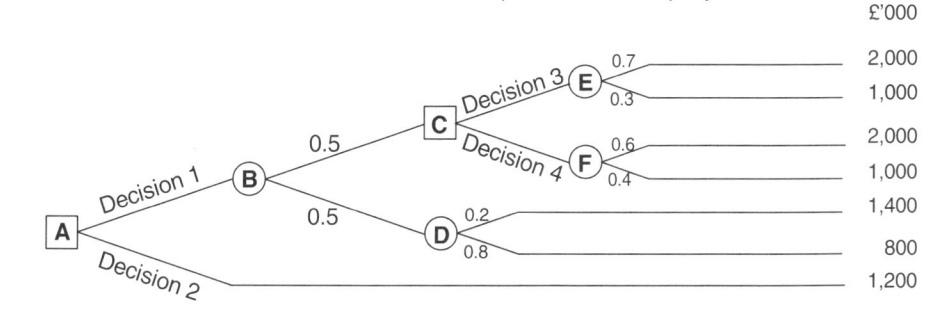

QUESTIONS

Which of the following statements are true for the above diagram?

A   At decision point C, decision 4 would be chosen.
B   The expected value at outcome point B is £680,000.
C   Decision 2 would be chosen over decision 1.
D   The expected value at outcome point D is £920,000.

(2 marks)

The following data relates to questions 1.6 and 1.7

X Ltd can choose from five mutually exclusive projects. The projects will each last for one year only and their net cash inflows will be determined by the prevailing market conditions. The forecast annual cash inflows and their associated probabilities are shown below.

Market Conditions	Poor	Good	Excellent
Probability	0.20	0.50	0.30
	£'000	£'000	£'000
Project L	500	470	550
Project M	400	550	570
Project N	450	400	475
Project O	360	400	420
Project P	600	500	425

6   Determine, based on the expected value of the net cash inflows, which project should be undertaken.

(2 marks)

7   Calculate the value of perfect information about the state of the market. (3 marks)

The following data relates to questions 1.8 and 1.9

The owner of a boat building company is deciding whether or not to exhibit at a particular boat show, which is to be held early in the season. The total cost of exhibiting at the show will be £6,000. Sales will be dependent on the weather; there is a 0.3 chance that the weather will be dry and a 0.7 chance that the weather will be wet.

If the weather is dry, the owner expects to sell six yachts at the show. If the weather is wet, he expects to sell only 2 yachts at the show. The contribution per yacht sold is £10,000.

If the owner does not exhibit at this show, he believes that two of the yachts he expects to sell at this show would be sold at another show later in the year.

8   The expected net gain from exhibiting at the show is

A   £0
B   £6,000
C   £12,000
D   £26,000

(2 marks)

9   The owner can pay for a long-term weather forecast, which will be accurate 60% of the time.

The maximum amount that the owner would be prepared to pay for the forecast, compared with not purchasing a weather forecast and not exhibiting at the show is

A   £0
B   £6,000
C   £20,000
D   £26,000

(2 marks)

(Total = 20 marks)

If you struggled with these OT questions, go back to your BPP Study Text for Paper P2 and revise Chapter 14 before you tackle the 10-mark and 25-mark questions on risk and uncertainty in decision making.

2 Ice cream manufacturer   18 mins

An ice cream manufacturer sells soft scoop ice cream in special pressurised containers and is planning production for the summer, which is the peak period.

The company wishes to ensure that it has the quantity of containers on hand: too few and sales will be lost; too many and the surplus will have to be stored over the winter at a substantial cost. The containers can only be purchased in lots of 500.

The following table shows the estimated lost contributions for various ordering patterns.

	Number of new containers bought			
	0	500	1,000	1,500
	£'000	£'000	£'000	£'000
Poor summer – low sales	0	20	20	30
Fair summer – reasonable sales	15	0	15	20
Good summer – good sales	20	20	0	15
Very good summer – very high sales	30	25	15	0

Based on past data, the probabilities of the different types of weather are as follows.

Poor	0.3
Fair	0.4
Good	0.2
Very good	0.1

The firm has obtained a copy of the long-range weather forecast for the summer which indicates that there will be a good summer, but past experience indicates that the forecasts are not 100% accurate, as follows.

P (Forecast good but weather poor)	0.3
P (Forecast good but weather fair)	0.4
P (Forecast good and weather good)	0.7
P (Forecast good but weather very good)	0.2

Required

Calculate the number of containers that should be purchased if the forecast is taken into account. **(10 marks)**

3 Sporting simulator   18 mins

A sports goods manufacturer, in conjunction with a software house, is considering the launch of a new sporting simulator based on videotapes linked to a personal computer enabling much greater realism to be achieved. Two proposals are being considered. Both use the same production facilities and, as these are limited, only one product can be launched.

The following data are the best estimates the firm has been able to obtain.

	Football simulator	*Cricket simulator*
Annual volume (units)	40,000	30,000
Selling price	£130 per unit	£200 per unit
Variable production costs	£80 per unit	£100 per unit
Fixed production costs	£600,000	£600,000
Fixed selling and administration costs	£450,000	£1,350,000

QUESTIONS

The higher selling and administrative costs for the cricket simulator reflect the additional advertising and promotion costs expected to be necessary to sell the more expensive cricket system.

The firm has a minimum target of £200,000 profit per year for new products. The management recognises the uncertainty in the above estimates and wishes to explore the sensitivity of the profit on each product to changes in the values of the variables (volume, price, variable cost per unit, fixed costs).

Required

(a) Calculate the critical value for each variable (the value at which the firm will earn £200,000), assuming that all other variables are as expected (express this as an absolute value and as a percentage change from the expected value). **(7 marks)**

(b) Discuss the factors which should be considered in making a choice between the two products. **(3 marks)**

(Total = 10 marks)

4 Homelathe   45 mins

H Ltd is a small company that manufactures a lathe attachment for the DIY market called the 'Homelathe'.

The data for manufacturing the attachment are as follows.

For each batch of ten Homelathes

Components	A	B	C	D	E	Total
Machine hours	10	14	12			36
Labour hours				2	1	3
	£	£	£	£	£	£
Variable cost	32	54	58	12	4	160
Fixed cost (apportioned)	48	102	116	24	26	316
Total component costs	80	156	174	36	30	476

Assembly costs (all variable)   £40 per ten
Selling price   £600 per ten

General purpose machinery is used to make components A, B and C and is already working to the maximum capability of 4,752 hours and there is no possibility of increasing the machine capacity in the next period. There is labour available for making components D and E and for assembling the product.

The marketing department advises that there will be a 50% increase in demand next period so the company has decided to buy *one* of the machine-made components from an outside supplier in order to release production capacity and thus help to satisfy demand.

A quotation has been received from GM Ltd for the components, but because this company has not made the components before, it has not been able to give single figure prices. Its quotation is as follows.

Component	Pessimistic		Most likely		Optimistic	
	Price	Probability	Price	Probability	Price	Probability
	£		£		£	
A	96	0.25	85	0.5	54	0.25
B	176	0.25	158	0.5	148	0.25
C	149	0.25	127	0.5	97	0.25

It has been agreed between the two companies that audited figures would be used to determine which one of the three prices would be charged for whatever component is bought out.

As management accountant of H Ltd, it is your responsibility to analyse the financial and production capacity effects of the proposed component purchase.

Required

(a) Show in percentage form the maximum increased production availability from the three alternatives, that is buying A or B or C. **(5 marks)**

(b) Analyse the financial implications of the purchase and, assuming a risk neutral attitude, recommend which component to buy out, noting that the production availability will be limited to a 50% increase. **(7 marks)**

(c) Prepare a profit statement for the period assuming that the component chosen in (b) is bought out and that the extra production is made and sold (show your workings). **(8 marks)**

(d) State three other factors you would consider if you were advised that management had decided to avoid risk as much as possible when buying out a component. (Calculations are not required for this section.) **(5 marks)**

(Total = 25 marks)

5 Pharmacy
18 mins

QR Ltd operates two pharmacies, X and Z.

A Pareto analysis has been carried out on the retail sales and closing stock for the last trading year for the two pharmacies. The results of the analysis are shown below.

Sales in X and Z

		X					Z		
Rank	Category	Sales	Cumulative sales		Rank	Category	Sales	Cumulative sales	
		£'000	£'000	%			£'000	£'000	%
1	OTC	35	35	21.9	1	OTC	24	24	24
2	Toiletries	30	65	40.6	2	Toiletries	20	44	44
3	Photo	25	90	56.3	3	Food/drink	15	59	59
4	Food/drink	20	110	68.8	4	Photo	12	71	71
5	Baby	10	120	75.0	5	Cosmetic	6	77	77
5	Sanpro	10	130	81.3	6	Baby	5	82	82
5	Other	10	140	87.5	6	Sanpro	5	87	87
8	Foot	6	146	91.3	6	Other	5	92	92
9	Cosmetics	5	151	94.4	9	Foot	4	96	96
9	Hair	5	156	97.5	10	Hair	2	98	98
11	Perfume	4	160	100.0	11	Perfume	2	100	100

Stock in X and Z

		X					Z		
Rank	Category	Stock	Cumulative stock		Rank	Category	Stock	Cumulative stock	
		£'000	£'000	%			£'000	£'000	%
1	Toiletries	12.0	12.0	26.1	1	Toiletries	13.0	13.0	30.2
2	Cosmetics	8.0	20.0	43.5	2	Cosmetics	9.0	22.0	51.2
3	OTC	7.0	27.0	58.7	3	OTC	8.0	30.0	69.8
4	Photo	4.0	31.0	67.4	4	Food/drink	4.0	34.0	79.1
4	Food/drink	4.0	35.0	76.1	5	Photo	2.5	36.5	84.9
6	Other	2.6	37.6	81.7	6	Perfume	1.5	38.0	88.4
7	Baby	2.0	39.6	86.1	7	Baby	1.0	39.0	90.7
7	Sanpro	2.0	41.6	90.4	7	Sanpro	1.0	40.0	93.0
7	Hair	2.0	43.6	94.8	7	Foot	1.0	41.0	95.3
7	Perfume	2.0	45.6	99.1	7	Hair	1.0	42.0	97.7
11	Foot	0.4	46.0	100.0	7	Other	1.0	43.0	100.0

QUESTIONS

Required

On the basis of the Pareto analysis, write a concise report to QR Ltd's management on your findings, highlighting points of importance. **(10 marks)**

6 Purchase options   45 mins

Z Ltd is considering various product pricing and material purchasing options with regard to a new product it has developed. Estimates of demand and costs are as follows.

		Selling price of £15 per unit Sales volume ('000 units)	Selling price of £20 per unit Sales volume ('000 units)
Forecasts	*Probability*		
Optimistic	0.3	36	28
Most likely	0.5	28	23
Pessimistic	0.2	18	13
Variable manufacturing costs (excluding materials) per unit		£3	£3
Advertising and selling costs		£25,000	£96,000
General fixed costs		£40,000	£40,000

Each unit requires 3 kg of material and because of storage problems any unused material must be sold at £1 per kg. The sole suppliers of the material offer three purchase options, which must be decided at the outset, as follows.

- Any quantity at £3 per kg
- A price of £2.75 per kg for a minimum quantity of 50,000 kg
- A price of £2.50 per kg for a minimum quantity of 70,000 kg

Required

Assume that the company is risk neutral.

(a) Prepare calculations to show what pricing and purchasing decisions the company should make, clearly indicating the recommended decisions. **(18 marks)**

(b) Calculate the maximum price you would pay for perfect information as to whether demand would be optimistic or most likely or pessimistic. **(7 marks)**

(Total = 25 marks)

7 Holiday resort   45 mins

A holiday resort operates a clifftop cable car to transport tourists to and from the beach during the holiday season. During the 20X6 season the following operating information applied.

(a) Average variable cost per single cable car journey was £10.

(b) Total fixed cost for the season was £48,000.

(c) The fare structure incorporates a return fare which gives a 10% saving as compared to paying for two single journeys. The fares per single journey were as follows: adult £1.00; juvenile £0.60; senior citizen £0.50.

(d) The cable car has a maximum capacity of 30 passengers per journey. It operated for 100 journeys per day on each of 120 days during 20X6.

(e) Total passenger journeys represented 60% capacity utilisation per journey. The capacity utilised comprised 50% adult, 30% juvenile and 20% senior citizen journeys. For all passenger categories, 75% of the tickets sold were for single journey fares and the remainder for return fares.

(f) Advertising revenue from displays in the cable car totalled £20,000 This is a fixed annual sum from contracts which will apply each season up to and including 20X8.

It is anticipated that costs will increase by 5% due to inflation during the 20X7 season and that fares will also increase by 5% from the 20X6 levels. While the fare increase has been agreed and cannot be altered, it is possible that the inflation effect on costs may differ from the forecast rate of 5%.

Required

(a) Explain the meaning of the information in the two-way data table shown in the appendix which has been extracted from a spreadsheet model of the situation and comment on the range of values. **(6 marks)**

(b) Capacity utilisation and the rate of inflation have been identified as key variables for 20X7. Probabilities have been estimated for the level at which the key variables will occur. Capacity utilisation and inflation are independent of each other. The estimates are as follows.

Capacity utilisation %	Probability	Inflation %	Probability
80	0.15	2	0.2
60	0.60	5	0.5
40	0.25	8	0.3

(i) Prepare a summary which shows the range of possible net profit or loss outcomes, showing the combined probability of each outcome, using the Appendix as appropriate. **(8 marks)**

(ii) Calculate the expected value of net profit or loss. **(2 marks)**

(iii) Using your answer to (b)(i), calculate the cumulative probability of the net profit being greater than £30,000. **(3 marks)**

(c) Explain ways in which a spreadsheet model could be used to calculate the effect of *each* of the following variable data changes on profit for 20X7 where all other variables remain unchanged.

(i) Changes in customer mix
(ii) Changes in the overall fare increase between 1% and 10% in steps of 1%. (No calculations required.)

(6 marks)

(Total = 25 marks)

Appendix

Two-way data table monitoring changes in net profit for a range of levels of capacity utilisation and inflation.

		\multicolumn{5}{c}{Capacity utilisation (%)}
		20%	40%	60%	80%	100%
	1%	−104927	−35935	33058	102050	171043
	2%	−106847	−37855	31138	100130	169123
	3%	−108767	−39775	29218	98210	167203
	4%	−110687	−41695	27298	96290	165283
	5%	−112607	−43615	25378	94370	163363
Inflation (%)	6%	−114527	−45535	23458	92450	161443
	7%	−116447	−47455	21538	90530	159523
	8%	−118367	−49375	19618	88610	157603
	9%	−120287	−51295	17698	86690	155683
	10%	−122207	−53215	15778	84770	153763

QUESTIONS

8 Concert hall   45 mins

A ticket agent has an arrangement with a concert hall that holds pop concerts on 60 nights a year whereby he receives discounts as follows per concert.

For purchase of:	He receives a discount of:
200 tickets	20%
300 tickets	25%
400 tickets	30%
500 tickets or more	40%

Purchases must be in full hundreds. The average price per ticket is £3.

He must decide in advance each year the number of tickets he will purchase. If he has any tickets unsold by the afternoon of the concert he must return them to the box office. If the box office sells any of these he receives 60% of their price.

His sales records over a few years show that for a concert with extremely popular artistes he can be confident of selling 500 tickets, for one with less known artistes 350 tickets, and for ones with relatively unknown artistes 200 tickets.

His sales records show that 10% of the tickets he returns are sold by the box office.

His administration costs incurred in selling tickets are the same per concert irrespective of the popularity of the artistes.

There are two possible scenarios in which his sales records can be viewed.

Scenario 1

On average, he can expect concerts with lesser known artistes.

Scenario 2

The frequency of concerts will be as follows.

	%
Popular artistes	45
Lesser known artistes	30
Unknown artistes	25
	100

Required

(a) Calculate separately for each of Scenarios 1 and 2 the following.

    (i) The expected demand for tickets per concert

    (ii) (1) The level of his purchases of tickets per concert that will give him the largest profit over a long period of time

        (2) The profit per concert that this level of purchases of tickets will yield **(20 marks)**

(b) For Scenario 2 only, calculate the maximum sum per annum that the ticket agent should pay to a pop concert specialist for 100% correct predictions as to the likely success of each concert. **(5 marks)**

(Total = 25 marks)

9 MP Organisation (11/05) 45 mins

The MP Organisation is an independent film production company. It has a number of potential films that it is considering producing, one of which is the subject of a management meeting next week. The film which has been code named CA45 is a thriller based on a novel by a well respected author.

The script has already been written at a cost of $10,000 and preliminary discussions have been held with the lead actors. The MP Organisation has incurred travel and other incidental costs of $4,000 to date. The following additional costs have been estimated in order to produce the film:

	$'000
Production director's fee	100
Set design	10
Costumes and wardrobe	20
Actors' fees	50
Musician/songwriter for soundtrack	5
Camera and equipment hire	20
Actors' travel and accommodation costs	10
Other production costs	5

Production of the film is estimated to take 16 weeks, and all of the above costs would be incurred during this period, though there is some uncertainty about the accuracy of these cost estimates. These cost values are those most likely to be incurred. With the exception of the payment to the production director which is a fixed fee, the other costs could be up to 10% higher or lower than the values estimated.

In addition there will be advertising, promotion and marketing costs of $15,000 immediately, $10,000 in each of years 1 and 2, and then $5,000 during each of the next three years. These figures are not subject to any uncertainty.

The film is expected to have a life of five years. During the first three years the film will be sold to cinemas through distributors and MP will receive 25% of the gross revenues. The film will be sold as a DVD for the remaining two years and MP will receive 100% of these revenues. The expected gross revenues are as follows:

Year	Source	Gross revenue $	MP's share %
1	Cinema	400,000	25
2	Cinema	600,000	25
3	Cinema	450,000	25
4	DVD	50,000	100
5	DVD	30,000	100

However, it is thought that the gross revenues could vary by as much as 20% higher or lower than those stated, depending on the popularity of the film. The initial level of popularity will continue for all five years.

The MP Organisation evaluates new films using a cost of capital of 15% per year.

Required

(a) Prepare calculations for each combination of the most likely, optimistic and pessimistic cost and revenue values to revalue whether or not the MP Organisation should continue with the production of the film. Discuss your analysis and make a recommendation to MP. **(15 marks)**

(b) Prepare notes for the management meeting that explain how probabilities can be used:

(i) to calculate the expected NPV; and
(ii) in a simulation model to evaluate the risk of a long term decision. **(10 marks)**

(Total = 25 marks)

10 Question with answer plan: Health clinic (5/06) 45 mins

A health clinic is reviewing its plans for the next three years. It is a not for profit organisation but it has a financial responsibility to manage its costs and to ensure that it provides a value for money service to its clients. The health clinic uses the net present value technique to appraise the financial viability of delivering the service, but it also considers other non-financial factors before making any final decisions.

The present facilities, which incur an annual total cost of £300,000, are only sufficient to meet a low level of service provision so the manager is considering investing in facilities to meet potential higher levels of demand. For the purpose of evaluating this decision the possible levels of demand for the health clinic's services have been simplified to high, medium or low.

The possible demand for the services in the first year and the level of demand that could follow that specific level in the next years, and their expected probabilities, are as follows:

Year 1	Probability	Years 2 and 3	Probability
Low	30%	Low	40%
		Medium	60%
		High	0%
Medium	50%	Low	30%
		Medium	40%
		High	30%
High	20%	Low	0%
		Medium	30%
		High	70%

The level of demand will be the same in years 2 and 3.

The manager is considering two alternative investments in facilities:

Facility A has the capacity to meet the low and medium levels of demand and requires an investment at the start of year 1 of £500,000. Thereafter it incurs annual fixed costs of £100,000 and annual variable costs depending on the level of operation. These annual variable costs are expected to be £150,000 at the low level of operation and £250,000 at the medium level of operation.

Facility B has the capacity to meet all levels of demand and requires an investment at the start of year 1 of £800,000. Thereafter it incurs annual fixed costs of £200,000 and annual variable costs depending on the level of operation. These annual variable costs are expected to be £100,000 at the low level of operation, £150,000 at the medium level of operation and £200,000 at the high level of operation.

Neither of these alternative investments has any residual value at the end of year 3.

If the facilities of the health clinic are insufficient to meet the level of service demand that occurs, the clinic must obtain additional facilities on a yearly contract basis at the following annual costs:

Level of service provision available internally	Level of service provision demanded	Annual cost of additional facilities
Low	Medium	£100,000
Low	High	£250,000
Medium	High	£150,000

These additional facilities are not under the direct control of the health clinic manager.

Note. All monetary values used throughout the question have been stated in terms of their present value. No further discounting is required.

QUESTIONS

Required

(a) Prepare a decision tree to illustrate the investment decision that needs to be made by the manager of the health clinic. (Numerical values are NOT required.) **(6 marks)**

(b) Advise the manager of the health clinic which investment decision should be undertaken on financial grounds. **(15 marks)**

(c) Briefly discuss any non-financial factors that the manager should consider before making her final investment decision. **(4 marks)**

(Total = 25 marks)

11 Theatre (11/06)   45 mins

A theatre has a seating capacity of 500 people and is considering engaging MS and her orchestra for a concert for one night only. The fee that would be charged by MS would be $10,000. If the theatre engages MS, then this sum is payable regardless of the size of the theatre audience.

Based on past experience of events of this type, the price of the theatre ticket would be $25 per person. The size of the audience for this event is uncertain, but based on past experience it is expected to be as follows.

	Probability
300 people	50%
400 people	30%
500 people	20%

In addition to the sale of the theatre tickets, it can be expected that members of the audience will also purchase confectionery both prior to the performance and during the interval. The contribution that this would yield to the theatre is unclear, but has been estimated as follows.

Contribution from confectionery sales	*Probability*
Contribution of $3 per person	30%
Contribution of $5 per person	50%
Contribution of $10 per person	20%

Required

(a) Using expected values as the basis of your decision, advise the theatre management whether it is financially worthwhile to engage MS for the concert. **(5 marks)**

(b) Prepare a two-way data table to show the profit values that could occur from deciding to engage MS for the concert. **(5 marks)**

(c) Explain, using the probabilities provided and your answer to *(b)* above, how the two-way data table can be used by the theatre management to evaluate the financial risks of the concert, including the probability of making a profit. **(9 marks)**

(d) Calculate the maximum price that the theatre management should agree to pay for perfect information relating to the size of the audience and the level of contribution from confectionery sales. **(6 marks)**

(Total = 25 marks)

QUESTIONS

> **FINANCIAL INFORMATION FOR SHORT-TERM DECISION MAKING**
>
> Questions 12 to 47 cover financial information for short-term decision making, the subject of Part C of the BPP Study Text for Paper P2.

12 Section A questions: Relevant costs and short-term decisions
36 mins

1 S Ltd is considering adapting its assembly process so that products can also be moulded at the same time. The existing assembly process machinery would have to be removed, either now at a dismantling cost of £100,000 and with the sale of the machinery for £800,000, or in one year's time at a dismantling cost of £110,000 and with sale proceeds of £600,000. Alternative machinery would have to be leased. This would cost £80,000 per annum. The existing assembly process machinery originally cost £2,000,000 when purchased seven years ago. It is being depreciated at 5% per annum on a straight line basis. Analysing on an incremental opportunity cost basis and ignoring the time value of money, which of the following is correct?

   A Adapting now will produce savings of £130,000 more than adapting in one year.
   B Adapting now will cost £130,000 more than adapting in one year.
   C Adapting now will produce savings of £110,000 more than adapting in one year.
   D Adapting now will cost £110,000 more than adapting in one year.

   (2 marks)

2 D Ltd's entire machine capacity is used to produce essential components. The variable costs of using the machines are £150,000 and the fixed costs are £400,000. If all the components were purchased from an outside supplier, the machines could be used to produce other items which would earn a total contribution of £250,000.

   Required

   Calculate the maximum price that D Ltd should be willing to pay to the outside supplier for the components, assuming there is no change in fixed costs. **(3 marks)**

3 What is the relevant cost of the product units in a decision about the disposal of existing product units no longer required?

   A Net realisable value
   B Replacement cost
   C Variable cost
   D Full cost

   (2 marks)

4 BS plc has been asked to carry out a systems amendment for L Ltd. The amendment will require 400 programmer hours and BS plc has only one programmer who is capable of doing the job.

   The programmer is paid £40 per hour. Employers' NIC and pension contributions are 20% of salary. Other overheads are absorbed by adding 200% to direct salaries.

   The programmer is scheduled to start work on a project for another customer, M Inc, the revenue from which is £60,000 and non-salary direct costs are £1,500. This job will also take 400 hours. If the programmer is assigned to the L Ltd job, BS plc will have to hire another programmer to carry out the Mowlisly job at a cost of £22,000.

   The relevant cost of the programmer's time if BS plc carries out the systems amendment for L Ltd is £19,200. *True or false?* **(4 marks)**

5 Which of the following are non-relevant costs?

　　I　　Avoidable costs
　　II　　Opportunity costs
　　III　　Notional costs
　　IV　　Sunk costs

　　A　　All of them
　　B　　IV only
　　C　　None of them
　　D　　III and IV　　　　　　　　　　　　　　　　　　　　　　　　　　　　　　　(2 marks)

6 A Ltd has three options for machine B. One of these options involves modifying the machine now at a cost of £7,200, which will mean that the company does not have to hire an alternative machine at a cost of £19,800. This modification would mean that machine B would have to be disposed of in one year's time at a cost of £4,000. Ignoring the time value of money, calculate the relevant cost of this option. (3 marks)

7 C Ltd is in the process of preparing a quotation for a special job for a customer. The job will require 700 units of material N. 400 units are already in stock at a book value of £50 per unit. The net realisable value per unit is £20. The replacement price per unit is £60. The material is in stock as the result of previous over buying. No other use can be found for material N.

Required

Calculate the relevant cost of material N for this special job. (4 marks)

(Total = 20 marks)

If you struggled with these OT questions, go back to your BPP Study Text for Paper P2 and revise Chapters 2 and 3 before you tackle the 10-mark and 25-mark questions on relevant costs and short-term decisions.

The following scenario relates to questions 13 and 14.

MOV plc produces custom-built sensors. Each sensor has a standard circuit board (SCB) in it. The current average contribution from a sensor is £400. MOV plc's business is steadily expanding and in the year just ending (20X1/20X2), the company will have produced 55,000 sensors. The demand for MOV plc's sensors is predicted to grow over the next three years:

Year	Units
20X2/X3	58,000
20X3/X4	62,000
20X4/X5	65,000

The production of sensors is limited by the number of SCBs the company can produce. The present production level of 55,000 SCBs is the maximum that can be produced without overtime working. Overtime could increase annual output to 60,500, allowing production of sensors to also increase to 60,500. However, the variable cost of SCBs produced in overtime would increase by £75 per unit.

Because of the pressure on capacity, the company is considering having the SCBs manufactured by another company, CIR plc. This company is very reliable and produces products of good quality. CIR plc has quoted a price of £116 per SCB, for orders greater than 50,000 units a year.

QUESTIONS

MOV plc's own costs per SCB are predicted to be:

	£	
Direct material	28	
Direct labour	40	
Variable overhead	20	(based on labour cost)
Fixed overhead	24	(based on labour cost and output of 55,000 units)
Total cost	112	

The fixed overheads directly attributable to SCBs are £250,000 a year; these costs will be avoided if SCBs are not produced. If more than 59,000 units are produced, SCBs' fixed overheads will increase by £130,000.

In addition to the above overheads, MOV plc's fixed overheads are predicted to be:

Sensor production, in units:	54,001 to 59,000	59,001 to 64,000	64,001 to 70,000
Fixed overhead:	£2,600,000	£2,900,000	£3,100,000

MOV plc currently holds a stock of 3,500 SCBs but the production manager feels that a stock of 8,000 should be held if they are bought-in; this would increase stockholding costs by £10,000 a year. A purchasing officer, who is paid £20,000 a year, spends 50% of her time on SCB duties. If the SCBs are bought-in, a liaison officer will have to be employed at a salary of £30,000 in order to liaise with CIR plc and monitor the quality and supply of SCBs. At present, 88 staff are involved in the production of SCBs at an average salary of £25,000 a year: if the SCBs were purchased, 72 of these staff would be made redundant at an average cost of £4,000 per employee.

The SCB department, which occupies an area of 240 × 120 metres at the far end of the factory, could be rented out, at a rent of £45 per square metre a year. However, if the SCBs were to be bought-in, for the first year only MOV plc would need the space to store the increased stock caused by outsourcing, until the main stockroom has been reorganised and refurbished. From 20X3/X4, the space could be rented out; this would limit the annual production of sensors to 60,500 units. Alternatively, the space could be used for the production of sensors, allowing annual output to increase to 70,000 units if required.

13 MOV plc I (IDEC, 5/02, amended)   18 mins

Read the scenario above and then critically discuss the validity of the following statement. It was produced by Jim Elliott, the company's accountant, to show the gain for the coming year (20X2/X3) if the SCBs were to be bought-in.

Saving in:	£
Manufacturing staff – salaries saved: 72 staff × £25,000	1,800,000
Purchasing officer – time saved	10,000
Placing orders for SCB materials: 1,000 orders × £20 per order	20,000
Transport costs for raw materials for SCBs	45,000
Cost saved	1,875,000
Additional cost per SCB: (£116 – £112) × 58,000 units	232,000
Net gain if SCBs purchased	1,643,000

(10 marks)

14 MOV plc II (IDEC, 5/02, amended)   18 mins

Read the scenario above and then produce detailed calculations that show which course of action is the best financial option for the three years under consideration. (Ignore the time value of money.) **(10 marks)**

15 Z Ltd (5/05)   18 mins

Z Ltd manufactures three joint products (M, N and P) from the same common process. The following process account relates to the common process last month and is typical of the monthly results of operating this process:

COMMON PROCESS ACCOUNT

	Litres	$		Litres	$
Opening work in process	1,000	5,320	Normal loss	10,000	20,000
Materials	100,000	250,000	Output M	25,000	141,875
Conversion costs:			Output N	15,000	85,125
Variable		100,000	Output P	45,000	255,375
Fixed		180,000	Closing work in process	800	3,533
			Abnormal loss	5,200	29,412
	101,000	535,320		101,000	535,320

Each one of the products can be sold immediately after the common process, but each one of them can be further processed individually before being sold. The following further processing costs and selling prices per litre are expected:

Product	Selling price after common process $/litre	Selling price after further processing $/litre	Further variable processing cost $/litre
M	6.25	8.40	1.75
N	5.20	6.45	0.95
P	6.80	7.45	0.85

Required

(a) State the method used to apportion the common costs between the products M, N and P and comment on its acceptability. Explain why it is necessary to apportion the common costs between each of the products. **(5 marks)**

(b) Evaluate the viability of the common process, and determine the optimal processing plan for each of the three products, showing appropriate calculations. **(5 marks)**

(Total = 10 marks)

Helping hand. Part (b). Work out the basis of the common apportionment first. Then find out if the process makes a profit to the end of the common process and then calculate the further incremental costs and revenues after the common process.

15 Question with analysis: Z Ltd (5/05)   18 mins

Z Ltd manufactures three joint products (M, N and P) from the same common process. The following process account relates to the common process last month and is typical of the monthly results of operating this process:

COMMON PROCESS ACCOUNT

	Litres	$		Litres	$
Opening work in process	1,000	5,320	Normal loss	10,000	20,000
Materials	100,000	250,000	Output M	25,000	141,875
Conversion costs:			Output N	15,000	85,125
Variable		100,000	Output P	45,000	255,375
Fixed		180,000	Closing work in process	800	3,533
			Abnormal loss	5,200	29,412
	101,000	535,320		101,000	535,320

QUESTIONS

Each one of the products can be sold immediately after the common process, but each one of them can be further processed individually before being sold. The following further processing costs and selling prices per litre are expected:

Product	Selling price after common process $/litre	Selling price after further processing $/litre	Further variable processing cost $/litre
M	6.25	8.40	1.75
N	5.20	6.45	0.95
P	6.80	7.45	0.85

Required

(a) **State the method used** to apportion the common costs between the products M, N and P and **comment on its acceptability**. Explain why it is necessary to apportion the common costs between each of the products. **(5 marks)**

[Look at the requirements of the question]

(b) **Evaluate** the viability of the common process, and **determine** the optimal processing plan for each of the three products, showing appropriate calculations. **(5 marks)**

[Do calculations and comment on them]

(Total = 10 marks)

Helping hand. Part (b). Work out the basis of the common apportionment first. Then find out if the process makes a profit to the end of the common process and then calculate the further incremental costs and revenues after the common process.

16 Mixit Ltd   45 mins

(a) Mixit Ltd produces a range of four products simultaneously from a joint process consisting of 10,000 gallons of raw materials input costing £150,000. Joint process labour and material costs are £148,000. A normal loss of 2,000 gallons is expected. Output of product A is 2,000 gallons, product B 2,500 gallons, product C 2,500 gallons and product D 1,000 gallons.

Product A enters into process 2 incurring further costs of £125,500. The product is then sold for £75 per gallon.

Product B enters process 3, the costs of which amount to £149,375. Product B is then sold for £173 per gallon.

Product C enters process 4. Additional costs amount to £111,875. Product C is then sold for £138 per gallon.

Product D does not require any additional processing and may be sold for £50 per gallon.

There are no further processing losses.

Mixit's policy is to apportion the joint costs on an output basis.

The company is investigating the profit earned by each product and is concerned that product A appears to be making a loss.

Required

(i) Calculate the loss for product A and the overall profit or loss for the company. Suggest reasons why product A appears to be making a loss. **(5 marks)**

(ii) Identify another method of cost apportionment and show how the profit or loss for each product may be changed. **(8 marks)**

(b) Mixit Ltd has recently discovered that there is a market for its products at the split off point, that is, before going into further processing. The selling price for each product is as follows.

$$A - £50$$
$$B - £100$$
$$C - £75$$

(i) Explain the advice that you would give the company to enable it to maximise profits. Support your answer with appropriate calculations. **(7 marks)**

(ii) Explain the nature of a by-product. Describe the effect if product D was treated as a by-product. (No further calculations are required.) **(5 marks)**

(Total = 25 marks)

17 Exe (Pilot paper)   45 mins

You have received a request from EXE to provide a quotation for the manufacture of a specialised piece of equipment. This would be a one-off order, in excess of normal budgeted production. The following cost estimate has already been prepared:

		Note	$
Direct materials:			
Steel	10m² @ $5.00 per m²	1	50
Brass fittings		2	20
Direct labour:			
Skilled	25 hours @ $8.00 per hour	3	200
Semi-skilled	10 hours @ $5.00 per hour	4	50
Overhead	35 hours @ $10.00 per hour	5	350
Estimating time		6	100
			770
Administration overhead @ 20% of production cost		7	154
			924
Profit @ 25% of total cost		8	231
Selling price			1,155

Notes

1 The steel is regularly used, and has a current stock value of $5.00 per square metre. There are currently 100 square metres in stock. The steel is readily available at a price of $5.50 per square metre.

2 The brass fittings would have to be bought specifically for this job: a supplier has quoted the price of $20 for the fittings required.

3 The skilled labour is currently employed by your company and paid at a rate of $8.00 per hour. If this job were undertaken it would be necessary either to work 25 hours' overtime, which would be paid at time plus one half, OR in order to carry out the work in normal time, reduce production of another product that earns a contribution of $13.00 per hour.

4 The semi-skilled labour currently has sufficient paid idle time to be able to complete this work.

5 The overhead absorption rate includes power costs which are directly related to machine usage. If this job were undertaken, it is estimated that the machine time required would be ten hours. The machines incur power costs of $0.75 per hour. There are no other overhead costs that can be specifically identified with this job.

6 The cost of the estimating time is that attributed to the four hours taken by the engineers to analyse the drawings and determine the cost estimate given above.

7 It is company policy to add 20% to the production cost as an allowance for administration costs associated with the jobs accepted.

QUESTIONS

8   This is the standard profit added by your company as part of its pricing policy.

Required

(a) Prepare on a relevant cost basis, the lowest cost estimate that could be used as the basis for a quotation. Explain briefly your reasons for using *each* of the values in your estimate. **(12 marks)**

(b) Now that the cost estimate has been prepared, the engineers have considered the skilled labour rate and hourly power costs that have been used. They have now realised that the following alternative values may occur and they have estimated the probabilities of each value:

Skilled labour		Power costs	
$/hour	Probability	$/hour	Probability
10	0.3	0.90	0.25
8	0.6	0.75	0.55
7	0.1	0.65	0.20

The following two-way data table shows the effects of these possible changes on the lowest cost estimate (all values in $):

Skilled labour rate (per hour)	Power costs (per hour)		
	0.90	0.75	0.65
10	+76.50	+75.00	+74.00
8	+1.50	0.00	−1.00
7	−36.00	−37.50	−38.50

Required

Demonstrate and explain how the two-way data table may be used to assist the company in making a decision concerning the contract. **(13 marks)**

(Total = 25 marks)

18 CS Group (5/05)   45 mins

(a) The CS group is planning its annual marketing conference for its sales executives and has approached the VBJ Holiday company (VBJ) to obtain a quotation.

VBJ has been trying to win the business of the CS group for some time and is keen to provide a quotation which the CS group will find acceptable in the hope that this will lead to future contracts.

The manager of VBJ has produced the following cost estimate for the conference:

	$
Coach running costs	2,000
Driver costs	3,000
Hotel costs	5,000
General overheads	2,000
Sub total	12,000
Profit (30%)	3,600
Total	15,600

You have considered this cost estimate but you believe that it would be more appropriate to base the quotation on relevant costs. You have therefore obtained the following further information.

Coach running costs represent the fuel costs of $1,500 plus an apportionment of the annual fixed costs of operating the coach. No specific fixed costs would be incurred if the coach is used on this contract. If the contract did not go ahead, the coach would not be in use for eight out of the ten days of the conference. For the other two days a contract has already been accepted which contains a significant financial penalty clause. This contract earns a contribution of $250 per day. A replacement coach could be hired for $180 per day.

Driver costs represent the salary and related employment costs of one driver for 10 days. If the driver is used on this contract the company will need to replace the driver so that VBJ can complete its existing work. The replacement driver would be hired from a recruitment agency that charges $400 per day for a suitably qualified driver.

Hotel costs are the expected costs of hiring the hotel for the conference.

General overheads are based upon the overhead absorption rate of VBJ and are set annually when the company prepares its budgets. The only general overhead cost that can be specifically identified with the conference is the time that has been spent in considering the costs of the conference and preparing the quotation. This amounted to $250.

Required

Prepare a statement showing the total relevant cost of the contract. Explain clearly the reasons for each of the values in your quotation and for excluding any of the costs (if appropriate). **(10 marks)**

(b) Now that the quotation has been prepared, it is realised that there is some uncertainty concerning the hotel cost and the fuel cost. Further investigation has shown that these costs may be higher or lower than the original estimates. Estimated costs with their associated probabilities are as follows:

Estimated hotel cost $	Probability %	Estimated fuel cost $	Probability %
4,000	20	1,200	10
5,000	50	1,500	50
6,000	30	2,000	40

The following two-way data table shows the effect on the total relevant cost of these alternative values. All figures are in $:

		Hotel $4,000	Hotel $5,000	Hotel $6,000
Fuel	$1,200	−1,300	−300	+700
	$1,500	−1,000	0	+1,000
	$2,000	−500	+500	+1,500

Required

(i) Explain the meaning of the above two-way data table.

(ii) Produce and interpret a table that shows how the two-way data table may be used in conjunction with the probabilities to improve the information available to the manager of VBJ.

(15 marks)

(Total = 25 marks)

18 Question with analysis: CS Group (5/05)   45 mins

(a) The CS group is planning its annual marketing conference for its sales executives and has approached the VBJ Holiday company (VBJ) to obtain a quotation.

VBJ has been trying to win the business of the CS group for some time and is keen to provide a quotation which the CS group will find acceptable in the hope that this will lead to future contracts.

The manager of VBJ has produced the following cost estimate for the conference:

QUESTIONS

			$
Coach running costs	See the		2,000
Driver costs	requirements of		3,000
Hotel costs	the question.		5,000
General overheads	You will need to		2,000
Sub total	comment on		12,000
Profit (30%)	each of these		3,600
Total			15,600

You have considered this cost estimate but you believe that it would be more appropriate to base the quotation on relevant costs. You have therefore obtained the following further information.

Coach running costs represent the fuel costs of $1,500 plus an apportionment of the annual fixed costs of operating the coach. No specific fixed costs would be incurred if the coach is used on this contract. If the contract did not go ahead, the coach would not be in use for eight out of the ten days of the conference. For the other two days a contract has already been accepted which contains a significant financial penalty clause. This contract earns a contribution of $250 per day. A replacement coach could be hired for $180 per day.

Driver costs represent the salary and related employment costs of one driver for 10 days. If the driver is used on this contract the company will need to replace the driver so that VBJ can complete its existing work. The replacement driver would be hired from a recruitment agency that charges $400 per day for a suitably qualified driver.

Hotel costs are the expected costs of hiring the hotel for the conference.

General overheads are based upon the overhead absorption rate of VBJ and are set annually when the company prepares its budgets. The only general overhead cost that can be specifically identified with the conference is the time that has been spent in considering the costs of the conference and preparing the quotation. This amounted to $250.

Required

Prepare a statement showing the total relevant cost of the contract. Explain clearly the reasons for each of the values in your quotation and for excluding any of the costs (if appropriate). **(10 marks)**

(b) Now that the quotation has been prepared, it is realised that there is some uncertainty concerning the hotel cost and the fuel cost. Further investigation has shown that these costs may be higher or lower than the original estimates. Estimated costs with their associated probabilities are as follows:

Estimated hotel cost	Probability	Estimated fuel cost	Probability
$	%	$	%
4,000	20	1,200	10
5,000	50	1,500	50
6,000	30	2,000	40

The following two-way data table shows the effect on the total relevant cost of these alternative values. All figures are in $:

		Hotel		
		$4,000	$5,000	$6,000
	$1,200	−1,300	−300	+700
Fuel	$1,500	−1,000	0	+1,000
	$2,000	−500	+500	+1,500

Required

> Notice the requirements here

(i) **Explain** the meaning of the above two-way data table.

(ii) **Produce** and **interpret** a table that shows how the two-way data table may be used in conjunction with the probabilities to improve the information available to the manager of VBJ.

(15 marks)

(Total = 25 marks)

19 ML (11/05)   18 mins

ML is an engineering company that specialises in providing engineering facilities to businesses that cannot justify operating their own facilities in-house. ML employs a number of engineers who are skilled in different engineering techniques that enable ML to provide a full range of engineering facilities to its customers. Most of the work undertaken by ML is unique to each of its customers, often requiring the manufacture of spare parts for its customers' equipment, or the building of new equipment from customer drawings. As a result most of ML's work is short-term, with some jobs being completed within hours while others may take a few days.

To date ML has adopted a cost plus approach to setting its prices. This is based upon an absorption costing system that uses machine hours as the basis of absorbing overhead costs into individual job costs. The Managing Director is concerned that over recent months ML has been unsuccessful when quoting for work with the consequence that there has been an increase in the level of unused capacity. It has been suggested that ML should adopt an alternative approach to its pricing based on marginal costing since 'any price that exceeds variable costs is better than no work'.

Required

With reference to the above scenario:

(a) briefly explain absorption and marginal cost approaches to pricing;
(b) discuss the validity of the comment 'any price that exceeds variable costs is better than no work'.

(10 marks)

20 PK plc (11/05)   18 mins

You are the assistant management accountant within PK plc. PK plc manufactures high quality self-assembly furniture from raw materials utilising highly skilled labour within a computer-controlled manufacturing facility. The company produces a range of furniture, and because of the lead time to receive delivery of its raw materials, has a finished goods inventory policy of holding an average of two weeks estimated sales in inventory. Customer demand is seasonal and as a consequence, this finished goods inventory level fluctuates throughout the year. The company also holds inventories of raw materials based upon estimates of its production requirements. An absorption costing system is used to attribute all manufacturing costs to win customer orders.

Required

Prepare a report addressed to the Management Team of PK plc that explains the changing nature of cost structures in the modern manufacturing environment and the implications for PK plc's.

(a) Inventory valuation.
(b) Short-term decision making.

Note. There are two marks available for format and presentational style.

(10 marks)

21 QXY plc (11/06) — 18 mins

You are the assistant management accountant of QXY plc, a food manufacturer. The Board of Directors is concerned that its operational managers may not be fully aware of the importance of understanding the costs incurred by the business and the effect that this has on their operational decision making. In addition, the operational managers need to be aware of the implications of their pricing policy when trying to increase the volume of sales.

You are scheduled to make a presentation to the operational managers tomorrow to explain to them the different costs that are incurred by the business, the results of some research that has been conducted into the implications for pricing and the importance of understanding these issues for their decision making. **The diagram on the next page has already been prepared for the presentation.**

Required

You are required to interpret the diagram and explain how it illustrates issues that the operational managers should consider when making decisions. (*Note*: your answer must include explanations of the Sales Revenue, Total Cost and Fixed Cost lines, and the significance of each of the activity levels labelled A, B, C, D.) **(10 marks)**

(Total = 30 marks)

Diagram for Question 21 – Costs and Revenues over a range of activity levels.

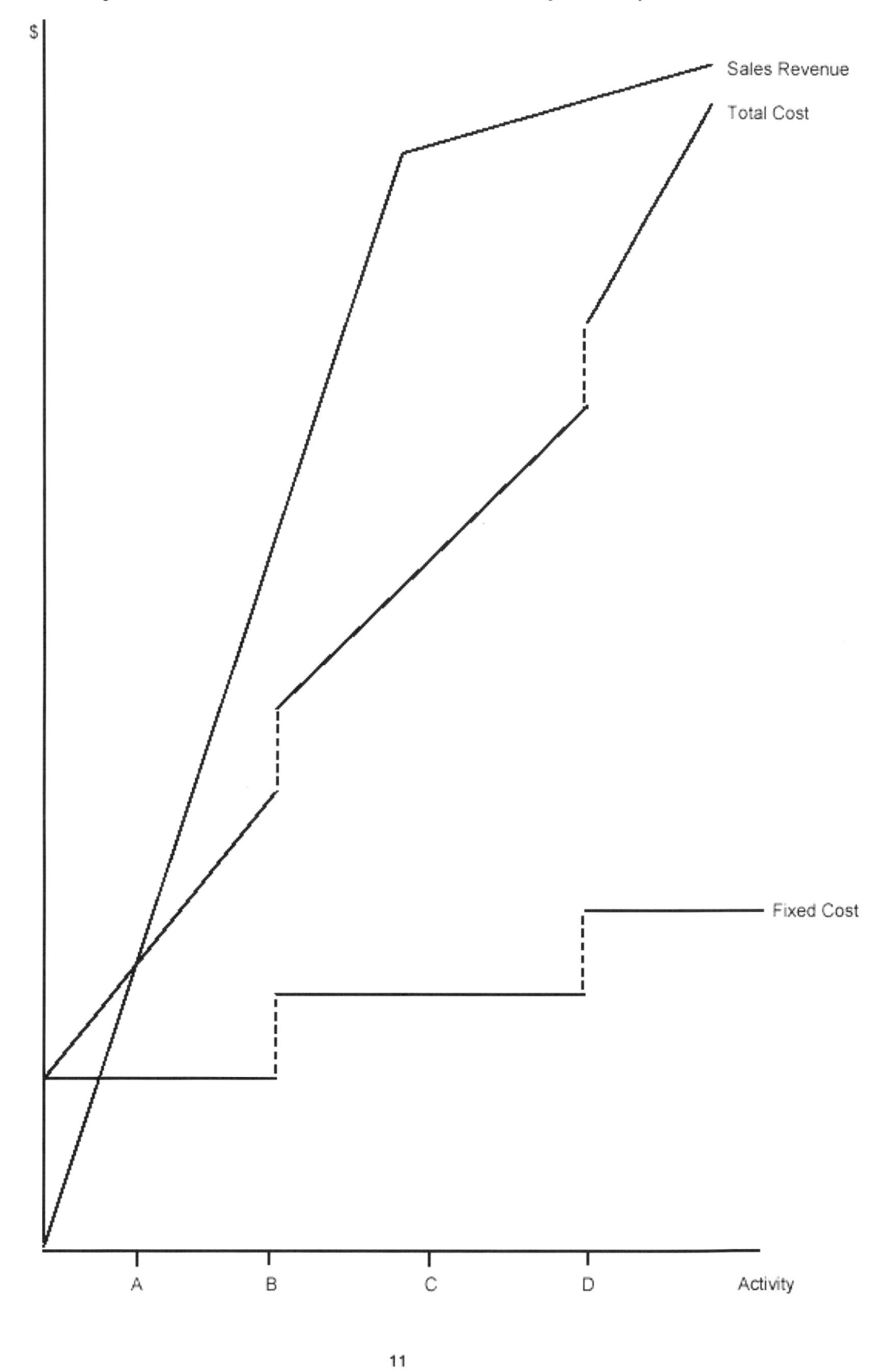

QUESTIONS

22 Z (5/07)   18 mins

Z is one of a number of companies that produce three products for an external market. The three products, R, S and T may be bought or sold in this market.

The common process account of Z for March 2007 is shown below:

	Kg	$		Kg	$
Inputs					
Material A	1,000	3,500	Normal loss	500	0
Material B	2,000	2,000	Outputs:		
Material C	1,500	3,000	Product R	800	3,500
Direct labour		6,000	Product S	2,000	8,750
Variable overhead		2,000	Product T	1,200	5,250
Fixed cost		1,000			
Totals	4,500	17,500		4,500	17,500

Z can sell products R, S or T after this common process or they can be individually further processed and sold as RZ, SZ and TZ respectively. The market prices for the products at the intermediate stage and after further processing are:

Market prices per kg:

	$
R	3.00
S	5.00
T	3.50
RZ	6.00
SZ	5.75
TZ	6.75

The specific costs of the three individual further processes are:

Process R to RZ	variable cost of $1·40 per kg, no fixed costs
Process S to SZ	variable cost of $0·90 per kg, no fixed costs
Process T to TZ	variable cost of $1·00 per kg, fixed cost of $600 per month

Required

(a) Produce calculations to determine whether any of the intermediate products should be further processed before being sold. Clearly state your recommendations together with any relevant assumptions that you have made. **(3 marks)**

(b) Produce calculations to assess the viability of the common process:

   (i) assuming that there is an external market for products R,S and T; and

   (ii) assuming that there is **not** an external market for products R,S and T. State clearly your recommendations. **(7 marks)**

(Total = 10 marks)

23 H (5/07)   45 mins

H, a printing company, uses traditional absorption costing to report its monthly profits.

It is seeking to increase its business by winning work from new customers. It now has the opportunity to prepare a quotation for a large organisation that currently requires a new catalogue of its services.

A technical report on the resource requirements for the catalogues has been completed at a cost of $1,000 and its details are summarised below:

Production period

It is expected that the total time required to print and despatch the catalogue will be one week.

Material A

10,000 sheets of special printing paper will be required. This is a paper that is in regular use by H and the company has 3,400 sheets in inventory. These originally cost $1·40 per sheet but the current market price is $1·50 per sheet. The resale price of the sheets held in inventory is $1·20 per sheet.

Material B

This is a special ink that H will need to purchase at a cost of $8 per litre. 200 litres will be required for this catalogue but the supplier has a minimum order size of 250 litres. H does not foresee any other use for this ink, but will hold the surplus in inventory. H's inventory policy is to review slow moving items regularly. The cost of any inventory item that has not been used for more than 6 months is accounted for as an expense of the period in which that review occurs.

Direct labour

Sufficient people are already employed by H to print the catalogue, but some of the printing will require overtime working due to the availability of a particular machine that is used on other work. The employees are normally paid $8 per hour, the order will require 150 hours of work and 50 of these hours will be in excess of the employees' normal working week. A rate of $10 per hour is paid for these overtime hours. Employees are paid using an hourly rate with a guaranteed minimum wage for their normal working week.

Supervision

An existing supervisor will take responsibility for the catalogue in addition to her existing duties. She is not currently fully employed and receives a salary of $500 per week.

Machinery

Two different types of machine will be required:

Machine A will print the catalogues. This is expected to take 20 hours of machine time. The running cost of machine A is $5 per hour. There is currently 30 hours of unused time on machine A per week that is being sold to other printers for $12 per hour.

Machine B will be used to cut and bind the catalogues. This machine is being used to full capacity in the normal working week and this is why there is a need to work overtime. The catalogue will require 25 machine hours and these have a running cost of $4 per hour.

Despatch

There will be a delivery cost of $400 to transport the catalogues to the customer.

Fixed overhead costs

H uses a traditional absorption costing system to attribute fixed overhead costs to its work. The absorption rate that it uses is $20 per direct labour hour.

QUESTIONS

Profit mark-up

H applies a 30% mark-up to its costs to determine its selling prices.

Required

(a) In order to assist the management of H in preparing its quotation, prepare a schedule showing the relevant costs for the production of the catalogues. State clearly your reason for including or excluding each value that has been provided in the above scenario. **(15 marks)**

(b) Explain how the use of relevant costs as the basis of setting a selling price may be appropriate for short-term pricing decisions but may be inappropriate for long-term pricing decisions. Your answer should also discuss the conflict between reporting profitability within a traditional absorption costing system and the use of relevant cost based pricing. **(10 marks)**

(Total = 25 marks)

24 Section A questions: Multi-product breakeven analysis
36 mins

1 Z plc currently sells products Aye, Bee and Cee in equal quantities and at the same selling price per unit. The contribution to sales ratio for product Aye is 40%, for product Bee it is 50% and the total is 48%. If fixed costs are unaffected by mix and are currently 20% of sales, the effect of changing the product mix to

  Aye 40% Bee 25% Cee 35%

  is that the total contribution/total sales ratio changes to:

  A 40%
  B 54%
  C 47.4%
  D 32% **(2 Marks)**

2 *Write as an answer the relevant words.*

  By convention, multiple products are usually shown on a P/V chart .... , from .... to ...., in order of .... size of C/S ratio. **(2 marks)**

3 J Ltd produces and sells two products. The O sells for £12 per unit and has a total variable cost of £7.90, while the H sells for £17 per unit and has a total variable cost of £11.20. For every four units of O sold, three of H are sold. J Ltd's fixed costs are £131,820 per period. Budgeted sales revenue for the next period is £398,500.

  Required

  Calculate the margin of safety. **(4 marks)**

4 A company makes and sells three products A, B and C. The products are sold in the proportions A: B: C = 1:1:4.

  Monthly fixed costs are £55,100 and product details are as follows.

Product	Selling price £ per unit	Variable cost £ per unit
A	47	25
B	39	20
C	28	11

  The company wishes to earn a profit of £43,000 next month. What is the required sales value of product A in order to achieve this target profit? **(3 marks)**

The following data relates to questions 24.5 and 24.6

HG plc manufactures four products. The unit cost, selling price and bottleneck resource details per unit are as follows.

	Product W £	Product X £	Product Y £	Product Z £
Selling price	56	67	89	96
Material	22	31	38	46
Labour	15	20	18	24
Variable overhead	12	15	18	15
Fixed overhead	4	2	8	7
	Minutes	Minutes	Minutes	Minutes
Bottleneck resource time	10	10	15	15

5 Assuming that labour is a unit variable cost, if the products are ranked according to their contribution to sales ratios, the most profitable product is

A W
B X
C Y
D Z

(2 marks)

6 Assuming that labour is a unit variable cost, if budgeted unit sales are in the ratio W : 2, X : 3, Y : 3, Z : 4 and monthly fixed costs are budgeted to be £15,000, the number of units of W that would be sold at the budgeted breakeven point is nearest to

A 106 units
B 142 units
C 212 units
D 283 units

(2 marks)

7 KEM Ltd produces and sells two products, the L and the E. The company expects to sell 2 L for every 5 E and have monthly sales revenue of £320,000. The L has a C/S ratio of 25% whereas the E has a C/S ratio of 35%. Budgeted monthly fixed costs are £90,000.

Required

Calculate the budgeted breakeven sales revenue. (3 marks)

8 PER plc sells three products. The budgeted fixed cost for the period is £648,000. The budgeted contribution to sales ratio (C/S ratio) and sales mix are as follows.

Product	C/S ratio	Mix
P	27%	30%
E	56%	20%
R	38%	50%

The breakeven sales revenue is nearest to

A £248,000
B £1,606,700
C £1,692,000
D £1,522,700

(2 marks)

(Total = 20 marks)

If you struggled with these OT questions, go back to your BPP Study Text for Paper P2 and revise Chapter 4 before you tackle the 10-mark and 25-mark questions on multi-product breakeven analysis.

QUESTIONS

25 POD and L **18 mins**

(a) POD Ltd makes and sells three products, X, Y and Z. The selling price per unit and costs are as follows.

	X	Y	Z
Selling price per unit	£80	£50	£70
Variable cost per unit	£50	£10	£20
Fixed costs per month	£160,000		

The maximum sales demand per month is 2,000 units of each product and the minimum sales demand is 1,000 of each.

Required

(i) Comment on the potential profitability of the company. **(2 marks)**

(ii) Suppose that there is a fixed demand for X and Y of 1,500 units per month, which will not be exceeded, but for which firm orders have been received. Calculate the number of units of Z that would have to be sold to achieve a profit of at least £25,000 per month. **(3 marks)**

(b) L Ltd achieved the following results in 20X1.

	£'000	£'000
Sales (200,000 units)		2,000
Cost of sales		
Direct materials	800	
Direct labour	400	
Overheads	600	
		1,800
Profit		200

Throughout 20X1, sales were £10 per unit, and variable overheads, which vary with the number of units produced, amount to £1 per unit.

Required

Using CVP analysis, calculate the sales volume necessary to achieve a profit of £330,000 in 20X2 if, at beginning of the year, the sales price is increased by £0.50 per unit, while the increases in costs above 20X1 levels are expected to be as follows. Comment on the result obtained.

Direct material	10%
Direct labour	15%
Variable overhead	10%
Fixed overhead	20%

(5 marks)

(Total = 10 marks)

26 RDF Ltd (IMPM, 5/04) **45 mins**

RDF Ltd offers four services to television companies The number of services provided is measured in service units and details of RDF Ltd's draft budget for its year ending 30 June 20X5 are as follows.

	Service K	Service L	Service M	Service N
Number of service units	1,000	2,300	1,450	1,970
Selling price per unit ($)	18	16	12	20
Variable cost per unit ($)	8	10	13	13
Fixed cost per unit ($)	2	3	2	4

The budgeted level of activity shown in the table above has been based on fully meeting the forecasted market demand for each type of service.

The following chart has been prepared based on the draft budget above.

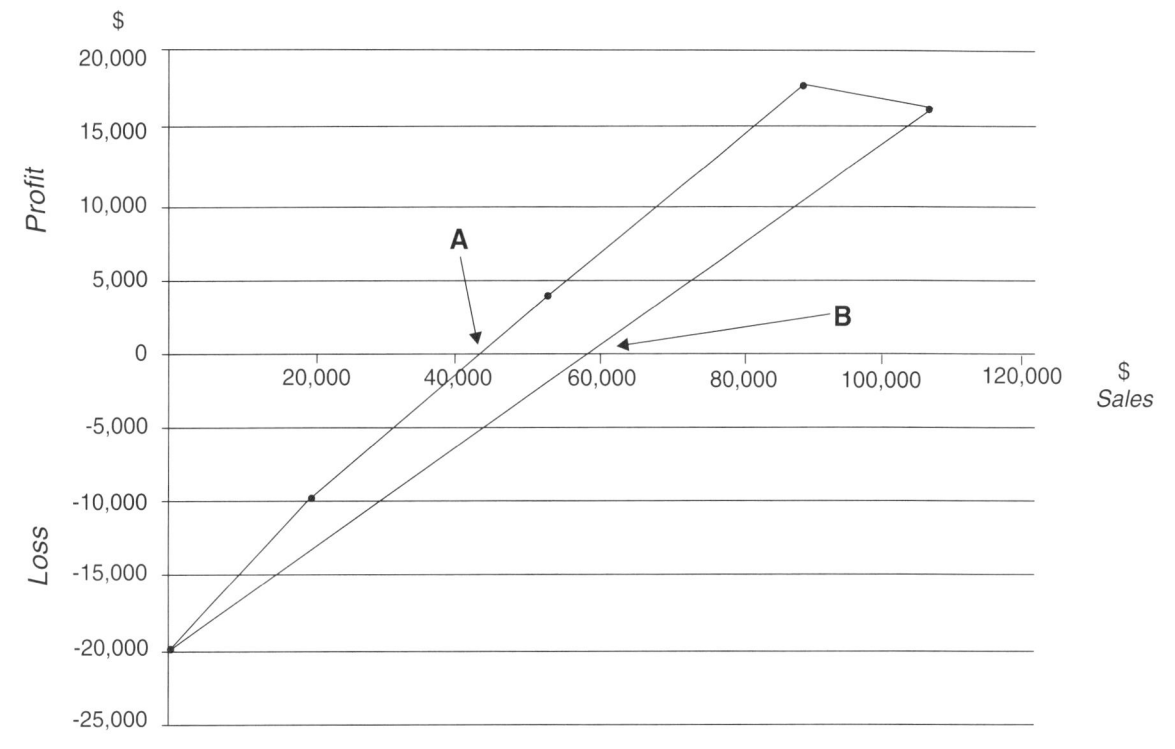

Required

(a) Explain the meaning of the values shown as points A and B on the chart. (*Note.* Calculations are not required.) **(4 marks)**

(b) Further investigation into the nature of the fixed costs has shown that some of those shown in the original budget are incurred as a direct result of providing specific services as follows.

	$
Service K	4,400
Service L	3,700
Service M	nil
Service N	2,650

The remaining budgeted fixed costs are general fixed costs that will be incurred regardless of the type and number of services provided.

RDF Ltd entered into a three-year contract in June 20X2 which requires it to provide 500 units of service M per year or suffer significant financial penalties. These services are included in the budgeted demand.

Required

(i) Evaluate the financial viability of each of the four services currently provided. **(6 marks)**

(ii) Recommend the operating plan that will maximise profit for the year ended 30 June 20X5 and state the resulting profit. Explain the assumptions that led to your decision and other factors that should be considered. **(5 marks)**

(iii) Calculate the overall breakeven sales value for the operating plan you have recommended in answer to (b)(ii), stating clearly the assumptions made in your calculations. **(5 marks)**

(iv) Comment on any limitations of using breakeven analysis for decision making purposes. **(5 marks)**

(Total = 25 marks)

27 Section A questions: Limiting factor analysis — 36 mins

1. Z plc manufactures three products which have the following selling prices and costs per unit.

		Z1 £	Z2 £	Z3 £
Selling price		15.00	18.00	17.00
Costs per unit:	Direct materials	4.00	5.00	10.00
	Direct labour	2.00	4.00	1.80
Overhead:	Variable	1.00	2.00	0.90
	Fixed	4.50	3.00	1.35
		11.50	14.00	14.05
Profit per unit		3.50	4.00	2.95

All three products use the same type of labour.

In a period in which labour is in short supply, the rank order of production is:

	Z1	Z2	Z3
A	First	Second	Third
B	Third	Second	First
C	Second	First	Third
D	First	Third	Second

(2 marks)

2. Z Ltd manufactures three products, the selling price and cost details of which are given below.

	Product X £	Product Y £	Product Z £
Selling price per unit	75	95	96
Costs per unit			
Direct materials (£5/kg)	10	5	15
Direct labour (£4/hour)	16	24	20
Variable overhead	8	12	10
Fixed overhead	24	36	30

In a period when direct materials are restricted in supply, the most and the least profitable uses of direct materials are

	Most profitable	Least profitable
A	Y	X
B	Y	Z
C	Z	X
D	Z	Y

(2 marks)

3. SW Ltd produces four products, A, B, C and D, and production capacity is limited. Product A has a C/S ratio of 27%, product B a C/S ratio of 22%, product C a C/S ratio of 19% and product D one of 11%.

Given unlimited demand for the four products, SW Ltd should concentrate on producing product A. *True or false?* (2 marks)

QUESTIONS

4 MNP plc produces three products from a single raw material that is limited in supply. Product details for period 6 are as follows.

	Product M	Product N	Product P
Maximum demand (units)	1,000	2,400	2,800
Optimum planned production	720	nil	2,800
Unit contribution	£4.50	£4.80	£2.95
Raw material cost per unit (£0.50 per kg)	£1.25	£1.50	£0.75

The planned production optimises the use of the 6,000 kgs of raw material that is available from MNP plc's normal supplier at the price of £0.50 kg. However, a new supplier has been found that is prepared to supply a further 1,000 kgs of the material.

Required

Calculate the maximum price that MNP plc should be prepared to pay for the additional 1,000 kgs of the material. **(3 marks)**

---

5 The following details relate to three services provided by JHN plc.

	Service J £	Service H £	Service N £
Fee charged to customers	84	122	145
Unit service costs:			
Direct materials	12	23	22
Direct labour	15	20	25
Variable overhead	12	16	20
Fixed overhead	20	42	40

All three services use the same type of direct labour which is paid £30 per hour.

The fixed overheads are general fixed overheads that have been absorbed on the basis of machine hours.

If direct labour is a scarce resource, the most and least profitable uses of it are

	Most profitable	Least profitable
A	H	J
B	H	N
C	N	J
D	N	H

(2 marks)

---

6 M Limited manufactures four products from different quantities of the same material which is in short supply. The following budgeted data relates to the products.

	Product M1 £/unit	Product M2 £/unit	Product M3 £/unit	Product M4 £/unit
Selling price	70	92	113	83
Materials (£4 per kg)	16	22	34	20
Conversion costs	39	52	57	43
	55	74	91	63
Profit	15	18	22	20
Machine time per unit in **minutes**	40	40	37.5	45

The conversion costs include general fixed costs that have been absorbed using a rate of £24 per machine hour.

The most profitable use of the raw materials is to make

A product M1
B product M2
C product M3
D product M4

(2 marks)

QUESTIONS

7 The following details relate to the four products made by EB Ltd.

	M £ per unit	V £ per unit	I £ per unit	F £ per unit
Selling price	17	22	10	38
Direct materials	3	12	1	20
Direct labour	4	1	2	2
Variable overhead	1	1	3	2
Fixed overhead	8	4	1	2
	16	18	7	26
Profit	1	4	3	12

All four products use the same labour and materials but in different quantities.

Complete the following.

In a period when the material used on these products is in short supply, the most profitable use of material is to make product ……......................, the least profitable is to make product …....................... . **(2 marks)**

---

8 J Ltd manufactures three products, the selling prices, maximum demand and cost details of which are as follows.

	X £	Y £	Z £
Unit selling price	150	190	190
Unit costs			
Direct materials (£10/kg)	20	10	30
Direct labour (£8/hr)	32	48	40
Variable overhead	16	24	20
Fixed overheads	48	72	60
Maximum demand	590	840	660

In the forthcoming period direct materials are restricted to 1,400 kgs and the company has contracted to supply 100 units of Z and 130 units of Y to a customer (included in the maximum demand figures above). What is the profit-maximising production plan?

A X 130 units;   Y 840 units;   Z 100 units
B X 280 units;   Y 840 units;   Z 0 units
C X 0 units;   Y 2 units;   Z 466 units
D X 1 unit;   Y 840 units;   Z 186 units   **(2 marks)**

---

9 *Choose the correct words from those highlighted in the statement below.*

The total costs of a company that has to subcontract work to make up a shortfall in its own in-house capabilities will be minimised if those units **made/bought** have the **lowest/highest** extra variable cost of **making/buying** per unit of scarce resource **used/saved**.   **(3 marks)**

(Total = 20 marks)

If you struggled with these OT questions, go back to your BPP Study Text for Paper P2 and revise Chapter 5 before you tackle the 10-mark and 25-mark questions on limiting factor analysis.

28 MN Ltd (IMPM, 5/03, amended) — 18 mins

The management team at MN Limited is considering the budgets it prepared for the year ending 31 December 20X3. It has now been revealed that in June 20X3 the company will be able to purchase only 10,000 litres of material Q (all other resources will be fully available). In the light of this new information, the management team wants to revise its plans for June to ensure that profits are maximised for that month.

MN Limited can produce three products from the same labour and main raw material Q, though different amounts are required for each product. The standard resource requirements, costs and selling prices, and the customer demand for delivery in June (including those orders already accepted) for each of its finished products are as follows.

	Product V	Product S	Product T
Resources per unit:			
Material Q	10 litres	8 litres	5 litres
Direct labour	8 hours	9 hours	6 hours
Selling prices and costs:	£ per unit	£ per unit	£ per unit
Selling price	145.00	134.00	99.00
Material Q	25.00	20.00	12.50
Other materials	10.00	4.00	8.50
Direct labour	40.00	45.00	30.00
Overheads:			
Variable	10.00	11.25	7.50
Fixed *	24.00	30.00	12.00
	109.00	110.25	70.50
Customer demand	1,100 units	950 units	1,450 units

* Based on budgeted costs of £95,000 per month

MN Limited has already accepted customer orders for delivery in June 20X3 as follows.

Product V	34 units
Product S	75 units
Product T	97 units

The management team has decided that these customer orders must be satisfied as the financial and non-financial penalties that would otherwise arise are very significant.

Given the shortage of material Q, the management team has now set the following stock levels for June.

	Opening stock	Closing stock
Material Q **	621 litres	225 litres
Product V	20 units	10 units
Product S	33 units	25 units
Product T	46 units	20 units

** This would mean that 10,396 litres of material Q would be available during the period.

Required

Prepare a production budget for June 20X3 that clearly shows the number of units of each product that should be produced to maximise the profits of MN Limited for June 20X3. **(10 marks)**

29 QP plc (11/05) — 45 mins

QP plc is a food processing company that produces pre-prepared meals for sale to consumers through a number of different supermarkets. The company specialises in three particular pre-prepared meals and has invested significantly in modern manufacturing processes to ensure a high quality product. The company is very aware of the importance of training and retaining high quality staff in all areas of the company and, in order to ensure their production employees' commitment to the company, the employees are guaranteed a weekly salary that is equivalent to their normal working hours paid at their normal hourly rate of £7 per hour.

The meals are produced in batches of 100 units. Costs and selling prices per batch are as follows.

QP plc has adopted throughput accounting for its short-term decisions.

Meal	TR £/batch	PN £/batch	BE £/batch
Selling price	340	450	270
Ingredient K (£5/kg)	150	120	90
Ingredient L (£10/kg)	70	90	40
Ingredient M (£15/kg)	30	75	45
Labour (£7/hour)	21	28	42
Factory costs absorbed	20	80	40

Required

(a) State the principles of throughput accounting and the effects of using it for short-term decision making.

(6 marks)

(b) QP plc is preparing its production plans for the next three months and has estimated the maximum demand from its customers to be as follows.

	Batches
TR	500
PN	400
BE	350

These demand maximums are amended figures because a customer has just delayed its request for a large order and QP plc has unusually got some spare capacity over the next three months. However, these demand maximums do include a contract for the delivery of 50 batches of each to an important customer. If this minimum contract is not satisfied then QP plc will have to pay a substantial financial penalty for non-delivery.

The production director is concerned at hearing news that two of the ingredients used are expected to be in short supply for the next three months. QP plc does not hold inventory of these ingredients and although there are no supply problems for ingredient K, the supplies of ingredients L and M are expected to be limited to.

	Kilos
Ingredient L	7,000
Ingredient M	3,000

The production director has researched the problem and found that ingredient V can be used as a direct substitute for ingredient M. It also costs the same as ingredient M. There is an unlimited supply of ingredient V.

Required

Prepare calculations to determine the production mix that will maximise the profit of QP plc during the next three months.

(10 marks)

(c) The World Health Organisation has now announced that ingredient V contains dangerously high levels of a chemical that can cause life-threatening illnesses. As a consequence it can no longer be used in the production of food.

As a result, the production director has determined the optimal solution to the company's production mix problem using linear programming. This is set out below.

Objective function value	110,714
TR value	500
PN value	357
BE value	71
TR slack value	0
PN slack value	43
BE slack value	279
L value	3
M value	28

Required

Explain the meaning of each of the values contained in the above solution. **(9 marks)**

(Total = 25 marks)

30 GHK plc (5/06)   45 mins

GHK manufactures four products from different combinations of the same direct materials and direct labour. An extract from the flexible budgets for next quarter for each of these products is as follows.

Product	G		H		J		K	
Units	3,000	5,000	3,000	5,000	3,000	5,000	3,000	5,000
	$'000	$'000	$'000	$'000	$'000	$'000	$'000	$'000
Revenue	30	50	60	100	45.0	75.0	90	150
Direct Material A (note 1)	9	15	12	20	4.5	7.5	18	30
Direct Material B (note 2)	6	10	6	10	13.5	22.5	36	60
Direct labour (note 3)	6	10	24	40	22.5	37.5	9	15
Overhead (note 4)	6	8	13	19	11.0	17.0	11	17

Notes

1 Material A was purchased some time ago at a cost of $5 per kg. There are 5,000 kgs in inventory. The costs shown in the flexible budget are based on this historical cost. The material is in regular use and currently has a replacement cost of $7 per kg.

2 Material B is purchased as required; its expected cost is $10 per kg. The costs shown in the flexible budget are based on this expected cost.

3 Direct labour costs are based on an hourly rate of $10 per hour. Employees work the number of hours necessary to meet production requirements.

4 Overhead costs of each product include a specific fixed cost of $1,000 per quarter which would be avoided if the product was to be discontinued. Other fixed overhead costs are apportioned between the products but are not affected by the mix of products manufactured.

QUESTIONS

GHK has been advised by the only supplier of material B that the quantity of material B that will be available during the next quarter will be limited to 5,000 kgs. Accordingly the company is being forced to reconsider its production plan for the next quarter. GHK has already entered into contracts to supply one of its major customers with the following:

    500 units of product G
  1,600 units of product H
    800 units of product J
    400 units of product K

Apart from this, the demand expected from other customers is expected to be

  3,600 units of product G
  3,000 units of product H
  3,000 units of product J
  4,000 units of product K

The major customer will not accept partial delivery of the contract and if the contract with this major customer is not completed in full, then GHK will have to pay a financial penalty of $5,000.

Required

(a) For each of the four products, calculate the relevant contribution per $ of material B for the next quarter.
(6 marks)

(b) It has been determined that the optimum production plan based on the data above is to produce 4,100 units of product G, 4600 units of product H, 800 units of product J, and 2,417 units of product K. Determine the amount of financial penalty at which GHK would be indifferent between meeting the contract or paying the penalty.
(5 marks)

(c) Calculate the relevant contribution to sales ratios for each of the four products. **(2 marks)**

(d) Assuming that the limiting factor restrictions no longer apply, prepare a sketch of a multi product profit volume chart by ranking the products according to your contribution to sales ratio calculations based on total market demand. Your sketch should plot the products using the highest contribution to sales ratio first.
(6 marks)

(e) Explain briefly, stating any relevant assumptions and limitations, how the multiproduct profit volume chart that you prepared in *(d)* above may be used by the manager of GHK to understand the relationships between costs, volume and profit within the business. **(6 marks)**

(Total = 25 marks)

31 Section A questions: Linear programming   36 mins

1   A company produces two types of orange juice, ordinary (X cartons per year) and premium (Y cartons per year).

Required

Determine the inequality that represents the fact that the amount of ordinary orange juice produced must be no more than twice the amount of premium orange juice produced. **(2 marks)**

2   In a linear programming problem, the constraints are $X \leq 41$ and $Y \geq 19$. Describe the feasible region, assuming where appropriate that the axes also constitute boundaries.

    A   A rectangle to the left of $X = 41$ and below $Y = 19$
    B   An infinite rectangle to the right of $X = 41$ and below $Y = 19$
    C   An infinite region above $Y = 19$ and to the right of $X = 41$
    D   An infinite rectangle to the left of $X = 41$ and above $Y = 19$ **(2 marks)**

3   In a linear programming problem the objective function is to maximise contribution given by 50X + 250Y.

    The feasible region has vertices (0, 160), (40, 140), (80, 120) and (140, 0).

    Write the answer.

    The vertex representing the optimal solution is .... **(2 marks)**

4   In a linear programming problem, contribution is 4X + 2Y and the vertices of the feasible region are P (0, 250), Q (50, 200) and R (100, 100). Which of the following statements is the full, correct statement about maximising contribution?

    A   Contribution is maximised at point P.
    B   Contribution is maximised at point Q.
    C   Contribution is maximised at point R.
    D   Contribution is maximised at point Q and R and all points on the straight line joining them. **(2 marks)**

5   A final simplex tableau has a top row with headings X, Y, a, b, c and Solution and a bottom row with values 0, 0, 5, 4, 0 and 17,000 corresponding to these headings. Which of the following is correct?

    A   In the solution given by this tableau, X = 5, Y = 4
    B   In the solution given by this tableau, X = Y = 0
    C   In the solution given by this tableau, a = 5
    D   The value of the objective function is 17,000 **(2 marks)**

6   Let X be the number of supervisors and Y be the number of other staff.

    Required

    Find the inequality to express the constraint that the number of supervisors must be no more than 20% of the total number of staff. **(2 marks)**

The following data relates to questions 31.7 and 31.8

PQ Ltd produces three products, A, B and C, from two processes. The slack/surplus variables for process 1 hours, process 2 hours and the maximum demand for product A are s4, s5 and s6 respectively.

The contribution per unit for each of the products is as follows:

A $400
B $200
C $100

The following linear programming solution has been determined in order to maximise contribution for the forthcoming period.

Simplex Tableau

	A	B	C	s4	s5	s6	Solution
B	0	1	0.83	0.33	0	−0.67	506.7
s5	0	0	0.33	−0.67	1	−1.67	586.7
A	1	0	0	0	0	1	200
Z	0	0	*	66.67	0	266.7	181333.3

*This box has been deliberately left blank.

QUESTIONS

7 If the company could increase production time in process 1 by 10 hours, the increase in total contribution would be nearest to

- A $700
- B $2,000
- C $2,700
- D $5,100

(2 marks)

8 If eight additional units of Product C were produced, the change in total contribution would be nearest to a

- A $500 decrease
- B $500 increase
- C $800 decrease
- D $800 increase

(2 marks)

9 The following final simplex tableau was obtained for a linear programming problem involving three variables (x, y, z) and three constraints (corresponding to slack variables a, b, c)

	x	y	z	a	b	c	Solution
X	1	0.75	0	1	0	-0.25	62.5
B	0	2.25	0	-1	1	0.25	17.5
Z	0	0.25	1	0	0	0.25	37.5
Solution	0	1.25	0	3	0	0.25	337.5

The values of x, y and z are quantities of output in kg per week of three different products.

If one more unit of the resource which is the subject of constraint c were to become available, which of the following would happen?

- A Output of x would fall by 0.25 kg and outputs of y and z would each rise by 0.25 kg.
- B Output of x would rise by 0.25 kg and output of y and x would each fall by 0.25 kg.
- C Output of x would fall by 0.25 kg, output of z would rise by 0.25 kg and an extra 0.25 units of the resource which is the subject of constraint b would go unused.
- D Output of x would fall by 0.25 kg, output of z would rise by 0.25 kg and an extra 0.25 units of the resource which is the subject of constraint b would be used.

(2 marks)

10 A spreadsheet package solution to a linear programming problem is shown below.

Objective function (c)   1,500,200

Variable	Value	Relative loss
A	72.00	0.00
B	29.00	0.00
C	0.00	120.00

Constraint	Slack/surplus	Worth
X	53.00	0.00
Y	3.00	0.00
Z	0.00	190.00

What products should be produced to maximise the objective function (c)?

- A 72 units of A and 29 units of B
- B 120 units of C
- C 190 units of Z
- D 53 units of X and 3 units of Y

(2 marks)

(Total = 20 marks)

QUESTIONS

> If you struggled with these OT questions, go back to your BPP Study Text for Paper P2 and revise Chapters 6 and 7 before you tackle the 10-mark and 25-mark questions on linear programming.

The following scenario relates to questions 32 and 33

A chemical manufacturer is developing three fertiliser compounds for the agricultural industry. The product codes for the three products are X1, X2 and X3 and the relevant information is summarised below.

	Chemical constituents: percentage make-up per tonne			
	Nitrate	Phosphate	Potash	Filler
X1	10	10	20	60
X2	10	20	10	60
X3	20	10	10	60

	Input prices per tonne
	£
Nitrate	150
Phosphate	60
Potash	120
Filler	10

	Maximum available input per month
	Tonnes
Nitrate	1,200
Phosphate	2,000
Potash	2,200
Filler	No limit

The fertilisers will be sold in bulk and managers have proposed the following prices per tonne.

X1	£83
X2	£81
X3	£81

The manufacturing costs of each type of fertiliser, excluding materials, are £11 per tonne.

32 Question with answer plan: Fertiliser I   18 mins

Formulate the above data into a linear programming model so that the company may maximise contribution.
Include slack variables.   (10 marks)

33 Fertiliser II   18 mins

Interpret the spreadsheet package output of the simplex solution given below.

Objective (Z)   284,000

Variable	Value	Relative loss
X1	4,000	0
X2	8,000	0
X3	0	22
Constraint	Slack/surplus	Worth
X4	0	170
X5	0	40
X6	600	0

(10 marks)

41

34 Staff uniforms (IMPM, 11/03) 45 mins

W plc provides two cleaning services for staff uniforms to hotels and similar businesses. One of the services is a laundry service and the other is a dry cleaning service. Both of the services use the same resources, but in different quantities. Details of the expected resource requirements, revenues and costs of each service are shown below.

		Laundry $ per service	Dry cleaning $ per service
Selling price		7.00	12.00
Cleaning materials	($10.00 per litre)	2.00	3.00
Direct labour	($6.00 per hour)	1.20	2.00
Variable machine cost	($3.00 per hour)	0.50	1.50
Fixed costs *		1.15	2.25
Profit		2.15	3.25

* The fixed costs per service were based on meeting the budget demand for December 20X3.

W plc has already prepared its budget for December based on sales and operational activities of 8,000 laundry services and 10,500 dry cleaning services, but it is now revising its plans because of forecast resource problems.

The maximum resources expected to be available in December 20X3 are

Cleaning materials	5,000 litres
Direct labour hours	6,000 hours
Machine hours	5,000 hours

W plc has one particular contract which it entered into six months ago with a local hotel to guarantee 1,200 laundry services and 2,000 dry cleaning services every month. If W plc does not honour this contract it has to pay substantial financial penalties to the local hotel.

Required

(a) Calculate the mix of services that should be provided by W plc so as to maximise its profit for December 20X3. **(9 marks)**

(b) The sales director has reviewed the selling prices being used by W plc and has provided the following further information.

- If the price for laundry were to be reduced to $5.60 per service, this would increase the demand to 14,000 services.

- If the price for dry cleaning were to be increased to $13.20 per service, this would reduce the demand to 9,975 services.

Required

Assuming that such selling price changes would apply to **all sales** and that the resource limitations continue to apply, and that a graphical linear programming solution is to be used to maximise profit:

(i) State the constraints and objective function. **(6 marks)**

(ii) Use a graphical linear programming solution to advise W plc whether it should revise its selling prices. **(10 marks)**

(Total = 25 marks)

35 MF plc (IMPM, 5/02, amended) — 45 mins

MF plc manufactures and sells two types of product to a number of customers. The company is currently preparing its budget for the year ending 31 December 20X3 which it divides into twelve equal periods.

The cost and resource details for each of the company's product types are as follows.

	Product type M £	Product type F £
Selling price per unit	200	210
Variable costs per unit		
Direct material P (£2.50 per litre)	20	25
Direct material Q (£4.00 per litre)	40	20
Direct labour (£7.00 per hour)	28	35
Overhead (£4.00 per hour)	16	20
Fixed production cost per unit	40	50
	Units	Units
Maximum sales demand in period 1	1,000	3,000

The fixed production cost per unit is based upon an absorption rate of £10 per direct labour hour and a total annual production activity of 180,000 direct labour hours. One-twelfth of the annual fixed production cost will be incurred in period 1.

In addition to the above costs, non-production overhead costs are expected to be £57,750 in period 1.

During period 1, the availability of material P is expected to be limited to 31,250 litres. Other materials and sufficient direct labour are expected to be available to meet demand.

It is MF plc's policy not to hold stocks of finished goods.

Required

(a) Calculate the number of units of product types M and F that should be produced and sold in period 1 in order to maximise profit. **(4 marks)**

(b) Using your answer to (a) above, prepare a columnar budgeted profit statement for period 1 in a marginal cost format. **(4 marks)**

(c) After presenting your statement to the budget management meeting, the production manager has advised you that in period 1 the other resources will also be limited. The maximum resources available will be:

Material P 31,250 litres
Material Q 20,000 litres
Direct labour 17,500 hours

It has been agreed that these factors should be incorporated into a revised plan and that the objective should be to make as much profit as possible from the available resources.

Required

Use graphical linear programming to determine the revised production plan for period 1. State clearly the number of units of product types M and F that are to be produced. **(9 marks)**

(d) Using your answer to part (c) above, calculate the profit that will be earned from the revised plan. **(3 marks)**

(e) Calculate and explain the meaning of the shadow price for material Q. **(5 marks)**

(Total = 25 marks)

36 Question with helping hand: Venture capital company (IDEC, 5/03)   45 mins

The management team of T Ltd, a small venture capital company, is planning its investment activities for the next five years. It has been approached by four start-up companies from the same industry sector which have presented their business plans for consideration. The forecast cash flows and resulting net present values (NPV) for each start-up company are as follows.

Company	Capital Year 0 $'000	Year 1 $'000	Year 2 $'000	Year 3 $'000	Year 4 $'000	Year 5 $'000	NPV $'000
A	(500)	(75)	(40)	50	400	650	60
B	(250)	(30)	(20)	(5)	250	247	0
C	(475)	(100)	(30)	(20)	400	750	77
D	(800)	(150)	(50)	50	900	786	80

The directors of T Ltd use a 12% cost of capital for appraising this type of investment.

You can assume that all investments are divisible and that they are not mutually exclusive.

Ignore tax and inflation.

Required

(a) Advise T Ltd which of the investments, if any, it should invest in. **(3 marks)**

(b) If capital for investment now is limited to $700,000 but T Ltd can raise further capital in one year's time and thereafter at a cost of 12% per annum.

 (i) Advise T Ltd how it should invest the $700,000. **(5 marks)**
 (ii) Discuss other factors which may affect the decision. **(4 marks)**

(c) T Ltd has now found out that funds will also be restricted in future years and that the constraints are absolute and cannot be removed by project generated incomes. The present values of cash that will be available for future investment are as follows.

	Present value $'000
Year 0	700
Year 1	80
Year 2	35

Required

Formulate the linear programming model that will maximise net present value and explain the meaning of each variable and the purpose of each constraint you have identified.

(You are not required to attempt a solution.) **(10 marks)**

(d) Briefly explain the benefits of using a linear programming format in this situation. **(3 marks)**

(Total = 25 marks)

QUESTIONS

> **Helping hand**
>
> - Look at the format required for the answer. Here you are advising T Ltd but no report/letter is required so straight forward short paragraphs and tables are fine.
>
> - Easy marks first – parts (a) and (d) can be answered straight away although the examiner prefers answers in sequence. So in your 20 minutes reading time, jot down prep answers for these two parts to use and answer (d) after (c) in the answer booklet.
>
> - Clearly this is a numerical question, with NPVs. What discount factor is to be used? Are there any tricky bits such as tax or uncertainty? Any sensitivity analysis? Check these off. No, but the question wants capital rationing). Answer part (b) separately.
>
> - Then onto part (c). The question asks for linear programming. Run through the stages in a linear programming formulation, from defining variables to objective function and constraints. If you have time, explain the meaning of the objective function and constraints – you will get marks but only on top of the actual calculation. So do that first.
>
> - Finally, copy your answer to part (d) into your answer booklet.
>
> Job done.

37 HT plc   45 mins

(a) HT plc produces and sells three products, HT01, HT02 and HT03.

The following details of prices and product costs have been extracted from HT plc's cost accounting records.

	HT01 £	HT02 £	HT03 £
Prices per unit	150	200	220
Costs per unit			
Direct labour at £4/hr	100	120	132
Direct material at £20/kg	20	40	40

Direct labour is regarded as a variable production cost.

A regression analysis had been carried out in order to estimate the relationship between overhead costs and production of the three products. Expressed in weekly terms the results of the analysis show the following.

$y = 4,000 + 0.5x_1 + 0.7x_2 + 0.8x_3$

where y   =   total overhead cost per week
       x_1 =   HT01, weekly direct labour hours
       x_2 =   HT02, weekly direct labour hours
       x_3 =   HT03, weekly direct labour hours

The company operates a 46-week year.

Required

Compute the total variable product costs for each of HT01, HT02 and HT03.   **(5 marks)**

(b) The material used by HT plc is also used in a wide variety of other applications and is in relatively limited supply. As business conditions improve in general, there will be pressure for the price of this material to rise, but strong competition in HT plc's sector of the market would make it unlikely that increased material costs can be passed on to customers in higher product prices. The position on material supplies is that HT plc can obtain 20,000 kgs at current prices.

QUESTIONS

In addition, reductions in the skilled labour force made during a recession mean that the number of available direct labour hours is estimated at no more than 257,600 hours for the next year.

Demand for each product over the year is forecast to be as follows.

HT01   16,000 units
HT02   10,000 units
HT03   6,000 units

Required

Formulate a linear programme from the above data in order to obtain the annual production/sales plan which will maximise HT plc's contribution earnings and profit. (You are not required to solve the problem.)

(12 marks)

(c)   The following is the final tableau, obtained as a result of running the linear programme.

Final tableau

HT01	HT02	HT03	S_1	S_2	S_3	S_4	S_5	Bij
0.0	0.0	1.0	0.0	0.0	0.0	0.0	1.0	6,000.0
1.0	1.2	1.3	0.0	0.0	0.0	0.0	0.0	10,304.0
0.0	−1.2	−1.3	−0.0	0.0	1.0	0.0	0.0	5,696.0
0.0	1.0	0.0	0.0	0.0	0.0	1.0	0.0	10,000.0
0.0	0.8	1.7	−0.0	1.0	0.0	0.0	0.0	9,696.0
0.0	2.0	1.5	0.7	0.0	0.0	0.0	0.0	180,320.0

where S_1, S_2, S_3, S_4, S_5 are the slack variables for labour, materials, HT01, HT02 and HT03 respectively.

Required

Provide as complete an interpretation of the final tableau as you can and give an estimate of the final net profit figure. **(8 marks)**

(Total = 25 marks)

38 Section A questions: Pricing   36 mins

1   Off-peak travel bargains are an example of differential pricing using which base?

     A   Time
     B   Market segment
     C   Product version
     D   Place   **(2 marks)**

2   Which of the following statements are incorrect?

     I   If there are no scarce resources and a company has spare capacity, the minimum price of a product is the full cost of making it.

     II   If there are scarce resources and a company makes more than one product, the minimum price of a product is the incremental cost of making it.

     III   Minimum prices are often charged in practice.

     IV   The minimum price simply has to cover the incremental costs of producing and selling an item.

     A   None of the above
     B   III only
     C   II and IV
     D   All of the above   **(2 marks)**

3   What type of market condition involves a large number of suppliers offering similar but not identical products?

    A   Perfect competition
    B   Monopoly
    C   Monopolistic competition
    D   Oligopoly   (2 marks)

4   Indicate on the answer paper which of the following conditions must hold if price discrimination is to be effective.

    A   There must be little or no chance of a black market developing.

    B   There must be little or no chance that competitors can and will undercut the firm's prices in the lower-priced market segments.

    C   Each of the sectors of the market must show similar intensities of demand.

    D   The cost of segmentation and administration should exceed the extra revenue derived from the price discrimination strategy.   (2 marks)

5   *Choose the correct word from those highlighted.*

    A market penetration pricing policy is appropriate when demand is **highly elastic/inelastic**.   (2 marks)

6   Which of the following are advantages of marginal cost plus pricing?

    I   It is simple and easy to use.
    II   The mark-up can be varied.
    III It pays attention to profit maximisation.
    IV   It ignores fixed overheads in the pricing decision.

    A   I only
    B   II and III
    C   II, III and IV
    D   I and II   (2 marks)

7   Market research by Company A has revealed that the maximum demand for product R is 50,000 units each year, and that demand will reduce by 50 units for every £1 that the selling price is increased. Based on this information, Company A has calculated that the profit-maximising level of sales for product R for the coming year is 35,000 units.

    Required

    Calculate the price at which these units will be sold.   (2 marks)

The following data relates to questions 38.8 and 38.9

RJD Ltd makes and sells a single product, Z. The selling price and marginal revenue equations for product Z are as follows:

Selling price   =   £50 – £0.001x
Marginal revenue   =   £50 – £0.002x

The variable costs are £20 per unit and the fixed costs are £100,000.

8   Calculate what the selling price should be in order to maximise profit.   (3 marks)

9   If the selling price was set to maximise **revenue**, calculate the resulting profit.   (3 marks)

                                                                                        (Total = 20 marks)

QUESTIONS

> If you struggled with these OT questions, go back to your BPP Study Text for Paper P2 and revise Chapters 8-9 before you tackle the 10-mark and 25-mark questions on pricing.

39 Elasticity *18 mins*

XYZ is the only manufacturer of a product called the X. The variable cost of producing an X is £1.50 at all levels of output.

During recent months the X has been sold at a unit price of around £6.25. Various small adjustments (up and down) have been made to this price in an attempt to find a profit-maximising selling price.

XYZ's commercial manager (an economics graduate) has recently commissioned a study by a firm of marketing consultants 'to investigate the demand structure for Xs and in particular to calculate the elasticity of demand for Xs produced by XYZ'.

(*Note.* The elasticity of demand for a product is the proportion by which demand changes divided by the proportional price change which causes it.)

The consultants have reported back that at a unit price of £10 there is no demand for Xs but that demand increases by 40 Xs for each 1p that the unit price is reduced below £10. They have also reported that 'when demand is at around half its theoretical maximum the elasticity of demand is approximately 1'.

Upon receiving this report the commercial manager makes the following statement.

'Recent experiences gained in adjusting the unit selling price of the X suggest that the product has quite an elastic demand structure. Small changes in the unit selling price produce far larger proportionate increases in demand. I find it difficult to accept that the elasticity of demand for the X is 1.'

Required

Write a memorandum to the commercial manager reconciling the consultants' report with his own observations on the elasticity of demand for the X. **(10 marks)**

The following scenario relates to questions 40 and 41

Just over two years ago, R Ltd was the first company to produce a specific 'off-the-shelf' accounting software packages. The pricing strategy, decided on by the managing director, for the packages was to add a 50% mark-up to the budgeted full cost of the packages. The company achieved and maintained a significant market share and high profits for the first two years.

Budgeted information for the current year (Year 3) was as follows.

Production and sales	15,000 packages
Full cost	£400 per package

At a recent board meeting, the finance director reported that although costs were in line with the budget for the current year, profits were declining. He explained that the full cost included £80 for fixed overheads. This figure had been calculated by using an overhead absorption rate based on labour hours and the budgeted level of production which, he pointed out, was much lower than the current capacity of 25,000 packages.

The marketing director stated that competitors were beginning to increase their market share. He also reported the results of a recent competitor analysis which showed that when R Ltd announced its prices for the current year, the competitors responded by undercutting them by 15%. Consequently, he commissioned an investigation of the market. He informed the board that the market research showed that at a price of £750 there would be no demand for the packages but for every £10 reduction in price the demand would increase by 1,000 packages.

The managing director appeared to be unconcerned about the loss of market share and argued that profits could be restored to their former level by increasing the mark-up.

Note. If price $= a - bx$
then marginal revenue $= a - 2bx$

40 Question with answer plan: Off-the-shelf I (IDEC, 5/03, amended) 18 mins

Discuss the managing director's pricing strategy in the circumstances described above. Your appraisal must include a discussion of the alternative strategies that could have been implemented at the launch of the packages.

(10 marks)

41 Off-the-shelf II (IDEC, 5/03, amended) 18 mins

(a) Based on the data supplied by the market research, calculate the maximum annual profit that can be earned from the sale of the packages from year 3 onwards. (4 marks)

(b) A German computer software distribution company, L, which is interested in becoming the sole distributor of the accounting software packages, has now approached R Ltd. It has offered to purchase 25,000 accounting packages per annum at a fixed price of €930 per package. If R Ltd were to sell the packages to L, then the variable costs would be £300 per package.

The current exchange rate is €1 = £0·60.

Required

Draw a diagram to illustrate the sensitivity of the proposal from the German company to changes in the exchange rate and then state and comment on the minimum exchange rate needed for the proposal to be worthwhile. (6 marks)

(Total = 10 marks)

42 W (11/06) 18 mins

W has recently completed the development and testing of a new product which has cost $400,000. It has also bought a machine to produce the new product costing $150,000. The production machine is capable of producing 1,000 units of the product per month and is not expected to have a residual value due to its specialised nature.

The company has decided that the unit selling prices it will charge will change with the cumulative numbers of units sold as follows.

Cumulative sales units	Selling price $ per unit in this band
0 to 2,000	100
2,001 to 7,000	80
7,001 to 14,500	70
14,501 to 54,500	60
54,501 and above	40

QUESTIONS

Based on these selling prices, it is expected that sales demand will be as shown below.

Months	Sales demand per month (units)
1 - 10	200
11 - 20	500
21 - 30	750
31 - 70	1,000
71 – 80	800
81 - 90	600
91 – 100	400
101 – 110	200
Thereafter	NIL

Unit variable costs are expected to be as follows.

	$ per unit
First 2,000 units	50
Next 12,500 units	40
Next 20,000 units	30
Next 20,000 units	25
Thereafter	30

W operates a Just in Time (JIT) purchasing and production system and operates its business on a cash basis.

A columnar cash flow statement showing the cumulative cash flow of the product after its Introduction and Growth stages has already been completed and this is set out below.

	Introduction	Growth	
Months	1-10	11-30	
Number of units produced and sold	2,000	5,000	7,500
Selling price per unit	$100	$80	$70
Unit variable cost	$50	$40	$40
Unit contribution	$50	$40	$30
Total contribution	$100,000	$425,000	
Cumulative cash flow	($450,000)	($25,000)	

Required

(a) Complete the cash flow statement for each of the remaining two stages of the product's life cycle. **Do not copy the Introduction and Growth stages in your answer.** Ignore the time value of money. **(5 marks)**

(b) Explain, using your answer to (a) above and the data provided, the possible reasons for the changes in costs and selling prices during the life cycle of the product. **(5 marks)**

(Total = 10 marks)

43 C1, C2, C3 (IDEC, 11/02, amended)   45 mins

X Ltd manufactures and distributes three types of car (the C1, C2 and C3). Each type of car has its own production line. The company is worried by the extremely difficult market conditions and forecasts losses for the forthcoming year.

Current operations

The budgeted details for the next year are as follows.

	C1	C2	C3
	£	£	£
Direct materials	2,520	2,924	3,960
Direct labour	1,120	1,292	1,980
Total direct cost per car	3,640	4,216	5,940
Budgeted production (cars)	75,000	75,000	75,000
Number of production runs	1,000	1,000	1,500
Number of orders executed	4,000	5,000	5,600
Machine hours	1,080,000	1,800,000	1,680,000

Annual overheads

	Fixed	Variable
	£'000	£
Set ups	42,660	13,000 per production run
Materials handling	52,890	4,000 per order executed
Inspection	59,880	18,000 per production run
Machining	144,540	40 per machine hour
Distribution and warehousing	42,900	3,000 per order executed

Proposed JIT system

Management has hired a consultant to advise them on how to reduce costs. The consultant has suggested that the company adopts a just-in-time (JIT) manufacturing system. The introduction of the JIT system would have the following impact on costs (fixed and variable):

Direct labour	Increase by 20%
Set ups	Decrease by 30%
Materials handling	Decrease by 30%
Inspection	Decrease by 30%
Machining	Decrease by 15%
Distribution and warehousing	Eliminated

Required

(a) Based on the budgeted production levels, calculate the total annual savings that would be achieved by introducing the JIT system. **(6 marks)**

(b) The following table shows the price/demand relationship for each type of car per annum.

C1		C2		C3	
Price	Demand	Price	Demand	Price	Demand
£		£		£	
5,000	75,000	5,750	75,000	6,500	75,000
5,750	65,000	6,250	60,000	6,750	60,000
6,000	50,000	6,500	45,000	7,750	45,000
6,500	35,000	7,500	35,000	8,000	30,000

Required

Assuming that X Ltd adopts the JIT system and that the revised variable overhead cost per car remains constant (as per the proposed JIT system budget), calculate the profit-maximising price and output level for each type of car. **(12 marks)**

(c) Write a report to the management of X Ltd which explains the conditions that are necessary for the successful implementation of a JIT manufacturing system. **(7 marks)**

(Total = 25 marks)

QUESTIONS

44 Mobile telephones (IDEC, 5/01, amended)   45 mins

VI plc produces a number of mobile telephone products. It is an established company with a good reputation that has been built on well-engineered, reliable and good quality products. It is currently developing a product called Computel and has spent £1.5 million on development so far. It now has to decide whether it should proceed further and launch the product in one year's time.

If VI plc decides to continue with the project, it will incur further development costs of £0.75 million straight away. Assets worth £3.5 million will be required immediately prior to the product launch, and working capital of £1.5 million would be required. VI plc expects that it could sell Computel for three years before the product becomes out of date.

It is estimated that the first 500 Computels produced and sold would cost an average of £675 each unit, for production, marketing and distribution costs. The fixed costs associated with the project are expected to amount to £2.4 million (cash out flow) for each year the product is in production.

Because of the cost estimates, the chief executive expected the selling price to be in the region of £950. However, the marketing director is against this pricing strategy; he says that this price is far too high for this type of product and that he could only sell 6,000 units in each year at this price. He suggests a different strategy: setting a price of £425, at which price he expects sales to be 15,000 units each year.

VI plc has found from past experience that a 70% experience curve applies to production, marketing and distribution costs. The company's cost of capital is 7% a year.

Required

(a) The chief executive has asked you to help sort out the pricing dilemma. Prepare calculations that demonstrate the following:

    (i) Which of the two suggestions is the better pricing strategy
    (ii) The financial viability of the better strategy   **(15 marks)**

(b) Discuss other issues that VI plc should consider in relation to the two pricing strategies.   **(5 marks)**

(c) Calculate and comment on the sensitivity of the financially better pricing strategy to changes in the selling price.   **(5 marks)**

Note. The value of b in the learning curve formula is –0.515 when the rate of learning is 70%.

    (Total = 25 marks)

45 Q Organisation (5/05)   45 mins

(a) The Q organisation is a large, worldwide respected manufacturer of consumer electrical and electronic goods. Q constantly develops new products that are in high demand as they represent the latest technology and are 'must haves' for those consumers that want to own the latest consumer gadgets. Recently Q has developed a new handheld digital DVD recorder and seeks your advice as to the price it should charge for such a technologically advanced product.

Required

Explain the relevance of the product life cycle to the consideration of alternative pricing policies that might be adopted by Q.   **(10 marks)**

(b) Market research has discovered that the price demand relationship for the item during the initial launch phase will be as follows:

Price	Demand
£	Units
100	10,000
80	20,000
69	30,000
62	40,000

Production of the DVD recorder would occur in batches of 10,000 units, and the production director believes that 50% of the variable manufacturing cost would be affected by a learning and experience curve. This would apply to each batch produced and continue at a constant rate of learning up to a production volume of 40,000 units when the learning would be complete.

Thereafter, the unit variable manufacturing cost of the product would be equal to the unit cost of the fourth batch. The production director estimates that the unit variable manufacturing cost of the first batch would be £60 (£30 of which is subject to the effect of the learning and experience curve, and £30 of which is unaffected), whereas the average unit variable manufacturing cost of all four batches would be £52.71.

There are no non-manufacturing variable costs associated with the DVD recorder.

Required

(i) Calculate the rate of learning that is expected by the production director. **(4 marks)**

(ii) Calculate the optimum price at which Q should sell the DVD recorder in order to maximise its profits during the initial launch phase of the product. **(8 marks)**

(iii) Q expects that after the initial launch phase the market price will be £57 per unit. Estimated product specific fixed costs during this phase of the product's life are expected to be £15,000 per month. During this phase of the product life cycle Q wishes to achieve a target monthly profit from the product of £30,000.

Calculate the number of units that need to be sold each month during this phase in order that Q achieves this target monthly profit. **(3 marks)**

(Total = 25 marks)

45 Question with analysis: Q Organisation (5/05)   45 mins

(a) The Q organisation is a large, worldwide respected manufacturer of consumer electrical and electronic goods. Q constantly develops new products that are in high demand as they represent the latest technology and are 'must haves' for those consumers that want to own the latest consumer gadgets. Recently Q has developed a new handheld digital DVD recorder and seeks your advice as to the price it should charge for such a technologically advanced product.

Required

Explain the relevance of the product life cycle to the consideration of **alternative pricing policies** that might be adopted by Q. **(10 marks)**

[Annotation: Think about the stages of the product life cycle and appropriate pricing policies for each]

(b) Market research has discovered that the price demand relationship for the item during the initial launch phase will be as follows:

Price	Demand
£	Units
100	10,000
80	20,000
69	30,000
62	40,000

Production of the DVD recorder would occur in **batches of 10,000 units**, and the production director believes that **50%** of the variable manufacturing cost would be affected by a **learning and experience curve**. This would apply to each batch produced and continue at a constant rate of learning up to a production volume of **40,000 units** when the learning would be complete.

[Annotation: Learning curve]

QUESTIONS

Thereafter, the unit variable manufacturing cost of the product would be equal to the unit cost of the fourth batch. The production director estimates that the **unit variable manufacturing cost of the first batch would be £60 (£30 of which is subject to the effect of the learning and experience curve, and £30 of which is unaffected)**, whereas the **average unit variable manufacturing cost of all four batches would be £52.71**.

There are no non-manufacturing variable costs associated with the DVD recorder.

Required

(i) Calculate the rate of learning that is expected by the production director. **(4 marks)**

(ii) Calculate the optimum price at which Q should sell the DVD recorder in order to maximise its profits during the **initial launch phase** of the product. **(8 marks)**

> Note initial launch phase and after initial launch phase

(iii) Q expects that **after the initial launch phase** the market price will be £57 per unit. Estimated product specific fixed costs during this phase of the product's life are expected to be £15,000 per month. During this phase of the product life cycle Q wishes to achieve a **target monthly profit** from the product of **£30,000**.

Calculate the number of units that need to be sold each month during this phase in order that Q achieves this target monthly profit. **(3 marks)**

(Total = 25 marks)

46 TQ (Pilot paper) — 45 mins

(a) TQ manufactures and retails second generation mobile (cell) phones. The following details relate to one model of phone:

	$/unit
Budgeted selling price	60
Budgeted variable cost	25
Budgeted fixed cost	10

Period	1	2	3
Budgeted production and sales (units)	520	590	660
Fixed overhead volume variance	$1,200 (A)	$1,900 (A)	$2,600 (A)

There was no change in the level of stock during any of periods 1 to 3.

The Board of Directors had expected sales to keep on growing but, instead, they appeared to have stabilised. This has led to the adverse fixed overhead volume variances. It is now the start of period 4 and the Board of Directors is concerned at the large variances that have occurred during the first three periods of the year. The Sales and Marketing Director has confirmed that the past trend of sales is likely to continue unless changes are made to the selling price of the product. Further analysis of the market for the mobile phone suggests that demand would be zero if the selling price was raised to $100 or more.

Required

(i) Calculate the price that TQ should have charged for the phone assuming that it wished to maximise the contribution from this product.

Note. If price = a – bx
then marginal revenue = a – 2bx **(7 marks)**

(ii) Calculate the difference between the contribution that would have been earned at the optimal price and the actual contribution earned during period 3, assuming the variable cost per unit were as budgeted. **(3 marks)**

(b) TQ is currently developing a third generation mobile phone. It is a 'state of the art' new handheld device that acts as a mobile phone, personal assistant, digital camera (pictures and video), and music player. The Board of Directors seeks your advice as to the pricing strategy that it should adopt for such a product.

The company has incurred a significant level of development costs and recognises that the technology for these products is advancing rapidly and that the life cycle for the product is relatively short.

Required

Prepare a report, addressed to the Board of Directors, that discusses the alternative pricing strategies available to TQ. **(15 marks)**

(Total = 25 marks)

47 Question with answer plan: AVX plc (5/06) 45 mins

AVX plc assembles circuit boards for use by high technology audio video companies. Due to the rapidly advancing technology in this field, AVX Plc is constantly being challenged to learn new techniques.

AVX plc uses standard costing to control its costs against targets set by senior managers. The standard labour cost per batch of one particular type of circuit board (CB45) is set out below:

	£
Direct labour – 50 hours @ £10 /hour	500

The following labour efficiency variances arose during the first six months of the assembly of CB45:

Month	Number of batches assembled and sold	Labour Efficiency Variance £
November	1	Nil
December	1	170.00 Favourable
January	2	452.20 Favourable
February	4	1,089.30 Favourable
March	8	1,711.50 Favourable
April	16	3,423.00 Favourable

An investigation has confirmed that all of the costs were as expected except that there was a learning effect in respect of the direct labour that had not been anticipated when the standard cost was set.

Required

(a) (i) Calculate the monthly rates of learning that applied during the six months;

(ii) Identify when the learning period ended and briefly discuss the implications of your findings for AVX plc. **(10 marks)**

AVX plc initially priced each batch of CB45 circuit boards on the basis of its standard cost of £960 plus a mark up of 25%. Recently the company has noticed that, due to increasing competition, it is having difficulty maintaining its sales volume at this price.

The finance director has agreed that the long run unit variable cost of the CB45 circuit board is £672·72 per batch. She has suggested that the price charged should be based on an analysis of market demand. She has discovered that at a price of £1,200 the demand is 16 batches per month, for every £20 reduction in selling price there is an increase in demand of 1 batch of CB45 circuit boards, and for every £20 increase in selling price there is a reduction in demand of 1 batch.

Required

(b) Calculate the profit maximising selling price per batch using the data supplied by the Finance Director

Note. If Price (P) = a–bx then marginal revenue (MR) = a–2bx **(8 marks)**

The technical director cannot understand why there is a need to change the selling price. He argues that this is a highly advanced technological product and that AVX Plc should not reduce its price as this reflects badly on the company. If anything is at fault, he argues, it is the use of standard costing and he has asked whether target costing should be used instead.

QUESTIONS

Required

(c) (i) Explain the difference between standard costs and target costs;

    (ii) Explain the possible reasons why AVX plc needs to re-consider its pricing policy now that the CB45 circuit board has been available in the market for six months. **(7 marks)**

(Total = 25 marks)

QUESTIONS

> **FINANCIAL INFORMATION FOR LONG-TERM DECISION MAKING**
>
> Questions 48 to 75 cover financial information for long-term decision making, the subject of Part D of the BPP Study Text for Paper P2.

48 Section A questions: Basic principles of investment decision making
36 mins

1   B Ltd has identified two mutually exclusive projects which have an equivalent effect on the risk profile of the company. Project 1 has a payback period of 3.7 years, an NPV of £16,100, an internal rate of return of 15% and an average accounting rate of return of 16%. Project 2 has a payback period of 4.7 years, an NPV of £14,900, an internal rate of return of 19% and an average accounting rate of return of 17%. The cost of capital is 10%. Assuming that the directors wish to maximise shareholder wealth and no shortage of capital is expected, which project should the company choose?

    A   Project 1 because it has the shorter payback period
    B   Project 1 because it has the higher net present value
    C   Project 2 because it has the higher internal rate of return
    D   Project 2 because it has the higher accounting rate of return   **(2 marks)**

2   Indicate whether or not the methods of investment appraisal listed below are based on accounting profits.

    A   NPV
    B   IRR
    C   Payback
    D   ARR   **(3 marks)**

3   A project has a cash outflow of £7,000 at time 0 and cash inflows of £5,000 at time 1, £800 at time 2 and £2,700 at time 3.

    Required

    If the cost of capital is 15% per annum, calculate the net present value of the project.   **(3 marks)**

4   Indicate by writing true or false, whether or not the following statements about the DCF approach to investment appraisal are true.

    A   The method takes account of all cash flows relating to the project.
    B   It allows for the timing of the cash flows.
    C   There are universally-accepted methods of calculating the NPV and the IRR.
    D   It is the method favoured by the majority of companies.   **(2 marks)**

5   Indicate whether, in a comparison of the NPV and IRR techniques, the following statements are true or false.

    A   Both methods give the same accept or reject decision, regardless of the pattern of the cash flows.
    B   IRR is technically superior to NPV and easier to calculate.
    C   The NPV approach is superior if discount rates are expected to vary over the life of the project.
    D   NPV and accounting ROCE can be confused.   **(3 marks)**

6   What is the present value of £5,000 in perpetuity at a discount rate of 10%?

    A   £500
    B   £5,500
    C   £4,545
    D   £50,000   **(2 marks)**

57

QUESTIONS

7   What are the disadvantages of the payback method of investment appraisal?

    I   It tends to maximise financial and business risk.
    II   It is a fairly complex technique and not easy to understand.
    III   It cannot be used when there is a capital rationing situation.

    A   None of the above
    B   All of the above
    C   I only
    D   II and III   (2 marks)

8   An investment of £200,000 is required at the commencement of project X and £35,000 at the end of years 1 to 4. What is the net present value of the costs of project X if the cost of capital is 10%?   (3 marks)

(Total = 20 marks)

> If you struggled with these OT questions, go back to your BPP Study Text for Paper P2 and revise Chapters 10 and 11 before you tackle the 10-mark and 25-mark questions on the basic principles of investment decision making.

The following scenario relates to questions 49 and 50

P, a multinational organisation, is currently appraising a major capital investment project which will revolutionise its business. The investment involves the installation of a new intranet. *[An intranet is a private Internet reserved for use by employees and/or customers who have been given the authority and passwords necessary to use that network. It is a private network environment built around Internet technologies and standards.]*

You have recently been appointed as the management accountant for this project and have been charged with the responsibility of preparing the financial evaluation of the proposed investment. You have carried out some initial investigations and find that that management currently uses a target accounting rate of return of 25% and a target payback period of 4 years as the criteria for the acceptance or rejection of major capital investments.

You propose to use the net present value method of project appraisal and, having carried out some further investigations, you ascertain the following information for the project.

	£'000
Initial outlay	2,000
Cash savings	
Years 1 to 3	400 per annum
Years 4 to 5	500 per annum
Years 6 to 8	450 per annum
Years 9 to 10	400 per annum

At the end of the project's life, no residual value is expected for the project.

The company' cost of capital is 15% per annum. All cash savings are assumed to occur at the end of each year.

Ignore taxation and inflation.

QUESTIONS

49 Intranet I (IDEC, 11/02, amended)   18 mins

As management accountant for this project:

Write a report to the management of P which incorporates the following.

(a) A full analysis and evaluation of **either** of the existing methods of project appraisal

(b) A recommendation on a purely financial basis as to whether or not the project should be undertaken

(c) A discussion of the difficulties associated with the net present value method when appraising this type of investment   **(10 marks)**

50 Intranet II (IDEC, 11/02, amended)   18 mins

Describe how you would undertake a post-completion appraisal for this project and discuss the benefits and drawbacks which the management of P might expect when undertaking such an exercise.   **(10 marks)**

51 JLX plc (IDEC, 5/01, amended)   18 mins

JLX plc is a well-established manufacturing organisation that has recently expanded rapidly, by a series of acquisitions, in a period of favourable trading conditions. The need to integrate the management information and control systems of the rapidly expanding group has imposed a very large workload on the managerial and accounting teams. Consequently, some of the normal procedures at JLX plc have been neglected.

The company uses net present value (NPV) to assess and select investment projects. It used to be standard practice to assess and review all projects after implementation by a post-completion appraisal (PCA). However, PCA has been one area that has been neglected because of the increased workloads, and recently PCA has been applied only to those projects which have been considered unsuccessful.

PR035 is a major project recently implemented by division X. This project was controversial because of its large capital requirement and high risk level. The group finance director has stated that his department is now considerably under-staffed and that he requires more resources to operate effectively. In particular, he is using the need to carry out a PCA on PR035 as a lever to gain more funds. He as told the group chief executive that he thinks that PR035 should be subjected to a PCA as he considers that it should be generating a greater return given the continuing favourable trading conditions.

The group chief executive has responded to this by saying that he feels that a PCA for PR035 is unnecessary as it is generating the predicted net cash flow.

Required

(a) Evaluate whether it is advisable for JLX plc to carry out PCAs.   **(6 marks)**

(b) Discuss whether a PCA should be carried out on PR035, a project that appears to be performing satisfactorily.   **(4 marks)**

(Total = 10 marks)

(Total = 25 marks)

52 HPC Ltd   45 mins

HPC Ltd has constructed a collection platform at an oil and gas field known as Gibson 6. This field holds reserves of oil and gas, both of which may be extracted and carried to an onshore terminal along the same pipeline. Gas collected at the platform is converted into liquid petroleum gas (LPG) for transport.

Oil and LPG received at the terminal are processed and transported 300 miles by rail to refineries. Details of annual capacities are as follows.

(a) **Pipeline capacity**

If the pipeline is used exclusively to transport oil, then a maximum of 100,000 barrels of oil can be transported. 1.4 barrels of LPG can be transported in place of each barrel of oil.

(b) **Processing capacity**

If processing facilities are used exclusively to process oil, then a maximum of 150,000 barrels of oil can be processed. 0.5333 barrels of LPG can be processed instead of each 1 barrel of oil up to a maximum of 70,000 barrels of LPG. No more than 70,000 barrels of LPG can be processed.

(c) **Rail transport capacity**

If rail transport capacity is used exclusively to transport oil, then a maximum of 120,000 barrels of oil can be transported. 1 barrel of LPG can be transported, using specialised wagons, instead of each 1 barrel of oil, up to a maximum of 20,000 barrels of LPG. Transporting amounts of LPG in excess of 20,000 barrels involves transporting 0.65 barrels of LPG instead of each 1 barrel of oil, using general-purpose wagons.

The initial capital cost of developing extraction capabilities is £40,000 per 1,000 barrels of oil per year and £60,000 per 1,000 barrels of LPG per year. Once developed, an extraction capability can be operated for at least 10 years. Contribution generated by the two products is £8 per barrel for oil and £11.50 per barrel for LPG. HPC evaluates projects using a 12% per annum discount rate and a 10-year time horizon.

Required

(a) Using linear programming identify the annual output combination of oil and LPG at which net present value is maximised. **(15 marks)**

(b) State whether or not HPC should invest in a new pump to increase the capacity of the Gibson 6 pipeline by 10%. The pump costs £50,000. Support your answer with relevant calculations. **(10 marks)**

(Total = 25 marks)

53 Multiple choice questions: Further aspects of investment decision making   36 mins

1   A Ltd can invest in three out of the following four projects. The company's cost of capital is 8%.

Project	1	2	3	4
Investment (£)	66,000	72,000	60,000	43,000
Life (years)	3	6	8	4
Annual receipts (£)	31,000	20,000	16,000	17,000

Which project should be rejected? Show your workings.   **(4 marks)**

QUESTIONS

2   L Ltd is considering a project. The present value of the initial investment of the project is £714,000, the present value of the project's variable costs is £290,000, the present value of its cash inflows is £1,250,000 and the present value of its net cash flows is £246,000.

Required

Calculate the change required in the value of the initial investment to make L Ltd indifferent between accepting and rejecting the project. (3 marks)

3   B plc has purchased equipment which has the following costs and disposal values over its four-year life. The initial cost is £28,000. B plc's cost of capital is 8%.

Year	1	2	3	4
Operating costs (£)	(12,000)	(14,000)	(15,000)	(17,000)
Year-end disposal value (£)	20,000	18,000	12,000	6,000

How frequently should the equipment be replaced? (4 marks)

4   R Ltd is considering a project. The present value of the initial investment of the project is £32,000, the present value of the project's variable costs is £27,000, the present value of its cash inflows is £130,000 and the present value of its net cash flows is £71,000. The cost of capital is 10%. The project's IRR is 17%.

The change required in the cost of capital to make R Ltd indifferent between accepting and rejecting the project is 17%. *True or false?* (3 marks)

5   A company is evaluating a new product proposal. The proposed product selling price is £180 per unit and the variable costs are £60 per unit. The incremental cash fixed costs for the product will be £160,000 per annum. The discounted cash flow calculation results in a positive NPV.

		Cash flow £	Discount rate factor	Present value £
Year 0	Initial outlay	(1,000,000)	1.000	(1,000,000)
Year 1-5	Annual cash flow	320,000	3.791	1,213,120
Year 5	Working capital released	50,000	0.621	31,050
	Net present value			244,170

What percentage change in selling price would result in the project having a net present value of zero?

A   6.7 per cent
B   7.5 per cent
C   8.9 per cent
D   9.6 per cent (2 marks)

6   R Ltd is deciding whether to launch a new product. The initial outlay for the product is £20,000. The forecast possible annual cash inflows and their associated probabilities are shown below.

	Probability	Year 1 £	Year 2 £	Year 3 £
Optimistic	0.20	10,000	12,000	9,000
Most likely	0.50	7,000	8,000	7,600
Pessimistic	0.30	6,400	7,200	6,200

The company's cost of capital is 10% per annum.

Assume the cash inflows are received at the end of the year and that the cash inflows for each year are independent.

Required

Calculate the expected net present value for the product. (4 marks)

(Total = 20 marks)

54 Capital rationing 18 mins

(a) Define the term 'profitability index' and briefly explain how it may be used when a company faces a problem of capital rationing in any single accounting period. **(5 marks)**

(b) Explain the limitations of using a profitability index in a situation where there is capital rationing. **(5 marks)**

(Total = 10 marks)

55 Hypermarket (Pilot paper) 18 mins

A hypermarket now delivers to a significant number of customers that place their orders via the internet and this requires a fleet of delivery vehicles that is under the control of local management. The cost of the fleet is now significant and management is trying to determine the optimal replacement policy for the vehicle fleet. The total purchase price of the fleet is $220,000.

The running costs for each year and the scrap values of the fleet at the end of each year are:

	Year 1 $'000	Year 2 $'000	Year 3 $'000	Year 4 $'000	Year 5 $'000
Running costs	110	132	154	165	176
Scrap value	121	88	66	55	25

The hypermarket's cost of capital is 12% per annum.

Ignore tax and inflation.

Required

Prepare calculations that demonstrate when the hypermarket should replace its fleet of delivery vehicles from a financial perspective. **(10 marks)**

56 HP 45 mins

HP is considering purchasing a new machine to alleviate a bottleneck in its production facilities. At present it uses an old machine which can process 200 units of product P per hour. HP could replace it with machine AB, which is product-specific and can produce 500 units an hour. Machine AB costs £500,000. If it is installed, two members of staff will have to attend a short training course, which will cost the company a total of £5,000. Removing the old machine and preparing the area for machine AB will cost £20,000.

The company expects demand for P to be 12,000 units per week for another three years. After this, early in the fourth year, the new machine would be scrapped and sold for £50,000. The existing machine will have no scrap value. Each P earns a contribution of £1.40. The company works a 40-hour week for 48 weeks in the year. HP normally expects a payback within two years, and its after-tax cost of capital is 10 per cent per annum. The company pays corporation tax at 30 per cent and receives writing-down allowances of 25 per cent, reducing balance. Corporation tax is payable quarterly, in the seventh and tenth months of the year in which the profit is earned, and in the first and fourth months of the following year.

Required

(a) Prepare detailed calculations that show whether machine AB should be bought, and advise the management of HP as to whether it should proceed with the purchase.

Make the following assumptions.

(i) The company's financial year begins on the same day that the new machines would start operating, if purchased.

(ii) The company uses discounted cash-flow techniques with annual breaks only.

(iii) For taxation purposes, HP's management will elect for short-life asset treatment for this asset.

(18 marks)

(b) The investment decision in part (a) is a closely defined manufacturing one. Explain how a marketing or an IT investment decision might differ in terms of approach and assessment. **(7 marks)**

(Total = 25 marks)

57 MN plc (IDEC, 11/01)   45 mins

MN plc has a rolling programme of investment decisions. One of these investment decisions is to consider mutually exclusive investments A, B and C. The following information has been produced by the investment manager.

	Investment decision A £	Investment decision B £	Investment decision C £
Initial investment	105,000	187,000	245,000
Cash inflow for A: years 1 to 3	48,000		
Cash inflow for B: years 1 to 6		48,000	
Cash inflow for C: years 1 to 9			48,000
Net present value (NPV) at 10% each year	14,376	22,040	31,432
Ranking	3rd	2nd	1st
Internal rate of return (IRR)	17.5%	14%	13%
Ranking	1st	2nd	3rd

Required

(a) Prepare a report for the management of MN plc which includes the following.

- A graph showing the sensitivity of the three investments to changes in the cost of capital

- An explanation of the reasons for differences between NPV and IRR rankings – use investment A to illustrate the points you make

- A brief summary which gives MN plc's management advice on which project should be selected

(18 marks)

(b) One of the directors has suggested using payback to assess the investments. Explain to him the advantages and disadvantages of using payback methods over IRR and NPV. Use the figures above to illustrate your answer. **(7 marks)**

(Total = 25 marks)

58 CAF plc (IDEC, 5/02) 45 mins

CAF plc is a large multinational organisation that manufactures a range of highly engineered products/ components for the aircraft and vehicle industries. The directors are considering the future of one of the company's factories in the UK which manufactures product A. Product A is coming to the end of its life but another two years' production is planned. This is expected to produce a net cash inflow of £3 million next year and £2.3 million in the product's final year.

Product AA

CAF plc has already decided to replace product A with product AA which will be ready to go into production in two years' time. Product AA is expected to have a life of eight years. It could be made either at the UK factory under consideration or in an Eastern European factory owned by CAF plc. The UK factory is located closer to the markets and therefore if product AA is made in Eastern Europe, the company will incur extra transport costs of £10 per unit. Production costs will be the same in both countries. Product AA will require additional equipment and staff will need training; this will cost £6 million at either location. 200,000 units of product AA will be made each year and each unit will generate a net cash inflow of £25 before extra transport costs. If product AA is made in the UK, the factory will be closed and sold at the end of the product's life.

Product X

Now, however, the directors are considering a further possibility: product X could be produced at the UK factory and product AA at the Eastern European factory. Product X must be introduced in one year's time and will remain in production for three years. If it is introduced, the manufacture of product A will have to cease a year earlier than planned. If this happened, output of product A would be increased by 12.5% to maximum capacity next year, its last year, to build stock prior to the product's withdrawal. The existing staff would be transferred to product X.

The equipment needed to make product X would cost £4 million. 50,000 units of product X would be made in its first year; after that, production would rise to 75,000 units a year. Product X would earn a net cash flow of £70 per unit. After three years' production of product X, the UK factory would be closed and sold. (Product AA would not be transferred back to the factory in the UK at that stage; production would continue at the Eastern European site.)

Sale of factory

It is expected that the UK factory could be sold for £5.5 million at any time between the beginning of year 2 and the end of year 10. If the factory is sold, CAF plc will make redundancy payments of £2 million and the sale of equipment will raise £350,000.

CAF plc's cost of capital is 5% each year.

Required

(a) Prepare calculations that show which of the three options is financially the best. **(15 marks)**

(b) The directors of CAF plc are unsure whether their estimates are correct. Calculate and discuss the sensitivity of your choice of option in (a) to:

 (i) changes in transport costs; **(3 marks)**
 (ii) changes in the selling price of the factory. **(3 marks)**

(c) Briefly discuss the business issues that should be considered before relocating to another country. **(4 marks)**

(Total = 25 marks)

59 NP plc (IDEC, 5/02, amended) — 45 mins

NP plc is a company that operates a number of different businesses. Each separate business operates its own costing system, which has been selected to suit the particular needs of that business. Data is transferred to Head Office for weekly management control purposes.

NP plc is considering investing in a project named Fantazia, which is a pleasure park consisting of a covered dome and external fun rides. The cost of the dome, which is a covered frame that can be dismantled and erected elsewhere or stored, is £20 million. NP plc is considering two sites for the dome: London or Manchester. The cost of acquiring the land and installing the equipment is expected to be £20 million for the London site and £9 million for the Manchester site.

A market research survey shows that if Fantazia were to be situated in London, there is a 0.5 chance of getting 1.2 million visitors a year for the next four years and a 0.5 chance of getting only 0.8 million visitors a year. Each visitor to the London site is expected to spend £25 on average. This comprises a £10 entrance fee which includes access to the fun rides, £10 on souvenir merchandise and £5 on food and drink.

If Fantazia were to be situated in Manchester, there is a 0.4 chance of getting 1.2 million visitors a year for the next four years and a 0.6 chance of getting only 0.8 million visitors. Each visitor to the Manchester site is expected to spend £23 on average. This comprises £9 entrance fee, £10 on merchandise and £4 on food and drink.

The average cost of servicing each visitor (that is, providing rides, merchandise and food and drink) at both sites is estimated to be £10.

After four years, the dome could be kept in operation for a further four years or dismantled. If the dome is kept on the same site, it is estimated that visitor numbers will fall by 0.1 million a year. This means that London would have a 0.5 chance of 1.1 million visitors and a 0.5 chance of 0.7 million visitors in each of years 5 to 8, and Manchester a 0.4 chance of 1.1 million visitors and a 0.6 chance of 0.7 million visitors.

If the dome were to be dismantled after four years, it could be stored at a cost of £0.5 million a year, sold for £4 million or transferred to the other site. The number of visitors and revenue received at this site would be as predicted for years 1 to 4.

The cost of dismantling the dome and equipment would be £3 million and the cost of moving and re-erecting it would be £9 million.

The purchase or sale price of the land at the end of year 4 would be: London £14 million and Manchester £10 million. At the end of year 8, the dome's resale value would be zero and all land values would be as four years previously.

The final cost of dismantling the dome and equipment would be £2 million.

NP plc uses a discount rate of 10% when evaluating all projects.

Required

(a) Assuming that NP plc intends to terminate the Fantazia project *after four years*:

    (i) draw a decision tree to show the options open to NP plc; **(3 marks)**

    (ii) calculate which option would generate the highest net present value. (Use either the decision tree or another method.) **(4 marks)**

(b) Assuming that NP plc chose the most advantageous option for years 1 to 4, determined in your answer to (a)(ii) above,

    (i) draw a decision tree for years 5 to 8, showing the options open to NP plc if Fantazia is not terminated after 4 years; **(3 marks)**

    (ii) calculate which of these options generates the highest net present value over years 5 to 8. **(5 marks)**

(c) Advise the company which options it should select in order to maximise net present value over the full eight years of the project. State what that net present value would be. **(5 marks)**

QUESTIONS

(d) NP plc recommends that Fantazia adopts activity based costing (ABC) in order to cost its activities. Discuss whether this would be a suitable system for Fantazia to use in order to assess visitor profitability. If you feel that ABC is not an appropriate system for Fantazia, suggest alternative(s). **(5 marks)**

(Total = 25 marks)

60 Healthcare organisation   45 mins

EHI plc is a commercial healthcare organisation that undertakes the development and marketing of new treatments. EHI is based in the United Kingdom and receives patients from around the world. One possible new treatment is under review. The demand for this treatment is very uncertain.

Preliminary research has indicated that the treatment can be developed but there are two alternative approaches to its design. The details of these alternatives are as follows.

- A low-technology route using existing surgical treatment and drugs; this involves a development cost of £800,000 and a variable cost of £40,000 per treatment. This route will take one year to develop, with the development cost being paid for one year from now.

- A high-technology route using new surgical treatment, drugs and equipment; this involves a development cost of £6,300,000 and a variable cost of £18,000 per treatment. This route will take three years to develop, with development costs being paid for in three equal annual instalments, the first of which is one year from now.

EHI's managers are uncertain which of the two development alternatives to follow. They are considering an offer from a firm of strategic consultants to advise on the annual level of demand for treatments. For the purpose of appraising this offer it may be assumed that two levels of annual demand for treatments are possible – weak (30 treatments and 0.4 probability), and strong (65 treatments and 0.6 probability). It may be assumed that the consultants have a 92% chance of correctly forecasting each level of demand.

EHI appraises projects using cash flows over a period of ten years from now and a 10% annual discount rate. It is forecast that the selling price of each treatment will be £43,000.

Required

(a) (i) Calculate the minimum number of treatments demanded to make the low-technology route viable.

 (ii) Calculate the minimum number of treatments demanded to make the high-technology route viable.

 (iii) Calculate the number of treatments demanded annually to make the low- and high-technology routes equally viable. **(9 marks)**

(b) Draw a diagram to illustrate the relative sensitivity of the two alternative routes to the number of treatments demanded annually. **(7 marks)**

(c) Advise EHI's managers on the maximum amount they should pay for the forecast of the annual demand for treatments. In preparing your advice, you are advised to use decision-tree analysis. **(9 marks)**

(Total = 25 marks)

61 Training courses (IDEC, 5/03)   45 mins

All of the 100 accountants employed by X Ltd are offered the opportunity to attend six training courses per year. Each course lasts for several days and requires the delegates to travel to a specially selected hotel for the training. The current costs incurred for each course are as follows.

Delegate costs

	£ per delegate per course
Travel	200
Accommodation, food and drink	670
	870

It is expected that the current delegate costs will increase by 5% per annum.

Course costs

	£ per course
Room hire	1,500
Trainers	6,000
Course material	2,000
Equipment hire	1,500
Course administration	750
	11,750

It is expected that the current course costs will increase by 2.5% per annum.

The human resources director of X Ltd is concerned at the level of costs that these courses incur and has recently read an article about the use of the Internet for the delivery of training courses (e-learning). She decided to hire an external consultant at a cost of £5,000 to advise the company on how to implement an e-learning solution. The consultant prepared a report which detailed the costs of implementing and running an e-learning solution.

	Notes	£
Computer hardware	1	1,500,000
Software licences	2	35,000 per annum
Technical manager	3	30,000 per annum
Camera and sound crew	4	4,000 per course
Trainers and course material	5	2,000 per course
Broadband connection	6	300 per delegate per annum

Notes

1. The computer hardware will be depreciated on a straight-line basis over five years. The scrap value at the end of the five years is expected to be £50,000.

2. The company would sign a software license agreement which fixes the annual software license fee for five years. This fee is payable in advance.

3. An employee working in the IT department currently earning £20,000 per annum will be promoted to technical manager for this project. This employee's position will be replaced. The salary of the technical manager is expected to increase by 6% per annum.

4. The company supplying the camera and sound crew for recording the courses for Internet delivery has agreed to hold its current level of pricing for the first two years but then it will increase costs by 6% per annum. All courses will be recorded in the first quarter of the year of delivery.

5. The trainers will charge a fixed fee of £2,000 per course for the delivery and course material in the first year and expect to increase this by 6% per annum thereafter. The preparation of the course material and the recording of the trainers delivering the courses will take place in the first quarter of the year of delivery.

QUESTIONS

6 All of the accountants utilising the training courses will be offered £300 towards broadband costs which will allow them to access the courses from home. They will claim this expense annually in arrears. Broadband costs are expected to decrease by 5% per annum after the first year as it becomes more widely used by Internet users.

X Ltd uses a 14% cost of capital to appraise projects of this nature.

Ignore taxation.

Required

As the management accountant for X Ltd:

(a) Prepare a financial evaluation of the options available to the company and advise the directors on the best course of action to take, from a purely financial point of view. (Your answer should state any assumptions you have made.) **(16 marks)**

(b) (i) Using the annual equivalent technique, calculate the breakeven number of delegates per annum taking each of the six e-learning courses that is required to justify the implementation of the e-learning solution.

(Note that you should assume that the number of delegates taking the e-learning courses will be the same in each of the five years.) **(6 marks)**

(ii) Comment on the implications of the breakeven number you have calculated in your answer to (b) (i). **(3 marks)**

(Total = 25 marks)

62 CD Ltd   45 mins

CD Ltd has for some years manufactured a product called the C which is used as a component in a variety of electrical items. Although the C remains in demand, the technology on which its design is based has become obsolete. CD Ltd's engineers have developed a new product called the D which incorporates new technology. The D is smaller and more reliable than the C but performs exactly the same function.

The management of CD Ltd is considering whether to continue production of the C or discontinue the C and start production of the D. CD Ltd does not have the means to produce both products simultaneously.

If the C is produced then unit sales in year 1 are forecast to be 24,000, but declining by 4,000 units in each subsequent year. Additional equipment costing £70,000 must be purchased now if C production is to continue.

If the D is produced then unit sales in year 1 are forecast to be 6,000, but a rapid increase in unit sales is expected thereafter. Additional equipment costing £620,000 must be purchased now if D production is to start.

Relevant details of the two products are as follows.

	C £	D £
Variable cost per unit	25	50
Selling price per unit	55	105

CD Ltd normally appraises investments using a 12% per annum compound cost of money and ignores cashflows beyond five years from the start of investments.

Required

(a) Using CD Ltd's normal investment appraisal rules, advise CD Ltd's management on the minimum annual growth in unit sales of the D needed to justify starting D production now. Support your advice with a full financial evaluation **(11 marks)**

(b) Advise CD Ltd's management on the number of years to which its investment appraisal time horizon (currently five years) would have to be extended in order to justify starting D production now if the forecast annual increase in D sales is 2,800 units. **(7 marks)**

(c) State and explain any factors not included in your financial evaluation that CD Ltd should consider in making its decision.
(7 marks)

Note. You should ignore inflation and the residual values of equipment.
(Total = 25 marks)

63 3-Year project (5/06)   18 mins

A manager is evaluating a three year project which has the following relevant pre-tax operating cashflows:

Year	1	2	3
	$000	$000	$000
Sales	4,200	4,900	5,300
Costs	2,850	3,100	4,150

The project requires an investment of $2m at the start of year 1 and has no residual value.

The company pays corporation tax on its net relevant operating cashflows at the rate of 20%. Corporation tax is payable in the same year as the net relevant pre-tax operating cashflows arise. There is no tax depreciation available on the investment.

The manager has discounted the net relevant post-tax operating cashflows using the company's post-tax cost of capital of 7% and this results in a post-tax net present value of the project of $1·018m.

Required

(a) Briefly explain sensitivity analysis and how the manager may use it in the evaluation of this project.
(4 marks)

(b) Calculate the sensitivity of the project to independent changes in

 (i) the selling price;
 (ii) the cost of capital.
(6 marks)
(Total = 10 marks)

64 Canal boats (5/07)   18 mins

(a) A company operates a fleet of three canal boats that provide cruises for tourists around the canals of a city. The company seeks your advice as to whether it is better to replace its boats every year, every two years or every three years. The company has provided the following data:

	$
Annual sales revenue from operating each boat	800,000
Purchase cost of each boat	400,000

Operating costs, which include maintenance, servicing, and similar costs are paid at the end of each year. Operating costs and end of year trade-in values vary depending on the age of the boat and are as follows for each year of the boat's life:

Year	Operating Costs $	Trade-in values $
1	300,000	240,000
2	400,000	150,000
3	600,000	80,000

These costs do not include depreciation or any other fixed costs of providing the tourist service. These other fixed costs are a constant $100,000 per year regardless of the age of the boat.

The company uses an 8% cost of capital for its investment decisions.

QUESTIONS

Required

Produce calculations to determine the optimum replacement cycle of the boats and state clearly your recommendations. Ignore taxation. **(6 marks)**

(b) The same company is also considering investing in one of three marketing campaigns to increase its profitability. All three marketing campaigns have a life of five years, require the same initial investment and have no residual value. The company has already evaluated the marketing campaigns taking into consideration the range of possible outcomes that could result from the investment. A summary of the calculations is shown below:

Marketing Campaign

	J	K	L
	$	$	$
Expected Net Present Value	400,000	800,000	400,000
Standard Deviation of Net Present Value	35,000	105,000	105,000

Required

(i) Explain the meaning of the data shown above; and

(ii) Briefly explain how the data may be used by the company when choosing between alternative investments. **(4 marks)**

(Total = 10 marks)

65 Section A questions: Inflation and taxation   36 mins

The following data relates to questions 65.1 and 65.2

A company is considering investing in a project that requires an initial outflow of £500,000 and will generate expected cash inflows in terms of today's £ of £130,000 over each of the next four years. The company's monetary cost of capital is 7 per cent and inflation is predicted to be 4 per cent over the next four years.

1   Calculate the company's real cost of capital. **(2 marks)**

2   Calculate the company's present value of the cash inflow in year 3. **(2 marks)**

The following data relates to questions 65.3 and 65.4

A company is considering investing in a manufacturing project that would have a three-year life span. The investment would involve an immediate cash outflow of £50,000 and have a zero residual value. In each of the three years, 4,000 units would be produced and sold. The contribution per unit, based on current prices, is £5. The company has an annual cost of capital of 8%. It is expected that the inflation rate will be 3% in each of the next three years

3   Calculate the net present value of the project (to the nearest £500) **(3 marks)**

4   If the annual inflation rate is now projected to be 4%, the maximum monetary cost of capital for this project to remain viable is (to the nearest 0.5%)

     A   13.0%
     B   13.5%
     C   14.0%
     D   14.5%

(2 marks)

5   The details of an investment project are as follows.

Life of the project	10 years
Cost of asset bought at the start of the project	£100,000
Annual cash inflow	£20,000
Cost of capital, after tax	8% each year

Corporation tax is 30% and is paid in equal quarterly instalments in the 7th and 10th months of the year in which the profit was earned and in the 1st and 4th months of the following year.

Writing down allowances of 25% reducing balance will be claimed each year.

(Assume the asset is bought on the first day of the tax year and that the company's other projects generate healthy profits.)

(Round all cash flows to the nearest £ and discount end of year cash flows.)

Calculate the *present value* of the cash flows that occur in the *second* year of the project **(4 marks)**

6   IM Ltd hopes to purchase a machine for £80,000 on which it can claim writing down allowances of 25% on a reducing balance basis. The machine will have a life of four years and will be sold for £20,000. Corporation tax is 30% and is paid in equal quarterly instalments in the seventh and tenth months of the year in which the profit is earned and in the first and fourth months of the following year. On the assumption that the investment occurs on the first day of the tax year and that IM Ltd's other projects generate healthy profits, what tax savings will the investment produce in years 3 and 4? **(3 marks)**

7   Tree Cole Tarts plc is appraising an investment of £700,000 in plant, which will last four years and have no residual value. Fixed operating costs (excluding depreciation) will be £200,000 in the first year, increasing by 5% per annum because of inflation. The contribution in the first year is forecast at £620,000, increasing by 7% per annum due to inflation. The company's money cost of capital is 14%.

Required

Calculate the net present value of the investment, to the nearest £'000. **(4 marks)**

(Total = 20 marks)

If you struggled with these OT questions, go back to your BPP Study Text for Paper P2 and revise Chapter 12 before you tackle the 10-mark and 25-mark questions on inflation and taxation.

66 Compact discs   18 mins

R plc is contemplating investment in an additional production line to produce its range of compact discs. A market research study, undertaken by a well-known firm of consultants, has revealed scope to sell an additional output of 400,000 units pa. The study cost £0.1m but the account has not yet been settled.

The price and cost structure of a typical disc (net of royalties) is as follows.

	£	£
Price per unit		12.00
Costs per unit of output		
Material cost per unit	1.50	
Direct labour cost per unit	0.50	
Variable overhead cost per unit	0.50	
Fixed overhead cost per unit	1.50	
		(4.00)
Profit		8.00

QUESTIONS

The fixed overhead represents an apportionment of central administrative and marketing costs. These are expected to rise in total by £500,000 pa as a result of undertaking this project. The production line is expected to operate for five years and require a total cash outlay of £11m, including £0.5m of materials stocks. The equipment will have a residual value of £2m. Because the company is moving towards a JIT stock management policy, it is expected that this project will involve steadily reducing working capital needs, expected to decline at about 3% pa by volume. The production line will be accommodated in a presently empty building for which an offer of £2m has recently been received from another company. If the building is retained, it is expected that property price inflation will increase its value to £3m after five years.

While the precise rates of price and cost inflation are uncertain, economists in R plc's corporate planning department make the following forecasts for the average annual rates of inflation relevant to the project.

Retail Prices Index	6% pa
Disc prices	5% pa
Material prices	3% pa
Direct labour wage rates	7% pa
Variable overhead costs	7% pa
Other overhead costs	5% pa

Note. You may ignore taxes and capital allowances in this question.

Required

Given that R plc's shareholders require a real return of 8.5% for projects of this degree of risk, assess the financial viability of this proposal. **(10 marks)**

67 AB plc   18 mins

AB plc is considering a new product with a three-year life. The product can be made with existing machinery, which has spare capacity, or by a labour-saving specialised new machine which would have zero disposal value at the end of three years.

The following estimates have been made at current prices.

Sales volume	1 million units per annum
Selling price	£15 per unit
Labour costs (without new machine)	£6 per unit
Material cost	£2 per unit
Variable overheads	£2 per unit

Additional fixed overheads for the new product are estimated to be £3 million per year.

The new machine would cost £5 million now and would halve the labour cost per unit.

Because of competition, selling price increases will be limited to 2% per annum, although labour cost is expected to rise at 12% per annum and all other costs at 8% per annum.

The company's money cost of capital is 15% and, apart from the cost of the new machine, all other cash flows can be assumed to arise at year ends.

Required

(a) Calculate the NPV of the new product assuming that manufacture uses existing machinery. **(4 marks)**
(b) Calculate the NPV assuming that the new machine is purchased. **(4 marks)**
(c) Recommend what action should be taken, and comment on your recommendations. **(2 marks)**

(Total = 10 marks)

68 A Company (5/05)   18 mins

A company is considering the replacement of its delivery vehicle. It has chosen the vehicle that it will acquire but it now needs to decide whether the vehicle should be purchased or leased.

The cost of the vehicle is £15,000. If the company purchases the vehicle it will be entitled to claim tax depreciation at the rate of 25% per year on a reducing balance basis. The vehicle is expected to have a trade-in value of £5,000 at the end of three years.

If the company leases the vehicle, it will make an initial payment of £1,250 plus annual payments of £4,992 at the end of each of three years. The full value of each lease payment will be an allowable cost in the computation of the company's taxable profits of the year in which the payments are made.

The company pays corporation tax at the rate of 30% of its profits.

50% of the company's corporation tax is payable in the year in which profits are made and 50% in the following year. Assume that the company has sufficient profits to obtain tax relief on its acquisition of the vehicle in accordance with the information provided above.

The company's after tax cost of capital is 15% per year.

Note. Tax depreciation is not a cash cost but is allowed as a deduction in the calculation of taxable profits.

Required

Calculate whether the company should purchase or lease the vehicle and clearly state your recommendation to the company.   **(10 marks)**

> **Helping hand.** Two alternatives are being considered – purchase or lease. So you need to calculate NPVs for both. The question also has tax and WDA – the WDA can be calculated separately for the bought vehicle. Remember to include any tax deductible costs, eg leasing costs. Use the correct discount rate – if tax is a factor you need to use the post tax cost of capital. You can save time by using annuities for savings and costs repeated in future years.

68 Question with analysis: A Company (5/05)   18 mins

A company is considering the replacement of its delivery vehicle. It has chosen the vehicle that it will acquire but it now needs to decide whether the vehicle should be purchased or leased.

[Tax WDA] **The cost of the vehicle is £15,000**. If the company **purchases** the vehicle it will be entitled to **claim tax** depreciation at the rate of 25% per year **on a reducing balance basis**. The vehicle is expected to have a [Cash flow year 3] **trade-in value of £5,000 at the end of three years**.

[Tax deductible] If the company **leases** the vehicle, it will make an **initial payment of £1,250 plus annual payments of £4,992** at the end of each of three years. The **full value of each lease payment will be an allowable cost** in the computation of the company's taxable profits of the year in which the payments are made.

The company pays **corporation tax at the rate of 30%** of its profits.

[Tax assumptions] **50% of the company's corporation tax is payable in the year** in which profits are made and **50% in the following year**. Assume that the company has sufficient profits to obtain tax relief on its acquisition of the vehicle in accordance with the information provided above.

[Correct discount rate] The company's **after tax cost of capital is 15% per year**.

[ie WDA] *Note.* Tax depreciation is not a cash cost but is allowed as a deduction in the calculation of taxable profits.

QUESTIONS

Required

Calculate whether the company should purchase or lease the vehicle and clearly state your recommendation to the company. **(10 marks)**

> **Helping hand.** Two alternatives are being considered – purchase or lease. So you need to calculate NPVs for both. The question also has tax and WDA – the WDA can be calculated separately for the bought vehicle. Remember to include any tax deductible costs, eg leasing costs. Use the correct discount rate – if tax is a factor you need to use the post tax cost of capital. You can save time by using annuities for savings and costs repeated in future years.

69 RAD Enterprises (Pilot paper)   18 mins

RAD Enterprises (RAD) has signed a contract with LPC to supply accounting packages. However, there has been a fire in one of the software manufacturing departments and a machine has been seriously damaged and requires urgent replacement.

The replacement machine will cost £1 million and RAD is considering whether to lease or buy the machine. A lease could be arranged under which RAD would pay £300,000 per annum for four years with each payment being made annually in advance. The lease payments would be an allowable expense for taxation purposes.

Corporation tax is payable at the rate of 30% of profits in two equal instalments: one in the year that profits are earned and the other in the following year. Writing-down allowances are available at 25% each year on a reducing balance basis. It is anticipated that the machine will have a useful economic life of four years, at the end of which there will be no residual value.

The after-tax cost of capital is 12%.

Required

Evaluate the lease or buy considerations for acquiring the new machine from a financial viewpoint, assuming that RAD has sufficient profits to claim all available tax reliefs. **(10 marks)**

70 Print Co (5/05)   45 mins

A printing company is considering investing in new equipment which has a capital cost of £3 million. The machine qualifies for tax depreciation at the rate of 25% per year on a reducing balance basis and has an expected life of five years. The residual value of the machine is expected to be £300,000 at the end of five years.

An existing machine would be sold immediately for £400,000 if the new machine were to be bought. This existing machine has a tax written down value of £250,000.

The existing machine generates annual revenues of £4 million and earns a contribution of 40% of sales. The new machine would reduce unit variable costs to 80% of their former value and increase output capacity by 20%. There is sufficient sales demand at the existing prices to make full use of this additional capacity.

The printing company pays corporation tax on its profits at the rate of 30%, with half of the tax being payable in the year that the profit is earned and half in the following year.

The company's after tax cost of capital is 14% per year.

Required

(a) Evaluate the proposed purchase of the new printing machine from a financial perspective using appropriate calculations, and advise the company as to whether the investment is worthwhile.

(15 marks)

(b) Explain sensitivity analysis and prepare calculations to show the sensitivity of the decision to independent changes in each of the following:

    (i) Annual contribution
    (ii) Rate of corporation tax on profit. **(10 marks)**

(Total = 25 marks)

70 Question with analysis and student answer: Print Co (5/05)
45 mins

[WDA here]

[Balancing charge or allowance here]

[Note requirement refers to unit variable cost so not 80% of absolute costs]

A printing company is considering investing in new equipment which has a **capital cost of £3 million**. The machine qualifies for **tax depreciation at the rate of 25% per year** on a reducing balance basis and has an **expected life of five years**. The **residual value** of the machine is expected to be **£300,000** at the end of five years.

An **existing** machine would be sold immediately for **£400,000** if the new machine were to be bought. This existing machine has a **tax written down value of £250,000**.

The existing machine generates **annual revenues of £4 million** and earns a **contribution of 40% of sales**. The **new machine would reduce unit variable costs to 80% of their former value and increase output capacity by 20%**. There is sufficient sales demand at the existing prices to make full use of this additional capacity.

The printing company pays **corporation tax on its profits at the rate of 30%**, with **half of the tax** being **payable in the year that the profit is earned** and **half in the following year**.

The company's **after tax cost of capital is 14% per year**.

Required

[Note requirement to calculate and to comment on your findings]

(a) **Evaluate** the proposed purchase of the new printing machine from a financial perspective using appropriate calculations, and advise the company as to whether the investment is worthwhile.

(15 marks)

[Note requirements to both explain a concept and to do calculations]

(b) **Explain** sensitivity analysis and **prepare calculations** to show the sensitivity of the decision to independent changes in each of the following:

    (i) Annual contribution
    (ii) Rate of corporation tax on profit. **(10 marks)**

(Total = 25 marks)

71 CH Ltd (Pilot paper)
45 mins

CH Ltd is a swimming club. Potential exists to expand the business by providing a gymnasium as part of the facilities at the club. The directors believe that this will stimulate additional membership of the club.

The expansion project would require an initial expenditure of £550,000. The project is expected to have a disposal value at the end of five years which is equal to 10% of the initial expenditure.

The following schedule reflects a recent market research survey regarding the estimated annual sales revenue from additional memberships over the project's five-year life:

QUESTIONS

Level of demand	£'000	Probability
High	800	0.25
Medium	560	0.50
Low	448	0.25

It is expected that the contribution to sales ratio will be 55%. Additional expenditure on fixed overheads is expected to be £90,000 per annum.

CH Ltd incurs a 30% tax rate on corporate profits. Corporation tax is to be paid in two equal instalments: one in the year that profits are earned and the other in the following year.

CH Ltd's after-tax nominal (money) discount rate is 15.5% per annum. A uniform inflation rate of 5% per annum will apply to all costs and revenues during the life of the project.

All of the values above have been expressed in terms of current prices. You can assume that all cash flows occur at the end of each year and that the initial investment does not qualify for capital allowances.

Required

(a) Evaluate the proposed expansion from a financial perspective. **(13 marks)**

(b) Calculate and then demonstrate the sensitivity of the project to changes in the expected annual contribution. **(5 marks)**

(c) You have now been advised that the capital cost of the expansion will qualify for writing down allowances at the rate of 25% per annum on a reducing balance basis. Also, at the end of the project's life, a balancing charge or allowance will arise equal to the difference between the scrap proceeds and the tax written down value.

Required

Calculate the financial impact of these allowances. **(7 marks)**

(Total = 25 marks)

72 Question with analysis and answer plan: PK Glass plc (IDEC, 11/03, amended) 45 mins

W Ltd is a division of PK Glass plc. W Ltd produces commercial window glass. The glass is fragile and must be packaged very carefully. The packaging is done internally in W Ltd's packaging department by an automated packaging machine. The estimated annual cost, based on the current costs of the packaging department, is as follows:

	£'000
Prime cost	700
Departmental overhead	
Supervisors' salaries	70
Rent	50
Depreciation of machinery	190
Maintenance of machinery	100
Allocation of general overhead	140
	1,250

Although the machinery is only two years old, it has become unreliable and costly to maintain. The machinery cost £1 million and had an estimated useful life of five years, after which it could be sold as scrap for £50,000. If the machinery was scrapped today it would generate £70,000.

In order to reduce packaging costs, the management team of W Ltd is considering two alternatives from two external companies (X Packaging Ltd and Y Ltd):

Alternative 1 – Closure of the packaging department

X Packaging Ltd has offered to undertake all of the packaging for a fixed fee of £950,000 per annum for the next three years. If W Ltd accepts this offer, its packaging department would be closed down.

Details relating to the closure are as follows:

Buildings

The buildings currently used by W Ltd's packaging department would be used by another department in W Ltd that currently pays rent of £60,000 per annum for accommodation.

Direct labour

30% of the estimate for prime cost is direct labour. Redundancy payments of 10% of the annual wages will be paid.

Direct materials

The packaging materials currently held in stock have a book value of £100,000 and a scrap value of £20,000. The current replacement cost of the materials is £125,000.

Supervisors

The supervisors would be redeployed in another department within W Ltd.

Alternative 2 – Sub-contract the maintenance

Y Ltd has offered to maintain the machinery for a fixed fee of £80,000 per annum for the next three years.

Taxation

W Ltd incurs 30% tax on corporate profits. Tax allowances on the cost of the packaging machine are 25% per annum on a reducing balance basis. At the end of the machine's life, a balancing charge or allowance will arise equal to the difference between the scrap proceeds and the tax written-down value. Corporation tax is payable 50% in the year in which the profit is earned and 50% in the following year.

The group uses DCF techniques and the NPV approach in particular to appraise investment projects. The after-tax cost of capital is 12%.

Required

(a) Write a memorandum in response to a letter from one of PK Glass plc's directors which includes the following statement:

'Since cash flow and profit are the same thing in the long run, we should always adopt courses of action which maximise accounting profit. I do not understand the logic behind our investment appraisal policy.' **(5 marks)**

(b) Determine which of the alternatives is the best one from a financial point of view. (You should show all calculations and state any assumptions that you have made.) **(17 marks)**

(c) Briefly discuss any other issues which might affect the recommendation you have made in your answer to part (b). **(3 marks)**

(Total = 25 marks)

QUESTIONS

72 Question with analysis and answer plan: PK Glass plc (IDEC, 11/03, amended) 45 mins

W Ltd is a division of PK Glass plc. W Ltd produces commercial window glass. The glass is fragile and must be packaged very carefully. The packaging is done internally in W Ltd's packaging department by an automated packaging machine. The estimated annual cost, based on the current costs of the packaging department, is as follows:

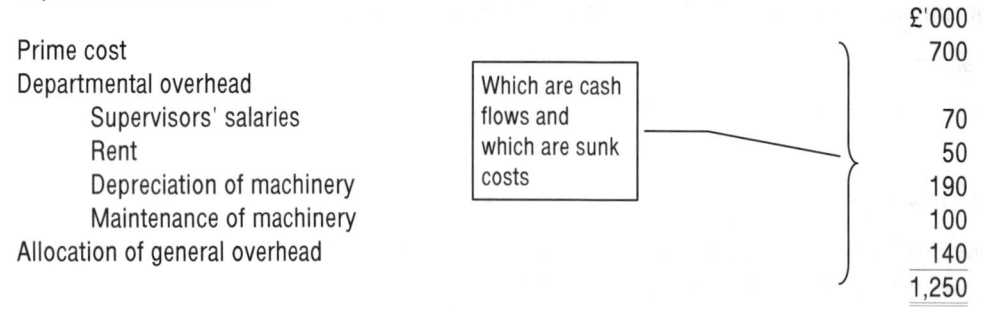

	£'000
Prime cost	700
Departmental overhead	
Supervisors' salaries	70
Rent	50
Depreciation of machinery	190
Maintenance of machinery	100
Allocation of general overhead	140
	1,250

[Annotation on overheads: *Which are cash flows and which are sunk costs*]

Although the machinery is only two years old, it has become unreliable and costly to maintain. The machinery cost £1 million and had an estimated useful life of five years, after which it could be sold as scrap for £50,000. **If the machinery was scrapped today it would generate £70,000**.

[Annotation: *Remember scrap value!*]

In order to reduce packaging costs, the management team of W Ltd is considering two alternatives from two external companies (X Packaging Ltd and Y Ltd):

Alternative 1 – Closure of the packaging department

X Packaging Ltd has offered to undertake all of the packaging for a fixed fee of £950,000 per annum for the next three years. If W Ltd accepts this offer, its packaging department would be closed down.

Details relating to the closure are as follows:

Buildings

The buildings currently used by W Ltd's packaging department would be used by another department in W Ltd that currently pays **rent of £60,000 per annum** for accommodation.

[Annotation: *Tax saving*]

Direct labour

30% of the estimate for prime cost is direct labour. Redundancy payments of 10% of the annual wages will be paid.

[Annotation: *Tax saving*]

Direct materials

The packaging materials currently held in stock have a **book value of £100,000** and a scrap value of £20,000. The current replacement cost of the materials is £125,000.

[Annotations: *Not a cash flow*; *Ignore any tax effect of writing off materials on book value*]

Supervisors

The supervisors would be **redeployed in another department** within W Ltd.

[Annotation: *Sunk cost*]

Alternative 2 – Sub-contract the maintenance

Y Ltd has offered to maintain the machinery for a fixed fee of £80,000 per annum for the next three years.

Taxation — [Annotation: *Note the features such as tax rate and timing of cash flows*]

W Ltd **incurs 30% tax on corporate profits**. **Tax allowances on the cost of the packaging machine are 25%** per annum on a reducing balance basis. At the end of the machine's life, a balancing charge or

QUESTIONS

allowance will arise equal to the difference between the scrap proceeds and the tax written-down value. **Corporation tax is payable 50% in the year in which the profit is earned and 50% in the following year**.

[*Is this the correct discount rate to use*]

The group uses DCF techniques and the NPV approach in particular to appraise investment projects. The **after-tax cost of capital is 12%**.

Required

[*Compare and contrast. Definitions too.*]

(a) Write a memorandum in response to a letter from one of PK Glass plc's directors which includes the following statement:

'**Since cash flow and profit are the same thing in the long run**, we should always adopt courses of action which maximise accounting profit. **I do not understand the logic behind our investment appraisal policy**.' [*Explain this in the memo*] **(5 marks)**

[*Obviously a NPV calculation*]

(b) Determine which of the alternatives is the best one from a financial point of view. (You should show all calculations and state any assumptions that you have made.) **(17 marks)**

(c) Briefly discuss any other issues which might affect the recommendation you have made in your answer to part (b). **(3 marks)**

(Total = 25 marks)

73 Taxi (11/05) 18 mins

The owner of a taxi company is considering the replacement of his vehicles. He is planning to retire in six years' time and is therefore only concerned with that period of time, but cannot decide whether it is better to replace the vehicles every two years or every three years.

The following data have been estimated (all values at today's price levels):

Purchase cost and trade-in values

	£
Taxi cost	15,000
Trade-in value of taxi: after two years	7,000
after three years	4,000

Annual costs and revenues

	Per year £
Vehicle running cost	20,000
Fares charged to customers	40,000

Vehicle servicing and repair costs

Vehicle servicing and repair costs depend on the age of the vehicle. In the following table, year 1 represents the cost in the first year of the vehicle's ownership; year 2 represents the cost in the second year of ownership, and so on:

	£
Year 1	500
Year 2	2,500
Year 3	4,000

Inflation

New vehicle costs and trade in-values are expected to increase by 5% per year. Vehicle running costs and fares are expected to increase by 7% per year. Vehicle servicing and repair costs are expected to increase by 10% per year.

QUESTIONS

Required

Advise the company on the optimum replacement cycle for its vehicles and state the net present value of the opportunity cost of making the wrong decision. Use a discount rate of 12% per year. All workings and assumptions should be shown. Ignore taxation.

(10 marks)

74 JK plc (11/06)   45 mins

JK plc prepares its accounts to 31 December each year. It is considering investing in a new computer controlled production facility on 1 January 2007 at a cost of £50m. This will enable JK plc to produce a new product which it expects to be able to sell for four years. At the end of this time it has been agreed to sell the new production facility for £1m cash.

Sales of the product during the year ended 31 December 2007 and the next three years are expected to be as follows:

Year ended 31 December 2007	2007	2008	2009	2010
Sales units (000)	100	105	110	108

Selling price, unit variable cost and fixed overhead costs (excluding depreciation) are expected to be as follows during the year ended 31 December 2007:

	£
Selling price per unit	1,200
Variable production cost per unit	750
Variable selling and distribution cost per unit	100
Fixed production cost for the year	4,000,000
Fixed selling and distribution cost for the year	2,000,000
Fixed administration cost for the year	1,000,000

The following rates of annual inflation are expected for each of the years 2008 - 2010:

	%
Selling prices	5
Production costs	8
Selling and distribution costs	6
Administration costs	5

The company pays taxation on its profits at the rate of 30%, with half of this being payable in the year in which the profit is earned and the remainder being payable in the following year. Investments of this type qualify for tax depreciation at the rate of 25% per annum on a reducing balance basis.

The Board of Directors of JK plc has agreed to use a 12% post-tax discount rate to evaluate this investment.

Required

(a) Advise JK plc whether the investment is financially worthwhile. **(17 marks)**

(b) Calculate the Internal Rate of Return of the investment. **(3 marks)**

(c) Define and contrast *(i)* the real rate of return and *(ii)* the money rate of return, and explain how they would be used when calculating the net present value of a project's cash flows. **(5 marks)**

(Total = 25 marks)

75 X (5/07) 45 mins

X operates in an economy that has almost zero inflation. Management ignores inflation when evaluating investment projects because it is so low as to be considered insignificant. X is evaluating a number of similar, alternative investments. The company uses an after tax cost of capital of 6% and has already completed the evaluation of two investments. The third investment is a new product that would be produced on a just-in-time basis and which is expected to have a life of three years. This investment requires an immediate cash outflow of $200,000, which does not qualify for tax depreciation. The expected residual value at the end of the project's life is $50,000. A draft financial statement showing the values that are specific to this third investment for the three years is as follows:

	Year 1 $	Year 2 $	Year 3 $
Sales	230,000	350,000	270,000
Production costs			
Materials	54,000	102,000	66,000
Labour	60,000	80,000	70,000
Other*	80,000	90,000	80,000
Profit	36,000	78,000	54,000
Closing receivables	20,000	30,000	25,000
Closing payables	6,000	9,000	8,000

* Other production costs shown above include depreciation calculated using the straight line method.

The company is liable to pay corporation tax at a rate of 30% of its profits. One half of this is payable in the same year as the profit is earned, the remainder is payable in the following year.

Required

(a) Calculate the net present value of the above investment proposal. **(10 marks)**

(b) Explain how the above investment project would be appraised if there were to be a change in the rate of inflation so that it became too significant to be ignored. **(5 marks)**

The evaluations of the other two investments are shown below:

Investment	Initial investment $	Net present value $
W	300,000	75,000
Y	100,000	27,000

The company only has $400,000 of funds available. All of the investment proposals are non-divisible. None of the investments may be repeated.

Required

(c) Recommend, with supporting calculations, which of the three investment proposals should be accepted. **(3 marks)**

(d) (i) Briefly explain gain sharing arrangements. **(3 marks)**

  (ii) Explain the reasons why X might not want to overcome its investment funding limitations by using a gain sharing arrangement. **(4 marks)**

(Total = 25 marks)

76 Section A questions: Forecasting and managing future costs
36 mins

1   T plc has developed a new product, the TF8. The time taken to produce the first unit was 18 minutes. Assuming that an 80% learning curve applies, the time allowed for the fifth unit (to 2 decimal places) should be

    A   5.79 minutes
    B   7.53 minutes
    C   10.72 minutes
    D   11.52 minutes

Note. For an 80% learning curve $Y = aX^{-0.3219}$ **(2 marks)**

2   The learning curve formula $Y = aX^{-0.322}$ applies to the production of product L,

    where Y = cumulative average time per unit
               a = time for the first unit
               X = number of units made to date

To date (the end of April year 4) 20 units of L have been produced. Budgeted production for May year 4 is 7 units. The time taken to produce the first unit of L, in January year 4, was 80 hours.

Required

Calculate the standard total labour time for May year 4.   **(3 marks)**

3   P Limited is considering taking account of a learning curve effect to derive the standard labour cost for output in department Y.

Indicate whether or not the following factors are likely to influence P Limited *against* taking account of the learning curve in preparing price quotations.

    A   Labour operations involve a complex set of repetitive activities.
    B   Labour is not a significant proportion of total cost.
    C   There is a high rate of labour turnover in department Y.
    D   There may be a long time delay between successive orders.   **(3 marks)**

4   Indicate which of the following methods can be used to move a currently-attainable cost closer to target cost.

    A   Using standard components wherever possible
    B   Acquiring new, more efficient technology
    C   Making staff redundant
    D   Reducing the quality of the product in question   **(2 marks)**

5   What are the four stages of the product life cycle?

    A   Introduction, growth, maturity, decline
    B   Growth, maturity, saturation, decline
    C   Introduction, growth, plateau, decline
    D   Growth, plateau, decline, obsolescence   **(2 marks)**

6   *Choose the correct terms from those highlighted.*

Within a system of target costing, target cost is calculated as **desired selling price/market price** minus **desired/actual/standard** profit margin. (2 marks)

7   A mobile phone manufacturer, C Ltd, is planning to produce a new model. The potential market over the next year is 1,000,000 units.

C Ltd has the capacity to produce 400,000 units and could sell 100,000 units at a price of £50. Demand would double for each £5 fall in the selling price.

The company has an 80% cost experience curve for similar products. The cost of the first batch of 1,000 phones was £103,000.

A minimum margin of 25% is required.

Required

Calculate C Ltd's target cost per unit, to the nearest £. (2 marks)

8   When are the bulk of a product's life cycle costs normally determined?

- A   At the design/development stage
- B   When the product is introduced to the market
- C   When the product is in its growth stage
- D   On disposal (2 marks)

9   Indicate whether or not the following aspects of 'value' should be considered in a value analysis exercise

- A   Sales value
- B   Replacement value
- C   Exchange value
- D   Disposal value (2 marks)

(Total = 20 marks)

If you struggled with these OT questions, go back to your BPP Study Text for Paper P2 and revise Chapter 15 before you tackle the 10-mark and 25-mark questions on forecasting and managing future costs.

77 Experience curve   18 mins

Discuss the usefulness of the experience curve in gaining market share. Illustrate your answer with specific instances/examples. (10 marks)

78 ML plc (IMPM, 11/01, amended)   18 mins

ML plc was formed three years ago to develop e-commerce systems and design web sites for clients. The company has expanded rapidly since then and now has a multi-site operation with bases in the UK and overseas.

Techniques that are used in order to improve an organisation's performance include cost reduction and value analysis.

Required

Explain these techniques and how they may be used by ML plc as part of its planning activities. (10 marks)

79 Wye hotel group (IMPM, 5/01, amended) — 18 mins

The Wye hotel group operates a chain of 50 hotels. The size of each hotel varies, as do the services that each hotel provides. However, all of the hotels operated by the group provide a restaurant, swimming pool, lounge bar, guest laundry service and accommodation. Some of the hotels also provide guest entertainment, travel bureaux and shopping facilities. The managing director of the group is concerned about the high level of running costs being incurred by the hotels.

Required

Explain how cost reduction and value analysis could be used by the WYE hotel group to improve the profitability of its hotels. **(10 marks)**

80 Question with answer plan: Cost management techniques (IDEC, 11/02, amended) — 18 mins

Traditional cost control systems focused on cost containment rather than cost reduction. Today, cost management focuses on process improvement and the identification of how processes can be more effectively and efficiently performed to result in cost reductions.

Required

Discuss how the cost management techniques of target costing and life cycle costing differ from the traditional cost containment approach and how each seeks to achieve cost reduction. **(10 marks)**

81 Telmat (IDEC, 11/01) — 45 mins

(a) 'Costing systems attempt to explain how products consume resources but do not indicate the joint benefits of having multiple products.'

Required

Explain the statement above and discuss the following.

(i) How the addition of a new product to the product range may affect the 'cost' of existing products
(ii) The consequences, in terms of total profitability, of decisions to increase/decrease the product range

(10 marks)

(b) Telmat is a company that manufactures mobile phones. This market is extremely volatile and competitive and achieving adequate product profitability is extremely important. Telmat is a mature company that has been producing electronic equipment for many years and has all the costing systems in place that one would expect in such a company. These include a comprehensive overhead absorption system, annual budgets and monthly variance reports and the balanced scorecard for performance measurement.

The company is considering introducing the following.

(i) Target costing
(ii) Life cycle costing systems

Required

Discuss the advantages (or otherwise) that this specific company is likely to gain from these two systems.

(15 marks)

(Total = 25 marks)

82 Question with answer plan: SY Ltd (IDEC, 11/03)   45 mins

SY Ltd, a manufacturer of computer games, has developed a new game called the MANPAC. This is an interactive 3D game and is the first of its kind to be introduced to the market. SY Ltd is due to launch the MANPAC in time for the peak selling season.

Traditionally SY Ltd has priced its games based on standard manufacturing cost plus selling and administration cost plus a profit margin. However, the management team of SY Ltd has recently attended a computer games conference where everyone was talking about life cycle costing, target costing and market-based pricing approaches. The team has returned from the conference and would like more details on the topics they heard about and how they could have been applied to the MANPAC.

Required

As management accountant of SY Ltd, do the following.

(a) Discuss how the following techniques could have been applied to the MANPAC.

- Life cycle costing
- Target costing   **(8 marks)**

(b) Evaluate the market-based pricing strategies that should have been considered for the launch of the MANPAC and recommend a strategy that should have been chosen.   **(6 marks)**

(c) Explain each stage in the life cycle of the MANPAC and the issues that the management team will need to consider at each stage. Your answer should include a diagram to illustrate the product life cycle of the MANPAC.   **(11 marks)**

(Total = 25 marks)

83 Financial advisors (5/06)   18 mins

A firm of financial advisors has established itself by providing high quality, personalised, financial strategy advice. The firm promotes itself by sponsoring local events, advertising, client newsletters, having a flexible attitude towards the times and locations of meetings with clients and seeking new and innovative ideas to discuss with its clients.

The senior manager of the firm has recently noticed that the firm's profitability has declined, with fewer clients being interested in the firm's new investment ideas. Indeed, many clients have admitted to not reading the firm's newsletters.

The senior manager seeks your help in restoring the firm's profitability to its former level and believes that the techniques of *Value Analysis* and *Functional Analysis* may be appropriate.

Required

(a) Explain the meanings of, and the differences between, Value Analysis and Functional Analysis.   **(4 marks)**

(b) Briefly explain the series of steps that you would take to implement Value Analysis for this organisation.   **(6 marks)**

(Total = 10 marks)

84 Learning curve (5/07) — 18 mins

A company is planning to launch a new product. It has already carried out market research at a cost of $50,000 and as a result has discovered that the market price for the product should be $50 per unit. The company estimates that 80,000 units of the product could be sold at this price before one of the company's competitors enters the market with a superior product. At this time any unsold units of the company's product would be of no value.

The company has estimated the costs of the initial batch of the product as follows:

	$'000
Direct materials	200
Direct labour ($10 per hour)	250
Other direct costs	100

Production was planned to occur in batches of 10,000 units and it was expected that an 80% learning curve would apply to the direct labour until the fourth batch was complete. Thereafter the direct labour cost per batch was expected to be constant. No changes to the direct labour rate per hour were expected.

The company introduced the product at the price stated above, with production occurring in batches of 10,000 units. Direct labour was paid using the expected hourly rate of $10 and the company is now reviewing the profitability of the product. The following schedule shows the actual direct labour cost recorded:

Cumulative number of batches	Actual cumulative direct labour costs
	$'000
1	280
2	476
4	809
8	1,376

Required

(a) Calculate the revised expected cumulative direct labour costs for the four levels of output given the actual cost of $280,000 for the first batch.

(b) Calculate the actual learning rate exhibited at each level of output.

(c) Discuss the implications of your answers to (a) and (b) for the managers of the company. **(10 marks)**

85 Section A questions: Activity based management — 36 mins

1   Which of the following is not a merit of activity based analysis?

   I   Activity based analysis recognises the complexity of modern business.
   II   Activity based analysis does not concern itself with all types of overhead cost.
   III   Some measure of arbitrary cost apportionment will still be required, even if such analysis is used.
   IV   Activity based analysis is based on the belief that it is always possible to improve.

   A   I only
   B   None of the above
   C   III and IV
   D   II, III and IV   **(2 marks)**

QUESTIONS

2   When building up the cost of a product or service using activity based costing, which of the following would NOT be used as levels of classification?

(i)   Unit
(ii)   Batch
(iii) Value added
(iv)   Product
(v)   Non-value added
(vi)   Facility

A   (ii) and (iii)
B   (iii) and (iv)
C   (iii) and (v)
D   (iii), (iv) and (vi)   (2 marks)

3   *Fill in the blank.*

    .... is the fundamental rethinking and radical redesign of business processes to achieve dramatic improvements in critical contemporary measures of performance such as cost, quality, service and speed.   (2 marks)

4   M Ltd is a furniture manufacturer. One of M Ltd's products is a chair which is produced in batches of 50.

    Chairs go through 11 separate production processes which necessitate a total of 18 materials movements per batch. 90 batches are produced each year.

    There are 30,000 materials movements each year, costing £75,000.

    Calculate the activity based cost of materials movements per chair, to the nearest £0.01.   (4 marks)

5   In activity based costing, what is a cost driver?

    A   An overhead cost that is incurred as a direct consequence of an activity
    B   Any direct cost element in a product's cost
    C   Any activity or product item for which costs are incurred
    D   Any factor which causes a change in the cost of an activity   (2 marks)

6   Which of the following definitions is correct?

    A   Activity based management uses activity-based cost information for a variety of purposes including cost reduction, cost modelling and customer profitability analysis.

    B   Activity based management is based on an activity framework and utilises cost driver data in the budget-setting and variances feedback processes.

    C   Activity based management involves the identification and evaluation of the activity drivers used to trace the cost of activities to cost objects. It may also involve selecting activity drivers with potential to contribute to the cost management function with particular reference to cost reduction.

    D   Activity based management involves tracing resource consumption and costing final outputs.
                                                                                                    (2 marks)

7   ABC Ltd manufactures two products, the D and the E. In 20X7, 264 units of the D were produced and 6,876 units of the E. Twenty eight production runs were required during the period, eight for the D and 20 for the E. The set-up costs during the period were £14,280. How should the set-up costs be divided between the two products if a system of activity based costing is used?   (4 marks)

QUESTIONS

8   The problem of producing a small number of products in volume against producing a large variety of products in small runs is known as volume versus variety. Which of the following graphs illustrates this?

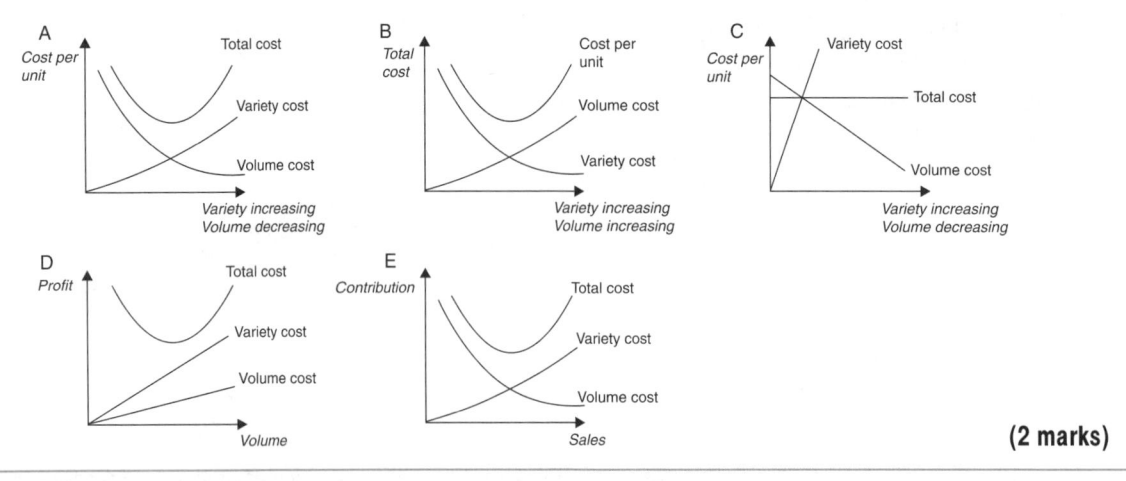

[Graph A: Cost per unit vs Variety increasing/Volume decreasing — showing Total cost, Variety cost, Volume cost]

[Graph B: Total cost vs Variety increasing/Volume increasing — showing Cost per unit, Volume cost, Variety cost]

[Graph C: Cost per unit vs Variety increasing/Volume decreasing — showing Variety cost, Total cost, Volume cost]

[Graph D: Profit vs Volume — showing Total cost, Variety cost, Volume cost]

[Graph E: Contribution vs Sales — showing Total cost, Variety cost, Volume cost]

(2 marks)

(Total = 20 marks)

If you struggled with these OT questions, go back to your BPP Study Text for Paper P2 and revise Chapter 16 before you tackle the 10-mark and 25-mark questions on activity based management.

86 BPR   18 mins

Explain the contribution the management accountant should make to the planning and implementation of a business process re-engineering programme.   (10 marks)

87 LM Hospital (IDEC, 5/01)   45 mins

LM Hospital is a private hospital, whose management is considering the adoption of an activity-based costing (ABC) system for the year 20X1/X2. The main reason for its introduction would be to provide more accurate information for pricing purposes. With the adoption of new medical technology, the amount of time that some patients stay in hospital has decreased considerably, and the management feels that the current pricing strategy may no longer reflect the different costs incurred.

Prices are currently calculated by determining the direct costs for the particular type of operation and adding a mark-up of 135%. With the proposed ABC system, the management expects to use a mark-up for pricing of 15% on cost. This percentage will be based on all costs except facility sustaining costs. It has been decided that the hospital support activities should be grouped into three categories – admissions/record keeping, caring for patients and facility sustaining.

The hospital has four operating theatres that are used for nine hours a day for 300 days a year. It is expected that 7,200 operations will be performed during the coming year. The hospital has 15 consultant surgeons engaged in operating theatre work and consultancy. It is estimated that each consultant surgeon will work at the hospital for 2,000 hours in 20X1/X2.

The expected costs for 20X1/X2

	£
Nursing services and administration	9,936,000
Linen and laundry	920,000
Kitchen and food costs (three meals a day)	2,256,000
Consultant surgeons' fees	5,250,000
Insurance of buildings and general equipment	60,000
Depreciation of buildings and general equipment	520,000
Operating theatre	4,050,000

Pre-operation costs	1,260,000
Medical supplies – used in the hospital wards	1,100,000
Pathology laboratory (where blood tests etc are carried out)	920,000
Updating patient records	590,000
Patient/bed scheduling	100,000
Invoicing and collections	160,000
Housekeeping activities, including ward maintenance, window cleaning etc	760,000

Other information for 20X1/X2

Nursing hours	480,000
Number of pathology laboratory tests	8,000
Patient days	44,000
Number of patients	9,600

Information relating to specific operations for 20X1/X2

	ENT (Ear, nose and throat)	Cataract
Time of stay in hospital	4 days	1 day
Operation time	2 hours	0.5 hour
Consultant surgeon's time (which includes time in the operating theatre)	3 hours	0.85 hour

Required

(a) Before making the final decision on the costing/pricing system, management has selected two types of operation for review: an ear, nose and throat (ENT) operation and a cataract operation.

  (i) Calculate the prices that would be charged under each method for the two types of operation. (Your answer should include an explanation and calculations of the cost drivers you have used.) **(10 marks)**

  (ii) Comment on the results of your calculations and the implications for the proposed pricing policy. **(5 marks)**

(b) Critically assess the method you have used to calculate the ABC prices by selecting two items/categories which you feel you should have been dealt with in a different way. **(5 marks)**

(c) Explain whether the concept of throughput accounting could be used in a hospital. **(5 marks)**

(Total = 25 marks)

88 ZP plc (11/05)   45 mins

ZP plc is a marketing consultancy that provides marketing advice and support to small and medium sized enterprises. ZP plc employs four full time marketing consultants who each expect to deliver 1,500 chargeable hours per year and each receive a salary of £60,000 per year. In addition the company employs six marketing support/administration staff whose combined total salary cost is £120,000 per year.

ZP plc has estimated its other costs for the coming year as follows:

	£'000
Office premises: rent, rates, heating	50
Advertising	5
Travel to clients	15
Accommodation whilst visiting clients	11
Telephone, fax, communications	10

ZP plc has been attributing costs to each client (and to the projects undertaken for them) by recording the chargeable hours spent on each client and using a single cost rate of £75 per chargeable hour. The same basis has been used to estimate the costs of a project when preparing a quotation for new work.

QUESTIONS

ZP plc has reviewed its existing client database and determined the following three average profiles of typical clients:

	Client profile		
	D	E	F
Chargeable hours per client	100	700	300
Distance (miles) to client	50	70	100
Number of visits per client	3	8	3
Number of clients in each profile	10	5	5

The senior consultant has been reviewing the company's costing and pricing procedures. He suggests that the use of a single cost rate should be abandoned and where possible, activities should be costed individually. With this is mind he has obtained the following further information:

- It is ZP plc's policy that where a visit is made to a client and the distance to the client is more than 50 miles, the consultant will travel the day before the visit and stay in local accommodation so that the maximum time is available for meeting the client the following day.

- The cost of travel to the client is dependent on the number of miles travelled to visit the client.

- Other costs are facility costs – at present the senior consultant cannot identify an alternative basis to that currently being used to attribute costs to each client.

Required

(a) Prepare calculations to show the cost attributed to each client group using an activity based system of attributing costs. **(7 marks)**

(b) Discuss the differences between the costs attributed using activity based costing and those attributed by the current system and advise whether the senior consultant's suggestion should be adopted. **(9 marks)**

(c) In a manufacturing environment activity based costing often classifies activities into those that are: unit; batch; product sustaining; and facility sustaining. Discuss, giving examples, how similar classifications may be applied to the use of the technique in consultancy organisations such as ZP plc. **(9 marks)**

(Total = 25 marks)

89 KL (11/06) — 45 mins

KL manufactures three products, W, X and Y. Each product uses the same materials and the same type of direct labour but in different quantities. The company currently uses a cost plus basis to determine the selling price of its products. This is based on full cost using an overhead absorption rate per direct labour hour. However, the managing director is concerned that the company may be losing sales because of its approach to setting prices. He thinks that a marginal costing approach may be more appropriate, particularly since the workforce is guaranteed a minimum weekly wage and has a three month notice period.

Required

(a) Given the managing director's concern about KL's approach to setting selling prices, discuss the advantages and disadvantages of marginal cost plus pricing **AND** total cost plus pricing. **(6 marks)**

The direct costs of the three products are shown below:

Product	W	X	Y
Budgeted annual production (units)	15,000	24,000	20,000
	$ per unit	$ per unit	$ per unit
Direct materials	35	45	30
Direct labour ($10 per hour)	40	30	50

In addition to the above direct costs, KL incurs annual indirect production costs of $1,044,000.

Required

(b) Calculate the full cost per unit of each product using KL's current method of absorption costing.

(4 marks)

An analysis of the company's indirect production costs shows the following:

	$	Cost driver
Material ordering costs	220,000	Number of supplier orders
Machine setup costs	100,000	Number of batches
Machine running costs	400,000	Number of machine hours
General facility costs	324,000	Number of machine hours

The following additional data relate to each product:

Product	W	X	Y
Machine hours per unit	5	8	7
Batch size (units)	500	400	1,000
Supplier orders per batch	4	3	5

Required

(c) Calculate the full cost per unit of each product using activity based costing. **(8 marks)**

(d) Explain how activity based costing could provide information that would be relevant to the management team when it is making decisions about how to improve KL's profitability. **(7 marks)**

(Total = 25 marks)

90 D (5/07)   45 mins

D provides a motorist rescue service to its members. At present all members pay a basic fee of $100 per year but D is considering the introduction of different fees for members depending on the data they provide when joining the service. The number of members, and therefore the fee income of D, is uncertain but the following estimates have been made:

Number of members	Probability
20,000	0·3
30,000	0·5
40,000	0·2

Required

(a) Calculate the expected annual fee income of D **(2 marks)**

The operating costs to be incurred by D have been analysed between call-out costs and administration costs. These operating costs have been assumed to vary in relation to the number of members and consequently the average costs per member for next year are expected to be:

Call-out cost per member for the year	$50
Administration cost per member for the year	$10

Each of these operating costs may vary by plus or minus 20%. There is equal probability of these costs being as expected, 20% higher, or 20% lower. In addition D expects to incur annual fixed costs of $1,100,000.

Required

(b) Using Expected Values, calculate the breakeven number of members. **(3 marks)**

(c) Prepare a two-way data table that shows the nine possible profit values. **(6 marks)**

(d) Explain the meaning of the table that you have produced in (c) above and, by including appropriate probability values, how it may be used by management. **(4 marks)**

Now that you have presented your calculations and explanations to the Management Team of D they have questioned the validity of the assumption that costs are caused by and therefore vary in relation to the number of members. They referred to the activities that are performed by the company:

- Processing applications for membership;
- Operating the call centre that deals with logging and scheduling rescues;
- Providing patrol vehicles and mechanics for breakdown assistance;
- Recording details of the time taken to respond to members' rescues;
- Recording details of the costs incurred in carrying out each rescue.

The Management Team collectively agreed that your assumption that operating costs are driven by the number of members was too simplistic and that in future the Administration department should request the following information from members:

- Member's date of birth;
- Member's address;
- Number of years the member has been a qualified driver;
- Age of vehicle;
- Make and model of vehicle;
- Average annual mileage.

Required

(e) Explain how and why the collection of this data from members might improve the information that would be available to the Management Team. **(10 marks)**

(Total = 25 marks)

91 Section A questions: Contemporary techniques   36 mins

1   Indicate which of the following is an aspect of JIT.

   A   The use of small frequent deliveries against bulk contracts
   B   The grouping of machines or workers by product or component instead of by type of work performed
   C   A reduction in machine set-up time
   D   Production driven by demand

   (3 marks)

2   A company manufactures four products: J, K, L and M. The products use a series of different machines but there is a common machine, X, which causes a bottleneck.

   The standard selling price and standard cost per unit for each product for the forthcoming year are as follows.

	J £	K £	L £	M £
Selling price	2,000	1,500	1,500	1,750
Cost				
Direct materials	410	200	300	400
Labour	300	200	360	275
Variable overheads	250	200	300	175
Fixed overheads	360	300	210	330
Profit	680	600	330	570
Machine X – minutes per unit	120	100	70	110

   Direct materials is the only unit-level manufacturing cost.

Using a throughput accounting approach, the ranking of the products would be

	J	K	L	M
A	1st	2nd	3rd	4th
B	1st	2nd	4th	3rd
C	2nd	1st	4th	3rd
D	2nd	3rd	1st	4th

(2 marks)

3   MN plc uses a JIT system and backflush accounting. It does not use a raw material stock control account. During April, 1,000 units were produced and sold. The standard cost per unit is £100: this includes materials of £45. During April, £60,000 of conversion costs were incurred.

Required

Calculate the debit balance on the cost of goods sold account for April. **(2 marks)**

4   *Fill in the blanks in the sentences below.*

(a)   The aim of TOC is to maximise .... while keeping..................................... and .... to a minimum.

(b)   An assumption in TOC is that all operational expenses except direct material cost are ....

(c)   An activity within an organisation which has a lower capacity than preceding or subsequent activities, thereby limiting throughput, is a .... or ....

(d)   Under TOC, the only inventory that a business should hold, with the exception of possibly a very small amount of finished goods inventory and raw materials that are consistent with the JIT approach, is a buffer inventory held .... **(4 marks)**

5   In 150 words or less, provide a comparison of Kaizen costing and standard costing. **(4 marks)**

6   Company X produces a single product with the following standard cost per unit.

	£
Material cost	10
Conversion cost	12
Total cost	22

The company operates a backflush costing system with a raw material stock control account. Details for the current month are as follows.

	£
Raw material stock control account opening balance	500
Raw materials purchased	4,600
Conversion costs incurred	5,200
Cost of goods sold at standard cost	8,998

Calculate the closing balance on the raw material stock control account. **(3 marks)**

7   A company operates a throughput accounting system. The details of product A per unit are as follows.

Selling price	£24.99
Material cost	£8.87
Conversion costs	£12.27
Time on bottleneck resource	6.5 minutes

Required

Calculate the return per hour for product A. **(2 marks)**

(Total = 20 marks)

If you struggled with these OT questions, go back to your BPP Study Text for Paper P2 and revise Chapter 17 before you tackle the 10-mark and 25-mark questions on contemporary techniques.

92 Question with helping hand: Standard costing, TQM and JIT (IDEC, 5/03, amended) — 18 mins

X Ltd has recently automated its manufacturing plant and has also adopted a Total Quality Management (TQM) philosophy and a Just in Time (JIT) manufacturing system. The company currently uses a standard absorption costing system for the electronic diaries which it manufactures.

Required

Explain why and how X Ltd may have to adapt its standard costing system now that it has adopted TQM and JIT in its recently automated manufacturing plant. **(10 marks)**

> **Helping hand.** Do not fall into the trap of repeating all you know about JIT and TQM. This is a written question but look at three aspects: JIT; TQM; and Standard costing. The question wants you to extract the features of JIT and TQM that would affect the usefulness of a standard costing system. Think about what a standard costing system tries to measure and whether the variances thrown by monitoring are in conflict with JIT. For instance, efficiency variables and material price variances.
>
> Likewise, do the aims of standard costing, ie quantity come into conflict with those of TQM which focuses on quality.
>
> You will also need to consider how the use of automated production will change the way products are costed and so measured under standard costing.
>
> Think about what changes to the cost of a product will occur if automation takes place, for instance direct variable costs will change.
>
> Our answer covers 1½ pages. You should think of three to four clear points for each aspect.

93 Cost management techniques again (IDEC, 11/02, amended) — 18 mins

Traditional cost control systems focused on cost containment rather than cost reduction. Today, cost management focuses on process improvement and the identification of how processes can be more effectively and efficiently performed to result in cost reductions.

Required

Discuss how the cost management techniques of (a) just-in-time and (b) activity based management differ from the traditional cost containment approach and how they seek to achieve cost reduction. **(10 marks)**

94 Exe plc (IMPM, 5/01, amended) 18 mins

Exe plc is a motor car manufacturer. Exe plc has been in business for many years, and it has recently invested heavily in automated processes.

Exe plc is currently experiencing difficulties in maintaining its market share. It is therefore considering various options to improve the quality of its motor cars, and the quality of its service to its customers.

Required

Discuss the significance to Exe plc of developing and maintaining communications with suppliers and customers.

(10 marks)

95 Backflush costing 18 mins

PSA Ltd is a jobbing concern and uses a conventional cost accounting system. The company reports cost variances at the end of each month, with labour and material variances split into operational and planning components. There is significant work in progress at any point in time, but PSA Ltd holds minimal stocks of finished goods and raw materials.

Required

Explain what backflush costing is and (as far as you can on the basis of available information) comment on the suitability of PSA Ltd's operation for backflush costing. **(10 marks)**

96 Question with answer plan: SWAL (Pilot paper) 18 mins

SW is a member of the SWAL Group of companies. SW manufacturers cleaning liquid using chemicals that it buys from a number of suppliers. In the past SW has used a periodic review stock control system with maximum and re-order levels to control the purchase of the chemicals and the economic order quantity model to minimise its costs.

The managing director of SW is considering a change by introducing a Just in Time (JIT) system.

Required

As management accountant, prepare a report to the managing director that explains how a JIT system differs from the system presently being used and the extent to which its introduction would require a review of SW's quality control procedures. **(10 marks)**

97 X Group (5/05) 18 mins

The X Group is a well-established manufacturing group that operates a number of companies using similar production and inventory holding policies. All of the companies are in the same country though there are considerable distances between them.

The group has traditionally operated a constant production system whereby the same volume of output is produced each week, even though the demand for the group's products is subject to seasonal fluctuations. As a result there is always finished goods inventory in the group's warehouses waiting for customer orders. This inventory will include a safety inventory equal to two weeks' production.

Raw material inventories are ordered from suppliers using the Economic Order Quantity (EOQ) model in conjunction with a computerised inventory control system which identifies the need to place an order when the re-order level is reached. The purchasing department is centralised for the group. On receiving a notification from the computerised inventory control system that an order is to be placed, a series of quotation enquiries are issued to prospective suppliers so that the best price and delivery terms are obtained

QUESTIONS

for each order. This practice has resulted in there being a large number of suppliers to the X Group. Each supplier delivers directly to the company that requires the material.

The managing director of the X Group has recently returned from a conference on World Class Manufacturing and was particularly interested in the possible use of Just in Time (JIT) within the X Group.

Required

Write a report, addressed to the managing director of the X Group, that explains how the adoption of JIT might affect its profitability. **(10 marks)**

97 Question with analysis: X Group (5/05)   18 mins

[Current features that will be affected by JIT]

The X Group is a well-established manufacturing group that **operates a number of companies** using **similar production and inventory holding policies**. All of the companies are in the same country though there are considerable distances between them.

The group has **traditionally operated a constant production system** whereby the **same volume of output is produced each week**, even though the demand for the group's products is subject to seasonal fluctuations. As a result there is **always finished goods inventory** in the group's warehouses waiting for customer orders. This inventory will **include a safety inventory equal to two weeks' production**.

Raw material inventories are ordered from suppliers **using the Economic Order Quantity (EOQ)** model in conjunction with a computerised inventory control system which identifies the need to place an order when the re-order level is reached. **The purchasing department is centralised for the group**. On receiving a notification from the computerised inventory control system that an order is to be placed, a series of quotation enquiries are issued to prospective suppliers so that the best price and delivery terms are obtained for each order. This practice has resulted in there being a large number of suppliers to the X Group. Each supplier delivers directly to the company that requires the material.

[Implement JIT across the group]

The managing director of the X Group has recently returned from a conference on World Class Manufacturing and was particularly interested in the **possible use of Just in Time (JIT) within the X Group**.

[Note format required]

Required

[Note requirements to explain how JIT would affect profitability]

Write a report, addressed to the managing director of the X Group, that **explains how the adoption of JIT might affect its profitability**. **(10 marks)**

98 MN Ltd   45 mins

MN Ltd manufactures automated industrial trolleys, known as TRLs. Each TRL sells for £2,000 and the material cost per unit is £600. Labour and variable overhead are £5,500 and £8,000 per week respectively. Fixed production costs are £450,000 per annum and marketing and administrative costs are £265,000 per annum.

The trolleys are made on three different machines. Machine X makes the four frame panels required for each TRL. Its maximum output is 180 frame panels per week. Machine X is old and unreliable and it breaks down from time to time – it is estimated that, on average, between 15 and 20 hours of production are lost per month. Machine Y can manufacture parts for 52 TRLs per week and machine Z, which is old but reasonably reliable, can process and assemble 30 TRLs per week.

The company has recently introduced a just-in-time (JIT) system and it is company policy to hold little work-in-progress and no finished goods stock from week to week. The company operates a 40-hour week, 48 weeks a year

(12 months × 4 weeks) but cannot meet demand. The demand for the next year is predicted to be as follows and this is expected to be typical of the demand for the next four years.

	Units per week		Units per week
January	30	July	48
February	30	August	45
March	33	September	42
April	36	October	40
May	39	November	33
June	44	December	30

The production manager has suggested that the company replaces machine Z with machine G which can process 45 TRLs per week. The maintenance manager is keen to spend £100,000 on a major overhaul of machine X as he says this will make it 100% reliable.

Required

(a) Calculate the throughput accounting ratio (defined below) for the key resource for an average hour next year.

$$\text{Throughput accounting ratio} = \frac{\text{return per factory hour}}{\text{cost per factory hour}}$$

where $\text{return per factory hour} = \dfrac{\text{sales price} - \text{material cost}}{\text{time on key resource}}$ **(5 marks)**

(b) Briefly describe the uses to which advocates of throughput accounting suggest that the ratio be put. **(4 marks)**

(c) Suggest two other ratios which may be used by a company operating throughput accounting and explain the use to which they may be put. **(5 marks)**

(d) Explain how the concept of contribution in throughput accounting differs from that in marginal costing. **(6 marks)**

(e) Machine G is purchased and Machine X is overhauled. Describe the impact that this should have on monitoring and reporting production activities. **(5 marks)**

(Total = 25 marks)

99 SG plc (IMPM, 11/02) — 45 mins

SG plc is a long-established food manufacturer which produces semi-processed foods for fast food outlets. While for a number of years it has recognised the need to produce good quality products for its customers, it does not have a formalised quality management programme.

A director of the company has recently returned from a conference, where one of the speakers introduced the concept of Total Quality Management (TQM) and the need to recognise and classify quality costs.

Required

(a) Explain what is meant by TQM and use examples to show how it may be introduced into different areas of SG plc's food production business. **(12 marks)**

(b) Explain why the adoption of TQM is particularly important within a Just-in-Time (JIT) production environment. **(5 marks)**

(c) Explain four quality cost classifications, using examples relevant to the business of SG plc. **(8 marks)**

(Total = 25 marks)

100 Quality costs (5/06)   18 mins

The Managing Director of a manufacturing company based in Eastern Europe has recently returned from a conference on modern manufacturing. One of the speakers at the conference presented a paper entitled 'Compliance versus Conformance – the quality control issue'. The Managing Director would like you to explain to her some of the concepts that she heard about at the conference.

Required

Prepare a report, addressed to the Managing Director, that discusses quality costs and their significance for the company. Your report should include examples of the different quality costs and their classification within a manufacturing environment. **(10 marks)**

Note: 2 marks are available for report format

101 Section A questions: Externally-orientated techniques
36 mins

1   In Pareto analysis, what is the 80/20 rule?

    I   An approximate rule to the effect that 20% of the products will provide 80% of sales.

    II   An approximate rule to the effect that an increase of 80% in costs will be reflected by a 20% decline in sales.

    III An approximate rule to the effect that 80% of wealth is held by 20% of the population.

    IV An approximate rule to the effect that the wealth of the richest 20% of the population equals that of the other 80%.

    A   II and III
    B   II only
    C   I only
    D   I and III **(2 marks)**

2   Explain, in no more than 100 words, within which areas of a contract or associated supply chain gain-sharing opportunities can exist. **(4 marks)**

3   In pain-/gain-sharing arrangements, cost overruns are the responsibility of the contractor while the customer receives only cost savings. *True or false?* **(2 marks)**

4   S Ltd manufactures components for the aircraft industry. The following annual information regarding three of its key customers is available.

	W	X	Y
Gross margin	£1,100,000	£1,750,000	£1,200,000
General administration costs	£40,000	£80,000	£30,000
Units sold	1,750	2,000	1,500
Orders placed	1,000	1,000	1,500
Sales visits	110	100	170
Invoices raised	900	1,200	1,500

The company uses an activity based costing system and the analysis of customer-related costs is as follows.

Sales visits	£500 per visit
Order processing	£100 per order placed
Despatch costs	£100 per order placed
Billing and collections	£175 per invoice raised

Using customer profitability analysis, write the ranking of the customers. **(4 marks)**

5   AB plc is a supermarket group which incurs the following costs.

   (i)   The bought-in price of the good
   (ii) Inventory financing costs
   (iii) Shelf refilling costs
   (iv) Costs of repacking or 'pack out' prior to storage before sale

   AB plc's calculation of direct product profit (DPP) would include

   A   all of the above costs
   B   all of the above costs except (ii)
   C   all of the above costs except (iv)
   D   cost (i) only   (2 marks)

6   Explain, in no more than 100 words, how an organisation chooses which activities (if any) to outsource.
                                                                                        (4 marks)

7   Indicate in which of the following situations Pareto analysis might be useful.

   A   When reviewing stock control procedures
   B   When conducting a comparative customer profitability analysis
   C   When calculating direct product profit   (2 marks)

                                                                                  (Total = 20 marks)

If you struggled with these OT questions, go back to your BPP Study Text for Paper P2 and revise Chapter 18 before you tackle the 10-mark and 25-mark questions on externally-orientated techniques.

102 AVN (11/06)   18 mins

AVN designs and assembles electronic devices to allow transmission of audio / visual communications between the original source and various other locations within the same building. Many of these devices require a wired solution but the company is currently developing a wireless alternative. The company produces a number of different devices depending on the number of input sources and the number of output locations, but the technology used within each device is identical. AVN is constantly developing new devices which improve the quality of the audio / visual communications that are received at the output locations.

The managing director recently attended a conference on world class manufacturing entitled 'The extension of the value chain to include suppliers and customers' and seeks your help.

Required

Explain

(a)   the components of the extended value chain; and   (3 marks)

(b)   how each of the components may be applied by AVN.   (7 marks)

                                                                                     (Total 10 marks)

103 Offshoring   18 mins

Briefly discuss the reasons for the trend of offshoring in outsourcing, and its disadvantages.   (10 marks)

104 Chains   18 mins

Your managing director remarks to you that he is aware of a number of business initiatives about which he knows embarrassingly little. He mentions in particular that a management consultant keeps talking to him about the supply chain and the value chain, and how they should be managed to add value. He is vaguely aware that initiatives such as e-procurement and outsourcing are examples of improvements the consultant has in mind.

Required

Explain what is meant by the terms 'supply chain' and 'value chain', and the purpose of supply chain management and value chain management. As part of your explanation, suggest how e-procurement and outsourcing are initiatives that might feature in supply chain management as a means of improving performance. **(10 marks)**

105 Preferred suppliers   18 mins

A preferred supplier is one to whom a buyer gives advantages over other suppliers, usually in the form of regular purchases, perhaps for a guaranteed future period. The major reason for choosing to have preferred suppliers is that they can provide the customer with a competitive advantage – they can provide a unique product or service, or a degree of quality or value that is not made available to the customer's competitors, or is not available from other suppliers.

Required

Briefly discuss the issues that an organisation should consider if preferred supplier status is being sought with a customer. **(10 marks)**

106 Partnering   18 mins

'In contrast with traditional "arms-length" procurement and contract management approaches, partnering is characterised by a greater degree of openness, communication, mutual trust and sharing information. The aims of partnering arrangements are often expressed in terms of business outcomes rather than specific outputs or improvements; their success is particularly dependent on the people and relationship aspects.'

(from the Office of Government Commerce website)

Required

(a) Briefly describe the circumstances in which partnering is appropriate, and those when it is unsuitable.
(b) Briefly describe some of the common pitfalls associated with partnering. **(10 marks)**

107 RS plc (IDEC, Pilot paper)   45 mins

RS plc is a retail organisation. It has fifteen supermarkets, all of which are the same size. Goods are transported to RS plc's central warehouse by suppliers' vehicles, and are stored at the warehouse until needed at the supermarkets – at which point they are transported by RS plc's lorries.

RS plc's costs are:

	£'000
Warehouse costs, per week	
Labour costs	220
Refrigeration costs	160
Other direct product costs	340
	720

	£'000
Head office costs, per week	
Labour costs	80
Other costs	76
	156

	£'000
Supermarket costs per shop, per week	
Labour costs	16
Refrigeration costs	24
Other direct product costs	28
	68

	£
Transport costs per trip	
Standard vehicles	3,750
Refrigerated vehicles	4,950

The company has always used retail sales revenue less bought-in price to calculate the relative profitability of the different products. However, the chief executive is not happy with this method and has asked for three products – baked beans, ice cream and South African white wine – to be costed on a direct product profit basis. The accountant has determined the following information for the supermarket chain.

	Baked beans	Ice cream	White wine
No of cases per cubic metre (m^3)	28	24	42
No of items per case	80	18	12
Sales per week – items	15,000	2,000	500
Time in warehouse – weeks	1	2	4
Time in supermarket – weeks	1	2	2
Retail selling price per item	£0.32	£1.60	£3.45
Bought-in price per item	£0.24	£0.95	£2.85

Additional information:

Total volume of all goods sold per week	20,000 m^3
Total volume of refrigerated goods sold per week	5,000 m^3
Carrying volume of each vehicle	90 m^3
Total sales revenue per week	£5m
Total sales revenue of refrigerated goods per week	£650,000

Required

(a) Calculate the profit per item using the direct product profitability method. **(13 marks)**

(b) Discuss the differences in profitability between the company's current method and the results of your calculations in (a), and suggest ways in which profitability could be improved. **(7 marks)**

(c) Explain how the direct product profit method differs from traditional overhead absorption. **(5 marks)**

(Total = 25 marks)

107 Question with analysis: RS plc (IDEC, Pilot paper) 45 mins

RS plc is a retail organisation. It has fifteen supermarkets, all of which are the same size. Goods are transported to RS plc's central warehouse by suppliers' vehicles, and are stored at the warehouse until needed at the supermarkets – at which point they are transported by RS plc's lorries.

QUESTIONS

RS plc's costs are:

[Costs are per week]

	£'000
Warehouse costs, **per week**	
Labour costs	220
Refrigeration costs	160
Other direct product costs	340
	720

	£'000
Head office costs, **per week**	
Labour costs	80
Other costs	76
	156

	£'000
Supermarket costs per shop, **per week**	
Labour costs	16
Refrigeration costs	24
Other direct product costs	28
	68

[Costs are per trip]

	£
Transport costs **per trip**	
Standard vehicles	3,750
Refrigerated vehicles	4,950

The company has always used **retail sales revenue less bought-in price to calculate the relative profitability** of the different products. **However, the chief executive is not happy with this method and has asked for three products – baked beans, ice cream and South African white wine – to be costed on a direct product profit basis**. The accountant has determined the following information for the supermarket chain.

[Requirement to cost using DPP]

	Baked beans	Ice cream	White wine
No of cases per cubic metre (m³)	28	24	42
No of items per case	80	18	12
Sales per week – items	15,000	2,000	500
Time in warehouse – weeks	1	2	4
Time in supermarket – weeks	1	2	2
Retail selling price per item	£0.32	£1.60	£3.45
Bought-in price per item	£0.24	£0.95	£2.85

Additional information:

Total volume of all goods sold per week	20,000 m³
Total volume of refrigerated goods sold per week	5,000 m³
Carrying volume of each vehicle	90 m³
Total sales revenue per week	£5m
Total sales revenue of refrigerated goods per week	£650,000

Required [You need to remember how to do this from your notes]

[Compare and contrast]

(a) Calculate the profit per item using the direct product profitability method. **(13 marks)**

(b) **Discuss the differences** in profitability between the company's current method and the **results** of your calculations in (a), and **suggest** ways in which profitability could be improved. **(7 marks)**

[Write what you know about DPP and how it compares to traditional method]

(c) **Explain** how the direct product profit method differs from traditional overhead absorption. **(5 marks)**

[2 requirements here]

(Total = 25 marks)

102

108 S&P Products plc (IDEC, 11/01, amended) 45 mins

S&P Products plc purchases a range of good quality gift and household products from around the world; it then sells these products through 'mail order' or retail outlets. The company receives 'mail orders' by post, telephone and Internet. Retail outlets are either department stores or S&P Products plc's own small shops. The company started to set up its own shops after a recession in the early 1990s and regards them as the flagship of its business; sales revenue has gradually built up over the last ten years. There are now 50 department stores and ten shops.

The company has made good profits over the last few years but recently trading has been difficult. As a consequence, the management team has decided that a fundamental reappraisal of the business is now necessary if the company is to continue trading.

Meanwhile the budgeting process for the coming year is proceeding. S&P Products plc uses an activity based costing (ABC) system and the following estimated cost information for the coming year is available.

Retail outlet costs

		Rate per cost driver	Number each year Department store	Own shop
Activity	Cost driver	£		
Telephone queries and requests to S&P	Calls	15	40	350
Sales visits to shops and stores by S&P sales staff	Visits	250	2	4
Shop orders	Orders	20	25	150
Packaging	Deliveries	100	28	150
Delivery to shops	Deliveries	150	28	150

Staffing, rental and service costs for each of S&P Products plc's own shops cost on average £300,000 a year.

Mail order costs

		Rate per cost driver		
Activity	Cost driver	Post	Telephone	Internet
		£	£	£
Processing 'mail orders'	Orders	5	6	3
Dealing with 'mail order' queries	Orders	4	4	1
		Number of packages per order		
Packaging and deliveries for 'mail orders' - cost per package £10	Packages	2	2	1

The total number of orders through the whole 'mail order' business for the coming year is expected to be 80,000. The maintenance of the Internet link is estimated to cost £80,000 for the coming year.

The following additional information for the coming year has been prepared.

	Dept store	Own shop	Post	Telephone	Internet
Sales revenue per outlet	£50,000	£1,000,000			
Sales revenue per order			£150	£300	£100
Gross margin: mark-up on purchase cost	30%	40%	40%	40%	40%
Number of outlets	50	10			
Percentage of 'mail orders'			30%	60%	10%

QUESTIONS

Expected head office and warehousing costs for the coming year are as follows.

	£
Warehouse	2,750,000
IT	550,000
Administration	750,000
Personnel	300,000
	4,350,000

Required

(a) (i) Prepare calculations that will show the expected profitability of the different types of sales outlet or order for the coming year. **(13 marks)**

(ii) Comment briefly on the results of the figures you have prepared. **(3 marks)**

(b) In relation to the company's fundamental reappraisal of its business, do the following.

(i) Discuss how helpful the information you have prepared in (a) is for this purpose and how it might be revised or expanded so that it is of more assistance. **(5 marks)**

(ii) Advise what other information is needed in order to make a more informed judgement. **(4 marks)**

(Total = 25 marks)

109 FF plc (IDEC, 11/03, amended)   45 mins

(a) FF plc is a bank that offers a variety of banking services to its clients. One of the services offered is aimed at high net worth individuals and the bank is currently reviewing the performance of its client base.

The high net worth clients are classified into four groups based on the value of their individual liquid assets deposited in FF plc. The following annual budgeted information has been prepared:

Group	W	X	Y	Z
Individual value ('000s)	$500-$999	$1,000-$2,999	$3,000-$5,999	$6,000-$9,999
Number of clients	1,000	1,500	2,000	1,800

	$'000	$'000	$'000	$'000	Total $'000
Total contribution	500	900	1,400	2,500	5,300
Overheads:					
Share of support costs	285	760	790	1,165	3,000
Share of facility costs	100	160	240	500	1,000
Profit/(loss)	115	(20)	370	835	1,300

FF plc is about to implement an activity based costing (ABC) system. The implementation team recently completed an analysis of the support costs. The analysis revealed that these costs were variable in relation to certain drivers. The details of the analysis are shown below.

Group	W	X	Y	Z	Total
Activity	000s	000s	000s	000s	000s
Number of telephone enquiries	200	150	220	300	870
Number of statements prepared	120	120	240	480	960
Number of client meetings	60	100	110	200	470

Activity	Support costs/overheads
	$'000
Telephone enquiries	1,000
Statements prepared	250
Client meetings	1,750
Total	3,000

The bank manager feels that the low profitability from client Group W and the losses from client Group X need to be investigated further and that consideration should be given to discontinuing these services and concentrating the marketing and sales effort on increasing the number of clients within Group Y and Group Z. He has outlined two proposals, as follows:

Proposal 1

Discontinue both of Groups W and X in order to concentrate on Groups Y and Z (so that the bank would have only two client groups). If this option were implemented, it is expected that the facility costs would increase by 10%.

The marketing manager has calculated the probability of the number of clients the bank would serve to be as shown below.

Projected revised numbers of clients in Groups Y and Z

Group Y		Group Z	
Client numbers	Probability	Client numbers	Probability
2,250	0.30	2,000	0.20
2,500	0.40	2,200	0.50
2,750	0.30	2,500	0.30

Proposal 2

Discontinue either Group W or Group X in order to concentrate on Groups Y and Z (so that the bank would have three client groups). If this option were implemented, it is expected that the facility costs would increase by 8%.

If this proposal is implemented, the marketing manager estimates that the **increase** in client numbers in Groups Y and Z would be reduced by 75%, compared with proposal 1.

Required

(i) Prepare a customer profitability statement based on the ABC analysis and comment on your results.
(8 marks)

(ii) Using the ABC details, evaluate the proposal of the bank manager (your answer must be supported by calculations). **(10 marks)**

(b) M Ltd has two divisions, X and Y. Division X is a chip manufacturer and Division Y assembles mobile phones.

The accountant of M Ltd has recently attended a course on activity based costing (ABC) and has recommended that the divisions should implement an ABC system rather than continue to operate the traditional absorption costing system.

Required

The management team of M Ltd has decided to implement ABC in all of the divisions. Discuss any difficulties which might be experienced when implementing ABC in the divisions. **(7 marks)**

(Total = 25 marks)

QUESTIONS

110 Section A questions: Mixed bank 1   36 mins

1   LEFM Ltd is considering the purchase of a machine for £1,200,000. It would be sold after five years for an estimated realisable value of £450,000. By this time capital allowances of £950,000 would have been claimed. The rate of corporation tax is 30%.

   Required

   Calculate the cash flow arising as a result of the tax implications on the sale of the machine at the end of the five years.   **(3 marks)**

2   A supermarket is trying to determine the optimal replacement policy for its fleet of delivery vehicles. The total purchase price of the fleet is £220,000.

   The running costs and scrap values of the fleet at the end of each year are:

	Year 1	Year 2	Year 3	Year 4
	£	£	£	£
Running costs	110,000	132,000	154,000	165,000
Scrap value	121,000	88,000	66,000	55,000

   The supermarket's cost of capital is 12% per annum.

   Ignore taxation and inflation.

   Indicate when the supermarket should replace its fleet of delivery vehicles.   **(4 marks)**

3   RT plc sells three products.

   Product R has a contribution to sales ratio of 30%.
   Product S has a contribution to sales ratio of 20%.
   Product T has a contribution to sales ratio of 25%.

   Monthly fixed costs are £100,000.

   If the products are sold in the ratio:

   R: 2   S: 5   T: 3

   the monthly breakeven sales revenue, to the nearest £1, is

   A   £400,000
   B   £411,107
   C   £425,532
   D   Impossible to calculate without further information   **(2 marks)**

4   ABC plc is about to launch a new product. Facilities will allow the company to produce up to 20 units per week. The marketing department has estimated that at a price of £8,000 no units will be sold, but for each £150 reduction in price one additional unit per week will be sold.

   Fixed costs associated with manufacture are expected to be £12,000 per week.

   Variable costs are expected to be £4,000 per unit for each of the first 10 units; thereafter each unit will cost £400 more than the preceding one.

   The most profitable level of output per week for the new product is 11 units. *True or false?*   **(3 marks)**

5   When analysing whether to replace an asset, which ONE of the following is not relevant?

   A   Balancing charge or allowance on the old asset
   B   Book value of the old asset
   C   Changes in working capital
   D   Removal costs of the old asset   **(2 marks)**

The following data relates to questions 110.6, 110.7, and 110.8

T plc manufactures a component D12, and two main products F45 and P67. The following details relate to each of these items.

	D12 $ per unit	F45 $ per unit	P67 $ per unit
Selling price	–	146.00	159.00
Material cost	10.00	15.00	26.00
Component D12 (bought-in price)		25.00	25.00
Direct labour	5.00	10.00	15.00
Variable overhead	6.00	12.00	18.00
Total variable cost per unit	21.00	62.00	84.00

	$ per annum	$ per annum	$ per annum
Fixed overhead costs			
Avoidable *	9,000	18,000	40,000
Non-avoidable	36,000	72,000	160,000
Total	45,000	90,000	200,000

* The avoidable fixed costs are product specific fixed costs that would be avoided if the product or component were to be discontinued.

6 Assuming that the annual demand for component D12 is 5,000 units and that T plc has sufficient capacity to make the component itself, the maximum price that should be paid to an external supplier for 5,000 components per year is

    A $105,000
    B $114,000
    C $141,000
    D $150,000

(2 marks)

7 Assuming that component D12 is bought from an external supplier for $25.00 per unit, the number of units of product F45 that must be sold to cover its own costs without contributing to T plc's non-avoidable fixed costs is closest to

    A   188 units
    B   214 units
    C   228 units
    D   261 units

(2 marks)

8 Assuming that component D12 is bought from an external supplier for $25.00 per unit and assuming that units of products F45 and P67 are to be sold in the ratio of 4:3 respectively, the breakeven sales value (to the nearest $'000) is

    A $506,000
    B $549,000
    C $616,000
    D $624,000

(2 marks)

(Total = 20 marks)

111 Section A questions: Mixed bank 2   36 mins

1   A company can invest in one of three solutions to a waste treatment problem. The cashflows are set out below.

Year	Option 1 £	Option 2 £	Option 3 £
0	19,500	28,000	31,000
1	30,000	16,000	27,000
2	63,000	50,000	32,000
3	15,000		41,000
4			26,000

The company's cost of capital is 15%.

Rank the three options in terms of their financial attractiveness. (4 marks)

2   BG plc has recently developed a new product. The nature of BG plc's work is repetitive, and it is usual for there to be an 80% learning effect when a new product is developed. The time taken for the first unit was 22 minutes. Assume that an 80% learning effect applies.

Required

Calculate the time taken for the fourth unit. (3 marks)

The following data relates to questions 111.3 and 111.4

An education authority is considering the implementation of a CCTV (closed circuit television) security system in one of its schools. Details of the proposed project are as follows.

Life of project   5 years
Initial cost   £75,000

Annual savings:
Labour costs   £20,000
Other costs   £5,000
Cost of capital   15% per annum

3   The internal rate of return for this project is nearest to

   A   10.13%
   B   14.87%
   C   15.64%
   D   19.88%   (2 marks)

4   Calculate the percentage change in the annual labour cost savings that could occur before the project ceased to be viable. (3 marks)

The following data relates to questions 111.5 and 111.6

P Ltd currently sells 90,000 units of product Y per annum. At this level of sales and output, the selling price and variable cost per unit are £50 and £21 respectively. The annual fixed costs are £1,200,000. The management team is considering lowering the selling price per unit to £45.

The estimated levels of demand at the new price, and the probabilities of them occurring, are:

Selling price of £45

Demand	Probability
100,000 units	0.45
120,000 units	0.55

It is thought that at either of the higher sales and production levels, the variable cost per unit, and the probability of it occurring, will be as follows:

Variable cost (per unit)	Probability
£20	0.40
£18	0.60

5   Calculate the probability that lowering the selling price to £45 per unit would increase profit. **(4 marks)**

6   The expected value of the company profit if the selling price is reduced to £45 per unit is £639,000. *True or false?* **(4 marks)**

(Total = 20 marks)

112 Section A questions: Mixed bank 3   36 mins

1   Indicate which of the following items would be included in the calculation of the life cycle costs of a product.

    A   Planning and concept design costs
    B   Preliminary and detailed design costs
    C   Testing costs
    D   Production costs
    E   Distribution and customer service costs   **(2 marks)**

2   KLQ plc sells three products. The ratio of their total sales values is K2:L3:Q5. The contribution to sales ratios of the products are

    K   30%
    L   25%
    Q   40%

If fixed costs for the period are expected to be £120,000, the revenue (to the nearest £1,000) needed to earn a marginal costing profit of £34,000 is

    A   £392,000
    B   £413,000
    C   £460,000
    D   £486,000   **(2 marks)**

3   A company produces two products, A and B, which pass through two production processes, J and K. The time taken to make each product in each process is as follows.

	Product A	Product B
Process J	6 ½ mins	9 mins
Process K	22 mins	15 mins

The company operates a 16-hour day and the processes have an average downtime each day as follows.

Process J	2½ hours
Process K	2 hours

The costs and revenue for each unit of each product are as follows.

QUESTIONS

	Product A	Product B
	£	£
Direct materials	15.00	15.00
Direct labour	17.00	12.00
Variable overhead	8.00	6.00
Fixed costs	8.00	6.00
Total cost	48.00	39.00
Selling price	87.50	72.50

Sales demand restricts the output of A and B to 40 and 60 units a day respectively.

Calculate the daily production plan that would maximise the THROUGHPUT contribution. **(3 marks)**

The following data relates to questions 112.4, 112.5 and 112.6

HG plc manufactures four products. The unit cost, selling price and bottleneck resource details per unit are as follows.

	Product W	Product X	Product Y	Product Z
	£	£	£	£
Selling price	56	67	89	96
Material	22	31	38	46
Labour	15	20	18	24
Variable overhead	12	15	18	15
Fixed overhead	4	2	8	7
	Minutes	Minutes	Minutes	Minutes
Bottleneck resource time	10	10	15	15

4 Assuming that labour is a unit variable cost, if the products are ranked according to their contribution to sales ratios, the most profitable product is

  A W
  B X
  C Y
  D Z

(2 marks)

5 Assume that labour is a unit variable cost, budgeted unit sales are in the ratio W : 2, X : 3, Y : 3, Z : 4 and monthly fixed costs are budgeted to be £15,000.

  Required

  Calculate the number of units of W that would be sold at the budgeted breakeven point. **(2 marks)**

6 If the company adopted throughput accounting and the products were ranked according to 'product return per minute', the highest ranked product would be product X. *True or false?* **(2 marks)**

7 A company is about to commence work on a repeat order for a customer. The item to be manufactured is identical to the first order, and it is expected that a 90 per cent learning curve will apply to the labour operations. The time taken to produce the first item was 100 hours. If labour is paid at the rate of £7 per hour, the labour cost of manufacturing the second item will be

  A £560
  B £630
  C £700
  D £1,260

(2 marks)

8   CC Ltd is in the process of preparing a quotation for a special job for a customer. The job will require 510 units of material S. 420 units are already in stock at a book value of £50 per unit. The net realisable value per unit is £30. The replacement price per unit is £72. The material is in stock as a result of previous over buying. The units in stock could be used on another job as a substitute for 750 units of material V, which are about to be purchased at a price of £25 per unit.

   Required

   Calculate the relevant cost of material S for this special job for the customer. **(3 marks)**

9   A company is calculating the relevant cost of the material to be used on a particular contract.

   The contract requires 4,200 kgs of material H and this can be bought for $6.30 per kg.

   The company bought 10,000 kgs of material H some time ago when it paid $4.50 per kg. Currently 3,700 kgs of this remains in stock. The stock of material H could be sold for $3.20 per kg.

   The company has no other use for material H other than on this contract, but it could modify it at a cost of $3.70 per kg and use it as a substitute for material J. Material J is regularly used by the company and can be bought for $7.50 per kg.

   The relevant cost of the material for the contract is

   A $17,210
   B $19,800
   C $26,460
   D $30,900 **(2 marks)**

   (Total = 20 marks)

113 Section A questions: Mixed bank 4 (5/05) 36 mins

1   The following details relate to ready meals that are prepared by a food processing company:

Ready meal	K $/meal	L $/meal	M $/meal
Selling price	5.00	3.00	4..40
Ingredients	2.00	1.00	1.30
Variable conversion costs	1.60	0.80	1.85
Fixed conversion costs*	0.50	0.30	0.60
Profit	0.90	0.90	0.65
Oven time (minutes per ready meal)	10	4	8

   Each of the meals is prepared using a series of processes, one of which involves cooking the ingredients in a large oven. The availability of cooking time in the oven is limited and, because each of the meals requires cooking at a different oven temperature, it is not possible to cook more than one of the meals in the oven at the same time.

   * The fixed conversion costs are general fixed costs that are not specific to any type of ready meal.

   The most and least profitable use of the oven is

	Most profitable	Least profitable
A	Meal K	Meal L
B	Meal L	Meal M
C	Meal L	Meal K
D	Meal M	Meal L	**(2 marks)**

QUESTIONS

2 A company provides three different levels of customer service support for one of its software products.

The following data relate to these three levels of support:

Support level	Superior $ per contract	Standard $ per contract	Basic $ per contract
Annual fee	1,000	750	400
Annual variable costs	450	250	180
Annual fixed costs (see note below)	200	100	50
Profit	350	400	170

Note. The total annual fixed costs are budgeted to be $1,000,000. None of these costs are specific to any type of customer service support.

Assuming that the number of customer service support contracts sold are in the proportion:

Superior 20%   Standard 30%   Basic 50%

The annual revenue needed to be generated to break even is closest to

- A $1,690,000
- B $1,695,000
- C $1,710,000
- D $2,270,000

(2 marks)

3 A company is preparing a quotation for a one-month consultancy project and seeks your help in determining the relevant cost of one of the members of its project team. Currently the company employs the consultant on an annual salary of £36,000. In addition, the company provides the consultant with a company car which incurs running costs of £6,000 each year. The car will continue to be provided to the consultant whether this project is undertaken by the company or not.

This consultant is fully employed on current projects and, if she were to be transferred to this new project, then an existing junior consultant would be used to cover her current work. The junior consultant would be paid a bonus of £5,000 for undertaking this additional responsibility.

Another alternative that the company is considering is hiring an external consultant who has the necessary technical knowledge to work on the new consultancy project on a one month contract at a cost of £4,500.

The relevant cost to be used in preparing the quotation is

- A £3,000
- B £3,500
- C £4,500
- D £5,000

(2 marks)

4 A company has determined that the net present value of an investment project is $12,304 when using a 10% discount rate and $(3,216) when using a discount rate of 15%.

Calculate the Internal Rate of Return on the project to the nearest 1%. **(2 marks)**

5 A company has a nominal (money) cost of capital of 18% per annum. If inflation is 6% each year, calculate the company's real cost of capital to the nearest 0.01%. **(2 marks)**

6 A company is considering the price that it should charge for a repeat order. Fifteen units of the product have already been made and supplied to the customer and the company has experienced an 80% learning curve so far. The first unit required 54 hours of labour to complete the manufacture, assembly and testing processes.

Assuming that the 80% learning curve continues, calculate the expected time to be taken for the 16th unit.

Note. The learning index for an 80% learning curve is –0.3219. **(3 marks)**

7   A company has estimated the selling prices and variable costs of one of its products as follows:

Selling price per unit		Variable cost per unit	
$	Probability	$	Probability
40	0.30	20	0.55
50	0.45	30	0.25
60	0.25	40	0.20

Given that the company will be able to supply 1,000 units of its product each week irrespective of the selling price, and variable costs per unit are independent of each other, calculate the probability that the weekly contribution will exceed $20,000. **(3 marks)**

8   A company is considering the pricing of one of its products. It has already carried out some market research with the following results:

The quantity demanded at a price of $100 will be 1,000 units.

The quantity demanded will increase/decrease by 100 units for every $50 decrease/increase in the selling price.

The marginal cost of each unit is $35.

Note that if selling price (P) = a – bx then marginal revenue = a – 2bx

Calculate the selling price that maximises company profit. **(4 marks)**

(Total = 20 marks)

114 Section A questions: Mixed bank 5 (Pilot paper)   36 mins

1   The following details relate to three services provided by JHN.

	Service J $	Service H $	Service N $
Fee charged to customers for each unit of service	84	122	145
Unit service costs			
Direct materials	12	23	22
Direct labour	15	20	25
Variable overhead	12	16	20
Fixed overhead	20	42	40

All three services use the same type of direct labour which is paid at $30 per hour.

In a period when the availability of the direct labour is limited, the most and least profitable use of the direct labour are:

	Most profitable	Least profitable
A	H	J
B	H	N
C	N	J
D	N	H

(2 marks)

QUESTIONS

2 The following equations have been taken from the plans of DX for the year ending 31 December 20X5:

Contribution (in dollars) = 12 × 1 + 5 × 2 + 8 × 3

2 × 1 + 3 × 2 + 4 × 3 + s1 = 12,000 kilos
6 × 1 + 4 × 2 + 3 × 3 + s2 = 8,000 machine hours

$0 \leq x1 \leq 2,000$
$100 \leq x2 \leq 500$
$5 \leq x3 \leq 200$

where: x1, x2 and x3 are the number of units of products produced and sold,
s1 is raw material still available, and
s2 is machine hours still available.

If an unlimited supply of raw material s1 could be obtained at the current price, the product mix that maximises the value of DX plc's contribution is

	X1	X2	X3
A	1,333	0	0
B	1,233	0	200
C	1,166	100	200
D	1,241	100	50

(2 marks)

3 An organisation is considering the costs to be incurred in respect of a special order opportunity. The order would require 1,250 kgs of material D. This is a material that is readily available and regularly used by the organisation on its normal products. There are 265 kgs of material D in stock which cost $795 last week. The current market price is $3.24 per kg.

Material D is normally used to make product X. Each unit of X requires 3 kgs of material D, and if material D is costed at $3 per kg, each unit of X yields a contribution of $15.

The relevant cost of material D to be included in the costing of the special order is nearest to

A $3,990
B $4,050
C $10,000
D $10,300

(2 marks)

The following data relates to both questions 114.4 and 114.5

TX Ltd can choose from five mutually exclusive projects. The projects will each last for one year only and their net cash inflows will be determined by the prevailing market conditions. The forecast net cash inflows and their associated probabilities are shown below.

	Market conditions		
	Poor	Good	Excellent
Probability	0.20	0.50	0.30
	$'000	$'000	$'000
Project L	500	470	550
Project M	400	550	570
Project N	450	400	475
Project O	360	400	420
Project P	600	500	425

4 Based on the expected value of the net cash inflows, which project should be undertaken? **(2 marks)**

5 The value of perfect information about the state of the market is calculated as: **(3 marks)**

6   An organisation manufactures four products – J, K, L and M. The products use a series of different machines but there is a common machine, X, which causes a bottleneck.

The standard selling price and standard cost per unit for each product for the forthcoming year are as follows:

	J £/unit	K £/unit	L £/unit	M £/unit
Selling price	2,000	1,500	1,500	1,750
Cost Direct materials	410	200	300	400
Labour	300	200	360	275
Variable overheads	250	200	300	175
Fixed overheads	360	300	210	330
Profit	680	600	330	570
Machine X – minutes per unit	120	100	70	110

Direct materials is the only unit-level manufacturing cost.

Using a throughput accounting approach, the ranking of the products would be: **(3 marks)**

7   BG has recently developed a new product. The nature of BG's work is repetitive, and it is usual for there to be an 80% learning effect when a new product is developed. The time taken for the first unit was 22 months. Assuming that an 80% learning effect applies, the time to be taken for the fourth unit is: **(3 marks)**

8   XJ, a manufacturing company, has two divisions: Division A and Division B. Division A produces one type of product, Prod X, which it transfers to Division B and also sells externally. Division B has been approached by another company which has offered to supply 2,500 units of Prod X for $35 each.

The following details for Division A are available:

	$'000
Sales revenue	
Sales to Division B @ $40 per unit	400
External sales @ $45 per unit	270
Less: variable cost @ $22 per unit	352
Fixed costs	100
Profit	218

If Division B decides to buy from the other company, the impact of the decision on the profits of Division A and XJ, assuming external sales of Product X cannot be increased will be: **(3 marks)**

115 Section A questions: Mixed bank 6 (11/05)   36 mins

1   A five-year project has a net present value of $160,000 when it is discounted at 12%. The project includes an annual cash outflow of $50,000 for each of the five years. No tax is payable on projects of this type.

The percentage increase in the value of this annual cash outflow that would make the project no longer financially viable is closest to:

A   64%
B   89%
C   113%
D   156%   **(2 marks)**

The following data are to be used when answering questions 115.2 and 115.3

A company expects to sell 1,000 units per month of a new product but there is uncertainty as to both the unit selling price and the unit variable cost of the product. The following estimates of selling price, variable costs and their related probabilities have been made:

QUESTIONS

	Selling price £ per unit	Unit variable cost probability %	£ per unit	Probability %
	20	25	8	20
	25	40	10	50
	30	35	12	30

There are specific fixed costs of £5,000 per month expected for the new product.

2   The expected value of monthly contribution is

    A   £5,890
    B   £10,300
    C   £10,890
    D   £15,300   **(2 marks)**

3   The probability of monthly contribution from this new product exceeding £13,500 is

    A   24.5%
    B   30.5%
    C   63.0%
    D   92.5%   **(2 marks)**

4   PT has discovered that when it employs a new test engineer there is a learning curve with a 75% rate of learning that exists for the first 12 customer assignments. A new test engineer completed her first customer assignment in 6 hours.

Calculate the time that she should take for her seventh assignment to the nearest 0.01 hours.

Note. The index for a 75% learning curve is −0.415.   **(2 marks)**

The following data are to be used when answering questions 115.5 and 115.6

JKL plc has $1 million available for investment. It has identified three possible investments, J K and L, which each have a life of three years. The three-year period coincides with JKL plc's investment plans. JKL plc uses a 15% cost of capital when appraising investments of this type. Details of these investments are set out below

	J $'000	K $'000	L $'000
Initial investment	400	500	300
Net positive cashflows			
Year 1	40	70	50
Year 2	80	90	50
Year 3	510	630	380
Net present value	31	43	31

5   Assuming that each of the investments is divisible, they are not mutually exclusive and cannot be invested in more than once, state the optimum investment plan for JKL plc.   **(2 marks)**

6   Calculate the Internal Rate of Return of an investment in project K to the nearest 0.01%.   **(3 marks)**

7   FH is an electronics company that has developed a new product for the video conferencing market. The product has successfully completed its testing phase and FH has now produced the first four production units. The first unit took three hours of labour time and the total time for the first four units was 8.3667 hours.

Calculate the learning curve improvement rate (rate of learning) to the nearest 0.1%. **(3 marks)**

8   A baker is trying to decide the number of batches of a particular type of bread that he should bake each day. Daily demand ranges from 10 batches to 12 batches. Each batch of bread that is baked and sold yields a positive contribution of £50, but each batch of bread baked that is not sold yields a negative contribution of £20.

Assuming the baker adopts the minimax regret decision rule, calculate the number of batches of bread that he should bake each day. You must justify your answer. **(4 marks)**

(Total = 20 marks)

116 Section A questions: Mixed bank 7 (5/06)   36 mins

1   X plc intends to use relevant costs as the basis of the selling price for a special order: the printing of a brochure. The brochure requires a particular type of paper that is not regularly used by X plc although a limited amount is in X plc's inventory which was left over from a previous job. The cost when X plc bought this paper last year was $15 per ream and there are 100 reams in inventory. The brochure requires 250 reams. The current market price of the paper is $26 per ream, and the resale value of the paper in inventory is $10 per ream.

The relevant cost of the paper to be used in printing the brochure is

  A $2,500
  B $4,900
  C $5,400
  D $6,500   **(2 marks)**

2   A farmer grows potatoes for sale to wholesalers and to individual customers. The farmer currently digs up the potatoes and sells them in 20kg sacks. He is considering a decision to make a change to this current approach. He thinks that washing the potatoes and packaging them in 2kg cartons might be more attractive to some of his individual customers. Which of the following is relevant to his decision?

  (i)   The sales value of the dug potatoes
  (ii)   The cost per kg of growing the potatoes
  (iii) The cost of washing and packaging the potatoes
  (iv)   The sales value of the washed and packaged potatoes

  A   (ii), (iii) and (iv) only
  B   (i), (ii) and (iii) only
  C   (i), (ii) and (iv) only
  D   (i), (iii) and (iv) only   **(2 marks)**

QUESTIONS

3 A company makes and sells three products, R, S, and T. Extracts from the weekly profit statements are as follows.

	R	S	T	Total
	$	$	$	$
Sales	10,000	15,000	20,000	45,000
Variable cost of sales	4,000	9,000	10,000	23,000
Fixed costs*	3,000	3,000	3,000	9,000
Profit	3,000	3,000	7,000	13,000

* general fixed costs absorbed using a unit absorption rate

If the sales revenue mix of products produced and sold were to be changed to: R 20%, S 50%, T 30% then the new average contribution to sales ratio

A would be higher.
B would be lower.
C would remain unchanged.
D cannot be determined without more information. (2 marks)

4 Z Limited is a hotel that serves cakes and gateaux in its coffee shop. An analysis of its internal costs has revealed that the variable cost of preparing its own gateaux is £5·50 per gateau compared to the price of £8·00 per gateau that would be charged by an external bakery. Z Limited employs a chef to prepare the gateaux at a salary of £1,000 per month. This chef is not able to carry out any other work in the hotel and is the only employee capable of preparing the gateaux.

Calculate the minimum monthly number of sales of gateaux at which it is worthwhile preparing the gateaux in the hotel. (2 marks)

The following data are to be used when answering questions 116.5 to 116.7

M plc is evaluating three possible investment projects and uses a 10% discount rate to determine their net present values.

Investment	A	B	C
	£'000	£'000	£'000
Initial Investment	400	450	350
Incremental cash flows			
Year 1	100	130	50
Year 2	120	130	110
Year 3	140	130	130
Year 4	120	130	150
Year 5*	100	150	100
Net present value	39	55	48

*includes £20,000 residual value for each investment project.

5 Calculate the payback period of investment A. (2 marks)

6 Calculate the discounted payback period of investment B. (3 marks)

7 Calculate the Internal Rate of Return (IRR) of investment C. (3 marks)

8   A company is preparing a quotation for a new product. The time taken for the first unit of the product was 30 minutes and the company expects an 85% learning curve. The quotation is to be based on the time taken for the final unit within the learning period which is expected to end after the company has produced 200 units.

Calculate the time per unit to be used for the quotation.

Note. The learning index for an 85% learning curve is -0.2345 (4 marks)

(Total = 20 marks)

117 Section A questions: Mixed bank 8 (11/06)   36 mins

1   A processing company operates a common process from which three different products emerge. Each of the three products can then either be sold in a market that has many buyers and sellers or further processed independently of each other in three other processes. After further processing each of the products can be sold in the same market for a higher unit selling price. Which of the following is required to determine whether or not any of the products should be further processed?

(i)   Total cost of the common process

(ii) The basis of sharing the common process cost between the three products

(iii) The total cost of each of the three additional processes

(iv) The unit selling price of each product after further processing

(v)   The unit selling price of each product before further processing

(vi) The percentage normal loss of each further process

(vii) The actual units of output of each product from the common process.

A   (iii), (iv), (vi) and (vii) only
B   (i), (ii), (iii), (iv), (vi) and (vii) only
C   (i), (ii), (v) and (vii) only
D   (iii), (iv), (v), (vi) and (vii) only (2 marks)

2   Z plc is preparing a quotation for a one off contract to manufacture an item for a potential customer. The item is to be made of steel and the contract would require 300 kgs of steel. The steel is in regular use by Z plc and, as a consequence, the company maintains an inventory of this steel and currently has 200 kgs in inventory. The company operates a LIFO basis of inventory valuation and its most recent purchases were as follows:

20 November 2006 150 kgs costing £600

3 November 2006 250 kgs costing £1,100

The steel is easily available in the market where its current purchase price is £4.25 per kg. If the steel currently held in inventory was to be sold it could be sold for £3.50 per kg. The relevant cost of the steel to be included in the cost estimate is

A   £1,050
B   £1,260
C   £1,275
D   £1,300 (2 marks)

QUESTIONS

3 X is considering the following five investments:

Investment	J $000	K $000	L $000	M $000	N $000
Initial investment	400	350	450	500	600
Net Present Value	125	105	140	160	190

Investments J and L are mutually exclusive, all of the investments are divisible and none of them may be invested in more than once. The optimum investment plan for X assuming that the funding available is limited to $1m is

- A $400,000 in J plus $600,000 in N.
- B $400,000 in M plus $600,000 in N.
- C $500,000 in M plus $500,000 in N.
- D $350,000 in K plus $600,000 in N plus $50,000 in M.

(2 marks)

4 A hospital is considering investing $80,000 in a new computer system that will reduce the amount of time taken to process a patient's records when making an appointment. It is estimated that the cash benefit of the time saved will be $20,000 in the first year, $30,000 in the second year and $50,000 in each of the next three years. At the end of five years the computer system will be obsolete and will need to be replaced. It is not expected to have any residual value.

Calculate the payback period to one decimal place of one year. (2 marks)

5 An investment company is considering the purchase of a commercial building at a cost of £0·85m. The property would be rented immediately to tenants at an annual rent of £80,000 payable in arrears in perpetuity.

Calculate the net present value of the investment assuming that the investment company's cost of capital is 8% per annum.

Ignore taxation and inflation. (2 marks)

6 A bakery produces three different sized fruit pies for sale in its shops. The pies all use the same basic ingredients. Details of the selling prices and unit costs of each pie are as follows:

	Small $ per pie	Medium $ per pie	Large $ per pie
Selling price	3.00	5.00	9.00
Ingredients	1.80	2.40	4.60
Direct labour	0.40	0.50	0.60
Variable overhead	0.30	0.50	0.80
Weekly demand (pies)	200	500	300
Fruit (kgs per pie)	0.2	0.3	0.6

The fruit used in making the pies is imported and the bakery has been told that the amount of fruit that they will be able to buy for next week is limited to 300 kgs. The bakery has established its good name by baking its pies daily using fresh fruit, so it is not possible to buy the fruit in advance.

Determine the mix of pies to be made and sold in order to maximise the bakery's contribution for next week.

(3 marks)

7   H is launching a new product which it expects to incur a variable cost of $14 per unit. The company has completed some market research to try to determine the optimum selling price with the following results. If the price charged was to be $25 per unit then the demand would be 1,000 units each period. For every $1 increase in the selling price, demand would reduce by 100 units each period. For every $1 reduction in the selling price, the demand would increase by 100 units each period.

Calculate the optimum selling price.

Note: If Price (P) = a – bx; then Marginal Revenue = a – 2bx

(3 marks)

8   A company sells three different levels of TV maintenance contract to its customers: Basic, Standard and Advanced. Selling prices, unit costs and monthly sales are as follows:

	Basic £	Standard £	Advanced £
Selling price	50	100	135
Variable cost	30	50	65
Monthly contracts sold	750	450	300

Calculate the average contribution to sales ratio of the company

(i)   based on the sales mix stated above; and

(ii) if the total number of monthly contracts sold remains the same, but equal numbers of each contract are sold.

(4 marks)

(Total = 20 marks)

118 Section A questions: Mixed bank 9 (5/07)   36 mins

1   An investment project that requires an initial investment of $500,000 has a residual value of $130,000 at the end of five years. The project's cash flows have been discounted at the company's cost of capital of 12% and the resulting net present value is $140,500. The profitability index of the project is closest to:

A   0.02
B   0.54
C   0.28
D   0.26

(2 marks)

2   A project has a net present value of $320,000.

The sales revenues for the project have a total pre-discounted value of $900,000 and a total present value of $630,000 after tax.

The sensitivity of the investment to changes in the value of sales is closest to:

A $310,000
B $580,000
C   51%
D   36%

(2 marks)

QUESTIONS

3 A company provides a number of different services to its customers from a single office. The fixed costs of the office, including staff costs, are absorbed into the company's service costs using an absorption rate of $25 per consulting hour based on a budgeted activity level of 100,000 hours each period.

Fee income and variable costs are different depending on the services provided, but the average contribution to sales ratio is 35%. The breakeven fee income each period is closest to:

A $1,400,000
B $11,500,000
C $875,000
D $7,143,000   (2 marks)

4 A company has recently completed the production of the first unit of a new product. The time taken for this was 12 minutes. The company expects that there will be a 75% learning rate for this product.

Calculate the total time expected to produce the first four units.   (2 marks)

The following data are given for sub-questions 118.5 and 118.6 below

An investment project with no residual value has a net present value of $87,980 when it is discounted using a cost of capital of 10%. The annual cash flows are as follows:

Year	$
0	(200,000)
1	80,000
2	90,000
3	100,000
4	60,000
5	40,000

5 Calculate the Accounting Rate of Return of the project using the average investment value basis. (2 marks)

6 Calculate the Internal Rate of Return of the project.   (3 marks)

7 A company manufactures three products. Each of these products use the same type of material but in different quantities. The unit selling prices, cost and profit details are as follows:

Product	X	Y	Z
	$/unit	$/unit	$/unit
Selling price	23	26	28
Direct materials	6	8	6
Direct labour	8	6	8
Variable overhead	2	3	3
Fixed overhead	4	5	6
Profit	3	4	5

The direct material used on all three products costs $10 per kg. The material available is expected to be limited to 600 kgs for the next accounting period. The maximum demand for each of the products during the next accounting period is expected to be as follows:

X 240 units
Y 600 units
Z 400 units

No inventories of finished products are held.

Calculate the optimum product mix for the next accounting period.   (3 marks)

8   A company is launching a new product. Market research shows that if the selling price of the product is $100 then demand will be 1,200 units, but for every $10 increase in selling price there will be a corresponding decrease in demand of 200 units and for every $10 decrease in selling price there will be a corresponding increase in demand of 200 units. The estimated variable costs of the product are $30 per unit. There are no specific fixed costs but general fixed costs are absorbed using an absorption rate of $8 per unit.

Calculate the selling price at which profit is maximised.

Note: When Price = a − bx then Marginal Revenue = a − 2bx **(4 marks)**

(Total = 20 marks)

Answers

ANSWERS

1 Section A answers: Uncertainty in decision making

1 EV = (500 × 0.5) + (600 × 0.1) + (400 × (1 − 0.5 − 0.1))= 470

2 Perfect information is calculated by taking the difference between the EV of the best decision option (predicted on the basis of the perfect information) and the highest EV of profit if the perfect information is not available.

3 A The method is too concerned with the need to avoid losses – **no**
   B The method is concerned only with making the greatest possible profit – **no**
   C The method ignores less likely outcomes – **no**
   D The method takes no account of risk aversion – **yes**

   A is not a drawback because the expected value averages out losses and profits according to their probabilities and so does not concentrate on avoiding losses.

   B is not a drawback because the expected value averages all the outcomes of a particular course of action and so is not solely concerned with the highest profit.

   C is not a drawback because, as far as is practical, the expected value will take into account all outcomes, though the importance it then allocates to them does depend on the likelihood of occurrence.

   D is a drawback because the calculation of expected value rates losses at their numerical value but in some circumstances making a loss might be disastrous to the decision maker, out of all proportion to the actual sum involved.

4 C A profit of £1,000 and a loss of £3,000 are less than or equal to a profit of £1,000 and so the overall probability of a profit of £1,000 or less is 0.3 + 0.21 = 0.51.

   If you chose **option A**, you do not appear to have taken the loss of £3,000 into account.

   If you chose **option B** you have worked out the probability of there being a profit greater than £1,000.

   If you chose **option D** you do not appear to have taken the profit of £1,000 into account.

5 A At decision point C, decision 4 would be chosen – **true**
   B The expected value at outcome point B is £680,000 – **false**
   C Decision 2 would be chosen over decision 1 – **true**
   D The expected value at outcome point D is £920,000 – **true**

   A: The EV at E is £1,700,000, whereas the EV at F is £1,600,000. Cost of sales should be minimised, so decision 4 would be chosen.

   B: The EV at C would be £1,600,000 (the *lower* of £1,700,000 and £1,600,000) while the EV at D is £920,000 and so the EV at B is (£1,600,000 × 0.5) + (£920,000 × 0.5) = £1,260,000.

   C: The EV of decision 1 is £1,260,000, whereas the known value of decision 2 is £1,200,000. The lower figure is taken because the figures relate to cost of sales.

   D: The EV at D = (£1,400,000 × 0.2) + (£800,000 × 0.8) = £920,000

6 EV of L = £'000 (0.2 × £500 + 0.5 × £470 + 0.3 × £550) = £500,000
   EV of M = £'000 (0.2 × £400 + 0.5 × £550 + 0.3 × £570) = £526,000
   EV of N = £'000 (0.2 × £450 + 0.5 × £400 + 0.3 × £475) = £432,500
   EV of O = £'000 (0.2 × £360 + 0.5 × £400 + 0.3 × £420) = £398,000
   EV of P = £'000 (0.2 × £600 + 0.5 × £500 + 0.3 × £425) = £497,500

   Project M should be undertaken as it has the highest EV.

ANSWERS

7 Value of perfect information = EV with perfect information – EV without information

With no information, EV would be £526,000

With perfect information

Forecast market conditions	Probability	Project chosen	Net cash inflow £'000	EV of inflow £'000
Poor	0.2	P	600	120
Good	0.5	M	550	275
Excellent	0.3	M	570	171
EV with perfect information				566

∴ Value of perfect information = £'000 (566 – 526)
= £40,000

8 B

	£
EV if dry = 6 × 0.3 × £10,000 =	18,000
EV if wet = 2 × 0.7 × £10,000 =	14,000
	32,000
Costs	(6,000)
Yachts sold at later show	(20,000)
	6,000

9 A

		Actual outcome		
		Dry	Wet	Total
	Dry	18[2]	28[3]	46[3]
Forecast	Wet	12[3]	42[2]	54[3]
	Total	30[1]	70[1]	100[3]

[1] – given
[2] – 60% × 30/60% × 70
[3] – balancing fig

p (forecast dry) = 0.46

p (forecast wet) = 0.54

p (dry/forecast dry) = $\frac{18}{46}$ p (wet/forecast dry) = $\frac{28}{46}$

p (wet/ forecast wet) = $\frac{42}{54}$ p (dry/forecast wet) = $\frac{12}{54}$

EV of exhibiting if forecast is dry: ($\frac{18}{46}$ × £60,000) + ($\frac{28}{46}$ × £20,000) – £6,000 = £29,652

EV of exhibiting if forecast is wet: ($\frac{12}{54}$ × £60,000) + ($\frac{42}{54}$ × £20,000) – £6,000 = £22,889

EV of forecast = ($\frac{46}{100}$ × £29,652) + ($\frac{54}{100}$ × £22,889) = £26,000

This is the same as the EV without the forecast (see question 1.8 above) and so the company would pay £0 for the information.

BPP note. The correct distractors did not appear in the actual exam question. All candidates who attempted the question were given full credit whatever answer they gave.

2 Ice cream manufacturer

> **Top tips.** The difficulty in this question arises in calculating the appropriate probabilities for use in the payoff table and it is compounded by the rather ambiguous manner in which the conditional probabilities are stated in the question. The student could be forgiven for thinking that P (forecast good but weather poor) means P (the weather turned out to be poor given that the forecast was for good weather). Were this the correct interpretation, however, the probabilities would have to total 1, since all possible outcomes consequent on a good forecast would be covered.
>
> P (forecast good but weather poor) is intended by the examiner to mean P (forecast was good given that we now know that the weather has in fact turned out to be poor). Bayes' rule is required to calculate the correct probabilities for use in the payoff table.

The probabilities given do not total to 1 and so, for example, **P (forecast good but weather poor)** cannot mean P (weather poor given that forecast was good) but must **mean P (forecast was good given that weather turned out to be poor)**.

We can use a table to determine the required probabilities. **Suppose that the weather was recorded on 100 days**.

Forecast	Poor	Fair	Good	Very good	Total
Good	**9	16	14	2	41
Other	21	24	6	8	59
	*30	40	20	10	100

How these figures were calculated

* From past data, poor weather occurs with probability 0.3 of the time, that is, on 0.3 of the 100 days in the sample = 0.3 × 100 = 30 days. Similarly other percentages along the bottom row are derived from past data.

** If the actual weather is poor, there is a 0.3 probability that good weather had been forecast. This will occur on 0.3 of the 30 days on which the weather was poor = 0.3 × 30 = 9 days. Similarly 16 = 0.4 × 40, 14 = 0.7 × 20 and 2 = 0.2 × 10.

The probabilities we require are

P (poor given forecast good) = 9/41
P (fair given forecast good) = 16/41
P (good given forecast good) = 14/41
P (very good given forecast good) = 2/41

Given that forecast is for good weather:

Number of new containers bought

Weather	p	0 x	0 px	500 x	500 px	1,000 x	1,000 px	1,500 x	1,500 px
poor	9/41	0	0.00	20	4.39	20	4.39	30	6.59
fair	16/41	15	5.85	0	0.00	15	5.85	20	7.80
good	14/41	20	6.83	20	6.83	0	0.00	15	5.12
very good	2/41	30	1.46	25	1.22	15	0.73	0	0.00
Expected loss			14.14		12.44		10.97		19.51

The decision which will **minimise the expected lost contribution** is to **order 1,000 new containers** giving an expected lost contribution of £10,970.

ANSWERS

3 Sporting simulator

> **Top tips.** One item in the Paper P2 syllabus is 'The importance of strategic, intangible and non-financial judgements in decision-making'. You must therefore be prepared for requirements such as that in part (b).
>
> When this question was set a number of years ago, the examiner at the time commented that it was often answered vaguely. You need to answer the question set and briefly plan your answer.

(a) **Critical values**

The variables stand in the following relationship:

Selling price × volume	SP
Variable costs × volume	(VC)
Contribution/unit × volume	C
Fixed costs	(FC)
Profit	P

We are told that P = £200,000

Annual volume

				Absolute value	% change
Football					
P	=	C × volume − FC			
200,000	=	50 × volume − 1,050,000			
Volume	=	$\frac{1,250,000}{50}$	=	25,000 units	− 37.5%
Cricket					
Volume	=	$\frac{2,150,000}{100}$	=	21,500 units	− 28.3%

Selling price

Football					
P	=	SP × 40,000 − (VC × 40,000 + FC)			
200	=	40 SP − (3,200 + 1,050)			
SP	=	$\frac{4,450}{40}$	=	£111.25	−14.4%
Cricket					
SP	=	$\frac{5,150}{30}$	=	£171.67	−14.2%

Variable production costs

				Absolute value	% change
Football					
P	=	SP × 40,000 − (VC × 40,000 + FC)			
200	=	5,200 − (40VC + 1,050)			
VC	=	$\frac{3,950}{40}$	=	£98.75	+ 23.4%
Cricket					
VC	=	$\frac{3,850}{30}$	=	£128.33	+ 28.3%

Fixed costs

Football
P	=	C × 40,000 − FC		
200	=	2,000 − FC		
FC	=	2,000 − 200	£1,800	+71.4%

Cricket
FC	=	3,000 − 200	£2,800	+ 43.6%

(b) **Factors to consider**

From (a) the most critical factor is **price** where a very small percentage variation for either product reduces profits significantly. The **variable cost per unit** is also fairly sensitive for both products, and so is **volume** for the cricket simulator.

In each of these cases the management therefore needs to be **more confident** in the estimates than it appears to be at present, judging from the wording of the question.

Further considerations in making a choice are as follows.

(i) The company already manufactures sports goods. One product may be a better fit with existing products than the other, or the company may be better placed to manufacture new spin-off products for one type of simulator rather than the other.

(ii) Sales of the products are likely to be stimulated by major sporting events: the football simulator would seem the most promising product in a football World Cup year.

(iii) Production facilities may be limited but if the company launches only one of the products a competitor might steal the potential market for the other one. A longer-term view needs to be taken, considering the future growth of the markets, the possibility of foreign markets and the threat of cheap (illegal) imitations.

4 Homelathe

Text references. Parts (b) and (d) can be answered from Chapter 14.

Top tips. A feature of the question which might have perplexed or confused you is the use of the term 'risk neutral attitude' in part (b) and 'had decided to avoid risk' in part (d).

'Risk neutral' refers to decisions that are taken without considering the size of the possible variations in the outcome. For example, the two outcomes X and Y below would be equally acceptable to someone with a risk neutral attitude, because they have the same expected value, even though X involves a greater variation in possible outcomes and so is more risky.

	X Outcome £	Y Outcome £
Probability 0.5	+ 2,000	+ 1,100
Probability 0.5	0	+ 900
Expected value	+ 1,000	+ 1,000

The requirement of part (b) of the question is simply to use EVs. Part (d) then goes on to ask how the decision ought to be approached if risk were taken into consideration.

(a) **Current capacity**, in batches $= \dfrac{4{,}752}{(10 + 14 + 12)}$

= 132 batches

ANSWERS

If **component A is bought outside**, the machine hours needed per batch of B and C would be (14 + 12) = 26 hours. Capacity in batches would be

$$\frac{4{,}752}{26} = 182.8 \text{ batches.}$$

This represents an **increase** in capacity of 50.8 batches or

$$\frac{50.8}{132} \times 100\% = 38.5\%$$

If **component B is bought outside**, the machine hours needed per batch of A and C would be (10 + 12) = 22 hours. Capacity in batches would be

$$\frac{4{,}752}{22} = 216 \text{ batches}$$

This represents an **increase** in capacity of 84 batches or

$$\frac{84}{132} \times 100\% = 63.6\%$$

If **component C is bought outside**, the machine hours needed per batch of A and B would be (10 + 14) = 24 hours. Capacity in batches would be

$$\frac{4{,}752}{24} = 198 \text{ batches}$$

This represents an **increase** in capacity of 66 batches or

$$\frac{66}{132} \times 100\% = 50\%$$

(b) **Fixed costs** are assumed to be the same regardless of which course of action is taken, and so should be **ignored**.

The expected value of the price per component from GM Ltd is as follows.

Probability	Component A Price £	EV of price £	Component B Price £	EV of price £	Component C Price £	EV of price £
0.25	96	24.0	176	44.0	149	37.25
0.50	85	42.5	158	79.0	127	63.50
0.25	54	13.5	148	37.0	97	24.25
EV		80.0		160.0		125.00

	If component A is bought outside £ £	If component B is bought outside £ £	If component C is bought outside £ £
Sales price per batch	600	600	600
Variable costs			
Component A	80	32	32
B	54	160	54
C	58	58	125
D	12	12	12
E	4	4	4
Assembly costs	40	40	40
Total variable cost per batch	248	306	267
Contribution per batch	352	294	333
Number of batches	182.8	* 198	198
Total contribution	£64,345.6	£58,212	£65,934

* Maximum, given expected increase in sales

ANSWERS

Recommendation. Component C should be bought out from GM Ltd, in order to maximise the EV of contribution and profit.

(c) **Profit statement**

		Per batch £	£	198 batches Total £
Sales		600		118,800
Variable costs				
Component	A	32	6,336	
	B	54	10,692	
	C	125	24,750	
	D	12	2,376	
	E	4	792	
Assembly costs		40	7,920	
Total variable costs		267		52,866
Contribution				65,934
Fixed costs (see working)				41,712
Profit				24,222

Working. Fixed costs are the same as at the current capacity of 132 batches, and from data given in the question are therefore 132 × £(48 + 102 + 116 + 24 + 26) = £41,712.

(d) (i) If management wish to avoid risk as much as possible, they should **consider** the **worst possible outcomes**, and calculate the expected profit from buying out A, B or C in the event that the actual component price turns out to be the pessimistic figure. The decision about which component to buy out might then be to select the component for buying out (A, B or C) with which the worst possible profit would be the least bad (a **maximum criterion** could be applied to the decision).

(ii) It is noticeable that the contribution per batch is highest if A is bought out. The preference for buying out C is based on the assumption that sales demand will increase by 50%. A risk averse management might **question the accuracy of this sales forecast**, and so perhaps prefer to buy out component A rather than C.

(iii) Another risk factor in the decision is the **lack of experience** of GM Ltd in producing any of the components before.

(1) Should H Ltd rely on a single inexperienced supplier? If the supplier fails to supply components to specification, the entire production line at H Ltd might be brought to a halt.

(2) Is there one component which is likely to be easier to make? If so, should this be the component bought out from GM Ltd?

5 Pharmacy

Text references. Chapter 18 covers Pareto analysis in detail.

Top tips.. The report in (b), the types of comment which usually result from a Pareto analysis (on the lines that 'these categories account for X% of sales but only Y% of stock') are not really appropriate in this case and you are advised to concentrate on the rankings of the different categories. Focus on the range of discussion points raised when reviewing the answer. Interpretation of results will be where marks are awarded in exam questions.

ANSWERS

REPORT

To: Management
From: Management accountant
Date: XX November 20X7
Subject: **Sales and stock in pharmacies X and Z**

1 Introduction

1.1 A **Pareto analysis** has been carried out using last year's sales and stock figures for pharmacies X and Z. The findings and some comments on points of importance are given below.

2 Findings

2.1 There is a **marked difference** between the two pharmacies in terms of the **amount of stock held relative to sales**.

Pharmacy	Sales £'000	Stock £'000	%
X	160	46	29
Z	100	43	43

2.2 The table below shows the **sales rank minus the stock rank** for each category.

Category	Difference in ranks of sales and stock	
	X	Z
OTC	−2	−2
Toiletries	1	1
Photo	−1	−1
Food/drink	0	−1
Baby	−2	−1
Sanpro	−2	−1
Other	−1	−1
Foot	−3	2
Cosmetics	7	3
Hair	2	3
Perfume	4	5

As can be seen from the table, the rankings for sales are **broadly similar** to **those for stock** in both pharmacies, with three **exceptions**.

2.3 **Exception 1. Cosmetics** stands out as the category which has particularly **high stock levels** compared to sales. This is the case in both pharmacies but is specially marked in X where the category is second in stock and only ninth in sales.

2.4 **Exception 2. Perfumery** is another category which has quite markedly **high stock levels** compared to sales, being eleventh in sales and sixth in stock in Z and, to a lesser extent, hair-care products also seem to involve high stock levels.

2.5 **Exception 3.** The categories which require lower stock levels than might be expected from their sales are shown by the negatives in the table and are not specially marked. In both pharmacies, OTC has a sales level ranked two points better than its stock level.

2.6 Comparing the two pharmacies, aside from the points made above, the **rankings of sales and stock are broadly similar.**

3 Recommendations

3.1 Management should give further consideration to a number of issues.

3.2 **Issue 1. The proportionately high level of stock being held in Z**. Can it be reduced to something closer to the 29% of pharmacy X?

3.3 **Issue 2. Cosmetics, perfumery and hair-care all seem to require, to different extents, high stock levels**. Is this necessary or can stock levels be reduced?

3.4 **Issue 3.** It might be a useful exercise, prior to taking action over the 'problem' categories, to **investigate the categories**, such as OTC, **which have low stock levels**.

Signed: Management accountant

6 Purchase options

Text references. Chapter 14 is the place to go if you want help with probabilities.

Top tips. In (a), for each purchase option you need to calculate the unit contribution at each selling price, then total contribution at each forecast level, and then, taking probability into account, expected profit.

Under purchase option 2 you need to check whether material requirements exceed 50,000 kg. If not, excess material will have to be purchased, but can then be sold on.

Likewise, under purchase option 3 you need to check whether material requirements exceed 70,000 kg.

In (b) you need to calculate the difference between profit expected with no knowledge (your answer to (a)) and the profit expected if the company knew what demand was going to be.

(a) **Purchase option 1**

	£			£		
Selling price	15			20		
Variable manufacturing costs	3			3		
'Contribution' to material and fixed costs	12			17		
Materials (£3 × 3 kg)	9			9		
Contribution	3			8		

Sales ('000)	36	28	18	28	23	13
	£'000	£'000	£'000	£'000	£'000	£'000
Contribution	108.0	84.0	54.0	224.0	184.0	104.0
Fixed costs	65.0	65.0	65.0	136.0	136.0	136.0
Conditional profit	43.0	19.0	(11.0)	88.0	48.0	(32.0)
Probability	0.3	0.5	0.2	0.3	0.5	0.2
	12.9	9.5	(2.2)	26.4	24.0	(6.4)
Expected profit (£'000)		20.2			44.0	

Purchase option 2

	£			£		
'Contribution' from above	12.00			17.00		
Materials (£2.75 × 3)	8.25			8.25		
Contribution	3.75			8.75		

Sales ('000)	36	28	18	28	23	13
	£'000	£'000	£'000	£'000	£'000	£'000
Contribution	135.0	105.0	67.5	245.0	201.250	113.75
Fixed costs	65.0	65.0	65.0	136.0	136.000	136.00
Purchase of excess material Less £1 revenue	–	–	–	–	–	*19.25
Conditional profit	70.0	40.0	2.5	109.0	65.250	(41.50)
Probability	0.3	0.5	0.2	0.3	0.500	0.20
	21.0	20.0	0.5	32.7	32.625	(8.30)
Expected profit (£'000)		41.5			57.025	

*(50,000 − (3 × 13,000)) × £1.75

ANSWERS

Purchase option 3

	£			£		
'Contribution' from above	12.00			17.00		
Materials £2.50 × 3	7.50			7.50		
Contribution	4.50			9.50		

Sales ('000)	36	28	18	28	23	13
	£'000	£'000	£'000	£'000	£'000	£'000
Contribution	162.0	126.0	81.0	266.0	218.5	123.5
Purchase of excess material Less £1 revenue	–	–	*24.0	–	**1.5	***46.5
Fixed costs	65.0	65.0	65.0	136.0	136.0	136.0
Conditional profit	97.0	61.0	(8.0)	130.0	81.0	(59.0)
Probability	0.3	0.5	0.2	0.3	0.5	0.2
	29.1	30.5	(1.6)	39.0	40.5	(11.8)
Expected profit (£'000)		58.0			67.7	

*   (70,000 – (3 × 18)) × £1.50
** (70,000 – (3 × 23)) × £1.50
*** (70,000 – (3 × 13)) × £1.50

Optimum expected profit = £67,700 and so the company should use a **selling price of £20 and purchase a minimum quantity of 70,000 kg at a price of £2.50 per kg.**

(b)

	£'000
If demand is optimistic, best expected profit =	39.0
If demand is most likely, best expected profit =	40.5
If demand is pessimistic, best expected profit =	0.5
Total expected profit with perfect knowledge	**80.0**
Expected profit without information	**67.7**
Maximum price to pay for perfect information	**12.3**

7 Holiday resort

> **Text references.** Look at the material in Chapter 14 to handle probabilities and EVs. Data tables are also found in Chapter 14 as is 'what if' analysis.
>
> **Top tips.** The interpretation of data tables appeared in the pilot paper and so make sure that you read through our answer to (a) if you are unable to analyse the one in the appendix.
>
> In part (b), the combined probability is calculated by multiplying the two probabilities at each level together, for example 0.15 × 0.2 = 0.030. The profit or loss is read from the two-way data table in the appendix for each capacity utilisation level/rate of inflation. The expected value is calculated by multiplying the profit or loss by the combined probability.

(a) The **two-way data table** shows what **net profit or loss will be made at rates of inflation** between 1% and 10% (in steps of 1%) **and at capacity utilisation levels** of between 20% and 100% (in steps of 20%). The **best possible outcome** (in the ranges shown) is a net profit of £171,043 (when the rate of inflation is 1% and capacity utilisation is 100%). The **worst possible outcome** is a loss of £122,207 (when the rate of inflation is 10% and capacity utilisation is 20%).

The **current situation** is a rate of inflation of 5% and capacity utilisation of 60%. The data table shows a profit of £25,378.

The table shows that a **capacity utilisation percentage** of somewhere between 40% and 60% will be necessary if the cable car service is to **breakeven whatever the rate of inflation**. The service will **breakeven near 50% capacity utilisation if the rate of inflation is low but a utilisation rate nearer 60% will be required if the rate of inflation is high.**

ANSWERS

(b) (i)

Capacity Utilisation %	Probability	Inflation %	Probability	Combined Probability	Profit/ (loss) £	Expected value £
80	0.15	2	0.2	0.030	100,130	3,003.90
	0.15	5	0.5	0.075	94,370	7,077.75
	0.15	8	0.3	0.045	88,610	3,987.45
60	0.60	2	0.2	0.120	31,138	3,736.56
	0.60	5	0.5	0.300	25,378	7,613.40
	0.60	8	0.3	0.180	19,618	3,531.24
40	0.25	2	0.2	0.050	(37,855)	(1,892.75)
	0.25	5	0.5	0.125	(43,615)	(5,451.88)
	0.25	8	0.3	0.075	(49,375)	(3,703.13)
				1.000		17,902.54

(ii) The **expected value** is a profit of £17,902.54.

(iii) From part (i) we can find four instances of net profit being greater than £30,000.

Profit £	Combined probability
100,130	0.030
94,370	0.075
88,610	0.045
31,138	0.120
	0.270

(c) A spreadsheet model could be used to carry out a **'what if' analysis**, whereby the value of one or more variables is changed and the effect on profit/loss noted.

(i) For example, the **passenger mix could be changed** to, say, adults 45%, juveniles 35%, senior citizens 20% and the amended profit noted, all other variables remaining the same.

(ii) Likewise, all other variables including the passenger mix, could remain unchanged, but the **fare increase could be changed** to 4% and the amended profit noted. If all other variables remain the same but the fares are increased in steps of 1% between rates of 1% and 10%, the resulting profits/losses would form a one-way data table.

8 Concert hall

Text references. Draw on material in Chapter 14 to answer this question, especially calculating EVs and working out the value of perfect information.

Top tips. In part (a) you must carry out (i) and (ii) for each scenario. For part (b) you need to compare the expected profit from making the correct decision with the expected profit found in part (a). There would undoubtedly be marks for good layout.

Note the layout of the payoff matrix – it could prove useful in future questions.

Part (b) is asking for the value of perfect information – notice the language used in the requirements to express this.

(a) Two way data table

Variable Demand	Probability	Decision Purchases			
		200	300	400	500
200	0.25	120	(57)[1]	(204)[3]	(246)[6]
350	0.30	120	225 [2]	219 [4]	177 [7]
500	0.45	120	225 [20]	360 [5]	600 [8]
	EV	120	154.50	176.70	261.60

ANSWERS

Workings

Summary

(i)

	Scenario one	Scenario 2
EU demand	350	500 × 0.45 = 225
		350 × 0.30 = 105
		200 × 0.25 = 50
		380

For 200 units purchased

Buy and sell 200 @ 60p profit £120

For 300 units purchased

(1) Buy 300 × £2.25 .... (675)
     Sell 200 × £3.00 600
     Sell 10 × £3.00 × 60% 18
                                                                          £(57)

(2) Buy 300 × £2.25 .... (675)
     Sell 300 × £3.00 900
                                                                          £225

For 400 units purchased

(3) Buy 400 × £2.10 .... (840)
     Sell 200 × £3.00 600
     Sell 20 × £3.00 × 60% 36
                                                                          (204)

(4) Buy 400 × £2.10 .... (840)
     Sell 350 × £3.00 1,050
     Sell 5 × £3.00 × 60% 9
                                                                          219

(5) Buy 400 × £2.10 .... (840)
     Sell 400 × £3.00 1,200
                                                                          360

For 500 units purchased:

(6) Buy 500 × £1.80 .... (900)
     Sell 200 × £3.00 600
     Sell 30 × £3.00 × 60% 54
                                                                          (246)

(7) Buy 500 × £1.80 .... (900)
     Sell 350 × £3.00 1,050
     Sell 15 × £3.00 × 60% 27
                                                                          177

(8) Buy 500 × £1.80 .... (900)
     Sell 500 × £3.00 1,500
                                                                          600

			Scenario one	Scenario 2
(ii)	(1) Tickets purchased for concert		£300	£500
	(2) Profit per concert		£225	£261.60

(b) If the agent **knew the outcome** he would **buy only as many tickets as he could sell**.

	Purchases	Sales	Profit £	Probability	Expected profit £
Popular	500	500	600	0.45	270.00
Less popular*	300	300	225	0.30	67.50
Unknown	200	200	120	0.25	30.00
					367.50
Previous profit per (a)(ii)(2)					261.60
Gain					105.90

The **maximum sum** to be paid each year for perfect information is £105.90 × 60 concerts = £6,354.

* Buying and selling 300 yields slightly more profit than buying 400 and selling 350, though as the difference is small the ticket agent might prefer to meet the extra demand.

9 MP Organisation

Text references. Refer to Chapters 11 and 14 to help answer this question.

Top tips. There are two parts to this question. Part (a) requires you to calculate NPVs based on a range of outcomes which means you need to take the PV for cost and revenues based on the expected costs and revenues and flex these for the anticipated variations in sales and costs.

In part (a), nine marks were available for calculating the PV of relevant production costs, non-production costs and revenues at the three levels of sales demand.

Another four marks could be earned for drawing up a table of the combinations of revenues and costs and NPV.

The remaining marks were available for discussion and recommendations. In part (b), five marks each were possible for discussing probabilities and simulation as techniques applied to problem solving of this type.

Easy marks. It is easiest to approach the question this way so you can draw up a table as we have done below with all of the possible combinations. There are nine in all which you would expect with three possible levels of sales and three possible levels of costs.

Remember to discuss your findings and make a recommendation to MP.

The second part of the question requires a written answer on expected NPVs and simulation as these are used in estimating probabilities. You will find it easier if you use illustrations from your calculations in part (a) to explain how ENPV and simulation models work.

See that the question requires two formats – in part (a), it requires a calculation and in part (b), it requires notes. Always look at what the required output is and tailor your approach to that.

Examiner's comments. Candidates didn't always stop to think how this question should be answered. So many answers to part (a) included unnecessary and duplicated calculations. Part (b) was very badly answered and most candidates showed little knowledge of simulation. Also, the question required answers for all 9 outcomes but many answers just calculated pessimistic, most likely and optimistic.

ANSWERS

(a) **Projected cash flows – project at 100% revenues and costs**

	Year 0 $'000	Year 1 $'000	Year 2 $'000	Year 3 $'000	Year 4 $'000	Year 5 $'000	Total PV $'000
Sales (W1)		100	150	112.50	50	30	
Discount factor at 15%		x 0.870	x 0.756	x 0.658	x 0.572	x 0.497	
PV of cash in flow		87	113	74	29	15	318
Certain costs							
Fixed costs (director's fees)	(100)						
Advertising and PR	(15)	(10)	(10)	(5)	(5)	(5)	
	(115)	(10)	(10)	(5)	(5)	(5)	
Discount factor at 15%	x 1.000	x 0.870	x 0.756	x 0.658	x 0.572	x 0.497	
PV of cash out flow	(115)	(9)	(8)	(3)	(3)	(2)	(140)
Uncertain costs (W2)	(120)						
Discount at 15%	x 1.000						
PV of cash flow	(120)						(120)
NPV of cash flow							58

Note that the script cost of $10,000 and the travel costs of $4,000 are sunk costs as these have been incurred already and are irrelevant to the decision being made in our analysis here.

Projected cash flows – project with varying revenues and costs

Present value at	$'000 100%	$'000 100%	$'000 100%	$'000 120%	$'000 120%	$'000 120%	$'000 80%	$'000 80%	$'000 80%
Sales	318	318	318	382	382	382	254	254	254
Costs									
Certain	(140)	(140)	(140)	(140)	(140)	(140)	(140)	(140)	(140)
Uncertain									
90%	(108)			(108)			(108)		
100%		(120)			(120)			(120)	
110%	–	–	(132)	–	–	(132)	–	–	(132)
NPV of cash flow	70	58	46	134	122	110	6	(6)	(18)

This analysis shows that there are a range of possible NPVs depending on the combination of expected sales and cost increases or decreases. The range is between a negative NPV of $18,000 which is definitely not acceptable to a positive NPV of $134,000 which would be acceptable. So the most likely optimistic and pessimistic cost and revenue values are as follows.

Outcome	NPV $000
pessimistic	(18)
optimistic	134
most likely	58

It is also possible to use sensitivity analysis to look at the cashflows that are most vulnerable to change and that would need to change the least to make the NPV dip to zero.

(b) **Notes for the management meeting on expected NPV and simulation**

Notes

1. The easiest way to explain expected NPVs (ENPVs) is to show an example of how these are calculated using the film project as our example. What ENPVs show is the expected NPV where a range of outcomes exist that have known probabilities. Therefore it measures risk which can be quantified rather than uncertainty which cannot.

Thus, taking our earlier example.

Sales revenue		318	254	382
Probability		0.5	0.1	0.4
Costs	Probability			
260	0.6	58[1]	(6)[1]	122[1]
248	0.3	70[2]	6[2]	134[2]
272	0.1	46[3]	(18)[3]	110[3]
	EV[4]	30.20	(0.36)	49.76

Expected NPV = $79.600

Workings

(1) When costs = 260 and
    (a) Sales = 318 : Contribution = 58 (318 − 260)
    (b) Sales = 254 : Contribution = (6) (254 − 260)
    (c) Sales = 382 : Contribution = 122 (382 − 260)

(2) When costs = 248 and
    (a) Sales = 318 : Contribution = 70
    (b) Sales = 254 : Contribution = 6
    (c) Sales = 382 : Contribution = 134

(3) When costs = 272 and
    (a) Sales = 318 : Contribution = 46
    (b) Sale = 254 : Contribution = (18)
    (c) Sales = 382 : Contribution = 110

(4) Expected value = Σ(contribution × probability of sales revenue × probability of costs)

    (i) (58 × 0.5 × 0.6) + (70 × 0.5 × 0.3) + (46 × 0.5 × 0.1) = 30.20
    (ii) ((6) × 0.1 × 0.6) + (6 × 0.1 × 0.3) + ((18) × 0.1 × 0.1) = (0.36)
    (iii) (122 × 0.4 × 0.6) + (134 × 0 4 × 0.3) + (110 × 0.4 × 0.1) = 49.76
    Expected NPV = 79.60

Of course with other probabilities the ENPV would be quite different and so it does depend very much on the expected probabilities assigned to each outcome.

2   Simulation models can be used to assess risk using random numbers assigned to probabilities. These are particularly suitable where there are many variables with uncertain outcomes. Continuing with our example:

Sales revenue has three possible outcomes based on probabilities of 50%, 10% and 40%.

Sales revenue PV $'000	Probability (say)	Assign random numbers
254	0.10	00–09
318	0.50	10–59
382	0.40	60–99

A random number generator could give numbers say 19007174604721296802. These would then be matched to the random numbers assigned to each probability and values assigned to PV based on this.

Likewise, costs have three possible outcomes being $248k, $260k and $272k. In the same way probabilities could have random numbers assigned and so combinations of both sales and costs generated for cash flow outcomes.

ANSWERS

Costs PV $'000	Probability (say)	Assign random numbers
248	0.30	00 – 29
260	0.60	30 – 89
272	0.10	90 – 99

As the random numbers generated give 10 possible outcomes, this gives ten periods of sales and costs on which to base data. Thus

Random number	Sales revenue PV $'000	Costs PV $'000	NPV $'000
19	318	248	70
00	254	248	6
71	382	260	122
74	382	260	122
60	382	260	122
47	318	260	58
21	318	248	70
29	318	260	58
68	382	260	122
02	254	248	6

10 Question with answer plan: Health Clinic

Text references. You can refer to Chapter 14 for help in drawing up the decision tree and EVs.

Top tips. Part (a) requires a decision tree so you need to consider the alternative decisions and plot these based on the levels of demand for each alternative and for the three years. The examiner remarked in his feedback that many candidates demonstrated a lack of understanding of decision trees. We suggest that if you feel this applies to you that you go back to Chapter 2 of the Study Text, read the relevant topic and practise the examples we've included there. Then attempt the question '**Pharmacy**' in the Kit to get used to the method and increase your confidence.

Remember that a **decision point** (eg to launch or not to launch) **is shown as a square. The outcomes** from this decision are **shown with their probabilities** [these must always add up to 1!] and any values which are attached. **Outcomes are shown as circles.**

The examiner gave one mark for identifying the three alternatives, two marks for plotting year 1 outcomes and three marks for plotting the outcomes of the rest of the project.

Part (b) carries 15 marks so represents the bulk of marks on this question. You need to cost out the three alternatives using the cost data in the question and determine expected values for the three levels of demand. See our table below for a suggested layout to this part of the question. A clear table of workings is vital in these Section C questions.

Let's have a look at a couple of the tricky bits. You may find it difficult to understand where the probabilities for years 2 and 3 come from. Let's take the probability for a low outcome. In years 2 and 3 there are three probabilities of a low demand, 40%, 30% and 0%. However these follow three possible outcomes in year 1 being 30%, 50% and 20%. So the combinations are:

Low outcome year 1, low outcome years 2 and 3 gives 30% x 40% = 12%

Medium outcome year 1, low outcome years 2 and 3 gives 50% x 30% = 15%

> High outcome year 1, low outcome years 2 and 3 gives 20% x 0% = 0%
>
> The total of course is 27%. Try this for yourself with the other outcomes for years 2 and 3.
>
> Secondly, with the investment decision for Facility A, although there is no capacity to meet demand at the high level, remember that this demand is still an outcome and may need to be met. So you need to use the figures for the cost of providing additional facilities on a yearly contract basis (which is how the demand would be met). Therefore the cost at the high level of demand would be £150,000 + £350,000 = £500,000.
>
> Finally, remember to multiply the EV for years 2 and 3 in the table by two as there are two years.
> The examiner remarked that candidates' answers to this part of the question were better than answers to part (a). Five marks were awarded for identifying the costs under each alternative, three marks each for the probability of each outcome and expected cost of each outcome and the balance for stating the investment required.
>
> Part (c) requires you to briefly list and discuss non-financial factors for four marks so a couple of well made points should suffice. However the examiner remarked that most candidates gave general answers and did not apply their analysis to the scenario.
>
> **Easy marks.** If you feel a bit unsteady start with part (c), where you should be able to pick up a couple of marks. In theory there should be some easy marks to be had on part (a), as no analysis is required on the decision tree – you simply have to draw it. Just using the correct symbols and drawing it from left to right - starting with the decision being considered and then the options arising from this – will get you some marks.
>
> **Examiner's comments.** Part (a) was, on the whole, badly answered and few candidates showed a good knowledge of decision trees.
>
> Part (b) could be answered in a variety of ways but candidates often just presented a page of figures without any clear analysis.
>
> Part (c) was often answered generally, without reference to the scenario in the question.

Answer plan

(a) Draw a decision tree
 - three outcomes
 - year 1 demand
 - years 2 and 3 demand

(b) Calculate PV for each alternative
 - outlay Y_0
 - costs Y_1 and Y_2
 - probabilities Y_1 and Y_2
 - PV
 - recommendation

(c) Comments on non-financial factors to consider
 - political
 - social
 - employee concerns

ANSWERS

(a) Decision tree

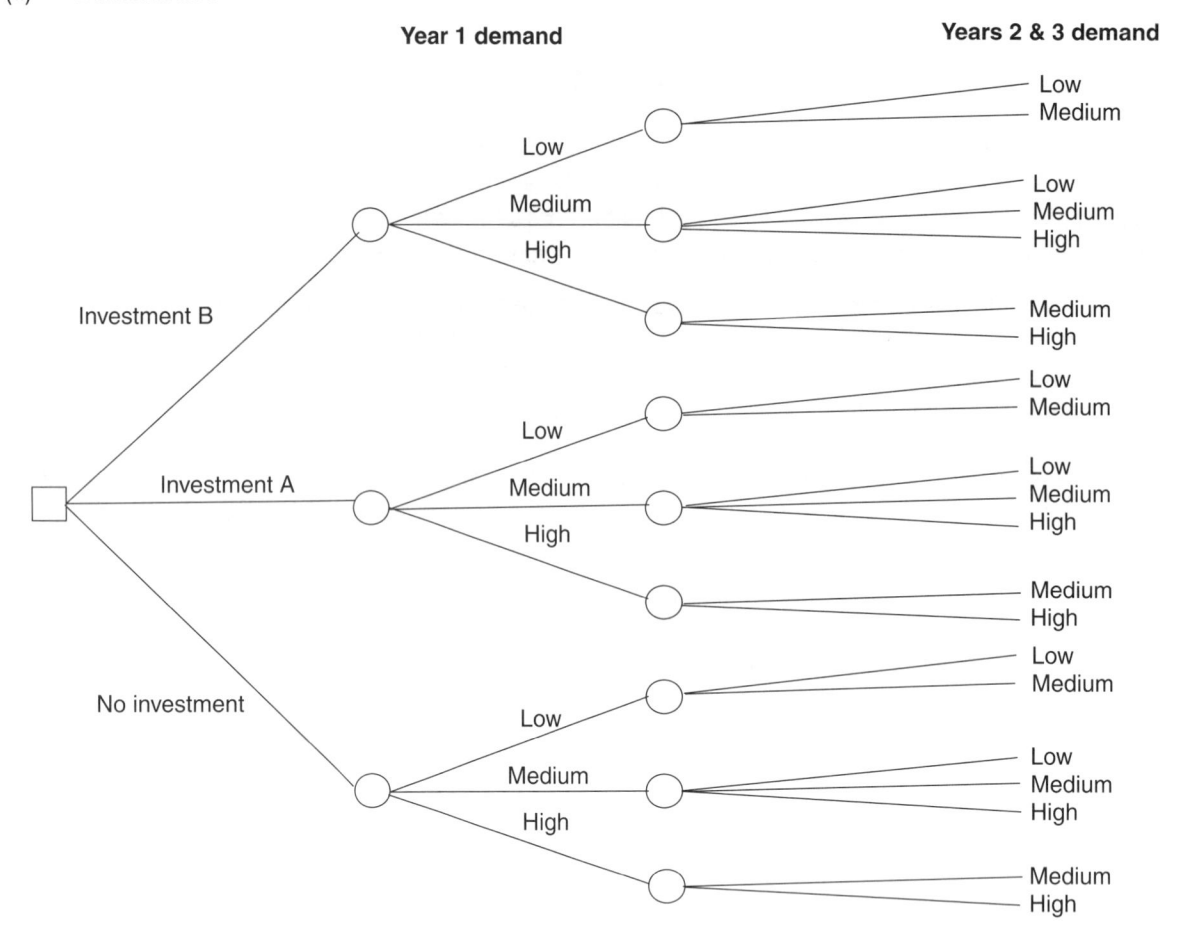

Year 1 demand — Years 2 & 3 demand

Investment B
- Low → Low, Medium
- Medium → Low, Medium, High
- High → Medium, High

Investment A
- Low → Low, Medium
- Medium → Low, Medium, High
- High → Medium, High

No investment
- Low → Low, Medium
- Medium → Low, Medium, High
- High → Medium, High

(b) Investment decision

Facility A

Demand	Probability	Year 1 Cost £'000	EV £'000	Probability	Years 2 and 3 Cost £'000	EV £'000	Total £'000
Low	0.3	250	75	0.27	250	67.50	
Medium	0.5	350	175	0.44	350	154.00	
High	0.2	500	100	0.29	500	145.00	
						366.50	
			350	Multiply EV by 2, as this EV occurs in both years		733.00	1,083
					Investment		500
					Total PV of cost		1,583

Facility B

Demand	Probability	Year 1 Cost £'000	EV £'000	Probability	Years 2 & 3 Cost £'000	EV £'000	Total £'000
Low	0.3	300	90	0.27	300	81	
Medium	0.5	350	175	0.44	350	154	
High	0.2	400	80	0.29	400	116	
						351	
			345	Multiply EV by 2, as this EV occurs in both years		702	1,047
					Investment		800
					Total PV of cost		1,847

No further investment

Demand	Probability	Year 1 Cost £'000	EV £'000	Probability	Years 2 & 3 Cost £'000	EV £'000	Total £'000
Low	0.3	300	90	0.27	300	81.00	
Medium	0.5	400	200	0.44	400	176.00	
High	0.2	550	110	0.29	550	159.50	
						416.50	
			400		X 2 years Investment	833	1,233
					Total PV of cost		1,233

On the basis of the calculations shown above, the **decision** that should be made is **not to invest** but to take on additional facilities on a yearly contract basis as this option has the **lowest PV of cost**.

(c) In the context of this organisation, which is a **not for profit** organisation, the manager must consider the **objectives** of the organisation and how these all balance with each other.

One important objective is the **service** provided by the clinic. For instance, does it aim to offer **free treatment** to anyone who turns up, whatever the cost? If this were the overriding objective then Facility B would be the better choice despite the calculations made above, as this enables all levels of demand to be met.

The manager may call upon the **additional facilities** as a top-up should levels of demand exceed those catered for by other means. If this is the case, this would allow **greater flexibility but with a loss of control**. This could mean problems with **quality and reliability** with if services are outside management's control.

Furthermore, if the **yearly contract** was chosen, this could have an **adverse motivational effect** on employees. They may regard this as short-termism (ie that the clinic considers short-term cost objectives above longer-term operations and investment).

11 Theatre

Text references. The information to answer this question can be found in Chapter 14 of the Study Text.

Top tips. This question is testing your knowledge of **uncertainty in decision-making**. This is a major area of the syllabus and is usually examined in a longer question. The question is testing three main techniques that can be used. These are expected values, two-way data tables and the value of perfect information.

Part (a) wants you to use **expected values (EV)** to make a decision. The calculation involves **two** variables, audience size and the contribution from confectionery sales. So you need to set out your calculations in a table like the one we have used. Remember that the probabilities used should add up to 1. If they don't you have missed something out.

Part (b) asks you to use a **two-way data table** to show the profit values that could arise. If you don't know what two variables to use think what factors in the scenario affect profit. Of course the relevant factors will be the fee, the audience size and the confectionery sales. The price of the ticket is fixed.

Part (c) wants you to combine your answer from part (b) with the probabilities given to evaluate financial risks including **the probability of making a profit.** Set out your workings like we have done below so you can easily distinguish the probabilities asked for.

Part (d) requires you to calculate the **value of perfect information** that is the maximum that the management would be willing to pay for information to enable them to make the best decision possible.

Easy marks. Setting out your workings in tables as in our suggested answer will ensure that you don't miss vital information and lose marks through carelessness. The two-way data table should be easy enough to draw up.

ANSWERS

(a) Expected audience size:

Audience size	Probability	EV
300	0.5	150
400	0.3	120
500	0.2	100
		370

Expected value of confectionery sales

Contribution/person	Probability	EV
$3	0.3	0.90
$5	0.5	2.50
$10	0.2	2.00
		5.40

Expected spend per person
= Ticket price + EV of confectionery sales
= $25 + 5.40
= $30.40

Expected total spend
= $30.40 × expected number of people
= $30.40 × 370
= $11,248

Expected profit
= $11,248 – fixed costs of $10,000
= $1,248

As the theatre is expected to make a profit of $1,248, it is financially worthwhile to engage MS for the concert.

(b) **Two-way data table for profit values**

We need to know what the likely profit values are from the likely audiences.

We therefore need to examine the effects of both the three possible audience sizes and the related contribution from confectionery sales. Remember that the question asks for **profit** so you will need to deduct the fee of $10,000 from each possible total revenue. Take this information from the table in part (a).

Two-way data table showing profit for a range of audience size based on $25 ticket per head, and confectionery sales.

		Audience size		
		300	400	500
		$'000	$'000	$'000
	$3/head	(1,600)	1,200	4,000
Confectionery sales	$5/head	(1,000)	2,000	5,000
	$10/head	500	4,000	7,500

(c) **Using the two-way data table**

If a probability distribution can be applied to either or both of the variables in our data table, a revised table can be prepared to provide improved management information.

Table of total contributions

The shaded area on this table shows the possible total contributions and the associated joint probabilities. We have also calculated the EV for each outcome. (This will be used in part (d) of the question when we calculate the value of perfect information.)

146

Audience size			300	400	500
Probability			0.5	0.3	0.2

Contribution from confectionery sales	Probability	EV			
$3	0.3		$(1,600)k	$1,200k	$4,000k
			0.15	0.09	0.06
		EV	(240)	108	240
$5	0.5		$(1,000)k	$2,000k	$5,000k
			0.25	0.15	0.10
		EV	(250)	300	500
$10	0.2		$500k	$4,000k	$7,500k
			0.10	0.06	0.04
		EV	50	240	300

We have taken the data from the table in part (b) and applied the probabilities given in the question to each possible combination of audience size and confectionery contribution. This table shows us some useful information.

Thus, taking the combinations where the outcome is negative and adding the associated probabilities we can work out the likelihood of making a loss. This is 0.15 + 0.25 = 0.40 or 40% and **so the probability of breaking even and making a profit is 60%.**

(d) **Maximum price for perfect information that management should pay**

The requirements of this part of the question are a bit unclear. Let's explain. When a decision is made involving perfect information, the best decision option will always be chosen. The best decision option is not known but is calculated by taking the best outcome for a variety of decisions, then calculate their EVs and compare with the EV without perfect information. In our case that has already been calculated in part(a) as $1,248.

We believe that the examiner wants you to calculate the likelihood of **the management making a profit**. With perfect information, the theatre would not engage MS if 300 people attend and the contribution was $3 or $5 from confectionery. This would be the best outcome and **one that is not already known**. Look back at the two-way data table you have drawn up in part(c). This should provide you with the information you need.

So to do this, you would need to add up the combinations of confectionery sales and audience size that result in a profit and use their EVs to get the value of perfect information based on profit.

So using the box above:

Audience size			300	400	500
Probability			0.5	0.3	0.2

Contribution from confectionery sales	Probability	EV	EV	EV
$3	0.3	0*	108	240
$5	0.5	0*	300	500
$10	0.2	50	240	300

* These EVs are entered as 0 rather than the negative contributions shown in the box above as the business would not run the concerts with negative contributions and would therefore avoid losses.

Total EV =	$1,738
Less: EV of contribution From part (a)	(1,248)
Value of perfect information	$ 490

ANSWERS

12 Section A answers: Relevant costs and short-term decisions

1   A   **By adapting now instead of in one year's time**

           Sale of machinery would produce additional income of £800,000 – £600,000 = £200,000

           Removal of machinery would save £100,000 – £110,000 = £10,000

           Leasing machinery would cost an additional £80,000 – £0 = £80,000

           There will therefore be additional savings of £200,000 + £10,000 – £80,000 = £130,000.

           If you chose **option B**, you calculated the correct amount but you got your costs and savings muddled up.

           If you chose **option C**, you probably deducted the savings on the removal of machinery instead of adding it.

           If you chose **option D**, you probably deducted the savings on the removal of machinery instead of adding it and got the direction of the cash flow the wrong way round.

2   Price = variable costs saved of £150,000 + contribution earned on other products of £250,000 = £400,000

3   A   Their net realisable value will, of course, depend on the manner in which they are to be disposed. It might be scrap value less any disposal costs or, if they are sold for an alternative use once work has been carried out on them, the net realisable value will be selling price less the costs of the further work.

           Option B is incorrect because replacement cost is not an appropriate relevant cost as the units are no longer required.

           Option C is incorrect because variable cost is only relevant in certain circumstances (if net realisable value is the same as variable cost).

           Option D is incorrect because full cost includes absorbed fixed overheads, which are not relevant.

4   **False**. The hire of a programmer is the incremental cost which would be incurred if the programmer works on the L job. It is therefore £22,000.

5   D   **I** is incorrect because this term is used to describe a cost which will differ under some or all of the decision options.

           II is incorrect because relevant costs can be expressed as opportunity costs.

           Notional cost (**III**) is a hypothetical accounting cost used to reflect the benefit from the use of something for which no actual cash expense is incurred.

           Sunk cost (**IV**) is a term is used to describe a cost that has already been incurred or committed and which is therefore not relevant to subsequent decisions.

6   Modification = £7,200, hire costs avoided = £(19,800) and disposal costs = £4,000 and so the relevant cost is a saving of £8,600.

7   400 of the units required are already in stock. They have no other use and if not used for this job they could be sold. The opportunity cost of using these 400 units is therefore the sales revenue forgone. The remaining 300 units would have to be purchased. The relevant cost is therefore (400 × £20) + (300 × £60) = £26,000

ANSWERS

13 MOV plc I

> **Top tips.** There is not an increase in stocks of sensors from 3,500 to 8,000, but an increase in stocks of SCBs, so the production volume remains at 58,000 units in 20X2/3. You could include the cost of producing the additional stock in your calculations, but the cost would be removed via closing stock and so there is little point.
>
> **Easy marks.** With two questions based on one scenario such as 12 and 13, you can do question 13 first as the answer to 12 doesn't affect 13. In fact, in this case, it makes answering 12 easier as 13 is the 'model answer'. Also 13 is easier to answer.

General problems with the statement

(a) The statement should not solely just on 20X2/3 given that the figures are not typical (because of the redundancy costs, for example) and because of the changing demand patterns.

(b) The statement makes no attempt to account for the gain in selling more sensors.

(c) The layout of the statement is not particularly helpful and does not compare like with like. Relevant costs saved (although they are not all saved) are compared with additional costs.

Specific problems with the statement

(a) £1.8m of salaries would be saved but the statement does not include the 72 × £4,000 = £288,000 redundancy cost.

(b) The saving of £10,000 due to the purchasing officer's time saved is not relevant. The annual salary of £20,000 will still be incurred regardless of whether SCBs are bought-in *unless* the purchasing officer's hours and hence salary are reduced.

(c) Assuming the cost of placing orders for SCB materials is correct, it should be included as a relevant saving within the statement. (It might have been more appropriate to include any relevant saving of the purchasing officer's salary within the cost of placing an order, however.)

(d) Assuming the saving in transport costs for raw materials for SCBs is correct, it should be included as a relevant saving within the statement. It might have been more appropriate to include the cost within the direct material cost of SCBs, however, and hence in the calculation of the additional cost per SCB.

(e) The additional cost per SCB has been calculated incorrectly. It should be based on bought-in price (£116 has been correctly included) less marginal cost (£88) and not full cost, which has been used.

(f) The statement does not include the cost of the new liaison officer's salary.

14 MOV plc II

> **Top tips.** There are two principal approaches to this question. You could calculate the profit earned under each option over the three years or you could work out the incremental profit earned under each option over the three years (against profit based on no changes). We have taken the first approach but also show the figures you should have calculated using the second.
>
> Note that in the first approach you do not need to include the cost savings relating to production staff made redundant or fixed costs saved, as this approach is based on calculating total profits rather than incremental costs/benefits. They would be included in the alternative approach, however.
>
> **Easy marks.** See comments on 12 above.

Options

1   Maintain current position and continue to produce SCBs in-house (using overtime)
2   Buy-in SCBs and expand production of sensors
3   Buy-in SCBs and rent out storage space

ANSWERS

Option 1

	20X2/3	20X3/4	20X4/5	Total
Production (max 60,500) units	58,000	60,500	60,500	
	£'000	£'000	£'000	£'000
Contribution (× £400)	23,200	24,200.0	24,200.0	
Additional variable cost				
(on production 55,000+) @ £75/unit	(225)	(412.5)	(412.5)	
Fixed costs				
SCB attributable	(250)	(380.0)	(380.0)	
MOVs	(2,600)	(2,900.0)	(2,900.0)	
	20,125	20,507.5	20,507.5	61,140

Option 2

	20X2/3	20X3/4	20X4/5	Total
Production	58,000	62,000	65,000	
	£'000	£'000	£'000	£'000
Contribution (× £400)	23,200	24,800	26,000	
Excess of CIR plc's cost over MOV				
plc's variable cost for SCBs (£(116 – 88))	(1,624)	(1,736)	(1,820)	
Fixed costs	(2,600)	(2,900)	(3,100)	
Additional costs:				
Stock holding	(10)	(10)	(10)	
Liaison officer	(30)	(30)	(30)	
Redundancy (see Q12(a))	(288)	–	–	
	18,648	20,124	21,040	59,812

Option 3

	20X2/3	20X3/4	20X4/5	Total
Production	58,000	60,500	60,500	
	£'000	£'000	£'000	£'000
Contribution (× £400)	23,200	24,200	24,200	
Excess of CIR plc's cost over MOV				
plc's variable cost for SCBs (£(116 – 88))	(1,624)	(1,694)	(1,694)	
Fixed costs	(2,600)	(2,900)	(2,900)	
Rental income (240m × 120m × £45)	–	1,296	1,296	
Additional costs:				
Stockholding	(10)	(10)	(10)	
Liaison officer	(30)	(30)	(30)	
Redundancy	(288)	–	–	
	18,648	20,862	20,862	60,372

Conclusion

Using the time horizon in question, the best financial option is to continue producing SCBs in-house, using overtime to increase capacity. This produces £(61,140 – 60,372) = £768,000 more profit than the second best option, that of renting.

Alternative approach – incremental profit				
	20X2/3	20X3/4	20X4/5	Total
	£'000	£'000	£'000	£'000
Option 1	975	1,357.5	1,357.5	3,690
Option 2	(502)	974	1,890	2,362
Option 3	(502)	1,712	1,712	2,922

ANSWERS

15 Question with analysis: Z Limited

> **Top tips.** Think about the possible methods for apportioning joint costs and see if there is any relationship between the cost per litre for the three products. This should tell you that litres is the basis of apportionment.
>
> In part (b) remember to only look at the incremental revenues and costs after the common process.
>
> **Easy marks.** This question requires very simple calculations. Therefore, work out the basis of the common apportionment first.
>
> **Examiner's comments.** This question was poorly answered, particularly part (a). Only one to two percent of candidates attempted to explain why it was necessary to apportion the common costs.
>
> Many students did not appreciate the simplicity of part (b).
>
> Common errors noted by the examiner include:
>
> - Misreading part (a) and answering that the method used to apportion meant absorption costing or ABC.
> - In part (b) calculating full profitability statements rather than simply comparing incremental costs and revenue.
> - Ignoring or misunderstanding the viability of the common process and whether it generated an overall profit.

(a)

Product	Value at end of process (i) $	Litres (ii)	Value per litre from process ((i)/(ii)) $
M	141,875	25,000	5.675
N	85,125	15,000	5.675
P	255,375	45,000	5.675
	482,375	85,000	

State the method used — As $482,375/85,000 = $5.**675 the method used to apportion common costs between the joint products is litres produced**.

Comment on its acceptability — **This method is only suitable when products remain in the same state** that is don't separate into liquid and gas products. It also doesn't take into account the relative income earning potential of each product.

However, it does allow values to be put on the products for stock and financial reporting purposes.

It is necessary to apportion the common costs between each product to put a value on stock for financial reporting and so sales can be matched with the cost the of sales.

(b) (i) **Viability of the common process**

Product	Selling price after common process $/litre	Litres	Total revenue $
M	6.25	25,000	156,250
N	5.20	15,000	78,000
P	6.80	45,000	306,000
			540,250

Less costs at end of common process (per (a) above) (482,375)
Net revenue at the end of the common process 57,875

Evaluate the viability of the common process — **Therefore the common process is viable** as net revenue is positive.

(ii) **Optimal processing plan for each product**

Product	Further revenues $/litre	Further costs $/litre	Net revenue $/litre
M	2.15	1.75	0.40
N	1.25	0.95	0.30
P	0.65	0.85	(0.20)

Optimal processing plan — **Therefore products M and N make additional profit and so should be processed further.**

Product P should not be processed beyond the common stage as net revenue is negative.

ANSWERS

16 Mixit Ltd

> **Text references.** Look at Chapter 3 for an explanation of how to allocate joint costs.
>
> **Top tips.** This is a nice straightforward question and perfect for revision. Work through our answer very carefully if you get parts wrong to make sure that you really understand the principles involved in joint cost allocations.

(a) **First calculate the joint costs per gallon.**

	£
Materials	150,000
Process labour and materials	148,000
	298,000

Output (10,000 – 2,000)　　　　　　　　　　　　　　　　　　　　　　8,000 gallons

Cost per gallon　　　　　　　　　　　　　　　　　　　　　　　　　　　£37.25

(i)

	A	B	C	D	Total
Output (gallons)	2,000	2,500	2,500	1,000	8,000
	£	£	£	£	£
Joint costs @ £37.25 per gallon	74,500	93,125	93,125	37,250	298,000
Further costs	125,500	149,375	111,875	-	386,750
	200,000	242,500	205,000	37,250	684,750
Output × selling price per gallon	(150,000)	(432,500)	(345,000)	(50,000)	(977,500)
Profit/(loss)	(50,000)	190,000	140,000	12,750	292,750

Product A appears to be making a loss of £50,000 **because of the way in which joint costs are allocated.** Product A represents **25% of all output but only generates 15% of total sales.** (By comparison product B represents 31¼% of output but generates about 44% of total sales.) The **further processing costs** of product A amount to (£125,000/2,000) = £62.75 per gallon and with a selling price of only £75 it can clearly bear a very small proportion of the joint costs.

(ii) It would be more equitable to **split joint costs on the basis of final sales value less further processing costs.**

Product	Final sales value £	Further processing costs £	Ratio for split £
A	150,000	125,500	24,500
B	432,500	149,375	283,125
C	345,000	111,875	233,125
D	50,000	-	50,000
			590,750

Reallocation of joint costs

Product	Ratio	Joint costs £
A	24,500/590,750 ⎫	12,359
B	283,125/590,750 ⎬ × 298,000	142,821
C	233,125/590,750 ⎪	117,598
D	50,000/590,750 ⎭	25,222
		298,000

ANSWERS

	A	B	C	D	Total
Joint costs	12,359	142,821	117,598	25,222	298,000
Further costs	125,500	149,375	111,875	-	386,750
	137,859	292,196	229,473	25,222	684,750
Sales value	(150,000)	(432,500)	(345,000)	(50,000)	(977,500)
Profit	12,141	140,304	115,527	24,778	292,750

Using this method **each product shows a profit**, although the overall profit is **unchanged**.

(b) (i) The **further processing decision compares the extra revenue obtainable from processing the product further with the extra costs involved**.

	A	B	C
Output (gallons)	2,000	2,500	2,500
Extra revenue from further processing	£25	£73	£63
Total extra revenue	50,000	182,500	157,500
Total extra cost	(125,500)	(149,375)	(111,875)
Additional profit/(loss)	(75,500)	33,125	45,625

The company should **sell product A at split-off point** with a net increase in profit of £75,500. Products **B and C should continue to be processed further**.

(ii) A **by-product** is one which is **produced at the same time and from the same process** as the main product or products. Its distinguishing feature is its **relatively low sales value** in comparison to the large value of the main product.

Unlike a joint product a by-product is **not important as a saleable item** and any revenue it earns is considered a **'bonus'** for the organisation.

There are **various methods** of accounting for by-products, as follows.

(1) Income (minus any post-separation further processing or selling costs) from the sale of the by-product may be added to sales of the main product, thereby increasing sales turnover for the period.

(2) The sales of the by-product may be treated as a separate, incidental source of income against which are set only post-separation costs (if any) of the by-product. The revenue would be recorded as 'other income' in the P&L account.

(3) The sales income of the by-product may be deducted from the cost of production of the main products.

(4) The 'net realisable value' of the by-product may be deducted from the cost of production of the main products. The net realisable value is the final saleable value minus any post-separation costs. Any closing stock valuation of the main product(s) would therefore be reduced.

Treating D as a by-product would therefore mean that it is not allocated any common costs, which would therefore be split between the three main products.

ANSWERS

17 Exe

Text references. Refer to Chapter 2 for the basis for making decisions based on relevant cash flows. Chapter 14 explains Expected Values.

Top tips. Don't forget to provide your reasons for using each of the values in your estimate.

Easy marks. In part (a) You should be able to identify that most overheads will not be relevant costs as they are incurred anyway irrespective of an individual job. Costs that are specifically incurred for this job, for instance the brass fittings would be relevant costs. Costs that have already been incurred such as estimating time are sunk costs.

(a)
	Notes	$
Direct materials		
Steel	1	55.00
Brass fittings		20.00
Direct labour		
Skilled	2	300.00
Semi-skilled	3	–
Overhead	4	7.50
Estimating time	5	–
		382.50
Administration overhead	6	–
Profit	7	–
Selling price		382.50

Lowest cost estimate = £382.50

Notes

1. 10m^2 × $5.50 (the replacement cost)

2. Overtime option – 25 hrs × $8 × 1.5 = £300

    Reduction in production of another product option = 25 × $(8 + 13) = £525

    ∴ It is cheaper to work overtime and hence this will be the relevant cost.

3. There is no incremental cost involved since the employees are currently being paid to be idle.

4. General fixed costs will be incurred regardless of whether or not the order is accepted and so are not relevant. The relevant cost therefore relates to the machine usage and is 10 hrs × $0.75.

5. This is a sunk cost and is therefore not relevant.

6. Administration costs will be incurred regardless of whether or not the order is accepted and so are not relevant.

7. We are asked to produce a lowest cost estimate which is one which just covers incremental costs and makes no profit. The profit mark up is therefore not relevant.

(b)

Top tips. The problem with this part of the question was knowing exactly what you had to cover. You may not have thought to cover all the points we have made, but the fact that two sets of linked probabilities were provided should have given you a bit of a hint that joint probabilities could be calculated.

ANSWERS

The two-way data table shows the **effect on the cost estimate of alternative combinations of three values for each of two variables** (skilled labour rate and hourly power costs).

In a scenario in which the two variables are at the values stated in part (a) ($8 per hour for labour and $0.75 per hour for power) the effect on the estimate is 0.00.

If alternative values for these variables are considered, however, the cost estimate will increase or decrease. For example, if the labour rate is $7 and the power cost is $0.65, the cost estimate falls by $38.50.

The table therefore **illustrates the range of possible impacts on the estimate** given the uncertainty in the value of the two variables under consideration. Given the information in the table, the cost estimate may be **as low as $344** ($(382.50 − 38.50)) or **as high as $459** ($(382.50 + 76.50)).

The introduction of the probabilities of the various values of the variables occurring makes it possible to **determine the probability of the minimum cost being more or less than the original estimate by calculating joint probabilities**. By applying these joint probabilities to the possible cost effects as shown in the data table, **an EV of the possible cost effect can be calculated and an EV of the minimum cost price established**. This is shown in the table below.

Skilled labour rate per hour $	Power costs per hour $	Joint probability	Effects (from data table) $	EV of effects $
10	0.90	0.3 × 0.25 = 0.075	+76.5	+5.7375
10	0.75	0.3 × 0.55 = 0.165	+75.0	+12.3750
10	0.65	0.3 × 0.20 = 0.060	+74.0	+4.4400
8	0.90	0.6 × 0.25 = 0.150	+1.5	+0.2250
8	0.75	0.6 × 0.55 = 0.330	0.0	0.0000
8	0.65	0.6 × 0.20 = 0.120	−1.0	−0.1200
7	0.90	0.1 × 0.25 = 0.025	−36.0	−0.9000
7	0.75	0.1 × 0.55 = 0.055	−37.5	−2.0625
7	0.65	0.1 × 0.20 = 0.020	−38.5	−0.7700
		1.000		+18.9250

If the **costs are to be higher than the original estimate** the EV of effects must be positive. The probability of this occurring is (0.075 + 0.165 + 0.06 + 0.15) 0.45, the individual probabilities being summed being the joint probabilities associated with positive effects.

If the **costs are to be lower than the original estimate** the EV of effects must be negative. The probability of this occurring is (0.12 + 0.025 + 0.055 + 0.02) 0.22, the individual probabilities being summed being the joint probabilities associated with positive effects.

The probability of **cost being the same** as the original estimate is 0.33.

The sum of the expected values of +$18.925 is the expected increase in cost compared with the original estimate.

The **EV of the minimum cost** is therefore $(382.50 + 18.925) = $401.43

Summary. Given the most likely combination of skilled labour rate per hour and power cost per hour, the minimum cost price is expected to be $401.43. Given the range of possible alternative values for these variables, however, the minimum cost could be as low as $344 or as high as $459.

ANSWERS

18 Question with analysis: CS Group

> **Text references.** Look at Chapter 2 if you need background to relevant cash flows, which is an important syllabus area. Chapter 14 should provide material to answer part (b) on EVs.
>
> **Top tips.** This question took one side of A4 for BPP to answer! Therefore, there isn't a large amount of writing or calculating required.
>
> Part (b)(i) is a straightforward explanation of the figures in the two way table.
>
> Part (b)(ii) requires more calculation but you should be able to get the figures straight from the data in part (b). Remember the probabilities should add up to 1!
>
> **Easy marks.** In part (a) overheads are usually not relevant costs but do read the specific text to confirm this. In part (b) set out a table to calculate EVs.
>
> **Examiner's comments.** This was generally well answered.
>
> Common errors noted by the examiner include:
>
> - Poor or non existent reasons for including and excluding figures (part a)
> - Incorrect reasons for including and excluding figures (part a)
> - Poorly tabulated tables (part b)
> - Incorrect interpretation of tables (part b)
> - Poor advice on how the information from the table would be useful to the recipient (part b)
> - Not relating parts (a) and (b)

(a) *Relevant costs*

	Notes	$
Coach running (fuel)	1	1,500
Driver	2	4,000
Hotel	3	5,000
Coach required under the contract	4	360
General overheads	5	0
		10,860

Notes [Comment on each of the costs included in the cost estimate.]

1 Fuel for the coach only. No overhead apportioned as not relevant.
2 A replacement driver at $400 day for 10 days.
3 Specific to this contract.
4 Other contract costs – replacement coach at $180 × 2 days.
5 General overheads are not relevant to this specific contract. The time in preparing a contract quotation, of $250, is a sunk cost.

(b) (i) [Explaining the meaning of the two-way data table in the question]

The data table shows the effect on the relevant cost of $10,860 of changes in the hotel cost and/or fuel cost.

There are a range of outcomes from a minimum relevant cost of $9,560 if hotel costs fall to $4,000 and fuel costs to $1,200. This is calculated as $10,860 + $1,500 from the table. A maximum relevant cost of $12,360 applies if fuel costs increase to $2,000 and hotel costs to $6,000.

ANSWERS

(ii) By including the probabilities of the costs, the likelihood of various cost outcomes identified in the two-way table can be calculated.

[Produce a table]

Hotel $	Fuel $	Probability	Adjustment to relevant cost $	EV of costs $
4,000	1,200	0.02	(1,300)	(26)
4,000	1,500	0.10	(1,000)	(100)
4,000	2,000	0.08	(500)	(40)
5,000	1,200	0.05	(300)	(15)
5,000	1,500	0.25	–	–
5,000	2,000	0.20	500	100
6,000	1,200	0.03	700	21
6,000	1,500	0.15	1,000	150
6,000	2,000	0.12	1,500	180
		1.00		270

[Interpret this table]

This table shows that the expected value of the total of hotel and fuel costs is $270 more than initially expected and hence the relevant cost is likely to be $270 higher.

However the use of EV does not distinguish the outcome of individual variances such as downside variances eg when the hotel and fuel costs are $1,500 more and there is a 12% likelihood of this outcome.

The table can be used to show the likelihood of costs exceeding $10,860. Therefore by summing the relevant probabilities:

- a 50% chance of cost exceeding $10,860 (sum the probabilities where the adjustment to relevant cost is positive).

- a 25% chance of cost being below $10,860 (sum the probabilities where the adjustment to relevant cost is negative).

19 ML

Top tips. This was a reasonable written question on pricing methods. You need to read through the scenario and refer to the pertinent characteristics of ML that would add to your discussion. The examiner gave up to three marks for explaining the differences between the two costing methods and another two marks for how the system would affect pricing decisions. The remainder of the marks could be earned for your comments in part (b).

Easy marks. You could earn useful marks by just repeating from memory what you know of the approaches to pricing. Better marks would accrue from applying these to the scenario but put down your general points first and then expand on these in the 18 minutes.

Examiner's comments. The general theme of the examiner's comments were that the specific question was not answered and many candidates addressed only the more basic points. Common errors included explanations of pricing that started with a selling price and deducting costs to arrive at a profit. Also excluding variable costs under the absorption costing method. Finally, failing to consider the specific business when discussing pricing.

(a) (i) **Absorption costing**

Traditionally the costing of production has included a 'fair share' of overheads. This is justified by the argument that all production overheads arise as a result of production and so each unit produced should incur some overhead costs. This includes both variable and fixed overheads.

By adding a margin for profit to the full cost of production, the sale price can be calculated. This is known as 'full cost plus' pricing. This method is particularly appropriate for companies who do jobbing or contract work where no standard sales prices can be fixed.

ANSWERS

ML has used a cost plus approach to pricing based on absorption costing. This approach is appropriate to a company, which like ML, undertakes ad hoc work that may need to be individually priced.

An absorption costing basis may be inappropriate when overheads apportioned to a job do not reflect the overheads a job has caused. Thus ML uses a machine hours basis but a labour hours basis may be more appropriate given the skilled engineers appear to drive the work carried out. Alternatively, activity based costing may be more appropriate. ML may be losing work because they have set the profit margin too high and hence quoted prices too high.

It is not clear if they are using the same margin on all products, but ML could consider varying the margin depending on the type of work and/or customers. Because there is unused capacity, the use of absorption costing does not necessarily imply fixed costs are covered.

(i) **Marginal costing**

Marginal costing values inventory at its variable cost thereby excluding fixed overheads, which are treated as a cost of the accounting period rather than being apportioned to production. There is a direct relationship between output and profitability as contribution varies directly with sales. Fixed overheads are charged as they are incurred.

Marginal costing is simple and easy to use. It is most appropriate when there is a readily identifiable unit cost, for instance in retail industries which is not the case with ML. However, it ignores fixed costs and so the mark-up must be sufficiently high to ensure they are covered.

Nonetheless the mark-up % can be varied so management can use their discretion when quoting for individual jobs. This may help ML win more quotes.

(b) **Comment on the Managing Director's remark**

A price based on variable costs reflects the marginal costing approach to pricing.

Any price that exceeds variable cost will at least offer some contribution toward fixed costs, but in the long term, this approach is not sustainable. The price must at least cover fixed costs for a profit to be made.

In the short term, ML could consider this approach in an effort to win business, but it may prove difficult to raise prices in the future without again losing business. In addition, low prices might give the impression that work is of an inferior quality to that of competitors.

20 PK plc

Top tips. This question required you to discuss three points being the changing nature of cost structures in modern manufacturing, the implications for PK plc's inventory valuation, and for PK plc's short term decision making. It awarded two points for format and presentation, which seemed to suggest there are only two or three marks for each point you need to discuss.

As suggested in the question, there were two marks for the report format. The remaining eight marks were split 50:50 between explaining traditional cost structures and how these have changed, and the importance of these to valuing stock and short-term decision making.

Easy marks. Make sure you use the appropriate headers and so on for a report. Lay out the body of your answer in a report format and end the report appropriately, and there's two marks straight away.

Divide up your report with headings so that it is clear you have covered the three points you need to discuss.

Examiner's comments. The examiner remarked that this question was badly answered. Unfortunately, most candidates did not identify that the main issue was how cost structure ie labour to overheads, had changed in recent times.

So errors included advising the company to use JIT, and not understanding what 'inventory valuation' meant.

ANSWERS

REPORT

To: Management Team of PK plc
From: Assistant management accountant
Date: 23 November 20X5
Subject: **Cost structures in the modern manufacturing environment**

1 Introduction

This report explains the changing nature of cost structures in the modern manufacturing environment and then considers the implications for PK's inventory valuation and short term decision making.

2 Changing nature of cost structures in the modern manufacturing environment

The traditional **absorption costing** approach to dealing with overheads was developed at a time when most organisations produced only a **narrow range of products** and when **overhead costs** were only a very **small fraction of total costs**, direct labour and direct material costs accounting for the largest proportion of the costs. Errors made in attributing overheads to products were therefore not too significant.

Nowadays, however, the situation is very different and it has been argued that traditional absorption costing is unsuitable for the modern business environment.

(i) **Direct labour may account for as little as 5% of a product's cost**. With the advent of advanced manufacturing technology, **support activities** such as setting-up, production scheduling, first item inspection and data processing have increased. These support activities assist the efficient manufacture of a wide range of products and are not, in general, affected by changes in production volume. To allocate them to products on the basis of some measure of production volume (as would be the case if absorption costing were used) would therefore be entirely inappropriate. The level of such activities tends to vary in the long term according to the **range** and **complexity of the products** manufactured. The wider the range and the more complex the product, the more support services will be required.

(ii) The current business environment is characterised by high levels of **competition**. Management's need for an accurate indication of how much it costs to take on competitors cannot be met by traditional costing systems.

(iii) **Support department costs** have a tendency to increase. Management therefore need additional information to enable them to **manage and control** these costs.

(iv) Traditionally, the management accounting cost object has been the product. Information about the **profitability of customers and market segments** is now vital, however, if organisations wish to compete in the modern business environment.

Given the accessibility of and improvement in **information technology**, and the need for more appropriate information, the reason for the development of new costing approaches, such as activity based costing (ABC), is obvious.

3 Inventory valuation

Absorption costing is used to value inventory for financial reporting purposes where the requirement is to include all costs in 'bringing the product to its present location and condition'. So this would include related production overheads.

However, absorption costing may give an inaccurate record of profit if the absorption basis used is inappropriate in the modern manufacturing environment.

In many circumstances, in the modern manufacturing environment, ABC allocates overheads to products using more relevant cost drivers. ABC therefore produces more realistic product costs and so more realistic inventory valuation.

ANSWERS

4   **Short-term decision making**

Some commentators argue that only marginal costing provides suitable information for decision making. This is untrue. Marginal costing provides a crude method of differentiating between different types of cost behaviour by splitting costs into their variable and fixed elements. **Marginal costing** can only be used for **short-term decisions** and usually even these have longer-term implications which ought to be considered.

ABC spreads costs across products or other cost units according to a number of different bases. The analysis may show that one activity which is carried out for one or two products is expensive. If costs have been apportioned using the traditional method prior to this the cost of this activity is likely to have been spread across all products, thus hiding the fact that the products using this activity may be loss making. If these costs are not completely variable costs but are, for example, batch costs, marginal costing would not have related them to the products at all. Therefore **ABC** can be used to make **decisions about pricing, discontinuing products**, and so on which are short-term. However, ABC is particularly suited in fact to long term and strategic decisions.

I hope this information has proved useful but if I can be of any further assistance please do not hesitate to contact me.

Signed: Assistant accountant

21 QXY plc

> **Top tips.** This question wants you to **apply** some basic and some more advanced knowledge to the particular scenario. What we mean by this is the interpretation of the diagram relies in some respects on knowledge you should have brought forward from earlier studies. So what types of costs and revenues are illustrated will gain you some marks. However, you still need to **apply** principles of pricing and decision making to your analysis and these are P2 subject areas.
>
> We have set out our answer in a headed note form. There is no need to do this but it helps you focus on using headers and the flow of your discussion.
>
> **Easy marks.** You should get a couple of marks for explaining sales revenue, total cost and fixed cost and the significance of the four activity levels. Remember that your audience are not accountants so keep your technical language simple.

The diagram

The **diagram** is what is known as a breakeven chart, and shows revenue, fixed cost and total cost for a range of activity levels.

The **vertical distance** between the sales revenue line and the total cost line at a certain activity level is the **profit** at that activity level.

Sales revenue line

This shows the revenue **at various levels of activity**. The **slope** of the line indicates the **unit selling price**. So the **steeper** the line, the **higher** the selling price. In the diagram the selling price is constant at activity levels up to C, and then reduces at higher levels of activity. We know that the selling price reduces after point C because the sales revenue line **flattens** after this point.

Operational managers should therefore bear in mind that at activity levels in excess of C, revenue per unit will fall.

Fixed cost line

The **fixed cost line** shows that QXY's fixed costs behave in **a stepped** fashion. They are fixed between certain activity levels (A and B, B and D) and then increase by what appears to be a constant amount each time. An example of a stepped cost would be factory rent. Additional factory premises may be required when activity levels exceed a certain amount.

Operational managers therefore need to bear in mind that an **increase in activity** from just less than B to just more than B, for example, will result in a significant increase in costs.

Total costs line

The **total cost line** shows the **sum** of both **fixed** and **variable** costs over a range of activity levels. The impact of the steps in the level of fixed costs at B and D is clear, with identical steps in the total cost line at these points.

The **slope** of the line indicates the **variable cost per unit**. Thus, the **steeper** the slope, the **higher** the unit cost. The unit cost is lowest for activity levels between B and D (presumably when QXY plc is operating most efficiently) and highest for activity levels in excess of D.

Variable costs are costs which **vary directly** with **activity.** They have the same unit cost across a range of activity. An example of these would be direct material costs in manufacturing.

Point A

At this activity level, **sales revenue equals total cost**. This is the **breakeven point**. Below activity level A QXY is making a loss, above this point it is making a profit.

Point B

At this activity level there is **a step increase in fixed cost** and hence in total cost. **Unit variable costs begin to fall** (as can be seen from the slope of the total cost line). **Profit drops** at point B because of the fixed cost increase, but then starts to **increase again**, helped by the fall in variable cost per unit.

Point C

At point C, QXY is achieving **maximum profit** (as the vertical distance between the sales revenue and total cost lines is greatest). This is also the point at which the unit selling prices changes (the slope of the sales revenue line becomes shallower), and so contribution starts to fall after this.

Point D

There is another **step in fixed costs** at this point and so profits drop sharply. After this point profits continue to fall given the **increase** in **variable cost per unit** (the slope of the total cost line becomes steeper) and the fall in unit selling price at C.

Implications for decision making

The diagram enables operational managers to **determine profitability** (or loss) at various levels of output. For instance, it is clear that activity must be greater than A to ensure a profit is made.

It highlights the **impact on profitability of increasing activity levels** (given the stepped nature of the fixed costs).

It shows **the profit-maximising activity level** (point C). It is clear that activity in excess of C is not worthwhile as profits will fall. Managers should aim for activity at level C.

The diagram can be used in conjunction with **sensitivity analysis**. Various revenue lines could be plotted for instance, based on different selling prices, to determine the effect on the breakeven point.

ANSWERS

22 Z

> **Text reference.** Read Chapter 3 if you get stuck with this question.
>
> **Top tips.** The examiner is testing how you make decisions. He asks you to **state recommendations** and **state assumptions** in parts(a) and (b). **So don't just tackle this as a calculation exercise.** You will need to produce calculations but also be able to explain these.
>
> **Easy marks.** The calculations in part(a) are quite simple. You need to compare the **incremental revenue** from the later products with the **incremental cost** to make these products. You can take much of this data straight from the question.

(a) **Further processing decision**

	Product		
	RZ	SZ	TZ
Incremental revenue	$	$	$
RZ/SZ/TZ	6.00	5.75	6.75
R/S/T	3.00	5.00	3.50
	3.00	0.75	3.25
Incremental cost (W)	1.40	0.90	1.00
Net revenue/loss	1.60	(0.15)	2.25

Working

Product TZ has fixed costs of $600/month. These are **relevant costs** as they are specific to the further processing of T into TZ. We discuss these further in the recommendations made just below.

Recommendations

The table shows that the further processing of products R and T into RZ and TZ will be profitable as these result in additional net revenue. Let's assume that the monthly output of product TZ remains at 1,200kg (no loss in further processing for instance). It is clear that even by accounting for these fixed costs it is profitable to convert T into TZ. So:

1,200 kg × $2.25 − $600 = $2,100

However, it is not profitable to process S further into product SZ. Nonetheless, other factors must also be considered. We do also need to consider whether the sales of these products are related so that, say, the sale of product T depends on that of S. So it may be necessary to continue selling a loss-making product to maintain a market presence.

(b) **Validity of the common process**

(i) *Assuming an external market for products R, S and T*

We are considering the **validity of the common process.** So we need to compare the combined cost of producing the three products with the combined market prices for each as given in the question.

	Product			
	R	S	T	Total
Revenue	$	$	$	$
R/S/T (W1)	2,400	10,000	4,200	16,600
Cost (W2)				17,500
Net revenue/loss				(900)

ANSWERS

Working

(1) Take the output from the common process for each product and multiply by the unit market prices given. So for product R, this would be 800kg × $3.00/kg.

(2) Total cost taken from process account in question.

Recommendation

The calculations in the table tell us that the common process is not viable given the costs and/or current market prices for the products.

(ii) *Assuming no external market for products R, S and T*

We need to work out a **notional sales value** for each product if there isn't a market price. This can be achieved by working backwards from the further products which do have a sales value.

	Product			
	RZ	SZ	TZ	Total
	$	$	$	$
Revenue RZ/SZ/TZ (W1)	4,800	11,500	8,100	24,400
Common costs				17,500
Further costs (W2)	1,120	1,800	1,800	4,720
Net revenue/loss				2,180

Workings

(1) Take the unit market prices in the question and multiply by the outputs from the common process. So taking product R/RZ, 800kg × $6/kg = $4,800.

(2) Take the output from the common process and multiply by the specific costs in the question. Remember to include the fixed costs relating to product TZ.

Recommendation

The calculations in the table tell us that the common process is viable given the costs and/or notional market prices for the products. However this does of course depend on how reliable the notional prices are in reflecting market prices for the products.

23 H

Text reference. You will find most of the information to answer this question in Chapters 2 and 3.

Top tips. To tackle part (a), we suggest you list the costs and profit mark-up in a table with a space for the reasons why you consider each to be relevant or non-relevant costs. Keep any workings that you need to do separate and cross reference these to your main table. Remember that relevant costs are **future, incremental cash flows** and frame your reasons with this definition in mind. Other terms you could use to describe relevant costs are **differential, avoidable** or **opportunity** costs.

In part(b), the examiner is testing how well you understand the differences between **relevant costing** and **absorption costing**. Make sure you use the data you have already calculated to make your points illustrating the differences.

Easy marks. You should be able to get a couple of easy marks in part (a). At least some of the costs are clearly relevant or non-relevant.

ANSWERS

(a) **Relevant costs**

	Cost $	Reason
Technical report	0	This is a sunk cost.
Material A	15,000	3,400 sheets in existing inventory that have an existing use so they will need to be replaced if they are used in this contract. Also 6,600 new sheets are needed. The current market price is $1.50/sheet.
Material B	2,000	250 litres of ink need to be bought in at $8/litre to provide 200 litres for this contract. There is no foreseen alternative use for the excess 50 litres which were brought in to fulfil this contract.
Direct labour	500	50 hours at the overtime rate only are **differential costs**. The other hours are paid under a guaranteed minimum wage.
Supervision	0	Existing supervisor and no suggestion that this work will require overtime or taking her off other duties.
Machine A	240	There are 30 unused hours of capacity that have an alternative market so an **opportunity cost** arises at 20 hours × $12/hour.
Machine B	100	This machine will need to be run at overtime rates so this is an **incremental cost** of 25 machine hours at $4/hr
Despatch	400	This is a specific cost relating to this contract.
Fixed overheads	0	Fixed overheads which aren't specifically attributable to this contract as they are general fixed overheads.
Profit mark-up	0	Profit is not a relevant cost.
	18,240	

(b) **Relevant costing, absorption costing, selling prices and profitability**

Short-term pricing

In the short-term, a product or service can be priced using **relevant cost** to enable a contract to be won on a one-off basis. However in the longer term, organisations will need to cover costs that don't fall under the 'relevant' category but are nonetheless still incurred. In the example in (a) above, the organisation needs to set prices in the longer term to cover the sunk costs and overheads that arise but aren't deemed relevant to this contract.

Profitability and absorption costing

Absorption costing attributes **full costs** to inventory using an agreed basis of allocation such as labour hours. Therefore non-relevant costs will be attributed to the catalogues as part of the absorption of overheads based on a measure such as labour hours taken or machine hours used. The cost of the materials included in the catalogues will also be based on a standard LIFO, FIFO or AVCO valuation.

If we take the cost of **material A,** this will be calculated at the original cost of $1.40/sheet for the existing inventory plus the cost of buying in the extra sheets at $1.50 each.

So total cost will be $1.40 × 3,400 + $1.50 × 6,600 = $14,660 instead of $15,000 under the relevant cost basis.

Material B will be costed based on the **materials used**. Therefore the cost will be $1,600 instead of $2,000.

The **direct labour** will be charged at the full cost of employee time and wages spent on the catalogues so at $8 × 150 hours or $1,200 compared to $500.

Overheads will be charged to the catalogues at $20 per direct labour hour. At 150 hours this results in an absorption of $3,000 of overheads.

ANSWERS

In summary the differences are:

Materials $(740) less
Labour $700 more
Overheads $3,000 more

If management have based their pricing of the catalogues on a relevant cost of $18,240 it is likely that then using an absorption costing system to attribute costs will see a loss on the contract as costs are nearly $3,000 higher.

24 Section A answers: Multi-product breakeven analysis

1   C

	Aye	Bee	Cee	Total
C/S ratio	0.4	0.5	*0.54	
Market share	× 1/3	× 1/3	× 1/3	
	0.133	0.167	0.18	0.48

* balancing figure

With revised proportions:

	Aye	Bee	Cee	Total
C/S ratio	0.40	0.500	0.540	
Market share	0.40	0.250	0.350	
	0.16	0.125	0.189	0.474

If you chose **option A,** you have selected the C/S ratio of the Aye.

If you chose **option B,** you have selected the C/S ratio of the Cee.

If you chose **option D,** you incorrectly calculated Cee's C/S ratio as 0.1 (possibly because you thought the sum of the C/S ratios should be 1.0).

2   By convention, multiple products are usually shown on a P/V chart **individually**, from **left** to **right**, in order of **decreasing size of C/S ratio.**

3   **Contribution per unit**

   O   £(12 − 7.90) = £4.10
   H   £(17 − 11.20) = £5.80

   Contribution per mix

   (£4.10 × 4) + (£5.80 × 3) = £33.80

   Breakeven point in terms of mixes

   Fixed costs/contribution per mix = £131,820/£33.80 = 3,900 mixes

   Breakeven point in units

   O   3,900 × 4   = 15,600
   H   3,900 × 3   = 11,700

   Breakeven point in revenue

			£
O	15,600 × £12 =		187,200
H	11,700 × £17 =		198,900
			386,100

   Margin of safety

   Budgeted sales − breakeven sales = £(398,500 − 386,100) = £12,400

ANSWERS

4 **Contribution per unit**

A   £22
B   £19
C   £17

Contribution per mix

(£22 × 1) + (£19 × 1) + (£17 × 4) = £109

Required number of mixes

(Fixed costs + required profit)/contribution per mix
= £(55,100 + 43,000)/£109
= 900 mixes

Required sales of A

900 × 1 = 900 units
900 × £47 = £42,300 revenue

5 **C**

	W	X	Y	Z
	£ per unit	£ per unit	£ per unit	£ per unit
Selling price	56	67	89	96
Variable costs	49	66	74	85
Contribution	7	1	15	11
C/S ratios	$7/56$ = 0.125	$1/67$ = 0.015	$15/89$ = 0.169	$11/96$ = 0.115
Ranking	2	4	1	3

6 **D** Contribution per mix

= (2 × £7) + (3 × £1) + (3 × £15) + (4 × £11) = £106

∴ Breakeven point in number of mixes = £15,000/£106 = 141.5

∴ Number of W sold at breakeven point = 2 × 141.5 = 283 units

7 Average C/S ratio = $\dfrac{(2 \times 25\%) + (5 \times 35\%)}{7}$

= 32%

Sales revenue at breakeven point = $\dfrac{\text{fixed costs}}{\text{C/S ratio}}$

= £90,000/0.32

= £281,250

8 **C** Average C/S ratio = $\dfrac{(3 \times 27\%) + (2 \times 56\%) + (5 \times 38\%)}{(3 + 2 + 5)}$ = 38.3%

At breakeven point, contribution = fixed costs

∴ $\dfrac{£648,000}{\text{Breakeven sales revenue}}$ = 0.383

∴ Breakeven sales revenue = £1,691,906

ANSWERS

25 POD and L

> **Top tips.** When there is no indication about whether marginal costing or absorption costing is in use, it is simpler (and more informative too) to assess profitability with contribution analysis and marginal costing. This is the requirement in part (a)(i) of the problem. The obvious analysis to make is a calculation of the worst possible and best possible results.
>
> The second part of the problem (a)(ii) is a variation of a 'target profit' calculation.

(a) (i)

	\multicolumn{3}{c}{Best possible}	\multicolumn{3}{c}{Worst possible}
	Sales units	Cont'n per unit £	Total cont'n £	Sales units	Cont'n per unit £	Total cont'n £
X	2,000	30	60,000	1,000	30	30,000
Y	2,000	40	80,000	1,000	40	40,000
Z	2,000	50	100,000	1,000	50	50,000
Total contribution			240,000			120,000
Fixed costs			160,000			160,000
Profit/(loss)			80,000			(40,000)

The company's **potential profitability ranges** from a profit of **£80,000 to a loss of £40,000 per month**.

(ii)

	£	£
Required (minimum) profit per month		25,000
Fixed costs per month		160,000
Required contribution per month		185,000
Contribution to be earned from:		
product X 1,500 × £30	45,000	
product Y 1,500 × £40	60,000	
		105,000
Contribution required from product Z		80,000
Contribution per unit of Z		**£50**
Minimum required sales of Z per month		**1,600 units**

(b) In 20X1 sales were 200,000 units. **The variable cost per unit** is therefore as follows.

	20X1 £	20X2 prediction £
Direct materials	4	4.40
Direct labour	2	2.30
Variable overhead	1	1.10
Per unit	7	7.80

Fixed costs

	£
20X1 total overhead (fixed plus variable)	600,000
Variable overhead in 20X1 (200,000 × £1)	200,000
Fixed overhead in 20X1	400,000
Add 20%	80,000
Estimated fixed overhead in 20X2	480,000

In 20X2, a **profit of £330,000 is required.**

	£
Required profit	330,000
Fixed costs	480,000
Required contribution	810,000

Contribution per unit in 20X2 (£10.50 − £7.80) = £2.70

167

ANSWERS

Required sales $\frac{£810,000}{£2.70}$ = 300,000 units

This is an increase of 50% on 20X1 volumes. It is first of all **questionable** whether such a **large increase** could be **achieved** in one year. Secondly, given such an increase, it is likely that **output** will be **outside** the **relevant range** of output. Thirdly, **estimates** of fixed costs and variable costs are **unlikely to be reliable**.

26 RDF Ltd

Text references. Refer to Chapter 4 for information to answer part (a). Part (b) draws on prior knowledge as in Chapter 1, and Chapter 4 for the C/S ratio.

Top tips. You should have been able to interpret the graph in (a) as details are provided in the BPP Study Text. Remember that on a multi-product P/V chart, products (or services) are plotted from left to right, starting with the product/service with the highest C/S ratio. These ratios were not provided but you should have been able to compute and compare them in your head.

Part (b)(i) was very straightforward – so straightforward, in fact, that you might have thought you had misunderstood the requirements. For both this part of the question and part (b)(iii) you had to apply marginal costing principles so that you arrived at figures for contribution which can be used for decision making.

In part (b)(ii) it was vital to take account of the financial penalty that would be incurred if RDF Ltd did not honour the contract to supply 500 units of service M per annum, as this had a significant impact on the profit-maximising operating plan.

In the text we use the C/S ratio of one standard mix of products to determine the breakeven point. In part (b)(iv) we assume that just one mix is sold, that being the total sales mix.

Part (b)(iv) requires knowledge of the assumptions underlying breakeven analysis and the limitations of these assumptions.

(a) **Point A** is the company's **breakeven point** on the **assumption that the services are sold in order of their C/S ratio**, all of the service with the highest C/S ratio (service K) being sold first, all of the service with the second highest C/S ratio (service L) second, and so on until the breakeven sales value is reached. We base the ratio on gross contribution (ie before any fixed costs).

Point B is the **average breakeven point** for RDF Ltd on the **assumption that the services are sold in the ratio 1,000: 2,300: 1,450, 1,970** until the breakeven sales value is reached.

(b) (i)

	K Per service $	K Total $	L Per service $	L Total $	M Per service $	M Total $	N Per service $	N Total $	Overall total $
Selling price	18		16		12		20		
Variable cost	8		10		13		13		
Gross contribution	10	10,000	6	13,800	(1)	(1,450)	7	13,790	36,140
Attributable fixed costs		4,400		3,700		-		2,650	10,750
Net contribution		5,600		10,100		(1,450)		11,140	25,390
General fixed costs (W)									8,930
Profit									16,460

Working

Total fixed costs = (1,000 × $2) + (2,300 × $3) + (1,450 × $2) + (1,970 × $4) = $19,680

General fixed costs = $(19,680 – 4,400 – 3,700 – 2,650) = $8,930

The above table shows that **services K, L and N are financially viable** as they make a **positive contribution** towards the organisation's general fixed costs. Each unit of **service M** provided results in a **negative contribution** of $1, however, and hence the service **should not be offered unless there are other business reasons** for continuing to provide it, such as the three-year **contract** already in force.

(ii) The **contract** for the 500 units of product M should be **fulfilled** to avoid the significant financial penalties that RDF Ltd would incur if it were to break the terms.

This level of provision is below the budgeted number of 1,450 service units and so leaves spare resources that can be employed in the provision of additional units of the other three services if there is demand for them.

Insufficient data has been provided to determine how these spare resources should be used, however, and so they have not been taken into account in the budget profit statement below.

(iii) We can calculate the breakeven point using the average C/S ratio. We assume that one 'mix' of products is sold (which represents the budgeted volumes as per the budget profit statement in (iii) above).

Total sales revenue = $(1,000 \times \$18) + (2,300 \times \$16) + (500 \times \$12) + (1,970 \times 20) = \$100,200$

Total gross contribution (from profit statement in (iii)) is $37,090.

Average C/S ratio = $(37,090/100,200) \times 100\% = 37\%$

Breakeven point in sales revenue = fixed costs/ C/S ratio = $\$(10,750 + 8,930)/ 0.37 = \$53,189$

(iv) Although breakeven analysis can give firms an indication of the minimum sales revenue or sales units that are required to cover total costs, it is based on a number of assumptions that really form the basis for its limitations.

(i) It is assumed that units are sold in a constant mix which is unlikely to be the case in reality. The proportions in which products are sold vary according to such factors as changing consumer tastes, availability of substitute products, changes in prices and so on.

(ii) Selling price is assumed to remain constant regardless of the number of units sold. This is unrealistic for most 'normal' products as consumers are often only persuaded to purchase more if prices are reduced. As soon as selling prices change, the breakeven point will change, which makes it necessary to conduct the analysis again.

(iii) Inventory levels are ignored as it is assumed that production and sales are the same. Although firms are increasingly striving to carry less inventory, it is unlikely that production and sales will exactly match.

(iv) The analysis suggests that any activity level above the breakeven point will result in profits being made. This is not necessarily the case in reality, as changes in costs and revenues as more units are sold may result in a second breakeven point after which losses may be made. This is particularly true of electronic products such as computer games that have a very short shelf life.

(v) Costs are expected to behave in a linear fashion. Unit variable costs are expected to remain constant regardless of activity levels and fixed costs are not expected to change. This assumption ignores the possibility of economies of scale that could result in lower unit variable costs, or the fact that fixed costs may have to increase after a certain level of activity due to, for example, the need to rent additional premises.

ANSWERS

27 Section A answers: Limiting factor analysis

1 D

	Z1	Z2	Z3
	£	£	£
Selling price per unit	15	18	17.00
Variable costs per unit	7	11	12.70
Contribution per unit	8	7	4.30
Labour cost per unit	£2	£4	£1.80
Contribution per £1 of labour	£4	£1.75	£2.39
Rank order of production	1	3	2

If you chose **option A**, you ranked according to contribution per unit.
If you chose **option B**, you ranked according to variable cost per unit.
If you chose **option C**, you ranked according to labour cost per unit.

2 B The products must be ranked in order of their contribution per kg of direct material.

	X	Y	Z
	£ per unit	£ per unit	£ per unit
Selling price	75	95	96
Variable cost	34	41	45
Contribution	41	54	51
Kg of material used per unit	2	1	3
Contribution per kg	£20.50	£54	£17
Ranking	2	1	3

If you chose **option A**, you ranked according to unit contribution.
If you chose **option C**, you ranked according to selling price.
If you chose **option D**, you ranked according to usage of material.

3 True. The company should concentrate on the product with the highest C/S ratio.

4 Limiting factor is raw material.

	M	N	P
Contribution per kg of limiting factor			
£4.50/(£1.25 ÷ £0.50)	£1.80		
£4.80/(£1.50 ÷ £0.50)		£1.60	
£2.95/(£0.75 ÷ £0.50)			£1.97
Ranking	2	3	1

Usage of the 6,000 kg

	Kg
2,800 units of P (× (£0.75/£0.50))	4,200
720 units of M (× (£1.25/£0.50))	1,800
	6,000

Optimum production with additional 1,000 kg

	Kg
(1,000 – 720) units of M (× (£1.25/£0.50))	700
100 units of N (× (£1.50/£0.50))	300
	1,000

Contribution obtainable

	£
280 units of M (× £4.50)	1,260
100 units of N (× £4.80)	480
	1,740

This contribution is after charging £0.50 per kg.

∴ Contribution before material cost = £1,740 + (1,000 × £0.50) = £2,240 = maximum amount that should be paid.

ANSWERS

5 A

	Service J	Service H	Service N
Contribution per unit	£45	£63	£78
Labour hours required per unit	½	⅔	⅚
Contribution per labour hour	£90	£94.50	£93.60
Ranking	3	1	2

6 A

	M1	M2	M3	M4
	£	£	£	£
Selling price	70	92	113	83
less: materials	(16)	(22)	(34)	(20)
conversion costs	(39)	(52)	(57)	(43)
plus: general fixed costs (W)	16	16	15	18
Contribution	31	34	37	38
Kg of material	4	5.5	8.5	5
Contribution per kg	£7.75	£6.18	£4.35	£7.60
Ranking	1	3	4	2

Working

M1   £24 × 40/60   = £16
M2   £24 × 40/60   = £16
M3   £24 × 37.5/60 = £15
M4   £24 × 45/60   = £18

7 In a period when the material used on these products is in short supply, the most profitable use of material is to make product **I**, the least profitable is to make product **V**.

	M	V	I	F
Contribution per unit	£9	£8	£4	£14
Material cost per unit	£3	£12	£1	£20
Contribution per £ of material	£3	£0.67	£4	£0.70
Ranking	2	4	1	3

8 A

	X	Y	Z
Unit contribution	£82	£108	£100
Kgs required per unit	2 kgs	1 kg	3 kgs
Contribution per kg	£41	£108	£33.33
Ranking	2	1	3

	Kgs used
Produce 100 units of Z (× 3 kgs)	300
Produce 130 units of Y (× 1 kg)	130
	430
Produce remaining (840 – 130) units of Y (× 1 kg)	710
Use balance to produce 130 units of X (× 2 kgs)	260
	1,400

Option B takes no account of the requirement to produce 100 units of Z.

Option C has ranked on the basis of unit profit and has taken no account of the contract requirements.

Option D has ranked on the basis of contribution per unit and has taken no account of contract requirements.

9 The total costs of a company that has to subcontract work to make up a shortfall in its own in-house capabilities will be minimised if those units **bought** have the **lowest** extra variable cost of **buying** per unit of scarce resource **saved**.

ANSWERS

28 MN Ltd

> **Top tips.** You need to carry out a limiting factor analysis, although there is restricted freedom of action as existing sales orders need to be met before the remaining resource can be allocated to products.
>
> The twist in this question relates to the stock level information provided. Because the stock levels of finished goods reduce over the period, the actual production levels required to meet the orders accepted can be less than the order levels.
>
> **Easy marks.** To calculate contribution per unit you could simply add fixed overheads back to unit profit as we have done, or list out the variable costs and deduct them from selling price.

Step 1 **Ascertain whether material Q is a scarce resource**

Production levels

	V Units	S Units	T Units
Opening stock	(20)	(33)	(46)
Demand	1,100	950	1,450
Closing stock	10	25	20
Production	1,090	942	1,424

Material Q required to meet production

		Litres
V	1,090 units × 10 litres	10,900
S	942 units × 8 litres	7,536
T	1,424 units × 5 litres	7,120
		25,556
Material available (litres)		10,396
Shortfall		15,160

∴ Material Q is a limiting factor.

Step 2 **Rank the products**

	V £	S £	T £
Standard/budgeted profit per unit *	36	23.75	28.50
Fixed overheads per unit	24	30.00	12.00
Contribution per unit	60	53.75	40.50
Litres of Q per unit	10	8	5
Contribution per litre of Q	£6	£6.72	£8.10
Ranking	3	2	1

* Sample: £(145 – 109)

Step 3 Determine a production plan

Product	Customer orders accepted Units	Reduction in finished stock levels Units	Production to meet accepted orders Units		Material Q required Litres
V	34	10	24	(× 10)	240
S	75	8	67	(× 8)	536
T	97	26	71	(× 5)	355
					1,131

Available material Q   10,396
Remaining material   9,265

Product	Demand net of accepted orders Units	Demand that can be met Units		Material Q required Litres	Remaining material Q available Litres
					9,265
T	1,353*	1,353	(× 5)	6,765	2,500
S	875**	312***	(× 8)	2,496	4

Production

		Units
V		24
S	(67 + 312)	379
T	(71 + 1,353)	1,424

*   1,450 – 97
**   950 – 75
*** 2,500 ÷ 8

29 QP plc

Text references. Chapter 17 should give you enough information to answer part (a). Then use Chapter 6 to answer the limiting factor calculation. Finally, refer to Chapter 7 for the simplex method.

Top tips. This question covered throughput accounting and decision making with both one and two limiting factors. Remember that throughput accounting takes contribution to be sales revenue less directly attributable variable costs. In the modern manufacturing environment the only truly variable cost in the short term is materials. Part (c) could be answered in isolation. Part (b) needed you to read the question carefully as two limiting factors then become one.

In part (a) two thirds of the six marks available are for explaining the effect of throughput accounting on constraints and scarce resources and the remainder for its impact on contribution.

In part (b) the marks were evenly spread (ie five marks each) for calculating the contribution per kg of material L, and for the product mix that maximises the value of contribution.

In part (c) one mark per value was awarded with a maximum of nine marks.

Easy marks. Part (c) should be easy enough if you remember what all the simplex values represent.

Examiner's comments. In general, the question was well answered although there were two common errors:

- Including labour costs in the calculation of the contribution

ANSWERS

> - Describing production processes and bottle-necks in detail. This relates to the theory of constraints rather than throughput accounting.

(a) **Throughput accounting**

Throughput accounting (TA) is a **cost and management system** used in a **JIT environment**. It emphasises **throughput**, **minimisation of inventory** and **cost control**.

TA is based on three concepts:

(i) In the short run most costs apart from materials are fixed.

(ii) The ideal inventory level is zero (given the assumption of a JIT environment).

(iii) Profitability is determined by the rate at which sales are made, which in a JIT environment is how quickly orders are produced for customers.

It aims to identify and eliminate bottleneck resources, which inhibit throughput and therefore hinder conversion of WIP to finished goods and hence to sales.

TA uses a series of measures to rank products in order to allocate scarce resources for short-term decision making purposes. One of these is the TA ratio which is (sales price- material cost)/(labour + overhead).

Because TA differentiates between fixed and variable costs it is often compared with marginal costing and **some people argue that there is no difference between marginal costing and throughput accounting.** In marginal costing direct labour costs are usually assumed to be variable costs. Years ago this assumption was true, but employees are not usually paid piece rate today and they are not laid off for part of the year when there is no work, and so labour cost is not truly variable. If this is accepted the two techniques are identical in some respects, but **marginal costing is generally thought of as being purely a short-term decision-making technique** while **TA, or at least TOC, was conceived with the aim of changing manufacturing strategy to achieve evenness of flow. It is therefore much more than a short-term decision technique.**

Because **TA combines all conversion costs** together and does not attempt to examine them in detail it is particularly **suited to use with ABC**, which examines the behaviour of these costs and assumes them to be variable in the long-run.

In throughput accounting, the limiting factor is the bottleneck. The return per time period measure can be adapted and used for **ranking products to optimise production** in the **short term**.

Product return per minute = $\dfrac{\text{sales price} - \text{material costs}}{\text{minutes on key/bottleneck resource}}$

Ranking products on the basis of throughput contribution per minute (or hour) on the bottleneck resource is **similar in concept to maximising contribution per unit of limiting factor**. Such product rankings are for **short-term production scheduling only**. In throughput accounting, bottlenecks should be eliminated and so rankings may change quickly. Customer demand can, of course, cause the bottleneck to change at short notice too.

Rankings by TA product return and by contribution per unit of limiting factor may be different. Which one leads to profit maximisation? The correct approach depends on the variability or otherwise of labour and variable overheads, which in turn depends on the time horizon of the decision. Both are short-term profit maximisation techniques and given that labour is nowadays likely to be fixed in the short term, it could be argued that TA provides the more correct solution. An analysis of variable overheads would be needed to determine their variability.

(b) **Calculations for the production mix that will maximise QP's profit**

This is an example of production with a scarce resource (ingredient L) and so limiting factor analysis should be used. Note that ingredient M is not scarce by virtue of the existence of a non-scarce substitute ingredient.

ANSWERS

If resources are limiting factors, then contribution is maximised by earning the biggest possible contribution per unit of limiting factor.

Step 1 Ascertain whether material L is the limiting factor

Product	TR	PN	BE	Total
Kgs of L per batch (kg)	7	9	4	
Kgs of L needed to meet sales demand	3,500	3,600	1,400	8,500
Kgs available				7,000
Shortfall				1,500

Step 2 Calculate contribution per unit of scarce resource and rank ingredients

Product	TR	PN	BE
Contribution per batch (£)	90	165	95
Kgs per batch	7	9	4
Contribution per kg (£)	12.86	18.33	23.75
Ranking	3	2	1

Step 3 Determine the optimum product mix

Product	Demand Batches	Ingredient L required kgs	Ingredient L available kgs*	Batches produced
			7,000	
BE	350 (× 4)	1,400	(1,400)	350
			5,600	
PN	400 (×9)	3,600	(3,600)	400
			2,000	
TR	500 (×7)	3,500	(1,995)	285
			5	

* Demand includes a requirement to produce 50 batches as a minimum.

(c) This is a linear programming solution using the simplex method because there are more than two decision variables.

(i) **Objective function value**. This is the optimal contribution of £110,714 (on the assumption the value is not in £'000).

(ii) **TR value**. This is the optimal number of batches of TR that should be produced, being 500.

(iii) **PN value**. Likewise, the optimum batch quantity is 357.

(iv) **BE value**. Likewise, 71 batches of BE should be produced.

(v) **TR slack value** of 0 represents the unsatisfied demand in batches.

(vi) **PN slack value** of 43 represents the unsatisfied demand in batches.

(vii) **BE slack value** of 279 represents the unsatisfied demand in batches.

(viii) **L value** is the shadow price of material L which indicates the amount by which the optimal contribution would increase if an extra kg of material L was available at its normal variable cost.

(ix) **M value** is the shadow price for material M and indicates that contribution would increase by this amount if an extra kg of M were available.

ANSWERS

30 GHK plc

> **Text references.** Chapter 2 for relevant costs, Chapter 4 for C/S ratios and P/V charts, and Chapter 5 for limiting factors.
>
> **Top tips.** Part (a) requires you to calculate the relevant contribution per $ for six marks (five marks for calculating the relevant contributions for each product and one for the relevant contribution per $ for material B).
>
> Just be a bit careful and don't calculate contribution per kg instead. This was a common mistake according to the examiner, who also remarked that this part of the question was poorly answered.
>
> Set out your workings in a table like the one we have prepared. You need to use the high-low method for the overhead costs. Deduct the specific fixed costs first and then work out the variable cost per unit. Use the replacement cost of materials for Material A.
>
> Part (b) basically requires you to do the following.
>
> **Step 1.** Calculate the contribution from the contract to supply the major customer. This uses the relevant contributions calculated in part (a) for each product. There were two marks for this.
>
> **Step 2.** Calculate the contribution from the alternative use of resources (ie fulfilling other demand expected as stated in the question). You need to compare demand and the optimum production plan capacity. There are two products where demand is more than capacity (J and K) and so you would look at switching capacity to produce these. Note however that one product (J) has a negative contribution so you wouldn't want to produce any more of this product. So look at switching resources from the minimum contract to satisfy the demand for product J. There were two marks for this part.
>
> **Step 3.** Lastly, compare the contribution from the contract with the contribution from the alternative use of resources and state the financial penalty at which the company would be indifferent between meeting the contract or paying the penalty. There was one mark for this part.
>
> Part (c) was well answered according to the examiner, which is not surprising given how easy it is!
>
> The examiner reported that part (d) was not well answered as many candidates could not sketch the graph. We take you through how to do this in our answer below but we also have a nice example in Chapter 5 of the Study Text which you can work through and practise sketching a graph yourself. Make sure that you don't lose marks for not labelling axes. There were two marks for plotting the fixed costs and four marks for plotting the products by their contribution/sales ratios from lowest to highest.
>
> Part (e) was also not well answered and many answers failed to relate to the scenario in the question.
>
> The marks are spread evenly across the five parts to the question so there are plenty of possibilities for at least a couple of marks in each part.
>
> **Easy marks.** You should have found part (a) easy and should have been able to pick up at least a couple of marks. Part (c) can be answered very, very easily straight from your answer to part (a) and just applying the C/S ratios. Part (d) also uses some of the calculations done in part (a) for overhead costs.
>
> **Examiner's comments.** The examiner gave specific comments for each of the five parts to the question. These are as follows:
>
> (a) Was poorly answered. In most cases, overhead was forgotten and contributions incorrectly expressed
> (b) Was better but few completely correct answers
> (c) Fine
> (d) Few candidates could sketch the graph or correct proportions
> (e) Most answers were poor and few referred to the actual scenario

ANSWERS

(a)

Product	G $	H $	J $	K $
Selling price (w1)	10.00	20.00	15.00	30.00
Material A (w2)	4.20	5.60	2.10	8.40
Material B (w3)	2.00	2.00	4.50	12.00
Direct labour (w4)	2.00	8.00	7.50	3.00
Overhead (w5)	1.00	3.00	3.00	3.00
Total costs	9.20	18.60	17.10	26.40
Relevant contribution per unit	0.80	1.40	(2.10)	3.60
Relevant contribution per $ of Material B (w6)	0.40	0.70	(0.47)	0.30

Workings

1. Take the revenue in $ as stated in the question and divide by the number of units. So for product G, take $30,000 and divide by 3,000 units to get $10 per unit selling price.

2. Costs shown in the budget are based on $5 per kg but the relevant cost will be the $7 replacement cost of material A. So taking Product G as an example:

    Cost of material A per unit of G was $9,000/3,000 units = $3

    Kgs of material A per unit of G = $3/$5

    Revised cost of material A per unit of G = ($3/$5) x $7 = $4.20

3. The relevant cost here is based on the $10 per kg replacement cost so there is no need to substitute a replacement cost as in working 2 above and you can use the figures straight from the budget.

4. Likewise, the relevant cost here is the $10 hourly rate and you can take the cost from the budget.

5. You need to use the high-low method to calculate the variable element of the overheads, after deducting the specific fixed cost of $1,000.

Product	G		H		J		K	
	$	Units	$	Units	$	Units	$	Units
High volume	5,000	3,000	12,000	3,000	10,000	3,000	10,000	3,000
Low volume	7,000	5,000	18,000	5,000	16,000	5,000	16,000	5,000
Difference	2,000 (1)	2,000 (2)	6,000	2,000	6,000	2,000	6,000	2,000
Variable cost per unit ((1)/(2))	2,000/2,000 = $1		$3		$3		$3	

6. Let's consider product G again. The cost of material B per the table above is $2 per unit. Apply this to the relevant contribution per unit you have already worked out and you will get the relevant contribution per $ of material B.

(b) **Optimum production plan and financial penalty**

In our Top tips above, we suggest the steps that you should take to work through this part of the question. So here goes......

Step 1 Calculate the contribution from the contract to supply the major customer.

The data for units comes straight from the question and you should then use the relevant contributions calculated in part (a) for each product.

	G	H	J	K	Total
Units in the contract	500	1,600	800	400	
Relevant contribution per unit ($)	0.80	1.40	(2.10)	3.60	
Total contribution ($)	400	2,240	(1,680)	1,440	2,400

ANSWERS

Step 2 Calculate the contribution from the alternative use of resources.

First, you need to compare demand and the optimum production plan for each product. These are stated in the question in the body of the question and in part (b). Clearly you will only want to produce more where demand is greater than capacity, and you can look at switching resources to meet this demand.

Product	G	H	J	K
Demand for Units	3,600	3,000	3,000	4,000
Optimum production plan	4,100	4,600	800	2,417
Therefore spare capacity	0 (W1)	0 (W1)	2,200(W2)	1,583(W3)
Plus additional spare capacity if no contract				400
Total useful spare capacity				1,983

Workings

1 There are two products where demand is more than capacity, so there is no spare capacity.

2 You would not want to produce more of product J as this has a negative contribution, so look at producing more of product K.

3 The demand from other customers for product K is 4,000 units but the optimum production plan recommends a production level of 2,417 units. Without the contract, the production level would be 2,417 – 400 = 2,017 units, so there are 1,983 units of unsatisfied demand.

Then look at switching resources from the minimum contract to satisfy the demand for product K.

Product	G	H	J	K	Total
Units in the contract	500	1,600	800	400	
Material B (kg) per unit (w)	0.20	0.20	0.45	1.20	
Total kg released	100	320	360	480	1,260

Working

Refer to the budget in the question. For product K, for example, at 3,000 units the cost of material B is $36,000 so the cost per unit is $12.00. Divide by the expected cost per unit for material B of $10 to give 1.20 kg of material B per unit of K.

Contribution from alternative use of resources

This all relates to product K

Capacity in units (see above)	1,983
Material B (kg) per unit(see above)	1.20
Total kg required (1,983 × 1.2 kgs)	2,380
Available kg from switching (See above)	1,260
Additional units from available kgs (1,260 kgs /1.2 kgs per unit) (W)	1,050
Contribution from alternative use of resources (1,050 × $3.60)	$3,780

Working

The 1,983 units would require (x 1.2 kgs) 2,379.6 kgs of material B, which is more than the 1,260 made available if the contract does not go ahead. Therefore the additional units are limited by the 1,260 kgs made available.

With the extra 1,260 kgs, an extra 1,050 units of K can be produced (divide by 1.2).

Step 3 Lastly, compare the contribution from the contract with the contribution from the alternative use of resources and state the financial penalty at which the company would be indifferent between meeting the contract or paying the penalty.

	$
Minimum contract	
Total contribution (Step 1 above)	2,400
Less fixed cost not incurred (w)	(1,000)
Net contribution from the minimum contract	1,400
Contribution from alternative use of resources	3,780
Difference between two options ($(3,780 – 1,400))	$2,380

Working

If the contract did not go ahead product J would not be produced (because it has a negative contribution) and specific fixed costs of $1,000 would be saved, so the contribution from the contract is a net figure of $1,400.

Conclusion. The penalty at which it is worthwhile to switch from the contract to other production is therefore $2,380.

Alternatively:

If GHK is indifferent between meeting the contract and paying the penalty:

Penalty + lost contribution from contract = extra contribution from production of additional product K

Therefore penalty = $3,780 - $1,400 = $2,380

(c) **Relevant contribution to sales ratios for all four products**

Take the information calculated in part (a) above and use to calculate C/S ratios for each product.

Product	G	H	J	K
	$	$	$	$
Selling price	10.00	20.00	15.00	30.00
Relevant contribution	0.80	1.40	(2.10)	3.60
Contribution to sales ratios (%)	8%	7%	(14%)	12%

(d) **Sketch a graph showing multi product profit volume (PV) chart**

Step 1 A P/V chart has revenue on the x axis and profit on the y axis, and so for each product you need to know the revenue that can be earned from total market demand (contract + other customers) and the profit from this level of revenue. Remember that the limiting factor restriction on material B no longer applies as demand will be the sum of that for the minimum contract plus the demand expected from other customers.

Product	G	H	J	K	Total
Total demand (units) (w1)	4,100	4,600	3,800	4,400	
	$	$	$	$	$
Sales revenue (w2)	41,000	92,000	57,000	132,000	322,000
Contribution to sales ratios (%) (w3)	8%	7%	(14%)	12%	
Contribution	3,280	6,440	(7,980)	15,840	17,580

Workings

1. You need to add the demand from the minimum contract to the other demand stated, for each product. All information is in the question.

2. Use the selling price you calculated in part (a) × total demand for units

3. From part (c)

ANSWERS

Step 2 You need a 'starting point' for the graph (ie at the point of nil revenue on the x axis) and so you need to determine the profit when revenue is nil (the point on the y axis). Profit – or loss - when revenue is nil = fixed costs.

Product	G	H	J	K	Total
	$	$	$	$	$
Overhead costs per the question	6,000	13,000	11,000	11,000	
Units	3,000	3,000	3,000	3,000	
Variable overhead cost per unit (from (a))	$1	$3	$3	$3	
Total variable costs (units x variable cost per unit)	3,000	9,000	9,000	9,000	
Fixed cost (total overhead costs – total variable costs)	3,000	4,000	2,000	2,000	11,000
Less avoidable fixed cost (from note 4 of question)					(4,000)
Fixed cost at which sales are nil					7,000

Step 3 The question states that the products are to be plotted in order of their C/S ratios so (from (c) they need to be plotted in the order KGHJ

You now need to work out cumulative revenues and profits

As each product is produced, a directly attrib fixed cost is incurred - we'll assume – immediately ie at zero revenue

Products	Revenue	Cumulative revenue (x axis coordinate)	Profit	Cumulative profit (y axis coordinate)
	$	$	$	$
None	None	None	(7,000)	(7,000)
Start selling K	None	None	(1,000)	(8,000)
Finish selling K	132,000	132,000	15,840	7,840
Start selling G	None	132,000	(1,000)	6,840
Finish G	41,000	173,000	3,280	10,120
Start selling H	None	173,000	(1,000)	9,120
Finish selling H	92,000	265,000	6,440	15,560
Start selling J	None	265,000	(1,000)	14,560
Finish selling J	57,000	322,000	(7,980)	6,580

Multi product profit volume chart

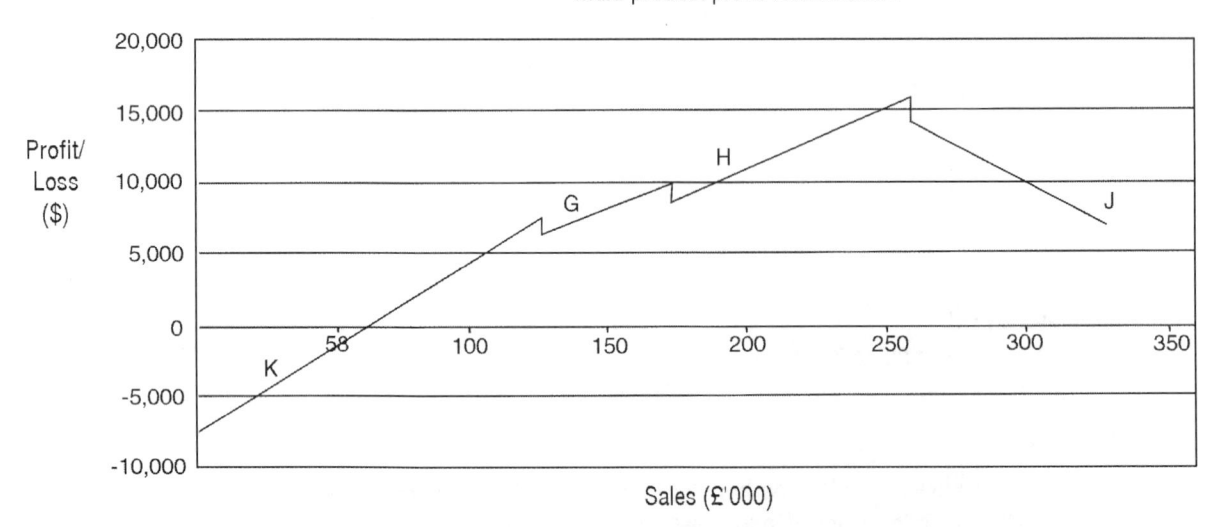

(e) The chart would **show further information about the contribution earned by each product individually**, so that their performance and profitability can be compared.

By convention, the **products are shown individually** on a P/V chart from **left to right**, in **order of the size of their C/S ratio**. In the question, product K will be plotted first, then products G and H and finally product J. The **jagged line** is used to show the **cumulative profit/loss and the cumulative sales** as each product's sales and contribution in turn are added to the sales mix.

It is also possible to plot a single line from the two end points on the **line** to indicate **the average profit, which** will be earned from sales of the products in this mix.

The diagram **highlights** the following points.

(i) Since K is the most profitable in terms of C/S ratio, it might be worth considering an increase in the sales of K, at the expense of less profitable products such as J.

(ii) Alternatively, the pricing structure of the products should be reviewed and a decision made as to whether the price of product J should be raised so as to increase its C/S ratio (although an increase is likely to result in some fall in sales volume).

The **multi-product P/V chart** therefore helps to **identify** the following.

(i) The overall company breakeven point.

(ii) Which products should be expanded in output and which, if any, should be discontinued.

(ii) What effect changes in selling price and sales volume will have on the company's breakeven point and profit.

Assumptions

1 The technique assumes that all variable costs are the same per unit at all levels of output and that fixed costs are the same in total.

2 It also assumes that sales price will be the same across all levels of activity.

3 There are no changes in levels of inventory so the consequences of increases and decreases in inventory levels are ignored.

31 Section A answers: Linear programming

1 This inequality should be that X must be at most 2Y, ie $X \leq 2Y$.

2 D The region to the left of X = 41 satisfies $X \leq 41$ while that above Y = 19 satisfies $Y \geq 19$.

Option A is incorrect because the region you have described is bounded by $X \leq 41$, but $Y \leq 19$ instead of $Y \geq 19$.

Option B is incorrect because the region you have described is bounded by $X \geq 41$ and $Y \leq 19$ instead of by $X \leq 41$ and $Y \geq 19$.

Option C is incorrect because the region you have described is bounded by $Y \geq 19$ but by $X \geq 41$ instead of $X \leq 41$.

3 The vertex representing the optimal solution is (0,160).

Evaluating contribution at the vertices gives 40,000 at (0, 160), 37,000 at (40, 140), 34,000 at (80, 120) and 7,000 at (140, 0) and so (0, 160) represents the optimal solution.

4 D Contribution is 500 at P, 600 at Q and 600 at R. This means that the outcomes represented by Q and R and all points on the straight line joining them will all lead to the optimal contribution of 600.

For **option A,** you have chosen the vertex which gives minimum contribution.

For **option B**, it is not sufficient to claim that Q is optimal since this is not the full solution.

For **option C**, it is not sufficient to claim that R is optimal since this is not the full solution.

ANSWERS

5 D The quantity in the bottom right hand corner always gives the value of the objective function.

Option A. The values of X and Y cannot be determined from figures in the bottom row.

Option B. Zeros in the bottom row mean that those variables do not have zero values. Their values are given by reading up to the 1 in the column and then across to the value in the solution row.

Option C. A non-zero in the bottom row, with the exception of the value of the objective function, means that that variable has a zero value. So a = 0.

6 The constraint requires that $X \leq (X+Y)/5$ and so $5X \leq X + Y$. Hence $4X \leq Y$.

7 A Shadow price of process 1 hours is $66.67 per hour.
If 10 extra hours were available, contribution would rise by 10 × $66.67 = $666.67.

8 A First use **common sense**: product C gives a **lower contribution** than either of the other products so contribution will certainly **decrease** if some production of A or B is sacrificed in order to make eight units of product C. This **eliminates** letters **B** and **D**, both of which suggest the answer is an increase.

Then look at the **C column in the tableau**. This tells us that for every unit of C made 0.83 fewer units of B can be made and 0.33 fewer units of s5 (process 2 time) will be available. There will be no effect on A.

Again this makes complete sense: units of B would be sacrificed if C is made because A gives a higher contribution ($400) than B ($200) and we also know that there is still plenty more demand (s6) for A (266.7 units).

If eight additional units of product C were produced, (8 × 0.83) fewer units of product B would be made.

	$
Increase in contribution from additional C (8 × $100)	800
Decrease in contribution from fewer B (8 × 0.83 × $200)	(1,328)
Decrease in contribution	(528)

9 C The effects of making available an extra unit of a resource are shown by the figures in the column of the corresponding slack variable.

–0.25 in the row labelled 'x' shows that there would be a fall in the output per week of x of 0.25kg.

+0.25 in the row labelled 'z' indicates the opposite: output per week of z would rise by 0.25 kg.

+0.25 in the row labelled 'b' indicates a rise in the unused units of the resource which is the subject of constraint b. This resource has a dual price of 0, so this resource is already not fully used.

10 A **Option B.** No units of C should be made (0.00 in the value column).
Option C. C would increase by 190 if constraint Z were changed by 1 unit.
Option D. 53 units of X and 3 units of Y are unused in the optimal solution.

ANSWERS

32 Question with answer plan: Fertiliser I

Top tips. Provided you work carefully through the steps required to formulate a linear programming model you should be able to pick up the majority of the ten marks on offer for this question.

Easy marks. There are three products so a simplex method is needed.

Answer plan

Linear programming questions require a set method of answer whether using graphs for two products, or simplex for more than two products. These methods are explained in the Study Text chapters 7 and 8. The way to approach this question therefore is as follows:

Step 1 Define variables.

Step 2 Establish the objective functions – what is the profit maximising contribution? You need to calculate the unit contribution first to write this function.

Step 3 Establish the constraints ie the limiting factors.

Step 4 Introduce slack variables and redefine the constraints.

Step 5 Then you will need to redefine the objective function.

Note that you may be requested to draw an initial simplex table or interpret a final ie optimum table. However, you do not have to calculate the final table.

Calculate contribution per tonne

	X_1 £ per tonne	X_2 £ per tonne	X_3 £ per tonne
Nitrate, at £150 per tonne	15	15	30
Phosphate, at £60 per tonne	6	12	6
Potash, at £120 per tonne	24	12	12
Filler, at £10 per tonne	6	6	6
Other manufacturing costs	11	11	11
	62	56	65
Sales price	83	81	81
Contribution	21	25	16

The **linear programming model** is formulated as follows.

Define variables

The three products are X_1, X_2 and X_3

Establish objective function

Maximise contribution (C) = $21X_1 + 25X_2 + 16X_3$

Establish constraints

Nitrate $0.1X_1 + 0.1X_2 + 0.2X_3 \leq 1,200$
Phosphate $\quad 0.1X_1 + 0.2X_2 + 0.1X_3 \leq 2,000$
Potash $0.2X_1 + 0.1X_2 + 0.1X_3 \leq 2,200$
Non-negativity $\quad\quad X_1, \quad X_2, \quad X_3 \geq 0$

183

ANSWERS

Introduce slack variables X4, X5 and X6 and redefine constraints

(a) Slack variable X4 represents the amount of unused nitrate, in tonnes, so that

0.1X1 + 0.1X2 + 0.2X3 + X4 = 1,200

(b) Slack variable X5 represents the amount of unused phosphate, in tonnes, so that

0.1X1 + 0.2X2 + 0.1X3 + X5 = 2,000

(c) Slack variable X6 represents the amount of unused potash, in tonnes, so that

0.2X1 + 0.1X2 + 0.1X3 + X6 = 2,200

Redefine objective function

C − 21X1 − 25X2 − 16X3 + 0X4 + 0X5 + 0X6 = 0

33 Fertiliser II

> **Top tips.** The interpretation required is relatively straightforward, especially if you have worked through a number of examples.
>
> Attempted in conjunction with Fertiliser I, these questions provide an excellent example of simplex. Work through them again and again until you are 100% confident.

The **optimal solution** is to make and sell:

(a) 4,000 tonnes of X1
(b) 8,000 tonnes of X2
(c) nothing of X3

There will be 600 tonnes of unused potash (X6). Total contribution will be £284,000.

X4 and X5 (nitrate and phosphate) will be fully used up, with means that they have a **shadow price**, as follows.

(a) For each **extra tonne of nitrate (X4)** that could be made available, the production plan could be rearranged so as to **increase total contribution by £170**.

(b) Similarly, for each **extra tonne of phosphate** (X5) that could be made available, the production schedule could be re-arranged so as to **increase total contribution** by £40.

(c) The **shadow price of X3** is £22. If a decision were taken to increase production of X3 from zero tonnes, total contribution would fall by £22 per tonne of X3 made and sold, given existing constraints on materials supply. The contribution per tonne of X3 would have to rise by £22 or more to make production of X3 worthwhile.

ANSWERS

34 Staff uniforms

> **Text references.** Look at Chapter 5, which should give you steps for working out the limiting factor. Chapter 6 will give you a plan for working out the optimal solution to part (b) and graphing this.
>
> **Top tips.** The question was slightly ambiguous as it was not completely clear whether the previously accepted contract was included in the demand figures. It was!
>
> In Step 2 of part (a) you could have worked out the contribution per $1 of machine cost instead of per hour of machine time.
>
> In (b), you had to calculate revised contribution figures as the selling prices had changed. If you are not sure about the accuracy of your graph, verify your answer by solving simultaneous equations.
>
> **Easy marks.** Part (a) is a straightforward limiting factor analysis with limited freedom of action. You needed to begin by checking which of the resources, if any, were scarce. Label graph and draw neatly for presentation. State whether selling prices should be revised in (b)(ii) for a mark.

(a) **Step 1** Establish which of the resources, if any, are scarce

		Litres
Cleaning materials		
Required	Laundry (2/10 × 8,000)	1,600
	Dry cleaning (3/10 × 10,500)	3,150
		4,750
Available		5,000
Spare		250

∴ **Not scarce**

		Hrs
Direct labour hours		
Required	Laundry (1.2/6 × 8,000)	1,600
	Dry cleaning (2/6 × 10,500)	3,500
		5,100
Available		6,000
Spare		900

∴ **Not scarce**

		Hrs
Machine hours		
Required	Laundry (0.5/3 × 8,000)	1,333.3
	Dry cleaning (1.5/3 × 10,500)	5,250.0
		6,583.3
Available		5,000.0
Shortfall		1,583.3

∴ **Scarce**

Step 2 Rank the services in terms of contribution per hour of machine time

	Laundry	Dry cleaning
Unit contribution		
$(2.15 + 1.15)	$3.30	
$(3.25 + 2.25)		$5.50
Machine hours per service		
($0.5/$3)	1/6	
($1.5/$3)		1/2
Contribution per hour of machine time	$19.80	$11
Ranking	1	2

185

ANSWERS

Step 3 Determine a production plan.

	Demand		Machine hrs required	Machine hrs available
				5,000
Contracted services				
Laundry	1,200	(× 1/6)	200	4,800
Dry cleaning	2,000	(× 1/2)	1,000	3,800
Non-contracted services				
Laundry	6,800*	(× 1/6)	1,133 1/3	2,666 2/3
Dry cleaning	5,333**	(× 1/2)	2,666 2/3	

* 8,000 – 1,200
** 2,666 2/3 ÷ 1/2

Profit-maximising mix of services

Laundry   8,000 services
Dry cleaning   7,333 services

(b) (i) **Define variables**

Let l = number of laundry services provided
Let d = number of dry cleaning services provided

Establish objective function

Fixed costs will be the same irrespective of the optimal mix and so the objective is to maximise contribution (c).

Laundry: revised contribution   = $5.60 – $(2 + 1.2 + 0.5)
                  = $1.90
Dry cleaning: revised contribution = $13.20 – $(3 + 2 + 1.5)
                  = $6.70

Maximise c = 1.9l + 6.7d, subject to the constraints below.

Establish constraints

Cleaning materials: $^{2}/_{10}l + {}^{3}/_{10}d \le 5,000$
            $^{1}/_{5}l + {}^{3}/_{10}d \le 5,000$

Direct labour: $^{1.2}/_{6}l + {}^{2}/_{6}d \le 6,000$
            $^{1}/_{5}l + {}^{1}/_{3}d \le 6,000$

Variable machine cost: $^{0.5}/_{3}l + {}^{1.5}/_{3}d \le 5,000$
            $^{1}/_{6}l + {}^{1}/_{2}d \le 5,000$

Maximum and minimum services (for contract): $14,000 \ge l \ge 1,200$
                          $9,975 \ge d \ge 2,000$

(ii) Establish coordinates to plot lines representing the inequalities.

Cleaning materials: If l = 0, d = 16,667
             If d = 0, l = 25,000

Direct labour: If l = 0, d = 18,000
             If d = 0, l = 30,000

Variable machine cost: If l = 0, d = 10,000
             If d = 0, l = 30,000

Also plot the lines l = 1,200 and d = 2,000, and l = 14,000 and d = 9,975

ANSWERS

Construct an iso-contribution line

$c = 1.9l + 6.7d$

If $c = (1.9 \times 6.7 \times 1,000) = 12,730$, then:

if $l = 6,700, d = 0$
if $d = 1,900, l = 0$

Draw the graph

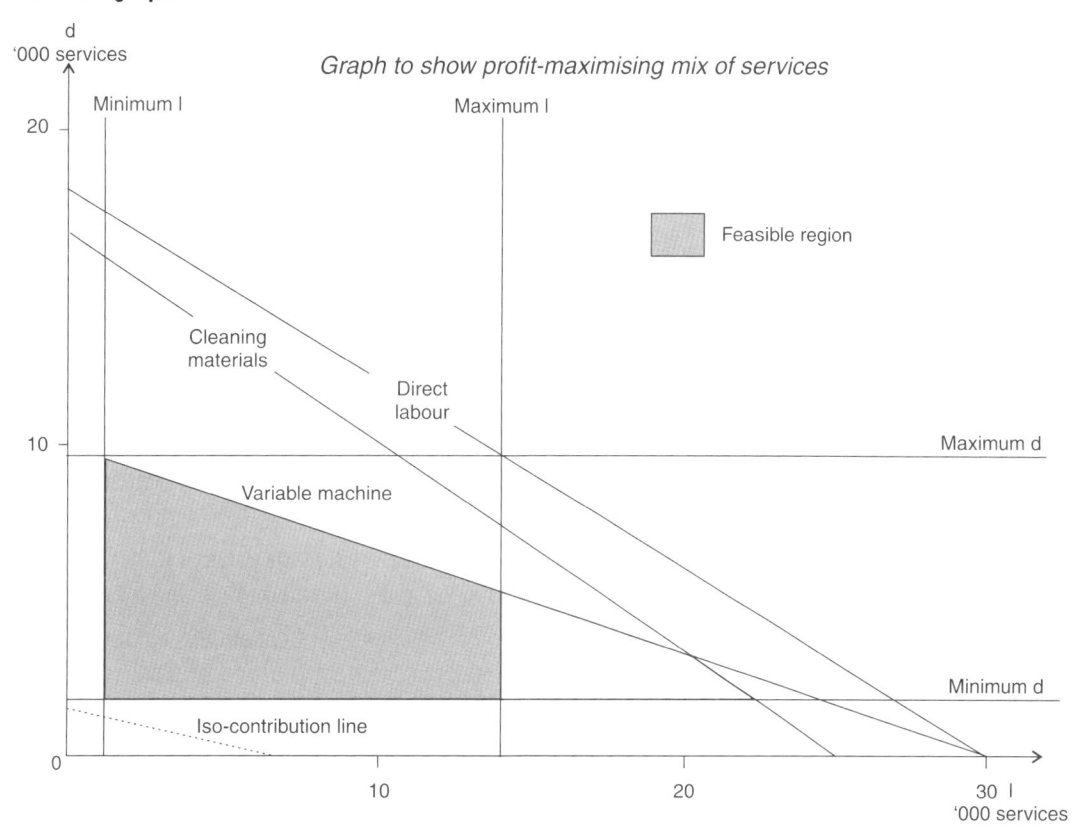

Graph to show profit-maximising mix of services

Find the optimal solution

By moving the iso-contribution line out across the graph, it is clear that the optimal solution lies at the intersection of lines representing the constraints for minimum number of laundry services and machine hours.

∴ Optimal solution occurs when:

$l = 1,200$ and $1/6 l + 1/2 d = 5,000$

If $l = 1,200$, then $d = (5,000 - 200) \times 2 = 9,600$

The **optimal solution** is to carry out 1,200 laundry services and 9,600 dry cleaning services.

Check the validity of revising selling prices

Maximum profit per mix in (a)

		$
Contribution		
Laundry:	8,000 × unit contribution of $3.30	26,400.0
Dry cleaning:	7,333 × unit contribution of $5.50	40,331.5
		66,731.5
Less: fixed costs ((8,000 × $1.15) + (10,500 × $2.25))		(32,825.0)
		33,906.5

ANSWERS

Maximum profit based on revised selling prices

		$
Contribution		
Laundry:	1,200 × unit contribution of $1.90	2,280
Dry cleaning:	9,600 × unit contribution of $6.70	64,320
		66,600
Less: fixed costs		32,825
		33,775

By revising the selling prices, maximum profit achievable falls by $(33,906.5 – 33,775) = $131.50

∴ In theory, **prices should not be revised** but the difference is so small that management should check carefully the reasonableness of the estimates used.

35 MF plc

> **Text references.** You will see from our answers that we have taken the methods in the text from Chapters 5 and 6 to answer the question.
>
> **Top tips.** In part (a), you are given a fairly strong hint that you need to use limiting factor analysis by a limit being placed on the availability of material P.
>
> The requirements in part (b) to present the profit statement in marginal cost format means that you need to separate fixed costs from variable costs and highlight contribution. Because marginal costing is applied you do not need to allocate fixed overheads to products, simply deduct them in full from total contribution.
>
> When establishing a sample objective function in part (c), make sure that the value of C that you choose can be divided 'nicely' by the values (ie unit contributions) of the variables. This makes plotting it easier.
>
> When your answer to a linear programming problem is not in whole numbers of units, you need to check that you can round up: substitute rounded up values into constraints to ensure that the constraints still hold. In this question, constraint (2) does not hold if m is rounded up (and f is rounded down) whereas constraint (1) does not hold if f is rounded up (and m is rounded down).
>
> **Easy marks.** Don't forget to rank in terms of contribution per unit of limiting factor instead of, say, selling price or unit contribution. This might seem obvious now but in the heat of the exam it's just the sort of thing that's easy to forget to do.

(a) **Step 1** Calculate contribution per unit

	M	F
	£	£
Selling price per unit	200	210
Variable costs per unit	104	100
Contribution per unit	96	110

Step 2 Calculate contribution per unit of limiting factor

	M	F
Contribution	£96	£110
Litres of P required per unit		
£20/£2.50	8	
£25/£2.50		10
Contribution per litre of P	£12	£11

Step 3 Rank products

	M	F
Ranking	1	2

Step 4 Production and sales budget

Product	Demand Units	Litres required	Litres available		Production Units
M	1,000	8,000	8,000	(÷8)	1,000
F	3,000	30,000	23,250 (bal)	(÷ 10)	2,325
			31,250		

> **Top tips.** A correct answer at Step 1 would probably earn you one mark, a correct answer at Step 3 another two marks. The fourth mark for part (a) would probably be awarded for a correct answer at Step 4.

(b)

	Product type M £'000	Product type F £'000	Total £'000
Revenue			
(1,000 × £200)	200		
(2,325 × £210)		488.250	
			688.250
Variable costs			
Direct material P			
(1,000 × £20)	20		
(2,325 × £25)		58.125	
			78.125
Direct material Q			
(1,000 × £40)	40		
(2,325 × £20)		46.500	
			86.500
Direct labour			
(1,000 × £28)	28		
(2,325 × £35)		81.375	
			109.375
Overhead			
(1,000 × £16)	16		
(2,325 × £20)		46.500	
			62.500
	104	232.500	336.500

	Product type M £'000	Product type F £'000	Total £'000
Contribution	96	255.750	351.750
Fixed costs			
Production (W)			150.000
Non-production			57.750
			207.750
Profit			144.000

Working

Total budgeted fixed cost = 180,000 hrs × £10 = £1,800,000
Budget for period 1 = £1,800,000/12 = £150,000

> **Easy marks.** The contribution values for each product and in total would probably be worth two marks, the fixed costs values in total another two marks.

(c) ## Step 1 Define variables

Let m be the number of product M produced
Let f be the number of product F produced

ANSWERS

Step 2 **Establish objective function**

Maximise contribution (C) = 96m + 110f
where the unit contribution figures are as calculated in (a)

Step 3 **Establish constraints**

(1) **Material P:** $0 \leq 8m + 10f \leq 31{,}250$
(2) **Material Q:** $0 \leq 10m + 5f \leq 20{,}000$
(3) **Labour:** $0 \leq 4m + 5f \leq 17{,}500$
(4) **Maximum M demand:** $0 \leq m \leq 1{,}000$
(5) **Maximum F demand:** $0 \leq f \leq 3{,}000$

Step 4 **Graph the problem**

Constraint (1) If m = 0, f = 3,125
 If f = 0, m = 3,906.25

Constraint (2) If m = 0, f = 4,000
 If f = 0, m = 2,000

Constraint (3) If m = 0, f = 3,500
 If f = 0, m = 4,375

Sample objective function:

C = 96 × 110 × 20 = 211,200 = 96m + 110f

∴ When m = 0, f = 1,920
 When f = 0, m = 2,200

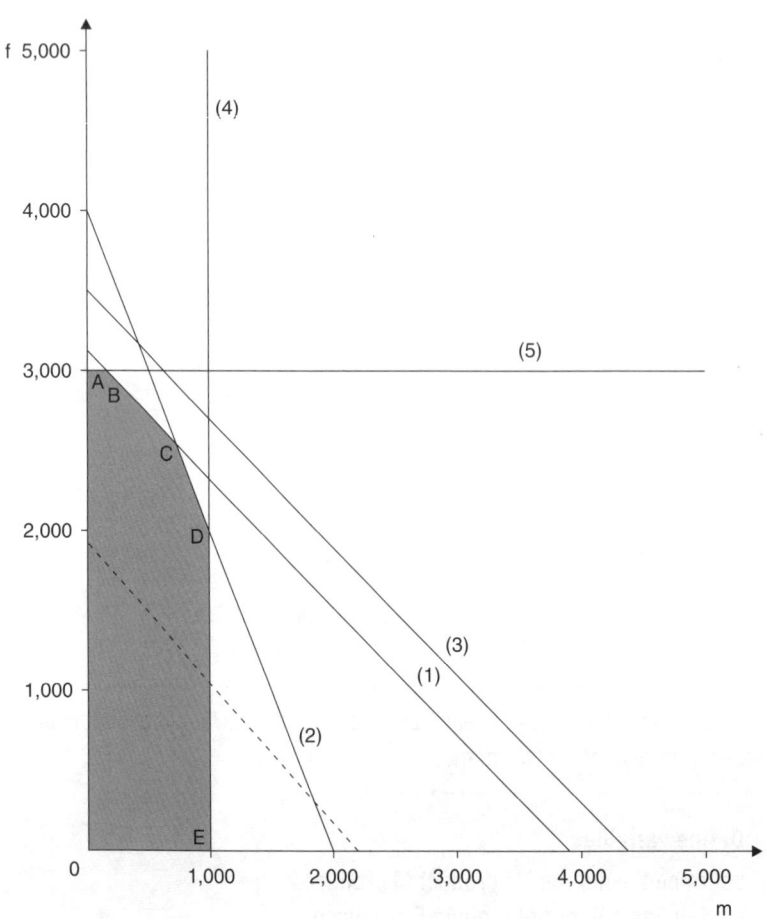

ANSWERS

Step 5 **Define feasible area**

The feasible area is OABCDE

Step 6 **Determine optimal solution**

Using the sample contribution line, the optimal solution can be seen to be at point C, where constraints (1) and (2) are equal.

We can find the coordinates using simultaneous equations:

8m + 10f = 31,250	(1)	
10m + 5f = 20,000	(2)	
20m + 10f = 40,000	(3)	(2) × 2
12m = 8,750	(3) – (1)	
∴ m = 729.17		
∴ f = 2,541.67	Sub into (2)	

The **optimal solution** is to produce 729 units of M and 2,541 units of F.

Top tips. A correct answer to the end of Step 3 would be worth about five marks, Step 4 would be worth about 3 marks, while the correct optimal mix would probably be worth the final one mark.

(d) Revised profit = (729 × unit contribution of M) + (2,541 × unit contribution of F) – fixed costs (from (b))
= (729 × £96) + (2,541 × £110) – £207,750
= £141,744

(e) The shadow price of material Q is the amount by which contribution would fall if availability of material of Q were reduced by one litre.

To calculate the shadow price we need to compare contribution when availability is 20,000 litres with contribution when availability is 19,999 litres.

Availability = 20,000 litres

Using the actual figures determined in (c), and the objective function C = 96m + 110f, contribution would be [8,750/12 × £96] + *[(20,000 – (8,750 × 10)/12)/5 × £110] = £349,583.33

* Value of f determined by substitution of value of m into equation (2) in Step 6 of (c).

Availability = 19,999 litres

If one less litre were available constraint (2) would become 0 ≤ 10m + 5f ≤ 19,999

We can now recalculate revised values for f and for m using simultaneous equations.

8m + 10f = 31,250	(1)	
10m + 5f = 19,999	(2)	
20m + 10f = 39,998	(3)	(2) × 2
12m = 8,748	(3) – (1)	
∴ m = 729		
∴ f = 2,541.8	Sub into (2)	

∴ C = (729 × £96) + (2,541.8 × £110) = £349,582

Difference in contributions = £1.33 = shadow price of a litre of material Q.

Top tips. The explanation would probably be worth one mark, the calculation four marks.

ANSWERS

> **Alternative approach**
>
> The CIMA model solution takes an alternative approach. This involves comparing the profit achieved when material Q is not a binding constraint (answer (b)) with that achieved when it is (answer (d)). The difference is profits is the shadow price of the difference in litres of material Q used.
>
> The value of the shadow price is largely affected by the accuracy of rounding carried out to determine the optimal solution in (c), however.

36 Question with helping hand: Venture capital company

> **Text references.** Part (b) draws on material in Chapter 11. Part (c) can be answered from Chapter 7.
>
> **Top tips.** Part (a) was a gift (unless you made your answer unnecessarily complicated). You did not even have to calculate the NPVs.
>
> Part (b) was a capital rationing situation. Products are ranked on the basis of the profitability index (PV of project's future cash flows not including the capital investment/PV of total capital outlay). It was vital to have noticed the stated assumption in the question that all investments are divisible.
>
> Part (c) was a bit trickier as it required the use of Simplex linear programming in an unusual scenario. The variables (things that could vary) were the proportions of the investments undertaken, as they were divisible. You were told that the objective was to maximise NPV and so the objective function was based on the proportions of the NPVs realised.
>
> When drawing up the funds constraints you had to notice that the available funds were given in PV terms (the cash flows were not) and so you had to convert the PV figures to actual figures. You also had to provide a constraint that ensured proportional investment was possible but ensured investments could not be undertaken twice.
>
> **Easy marks.** Part (d) is easy if you have to learnt the benefits asked for in the question. Part (c) requires you to trot through the correct format for the model (see top tips comment).

(a) Given that **investment in companies A, C and D** would result in **positive NPVs**, they provide a return in excess of the cost of capital. Hence T Ltd should **invest** in these companies as they fulfil the company's assumed objective of maximising shareholder wealth.

T Ltd will be **indifferent** to investment in **company B** as it would result in a **zero NPV**, and hence provide a return of the cost of capital and no more.

(b) (i)

Project	Investment required $'000	NPV $'000	PV of cash flows (W1) $'000	Profitability index PI (W2)	Ranking
A	(500)	60	560	1.120	2
B	(250)	0	250	1.000	4
C	(475)	77	552	1.162	1
D	(800)	80	880	1.100	3

Workings

1. As the investment is at year 0, the PV of cash flows is simply the NPV minus the investment.

    eg A:$'000 (60 – (500)) = $560,000

2. PV of cash flows/PV of investment required

Investment analysis

		$
Total investment		700,000
Investment C		475,000
		225,000
Investment A (part of)		225,000
		–

T Ltd should therefore **invest $475,000 in company C** (the whole of the requested investment) and **$225,000 in company A** (a proportion of the requested $500,000).

(ii) **Other factors which may affect the decision**

(1) **T Ltd's attitude to risk**

The mix of investments in T Ltd's current portfolio will impact on the decision. If it already contains a high proportion as high-risk investments, the company may wish to lower their overall exposure by taking on a number of less risky investments.

(2) **Divisibility of investments**

It may be that benefits from investment do not occur in line with the proportion of the total investment made. Investment of $225,000 in company A may not produce (($225,000/$500,000) × 100%) 45% of the expected total cash inflows.

(3) **Strategic implications**

The decision made takes no account of the possible strategic value of individual investments in the context of the overall objectives of T Ltd.

(4) **Cashflow/payback**

The decision takes no account of the differing cash flow patterns of the investments. These patterns may be important as they will affect the timing and availability of funds to T Ltd.

(5) **The risk of the product/service being offered by the start-up companies**

Innovative and untested products/services are inherently more risky than those for which there are competitors' versions. Companies C and A may be introducing new products with no track record whereas company D may be hoping to enter an established market.

(6) **The experience of the management/staff of the start-up companies**

This will impact on the success of the investment.

> **Easy marks.** You could probably earn one mark for each valid point made up to a maximum of four.

(c) **Define variables**

Let a = proportion of investment in A undertaken
Let b = proportion of investment in B undertaken
Let c = proportion of investment in C undertaken
Let d = proportion of investment in D undertaken

Establish objective function

Maximise NPV = 60a + 0b + 77c + 80d, subject to the constraints below.

Establish constraints

The funds available for future investment are shown in present value terms. We therefore need to convert these to 'actual' amounts in order to compare them with the investment cash flows.

ANSWERS

Year 1: funds available = $80,000 \times 1.12 = $89,600
Year 2: funds available = $35,000 \times (1.12)^2 = $43,904

The **period 0 constraint** must show that the available funds are greater than or equal to the sum of the proportions of the capital required.

The **periods 1 and 2 constraints** must show that the available funds are greater than or equal to the sum of the relevant proportions of the cash outflows

Year 0: $700,000 $\leq$ 500a + 250b + 475c + 800d
Year 1: $89,600 $\leq$ 75a + 30b + 100c + 150d
Year 2: $43,904 $\leq$ 40a + 20b + 30c + 50d

Investment proportions: $0 \leq a, b, c, d, \leq 1$ (which ensures that no investment is undertaken more than once, but allows for partial investments)

Introduce slack variables

These represent unused funds in each period.

Let S_0 = the available funds not invested in year 0
Let S_1 = the available funds not invested in year 1
Let S_2 = the available funds not invested in year 2

Redefine constraints

Year 0: $700,000 = 500a + 250b + 475c + 800d + S_0
Year 1: $89,600 = 75a + 30b + 100c + 150d + S_1
Year 2: $43,904 = 40a + 20b + 30c + 50d + S_2

Redefine objective function

Maximise NPV given by NPV − 60a − 0b − 77c − 88d = 0

> **Top tips.** There would probably be four marks available for explanation of the meaning of the objective function and the constraints, and of the variables and slack variables. Formulation of the model would probably be worth six marks.

(d) **Benefits of using a linear programming format in this situation**

(i) If a computer program is used to solve the problem, the investment decision can be made **quickly** and **efficiently**. Programs usually also provide **sensitivity analysis** indicating by how much key variables can change.

(ii) Solutions should show **opportunity costs** for the scarce resources (investment funds in this situation), which is useful information for planning, control and decision making.

(iii) The approach provides the best solution in the given circumstances and hence gives a **clear plan of action**.

37 HT plc

> **Text references.** If you get stuck or want some help, look at Chapter 7 which will give you material for answering the question.
>
> **Top tips.** Notice the checking we have performed in part (c). It may boost your confidence to know that your interpretation is correct!
>
> **Easy marks.** If you are confident with manipulating functions and following the steps involved, these are standard and so practice is key to gain confidence here.

ANSWERS

(a) The regression equation indicates that HT plc's overheads consist of:

£4,000 per week fixed overhead
£0.50 per hour spent on production of HT01
£0.70 per hour spent on production of HT02
£0.80 per hour spent on production of HT03

The **total variable product costs** are therefore as follows.

	HT01 £	HT02 £	HT03 £
Direct labour	100.0	120	132.0
Direct materials	20.0	40	40.0
Variable overhead:			
HT01 (£100/£4 × £0.50)	12.5		
HT02 (£120/£4 × £0.70)		21	
HT03 (£132/£4 × £0.80)			26.4
	132.5	181	198.4

(b) **Contribution earned by each product**

	HT01 £	HT02 £	HT03 £
Price	150.0	200	220.0
Variable production costs (see part (a))	132.5	181	198.4
	17.5	19	21.6

Define variables

Let a, b, c be the number of HT01, HT02 and HT03 produced respectively.

Establish objective function

The objective function is to maximise contribution C, given by:

C = 17.5a + 19b + 21.6c

Establish constraints

The constraints are as follows.

$25a + 30b + 33c \leq 257{,}600$ (labour hours)
$a + 2b + 2c \leq 20{,}000$ (materials)
$a \leq 16{,}000$ (demand for HT01)
$b \leq 10{,}000$ (demand for HT02)
$c \leq 6{,}000$ (demand for HT03)
$a, b, c \geq 0$

Introduce slack variables

Let S_1 be the number of unused labour hours.

Let S_2 be the number of unused kilograms of material.

Let S_3, S_4, S_5 respectively be the number of units produced of HT01, HT02 and HT03 less than the maximum demand.

Reformulate constraints

$25a + 30b + 33c + S_1 = 257{,}600$
$a + 2b + 2c + S_2 = 20{,}000$
$a + S_3 = 16{,}000$
$b + S_4 = 10{,}000$
$c + S_5 = 6{,}000$
$a, b, c \geq 0$

ANSWERS

Reformulate objective function

The objective function is to maximise C, given by:

$C - 17.5a - 19b - 21.6c + 0S_1 + 0S_2 + 0S_3 + 0S_4 + 0S_5 = 0$

(c) In the final tableau the **variables** represented in the **solution column** are respectively S_5, HT01, S_3, S_4, S_2. The **optimal solution** is therefore to produce 10,304 units of HT01, with no production of HT02 or HT03. The contribution arising from this policy is given in the solution row as £180,320 (check: 10,304 × £17.50 = £180,320).

The **remaining figures in the solution column** indicate the following.

S_5 =	6,000	(production of HT03 should be 6,000 less than demand, ie nil)
S_3 =	5,696	(production of HT01 should be 5,696 less than demand ie 10,304 (16,000 – 5,696) as indicated above)
S_4 =	10,000	(production of HT02 should be 10,000 less than demand, ie nil)
S_2 =	9,696	(there will be 9,696 kilograms of unused material (check: 20,000 – (10,304 × 1) = 9,696)

Since there is **no value for S_1,** it follows that **labour hours will be fully utilised** (check: 10,304 × 25 = 257,600).

The **shadow prices of HT02 and HT03** are £2.00 and £1.50 respectively. This means that for every unit of HT02 or HT03 made, contribution would fall by £2 and £1.50 respectively. In other words, the contribution from HT02 and HT03 would need to rise by at least those respective amounts before it became profitable to manufacture them at the expense of HT01.

Adoption of the **optimum production plan** will lead to the following **results**.

	£
Contribution earned	180,320
Less: fixed overheads (46 × £4,000)	184,000
Net loss for year	3,680

The **shadow price of one hour of labour (S_1)** is £0.70. This means that for every extra hour of labour made available at its normal cost of £4 per hour, contribution could be increased by 70p. (Check: one hour of labour would produce 1/25th of a unit of HT01 at a contribution of £17.50/25 = £0.70.) This interpretation is only valid while labour hours are a constraint on production.

38 Section A answers: Pricing

1   A   Discriminating prices based on time attempt to increase sales revenue by covering variable but not necessarily average cost of provision.

2   D   **Statement I** is incorrect because if there are no scarce resources and a company has spare capacity, the minimum price of a product is the incremental cost of making it.

           Statement II is incorrect because if there are scarce resources and a company makes more than one product, minimum prices must include an allowance for the opportunity cost of using the scarce resources to make and sell the product.

           Statement III is incorrect because it is unlikely that a minimum price would be charged because it would not provide the business with any incremental profit.

           Statement IV is incorrect because the minimum price must also include the opportunity costs of making and selling an item.

3   C   This is monopolistic competition. The similarities ensure elastic demand whereas the slight differences give some monopolistic power to the supplier.

ANSWERS

4 A **Condition I** must hold because a black market would allow those in the lower-priced segment to resell to those in the higher-priced segment.

      Condition II is not necessary. Competitors must not be able to undercut the firm's prices in the higher-priced (and/or most profitable) market segments.

      Condition III is not necessary. Different sectors must show different intensities of demand.

      Condition IV is incorrect because the cost should *not* exceed the extra revenue.

5   If demand is highly **elastic** it would respond well to low prices.

6 D I: The same can be said of full cost plus pricing.

      II: The mark-up can be adjusted to reflect demand conditions.

      III: Although the size of the mark-up can be varied in accordance with demand conditions, it is not a method of pricing which ensures that sufficient attention is paid to demand conditions, competitors' prices and profit maximisation.

      IV: The price must be high enough to ensure that a profit is made after covering fixed costs.

7   When p = 0, demand (x) = 50,000
     When p = 1, demand (x) = 49,950

     ∴ **Demand (x) = 50,000 – 50p**, where p is the selling price in £ (because demand will drop by 50 for every increase (from £0) of £1 in the selling price).

     If x = 35,000, p = 1/50 (50,000 – 35,000) = £300

8   Marginal cost = £20
     Profits are maximised when marginal cost = marginal revenue
     ie when 20 = 50 – 0.002x
     ie when x = 15,000

     When x = 15,000, selling price = £50 – £(0.001 × 15,000) = £35

9   Maximum revenue occurs when marginal revenue = £0

     ie when 0 = £50 – £0.002x
     ie when x = 25,000

     When x = 25,000, selling price = £50 – (£0.001 × 25,000) = £25

     Profit = contribution – fixed costs
           = (25,000 × £(25 – 20)) – £100,000 = £25,000

39 Elasticity

> **Top tips**. This question required you to write a memorandum, so your answer should have been produced in memorandum form. You should have ensured that you did actually explain how the differing observations on elasticity of demand could be reconciled.

MEMORANDUM

To: Commercial manager
From: Management accountant
Date: 01.01.X1
Subject: **Elasticity of demand for product X**

Overview of report

The consultants' report which you recently commissioned stated that there would be no demand for X if the selling price were £10 and that for each 1p decrease in the selling price, demand would increase by 40 units of X.

ANSWERS

Implications for sales volume

The maximum number of units which could be sold is therefore 1,000 × 40 (that is, the maximum number of 1p decreases below £10 × increase in demand by 40 for each 1p decrease in price). The selling price of the 40,000 units would be 1p.

Report on elasticity of demand

The report also stated that the elasticity of demand for X would be approximately 1 at around half the theoretical maximum demand. We can calculate the elasticity of demand at this point as follows.

$$\text{Elasticity of demand} = \frac{\frac{q^2 - q^1}{q^1}}{\frac{p^2 - p^1}{p^1}} = \frac{q^2 - q^1}{q^1} \times \frac{p^1}{p^2 - p^1} = \frac{q^2 - q^1}{p^2 - p^1} \times \frac{p^1}{q^1}$$

$$= \frac{0 - 20{,}000}{£10 - £5} \times \frac{£5}{20{,}000} = 1$$

When the price per unit is £5 then a percentage change in the selling price produces an equal percentage change in the quantity demanded. Elasticity does, however, vary in value along a demand curve (the function relating quantity demanded to price) because the higher the price (and lower the demand), the larger p^1/q^1, and therefore the bigger the numerical value (ignoring the sign) of the elasticity. Similarly, the lower the price, the smaller the elasticity.

Reconciliation with your observations

This supports your observation that small changes in the current selling price of £6.25 produce larger proportionate increases in demand. The current selling price of £6.25 is not sufficiently close to the price when demand is around half the theoretical maximum for the elasticity to be 1.

At the current selling price of £6.25, the consultant would calculate sales to be 1,000 − 625 = 375 × 40 = 15,000 units of X. Elasticity of demand when the price is £6.25 and the demand is for 15,000 units is

$$\frac{0 - 15{,}000}{10 - 6.25} \times \frac{6.25}{15{,}000} = 1.67$$

An elasticity of demand of 1.67 at a selling price of £6.25 is in line with your observation that the elasticity of demand is not 1 at the current selling price.

Signed: Management accountant

40 Question with answer plan: Off-the-shelf I

> **Top tips.** This question should have given you no problems apart from deciding on the alternative pricing strategies to suggest. You may have included target pricing, for example. Each valid point made would probably earn you one mark.

Answer plan

Read the question carefully for what is required. Although the product has been in the market for over two years, the appraisal asks for pricing strategies relevant to new products.

Remember that the policy adopted was also intended to take advantage of being first in the market.

Step 1 Identify the current pricing strategy.

Step 2 Comment on its advantages and disadvantages.

ANSWERS

Step 3 List and comment on the relative merits and drawbacks of two or three other pricing strategies appropriate for first market entrants.

Managing director's pricing strategy

The managing director has adopted what is known as a **full cost plus** pricing strategy, which means that a profit margin (in this case, of 50%) is added to the budgeted full cost of the product.

Given the information in the question, the **selling price used by R Ltd** is calculated as follows.

	£
Full cost	400
50% mark up	200
Selling price	600

Disadvantages of this pricing strategy

(a) Its **focus** is **internal** – internal costs and internal targets.

(b) It therefore takes **no account of the market conditions** faced by R Ltd, which is why the company's selling price bears little resemblance to those of competitors.

(c) By adopting a fixed mark-up, **it does not allow the company to react to competitors'** pricing decisions.

(d) It is based on the **assumption** that demand for the company's software is **inelastic**. This means that a change in price will not lead to any significant change in demand. If this is the case, prices should be increased in order to increase total revenue and hence profit. The market research information does not support this view, however. It suggests that increasing prices will lead to a drop in demand and hence a reduction in profit.

(e) **Absorption bases** used when calculating the full cost are **decided arbitrarily**. The current basis of absorption is based on the budgeted level of production, which is lower than the current capacity.

(f) **Depending on the absorption basis** used in the calculation of total cost, the strategy can **produce different selling prices**.

Advantages of this pricing strategy

(a) It is **quick**, **cheap** and relatively **easy** to apply. Pricing can therefore be delegated to more junior management if necessary.

(b) It ensures that **all costs are covered** and that the organisation **makes a profit**, provided budget figures used in the pricing calculation are reasonably accurate. This was the case in the first two years for R Ltd.

(c) The **costs of collecting market information** on demand and competitor activity are **avoided**.

Alternative pricing strategies

(a) **Market penetration pricing**

Market penetration pricing is a policy of low prices when a product is first launched in order to achieve high sales volumes and hence gain a significant market share. If R Ltd had adopted this strategy it might have discouraged competitors from entering the market.

(b) **Market skimming**

This pricing strategy involves charging high prices when a product is first launched and spending heavily on advertising and promotion to obtain sales so as to exploit any price insensitivity in the market. Such an approach would have been particularly suitable for R Ltd's circumstances: demand for the software would have been relatively inelastic, customers being prepared to pay high prices for the software given its novelty appeal. As the product moves into later stages of its life cycle, prices can be reduced in order to remain competitive.

(c) **Demand based approach (optimal pricing)**

This approach is based on the assumption that there is a profit-maximising combination of price and demand because demand is elastic. The market research recently commissioned by the marketing director would have been needed if R Ltd were to have adopted such an approach. There are some significant **drawbacks** to optimal pricing, however.

ANSWERS

(i) It can be difficult to predict the demand curve (although the marketing director's investigations appear to have been successful).

(ii) It ignores the market research costs of acquiring knowledge of demand.

(iii) It assumes that price is the only influence on quantity demanded.

(iv) It is complicated by the issue of price discrimination.

(v) It assumes that R Ltd has no production constraints which prevent the equilibrium point between supply and demand being reached.

The **advantages** of the approach are that it forces managers to think about price/demand relationships and to consider the market in which the organisation operates.

41 Off-the-shelf II

Top tips. Hopefully you could see that you needed to use the information in the 'note' box in part (a) and could appreciate the link between the demand curve you derived and the price function provided. The simplest way of calculating maximum profit was to deduct fixed overheads from contribution otherwise you would have to deal with any under or over absorption of overheads. You did need a certain level of mathematical ability to answer this part of the question well.

The ability to draw graphs to carry out sensitivity analysis as required in part (b) is a key Paper P2 skill and if you had problems with this part of the question make sure you look at the topic again in the BPP Study Text.

(a) Demand curve, $P = a - bQ/\Delta Q$

a = price at which demand would be nil = £750
b = £10
ΔQ = 1,000

$\therefore P = 750 - 10Q/1,000 = 750 - 0.01Q$

We are told that if price = $a - bx$, **marginal revenue (MR)** = $a - 2bx$

(Here x is equivalent to Q in the demand curve formula above and so we will use MR = $a - 2bQ$.)
$\therefore$ If $P = 750 - 0.01Q$, $a = 750$ and $b = 0.01$ and MR = $750 - (2 \times 0.01)Q = 750 - 0.02Q$

We now need to **find marginal cost (MC)**

Full cost = £400

Absorbed fixed overheads = £80

$\therefore$ Variable cost = £320
$\therefore$ We take the variable cost of £320 to be MC

Profits are maximised when MC = MR
$\therefore$ Profits are maximised when $750 - 0.02Q = 320$ ie when $Q = 21,500$

Calculation of maximum profit

Price (when Q = 21,500) = $750 - (0.01 \times 21,500) = £535$
$\therefore$ Contribution per unit (when Q = 21,500) = £(535 - 320) = £215

Maximum profit

	£'000
Contribution (£215 × 21,500)	4,622.5
Fixed overheads (£80 × 15,000 units)	(1,200.0)
	3,422.5

200

(b) **Data for graph**

Rate of exchange €1=	Contribution per unit	Total contribution (per unit × 25,000) £'000
£0.30	(930 × £0.30) − £300 = −£21	(525)
£0.50	(930 × £0.50) − £300 = £165	4,125
£0.60	(930 × £0.60) − £300 = £258	6,450

Graph to show sensitivity of proposal to movements in €/£ exchange rate

[Graph: Contribution £m (y-axis) vs Exchange rate (€ = £?) (x-axis). Line passes through plotted points at 0.3 (≈ −£0.5m), 0.5 (≈ £4m), and 0.6 (≈ £6.5m). Dashed line indicates "Current contribution" intersecting the line between 0.5 and 0.6.]

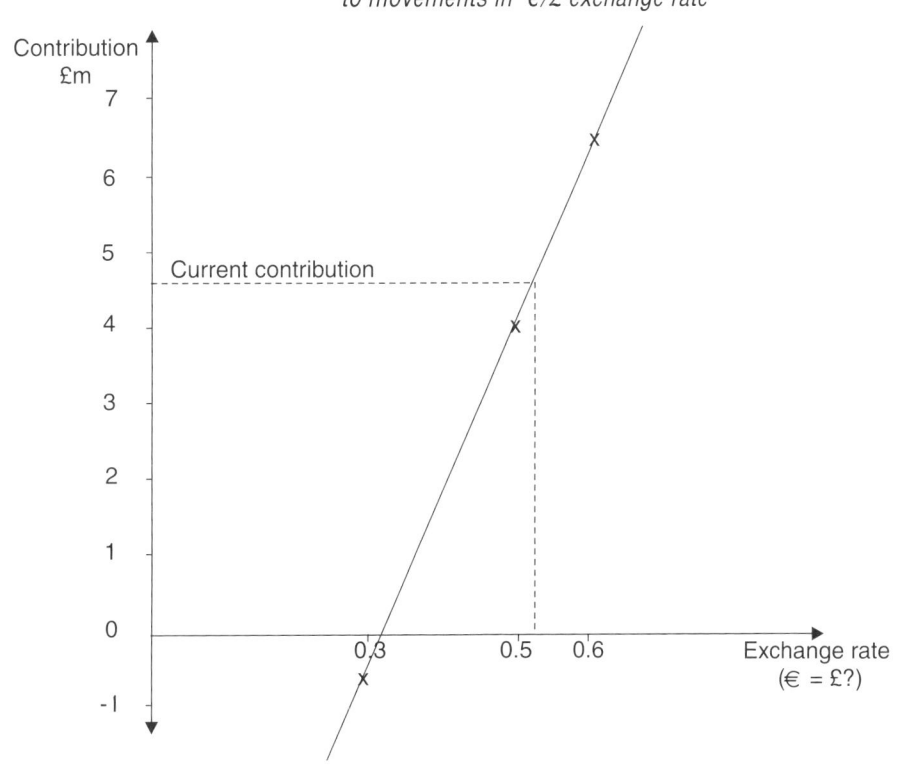

Analysis

	£
Maximum contribution if R Ltd sells package itself (from (a))	4,622,500
Contribution from exporting to L (with exchange rate of €1 = £0.60)	6,450,000
Increase in contribution from exporting	1,827,500

With an exchange rate of €1 = £0.60, the proposal is therefore worthwhile.

As can be seen from the graph, once the exchange rate falls below approximately €1 = £0.52, however (a fall of approximation 13.3%), the contribution for the proposal is less then the contribution that can be earned if R Ltd sells the packages itself. The proposal is therefore not worthwhile at exchange rates below this level.

R Ltd needs to assess the likelihood of falls in exchange rate before deciding on whether or not to accept L's offer.

ANSWERS

42 W

> **Top tips.** You will find the data you need scattered throughout the question. This makes it a bit difficult for you to remember to use it all but keep a clear head and cross off data as you use it. In part(a) you are required to complete the cash flow statement for the two remaining stages in the product life cycle. Remember that you need to produce a **cumulative statement** as well as stating cash flows for a period. You will need to remember the **four stages of the product life cycle** and their features so that you can select the **correct sales and cost characteristics** of the two remaining stages.
>
> Part (b) you need to make some clear points about the reasons why costs and sales change during the life cycle of a product. You must remember to **apply study text knowledge** to the scenario in the question. There are four stages in the lifecycle so you should score at least one mark for a comment on each stage.
>
> **Easy marks.** Part (a) is easy in principle. You are calculating a cash flow using data from the question and using the format suggested in the question. So you could earn a few useful marks by just setting out the format for the two remaining periods and slotting in some of the easier calculations such as sales demand for the maturity stage. In part (b) set out your answer with headings so the marker can pick out the four stages clearly and award marks more easily.

(a) (i)

	Maturity	Total	Decline	Total
Months	31-70		71-110	
Number of units produced and sold (W1)	20,000	20,000	20,000	
Selling price per unit ($)	60	60	40	
Unit variable cost ($)	30	25	30	
Unit contribution ($)	30	35	10	
Total Contribution($)	1,300,000		200,000	
Cumulative cash flow(w2)	1,275,000		1,475,000	

Workings

1. Months 31 –70. 1,000 units per month × 40 months = 40,000 units.

   Months 71-110 are calculated as follows:

   (10 × 800) + (10 × 600) + (10 × 400) +(10 × 200) = 20,000 units.

   The clue to knowing which sales demand applies to which life cycle stage is to look at the sales demand over the life cycle. Monthly sales levels continue to increase up to months 31-70. Thereafter they decline. The growth stage typically shows a **rapid increase** in sales and the maturity stage shows a slow down in sales **growth**. However, it is only at the decline stage that sales actually **decline**.

2. Cumulative cash flow brought forward = $(25,000).

(b) **The possible reasons for the changes in cost and selling prices during the life cycle of the product.** There are **four stages** in a product life cycle. Each stage has different features in relation to costs and sales. These are:

Introductory stage

The principal aim during this stage is to **introduce a product and build demand**. The organisation is likely to **spend significant amounts on advertising and distribution** to get the product or service known. Production costs ie **unit variable costs** are also likely to be high as the product has not yet achieved **economies of scale.** This is also the time in the product lifecycle where **research and development costs** are incurred. Prices are generally high if a **market skimming** policy is adopted to take advantage of being an early entrant to the market and so recoup costs. However an organisation may choose a **market penetration** strategy so prices are low to gain market share. For W, costs are high at $50/unit and the selling price is also (compared with those over the entire lifecycle) high at $100/unit. An unit contribution of $50/unit sold is the highest contribution over the product life cycle. W therefore appears to be seeking to recoup as much R&D expenditure and fixed asset expenditure as possible at this stage.

Growth stage

The aim during this stage is to **build market share**. **Costs will still be high** as more promotion is needed to advertise the product more widely. Distribution channels may be expanded to take up more market share. **The price will be high** but may need to fall if demand is seen as falling. W charges between $70 and $80/unit sold and the price drops over the period in response to market conditions. However, the unit variable cost is also falling. Margins are falling but volume has risen so the product is contributing more at this stage than the last one.

Maturity stage

This is the **most profitable stage** of the product's life cycle. **Costs will begin to fall** as economies of production are achieved. Advertising costs should fall as product awareness is stronger. Marketing is concentrated in reaching new customers. **The price will fall** in response to competition and to retain market share. Profitability is shown by the contribution of $1.3m that is the highest over the life cycle of the product despite a fall in selling price/unit. This is achieved by volume sales as well as the unit cost continuing to fall.

Decline stage

This is the stage at which the product is **losing popularity and market share is falling**. W can adopt a **choice of strategies** including running the product down or discontinuing it. Costs fall as marketing support is withdrawn but economies of scale begin to decline so the **unit variable cost actually rises** again to $30/unit. **Prices are reduced** to mop up market share.

43 C1, C2, C3

Text references. Part (a) should be brought forward knowledge but look at Chapter 1 if you need to reread cost controls and techniques. Part (b) can be answered by referring to Chapter 8 on Pricing decisions. Part (c) wants you to explain JIT which is covered in Chapter 17.

Top tips. In part (a) you are required to calculate the total savings that the company would make as a result of implementing a particular system (JIT).

Easy marks. You could have worked out the total budgeted cost of current operations and the total budgeted cost of JIT operations but it is quicker to consider the incremental changes in costs as we have done. If you took the alternative approach, the total cost of current operations is £1,770,670, the total cost when JIT has been implemented £1,604,110.

You need to tabulate your workings very carefully in part (b). You may have got to your answer in a slightly different way – for example the CIMA model answer calculated set-up costs, material handling costs, inspection costs and machinery costs per car. It was imperative, however, that your decision was based on variable cost and **not** full cost.

Do not make the obvious mistake of writing about JIT in general in part (c).

ANSWERS

(a) **Impact of JIT – savings in costs**

	£m
Direct labour [£(1,120 + 1,292 + 1,980) × 0.2 × 75,000]	(65.880)
Set-ups	
variable (£13,000 × 0.3 × 3,500)	13.650
fixed (£42.66m × 0.3)	12.798
Materials handling	
variable (£4,000 × 0.3 × 14,600)	17.520
fixed (£52.89m × 0.3)	15.867
Inspection	
variable (£18,000 × 0.3 × 3,500)	18.900
fixed (£59.88m × 0.3)	17.964
Machinery	
variable (£40 × 0.15 × 4.56m)	27.360
fixed (£144.54m × 0.15)	21.681
Distribution and warehousing	
variable (£3,000 × 14,600)	43.800
fixed	42.900
	166.560

(b) **Savings**

Car C1

Price £	Demand Cars	Revenue £m	Direct cost per car (W1) £	Total direct costs £m	Variable overhead cost per car (W2) £	Total variable overhead costs £m	Contribution £m
5,000	75,000	375.00	3,864	289.800	928	69.60	15.60
5,750	65,000	373.75	3,864	251.160	928	60.32	62.27
6,000	50,000	300.00	3,864	193.200	928	46.40	60.40
6,500	35,000	227.50	3,864	135.240	928	32.48	59.78

Therefore, profit-maximising price is £5,750 at output level of 65,000 cars.

Car C2

Price £	Demand Cars	Revenue £m	Direct cost per car (W1) £	Total direct costs £m	Variable overhead cost per car (W3) £	Total variable overhead costs £m	Contribution £m
5,750	75,000	431.25	4,474.4	335.580	1,292	96.90	(1.230)
6,250	60,000	375.00	4,474.4	268.464	1,292	77.52	29.016
6,500	45,000	292.50	4,474.4	201.348	1,292	58.14	33.012
7,500	35,000	262.50	4,474.4	156.604	1,292	45.22	60.676

Therefore, profit-maximising price is £7,500 at output level of 35,000 cars.

Car C3

Price £	Demand Cars	Revenue £m	Direct cost per car (W1) £	Total direct costs £m	Variable overhead cost per car (W4) £	Total variable overhead costs £m	Contribution £m
6,500	75,000	487.50	6,336	475.20	1,405	105.375	(93.075)
6,750	60,000	405.00	6,336	380.16	1,405	84.300	(59.460)
7,750	45,000	348.75	6,336	285.12	1,405	63.225	0.405
8,000	30,000	240.00	6,336	190.08	1,405	42.150	7.770

Therefore, profit-maximising price is £8,000 at output level of 30,000 cars.

Workings

1   **Revised direct cost per car**

	C1 £	C2 £	C3 £
Direct materials	2,520	2,924.0	3,960
Direct labour (× 120%)	1,344	1,550.4	2,376
	3,864	4,474.4	6,336

2   **Revised variable overhead costs for 75,000 C1 cars**

	£m
Set-ups (£13,000 × 1,000 × 70%)	9.10
Materials handling (£4,000 × 4,000 × 70%)	11.20
Inspection (£18,000 × 1,000 × 70%)	12.60
Machining (£40 × 1.08m × 85%)	36.72
Distribution and warehousing	–
	69.62

Therefore, cost per car = $\dfrac{£69.62m}{75,000}$ = £928

3   **Revised variable overhead costs for 75,000 C2 cars**

	£m
Set-ups (£13,000 × 1,000 × 70%)	9.1
Materials handling (£4,000 × 5,000 × 70%)	14.0
Inspections (£18,000 × 1,000 × 70%)	12.6
Machining (£40 × 1.8m × 85%)	61.2
Distribution and warehousing	–
	96.9

Therefore, cost per car = $\dfrac{£96.9m}{75,000}$ = £1,292

4   **Revised variable overhead costs for 75,000 C3 cars**

	£m
Set-ups (£13,000 × 1,500 × 70%)	13.65
Materials handling (£4,000 × 5,600 × 70%)	15.68
Inspection (£18,000 × 1,500 × 70%)	18.90
Machining (£40 × 1.68m × 85%)	57.12
Distribution and warehousing	–
	105.35

Therefore, cost per car = $\dfrac{£105.35m}{75,000}$ = £1,405

ANSWERS

(c)

REPORT

To: Management of X Ltd
From: Management accountant
Date: 17 December 20X2
Subject: Implementation of JIT manufacturing system

1 Introduction

1.1 Set out below are the conditions that are necessary for the successful implementation of a JIT manufacturing system.

2 Suppliers

2.1 Quality raw materials/components

Stocks of raw materials/components, work in progress and finished goods are kept at near zero levels under a JIT system. Raw materials/components must therefore be of **100% quality** as defects stop the production line and, with no buffer stocks available, they could possibly result in failure to meet delivery dates to customers.

2.2 Delivery on time

As well as being responsible for the quality of raw materials/components, suppliers must also guarantee to deliver on time so that there are no production delays.

2.3 Small deliveries

Order sizes should be small to avoid the build up of stocks and the costs associated with this.

2.4 Close relationships

You must therefore establish long-term commitments with a limited number of suppliers with whom you should deal exclusively in their component areas. They guarantee to deliver material of 100% quality on time. In return they are guaranteed demand for their product.

3 Production

3.1 Smooth production flow

The rate of production should be kept as smooth as possible as fluctuations can cause delays and lead to high levels of work in progress.

3.2 Pull system

Production in one process is only carried out when output of that process is needed by the next. Ultimately this means production is entirely based on customer demand for final output.

3.3 Set-ups

Because production runs are short, there are more of them, and set-ups need to be quick and inexpensive.

3.4 Machine maintenance

Routine preventative maintenance will avoid machine downtime.

4 Employees

4.1 Flexible and multi-skilled workers

Workers must be multi-skilled and flexible in order to be able to move between different production lines to maintain output.

ANSWERS

4.2 **Teamwork**

Teamwork will ensure high levels of efficiency and the elimination of non-value added costs.

5 **Summary**

5.1 If the conditions detailed above were established, the implementation of a JIT manufacturing system within X Ltd is likely to be successful.

5.2 If I can provide any further information, please do not hesitate to contact me.

44 Mobile telephones

Text references. Part (a) needs you to include material from Chapters 11 and 15. Part (b) draws on knowledge of pricing in Chapter 8. Finally, Chapter 14 contains sensitivity analysis, for part (c).

Top tips. Make sure you know which technique to use in investment appraisal questions. NPV is definitely needed to assess financial viability.

In part (a) it is important to note that the product will be launched in one year's time and so the first net revenues will not be received until year 2. Don't forget that you need to 'add back' the working capital released at the end of the project in year 4.

Part (b) requires you to 'discuss' so do not simply provide a bullet-point list. You would have received one to two marks for each point made so you would only need to include a maximum of five relevant points.

Answers to part (c) defining sensitivity or explaining how it could be generated are unlikely to gain marks.

Easy marks. Our approach to part (a) shows that you can get a fair way through the answer without having to deal with the tricky calculations involving the experience curve. If you had dealt with this more problematic area first you may have panicked and been unable to complete part (a). This is important in any question: **get the easy marks first**.

(a) **Pricing strategy**

Strategy 1: Price of £950

Workings

(i) Production costs

Calculate PV of 'production etc' costs

To determine the cost of making 6,000 units we need to apply the learning curve or experience curve formula $Y = aX^b$, where $b = -0.51457$.

We do not know the cost of making the first unit but we know the average cost per unit of the first batch of 500 units.

If $Y = aX^b$
£675 = $a \times 500^{-0.51457}$
∴ a = £16,523.908
∴ $Y = £16,523.908 \times X^{-0.51457}$

Over the three-year life of the project 6,000 units will be made each year and the experience effect applies to all of these units.

Year 1: cumulative production = 6,000 units

$Y_{6,000}$ = £16,523.908 × $6,000^{-0.51457}$ = **£187.927**

ANSWERS

Year 2: cumulative production = 12,000 units

$$Y_{12,000} = £16,523.908 \times 12,000^{-0.51457} = £131.549$$

Year 3: cumulative production = 18,000 units

$$Y_{18,000} = £16,523.908 \times 18,000^{-0.51457} = £106.777$$

Total and incremental costs for each year

Year	Cumulative production Units	Average unit cost £	Total cost £	Incremental cost £
1	6,000	187.927	1,127,562	
2	12,000	131.549	1,578,588	451,026
3	18,000	106.777	1,921,986	343,398

Alternative approach to calculating 'production etc' costs

We could consider output in terms of batches of 500 units.

Step 1 We know that the cost of the first batch of 500 = £675 × 500 = £337,500

$$\therefore Y = £337,500 \times X^{-0.51457}$$

Year 1: cumulative production = 12 batches of 500 units ∴ X = 12

$$Y_{12} = £337,500 \times 12^{-0.51457} = £93,964$$

Year 2: cumulative production = 24 batches

$$Y_{24} = £337,500 \times 24^{-0.51457} = £65,775$$

Year 3: cumulative production = 36 batches

$$Y_{36} = £337,500 \times 36^{-0.51457} = £53,388$$

Step 2

Year	Cumulative production batches of 500	Average batch cost £	Total cost £	Incremental cost £
1	12	93,964	1,127,568	
2	24	65,775	1,578,600	451,032
3	36	53,388	1,921,968	343,368

The same approach can be adopted for strategy 2

(ii) Revenue

Revenue will be £950 × 6,000 = £5,700,000

Net present value

Year	0 £'000	1 £'000	2 £'000	3 £'000	4 £'000
Cash flows:					
Revenue	-	-	5,700	5,700	5,700
Development costs	(750)	-	-	-	-
Assets	-	(3,500)	-	-	-
Working capital	-	(1,500)	-	-	1,500
Fixed costs	-	-	(2,400)	(2,400)	(2,400)
Production costs	-	-	(1,128)	(451)	(343)
Net cash flow	(750)	(5,000)	2,172	2,849	4,457
Discount factor (7%)	1.000	0.935	0.873	0.816	0.763
Present value	(750)	(4,675)	1,896	2,325	3,401

Net present value = £2,197,000.

Strategy 2: price of £425

Workings

(i) Production costs

Calculate PV of 'production etc' costs

$Y = £16,523.908 \times X^{-0.51457}$ as before

Year 1: cumulative production 15,000 units

$Y_{15,000} = £16,523.908 \times 15,000^{-0.51457} = £117.279$

Year 2: cumulative production 30,000 units

$Y_{30,000} = £16,523.908 \times 30,000^{-0.51457} = £82.096$

Year 3: cumulative production 45,000 units

$Y_{45,000} = £16,523.908 \times 45,000^{-0.51457} = £66.636$

(ii) Revenue

Revenue will be £425 × 15,000 = £6,375,000 per annum.

Net Present Value

Year	0	1	2	3	4
	£'000	£'000	£'000	£'000	£'000
Cash flows:					
Revenue	-	-	6,375	6,375	6,375
Development costs	(750)	-	-	-	-
Assets	-	(3,500)	-	-	-
Working capital	-	(1,500)	-	-	1,500
Fixed costs	-	-	(2,400)	(2,400)	(2,400)
Production costs	-	-	(1,759)	(704)	(536)
Net cash flow	(750)	(5,000)	2,216	3,271	4,939
Discount factor (7%)	1.000	0.935	0.873	0.816	0.763
Present value	(750)	(4,675)	1,935	2,669	3,768

Net Present Value = £2,947,000

Strategy 2 (price £425) is preferable as it has the higher NPV.

The strategy to sell at a price of £425 is financially viable as it results in a positive NPV.

(b) **Other issues to consider**

(i) Given the **fast-changing nature** of the product environment and expected **competition**, VI plc needs to consider whether the product would have a **three-year life**.

(ii) A **low price** should result in **increased market share**, which may prove useful when VI plc comes to market its next generation of products.

(iii) Will there be a **conflict** in the market between the **low price** of the product and the company's reputation for 'well-engineered, reliable and **good quality** products'?

(iv) The low price strategy will require **additional production facilities**. VI plc should consider whether **more profitable use** could be made of these facilities.

(v) The company should be satisfied that the **cost and demand estimates** are sufficiently **accurate** to ensure the comparison and viability exercises have value.

ANSWERS

(vi) VI plc should confirm that the **70% experience curve** is **applicable** to production of this product and that it is relevant to the entire production period.

(vii) The project requires **£5.75 million** before the product is launched in one year's time. VI plc needs to assess the **availability** of such funds.

(viii) The project will not **pay back** until year 4. Is this in line with current guidelines within the company?

(c) **Sensitivity analysis to changes in the selling price**

The sensitivity of individual variables is measured as follows:

$$\frac{\text{NPV of the project}}{\text{PV of the cash flow affected}}$$

At a selling price of £425 the project's **NPV is £2,947,000.** If the sales revenue in years 2 to 4 fell by more than this amount in present value terms, the project would no longer be financially viable.

Sales revenue in each of years 2 to 4 = £6,375,000.

This is (using cumulative PV factors at 7%) £6,375,000 × (3.387 – 0.935) = **£15,631,500 in PV terms.**

∴ The project is **no longer financially** viable if the **PV of sales revenue falls by (2,947,000/15,631,500)** × 100% = 18.9%

∴ The selling price can **fall by 18.9% to £345** before the project becomes unviable.

The financial viability of the project is therefore **not particularly sensitive** to changes in selling price. VI plc should bear in mind, however, that a **competing organisation**, able to take advantage of greater experience curve benefits, could **undercut prices**.

45 Question with analysis: Q Organisation

Text references. Chapter 8 explains the product life cycle and pricing. Chapter 15 explains the learning curve, Chapter 8 again should give you material to help you calculate an optimum price.

Top tips. Part (a) of the question requires you to identify the four stages of the product life cycle and the appropriate pricing policies for each stage. Think about the product and apply your knowledge to this specific product.

Part (b)(i) requires you to remember how to calculate a rate of learning and a learning curve.

Part (b)(ii) should just follow on: once you have total variable costs for each level of demand you can calculate the optimal contribution.

Part (b)(iii) requires a careful reading of the question – you need to calculate the average variable cost for each learning stage after the initial phase identified in part (ii).

Examiner's comments. Most students made a good attempt at this question but many did not actually answer the question. In part (b), too many candidates had only a basic understanding of the learning curve!

Common errors noted by the examiner include:

- Describing life cycle costing rather than the product life cycle
- Not relating appropriate pricing policies to the stage of the product life cycle
- Suggesting inappropriate pricing policies
- Not using initiative by introducing the figure calculated in part (b)(i) into part (b)(ii)
- Applying the learning curve formula incorrectly especially when the quantity being produced falls outside the 'doubling' process (part (b)(ii))
- Applying the learning curve effect to the full £60
- Not understanding what was required in part (iii)

ANSWERS

(a) The product life cycle comprises four stages:

- Introduction
- Growth
- Maturity
- Decline

> *In the answer, the key words and stages of the product life cycle are in bold*

> **Easy marks**. The examiner gave two marks for identifying the four stages correctly.

In the **introduction stage** the company needs to price the product to achieve its market strategy using either **penetration or skimming pricing policies**.

A **penetration policy** is used with the **objective of achieving a high level of demand very quickly by using a low price that is affordable to a large number of potential customers**. This has the effect of discouraging new suppliers to the market because the unit profitability is relatively low, but the high volume of sales enables the initial supplier to recover their development costs.

A **skimming policy** is particularly **appropriate to a product that has a novelty value or that is technologically advanced**. Such a policy uses a **price that is high and this restricts the volume of sales** since only high worth customers can afford the product, but **the high unit profitability enables the initial supplier to recover their development costs**. However, the high unit profitability attracts competitors to the market so that it is important for the initial supplier to be able to reduce the price and can prevent new entrants to the market from being able to reverse engineer the product and make significant profits from little or no development investment.

The Q organisation is launching a technologically advanced product which will be demanded by high worth customers who are proud to be amongst the first to own such a state of the art product. This is exactly the type of product for which a price skimming policy is appropriate.

The initial price will be high as this will quickly recover the development costs of the product. The high worth customers will not be deterred from buying the product as it will be sold on the basis of its technological value rather than its price.

Competitors will be attracted to the product by its high price and will seek to compete with it by introducing their own version of the product at much lower development costs (by reverse engineering Q's product) so it is important for Q to **reduce the price** during the **growth stage** of the product's life cycle There may be many price reductions during this phase so that the product gradually becomes more affordable to lower social economic groups.

As the product enters the **maturity stage** the price will need to be **lowered further**, though a profitable contribution ratio would continue to be earned. Oligopolistic competition is often found in this stage, but provided Q has gained market share and survived until this stage the opportunity to make profit and cash surpluses should exist. **However, in this type of market the price will tend to be set by the market and Q will have to accept that price**. Thus Q will need to focus on the control of its costs to ensure that the product will remain profitable.

When the product enters the **decline phase** a **loyal group of customers** may continue to be prepared to pay **a reasonable price** and at this price the product will continue to be profitable, especially as costs continue to reduce. **Eventually the price will be lowered to marginal cost or even lower in** order to sell off inventories of what is now an obsolete product as it has been replaced by a more technologically advanced item.

> **Top tips**. The examiner gave eight marks for discussing the pricing policies appropriate to each stage of the product life cycle.
>
> See the comments in bold – these are key phases that will get you marks.
>
> Remember to look at Q's specific product to determine which pricing policy applies.

ANSWERS

(b) (i)

Cumulative number of units	Total variable cost/unit £	Affected by learning £	Not affected by learning £
10,000	60.00	30.00	30.00
20,000	56.10 (W2)	26.10	30.00
30,000	54.06 (w3)	24.06	30.00
40,000	52.71	22.71	30.00

Workings

(1) Calculation of rate of learning

At 10,000 units, variable cost affected by learning = £30

At 40,000 units, variable cost affected by learning = £22.71

Let the rate of learning be r.

$30r^2$ = 22.71

r^2 = 0.757

r = 0.87

> **Easy marks**. The examiner gave four marks for just this calculation!

(2) We can now derive the variable cost affected by learning for 20,000 units,
= 30r = 30 × 0.87 = 26.10

The variable cost affected by learning for 30,000 units will require the use of a formula for the learning curve.

a = £30
= 3

b = log0.87/log2
= –0.201

Thus Y = aX^b
= 30 × $3^{-0.201}$
= 24.06

(ii) Optimum price at which the DVD recorder should be sold.

Demand in Units	Price/unit £	Variable cost /unit £	Contribution/ unit £	Total contribution £
10,000	100	60.00	40.00	400,000
20,000	80	56.10	23.90	478,000
30,000	69	54.06	14.94	448,200
40,000	62	52.71	9.29	371,600

The price which gives the optimum contribution is £80/unit.

> **Top tips**. Doing this calculation and identifying the best price would get you three marks.

(iii) The initial launch phase identified in (b)(ii) is up to a level of at 20,000 units.

The target contribution is £45,000 per month.

ANSWERS

To determine unit costs if after the initial phase, total volume is between 20,000 and 30,000 units, the average cost would be

$$\frac{30,000 \times 54.06 - 20,000 \times 56.10}{10,000} = £49.98$$

Likewise between 30,000 and 40,000 units, the average cost would be
$$\frac{40,000 \times 52.71 - 30,000 \times 54.06}{10,000} = £48.66$$

total volume

> After initial launch phase market price is £57/unit

Therefore, at between 20,000 and 30,000 units, the required sales level is calculated as:

£45,000 / £(57 – 49.98) = 6,410 units

Likewise between 30,000 and 40,000 units, required sales are:

£45,000 / £(57 – 48.66)
= 5,396 units

46 TQ (Pilot paper)

Text references. Chapter 8 covers profit-maximising price calculations. Chapter 9 will give you material to put in the report on different pricing strategies.

Top tips. You may have floundered around for a few minutes at the beginning of this question, not knowing quite how to start. Unless the examiner is being very mean and the information about the volume variance and the budgeted production and sales volumes are red herrings, you could always use it to find out actual volumes (given that the volume variance is the difference between budgeted and actual volumes). As the link between the demand curve and marginal revenue is provided, hopefully you realised that you had to derive the demand curve, which you couldn't do without the actual volumes. Part (i) certainly needed a fair amount of mathematical ability, but once you grasp the key steps in these questions you should find they become easier with practice.

Easy marks. Start part (b) first. Part (b) was far more straightforward although, as is the case with all written answers, there is no point simply regurgitating book knowledge. You must apply it to the details and circumstances described in the question scenario.

(a) (i) P = a – bx

When P = 100, x = 0

∴ using above equation, a = 100

Using fixed overhead volume variance to find actual sales units:

Fixed overhead volume variance =

(Budgeted units – actual units) × standard fixed overhead rate

Rearranging:

$$\text{Actual units} = \text{budgeted units} - \frac{\text{Fixed overhead volume variance}}{\text{Standard fixed overhead rate}}$$

Period	Budgeted units	−	Fixed overhead volume variance / Standard fixed overhead rate	−	Actual units
1	520	−	1,200/10	−	400
2	590	−	1,900/10	−	400
3	660	−	2,600/10	−	400

213

ANSWERS

Using high-low method to calculate b:

$$b = \frac{\text{Change in P}}{\text{Change in x}}$$

When P = 60, x = 400
P = 100, x = 0

$$b = \frac{(100 - 60)}{400}$$

$$= 0.10$$

So, we can now write equations as:

P = 100 − 0.1x

MR = 100 − 0.2x

To maximise contribution: MR = MC

We assume that MC = variable cost per unit of $25

100 − 0.2x = 25
x = 375

To sell 375 units:

P = 100 − (0.1 × 375)
P = $62.50 (this is the price at which contribution will be maximised).

(ii)

	Optimal price $	Actual price $
Selling price	62.50	60.00
Variable costs	25.00	25.00
Contribution per unit	37.50	35.00
Units sold	375 units	400 units
Total contribution	$14,062.50	£14,000

Difference in contribution = $62.50.

(b) **REPORT**

To: Board of directors
From: Management accountant
Date: 13 March 20X3
Subject: **Alternative pricing strategies**

Following our recent meeting to discuss pricing of our new mobile phone, I set out below a number of alternative strategies that we should consider.

Market skimming

This pricing strategy involves charging **high prices when a product is first launched** and spending heavily on advertising and promotion to obtain sales so as to exploit any price insensitivity in the market. As the product moves into **later stages of its life cycle**, **prices can be reduced** in order to remain competitive. The aim is therefore to gain high unit profits early in the product's life.

A **high price** makes it more likely that **competitors** will **enter** the market, however, and so there must be significant **barriers to entry** or the product must be **differentiated** in some way. The fact that our product is 'state of the art' should provide some level of differentiation.

Such a strategy could be **appropriate** for a number of reasons.

(i) Our product will be new and different and so high prices can be charged to take advantage of its **novelty appeal**.

(ii) Charging high prices in the early stages of the product's (expected) very short life cycle would generate the **high initial cash flows** needed to cover the significant level of development costs we have incurred.

(iii) Once the market has become **saturated**, the product's price could be **reduced** to attract that part of the market that has not been exploited.

Market penetration pricing

This is a policy of **low prices when a product is first launched** in order to **achieve high sales** volumes and hence **gain a significant market share**. If we adopt this strategy it might **discourage competitors** from entering the market. You should note that demand for our **product** is likely to be **inelastic**, however, whereas **penetration pricing** is most suited to products for which demand is **elastic** and so responds well to low prices.

Demand-based approach

This approach is based on the **assumption that there is a profit-maximising combination of price and demand** because demand is elastic. We would need to commission some market research if we were to adopt such a strategy, however, to obtain information about levels of demand at various prices.

There are some significant **drawbacks** to this approach to pricing, however.

(i) It can be difficult to predict the demand curve, even with market research.

(ii) It ignores the market research costs of acquiring the necessary information.

(iii) It assumes that price is the only influence on the quantity demanded. Other factors such as quality of the product, levels of after sales service and so on could also impact.

(iv) It assumes that we have no production constraints that prevent the equilibrium point between supply and demand being met.

The **advantages** of the approach are that if would force management to think about price/demand relationships and to consider the market in which we operate.

Premium pricing

This strategy would involve highlighting the product's 'state of the art' features as a **differentiating factor** to justify a **premium price**.

Price discrimination

A **different price** for the product would be charged to **different groups of buyers** if this strategy were adopted. For example, we could charge a different price if the product were bought on-line to the price charged in retail outlets.

I hope this information proves useful. If you would like to discuss any of the issues further, please get in touch.

ANSWERS

47 Question with answer plan: AVX plc

Text references. Look at Chapter 15 to answer part (a), Chapter 8 for part (b) and Chapters 9 and 15 for part (c).

Top tips. The examiner's post exam guide notes that part (a) was very poorly answered. Therefore we have given you a lot of information to help you answer this. What you need to do can be broken down into easily managed parts.

You may have struggled to know where to start with part (a)(i), and may not have known how to work out the rates of learning. So one approach is to look at the information in the question and see if you can work out what you need to do once you have established the information available. You have a table with batches that double in each subsequent month. What does this remind you of from reading your text? You have standard labour hours and you have labour efficiency variances from which you can work out actual hours.

First, what you need to do is work out the actual hours per month by deducting the favourable efficiency variance (translated into hours by dividing by £10/h) for each month from the standard labour hours for each month. Even if your knowledge of variances is a bit vague it should be possible to work out that a labour efficiency variance is measuring a **speeding up** in activity by labour and so it is measuring how much **quicker** workers become over the six months.

Then work out the cumulative actual hours. Up to this point, the examiner awarded three marks.

Use this to calculate the cumulative average actual hours. He indicated two marks just for this.

Finally divide each month's cumulative average actual hours by that of the following month and this should give the rate of learning. The examiner gave three marks for this. Remember that learning curve theory states that the cumulative average time per unit falls by a constant percentage [the rate of learning] every time total output of the product doubles.

Finally, he gave two marks for discussing the implications of the learning effect.

Part (b) was well answered so we don't need to dwell on this. Four marks could be earned for deriving the price equation and then the rest of the marks were for applying this equation to get a profit-maximising selling price.

Part (c) saw many candidates describing market skimming and penetration rather than identifying that the company needed to move from a cost plus price to a target price method. Up to four marks were possible for the differences between standard and target costs and three marks for explaining the reasons to reconsider pricing policy.

Easy marks. The second part of the question requires you to calculate a profit-maximising selling price using data from the question. The formula is given. If you know that MR = MC (and you should), you just need to slot the data into the formula to calculate the answer.

Then the final part of the question asked in part (i) for an explanation of the difference between standard and target costs. This is book knowledge and should have presented you with few problems.

Examiner's comments. A range of responses, thus part (a) was poorly answered and many candidates couldn't relate the efficiency variant to the learning aim. Part (b) was very well answered. Part (c) revealed basic flaws in understanding such as not being able to explain 'standard cost' and not picking up from c(i) that AVX needed to move from cost plus pricing to target selling.

Answer plan

Step 1   Set out a table   – batches, month and YID
                               – standard hours
                               – actual hours and YID

Calculate average actual hours for batch

Calculate rate of learning

216

ANSWERS

Step 2 Marginal cost – stated in question
Calculate price equation
Calculate MR equation
MR = MC = profit maximising price

Step 3 Standard cost
Target cost
Reasons why AVX should revisit pricing policy – new entrants
– competition

(a) (i) **Rates of learning**

We have drawn up the table below based on the method sketched out in our top tips above. The data has been worked out and set out sequentially as follows:

Step 1 Take the number of batches in each month and work out the cumulative batches to date.

Step 2 Work out the standard hours per month (standard hours per batch multiplied by the number of batches produced in the month).

Step 3 Work out the actual hours per month by deducting the appropriate labour efficiency variance **in hours** (divide the monetary variance by £10 to get the number of hours) from the standard hours per month. We deduct the variance because the actual hours are less than the standard hours, as indicated by the fact that the variance is favourable.

Step 4 Work out the cumulative actual hours by adding each month's actual hours to the total of preceding months.

Step 5 Work out the cumulative average actual hours by dividing the cumulative actual hours by the cumulative batches produced.

Step 6 Finally, work out the rate of learning, which is each month's cumulative average actual hours divided by that of the preceding month.

Month	Batches	Cumulative batches	Standard hours per month	Actual hours per month	Cumulative actual hours	Cumulative Average actual hours	Rate of learning
November	1	1	50.0	50.00	50.00	50.00	–
December	1	2	50.0	33.00	83.00	41.50	0.83
January	2	4	100.0	54.78	137.78	34.45	0.83
February	4	8	200.0	91.07	228.85	28.61	0.83
March	8	16	400.0	228.85	457.70	28.61	0
April	16	32	800.0	457.70	915.40	28.61	0

(ii) From the table it is clear that the **learning period ended** after February when the rate of learning was at 83%. This means that after February the production time taken is no longer decreasing and so labour efficiency savings are not being made. The company could look at training and review processes to see if the **learning process could be continued** or consider switching to a more mechanised process. This also means that the company should make **decisions** involving costs, for instance profit maximisation and pricing policy decisions, **based on this now constant labour time per batch**.

ANSWERS

(b) **Profit-maximising selling price per batch**

The formula as given in the question is P = a – bx and MR = a – 2bx, where a = price at which demand is nil.

Demand is 16 batches at a price of £1,200 (£960 + 25% mark up) and demand varies by 1 batch for every £20 change in price so b = 20.

Marginal cost is £672.72 from the question.

The price at which demand would be nil = £1,200 + £20 × 16 = £1,520.

So, putting these into the equation:

P = 1,520 – 20x

Price is maximised when MR = MC

MR = 1,520 – 40x = £672.72

Therefore x = 21.18

And P = 1,520 – 20 × 21.18

= £1,096.40.

This is the profit maximising selling price per batch for product CB45.

(c) (i) **The difference between standard costs and target costs**

A **standard cost** is an expected cost for a unit of product or service based on the resources required (materials, labour etc) and the expected prices for the resources. Standard costs are used in standard costing systems, which aim to control an organisation's costs.

A **target cost** is calculated by deducting a target profit from a predetermined selling price based on customers' views. Functional analysis, value engineering and value analysis are used to change production methods and/or reduce expected costs so that the target cost is met. This is all part of a target costing system.

Target costs are therefore based on the price set by the external market, a factor over which an organisation has no control. Standard costs, on the other hand, are internally-derived costs to be used as part of an internal control system.

(ii) **Review of pricing policy**

When the product was **new** and the price was first set, this was possibly the **only product of its kind in the market**. So the price charged was **high**. The price was based on earning a 25% margin on the cost, to ensure a profit was made. This strategy of setting high prices when a product is first launched is known as **market skimming**.

The product has now been on the market for six months. **Competitors** have entered the market with their own versions. They have able to work out how the product is made and hence **copy** it. AVX plc is therefore probably facing competition and is unable to sell at £1,200 per batch. The price therefore needs to be **successively lowered** in order to **maintain some market share** and continue to earn profits. By adopting **target costing** and applying continual pressure to ensure target costs are met, the organisation can charge prices that the market will pay and maintain profits.

ANSWERS

48 Section A answers: Basic principles of investment decision making

1   B   Net present value is the appraisal method to adopt when mutually exclusive projects exist.

2   NPV   – **not based on accounting profits**
      IRR   – **not based on accounting profits**
      Payback – **not based on accounting profits**
      ARR   – **based on accounting profits**

3   The NPV = £((7,000) × 1,000 + £5,000 × 0.870 + £800 × 0.756 + £2,700 × 0.658) = –£268.60.

4   A   The method takes account of all cash flows relating to the project – **true**
      B   It allows for the timing of the cash flows – **true**
      C   There are universally-accepted methods of calculating the NPV and the IRR – **true**
      D   It is the method favoured by the majority of companies – **false**

A: The method takes into account all the relevant cash flows that arise as a result of the project being undertaken.

B: The use of discount rates incorporates the effects of the time value of money into the calculations.

C: The universality of methods used means that projects can be compared widely.

D: Although many companies do use DCF techniques, the most universally-favoured approach is still the payback method.

5   A   Both methods give the same accept or reject decision, regardless of the pattern of the cash flows – **false**
      B   IRR is technically superior to NPV and easier to calculate – **false**
      C   The NPV approach is superior if discount rates are expected to vary over the life of the project – **true**
      D   NPV and accounting ROCE can be confused – **false**

A: The methods only give the same accept or reject decision when the cash flows are conventional. When the cash flow patterns are non-conventional, there may be several IRRs that decision makers must be aware of to avoid making the wrong decision.

B: On the contrary, NPV is technically superior to IRR and easier to calculate.

C: Variable discount rates can be incorporated easily into NPV calculations, but not into IRR calculations.

D: NPV is dissimilar to accounting ROCE, but IRR can be confused with ROCE since both measures are expressed in percentage terms.

6   D   The present value of £5,000 in perpetuity is calculated as £5,000/0.1.

           If you selected **option A,** you might have calculated £5,000 × 10%.

           If you selected **option B,** you might have calculated £5,000 × 110%.

           If you selected **option C,** you might have calculated £5,000/110%.

7   A   I is not a disadvantage because the fact that it tends to bias in favour of short-term projects means that it tends to minimise both financial and business risk.

           II is untrue. It is simple to calculate and simple to understand, which may be important when management resources are limited.

           III is not a disadvantage because it helps to identify those projects which generate additional cash for investment quickly.

8   The NPV is (£200,000 × 1.000) + (£35,000 × 3.170) = £310,950.

ANSWERS

49 Intranet I

> **Top tips.** This question examines the different methods of project appraisal used by organisations.
>
> You need to relate all aspects of your answer to the scenario, so include payback and ARR calculations for the Intranet project.
>
> In part (c) you need to consider investments in IT-related areas in particular.
>
> **Easy marks.** You will get a mark or so for using a report format.

REPORT

To: Management of P
From: Management accountant
Date: 3 December 20X2
Subject: **Investment in installation of an Intranet**

1 Introduction

1.1 This report will consider the existing methods of appraising capital investment projects within P and will provide a financial recommendation as to whether or not the project should be undertaken.

2 Existing methods of project appraisal (part (a))

2.1 Accounting rate of return method

2.1.1 The accounting rate of return (ARR) is based on **the ratio of average accounting profit from an investment to the average capital employed**. A project will be **undertaken** if its **estimated** ARR is **greater** than a **target** ARR, which in P's case is 25%.

2.1.2 **The ARR for this investment** is:

	£'000
Total cash savings	4,350
Less: depreciation	2,000
Accounting profit	2,350

Life of project	10 years
Average accounting profit	£235,000

∴ ARR = (235/1,000) × 100% = 23.5%

2.1.3 **Using ARR**, the project would therefore **not be given the go ahead** as its **ARR is less than the target rate**.

2.1.4 As a method of project appraisal its most serious **drawback** is that **it does not take account of the timing of the profits** from the project. Money tied up as an investment in one project cannot be invested elsewhere until it starts to earn profits.

2.1.5 And this is not its only **disadvantage**.

(i) It is based on accounting profits, which are subject to a number of different accounting treatments, making comparisons problematic.

(ii) It is a relative measure and so takes no account of the size of the investment.

(iii) It takes no account of the length of the project.

(iv) It ignores the time value of money.

2.1.6 Despite these criticisms, it is a **popular** method of project appraisal due to the fact that not only is it **quick** and **easy to calculate and understand,** but it produces a percentage rate of return, a concept with which non-finance managers are familiar. In addition it incorporates **profit flows from the entire life of the project**,

ANSWERS

which the payback method (see below) does not. And when applied to relatively minor short-run decisions it gives acceptable decision advice.

2.2 Payback method

2.2.1 The payback period is the **time taken for the cash inflows from a project to equal the cash outflows**. A **target** payback period is **set** (which for P is four years) and if the project's payback period **exceeds** this then it is **not acceptable**.

2.2.2 The **payback period for this investment** is:

Year	Cash flow £'000	Cumulative cash position £'000
0	(2,000)	(2,000)
1	400	(1,600)
2	400	(1,200)
3	400	(800)
4	500	(300)
5	500	200

Payback period = $4^{3}/_{5}$ years = 4 years 7 months

2.2.3 The **project** would therefore be **rejected** if payback were to be used as an initial screening test.

2.2.4 The method suffers from a number of serious disadvantages. It ignores the timing of cash flows within the payback period, the cashflows after the end of the payback period and therefore the total project return. And, like the ARR method, it ignores the time value of money.

2.2.5 There are also a number of other **problems** with using it to appraise projects.

(i) It cannot distinguish between projects with the same payback period.

(ii) The choice of cut-off period is arbitrary.

(iii) It can lead to excessive investment in short-term projects.

(iv) Although it takes account of the risk of the timing of cash flows, it does not take account of the variability of those cash flows.

2.2.6 It does have a number of **advantages**, however, especially if used as **an initial screening device.**

(i) It is quick and straightforward to calculate and is easily understood by non finance managers.

(ii) It focuses attention on early cash flows, indicating projects likely to improve liquidity positions.

(iii) By ignoring cash flows occurring further in the future, it can be said to reduce risk.

2.2.7 If a project gets through the first screening process provided by evaluation of payback, it should then be evaluated using a more sophisticated project appraisal technique.

2.2.8 **Discounted payback** (the time it takes before a project's cumulative NPV turns from negative to positive) can be used as an initial screening test to take account, to an extent, of the time value of money.

3 Financial analysis (part (b))

3.1 If either **ARR or payback** were used to appraise the project, it would have been **rejected**. This would have been an **incorrect decision**, however, as the **NPV** calculation shows.

3.2

Time	Cashflow £'000	Discount factor 15%	PV £'000
0	(2,000)	1.000	(2,000.00)
1-3	400	2.283	913.20
4-5	500	3.352 – 2.283 = 1.069	534.50
6-8	450	4.487 – 3.352 = 1.135	510.75
9-10	400	5.019 – 4.487 = 0.532	212.80
			171.25

ANSWERS

3.3 On a purely **financial basis** the project should therefore be **undertaken** as it has a positive NPV of £171,250. This means the return is greater than the 15% required return and that the project provides an additional £171,250 for shareholder wealth. Use of **discounted payback** in conjunction with the NPV calculation would ensure that the **speed of repayments** was also **considered**.

4 Difficulties associated with the NPV method when appraising investments such as the installation of an Intranet (part (c))

4.1 Investment in tangible manufacturing equipment will more than likely give rise to specific outflows of cash. **Cash flows** from an IT project are **less likely to be as easily identifiable or measurable**. Estimates of the financial impact of customer use of the Intranet, for example, can only be 'guesstimates'. Probabilities could be used to incorporate uncertainty into the appraisal process.

4.2 The **estimation of the future life** of an IT investment is made **difficult** by the **rapid rate of technological change** in this area. Benefits may materialise over the long term, outside the time period considered.

4.3 P's 15% cost of capital may not be entirely appropriate for discounting purposes. A **higher discount factor** could be used to reflect the risk associated with an IT project.

4.4 It is possible that a **negative NPV** will be generated from an IT project such as that currently being considered. The decision should be based on management's assessment of whether the negative NPV is a price worth paying for the intangible benefits of the system (enhanced corporate image, for example).

5 Conclusion

5.1 I would **recommend** this **project** be **undertaken** and that in future we **use NPV** methods and **discounted payback** to appraise capital investments.

5.2 If you have any questions or comments about the contents of this report please do not hesitate to contact me.

50 Intranet II

> **Top tips.** This should have been straightforward if you had worked through the questions in the back of the text and others in this Kit.
>
> Read the hints in the question! So 'describe' how 'discuss benefits' 'discuss drawbacks'. Three parts and 3–4 marks gives you the format for your answer.

Undertaking a post-completion appraisal for the Intranet project

A post-completion appraisal involves **comparing the actual results of the project with the estimated results** that were included in the investment appraisal. The comparison exercise should use the **same method of appraisal** as that used in making the investment decision. Where possible, actual cash flows to date plus estimated cash flows to the end of the project's life should be compared with the cash flows incorporated in the original appraisal. The ability to carry out such a comparison will depend on the ease and cost of estimating future cash flows, however. If **actual plus forecast flows are different (unfavourably) to those estimated, an investigation** will be required.

Benefits for management of P of undertaking such an exercise

Post-completion appraisal cannot reverse the decision to incur capital expenditure, because the expenditure will already have taken place, but it will have some **control value**.

(a) The **threat** of a post-completion audit will **motivate** managers to work to achieve the promised benefits from the project.

(b) If the appraisal takes place before the end of the project life, and if it is found that the benefits have been less than expected because of management inefficiency in promoting the Intranet to suppliers, say, steps can be taken to **improve efficiency**. Alternatively it might highlight the fact that the project should be discontinued.

(c) It can help to **highlight** those **mangers** that have been instrumental in making the Intranet a **success**.

(d) It might **identify weaknesses** in the **forecasting and estimating techniques** used to evaluate projects within P, and so should help to improve the discipline and quality of forecasting for future investment decisions that the company might make.

(e) Areas where **improvements** can be made in **methods to achieve better results in general** from capital investments might be revealed.

(f) **Original estimates** of cash flows might be **more realistic** if mangers are aware that they will be monitored, but post-completion audits should not be unfairly critical.

Possible drawbacks of undertaking a post-completion appraisal

As well as being **expensive** and **time consuming**, they also suffer from a number of other problems.

(a) It may **not be possible to identify separately** those **costs** and **benefits** associated with the Intranet project.

(b) The fact that it is an IT project increases the **uncontrollable factors** which impact on its success but which are outside management control. Obsolescence is one example.

(c) The exercise may lead **managers** to become **over cautious** and **unnecessarily risk averse** if they are unfairly punished for worse than expected outcomes.

(d) The **strategic effects** of a capital investment project may **take years to materialise** and it may never be possible to identify or quantify them effectively.

51 JLX plc

> **Top tips.** You do not need to include a definition and explanation of PCA in part (a). We have included it to help you with your revision.
>
> This is fairly straightforward question, the case details can be easily incorporated into your answers to make them relevant and there are no 'tricks' or complicating factors lurking under the surface.
>
> **Easy marks.** You would probably gain one mark simply for answering the question asked in part (a). Arguments supporting this (with reference to JLX plc) would probably earn one or two marks per point made.

(a) Post-completion appraisal (PCA) involves measurement of the success of a capital expenditure project in terms of **the realisation of anticipated benefits.** PCA should cover the implementation of the project from authorisation to commissioning and its **technical and commercial performance** after commissioning. The information provided by the appraisal can also be used by management as **feedback** to help with the implementation and control of future projects.

Reasons for carrying out PCAs

Given that JLX is a manufacturing organisation and therefore likely to make capital expenditure for new machinery, say, on a fairly regular basis, the claimed benefits of the use of PCA could be significant.

(i) **Learning aspect.** PCA should highlight areas where improvements can be made in methods that should help to achieve better results in general fro capital investment. This is particularly applicable if investments have similar characteristics, which could well be the case in the manufacturing environment within which JLX operates.

(ii) **Improved forecasting.** PCA might identify weaknesses in the forecasting and estimating techniques used to provide information for NPV calculations, and so should help to improve the discipline and quality of forecasting for future investments.

ANSWERS

(iii) **Behavioural implications**

(1) Following from (ii) above, PCA could highlight the fact that ambitious managers are being overoptimistic in their forecasting in order to be associated with high-profile projects. This is more likely to occur within an organisation structured on a divisional basis, with divisional managers competing against each other. The fact that managers know that projects are being subject to PCA should make their original estimates more accurate, however.

(2) The 'threat' of a PCA should motivate managers to work to achieve the benefits promised from the project.

(3) PCA should also help to identify those managers who have been good performers and those who have been poor performers.

(iv) **Improved efficiency**. If the appraisal takes place before the end of the project's life, and it finds that the benefits have been less than expected because of management inefficiency, steps can be taken to improve efficiency.

(v) **Discontinuance**. Following on from (iv) above, the appraisal could alternatively highlight those projects which should be discontinued.

Problems associated with PCAs

PCA is a costly and time consuming exercise, however, and the process does have other disadvantages.

(i) **Effect on managers**. It can lead managers to become over cautious and unnecessarily risk averse.

(ii) **Identification of costs/benefits.** It may not be possible to identify separately the costs and benefits of a particular project. The strategic implication of a capital investment project may take years to materialise and in fact it may never be possible to identify or quantify them effectively.

(iii) **Uncontrolled factors**. Management might not always be able to ensure a particular project achieves the anticipated benefits because of uncontrollable factors outside their control which arise in long-term decisions, such an environmental changes.

Given these problems, senior management at JLX need to weigh up the value that PCAs can bring to the organisations.

They also need to bear in mind that PCAs were **neglected** because of the increased workload but the group finance director is using PCA on PR035 as a **lever to gain more funds.** So does the group finance director consider them an essential control tool or is he simply using them to enhance his own position within the organisation?

Behavioural issues as well as monetary implications are therefore important.

(b) If an organisation operates a system of PCA, all projects should be submitted to scrutiny.

(i) Analysis of a successful project should highlight **the reason why the project was successful.** This knowledge can then be applied to future projects to increase their chances of success.

(ii) Some projects may appear to be **performing poorly** but are actually **relatively successful given actual circumstances**. For example, the occurrence of unexpected events such as the terrorist attack in New York in September 2001 can be significant unforeseen impact on projects. Yet projects might be performing satisfactorily given actual operating conditions.

(iii) Likewise, an **apparently successful project** might only **be performing well because of differences between predicted and actual circumstances.** The recent favourable trading conditions experienced by JLX could well be the reason for the success of PR035.

The application of a PCA will therefore ensure that **apparent success** does not lead to **complacency** and that **apparent failure** does not lead to management **aversion to risk, lack of motivation** and to **'punishment'** for not achieving expected returns.

… ANSWERS

52 HPC Ltd

> **Text references.** You need to draw on your study of Chapters 6 and 11 to give a good answer here.
>
> **Top tips.** You needed to rely on your knowledge of linear programming in this question. Part (a) was particularly tricky. Did you have problems defining the constraints? Perhaps you didn't know if 100,000 ≥ 1.4x + y, or x/1.4 + y, or x + y/1.4, or x + 1.4y. Imagine there is no output of LPG, so y = 0. Output of oil must be 100,000 and so the coefficient of x must be 1. Now, 1.4 barrels of LPG can be transported for each barrel of oil and so if x = 0, y must be greater than 100,000. And so the coefficient of y must be less than 1.
>
> The rail transport capacity constraint was very difficult to define. It needed to be split into two. The first part was fairly straightforward (when 0 ≤ y ≤ 20,000) but the second part had to cover the range when y > 20,000 and x < 100,000 (because 20,000 of the 120,000 barrels had already been allocated to y). So don't worry if you got this wrong. You would have got the majority of the marks for the derivation of the other constraints, the graph and so on.

(a) We begin by formulating the problem.

Define variables

Let x = annual output of oil
Let y = annual output of LPG

Establish objective function

We want to maximise NPV.

10 year 12% annuity factor = 5.650

∴ PV of contribution from one barrel of oil = 5.650 × £8 = £45.2
PV of contribution from one barrel of LPG = 5.650 × £11.50 = £64.975

Capital costs are £40 per barrel of oil (£40,000 ÷ 1,000) and £60 per barrel of LPG (£60,000 ÷ 1,000).

∴ NPV per barrel of oil = £(45.2 – 40) = £5.20
NPV per barrel of LPG = £(64.975 – 60) = £4.975

∴ Objective is to maximise NPV = £5.20x + £4.975y

Define constraints

- Pipeline capacity: 100,000 ≥ x + y/1.4
- Processing capacity (1): 150,000 ≥ x + y/0.5333
- Processing capacity (2): 70,000 ≥ y
- Rail transport capacity (1): 120,000 ≥ x + y (where 0 ≤ y ≤ 20,000)
- Rail transport capacity (2): 100,000 ≥ x + (y – 20,000)/0.65 (where x < 100,000 and y > 20,000)

Graph constraints and highlight feasible area

- Pipeline capacity: 100,000 ≥ x + y/1.4

  When x = 0, y = 140,000
  When y = 0, x = 100,000

- Processing capacity (1): 150,000 ≥ x + y/0.5333

  When x = 0, y = 79,995
  When y = 0, x = 150,000

- Processing capacity (2): 70,000 ≥ y

  Graph the line y = 70,000

- Rail transport capacity (1): 120,000 ≥ x + y

  When x = 0, y = 120,000
  When y = 0, x = 120,000
  When y = 20,000, x = 100,000

- Rail transport capacity (2): 100,000 ≥ x + (y – 20,000)/0.65

ANSWERS

When x = 0, y = 85,000
When y = 20,000, x = 100,000

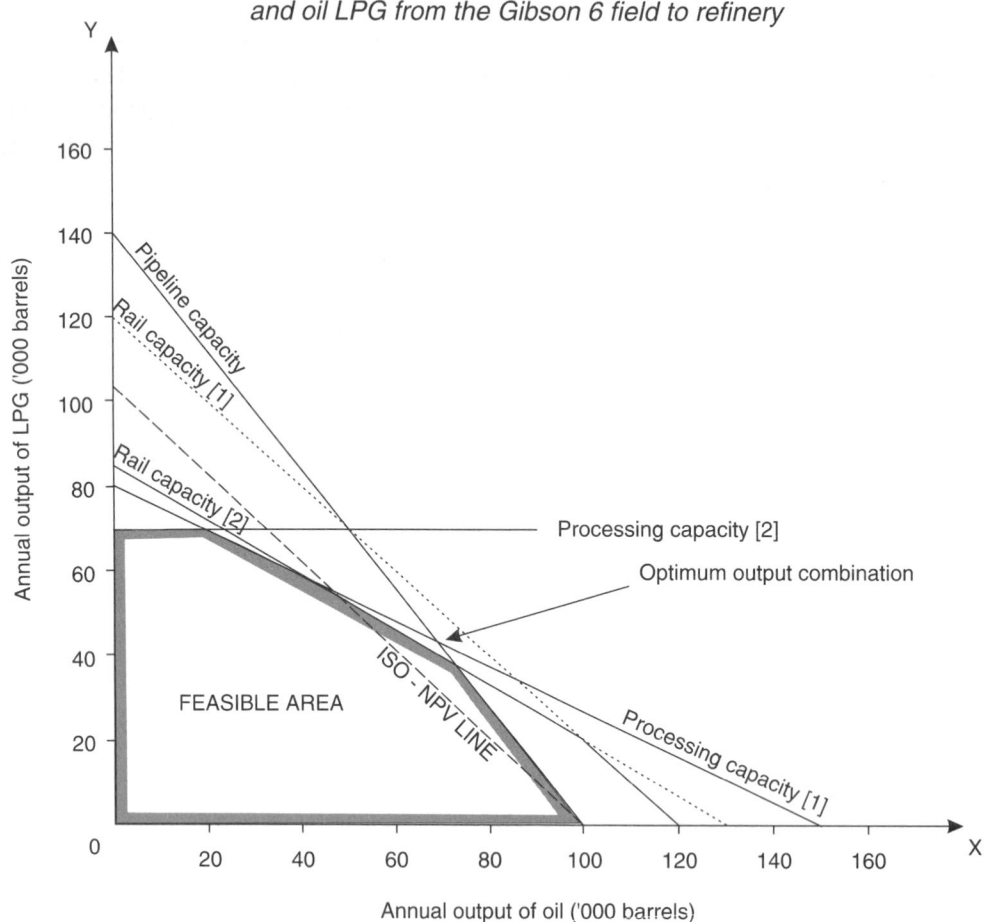

HPC - Constraints on the production and transport of oil and oil LPG from the Gibson 6 field to refinery

[Graph showing feasible area with constraints: Pipeline capacity, Rail capacity [1], Rail capacity [2], Processing capacity [1], Processing capacity [2], Iso-NPV line, and Optimum output combination. X-axis: Annual output of oil ('000 barrels), Y-axis: Annual output of LPG ('000 barrels)]

The feasible area is the area in which all the constraints are satisfied.

Add an iso-NPV line

The objective is to maximise 5.2x + 4.975y (or approx 5.2x + 5y)

Consider 5.2x + 5y = 520,000

If x = 0, y = 104,000
If y = 0, x = 100,000

Plot these points and join with a straight line.

Identify the optimal solution

Moving the iso-NPV line away from the origin, the furthest point within the feasible area touched by the line is the optimal solution. This appears to be the intersection of the pipeline capacity constraint and rail transport capacity constraint (2).

∴ At the optimal solution:
100,000 − x − y/1.4 = 100,000 − x − (y − 20,000)/0.65

∴ y/1.4 = y/0.65 − 20,000/0.65
37,333 = y

∴ Using pipeline capacity constraint:
100,000 = x + (37,333/1.4)

∴ 73,334 = x

Conclusion

The optimal solution is to produce 73,334 barrels of oil and 37,333 barrels of LPG.

(b) The **optimum profit is affected by pipeline capacity** and so the option should be considered. The **new pipeline capacity constraint** would be:

$$(100{,}000 \times 1.1) \geq x + y/1.4$$
ie $\quad 110{,}000 \geq x + y/1.4$

The **intersection of this constraint with the rail transport capacity** constraint can be found as follows.

$110{,}000 - x - y/1.4 = 100{,}000 - x - (y - 20{,}000)/0.65$
$10{,}000 - 20{,}000/0.65 = y/1.4 - y/0.65$
$25{,}200 = y$

∴ Using the revised pipeline capacity constraint:

$110{,}000 = x + (25{,}200/1.4)$
$92{,}000 = x$

The **revised optimal output** is 92,000 barrels of gas and 25,200 barrels of LPG.

Let's **compare the NPVs for the original optimal solution and the revised optimal** solution.

		Original solution £		Revised solution £
NPV from oil	(73,334 × £5.20)	381,336.800	(92,000 × £5.20)	478,400
NPV from LPG	(37,333 × £4.975)	185,731.675	(25,200 × £4.975)	125,370
				603,770
Less: additional capital costs		–		(50,000)
Total NPV		567,068.475		553,770

The **NPV has fallen by £13,298 and so the option should not be pursued.**

53 Section A answers: Further aspects of investment decision making

1 Project 4 has the lowest annualised equivalent and so should be rejected.

Project	1	2	3	4
Investment (£)	66,000	72,000	60,000	43,000
Life (years)	3	6	8	4
Annual receipts (£)	31,000	20,000	16,000	17,000
Cumulative discount factor	2.577	4.623	5.747	3.312
NPV	13,887	20,460	31,952	13,304
Annualised equivalent	5,389	4,426	5,560	4,017

2 The initial investment can rise by £246,000 before the project breaks even and so it may increase by $(246{,}000/714{,}000) \times 100\% = 34\%$.

ANSWERS

3 Lowest annualised equivalent cost is over a two-year replacement cycle.

Year	0	1	2	3	4
Discount factor	1.000	0.926	0.857	0.794	0.735
Outflows (£)	(28,000)	(12,000)	(14,000)	(15,000)	(17,000)
PV of outflows (£)	(28,000)	(11,112)	(11,998)	(11,910)	(12,495)
Year-end disposal value (£)		20,000	18,000	12,000	6,000
PV of disposal value (£)		18,520	15,426	9,528	4,410
NPV of replacement at year-end (£)		(20,592)	(35,684)	(53,492)	(71,105)
Cumulative 8% discount factor (£)		0.926	1.783	2.577	3.312
Annualised equivalent (£)		(22,238)	(20,013)	(20,757)	(21,469)

4 **False**. The cost of capital can increase by $((17 - 10)/10) \times 100\% = 70\%$.

5 C

	£
Annual cash flow	320,000
add fixed costs	160,000
Annual contribution	480,000

Contribution per unit = £120

∴ **Annual sales volume** = £480,000/£120 = 4,000 units

Permissible fall in present value of revenue =	£244,170
PV of revenue (4,000 × £180 × 3.791)	÷ £2,729,520
Percentage change in selling price = £244,170/£2,729,520	= 8.9 %

6 EV of year 1 cash flow = 0.2 × £10,000 + 0.5 × £7,000 + 0.3 × £6,400 = £7,420
   EV of year 2 cash flow = 0.2 × £12,000 + 0.5 × £8,000 + 0.3 × £7,200 = £8,560
   EV of year 3 cash flow = 0.2 × £9,000 + 0.5 × £7,600 + 0.3 × £6,200 = £7,460

Year	Cash flow £	Discount factor 10%	PV £
0	(20,000)	1.000	(20,000.00)
1	7,420	0.909	6,744.78
2	8,560	0.826	7,070.56
3	7,460	0.751	5,602.46
			(582.20)

54 Capital rationing

> **Top tips.** This question illustrates the fact that as well as being able to perform techniques, you need to be able to discuss them too, and consider their advantages and disadvantages.

(a) **Profitability index**

The **profitability index** (PI) is the ratio of the **present value** (PV) of the project's **future cash flows** (not including capital investment) **divided by** the PV of the **total capital outlays**.

$$\text{Profitability index} = \frac{\text{Present value of cash inflows}}{\text{Present value of capital outlays}}$$

This ratio measures the PV of future cash flows per £1 of investment, and so indicates **which investments** make the **best use** of the limited resources available.

Assumptions

The profitability index is based upon the following assumptions.

ANSWERS

(i) If a project is not accepted and undertaken during the period of capital rationing, the **opportunity** to undertake it is **lost**. It cannot be postponed until a subsequent period when no capital rationing exists.

(ii) There is **complete certainty** about the outcome of each project, so that the choice between projects is not affected by considerations of risk.

(iii) Projects are **divisible**, so that it is possible to undertake x% of a given project and earn x% of the expected return on that project.

In a capital rationing situation, the project with the **highest PI** will be selected first, and projects will continue to be selected on this basis until the supply of capital is used up.

(b) **Limitations of the PI approach in a capital rationing situation**

(i) The technique has little use when the projects are indivisible because it cannot be used to find the **best combination** of projects that will maximise the NPV.

(ii) It does not take account of differing levels of **risk** between projects. This must be dealt with separately, for example by adjusting the discount rates.

(iii) It does not take into account the **relative strategic importance** of the different projects and the degree to which they fit with the company's wider strategic objectives.

(iv) It ignores the **pattern** of **cash flows** associated with the different projects. This is because it is essentially a **single period model**. However, the speed with which a project starts to generate a positive cash flow may be important to the company's subsequent investment decisions.

(v) As with the internal rate of return method of project appraisal, this technique ignores the **relative size** of the different projects. A project that generates a **large overall return**, albeit over a longer period, may be **more valuable** to the company than one which shows a **high PI**, but a relatively **small absolute return**.

An alternative approach would be to use **linear programming**. This technique aims to maximise the overall level of NPV achieved, subject to defined constraints. However, it also has the problems associated with the assumption of project divisibility.

55 Hypermarket (Pilot paper)

Top tips. In the last year of the replacement cycle the cash flow is the difference between the running costs and the resale value. In all other years the cash flow is the running costs. So for a two-year cycle, the flow in year two is the difference between running costs and resale value, but in year 1 it is the year one running costs.

Easy marks. Remember to set out your workings in a proforma. It is easier for the examiner to mark and for you to use for your calculations.

	Replace after one year		Replace after two years		Replace after three years		Replace after four years		Replace after five years	
Year	Cash flow $'000	PV at 12% $'000	Cash flow $'000	PV at 12% $'000	Cash flow $'000	PV at 12% $'000	Cash flow $'000	PV at 12% $'000	Cash flow $'000	PV at 12% $'000
0	(220)	(220.000)	(220)	(220.000)	(220)	(220.000)	(220)	(220.000)	(220)	(220.000)
1	11	9.823	(110)	(98.230)	(110)	(98.230)	(110)	(98.230)	(110)	(98.230)
2			(44)	(35.068)	(132)	(105.204)	(132)	(105.204)	(132)	(105.204)
3					(88)	(62.656)	(154)	(109.648)	(154)	(109.648)
4							(110)	(69.960)	(165)	(104.940)
5									(151)	(85.617)
PV of cost over one replacement cycle (1)		(210.177)		(353.298)		(486.090)		(603.042)		(723.639)

ANSWERS

Cumulative PV factor (2)	0.893	1.690	2.402	3.037	3.605
Annualised equivalent cost (1)/(2)	$235,361	$209,052	$202,369	$198,565	$200,732

The lowest annualised equivalent cost occurs if the fleet is **replaced every four years**.

56 HP

> **Text references.** This is a very common type of examination question. Although Chapter 12 is a short chapter, the examiner is likely to test your knowledge of tax and inflation.
>
> **Top tips.** Remember to capitalise the installation and removal costs. When calculating incremental contribution look for constraints. Here demand is 12,000 units so the additional contribution of AB is limited to demand and not to its own production capacity. Although the tax sounds complicated, it is really just 50% in the current year and 50% in the following year.
>
> **Easy marks.** Do the WDA calculations first.

(a) **Initial workings**

1 **Capital allowances**

	£	Tax @30% £	Year 1 £	Year 2 £	Year 3 £	Year 4 £	Year 5 £
Machine cost	520,000						
WDA year 1, 25%	130,000	39,000	19,500	19,500			
	390,000						
WDA year 2, 25%	97,500	29,250		14,625	14,625		
	292,500						
WDA year 3, 25%	73,125	21,938			10,969	10,969	
	219,375						
Sale for scrap, year 4	50,000						
Balancing allowance	169,375	50,813				25,406	25,407
Tax payable on contribution (working 2)			(40,320)	(80,640)	(80,640)	(40,320)	
Tax relief on training costs (£5,000 × 30% × 0.5)			750	750			
Total tax recoverable/(payable)			(20,070)	(45,765)	(55,046)	(3,945)	25,407

2 **Incremental contribution**

Demand per week	12,000	units
Demand per hour (12,000/40)	300	units
Current capacity per hour	200	units
Incremental units per hour (300 – 200)	100	units
Contribution per unit	£1.40	
Hours available (40 hours × 48 weeks)	1,920	
Contribution per annum (100 × £1.40 × 1,920)	£268,800	
Tax @ 30%	£80,640	

ANSWERS

Cash flows from profit

Year	Acquisition/ disposal £	Contribution (W2) £	Tax (W1) £	Total cash flow £	Discount factor 10%	Present value £
0	(525,000)			(525,000)	1.000	(525,000)
1		268,800	(20,070)	248,730	0.909	226,096
2		268,800	(45,765)	223,035	0.826	184,227
3		268,800	(55,046)	213,754	0.751	160,529
4	50,000		(3,945)	46,055	0.683	31,456
5			25,407	25,407	0.621	15,778
Net present value						**93,086**

Payback period

Year	Cash flow £	Cumulative cash flow £
0	(525,000)	(525,000)
1	248,730	(276,270)
2	223,035	(53,235)

Payback period = 2 years + (£53,235/£213,754)
= 2.25 years, or approximately 2 years 3 months

The net present value (**NPV**) of the project is **positive** at £93,086 and on that basis it is recommended that the **project should go ahead** after consideration is given to the following.

(i) The company expects a **payback within two years**. In this instance payback is only reached after approximately 2 years and 3 months but this should be over-ridden by the positive NPV.

(ii) The £50,000 **recoverable value** should be reconsidered in light of the fact that the current machine would be scrapped at a cost of £20,000.

(iii) Consideration should be given to **alternatives** such as working overtime on the old machine as a way of alleviating the bottleneck, thus eliminating the need for this investment.

(iv) It is noted that the new machine would be **operating at 60% capacity**. Is there an alternative machine with a capacity matched to our needs of 300 units per hour at a correspondingly lower price? Alternatively, are there actions we could take which would stimulate demand to be closer to our potential 500 unit capacity (assuming there would be no other bottlenecks) which would make this a more attractive investment?

(b) There are a number of **reasons why investment decision making will be different when the investment involves a marketing or IT project rather than tangible manufacturing equipment**.

(i) Although most projects will have specific outflows of cash in the investing period, neither IT nor marketing will necessarily give rise to the same sorts of **identifiable and easily measurable cash flows** as manufacturing equipment. In the case of marketing it may be possible to forecast an expected value of additional revenues as an estimate of future cash inflows, but for IT projects there may not be any easily attributable cash inflow.

(ii) The **estimation of the expected future** life of an IT investment is made difficult by the rapid rate of technological change in this area, and estimating the time that a marketing campaign's impact may be felt is even more problematic.

(iii) In terms of approach it is often recommended that NPV is used as a way of assessing IT investments. A **high discount factor** should be used to reflect the fact that any identified cash inflows are subject to a high risk of obsolescence.

ANSWERS

(iv) It is possible that a **negative net present value** will be generated from an IT project. The investment decision will be based on management's assessment of whether the negative present value is a price worth paying for the intangible benefits of the system (increased user-friendliness, faster processing and so on).

(v) For marketing investments the decision-making approach will depend on the **value of marketing spend**.

(1) For small marketing campaigns it should be adequate merely to consider whether there are sufficient profits available to absorb the cost of the campaign and still leave an acceptable level of reported profit.

(2) For larger proposed expenditure an expected value of revenue increases should be calculated and compared to the campaign cost. The length of the campaign and its expected impact will often be so short that no discount factor will need to be applied to calculate the net present value of the campaign.

57 MN plc

> **Text references.** This question draws on a wide range of material in the syllabus area of long-term decision making. Look at Chapters 10, 11 and 13 for material.
>
> **Top tips.** Even if you found parts of (a) tricky, you should have been able to earn the majority of the marks available for the graph, for using a report format and for part (b).
>
> The examiner at the time this question was set under the previous syllabus version of Paper P2 made a number of interesting comments in her report on part (a). [Emphasis is BPP's.]
>
> - 'Candidates must learn to **read the question carefully** and **answer the question posed** – and only that.
> - The graph was well drawn on the whole, but many candidates felt unable to plot it with just the information given and **spent time** calculating two or three new points to plot per line/project.
> - Many candidates **wasted time** by spending the first page of their report with **lengthy headings** and introduction. Although a report was called for, the quicker the candidate gets to the main content the better.
> - No marks were given for definitions of NPV and IRR.'
>
> **Easy marks.** The question just asks for a graph so just use the information provided to plot this and no more.

(a)   **REPORT**

To: Management of MN plc
From: Management accountant   Date: 3 November 20X1
Subject: **Investments A, B and C**

1   **Introduction**

1.1   This report analyses information about mutually exclusive investments A, B and C provided by the investment manager and provides advice on which project should be accepted.

2   **Sensitivity of the investments to changes in the cost of capital**

2.1   The **graph** in appendix 1 illustrates how the net present value (**NPV**) of each project **varies** with changes in the **cost of capital**. The graph can be used to select the best project at a particular cost of capital. For example, at a cost of capital of 10%, project C is the best option followed by project B and then project A, while at a rate of 16% project A would be preferred.

ANSWERS

3 Reasons for differences between NPV and IRR rankings

3.1 The NPV and internal rate of return (IRR) methods have given completely different rankings for the three projects. There are a number of possible reasons why this has occurred.

3.2 Size of the initial investment

3.2.1 Suppose we were to consider the **size of the projects' NPVs in relation to the size of the initial investment**. The table below shows how the projects would be ranked on such a basis.

	A	B	C
NPV/initial investment	14,376/105,000	22,040/187,000	31,432/245,000
	= 13.7%	= 11.8%	= 12.8%
Ranking	1	3	2

3.2.2 **Project A** gives the **best return** but if project A were to be chosen, **what should the company do with the additional £(245,000 – 105,000) not invested in project C?**

3.2.3 As shown in the table below, the **additional positive net cash flow on this additional investment** is £17,056 **at the cost of capital**. The **return** on the additional investment is therefore **in excess of the cost of capital** (because its NPV is positive).

	Present value 10%		
	A	C	C – A
	£	£	£
Year 0	(105,000)	(245,000)	(140,000)
Years 1 – 3	119,376	119,376	–
Years 4 – 9	–	157,056	157,056
			17,056

3.2.4 If the company can **only reinvest at the cost of capital** during years 4 to 9, project **C** should therefore be **selected** because it offers a higher return. If the funds can be reinvested and earn a return greater than the IRR of the additional cash flow (approximately 12%), project A should be selected.

3.3 The length of the project

3.3.1 Project A lasts for just three years compared with the six-year life of project B and the nine-year life of project C.

3.3.2 An underlying **assumption** of the **NPV appraisal method** is that at the end of the project's life, the **funds released** simply **earn the cost of capital**. In year 4, for example, the funds released from project A are assumed to earn 10% whereas projects B and C are earning higher internal rates of return. For this reason the NPV method ranks project A in third place.

3.3.3 In reality, however, the funds could probably be reinvested at the beginning of year 4 in a project earning a return in excess of 10%, the cost of capital. And if the funds could be reinvested in a project with the same IRR as that of A at the beginning of year 4 and again at the beginning of year 7, the overall investment would be ranked first.

4 Advice

4.1 Project **A** is the best project **if similar investment opportunities exist in year 4 and in year 7**. If this is not the case, project C should be selected.

4.2 There is an additional advantage in selecting short-life project A given the **difficulty in predicting the future correctly**.

4.3 Project A also allows the organisation to keep its **options open** as **funds are only committed for three years**.

4.4 Finally, project A **returns** the initial **capital** outlay **quickly**, thus helping to keep MN plc **liquid**.

ANSWERS

5   I hope you have found this information useful, but if I can offer any further assistance please do not hesitate to contact me.

Signed: Management accountant

Appendix A

The graph of NPV against cost of capital will be a curve, but for our purposes we can approximate this curve to a straight line based on two plotted points.

Decision A

Discount rate %		NPV £
10	£(−105,000 + (2.487 × 48,000))	14,376
17.5	IRR	NIL

Decision B

Discount rate %		NPV £
10	£(−187,000 + (4.355 × 48,000))	22,040
14	IRR	NIL

Decision C

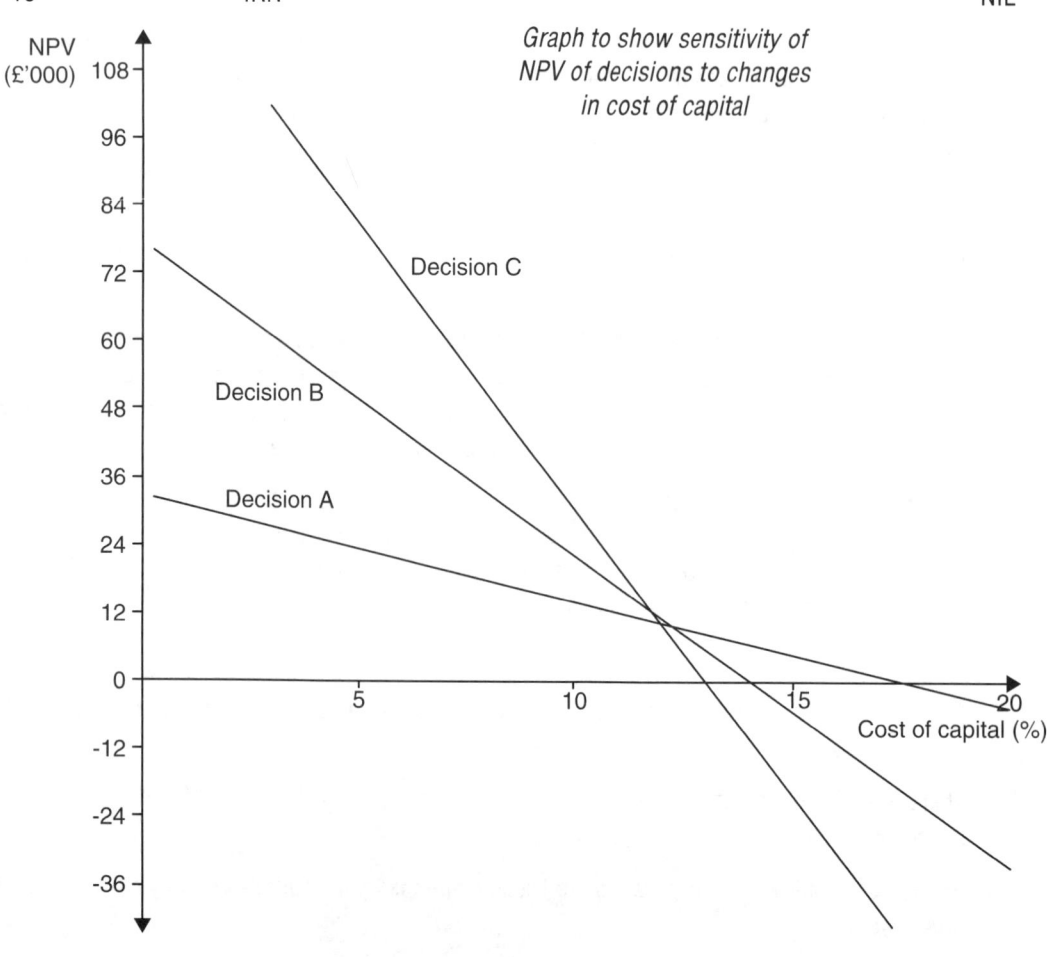

Discount rate %		NPV £
10	£(−245,000 + (5.759 × 48,000))	31,432
13	IRR	NIL

Graph to show sensitivity of NPV of decisions to changes in cost of capital

(b) **Advantages of payback over IRR and NPV**

(i) The calculation is **quicker** and **simpler.**

(ii) The concept of payback period is **more easily understood**. For example, project A pays back in about 2.2 years. Such a statement is easier for non-finance specialists to understand than 'Project A's internal rate of return is 17.5%'.

(iii) The payback period is crucial information when money is put at risk. It **focuses** on early cash flows, thereby indicating **projects** likely to **improve liquidity positions**. For this reason payback favours A, although A is not the most advantageous in terms of profit maximisation.

(iv) It **reduces risk by ignoring longer-term cash flows occurring further into the future that may be subject to higher risk**. For example, the cash inflows in the last three years of the nine-year life of C are ignored as the project has paid back.

Disadvantages of payback compared with IRR and NPV

(i) It **ignores** the **timing of cash flows within the payback period, the cash flows after the end of the payback period and therefore the total project return**. It therefore favours A, which pays back the relatively small investment relatively quickly, over the ultimately more profitable B and C (which have larger initial investments but which, over time, produce greater cash inflows).

(ii) It **ignores** the **time value of money**.

(iii) It is **unable to distinguish between projects with the same payback period**.

(iv) The **choice** of any **cut-off period** is **arbitrary**.

(v) It **may lead to excessive investment in short-term projects**. Project A has the shortest payback period but its life is only one third of that of project C.

(vi) Although it takes account of the risk of the timing of cash flows, it **does not take account of the variability of the cash flows**. An investment might produce an inflow of £100,000 in year one and then nothing until year 5. If an organisation depends on a constant cash inflow, acceptance of such an investment on the basis of payback would be a poor decision.

(vii) It **does not distinguish between investments of different sizes**. The investment in C is more than double the size of that required in A; if the annual cash inflows are identical C will take longer to pay back, but it will be more profitable.

Nowadays the **discounted payback** appraisal method is widely used. The table below shows the marked effect of discounting the payback at 10%.

	A	B	C
Payback	2.2 years	3.9 years	5.1 years
Discounted payback	2.6 years	5.2 years	7.5 years

For example, project C takes more than seven years to payback once the returns are discounted.

MN plc might therefore consider employing discounted payback as an initial screening cost as a replacement for IRR.

58 CAF plc

Text references. Chapters 11 and 13 should provide enough data to answer parts (a) and (b). Part (c) needs a bit more lateral thinking.

Top tips. It is a good idea to detail the three options before you begin part (a) just to get the scenario clear in your mind – you'll probably get a mark for doing this (which could be the difference between a pass and a fail).

ANSWERS

> We assumed in (a) that the costs relating to the additional equipment and staff for AA were incurred in year 2. Any reasonable assumption, logically explained, would have been acceptable, however.
>
> When appraising option 3, we assumed that the net inflow from A all occurred in year 1. CIMA's suggested solution included the 12.5% increase in year 2 but stated that either approach was acceptable. The choice of best option is not affected by the approach taken.

(a) **Options**

1. Produce product A for two years, replace it with product AA and produce product AA in the UK for eight years
2. Produce product A for two years, replace it with product AA, sell the UK factory and produce product AA in Eastern Europe for eight years
3. Produce product A for one year only, replace it with product X produced in the UK for three years, and produce product AA (starting in two years' time) in Eastern Europe for eight years.

Financial appraisal of option 1

Year	Cash flow £m		Disc factor 5%	PV £m	
1	3.00	Net inflow from A	0.952	2.856	⎫ 4.942
2	2.30	Net inflow from A	0.907	2.086	⎭
2	(6.00)	Additional equip/staff	0.907	(5.442)	
3-10	5.00**	Net inflow from AA	5.863*	29.315	
10	5.50	Sale of UK factory	0.614	3.377	
10	(2.00)	Redundancy payments	0.614	(1.228)	
10	0.35	Sale of equip	0.614	0.215	
				31.179	

* 7.722 − 1.859 = 5.863
** 200,000 × £25

Financial appraisal of option 2

Year	Cash flow £m		Disc factor 5%	PV £m
1–2		Net inflow from A		4.942 (see above)
2	(6.00)	Additional equip/staff	0.907	(5.442)
3–10	3.00*	Net inflow from AA	5.863	17.589
2	5.50	Sale of UK factory	0.907	4.989
2	(2.00)	Redundancy payments	0.907	(1.814)
2	0.35	Sale of equip	0.907	0.317
				20.581

* 200,000 × £15

Financial appraisal of option 3

Year	Cash flow £m		Disc factor 5%	PV £m
1	3.375	Net inflow from A*	0.952	3.213
1	(4.000)	Equipment for X	0.952	(3.808)
2	3.500	Net inflow from X**	0.907	3.175
3–4	5.250	Net inflow from X***	1.687****	8.857
4	5.500	Sale of factory	0.823	4.527
4	(2.000)	Redundancy payments	0.823	(1.646)
4	0.350	Sale of equip	0.823	0.288
2	(6.000)	Additional staff/equip for AA	0.907	(5.442)
3–10	3.000	Net inflow from AA	5.863	17.589
				26.753

* £3m × 1.125
** 50,000 × £70
*** 75,000 × £70
**** 3.546 – 1.859

> **Top tips.** Note that it would have been perfectly acceptable to include the cash inflow from the 12.5% increase in production of A in year 2, resulting in an NPV of £(26.754 – (0.375 × 0.952) + (0.375 × 0.907))m = £26.736m.

Conclusion. Option 1 is the best.

(b) (i) **Sensitivity to changes in transport costs**

Transport costs are the same in options 2 and 3 and so the analysis should be made between option 3 (the better of the two options) and option 1.

	£m
NPV of option 1 =	31.179
NPV of option 3 =	26.753
	4.426

∴ Transport costs can change by a PV of £4.426m before CAF plc should consider option 3 instead of option 1.

Current PV of transport costs = £10 × 200,000 × 5.863
= £11.726m

∴ PV of transport costs can change to £(11.726 – 4.426)m = £7.3m

This equates to a per annum change of £7.3m/5.863 = £1,245,267 (where 5.863 is the PV factor at 5% over years 3 to 10).

> **Alternative approach**
>
> The allowable drop is (£4.426m/£11.726m) × 100% = 37.75%

∴ Transport costs can fall by £1.245m or 37.75% before the choice of option 1 is invalid. Transport costs can therefore fall to ((£10 × 200,000) – £1,245,267) = £754,733.

Transport costs can change by a significant amount. The **result in (a)** is therefore **not sensitive to changes in transport costs.**

Transport costs do not affect the decision, which underlines the choice of option 1. Product X does not generate enough income to cover the extra transport costs of producing AA in Eastern Europe.

(ii) **Sensitivity to changes in the selling price of the factory**

If option 3 were to be preferred to option 1, the PV of the sale of the factory would need to change by £(31.179 – 26.753)m = £4.426m.

The difference in the PVs of the factory sale in the two options is £(4.527 – 3.377)m = £1.150m (the value being bigger in option 3). The difference in the PVs would therefore need to change by £(4.426 + 1.150)m = £5.576m, a (£(5.576 – 1.150)m/£1.150m) × 100% = 385% increase. This means the selling price would have to be £5.5m × 485% = £26.675m before option 3 were preferred.

The decision between options 1 and 3 is therefore not sensitive to changes in the selling price of the factory.

If option 2 were to be preferred to option 1, the PV of the sale of the factory would need to change by £(31.179 – 20.581)m = £10.598m. Such a massive change required means that the choice between options 1 and 2 is not sensitive to changes in selling price.

ANSWERS

(c) **Business issues that should be considered before relocating to another country**

A decision to relocate should be based on a number of issues including:

- The availability of skilled labour
- Lower taxation rates
- Shorter distance to market (so as to be able to respond more quickly to customers' needs)
- Lower costs (labour especially)
- Incentives/grants

There are risks in relocation to consider, however.

- Currency and exchange rate risk
- Political instability
- Lack of infrastructure (transport, power and so on)
- Cultural problems
- Operating a business that is geographically dispersed

59 NP plc

> **Text references.** Look at Chapter 14 if you need help with decision trees as these can be quite tricky to draw. Parts (a), (b) and (c) require simple NPV calculations which you can refer to in Chapter 11. Part (d) can be answered from Chapters 16 and 18.
>
> **Top tips.** The easiest mistake to make in part (a)(i) is to miss out the reject option at year 0: NP plc does not have to go ahead with the project. The tree is only meant to show the options open to the company in the first part of (a).
>
> In part (a)(ii) there is no need to include any costs of dismantling, storage, moving or any sales revenue as these are common to all options. It is only the purchase/sale price of the land that varies according to location.
>
> You needed to keep your head in part (b) so that you didn't miss any of the costs and revenues associated with each option. Allowance would be made for your decision from (a), so you would not be penalised for getting (a) incorrect. Don't forget to use PV factors for years 5-8 in (b)(ii).
>
> In part (c) you should not have included any sale of land figures at year 4 because the project was continuing in the same place. Provided you realised that you needed to consider the eight-years-in-London option because of the narrow margin in part (b)(ii), part (c) was straightforward.
>
> Part (d) does **not** require a general discussion of ABC. Instead you needed to consider the visitor/customer perspective and the information needs of this type of business.
>
> **Easy marks.** Part (a)(i) is a simple accept/reject decision. You can do part (d) without doing other parts.

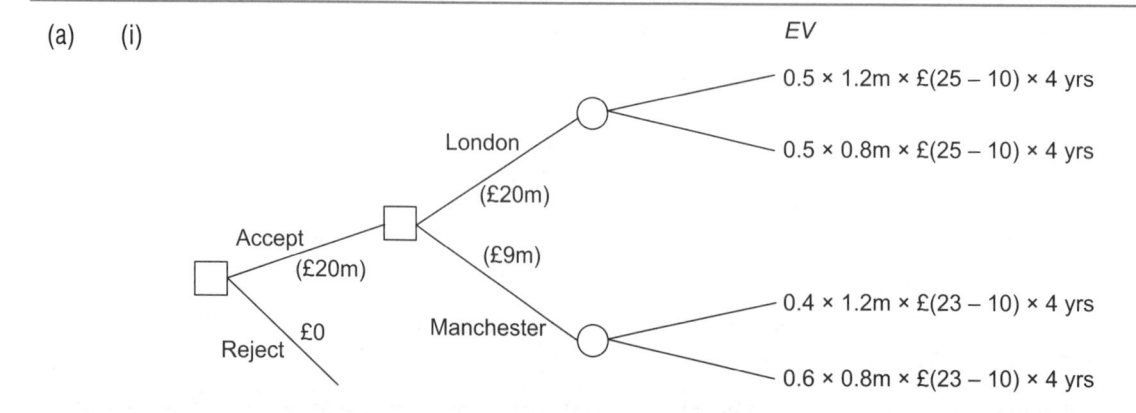

(a) (i)

```
                                                                    EV
                                                        ┌── 0.5 × 1.2m × £(25 − 10) × 4 yrs
                                    London ────○───────┤
                                    (£20m)             └── 0.5 × 0.8m × £(25 − 10) × 4 yrs
                    Accept   ┌──────┤
                    (£20m)   │      (£9m)
              ┌─────□────────┤      Manchester
              │               └──────○───────┬── 0.4 × 1.2m × £(23 − 10) × 4 yrs
        Reject│  £0                          │
                                             └── 0.6 × 0.8m × £(23 − 10) × 4 yrs
```

238

(ii)

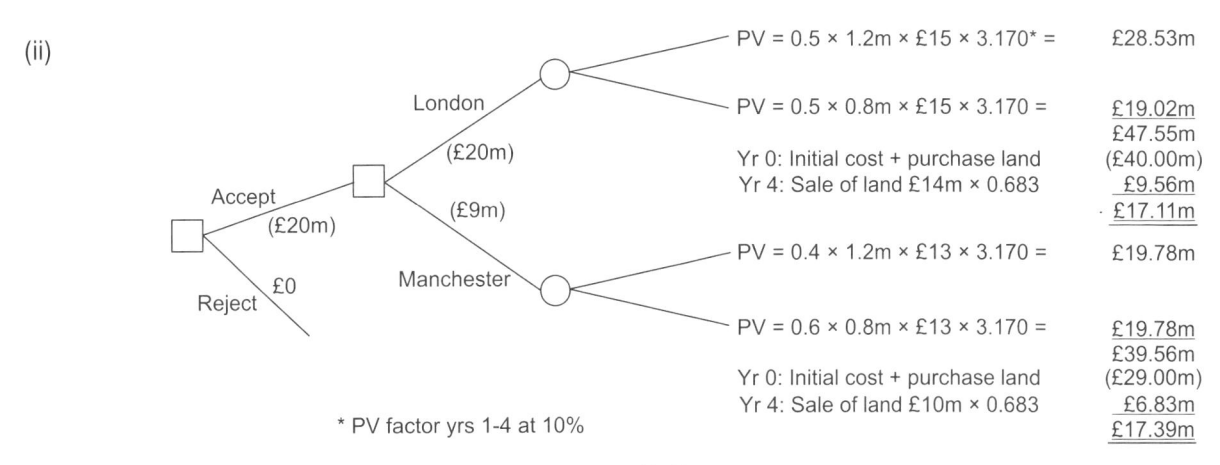

```
                                          ┌─ PV = 0.5 × 1.2m × £15 × 3.170* =    £28.53m
                              London      │
                                 ○────────┤                                       
                                ╱         └─ PV = 0.5 × 0.8m × £15 × 3.170 =     £19.02m
                               ╱                                                  £47.55m
                              ╱              Yr 0: Initial cost + purchase land  (£40.00m)
                    (£20m)   ╱               Yr 4: Sale of land £14m × 0.683      £9.56m
              Accept  ▢─────┤                                                     £17.11m
                     ╱(£20m) ╲(£9m)
                    ╱         ╲
            ▢                  Manchester  ┌─ PV = 0.4 × 1.2m × £13 × 3.170 =     £19.78m
                    ╲            ○─────────┤
             £0      ╲                     └─ PV = 0.6 × 0.8m × £13 × 3.170 =     £19.78m
           Reject                                                                 £39.56m
                                             Yr 0: Initial cost + purchase land  (£29.00m)
                                             Yr 4: Sale of land £10m × 0.683      £6.83m
                                                                                  £17.39m
```

* PV factor yrs 1-4 at 10%

Manchester is therefore the **better** option by £0.28m.

> **Top tips.** Alternatively you could have taken the standard approach to NPV calculations and simply tabulated the cashflows.

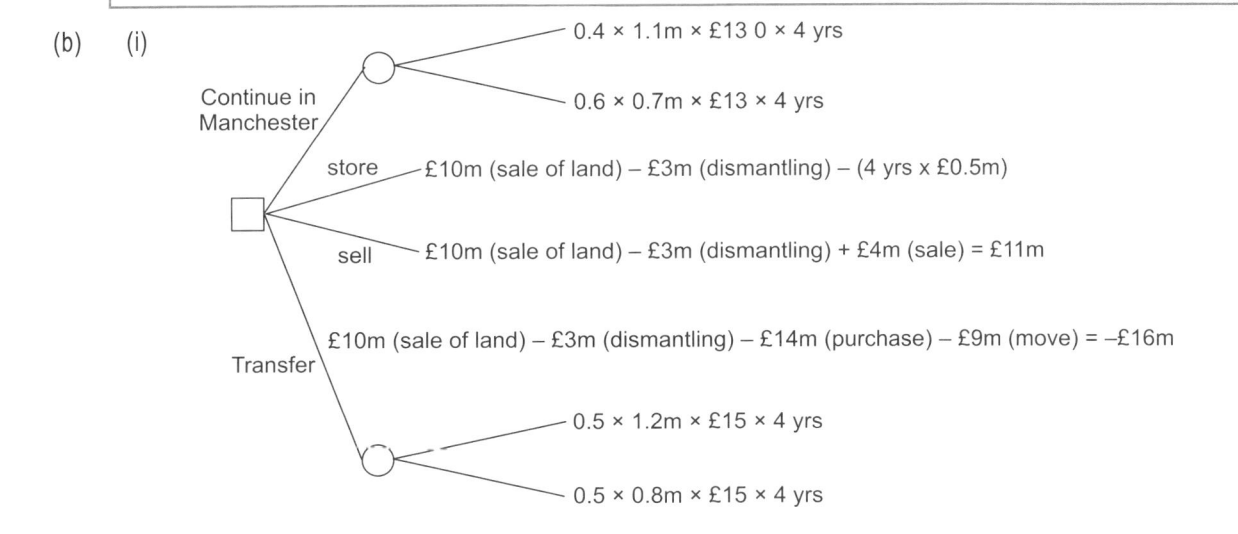

(b) (i)

```
                                    ┌─ 0.4 × 1.1m × £13 0 × 4 yrs
                   Continue in      ○
                   Manchester ╱     └─ 0.6 × 0.7m × £13 × 4 yrs
                             ╱
                            ╱  store   ┌─ £10m (sale of land) – £3m (dismantling) – (4 yrs × £0.5m)
                      ▢────┤
                            ╲  sell    └─ £10m (sale of land) – £3m (dismantling) + £4m (sale) = £11m
                             ╲
                              ╲  £10m (sale of land) – £3m (dismantling) – £14m (purchase) – £9m (move) = –£16m
                     Transfer  ╲
                                ╲    ┌─ 0.5 × 1.2m × £15 × 4 yrs
                                 ○───┤
                                     └─ 0.5 × 0.8m × £15 × 4 yrs
```

239

ANSWERS

(ii)

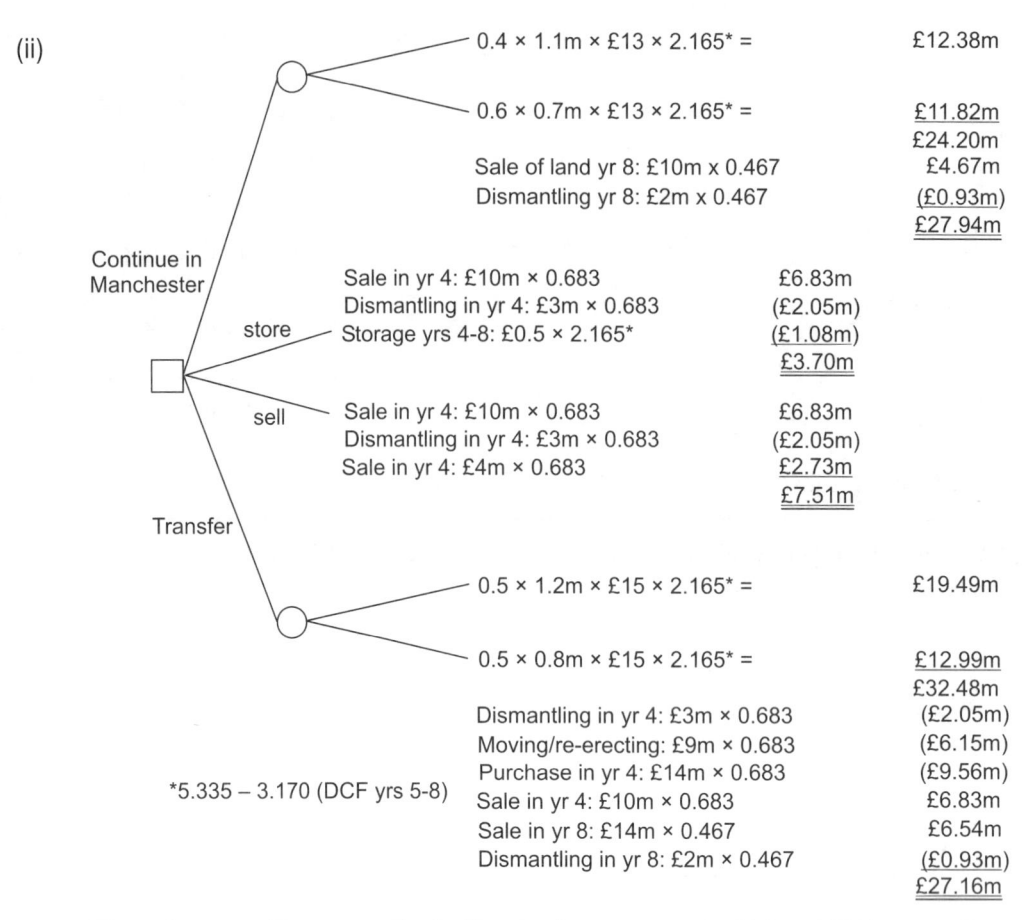

```
                                                                                    £12.38m
            ┌─── 0.4 × 1.1m × £13 × 2.165* =
           ○
            └─── 0.6 × 0.7m × £13 × 2.165* =                                        £11.82m
                                                                                    £24.20m
                 Sale of land yr 8: £10m × 0.467                                     £4.67m
                 Dismantling yr 8: £2m × 0.467                                      (£0.93m)
                                                                                    £27.94m
  Continue in
  Manchester /
           /      Sale in yr 4: £10m × 0.683              £6.83m
          /       Dismantling in yr 4: £3m × 0.683       (£2.05m)
     store        Storage yrs 4-8: £0.5 × 2.165*         (£1.08m)
        ┌─────                                            £3.70m
        □
        └─────
     sell         Sale in yr 4: £10m × 0.683              £6.83m
          \       Dismantling in yr 4: £3m × 0.683       (£2.05m)
           \      Sale in yr 4: £4m × 0.683               £2.73m
  Transfer  \                                             £7.51m
             \
              \
               \  ┌─── 0.5 × 1.2m × £15 × 2.165* =                                  £19.49m
               ○
                  └─── 0.5 × 0.8m × £15 × 2.165* =                                  £12.99m
                                                                                    £32.48m
                       Dismantling in yr 4: £3m × 0.683                             (£2.05m)
                       Moving/re-erecting: £9m × 0.683                              (£6.15m)
  *5.335 – 3.170 (DCF yrs 5-8)  Purchase in yr 4: £14m × 0.683                      (£9.56m)
                       Sale in yr 4: £10m × 0.683                                    £6.83m
                       Sale in yr 8: £14m × 0.467                                    £6.54m
                       Dismantling in yr 8: £2m × 0.467                             (£0.93m)
                                                                                    £27.16m
```

The option to **continue operating in Manchester** generates the highest NPV by a small margin.

(c) Based on (b), the option to continue operating in Manchester for eight years should be selected.

Total NPV over eight years

	NPV £m
Years 1 to 4 in Manchester *	10.56
Years 5 to 8 in Manchester ((b)(ii))	27.94
	38.50

* From (a)(ii) £(39.56 – 29.00)m = £10.56m, ie net of sale of land

Given the results in (b) (where the margin is very small), the only other possible alternative could be to site the project in London for the entire eight-year period.

Total NPV over eight years

		NPV £m	£m
Years 1 to 4 in London*			7.55
Years 5 to 8 in London			
Net revenue:	0.5 × 1.1m × £15 × 2.165	17.86	
	0.5 × 0.7m × £15 × 2.165	11.37	
Dismantling in yr 8:	£2m × 0.467	(0.93)	
Sale in yr 8:	£14m × 0.467	6.54	
			34.84
			42.39

∴ The **best** option is to site the **project in London** for the eight-year period.

*From (a)(ii), £(47.55 – 40)m = £7.55m, ie net of sale of land

(d)   **The value of ABC to the Fantazia project**

The project being considered by NP plc will run as a service. **ABC** has been **successfully implemented** in a wide range of **service** environments, but its value to the Fantazia project as a means of assessing visitor profitability is open to question. **ABC** is best applied to **individual** products/services, whereas **Fantazia** needs to be **considered as a whole** because rides are not priced individually and it is the totality of rides, merchandise, food and drink which attracts visitors to the dome.

A better option?

In the circumstances, a more appropriate system might be **customer profitability analysis (CPA)**.

CPA and customer segments

Whereas a manufacturing company supplying, say, ten main customers would cost each customer separately, Fantazia should attract a huge number of customers. There would be little value in assessing each customer individually, so **customers** should be **divided into different categories** such as families, teenagers and groups.

Once these groups have been identified, the rides they choose and their spending on merchandise, food and drink can be monitored and a **profitability per category** determined. **Strategies for attracting the most profitable group** and **promotions** to appeal to particular segments can then be adopted.

ABC and costs

ABC could be **used to cost the different activities** at Fantazia, however, thereby providing vital **information for CPA**, although the ease with which fixed costs could be apportioned to the various rides and so on using cost drivers is open to question.

Conclusion

Profitability will be largely determined by the type of customer segment attracted to Fantazia and so the costing system adopted should focus on assessing customer profitability rather than costing activities.

60 Healthcare organisation

Text references. Look at Chapters 11 and 13 for information on DCF analysis and sensitivity analysis. Draw on your knowledge of Chapter 2 to answer part (c) and probabilities.

Top tips. This question involves DCF analysis, sensitivity analysis and probability analysis. Quite a combination! In part (b), when you need to calculate the NPV of each alternative at various numbers of treatments, it is worth calculating the NPV for each alternative at 30 and 65 treatments per year as these values are needed for part (c).

Easy marks. Calculate the treatments in part (a) of the question. These are a type of PV calculation so remember to discount revenues.

(a) (i)   **Minimum number of treatments needed per year to make the low-technology route viable**

Contribution per treatment = £43,000 − £40,000 = £3,000

Present value (PV) of 1 treatment pa in years 2 to 10 = £3,000 × (6.145 − 0.909) = £3,000 × 5.236 = £15,708

PV of development costs = £800,000 × 0.909 = £727,200

∴ Minimum number of treatments needed = £727,200 ÷ £15,708 = 46.29, ie 47 per year

ANSWERS

(ii) **Minimum number of treatments needed per year to make the high-technology route viable**

Contribution per treatment = £43,000 − £18,000 = £25,000

Present value (PV) of 1 treatment pa in years 4 to 10 = £25,000 × (6.145 − 2.487) = £25,000 × 3.658 = £91,450

PV of development costs over years 1-3 = £2,100,000 × 2.487 = £5,222,700

∴ Minimum number of treatments needed = £5,222,700 ÷ £91,450 = 57.1, ie 58 per year

(iii) **Number of treatments needed per year to make both the low- and high-technology routes equally viable**

For both routes to be equally viable, they must have the same NPV.

Let X = the number of treatments per year

£91,450X − £5,222,700	=	£15,708X − £727,200
∴ 91,450X − 15,708X	=	5,222,700 − 727,200
75,742X	=	4,495,500
X	=	59.353

Number of treatments is 60

Top tips. Test using 59 and 60 treatments per year

		£
Low-technology route:	(59 × £15,708) − £727,200	199,572
High-technology route:	(59 × £91,450) − £5,222,700	172,850
Difference:		26,722

Low-technology route is preferable.

		£
Low-technology route:	(60 × £15,708) − £727,200	215,280
High-technology route:	(60 × £91,450) − £5,222,700	264,300
Difference:		(49,020)

High-technology route is preferable.

(b) **Relative sensitivity of the two routes**

We need to **calculate NPVs at various numbers of treatments**. We will use the NPV for each alternative at 30 and 65 treatments per year as these values will be needed for part (c) of the question.

		NPV £
Low-technology route:	(30 × £15,708) − £727,200	(255,960)
	(65 × £15,708) − £727,200	293,820
High-technology route:	(30 × £91,450) − £5,222,700	(2,479,200)
	(65 × £91,450) − £5,222,700	721,550

ANSWERS

Diagram to illustrate the relative sensitivity of the two alternative routes to the number of treatments demanded per year

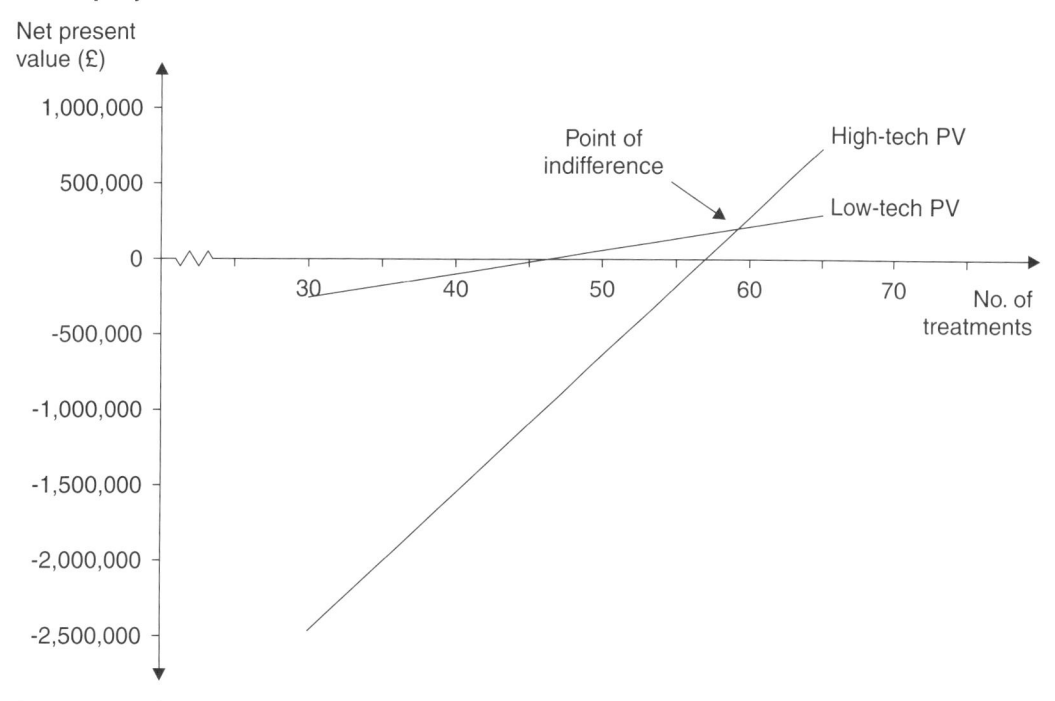

[Graph showing Net present value (£) on y-axis from -2,500,000 to 1,000,000, and No. of treatments on x-axis from 30 to 70. Two lines are shown: High-tech PV (steeper) and Low-tech PV (flatter), intersecting at a "Point of indifference" around 58 treatments.]

(c) **Maximum amount payable for forecast of the annual demand for treatments**

Step 1 Calculate expected treatments pa based on existing knowledge.

Demand	Treatments pa	Probability	Expected value
Weak	30	0.4	12
Strong	65	0.6	39
Total	N/A	1.0	51

In the absence of better information, EHI should choose the low-technology route. The expected value of 51 treatments per year will be less than the 58 pa minimum for the high-technology route to be viable, but be more than the 47 pa necessary for the low-technology route to be viable.

Step 2 Draw up a conditional probability table.

The probability of correctly forecasting each level of demand is 0.92. This information can be used to prepare a **conditional probability table** in order to establish the probabilities for use in a decision tree.

		Forecast Weak	Forecast Strong	Total
Actual	Weak	0.4 × 0.92 = 0.368	0.4 – 0.368 = 0.032	0.4
	Strong	0.6 – 0.552 = 0.048	0.6 × 0.92 = 0.552	0.6
	Total	0.368 + 0.048 = 0.416	0.032 + 0.552 = 0.584	1.0

Step 3 Determine probabilities.

If EHI decide to seek advice, the probability of a forecast of strong demand is 0.584 and the probability of a forecast of weak demand is 0.416.

If weak demand (ie 30 treatments pa) is forecast, EHI will not develop the treatment as it would be unprofitable under either option (see diagram in part (b)) as the NPV of both options is negative.

ANSWERS

If strong demand (ie 65 treatments pa) is forecast, EHI will select the high-technology option as this will be the most profitable (see diagram in part (b)). The high-technology option has the higher NPV.

If strong demand is forecast the probability of actual demand being strong is 0.552/0.584 = 0.9452 (see table), and the probability of actual demand being weak is 1 – 0.9452 = 0.0548.

Step 4 Calculate the expected value of a decision to adopt the low-technology route in the absence of better information.

Actual demand	NPV £	Probability	Expected value £
Weak (30 treatments pa)	(255,960)	0.4	(102,384)
Strong (65 treatments pa)	293,820	0.6	176,292
Total	N/A	1.0	73,908

Step 5 Calculate the expected value of a decision to adopt the high-technology route as a result of strong demand being forecast.

Actual demand	NPV £	Probability	Expected value £
Weak (30 treatments pa)	(2,479,200)	0.0548	(135,860)
Strong (65 treatments pa)	721,550	0.9452	682,009
Total	N/A	1.0000	546,149

As there is a 0.584 probability of strong demand being forecast, the expected value of the decision to employ consultants would be 0.584 × £546,149 = £318,951.

This figure exceeds that for not seeking a forecast by (£318,951 – £73,908) = £245,043.

Step 6 Advice

The maximum amount worth paying for the forecast is £245,000.

> **Top tips.** The question advises candidates to use decision-tree analysis. This is not strictly necessary, as it should be possible to identify the relevant decisions and outcomes in this case without difficulty.

61 Training courses

> **Text references.** Part (a) should be answerable based on Chapter 11 but you will need to read the chapter carefully so that you understand the timing of cash flows and what is included in a cash flow. Part (b) once again wants information on NPV.
>
> **Top tips.** It was absolutely vital in part (a) to state quite clearly your assumptions and to provide examples of your workings. You may have based your answer on different assumptions to ours, indeed the CIMA answer is different to ours, but it is a matter of interpretation. We have set out our thoughts and approach in the 'Notes' part of our answer.
>
> The CIMA answer, for example, when appraising the external courses option, has not inflated the cash flows until year 2. If you took this approach you should have got an NPV of £2,207,513.
>
> Because the question stated that the costs of camera/sound crew and trainers/course material were incurred in the first quarter of a year, you may have included a cost incurred in year N as a cash flow of year N–1. If you took this approach you should have got an NPV of £(1,971,616).
>
> You may have been completely unsure about how to tackle part (b)(i) – it took us a while to figure out what was required. Read our reasoning included in the question carefully to ensure you can understand the approach used.

ANSWERS

(a) **External courses v e-learning**

X Ltd should **go for the e-learning option** as this has the lower NPV of cost.

External training courses option

Year	Delegate costs (W1) £	Courses costs (W2) £	Total costs £	Discount factor 14%	PV £
1	(548,100)	(72,263)	(620,363)	0.877	(544,058)
2	(575,505)	(74,069)	(649,574)	0.769	(499,522)
3	(604,280)	(75,921)	(680,201)	0.675	(459,136)
4	(634,494)	(77,819)	(712,313)	0.592	(421,689)
5	(666,219)	(79,764)	(745,983)	0.519	(387,165)
				NPV =	(2,311,570)

Workings

1 **Delegate costs**

Assume current costs given are at time 'year 0' and so first increase applies to time 'year 1'.

Year 0 £870 × 100 delegates × 6 courses = £522,000
Year 1 £522,000 × 1.05
Year N £522,000 × 1.05^N

2 **Course costs**

Assume current costs given are at time 'year 0' and so first increase applies to time 'year 1'.

Year 0 £11,750 × 6 courses = £70,500
Year 1 £70,500 × 1.025
Year N £70,500 × 1.025^N

Assumptions

1 All costs incurred during a year are assumed to be incurred at the end of the year.
2 All costs start with one year of inflation included.
3 All costs are known with certainty.

E-learning option

	Notes	0 £'000	1 £'000	2 £'000	3 £'000	4 £'000	5 £'000
Hardware	2	(1,500)	-	-	-	-	50.000
Software licenses	3	(35)	(35.00)	(35.000)	(35.000)	(35.000)	-
Technical manager	4	-	(30.00)	(31.800)	(33.708)	(35.730)	(37.874)
Camera & sound crew	5	-	(24.00)	(24.000)	(25.440)	(26.966)	(28.584)
Trainers and course material	6	-	(12.00)	(12.720)	(13.483)	(14.292)	(15.150)
Broadband connection	7		(30.00)	(28.500)	(27.075)	(25.721)	(24.435)
		(1,535)	(131.00)	(132.020)	(134.706)	(137.709)	(56.043)
Discount factor (14%)		× 1.000	× 0.877	× 0.769	× 0.675	× 0.592	× 0.519
		(1,535)	(114.887)	(101.523)	(90.927)	(81.524)	(29.086)

NPV = £(1,952,947)

Notes

1 We do not include the consultant's fee as this has already been incurred and so is a sunk cost.

2 Depreciation is not a cash flow and so is not included.

ANSWERS

3   The fee is payable in advance so the fee for year N is paid at the end of year N – 1 and is included under year N – 1.

4   We do not include the salary of the replacement employee as this is not an incremental cost as we assume he/she is paid what the existing employee would have been paid.

We assume the technical manager's salary is £30,000 in year 1 (ie it does not need inflating for year 1) and hence is £30,000 × 1.06^{N-1} in year N.

5   The costs are incurred in the first quarter of year N but we include them as costs of year N.

Cost in year 1 = £4,000 × 6 = £24,000
Increases after two years by 6% pa.

6   The costs are incurred in the first quarter of year N but we include them as costs of year N.

Cost in year 1 = £2,000 × 6 = £12,000
Cost in year N = £12,000 × 1.06^{N-1}

7   Cost in year 1 = £300 × 100 = £30,000

Cost in year N = £30,000 × 0.95^{N-1}

Top tips. The 16 marks available for part (a) would probably be allocated 25% for the current approach, 75% for the e-learning option.

(b) (i) The variable cost per delegate is far lower for the e-learning option, although the fixed costs are much higher.

If **sufficient delegates** attend the courses so the **total savings in variable costs** (from using e-learning instead of external courses) are **greater** than the **increase in fixed costs**, the **e-learning option** is **viable**.

We therefore need to work out the extra annual fixed costs of the e-learning option, and divide this by the annual saving in variable costs per delegate to determine a breakeven number of delegates.

The calculation of the fixed and variable costs is not straightforward, however, as they **vary** over the five years **due to inflation**. However we can calculate **annual equivalents** of the fixed costs and the variable costs per delegate using the cumulative discount factor at 14% over five years of 3.433.

	PV of fixed costs £	Annual equivalent £	PV of variable costs £	Annual equivalent £	Annualised cost per delegate £
External courses	259,048 (W1)	75,458	2,052,522 (W2)	597,880	5,979
e-learning	1,858,535 (W3)	541,373	94,412 (W3)	27,501	275
Annualised savings		465,915			5,704

Breakeven number of delegates = £465,915/£5,704
= 81.68 delegates, say 82

Workings

1
Year	Course costs (from (a)) £	Discount factor 14%	PV £
1	72,263	0.877	63,375
2	74,069	0.769	56,959
3	75,921	0.675	51,247
4	77,819	0.592	46,069
5	79,764	0.519	41,398
PV of fixed costs			259,048

2   Total PV – PV of fixed costs = PV of variable costs

∴ PV of variable costs = £(2,311,570 – 259,048) = £2,052,522

3   The only variable costs are those associated with broadband.

Year	Broadband Costs £'000	Discount factor 14%	PV of broadband costs £'000	Total PV £'000	PV of fixed costs £'000
0	-	1.000	-	1,535.000	1,535.000
1	30.000	0.877	26.310	114.887	88.577
2	28.500	0.769	21.917	101.523	79.606
3	27.075	0.675	18.276	90.927	72.651
4	25.721	0.592	15.227	81.524	66.297
5	24.435	0.519	12.682	29.086	16.404
			94.412	1,952.947	1,858.535

(ii)   **82 out of the 100 accountants** would be required to adopt the e-learning approach. This is a **high proportion** and so X Ltd would need to ensure that all accountants were **in favour** of such a method of delivery before adopting it.

62 CD Ltd

> **Text references.** The background information is available from Chapter 11. However, the question is testing your confidence in manipulating data as much as background knowledge.
>
> **Top tips.** Once you get started this question is not as difficult as it seems at first sight.
>
> **Easy marks.** Do part (c) first as this is a standalone requirement.
>
> The best way to answer part (a) is to express annual sales growth as a certain number of units per year. A much more difficult approach is to express growth as a compound percentage rate. Another way of doing this is to start with part (b) and use your answer here to do part (a). This alternative approach is below.

(a)   Let the minimum required annual growth in unit sales of the D be x units. Each unit of the D contributes £55 (£105 – £50). The extra contribution from the sales growth in year 2 will therefore be £55x. The extra contribution from the sales growth in year 3 will be £55 × 2x, and so on.

The cash flows can now be investigated.

Year	Continue with C £	Produce D £	Difference £	Discount factor 12%		Present value £
0	(70,000)	(620,000)	(550,000)	1.000		(550,000)
1	720,000	330,000	(390,000)	0.893		(348,270)
2	600,000	330,000 + 55x	55x + (270,000)	0.797	43.835x	+ (215,190)
3	480,000	330,000 + 110x	110x + (150,000)	0.712	78.32x	+ (106,800)
4	360,000	330,000 + 165x	165x + (30,000)	0.636	104.94x	+ (19,080)
5	240,000	330,000 + 220x	220x + 90,000	0.567	124.74x	+ 51,030
				Net present value	351.835x	– 1,188,310

The **minimum required annual growth** is where   351.835x – 1,188,310 = 0

∴ x = 3,377

Recommendation

To justify starting D production now, the minimum expected annual growth in sales must be 3,400 units, to the nearest hundred units.

ANSWERS

(b) Using the **column for differential cash flows in part (a) and x = 2,800**, the present value of the differential cash flows is as follows.

Year	Differential cash flow £	Discount factor 12%	Present value £
0	(550,000)	1.000	(550,000)
1	(390,000)	0.893	(348,270)
2	(55 × 2,800) − 270,000 = (116,000)	0.797	(92,452)
3	(110 × 2,800) − 150,000 = 158,000	0.712	112,496
4	(165 × 2,800) − 30,000 = 432,000	0.636	274,752
5	(220 × 2,800) + 90,000 = 706,000	0.567	400,302
		Net present value	(203,172)
6	(275 × 2,800) + 210,000 = 980,000	0.507	496,860
		Net present value	293,688

An annual sales increase of 2,800 units is less than the amount recommended in part (a) and therefore the net present value after five years is negative. However, the addition of a further year to the investment appraisal time horizon produces a positive net present value.

The precise fraction of a year required to break even in present value terms, assuming even cash flows, is

$$\frac{£203,172}{£496,860} = 0.4 \text{ years.}$$

Recommendation

If the forecast annual increase in D sales is 2,800 units then CD's investment **appraisal time horizon must be increased to 5.4 years, or 6 years to the nearest whole year, in order to justify starting D production now**.

(c) **Other factors that CD should consider include the following.**

Competitors' actions

CD's competitors may be investing in new technology, enabling them to offer D or its equivalent to customers. The decline in sales of C may then be more rapid than expected. Competitors will be able to build up market share and experience ahead of CD, putting CD at a competitive disadvantage.

Technological changes

There may be further technological change in the near future that renders D obsolete. The anticipated sales increases may not then materialise.

Demand for D

D performs exactly the same function as C but is smaller and more reliable. The price structure is such that customers are expected to pay almost twice as much for D as for C. Is CD sure that customers value the reliability and smaller size sufficiently to be willing to pay the significantly higher price? Will it be necessary to reduce the selling price in order to attract the higher forecast sales volumes in later years?

Cost structure

The financial analysis has assumed that unit variable costs and total fixed costs remain unaltered over the whole range of output. It is unlikely that this would be the case and further investigation is needed into forecast cost behaviour patterns.

Risk analysis

This is a high technology project that exposes CD to a certain amount of risk. Some sort of risk analysis should be carried out as part of the financial evaluation. For example, a sensitivity analysis could be used to draw managers' attention to the most important of the forecast variables.

Alternative approach

(a) Calculate your answer as in (b) above. Where sales growth is 2,800, the NPV is negative, as (£203,172), therefore, growth must be more than 2,800.

Try another growth number, say 3,500 units.

Calculate the NPV with this growth rate, this is around £44k. Say this is positive, then you can apply an interpolation formula.

Thus: $2{,}800 + \left[\dfrac{203}{203 + 44} \times 3{,}500 - 2{,}800 \right] = \underline{3{,}375}$ units

This is much quicker and easier to do than the table in the other method but if you are happer with tables then use the first method!

63 3-Year project

Top tips. The examiner remarked that many candidates completely ignored the tax implications in their answers despite this being noted in the scenario. So don't lose marks by not reading the question carefully.

In sensitivity analysis of a project being appraised using DCF, the assessment of sensitivity is always based on the NPV of the project and how this is affected by changes. So remember the simple formula to calculate sensitivity in a variable: $\dfrac{\text{NPV of project}}{\text{PV of cashflow affected}} \times 100\%$.

In Part (b)(ii) we have shown two alternative approaches to calculating an IRR. Our first approach uses the BPP P2 Text formula for deriving an IRR (based on using a higher discount rate to determine a negative NPV). Our second approach shows that adopted in the CIMA model answer, which is based on using another positive NPV to determine the IRR, and involves subtracting the NPV at the higher rate of return from the NPV at the lower rate of return. Either method will earn you full marks as long as you apply your chosen method correctly.

Easy marks. You should have absolutely no problems in calculating the PV of sales in part (b)(i) and the second IRR needed in part (b)(ii). So even if you couldn't work out the sensitivities you should have picked up at least half of the six marks available. And you will have encountered sensitivity analysis in so many places during your P2 studies that your really should be able to earn at least a couple of marks in part (a).

Examiner's comments. To score highly, candidates needed to relate sensitivity analysis to the actual scenario given. Part (b) was poorly answered with many candidates ignoring tax and the time value of money.

(a) **Sensitivity analysis** is one method of analysing the risk surrounding a capital expenditure project and enables an assessment to be made of how responsive the project's NPV is to changes in the variables that are used to calculate that NPV.

The manager could use sensitivity analysis to look at how sensitive the project's NPV is to changes in the different variables (sales, costs, cost of capital etc) affecting the project. This analysis would identify those variables where the change is least before the NPV becomes negative and so need more regular monitoring.

(b) Using the formula as noted above:

(i) *Selling price*

Sensitivity = ($1.018m/$10.024m(w)) × 100%
= 10.16%

ANSWERS

Working

The PV of sales

Year	Cash flow $'000	Discount factor @ 7%	Present value $'000
1	4,200	0.935	3,927
2	4,900	0.873	4,278
3	5,300	0.816	4,325
			12,530

Tax is paid at 20% so the net PV after tax is $12,530,000 × 80% = $10,024,000.

(ii) *Cost of capital*

We need to calculate the IRR of the project. We know that the NPV using a discount rate of 7% is $1.018m.

To find IRR, we need to find another NPV at a higher rate than 7% and then use the IRR formula. Try to use a rate that is included in the present value tables provided in the exam so that you can obtain discount factors quickly.

Let's try a rate of 20%.

Year	Net cash flow $'000	Discount factor @ 20%	Present value $'000
1	1,350	0.833	1,125
2	1,800	0.694	1,249
3	1,150	0.579	666
			3,040

Tax is paid at 20% so the net PV after tax is $3,040,000 × 80% = $2,432,000.

Post tax NPV less initial investment = $'000(2,432-2,000)

$$= \$432,000$$

Then calculate the IRR of the project.

$$IRR = 7 + \left[\frac{1,018}{1,018 - 432} \times (20 - 7) \right]\% = 29.58\%$$

The cost of capital can therefore increase by 29.58 – 7 = 22.58 percentage points.

or: $\dfrac{22.58}{7} = 323\%$

Top tips. The mark allocation in part (b) was two marks for calculating the sensitivity of the project to changes in the selling price and four marks for the longer calculation of the sensitivity of the project to changes in the cost of capital.

ANSWERS

64 Canal boats

> **Text reference.** Chapter 13 will help you with annualised equivalents. Read Chapter 14 if you need help with expected NPVs and standard deviation.
>
> **Top tips.** In part (a) of the question, you are asked to compare the NPVs for three possible replacement cycles. So you are looking at comparing investments with unequal lives. Therefore you will need to use **annualised equivalents** here to be able to rank the investments. The examiner expects you to use your knowledge of **relevant costs** to exclude costs that are common or not cash flows. Part (b) is a separate requirement which tests your knowledge of risk and uncertainty. Use the data given in the question to illustrate your points and don't just write all that you know on expected values and standard deviation.
>
> **Easy marks.** You should be able to calculate present values easily for all three investment cycles as there are few costs and no tricky adjustments such as tax or inflation involved.

(a) **Optimum replacement cycle**

Year	Cost	Cash flow $	DF	PV $
0	Purchase cost	400,000	1.000	400,000
1	Operating costs	300,000	0.926	
1	Trade-in value	(240,000)		
		60,000	0.926	55,560
				PV = 455,560

Therefore the **annualised equivalent cost** for a replacement cycle of one year is:

$455,560/0.926 = $491,965.

Year	Cost	Cash flow $	DF	PV $
0	Purchase cost	400,000	1.000	400,000
1	Operating costs	300,000	0.926	277,800
2		400,000		
2	Trade-in value	(150,000)		
		250,000	0.857	214,250
				PV = 892,050

Therefore the **annualised equivalent cost** for a replacement cycle of two years is:

$892,050/(0.926 + 0.857) = $500,308.

Year	Cost	Cash flow $	DF	PV $
0	Purchase cost	400,000	1.000	400,000
1	Operating costs	300,000	0.926	277,800
2		400,000	0.857	342,800
3		600,000		
3	Trade-in value	(80,000)		
		520,000	0.794	412,880
				PV = 1,433,480

Therefore the **annualised equivalent cost** for a replacement cycle of three years is:

$1,433,480/(0.926 + 0.857 + 0.794) = $556,259. Note the examiner's answer is slightly different due to rounding.

ANSWERS

When we compare the three cycles we can see that the **lowest annualised equivalent cost** is that for a yearly replacement cycle at $491,965. Remember that annual sales revenues are the same for each replacement cycle and so the optimum replacement cycle overall including revenues will remain at one year.

(b) (i) **Explanation of expected net present value and standard deviation**

Expected net present value (ENPV). This measures the sum of the possible range of outcomes for each campaign multiplied by their probabilities. It does not tell management about the range of values however which would allow them to assess the likelihood of profit or loss. **Standard deviation (SD).** Risk can be measured by the possible range of outcomes around the ENPV of the campaigns. One way of doing this is by calculating the SD of the ENPV. Managers can then assess the campaigns looking at the riskiness as well as the single measure of ENPV.

(ii) **How would the company use this data to choose between investments**

One way of ranking the three campaigns is to compare their ENPVs and choose the campaign with the highest ENPV. This means that campaign K should be chosen with a ENPV of $800,000. Management may be risk averse in which case they would choose a campaign where the SD is smaller. This risk profile would be satisfied by choosing campaign J with a SD of $35,000. A more risk seeking management might opt for a campaign where the SD was higher but the outcomes were also higher. They would opt for campaign K which has a SD of $105,000 but also a higher ENPV. Management would not opt for campaign L as the ENPV is lower than campaign K and the SD is higher than campaign J.

65 Section A answers: Inflation and taxation

1   (1 + money or nominal rate) = (1 + real rate) × (1 + inflation rate)

$$(1 + 0.07) = (1 + r) \times (1 + 0.04)$$

$$r = \frac{1.07}{1.04} - 1$$

$$= 0.0288$$

$$= 2.88\%$$

2   Year 3 cash inflow   = £130,000 × 1.04^3
                                                         = £146,232
    Present value at discount rate of 7%   = £146,232 × 0.816
                                                         = £119,326

3

> **Top tips.** There are two possible approaches to answering this question.

Year	Annual cash flow inflated		Discount factor	PV
		£	8%	£
0		(50,000)	1.000	(50,000)
1	(4,000 × £5 × 1.03)	20,600	0.926	19,076
2	(4,000 × £5 × 1.03^2)	21,218	0.857	18,184
3	(4,000 × £5 × 1.03^3)	21,855	0.794	17,353
				4,613

> **Alternative approach**
>
> Here we discount using the real rate.
>
> (1 + money rate) = (1 + real rate) × (1 + inflation rate)
>
> ∴ 1.08/1.03 = 1 + real rate
>
> ∴ Real rate = 4.85%
>
> | Year | Annual cash flow £ | Discount factor 4.85% | | PV £ |
> |---|---|---|---|---|
> | 0 | (50,000) | 1.000 | | (50,000) |
> | 1 | 20,000 | 1/1.0485 | 0.954 | 19,080 |
> | 2 | 20,000 | $1/1.0485^2$ | 0.910 | 18,200 |
> | 3 | 20,000 | $1/1.0485^3$ | 0.868 | 17,360 |
> | | | | | 4,640 |

4   C   The rate required is the IRR (the rate at which the project breaks even).

Let the rate = r

∴ £50,000 = PV of (4,000 × £5) for years 1 to 3 at rate r

∴ £50,000 = (cumulative PV factor for years 1 to 3 at rate r) × £20,000

∴ £50,000/£20,000 = cumulative PV factor for years 1 to 3 at rate r

∴ 2.5 = cumulative PV factor for years 1 to 3 at rate r

In cumulative PV tables, this corresponds to a rate of approximately 9.7% over three years.

> **Top tips.** Because we are asked to give an answer to the nearest 0.5%, we need to assume that the PV factors behave in a linear fashion so as to determine a more accurate rate than 9% or 10%.

r	PV factor
9%	2.531
10%	2.487
	0.044

∴ r = 9% + ((2.531 − 2.5)/0.044)% = 9.7%

This 9.7% is the real cost of capital (because we did not inflate the cash flows).

Now (1 + money rate) = (1 + real rate) × (1 + inflation rate)

∴ Money rate = (1.097 × 1.04) − 1   = 0.14088
                                      = 14.1%

5   WDA in year 1 = £100,000 × 25% = £25,000

Tax saved in year 2 = £25,000 × 50% × 30% = £3,750

Reducing balance of asset at beginning of year 2 = £100,000 − £25,000 = £75,000

∴ WDA in year 2 = £75,000 × 25% = £18,750

Tax saved in year 2 = £18,750 × 50% × 30% = £2,813

	Cash flows £
Annual cash inflow	20,000
Tax on inflow *	(6,000)
Tax saved (year 1)	3,750
(year 2)	2,813
	20,563
× 8% discount factor for year 2	× 0.857
PV	17,622

*£3,000 of this relates to year 1 annual cash inflow, £3,000 to year 2 annual cash inflow.

ANSWERS

6

		Tax saved	Yr 1	Yr 2	Benefit received Yr 3	Yr 4	Yr 5
	£	£	£	£	£	£	£
Purchase price	80,000						
Yr 1 WDA	20,000	6,000	3,000	3,000			
	60,000						
Yr 2 WDA	15,000	4,500		2,250	2,250		
	45,000						
Yr 3 WDA	11,250	3,375			1,687.50	1,687.50	
	33,750						
Yr 4 sales price	20,000						
Balancing allowance	13,750	4,125				2,062.50	2,062.50
					3,937.50	3,750.00	

7

Since we are given a money cost of capital, the actual money cash flows must be used in the appraisal:

Yr	Investment	Fixed costs	Contribution	Net cash flow	14% factor	Present value
	£	£	£	£		£
0	(700,000)			(700,000)	1.000	(700,000)
1		(200,000)	620,000	420,000	0.877	368,340
2	+ 5%	(210,000) (+ 7%)	663,400	453,400	0.769	348,665
3	+ 5%	(220,500) (+ 7%)	709,838	489,338	0.675	330,303
4	+ 5%	(231,525) (+ 7%)	759,527	528,002	0.592	312,577
					Net present value	659,885

= £660,000 to the nearest £'000

66 Compact discs

> **Top tips.** In this question it is necessary to identify sunk costs, relevant costs and opportunity costs. Your treatment of these should be stated clearly. You also need to note that the price/cost structure provided in the question is based on price/cost at time 0.

In R plc's case, different elements of the cash flow are expected to inflate at different rates. It is therefore appropriate to use the first approach described above using the money rate in the DCF calculation. This can be found as follows.

(1 + nominal rate (n)) = (1 + real rate (r)) × (1 + inflation rate (i))
In this case: r = 8.5%
                 i = 6%
       (1 + n) = (1 + 8.5%) × (1 + 6%)
             n = 15%

It is also necessary to identify which costs are truly relevant to the project, and to exclude those which are sunk costs or which would be incurred whether or not the project is undertaken.

(a) **Property costs**

Although no additional expenditure will be incurred in finding a new building, the existing building could be sold for £2m. This is therefore an opportunity cost to R plc and should be included in the cash flow, as should the projected disposal value of £3m at the end of the period.

(b) **Market research report**

Although the account has not yet been settled, the work has been done and the debt incurred. This is therefore a sunk cost and should be excluded from the calculations.

ANSWERS

(c) **Fixed overheads**

Since the fixed overhead cost per unit represents an apportionment of central costs this should be excluded. However, the true incremental cost of £0.5m per year must be included.

(d) **Working capital**

The annual rate of reduction in the volume of stocks is exactly matched by the annual inflation in material prices. The value of working capital in money terms will therefore remain stable throughout the life of the project.

The calculations show that the project yields a positive NPV of £2.435m over five years. Provided that the terminal value assumptions are realistic, the project is therefore **acceptable** on financial grounds.

Projected cash flows

	Year 0 £'000	Year 1 £'000	Year 2 £'000	Year 3 £'000	Year 4 £'000	Year 5 £'000
Equipment	(10,500)					2,000
Working capital	(500)					500
Property	(2,000)					3,000
Sales (+ 5% pa)		5,040	5,292	5,557	5,834	6,126
Materials (+ 3% pa)		(618)	(637)	(656)	(675)	(696)
Labour (+ 7% pa)		(214)	(229)	(245)	(262)	(281)
Variable o/hds (+ 7% pa)		(214)	(229)	(245)	(262)	(281)
Fixed o/hd (+ 5% pa)		(525)	(551)	(579)	(608)	(638)
Net cash flow	(13,000)	3,469	3,646	3,832	4,027	9,730
Discount at 15%	1.000	0.870	0.756	0.658	0.572	0.497
PV of cash flow	(13,000)	3,018	2,757	2,521	2,303	4,836

Net present value of project = £2,435,000

67 AB plc

Top tips. The quickest way to get to the answer is to use the real rate for each cash flow as in method 1 below. If you used a more laborious approach your NPVs will probably be closer to those shown under method 2. The differences are due solely to rounding. They may seem significant but bear in mind the size of numbers that we are dealing with. There is even a case for deducting marks for too exact an answer: whatever method you use it is subject to uncertainty and calculating to the nearest pound, say, gives a spurious impression of accuracy. Fortunately there is no doubt as to the correct decision in this example.

Method 1

(a) Real rates of interest (r) are as follows, using the formula (1 + money rate) = (1 + real rate) × (1 + inflation rate)

Sales	1.15/1.02	= 1.13	∴ r = 13%
Labour	1.15/1.12	= 1.03	∴ r = 3%
Other costs	1.15/1.08	= 1.06	∴ r = 6%

Existing machinery

Year		Cash flow £'000	Cumulative discount factor	Present value £'000
1-3	Sales	15,000	2.361	35,415
1-3	Labour cost	(6,000)	2.829	(16,974)
1-3	Materials	(2,000)	2.673	(5,346)
1-3	Variable overheads	(2,000)	2.673	(5,346)
1-3	Fixed costs	(3,000)	2.673	(8,019)
NPV				(270)

ANSWERS

(b) **New machinery**

	£'000
NPV as calculated above	(270)
Add back half of labour cost	8,487
	8,217
Less cost of new machine	(5,000)
NPV	3,217

Alternative approach – method 2

(a) **Existing machinery**

		Year		
	Growth rate pa	1	2	3
	%	£'000	£'000	£'000
Sales	2	15,300	15,606	15,918
Labour	12	(6,720)	(7,526)	(8,430)
Materials	8	(2,160)	(2,333)	(2,519)
Variable overheads	8	(2,160)	(2,333)	(2,519)
Fixed costs	8	(3,240)	(3,499)	(3,779)
		1,020	(85)	(1,329)
Discount factor @ 15%		0.870	0.756	0.658
PV		887	(64)	(874)

NPV = £(887,000 – 64,000 – 874,000) = £(51,000)

(b) **New machinery**

	£'000
NPV as calculated in (a)	(51)
Add back half of labour cost	
½ × ((6,720 × 0.870) + (7,526 × 0.756) + (8,430 × 0.658))	8,542
	8,491
Less cost of new machine	5,000
NPV	3,491

(c) Very clearly, the **new machine** should be **purchased** as it gives a positive NPV as opposed to a negative NPV with the existing machinery. This decision is **subject** to the accuracy of the cost of capital percentage and the inflation percentages and it assumes that *all* costs are accounted for (so there are no redundancy costs or retraining costs, no changes to material usage, no alteration in fixed costs and so on).

68 Question with analysis: A Company

Top tips. Remember to split the calculation into manageable elements so do the tax depreciation on the purchase separately, then fit this into the calculation for the purchase NPV.

You can use annuities instead of individual discount factors to save a bit of time where cash flows are identical in later years.

ANSWERS

> **Easy marks.** Calculate WDAs first and slot these into your main workings. Remember to use proformas to set out your workings.
>
> **Examiner's comments.** This question was generally well answered.
>
> Common errors noted by the examiner include:
>
> - Calculating an incorrect figure for the balancing allowance on the purchase option
> - Calculating incorrect figures for the tax savings on both the purchase and the lease option
> - Showing no tax relief for the initial lease payment

1   **Purchase**

	Year 0 £	Year 1 £	Year 2 £	Year 3 £	Year 4 £
Initial investment	(15,000)	–	–	–	–
Tax saved (W)		563	985	937	516
Trade in value				5,000	
	(15,000)	563	985	5,937	516
Discount rate at 15%	× 1.000	× 0.870	× 0.756	× 0.658	× 0.572
PV	(15,000)	490	745	3,907	295

NPV = £(9,563)

Working

Tax depreciation and tax saved ← Tax WDA

		Tax at 30% £	Year 1 £	Year 2 £	Year 3 £	Year 4 £
Machine cost	15,000					
Year 1 – WDA at 25%	(3,750)	1,125	563	563		
	11,250					
Year 2 – WDA at 25%	(2,813)	844		422	422	
	8,437					
Year 3						
Disposal	(5,000)					
Balancing allowance	3,437	1,031			515	516
Tax saved			563	985	937	516

2   **Lease**

	Year 0 £	Year 1 £	Year 2 £	Year 3 £	Year 4 £
Payment ← Deductible costs	(1,250)	(4,992)	(4,992)	(4,992)	–
Tax deduction at 30%	**188**	**187**	**749**	**749**	
		749	**748**	**748**	**748**
	(1,062)	(4,056)	(3,495)	(3,495)	748
Discount rate at 15% ← Discount rate	**× 1.000**	**× 0.870**	**× 0.756**	**× 0.658**	**× 0.572**
PV	(1,062)	(3,529)	(2,642)	(2,300)	428

NPV = £ (9,105)

69 RAD Enterprises

> **Top tips.** It is vital in a question such as this, that requires lots of calculations, to show all your workings in case you make an arithmetical mistake. As there was no residual value, the balancing allowance is simply the brought forward written down value at the beginning of year 4.

ANSWERS

> **Easy marks.** Calculate WDAs first on the purchased machine. You could save a bit of time by using cumulative PV factors for years 1 to 3 on the lease option where cashflows are identical.

Lease v purchase

R Ltd should lease the machine as this option has the least negative NPV.

Lease option

Time	Cash outflow £'000	Tax savings (W) £'000	Net cash flow £'000	Discount factor 12%	PV £'000
0	300	45	(255)	1.000	(255,000)
1	300	90	(210)	0.893	(187,530)
2	300	90	(210)	0.797	(167,370)
3	300	90	(210)	0.712	(149,520)
4	–	45	45	0.636	28,620
					(730,800)

Working

Tax savings

	Year 0 £'000	Year 1 £'000	Year 2 £'000	Year 3 £'000	Year 4 £'000
Saving on year 0 payment	45	45			
Saving on year 1 payment		45	45		
Saving on year 2 payment			45	45	
Saving on year 3 payment				45	45
	45	90	90	90	45

Purchase option

Year	Cash flow £'000	Tax benefit (W) £'000	Discount factor 12%	PV £
0	(1,000,000)		1.000	(1,000,000)
1		37,500	0.893	33,488
2		65,625	0.797	52,303
3		49,219	0.712	35,044
4		84,375	0.636	53,663
5		63,282	0.567	35,881
				(789,621)

Working

WDAs

	Reducing balance £	Tax saved £	Year 1 £	Year 2 £	Benefit received Year 3 £	Year 4 £	Year 5 £
Purchase price	1,000,000						
Yr 1 WDA (25%)	250,000	75,000	37,500	37,500			
Value at start of yr 2	750,000						
Yr 2 WDA (25%)	187,500	56,250		28,125	28,125		
Value at start of yr 3	562,500						
Yr 3 WDA (25%)	140,625	42,188			21,094	21,094	
Value at start of yr 4	421,875						
Disposal value	–						
Balancing allowance	421,875	126,563				63,281	63,282
			37,500	65,625	49,219	84,375	63,282

ANSWERS

70 Question with analysis and student answer: Print Co

> **Text references.** The answer to this question draws very much on material from Chapters 12 and 13 of your Study Text.
>
> **Top tips.** Look at the incremental contribution from the new machine. Note the residual value of the new machine and adjustments to WDAs required on both the old and new machines.
>
> **Examiner's comments.** A good attempt was made by most students at part (a) but the standard of layout and presentation was often poor as was any reference to workings.
>
> Part (b). This was very poorly answered. Many students showed that they had an incomplete understanding of sensitivity analysis.
>
> Common errors noted by the examiner include:
>
> - Not appreciating that the calculations needed the additional contribution (£896k) and not the new contribution (£2,496k)
> - Incorrect phasing of tax relief and tax on the incremental contribution
> - Incorrect calculation of the balancing charge
> - Not discounting the contribution figures
> - Using the answer to part (a) as the numerator in the sensitivity tests

Working

(a) 1 Tax depreciation on the new machine

[*Don't bother with £ – round to £'000 – it saves time*]

	£'000	Tax at 30% £'000	Year 1 £'000	Year 2 £'000	Year 3 £'000	Year 4 £'000	Year 5 £'000	Year 6 £'000
Machine cost	3,000							
Year 1 WDA at 25%	(750)	225	112	113				
	2,250							
Year 2 WDA at 25%	(563)	169		84	85			
	1,687							
Year 3 WDA at 25%	(422)	127			63	64		
	1,265							
Year 4 WDA at 25%	(316)	95				47	48	
	949							
Year 5 Disposal	(300)							
Balancing allowance	649	195					97	98
			112	197	148	111	145	98

2 Balancing charge on old machine

	£'000	Tax at 30% £'000	Year 1 £'000	Year 2 £'000
Year 0 TWDV (tax written down value)	250			
Disposal	(400)			
	150	45	22	23

[*This is tax due not a refund*]

> **Easy marks.** Split the question into manageable chunks. Do the tax WDA parts first, then calculate the incremental contribution. The examiner gives eight marks for these two calculations.

3 Increased contribution from the new machine

(a) New sales £4m × 1.2 = £4.8m

[*Unit variable cost*]

ANSWERS

(b) **Reduced UNIT variable costs = 0.60 × 0.80 = 0.48 of sales**

(c) Therefore new contribution = £4.8m × 0.52 = £2.496m

(d) Existing contribution = £4m × 0.4 = £1.6m

Therefore improved contribution = £0.896m

4 Tax on this will be 30% × £0.896m × 50% year 1 to year 6

> **Top tips.** The examiner is asking for a sensitivity analysis on the annual contribution and the rate of corporation tax. Consider calculating the NPV on the tax cash flows separately and then add together for the final assessment of NPV. This means it is easier to pick out what figures you need for your answer to part (b).

5 NPV of cash flows

	Year 0 £'000	1 £'000	2 £'000	3 £'000	4 £'000	5 £'000	6 £'000
Capital cost	(3,000)	-	-	-	-	-	-
Increased contribution	-	896	896	896	896	896	-
Sales proceeds	400	-	-	-	-	300	-
Tax:							
Contribution (W3)	-	(134)	(268)	(268)	(268)	(268)	(134)
Old machine (W2)	-	(23)	(22)	-	-	-	-
New machine (W1)	-	112	197	148	111	145	98
Net cash flow	(2,600)	851	803	776	739	1,073	(36)
Discount factor 14% (after tax rate)	1.000	0.877	0.769	0.675	0.592	0.519	0.456
Present value	(2,600)	746	618	524	437	557	(16)

Or use cumulative PV factor for year 1-4 as cash flows are identical

NPV = £266,000

Comment on findings — The overall investment NPV is positive, therefore the investment is worthwhile.

(b) **Sensitivity analysis enables an analysis of risk in a capital expenditure project by testing the responsiveness of the NPV to changes in the variables that are used to calculate the NPV.**

Explanation as required in the question

The variables that are most sensitive are those critical to the project's outcome. These variables are those where the change in the variable is smallest. This sensitivity is measured by:

$$\frac{\text{NPV of the project}}{\text{PV of the cash flow affected}}$$

By analysing these variables managers can review the risks posed by an existing cost structure and allows them to consider alternative structures.

(i) Contribution

> **Top tips.** Note that the question asks for change in the annual contribution, which is different to the incremental contribution used in part (a).

… ANSWERS

	£'000
Pre-tax contribution	2,496
NPV of this contribution – (five years at a discount rate of 3.433)	8,569
Less: tax on this	
(i) Years 1–5 $2,496 \times 3.433 \times 30\% \times 50\%$	(1,285)
(ii) Years 2–6 $2,496 \times (3.889 - 0.877) \times 30\% \times 50\%$	(1,128)
NPV of annual contribution	6,156

Sensitivity of this factor: $\dfrac{\text{NPV of project}}{\text{PV of affected cash flow}} = \dfrac{266}{6,156} = \underline{4.3\%}$

So a reduction of 4.3% in the contribution would make the project NPV zero.

(ii) Rate of corporation tax on profits

$\dfrac{\text{NPV of project}}{\text{PV of affected cash flow}} = \dfrac{266}{365} = \underline{72.9\%}$

So tax rates would have to increase by nearly 73% to make the NPV zero. Thus the project is more sensitive to changes in contribution than it is to changes in the rate of tax.

> Good clear layout of workings in tables. This helps the marker see clearly what he needs to mark

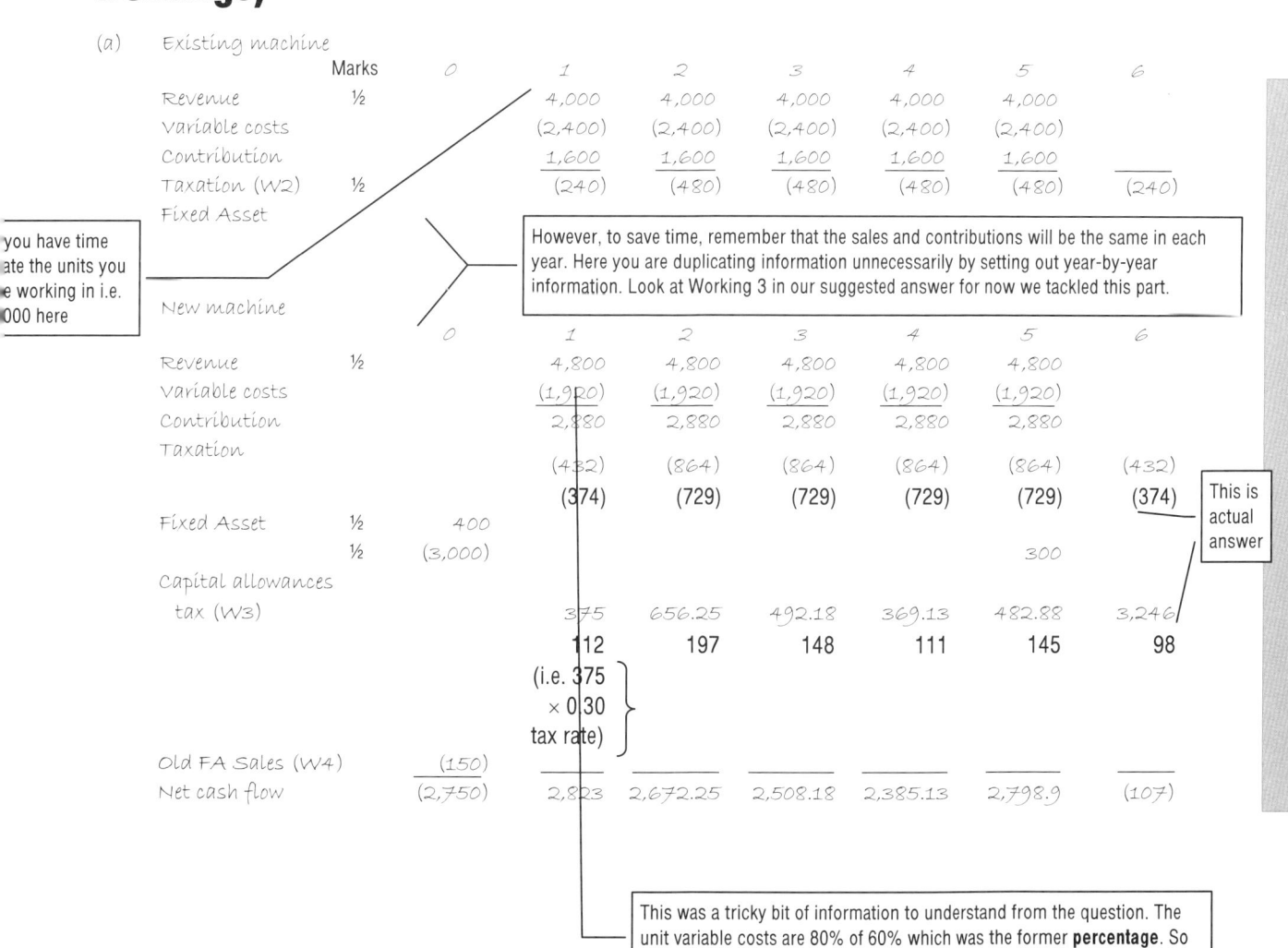

70 Student Answer (Marks awarded are shown next to workings)

(a) Existing machine

	Marks	0	1	2	3	4	5	6
Revenue	½		4,000	4,000	4,000	4,000	4,000	
Variable costs			(2,400)	(2,400)	(2,400)	(2,400)	(2,400)	
Contribution			1,600	1,600	1,600	1,600	1,600	
Taxation (W2)	½		(240)	(480)	(480)	(480)	(480)	(240)
Fixed Asset								

> If you have time state the units you are working in i.e. £000 here

> However, to save time, remember that the sales and contributions will be the same in each year. Here you are duplicating information unnecessarily by setting out year-by-year information. Look at Working 3 in our suggested answer for now we tackled this part.

New machine

		0	1	2	3	4	5	6
Revenue	½		4,800	4,800	4,800	4,800	4,800	
Variable costs			(1,920)	(1,920)	(1,920)	(1,920)	(1,920)	
Contribution			2,880	2,880	2,880	2,880	2,880	
Taxation			(432)	(864)	(864)	(864)	(864)	(432)
			(374)	(729)	(729)	(729)	(729)	(374)
Fixed Asset	½	400						
	½	(3,000)					300	
Capital allowances tax (W3)			375	656.25	492.18	369.13	482.88	3,246
			112	197	148	111	145	98
			(i.e. 375 × 0.30 tax rate)					
Old FA Sales (W4)		(150)						
Net cash flow		(2,750)	2,823	2,672.25	2,508.18	2,385.13	2,798.9	(107)

> This is actual answer

> This was a tricky bit of information to understand from the question. The unit variable costs are 80% of 60% which was the former **percentage**. So the variable costs will be £2.304 and the contribution is £2.496m

ANSWERS

Note on this answer

(i) The student would score around 7 to 8 out of 15 for part (a).

The marks awarded are shown here and include credit for correct method.

(ii) However, the student did not

- calculate the correct tax effect of the capital allowances and therefore lost easy marks
- finish their answer by discontinuing the net cash flows and making recommendations.

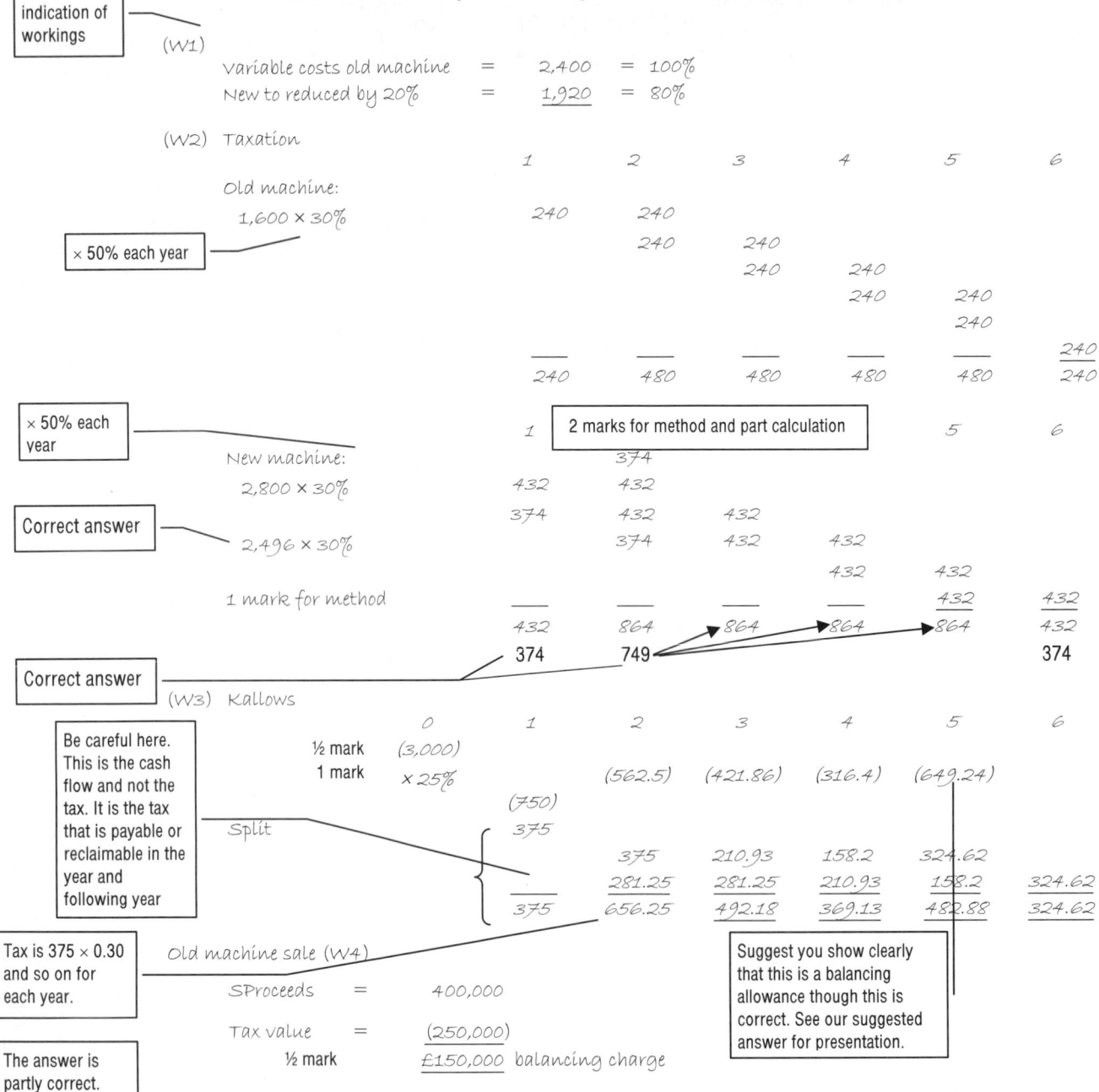

> **Nice, clear indication of workings**

(W1)

Variable costs old machine	=	2,400	= 100%
New to reduced by 20%	=	1,920	= 80%

(W2) Taxation

	1	2	3	4	5	6
Old machine:						
1,600 × 30%	240	240				
		240	240			
			240	240		
				240	240	
					240	240
						240
	240	480	480	480	480	240

> × 50% each year

> × 50% each year

New machine:

2,800 × 30%

	1	2	3	4	5	6
		374				
	432	432				
	374	432	432			
		374	432	432		
			374	432	432	
					432	432
	432	864	864	864	864	432
	374	749				374

2,496 × 30%

> **Correct answer**

1 mark for method

> 2 marks for method and part calculation

> **Correct answer**

(W3) Kallows

	0	1	2	3	4	5	6
½ mark	(3,000)						
1 mark × 25%			(562.5)	(421.86)	(316.4)	(649.24)	
Split	(750)						
	375						
		375	210.93	158.2	324.62		
			281.25	281.25	210.93	158.2	324.62
		375	656.25	492.18	369.13	482.88	324.62

> **Be careful here. This is the cash flow and not the tax. It is the tax that is payable or reclaimable in the year and following year**

> Tax is 375 × 0.30 and so on for each year.

Old machine sale (W4)

$Proceeds	=	400,000
Tax value	=	(250,000)
½ mark		£150,000 balancing charge

> Suggest you show clearly that this is a balancing allowance though this is correct. See our suggested answer for presentation.

> **The answer is partly correct. Look at key words such as risk and responsiveness of the NPV to changes in underlying variables.**

Sensitivity analysis calculates a percentage that determines the amount that revenue can decrease by before a loss is made against costs. **1 mark**

Sensitivity can be calculated based on after tax revenues and annual contribution.

$$\frac{\text{NPV of investment}}{\text{presvalue of affected cash flows}} = \frac{264}{3,520} = 7.5\% \quad \text{1 mark}$$

ANSWERS

	1	2	3	4	5	6
Contribution before	1,600	1,600	1,600	1,600	1,600	
Contribution after	2,304	2,304	2,304	2,304	2,304	
	704 × 5	= 3,520				

> Need to use pre-tax Contribution in this calculation. So use £2.496bn and work out the NPV of this over the time period of the investment See part (b)(i) of the suggested answer.

Note on this answer

(a) The student would obtain 2 marks for their answer here. To score higher marks they would need to

    (i) be more precise with the explanation in the first part of the question.

    (ii) evaluate the correct PVs for the denominator

    (iii) answer both b(i) and (ii).

71 CH Ltd

> **Text references.** Look at Chapter 12 if you get stuck on inflating the cash flows or need help with the calculation of tax benefits.
>
> **Top tips.** The costs and benefits given in the question are at current prices which means a real rate should be applied to them for discounting purposes. Such an approach does not allow for the benefit of the lag in the payment of taxation. You therefore need to inflate the values given so that they represent the actual number of pounds that will be received or paid, and then apply the money rate, as this takes account of this time lag of taxation. We have provided the alternative approach to discounting using the real rate of 10%, in case that is the method you adopted.
>
> Because part (b) so clearly requires sensitivity analysis of contribution, if you are planning your answer carefully you should aim to calculate the PV of the sensitive variable (contribution) separately in part (a) so that you can use your answer in part (b). In our alternative approach to (a) we dealt with them together to show the appropriate method if you did not deal with them separately.
>
> Because we are using the nominal rate of 15.5% you cannot use PV tables and so have to determine the discount factors using $(1/(1.155)^n)$ and your calculator.
>
> **Easy marks.** Part (c) of the question examines the preparation of project cash flows that take account of taxation and inflation. It was a fairly straightforward DCF/tax scenario except for one small point: the disposal value of £55,000 was a current value; the actual disposal value at year 5 needed to be included in the analysis. This part of the question is 'stand alone', in that it is unaffected by parts (a) and (b). If you have practised capital allowance workings then it might be better to tackle this part first before you make any attempt at the more complex and unfamiliar parts (a) and (b).
>
> Don't worry if your answer is slightly different due to the approach to rounding that you have adopted.

(a) As explained in top tips, we need to inflate the cash flows and use the nominal rate of 15.5%. And we are dealing with contribution separately, as discussed in top tips.

ANSWERS

Step 1 Calculate the PV of non-contribution items

Inflated fixed cost = £90,000 × 1.05^n (when n is for years 1 to 5)

Inflated disposal value = £55,000 × 1.05^5

Time	Cash flows £	Tax benefits (W) £	Net cash flow £	Discount factor 15.5%	PV £
0 Investment	(550,000)	–	(550,000)	1.000	(550,000)
1 Fixed costs	(94,500)	14,175	(80,325)	0.866	(69,561)
2 Fixed costs	(99,225)	29,059	(70,166)	0.750	(52,625)
3 Fixed costs	(104,186)	30,512	(73,674)	0.649	(47,814)
4 Fixed costs	(109,396)	32,037	(77,359)	0.562	(43,476)
5 Fixed costs	(114,865)	33,640	(81,225)	0.487	(39,557)
5 Disposal value	70,195		70,195	0.487	(34,185)
6 Fixed costs	–	17,230	17,230	0.421	7,254
					(761,594)

Working

Tax effect of fixed costs

Year	Cash flow £	Tax saved (30%) £	Yr 1 £	Yr 2 £	Yr 3 £	Yr 4 £	Yr 5 £	Yr 6 £
1	94,500	28,350	14,175	14,175				
2	99,225	29,768		14,884	14,884			
3	104,186	31,256			15,628	15,628		
4	109,396	32,819				16,409	16,410	
5	114,865	34,460					17,230	17,230
			14,175	29,059	30,512	32,037	33,640	17,230

Step 2 Calculate annual contribution

Estimated annual sales revenue = (£800,000 × 0.25) + (£560,000 × 0.5) + (£448,000 × 0.25) = £592,000

Contribution/ sales ratio = 55%

∴ Annual contribution = 0.55 × £592,000 = £325,600

Inflated contribution = £325,600 × 1.05^n (where n is for years 1 to 5)

Step 3 Calculate the PV of contribution

Year	Inflated contribution £	Tax payment (W) £	Net cash flow £	Discount factor 15.5%	PV £
1	341,880	(51,282)	290,598	0.866	251,658
2	358,974	(105,128)	253,846	0.750	190,385
3	376,923	(110,384)	266,539	0.649	172,984
4	395,769	(115,904)	279,865	0.562	157,284
5	415,557	(121,699)	293,858	0.487	143,109
6		(62,334)	(62,334)	0.421	(26,243)
					889,177

ANSWERS

	Working	Tax			Tax payments			
Year	Cash flow £	saved (30%) £	Yr 1 £	Yr 2 £	Yr 3 £	Yr 4 £	Yr 5 £	Yr 6 £
1	341,880	102,564	51,282	51,282				
2	358,974	107,692		53,846	53,846			
3	376,923	113,077			56,538	56,539		
4	395,769	118,731				59,365	59,366	
5	415,557	124,667					62,333	62,334
			51,282	105,128	110,384	115,904	121,699	62,334

Step 4 Determine overall NPV

NPV = £(889,177 − 761,594) = £127,583

The project should be undertaken as it results in a positive NPV.

Alternative approach.

(a) ### Step 1 Work out the real rate.

(1 + money rate) = (1 + real rate) × (1 + inflation rate)

∴ 1.155 = (1 + real rate) × 1.05

∴ Real rate = (1.155/1.05) − 1 = 10%

Step 2 Work out the annual cash flows.

Estimated annual sales revenue = (£800,000 × 0.25) + (£560,000 × 0.5) + (£448,000 × 0.25)
= £592,000
Contribution/sales ratio = 55%
∴ Annual contribution = 0.55 × £592,000 = £325,600

Step 3 Work out the tax effects.

Expected profit (cash flow) = Annual contribution − fixed costs

Year	Cash inflow £	Tax at 30% £	Year 1 £	Year 2 £	Year 3 £	Year 4 £	Year 5 £	Year 6 £
1	235,600	70,680	35,340	35,340				
2	235,600	70,680		35,340	35,340			
3	235,600	70,680			35,340	35,340		
4	235,600	70,680				35,340	35,340	
5	235,600	70,680					35,340	35,340
			35,340	70,680	70,680	70,680	70,680	35,340

ANSWERS

Step 4 **Perform DCF analysis.**

Year	Cash flow £	Discount factor 10%	PV £
0	(550,000) investment	1.000	(550,000)
1-5	235,600 inflow	3.791	893,160
1	(35,340) tax	0.909	(32,124)
2-5	(70,680) tax	2.882 *	(203,700)
5	55,000 disposal	0.621	34,155
6	(35,340) tax	0.564	(19,932)
			121,559

* 3.791 – 0.909

The project should be undertaken as it results in a positive NPV.

(b) NPV of after-tax contribution = £889,177 and overall NPV = £127,583

∴ The PV of after-tax contribution could fall by £127,583 before the recommendation above changes.

This represents a (127,583/889,177)×100% = 14.3% fall

(c) **Tax implications**

	Reducing balance £	Tax saved £	Year 1 £	Year 2 £	Year 3 £	Year 4 £	Year 5 £	Year 6 £
Purchase price	550,000							
Yr 1 WDA (25%)	(137,500)	41,250	20,625	20,625				
Value at start of Yr 2	412,500							
Yr 2 WDA (25%)	(103,125)	30,938		15,469	15,469			
Value at start of Yr 3	309,375							
Yr 3 WDA (25%)	(77,344)	23,203			11,602	11,601		
Value at start of Yr 4	232,031							
Yr 4 WDA (25%)	(58,008)	17,402				8,701	8,701	
Value at start of Yr 5	174,023							
Yr 5 scrap proceeds	(70,195)*							
Balancing allowance	103,828	31,148					15,574	15,574
			20,625	36,094	27,071	20,302	24,275	15,574

* The **disposal value** of 10% of initial expenditure (£55,000) is a current price. The actual disposal value therefore needs to be **inflated** to determine the actual tax effects. WDAs are based on current prices.

∴ Disposal value = £55,000 × 1.05^5 = £70,195

NPV implications

We **discount at the money rate** as we are **dealing with actual cash flows**.

Year	Cashflow £	Discount factor 15.5%	PV £
1	20,625	0.866	17,861
2	36,094	0.750	27,071
3	27,071	0.649	17,569
4	20,302	0.562	11,410
5	24,275	0.487	11,822
6	15,574	0.421	6,557
		NPV	92,290

The NPV of the project would therefore **increase** by £92,290 **due to savings from tax implications**.

72 Question with analysis and answer plan: PK Glass plc

Text references. Part (a) requires you to demonstrate knowledge of the pros and cons of DCF so refer to Chapter 11 when answering this. Part (b) can be answered using Chapter 12.

Top tips. Do not include the scrap value of the machine in the cash flow tax calculations for alternative 1. This must be dealt with separately using capital allowances.

Your calculations might have included the **second instalment** of the machinery's **WDA** for **last year** (time –1) since that will affect the tax charge for time 1. This would need to be taken into account for **both alternatives**, however, so it is not an incremental benefit and can be omitted from the comparative calculations altogether.

Note that maintenance applies in both consequences so can leave this out.

You could have included the loss of WDAs in your analysis of alternative 1 or, as we have done, included them as a benefit in alternative 2.

Easy marks. The calculation of writing down allowances is usually quite straightforward so begin with those as you deal with each alternative in part (b). This will give you a bit of confidence to cope with the rest of the question.

Answer plan

This question has a mix of requirements but parts (a), (b) and (c) can be answered separately and in any order. Remember however, if you wish to do this in the exam, leave enough space in your answer book so you can slot your answers in the right order.

So if you feel a bit uncertain about launching straight into a large NPV calculation, write the memo first.

However, if you love number crunching then get the majority of the marks by doing the NPV bits first. So (1) below could be your number (3) or vice versa.

(1) Write the memo. Use the correct format including addressee, date and subject. Compare and contrast between profit and cash flow used in DCF. Remember to apply this to the company also and explain why PK Glass use DCF.

(2) Then do the NPVs

    (a) There are two alternatives to calculate and then compare NPVs.

    (b) Taxation is an additional requirement

    (c) Set out your workings in a separate schedule and cross reference these to your main NPV calculation.

    (d) Do a table setting out years and cash flows for your main NPV calculation.

    (e) Remember capital costs of outlay and scrap values.

(3) Finally, three marks for a brainstorming look at what factors would affect the model.

ANSWERS

(a)

MEMORANDUM

To: PK Glass plc Director
From: Management accountant
Date: 19 November 20X7
Re: Investment appraisal policy

1 Introduction

> Note how the memo compares cash flow and profit to explain how they differ. So advantages and disadvantages of each.

1.1 Thank you for your letter of 16 November in which you suggested that, since cash flow and profit are the same thing in the long run, we should always adopt courses of action which maximise accounting profit.

2 Advantages of using profit

2.1 **Profit** is a more widely known and understood concept than discounted cash flow (DCF) analysis and it is perfectly **understandable** that **non-financial specialists** should be more ready to **accept decisions based on a concept with which they have familiarity**. **DCF analysis** is, however, the **commoner and correct approach to take when appraising investments**.

3 The unsuitability of profit

3.1 **Profit** has a number of **features which make it unsuitable as an appraisal measure**. For example, due to **different accounting conventions** that organisations might adopt, such as the depreciation method or stock valuation method, it is a **subjective** measure.

4 The advantages of DCF

4.1 DCF analysis, on the other hand, takes account of actual cash flows, the timing of those cash flows and the time value of money (the idea that £1 received now is worth more than £1 received in the future), all of which are vital components of the investment appraisal method adopted by an organisation.

4.2 **Although profit and cash flow might be the same in the long run, the timing of the short-term differences can have an impact on the acceptability of an investment** and so DCF analysis rather than measures of profit should be used to appraise investments.

5 DCF and PK Glass plc

5.1 The group uses the net present value (NPV) approach to DCF analysis. This means that we require the net cash flows from an investment project to produce a return greater than the cost of capital of the division considering the investment.

6

I hope you have found this explanation useful but if you do require any further information please do not hesitate to contact me.

Signed: Management accountant

(b) **Alternative 1 v alternative 2 – summary**

Alternative 2 is better by a present value of £129k and should therefore be chosen.

Alternative 1 – closure of the packaging department

Assume that all prime costs are avoidable.

ANSWERS

Step 1 **Determine writing down allowances (WDAs)**

	£'000
Current written down value of machine (based on two years WDAs received) (£1,000,000 × 75% × 75%)	563
Scrap value	70
Balancing allowance	493

Tax benefit at 30% = 147.9

We will incorporate the cash flow effects of this tax benefit in step 2 below.

Step 2 **Determine cash flows and hence NPV**

Time	0	1	2	3	4
	£'000	£'000	£'000	£'000	£'000
Savings					
Prime cost (W1)		700.000	700.0	700.0	
Rent (W3)		60.000	60.0	60.0	
Maintenance (W5)		100.000	100.0	100.0	
Costs					
X Packaging Ltd		(950.000)	(950.0)	(950.0)	
Net cash flow		(90.000)	(90.0)	(90.0)	
Other					
Redundancy (W1)	(21.000)				
Scrap value of materials (W7)	20.000				
Taxable cash flows	(1.000)	(90.000)	(90.0)	(90.0)	
Tax at 30% receivable in current year	0.150	13.500	13.5	13.5	
Tax at 30% receivable in following year		0.150	13.5	13.5	13.5
Capital					
Scrap value of machine	70.000				
Tax benefit of WDAs receivable (£147,750 × 50% in each year)	73.950	73.900			
Total cash flow	143.100	−2.450	−63.0	−63.0	13.5
Discount factor (12%)	× 1.000	× 0.893	× 0.797	× 0.712	× 0.636
Present value	143.100	−2.190	−50.210	−44.860	8.590

∴ **NPV = £54,430**

Workings

1   *Prime cost*

There will be an immediate (time 0) cost of 30% × £700,000 × 10% = £21,000 relating to redundancies. Thereafter the annual savings will be £700,000.

2   *Supervisors*

These will be redeployed so there is no cost or saving.

3   *Rent*

The cost of rent of the buildings for the packaging department (£50,000 per annum) will not be saved by the company overall, but the current cost (£60,000 per annum) of accommodation for the department that will use the packaging buildings in future presumably will be saved.

4 *Depreciation*

This is not a cash flow.

5 *Maintenance*

The machinery will be scrapped so the annual costs of maintenance will be saved.

6 *Allocated overhead*

Allocated costs are just a cost accounting device. Presumably the overheads will still be incurred so there is no cost or benefit.

7 *Packaging materials*

The original cost or book value of the stock is a sunk cost. The stock will not be needed and will not be replaced so the relevant cost is the scrap value.

Alternative 2 – sub-contract the maintenance

Assume that the only existing cost affected is the maintenance cost.

Step 1 **Determine WDAs**

	Reducing balance	*Tax saved*	*Benefit received* *Yr 1*	*Yr 2*	*Yr 3*	*Yr 4*
	£'000	£'000	£'000	£'000	£'000	£'000
Written down value at time 0						
(£1m × 75% × 75%)	562.5					
Yr 1 WDA (25%)	140.6	42.18	21.09	21.09		
Value at start of year 2	421.9					
Yr 2 WDA (25%)	105.5	31.65		15.83	15.82	
Value at start of year 3	316.4					
Sales proceeds	50.0					
Balancing allowance	266.4	79.92			39.96	39.96
			21.09	36.92	55.78	39.96

Step 2 **Determine cash flows and hence NPV**

Time	*1*	*2*	*3*	*4*
	£'000	£'000	£'000	£'000
Savings				
Maintenance	100.00	100.00	100.00	
Costs				
To Y Ltd	(80.00)	(80.00)	(80.00)	
Taxable cash flows	20.00	20.00	20.00	
Tax at 30% payable in current year	(3.00)	(3.00)	(3.00)	
Tax at 30% payable in following year		(3.00)	(3.00)	(3.00)
Capital				
Scrap value of machine			50.00	
Tax benefit of WDAs receivable (see step 1)	21.09	36.92	55.78	39.96
Total cash flow	38.09	50.92	119.78	36.96
Discount factor (12%)	× 0.893	× 0.797	× 0.712	× 0.636
Present value	34.01	40.58	85.28	23.51

∴ **NPV** = £183,380

(c) **Factors which might affect the recommendation made in (a)**

(i) The accuracy of the cost and revenue estimates, especially those for three years in the future.

(ii) The reliability/experience of Y Ltd. How will W Ltd's business be affected if the quality of Y Ltd's service is not high enough? The maintenance cost per annum might be less but overall there could be a drop in profit if the machine cannot be used.

(iii) The ease with which W Ltd could take over maintenance of the machine if Y Ltd proved unable to offer the appropriate level of service

(iv) The possibility of redundancies of W Ltd's own maintenance staff. This could lead to a loss of staff goodwill.

(v) The experience and reliability of X Packaging Ltd. If X Packaging Ltd were to carry out the packaging, the costs of glass breakage may well fall considerably given that it is a specialist packaging company. Incorporating this reduction in breakage costs into the analysis would improve alternative 1's NPV.

(vi) Mere maintenance (alternative 2) does not address the problem of the ongoing unreliability of the machine. Other costs might start to arise when the machine breaks down (from lost production and loss of quality, for example).

(vii) The difference in NPVs between the two alternatives emphatically favours alternative 2, so the conclusion is not sensitive to modest changes in variables such as cost of capital or tax rates and allowances.

73 Taxi

Top tips. This is a calculation question on asset replacement. However it included inflation and so you would not be able to use annualised equivalent costs. The principal things you would need to do to score well would be:

- Calculate cash flows including inflated values for both alternatives
- Comment on your findings as you are asked to advise the owner on the best alternative
- State the net present value of the opportunity cost of making the wrong decision

Four marks each were given for calculating the two year and three year replacement cycles. The remaining marks were awarded for advising management based on the results of your calculations of NPV.

Easy marks. There are lots of easy marks available here. You should have no problem inflating the costs and revenues providing you have set out workings tables as shown below.

Examiner's comments. A question not answered well and errors included:

- Discounting options over two and three years and applying the annualised equivalent method. This won't work because of inflation
- Incorrectly calculating inflated figures
- Including non-relevant costs including initial purchase cost and vehicle running costs

In the examiner's comments he remarks that candidates should not include non-relevant costs such as the initial purchase cost and annual costs and revenues, so these have been excluded from our answer.

Assumptions. Inflation applies from Year 0 to all costs and revenues, which are stated at their Year 0 values in the question.

ANSWERS

Incremental cash flows – 2 year trade-in

	Year 2 £	Year 3 £	Year 4 £	Year 5 £	Year 6 £
Taxi cost	(16,538)		(18,233)		
Trade-in value	7,718		8,509		9,381
Servicing and repair		(666)	(3,660)	(805)	(4,429)
Net cash flow	(8,820)	(666)	(13,384)	(805)	4,952
Discount factor 12%	0.797	0.712	0.636	0.567	0.507
Present value	(7,030)	(474)	(8,512)	(456)	2,511

NPV of incremental cash flows (2 year trade-in) = £(13,961)

Incremental cash flows – 3 year trade-in

	Year 3 £	Year 4 £	Year 5 £	Year 6 £
Taxi cost	(17,365)			
Trade-in value	4,631			5,360
Servicing and repair	(5,324)	(732)	(4,026)	(7,086)
Net cash flow	(18,058)	(732)	(4,026)	(1,726)
Discount factor 12%	0.712	0.636	0.567	0.507
Present value	(12,857)	(466)	(2,283)	(875)

NPV of incremental cash flows (3 year trade-in) = £(16,481)

Based on the NPV of the incremental cash flows of each of the replacement cycles, the two year cycle is preferable. The NPV of the opportunity cost of choosing the wrong cycle is the difference between the two NPVs, which is £2,520.

74 JK plc

Text reference. The information to answer this question can be found in Chapters 11, 12 and 13 of the Study Text.

Top tips. This question is asking you to evaluate an investment using **long-term decision making techniques**. This is a good question if you love calculations. **The actual calculations aren't difficult but there are lots of them.**

In part (a) you are asked to assess whether the investment is financially worthwhile. You should be familiar with NPV by now. You need to read the question closely to extract the information you need to perform your calculations. Split up the calculations into workings for tax, tax depreciation and the variable costs and revenues. This will help you manage the sheer volume of calculations needed.

Remember with the tax cash flows that 50% is paid or received in **the year after the year the profit arises.** This means that the cash flows will extend beyond Year 4. Don't forget to **advise** the company on whether the investment is worthwhile.

In part (b), you are asked to calculate the IRR of the investment. You will need to use the IRR formula and that is one you need to learn! The formula requires two NPVs so you will need to calculate the NPV of the net cash flows from part(a) at a different rate.

Easy marks. Set out a proforma for calculating the NPV in part (a). The fixed costs can be input straight into the main proforma calculation, but remember to inflate them. Keep your workings neat and the marker will be able to do their job more easily!

You can choose to do part (c) separately as this is a discrete question and could get you a few marks straight away.

ANSWERS

(a) **Projected cash flows for a computer controlled production facility**

	Year 0 £'000	Year 1 £'000	Year 2 £'000	Year 3 £'000	Year 4 £'000	Year 5 £'000
Sales (W1)		120,000	132,300	145,530	150,012	
Variable costs						
Production costs (W2)		(75,000)	(85,050)	(96,250)	(102,060)	
Selling/distribution costs(W3)		(10,000)	(11,130)	(12,320)	(12,852)	
Fixed costs (W4)						
Production costs		(4,000)	(4,320)	(4,666)	(5,039)	
Selling/distribution costs		(2,000)	(2,120)	(2,247)	(2,382)	
Administration costs		(1,000)	(1,050)	(1,103)	(1,158)	
Total costs		(92,000)	(103,670)	(116,586)	(123,491)	
Net cash inflow before tax		28,000	28,630	28,944	26,521	
Tax due on net cash flow (W5)		(4,200)	(8,494)	(8,637)	(8,319)	(3,978)
Tax saved (via WDA) (W6)		1,875	3,281	2,461	4,069	3,014
Capital cost (W7)	(50,000)				1,000	
Net cash inflow after tax	(50,000)	25,675	23,417	22,768	23,271	(964)
Discount factor at 12%	× 1.000	× 0.893	× 0.797	× 0.712	× 0.636	× 0.567
PV of cash out flow	(50,000)	22,928	18,663	16,211	14,800	(547)

NPV of cash flow = £22,055,000

Based on a positive NPV of £22.055 million the investment is worthwhile and should be undertaken.

Workings

1 *Sales revenue*

	Year 1	Year 2	Year 3	Year 4
Sales units ('000)	100	105	110	108
Sales price/unit (£)	1,200	1,260	1,323	1,389
Sales revenue (£'000)	120,000	132,300	145,530	150,012

Note. The sales price/unit is inflated by 5% pa.

2 *Production costs*

	Year 1	Year 2	Year 3	Year 4
Sales units ('000)	100	105	110	108
Variable cost price/unit (£)	750	810	875	945
Production costs (£'000)	75,000	85,050	96,250	102,060

Note. The variable production cost/unit is inflated by 8% pa

3 *Selling and distribution costs*

	Year 1	Year 2	Year 3	Year 4
Sales units ('000)	100	105	110	108
Variable cost price/unit (£)	100	106	112	119
Selling and distribution costs (£'000)	10,000	11,130	12,320	12,852

Note. The selling and distribution cost /unit is inflated by 6% pa

4 *Fixed costs*

These are inflated in accordance with the question as follows:

(a) production costs are inflated by 8% pa
(b) selling and distribution costs are inflated by 6% pa
(c) administration costs are inflated by 5% pa

ANSWERS

5 **Tax on net cash flows**

	Year 1 £'000	Year 2 £'000	Year 3 £'000	Year 4 £'000	Year 5 £'000
Net cash inflow before tax	28,000	28,630	28,944	26,521	
Tax at 30%	8,400	8,589	8,683	7,956	
Due 50% in year and 50% in the following year	4,200	4,200			
	0	4,294	4,295		
			4,342	4,341	
				3,978	3,978
Tax due on net cash flow (W5)	4,200	8,494	8,637	8,319	3,978

6 **Tax depreciation**

Year		£'000
0	Purchase	50,000
1	WDA	12,500
	Value at start of year 2	37,500
2	WDA	9,375
	Value at start of year 3	28,125
3	WDA	7,031
	Value at start of year 4	21,094
4	Sale	1,000
	Balancing allowance	20,094

Year of claim	Allowance £'000	Tax saved £'000	Year 1 £'000	Year 2 £'000	Year 3 £'000	Year 4 £'000	Year 5 £'000
1	12,500	3,750	1,875	1,875			
2	9,375	2,813		1,406	1,407		
3	7,031	2,109			1,054	1,055	
4	20,094	6,028	–	–	–	3,014	3,014
5			1,875	3,281	2,461	4,069	3,014

7 **Treatment of receipt on sale in Year 4**

The receipt on sale of the machine is a capital receipt and would not be taxed. Capital allowances are claimed instead.

(b) **Internal rate of return of the investment**

Cost of capital

We need to calculate the IRR of the project. We know that the NPV using a discount rate of 12% is £22.055 million.

As the NPV is fairly high at a rate of 12%, the rate to produce a negative NPV will need to be well in excess of 12%.

Let's try 35%.

Remember that where discount rates are not found in your tables, you can calculate these by taking the formula $1/(1+r)^n$ where n = 1, 2 or 3 in this situation and r = 35%.

ANSWERS

Year	Net cash flow £'000	Discount factor @ 35%	Present value £'000
0	(50,000)	1.000	(50,000)
1	25,675	0.741	19,025
2	23,416	0.549	12,855
3	22,769	0.406	9,244
4	23,270	0.301	7,004
5	(964)	0.223	(215)
			(2,087)

Then calculate the IRR of the project.

$$\text{IRR} = 12\% + \left[\frac{22{,}055}{22{,}055 + 2{,}087} \times (35 - 12)\right]\% = \mathbf{33.01\%}$$

(c) **Real rate of return and money rate of return**

The money rate or nominal rate measures the return in terms of the unit of currency that is, (usually due to inflation) falling in value.

The **real rate** measures the return in **constant price level** terms.

The two rates of return and the inflation rate are linked by an equation.

(1+ money rate of return) = (1 + real rate of return) × (1 + rate of inflation)

Money cash flows should be discounted at a money discount rate.

Real cash flows (ie adjusted for inflation) should be discounted at a real discount rate.

We must decide **which rate** to use for discounting, the **money rate** or the **real rate**. The rule is as follows.

(i) If the cash flows are expressed in terms of the **actual number of pounds** that will be received or paid on the various future dates, we **use the money rate for discounting**.

(ii) If the cash flows are expressed In terms of the value of the pound at time 0 (that is, in constant price level terms), we use the real rate.

The **cash flows** calculated in part(a) are expressed **in terms of the actual number of pounds** that will be received or paid at the relevant dates. We should, therefore, **discount** them using a **money rate of return**

75 X

Text reference. This question covers material found in Chapters 10 - 13 and 18.

Top tips.

In part (a), there are a few things that you need to remember to do. These include:

(i) Adjusting the draft statement for the receivables and payables figures to arrive at a true cash flow in each year.

(ii) Making sure that you adjust for the depreciation on the investment when calculating cash flows.

(iii) Ensuring that you get the correct profit figures for calculating tax. These are not the same as the cash flows calculated.

(iv) Allocating the correct timing on the tax payments as there will be a payment due in the year after the investment finishes.

You should also note that there are no writing down allowances available on the investment.

ANSWERS

> Part (b) wants you to mention money cash flows, and what effect this may have on the detail and type of information needed. You also need to discuss what discount factor is appropriate when inflation is included in cash flows.
>
> Part (c) considers a scenario where resources are scarce. The question makes clear that the projects are **non-divisible** and **none will be repeated**. There are only three marks so keep your calculations simple.
>
> In part (d) remember that gain sharing involves sharing **cost overruns as well as cost savings**. There might also be other reasons why X might not want to enter a gain sharing arrangement such as wanting to keep information confidential.
>
> **Easy marks.** Use lots of workings to break up your calculations especially in part(a) where there are quite a few adjustments to make. Using $'000 rather than $ saves a bit of time when doing calculations.

(a) **NPV of investment proposal**

	Y0 $'000	Y1 $'000	Y2 $'000	Y3 $'000	Y4 $'000
Investment	(200)	–	–	50.0	
Annual cash flows					
Sales (W1)		210.0	340	275.0	25.0
Production costs (W2)		(138.0)	(219)	(167.0)	(8.0)
Net pre-tax cash flow	(200)	72.0	121.0	158.0	17.0
Taxation (W3)	0	(12.9)	(32.1)	(34.8)	(15.6)
Net post-tax cash flow	(200)	59.1	88.9	123.2	1.4
Discount factor	1.000	0.943	0.890	0.840	0.792
PV	(200)	55.73	79.12	103.49	1.11
NPV	**39.45**				

Workings

1

	Y1 $'000	Y2 $'000	Y3 $'000	Y4 $'000
Sales				
Per statement	230	350	270	
Receivables				
Plus opening	0	20	30	25
Less closing	(20)	(30)	(25)	0
	(20)	(10)	5	25
Cash flow sales	210	340	275	25

2

	Y1 $'000	Y2 $'000	Y3 $'000	Y4 $'000
Production costs				
Per statement	194	272	216	
Less depreciation (W)	(50)	(50)	(50)	
	144	222	166	
Payables				
Plus opening	0	6	9	8
Less closing	(6)	(9)	(8)	0
	(6)	(3)	1	8
Cash flow costs	138	219	167	8

Working for depreciation

$$\frac{\text{(Cost of investment less residual value)}}{\text{Life}} = \$'000 \ \frac{(200-50)}{3} = \$50,000 \text{ pa}$$

ANSWERS

3

	Y1	Y2	Y3	Y4
	$'000	$'000	$'000	$'000
Tax				
Profit from main statement	36.0	78.0	54.0	
Adjusted for depreciation	50.0	50.0	50.0	
Profit for tax-purposes	86.0	128.0	104.0	
At 30% (Note)	25.8	38.4	31.2	
Payable	12.9	12.9		
		19.2	19.2	
	0.0	0.0	15.6	15.6
Total tax payable	12.9	32.1	34.8	15.6

Note. The company is liable to pay corporation tax on its accounting profits adjusted for various tax-related amendments. So we need to take the figures from the financial statement and adjust for depreciation only.

(b) **Inflation**

Inflation would affect the investment in a variety of ways.

(i) Cash flows would have to be inflated **where inflation applied** so each relevant cash flow for the investment would be inflated over three years. Rates of inflation may vary depending on the particular cash flow so these might have to be broken down further. These cash flows would be **money cash flows**.

(ii) Where **receipts and payments** relate to a previous year's sales and costs, these need to be inflated at the previous year's rate.

(ii) The discount factor or cost of capital would be at a **money rate**. This is expressed as follows

(1 + money rate) = (1 + real rate) × (1 + inflation rate)

(c) **Ranking three projects**

Investments	Initial investment	NPV
	$'000	$'000
W + investment	500	114
W+Y	400	102
Y+ investment	300	66

As funds are limited to $400,000 clearly W + new investment are not possible. Of the two remaining alternatives, W+Y has the larger total NPV and so should be chosen on this basis.

(d) (i) **Gain sharing arrangements**

In gain sharing arrangements **all cost savings and cost overruns are shared** between the customer and the contractor. A **target cost** is negotiated and agreed. Any savings on this target cost are shared in agreed proportions. However any cost overruns based on the target cost are also shared between the parties. Any financial gains are assessed by providing open access to relevant cost data. This is known as **open book accounting**.

(ii) **Why X might not want to use gain sharing arrangements**

It appears that a gain sharing arrangement would give X access to funds and maybe resources that would help lessen its shortfall in funding. A partner could take over funding one or more of the contracts. Although this sounds ideal, the arrangements for calculating the sharing of gains require some scrutiny of X's accounts which may not be desirable from X's viewpoint. These contain information that X may wish to keep confidential to protect its competitive position. The partner will also want some say over how their funding is used which may also be in conflict with X's plans for using the funds.

ANSWERS

76 Section A answers: Forecasting and managing future costs

1   B $Y = aX^{-0.3219}$

   $a = 18$ minutes

   If the cumulative number of units (X) = 5, the cumulative average time per unit (Y) = $18 \times 5^{-0.3219}$ = 10.722

   ∴ Total time for 5 units = 10.722×5 = 53.61 minutes

   If the cumulative number of units (X) = 4, the cumulative average time per unit (Y) = $18 \times 4^{-0.3219}$ = 11.520

   ∴ Total time for 4 units = 11.520×4 = 46.08 minutes

   ∴ Time for fifth unit = $53.61 - 46.08$ = 7.53 minutes

2   For 20 cumulative units, cumulative average time per unit = $80 \times 20^{-0.322}$
   = 30.49 hours

   For 27 cumulative units, cumulative average time per unit = $80 \times 27^{-0.322}$
   = 27.68 hours

	Cumulative units	Average time per unit Hours	Total time Hours
End of April	20	× 30.49	609.8
End of May	27	× 27.68	747.4
Total standard time for May			137.6

3   A   Labour operations involve a complex set of repetitive activities – **no**
    B   Labour is not a significant proportion of total cost – **yes**
    C   There is a high rate of labour turnover in department Y – **yes**
    D   There may be a long time delay between successive orders – **yes**

   If labour operations involve a complex set of repetitive activities (**factor A**), then a learning curve might apply.

   If labour is not a significant proportion of total cost (**factor B**) the effort involved in calculating the learning effect may not be worthwhile.

   A higher rate of labour turnover (**factor C**) may mean that employees do not stay in department Y long enough for the learning to be remembered.

   If there is a long time delay (**factor D**) then the learning curve should not be applied, because the learning will be forgotten.

4   A   Using standard components wherever possible – **can**
    B   Acquiring new, more efficient technology – **can**
    C   Making staff redundant – **can't**
    D   Reducing the quality of the product in question – **can't**

   To make improvements towards the target cost, technologies and processes must be improved (**B**). The use of standard components is a way of improving the production process (**A**).

   Making staff redundant will not improve technologies and processes (**C**).

   Reducing the quality of the product in question does not do this either (**D**).

ANSWERS

5　A　Remember that not all products will follow this life cycle. The concept can only be applied in general.

6　Within a system of target costing, target cost is calculated as **market price** minus **desired** profit margin.

7　Target cost = selling price at capacity – 25% profit margin

Price	Demand
£	Units
50	100,000
45	200,000
40	400,000

∴ Target cost = £40 – (25% × £40) = £30

8　A　The bulk of a product's life cycle costs will be determined at the design/development stage (being designed in at the outset during product and process design, plant installation and setting up of the distribution network).

9　A　Sales value – **no**
　　B　Replacement value – **no**
　　C　Exchange value – **yes**
　　D　Disposal value – **no**

The four aspects of value to consider are cost, exchange, use and esteem.

77 Experience curve

Top tips. You can increase your chances of being able to provide specific instances/examples by reading *Insider*, *Financial Management* and a quality newspaper on a regular basis.

The experience curve and pricing

From **previous experience** of production and sales of similar products within very similar conditions and markets, an organisation may be aware that an **experience curve** can be applied to the production of a new product. The price for that product can therefore be **based on a cost below that of the Initial cost if the cost will fall as the experience curve takes effect**.

The significance of low prices

A **low price when a product is first launched** can, in general, help a product to **gain a significant market share** within a particular period of time. Depending on the product, volume of sales can be the determining factor in attaining **profitability**. A policy of low pricing when a product is first launched in order to obtain sufficient penetration in the market is known as **penetration pricing** and is particularly **useful** in the following circumstances.

(a)　If the firm wishes to **discourage new entrants** into the market

(b)　If the firm wishes to **shorten the initial period** of the product's life cycle in order to enter the growth and maturity stages as quickly as possible

(c)　If there are significant **economies of scale** to be achieved from a high volume of output, so that quick penetration into the market is desirable in order to gain unit cost reductions

(d)　If **demand** is highly **elastic** and so would respond well to low prices

The **low price** is then often **raised** as the product moves into its growth stage. Such a tactic is designed to entice customers to use the product and hopefully become loyal to it.

Examples

Texas Instruments employed this strategy when it introduced its semiconductor chips for computers.

ANSWERS

Penetration pricing is also often used by organisations **introducing new credit cards**. In most cases the initial interest rate (the 'price') is lower than the 'going rate', so that prospective customers are encouraged to transfer balances from their existing credit cards to the new one. In many cases, once the credit card has become established in the market, the interest rate charged will start to rise towards the 'going rate'.

78 ML plc

> **Top tips.** You should have been able to score highly on this question as long as you applied your understanding of cost reduction and value analysis to the question scenario.

Cost reduction

Cost reduction is a **planned and positive approach** to **reducing** the unit cost of goods/services **below current budgeted or standard** levels **without impairing** the **suitability for the used intended** for the goods produced/services provided by the organisation. It should not be confused with cost control, which is all about keeping costs within acceptable (standard or budgeted) limits.

Cost reduction in ML plc

A cost reduction programme in ML plc would therefore look at how to reduce, for example, the costs of designing a web site, or even a particular part of a web site, without the customer perceiving any fall in the value of the service the company is providing.

Value analysis

Conventional cost reduction techniques try to achieve the lowest unit cost for a specific product design/way of providing a service. **Value analysis tries to find the least-cost method of making a product or providing a service that achieves the desired function/outcome.**

Value analysis in ML plc

Value analysis within ML plc of, say, the design of web sites for customers, would involve the systematic investigation of both the costs connected with it and the way in which it is provided, with **the aim of getting rid of all unnecessary costs**. An unnecessary cost is an additional cost incurred **without adding to the following aspects of value.**

- **Use value** – the purpose fulfilled by the service
- **Exchange value** – the market value of the service
- **Esteem value** – the prestige the customer attaches to the service

Example

Given that ML plc has a multi-site operation with bases in the UK and overseas, cost reduction and value analysis techniques could investigate possible duplication of activities that occur as a result.

It is important that duplicated activities are not eliminated in an effort to reduce costs if value is adversely affected, however.

For example, given the nature of its services, specialist teams could be based anywhere in the world. Maintaining a physical presence in different parts of the world should improve customers' perceptions of the value of ML plc's services, however; customers would feel they were dealing with a local organisation.

79 Wye hotel group

> **Top tips.** This is very, very similar to question 73 but we have included it so that you can see how to apply your knowledge to different scenarios.

Cost reduction

Cost reduction is a planned and positive approach to **reducing the unit cost** of goods/services below current budgeted or standard levels **without impairing their suitability for the use intended**. It should not be confused with cost control, which is all about keeping costs within acceptable (standard or budgeted) limits.

A cost reduction programme in the WYE hotel group would therefore look at how to reduce the cost of a guest staying a night in the hotel, a meal being served in the restaurant and so on, without the customer perceiving any fall in the value of the service provided.

How to reduce costs

The **improvement of efficiency levels** might be considered.

(a) Improving materials usage (eg the use of food in restaurants or guest supplies in bedrooms)

(b) Improving labour productivity (eg changing work methods to eliminate unnecessary procedures, perhaps in the work required to prepare rooms for new guests)

(c) Improving efficiency of equipment usage (eg allowing members of the public to use the swimming pool at certain times of the day/year for payment of a fee)

A programme could also consider ways to **reduce the costs of resources**.

(a) It might be possible to find cheaper suppliers for, say, wines and beers.

(b) Increased automation of certain guest services, say the travel bureaux, would reduce labour costs.

Other aspects of a cost reduction programme might include **increased control over spending decisions**.

Value analysis

Conventional cost reduction techniques try to achieve the lowest unit costs for a specific product design or specific way of providing a service. Value analysis tries to find the **least-cost method of making a product or providing a service that achieves the desired function/outcome**.

Value analysis of a particular service within the hotel group would involve the systematic investigation of both the costs connected with the service and the way in which it is provided, with the **aim of getting rid of all unnecessary costs**. An unnecessary cost is an **additional cost incurred without adding** to the following aspects of value.

- **Use value** – the purpose fulfilled by the service
- **Exchange value** – the market value of the service
- **Esteem value** – the prestige the guest attaches to the service

Applying value analysis

A value analysis of the guest entertainment provided might therefore pose the following questions.

(a) **Are all parts of the entertainment programme necessary?** Could the cabaret show be removed from the programme without affecting guests' perception of the quality of the overall programme?

(b) **Could the programme be provided at a lower cost without affecting its value?** For example, could children's films be shown instead of using a live entertainer?

From the analysis **a variety of options** can be **devised** and **the least cost alternative which maintains or improves the value of the service to the guests can be selected**.

80 Question with answer plan: Cost management techniques

> **Top tips.** To earn good marks for this question you would need to mention the traditional cost containment approaches.

Answer plan

- Two parts to the answer – target costing
  – life cycle costing
- Within each part refer to – traditional approach
  – modern approach
- Remember to mention cost reduction opportunities under each part

(a) **Target costing**

Traditional approach

The traditional approach to product costing, which is dominated by **standard costing**, is first to **develop a product**. An **expected standard cost is then determined** and a **selling price** (probably based on cost) is **set**, with a **resulting profit** or loss.

Costs are **controlled** at **monthly intervals through variance analysis**. The **standard cost**, once set, is **only revised for changes of a permanent or reasonably long-term nature**.

Target costing approach

This is to **develop a product concept** and then **determine the price** that **customers** would be **willing** to **pay** for it. A **desired profit margin** is then **deducted** from the price to **leave** a figure representing total **cost**. This is the **target** cost.

If the **target cost** is vastly **different** from the **cost at which the product can be produced**, the product may need to be **redesigned** or may even be **scrapped** if the target is impossible to achieve.

Management may decide to go ahead and manufacture a product with **a target cost well below the currently attainable cost**. In such circumstances they will set **benchmarks for improvement** towards the target cost, by specified dates. Reducing the number of components, cutting out non-value-added activities and so on are possible **cost reduction approaches.**

Once the product goes into production, the target cost will gradually be reduced, the reductions being incorporated into the budgeting process.

Target costing and cost reduction opportunities

To remain competitive, organisations must continually **redesign** their products. Far more so than in the past, when cost reduction during the production process was important, a product's **planning, development and design stages are therefore critical to an organisation's cost reduction process**. Target costing, by focusing on costs incurred at all steps of a product's life (not just the production stage), gives added emphasis to cost reduction at this vital stage.

(b) **Life cycle costing**

Traditional approach

Traditional management accounting practice is, in general, to **report costs at the physical production stage** of the life cycle of a product; cost are **not accumulated over the entire life cycle**. This means a product's **profitability** is not assessed over its entire life but rather on a **periodic basis**. Costs tend to be **accumulated according to**

ANSWERS

function; research, design, development and customer service costs incurred on all products during a period are totalled and are recorded as a period expense, effectively **hiding them from cost reduction opportunities.**

Life cycle approach

Using life cycle costing, however, such **costs** are **traced to individual products over complete life cycles** (from the product's inception to its decline). This **overview** of a product's profitability is of utmost importance when assessing cost reduction opportunities.

Life cycle costing and cost reduction

One of the principal ideas of life cycle costing is that the **profit generated by a product** must **cover** not only production costs, but the **costs associated with the pre- and post-production stages** (such as costs of research, design and testing, and costs of distribution and customer service). It has been claimed that up to **90% of a product's life cycle costs will be determined 'up front'** by decisions made very early within the life cycle (production costs are based on design decisions, for example). The application of **life cycle costing** will therefore ensure that **cost control and cost reduction** will be carried out at the **early stages**, as well as during the production stage.

81 Telmat

> **Text references.** Part (a) could be answered referring to Chapters 1, 16 and 17 for data on costing systems. Part (b) could be answered from Chapter 15.
>
> **Top tips.** Part (a) was rather vague and you may have found it difficult to produce enough material to warrant 10 marks. Make sure you referred to Telmat in your answer to (b). According to the examiner at the time this question was set under the previous syllabus version of Paper P2, the inclusion of the words 'joint benefits' in the quotation acted as a trigger for some candidates to focus on process costing, and as a consequence, by-products and joint products were much discussed.

(a) There are a **variety of costing systems** which the management accountant can use to establish the way in which products consume resources.

For example, **marginal costing** looks at the way in which those resources which can be directly allocated to products are consumed. **Throughput accounting,** on the other hand, examines the way in which products use scarce resources. **ABC** is probably the most accurate costing technique in this respect, as it attempts to link costs to activities/resources.

(i) **The effect of the addition of a new product to a product range**

The total **cost** of some activities or resources is **dependent** on the **number of batches** manufactured. An example of such an activity is the **setting-up** of machines. The greater the number of batches, the higher the cost of the setting-up activity. The addition of a new product would increase the number of batches and would therefore increase the cost.

Likewise, there is a strong **correlation** between the **costs** of some activities or resources and the **number of different products** produced. Set-up costs are not incurred if only one product is manufactured, but as more and more different products are made, the cost of setting-up increases.

The costs of some resources will therefore increase if an organisation manufactures multiple products.

Benefits

(1) The costs per unit of activities such as distribution and marketing may fall if such facilities are used more fully.

(2) Any production peaks and troughs caused by seasonal demand and/or economic conditions may be smoothed out by the existence of an additional product.

283

ANSWERS

(3) New products can be launched more cheaply by an organisation already selling a range of products under a brand name than by an organisation launching its first product.

(ii) **Effect on total profitability of increasing/decreasing a product range**

Although production costs could increase if a product range expands, scope for **cost reduction opportunities** could present themselves in the costs of product-line level activities such as marketing. The existence of a **complete product range** is almost certain to prove **advantageous** in terms of **marketing**.

A **full product range** is sometimes **necessary to attract/retain customers and maintain profitability**, however. An example is a supplier of study material for professional examinations. If students are unable to get study texts for all of the exams they are sitting, they may switch to an alternative supplier who can provide the entire range.

(b) (i)

> **Top tips.** A common error, according to the examiner at the time this question was set under the previous version of the Paper P2 syllabus, was 'a general discussion was summed up with the words "therefore Telmat could use target costing and life cycle costing". The nature of Telmat's product/business should have been considered and specific advantages mentioned.'

Target costing

To **compete** effectively in today's competitive markets, such as that for mobile phones, organisations must **continually redesign their products** (launching new and ever more sophisticated mobile phones, for example), with the result that **product life cycles** are becoming much **shorter**.

The planning, development and design stages of a product are therefore critical to an organisation's cost management process because it is here that a large proportion of a product's life cycle costs are determined. **Cost reduction** at these **early stages of a product's life cycle**, rather than during the production process, is now one of the most **important** issues facing management accountants in industry.

One possible costing system to cope with this change is target costing.

Traditional costing systems versus target costing

Traditionally, Telmat is likely to develop a particular mobile phone, work out its production cost and set what it believes to be an appropriate selling price. The profit or loss drops out as the balancing figure.

The target costing approach is radically different. If Telmat were to introduce it, a **mobile phone** would be **developed**, a **selling price based on capturing a target market share set** and a **profit based on the organisation's required levels of return established**. The **balancing figure** in the price/cost/profit relationship would be the product **cost**, a **target** that Telmat would have to aim to achieve.

Target costing and a customer focus

By considering the market and the price they are willing to pay, target costing therefore forces an organisation to **focus** more intently on **customers**. This contrasts with the traditional focus on suppliers.

Target costing and cost reductions

Using target costing, all ideas for **cost reduction** would be **examined during the product planning, research and development processes,** ensuring that quality, reliability and other **customer requirements were built into the product from the outset**. Given the short life of Telmat's products, minimum costs and customer satisfaction from product launch are of paramount importance to ensure maximum sales and maximum profit.

ANSWERS

Target cost management

Target costing is more **flexible** than traditional methods of control such as standard costing, which is likely to prove too rigid for a company such as Telmat.

For example, **initial production costs**, determined by Telmat's current technology and processes, would probably be **greater than the target cost**. But given the fast-moving nature of mobile phone technology, this could change rapidly. The company's management would therefore have to set **benchmarks** for improvement towards the target cost. The **learning effect** could be incorporated, probably an important factor in the manufacture of mobile phones.

These benchmarks, which could be incorporated into the **company's balanced scorecard,** would become increasingly more stringent as the target cost was reduced over the product life; cost savings would have to be actively sought and made continuously.

Limitations of target costing

If **unrealistic and hence unachievable targets** were set, however, the workforce would **not be committed to them** or else would be **demotivated** if unable to achieve them. If, on the other hand, Telmat management set them too low, the workforce would not be motivated to improve.

Telmat's **current costing systems** may **be unable to provide the data needed** to operate target costing effectively, but in time the company would be able to build up enough relevant data to create cost tables. **Cost tables** are a very sophisticated version of standard cost setting data and can be used to predict the costs of even new products with an acceptable degree of accuracy.

(ii) **Life cycle costing**

Life cycle costing is an alternative to the traditional approach to determining product profitability.

Traditional approach to determining product profitability

Traditional management accounting practice at Telmat would be **to report costs at the physical production stage** of the life cycle of a mobile phone; costs would not be accumulated over the entire life cycle. The **profitability** of a particular mobile phone would **not be assessed over its entire life but rather on a periodic basis. Costs** would tend to **be accumulated according to function;** research, design, development and customer service cost incurred on all products during a period would be totalled and **recorded as a period expense.**

The life cycle approach

Using life cycle costing, however, Telmat's **costs** would be **traced to individual products over complete life cycles.**

The advantages of life cycle costing to Telmat

(1) Traditional **comparisons** between budgeted and actual costs on a month by month basis could be replaced by **comparing actual plus projected costs and revenues with original (or revised) budgeted life cycle costs and revenues** for a particular mobile phone. Such comparisons would allow for improved future decisions about product design, and would **show whether expected savings** from using new production methods or technology had been **realised**.

(2) In the market within which Telmat is operating, the duration **of product life cycles is decreasing** as the pace of technological change increases and consumer demand becomes more sophisticated. Increasing automation means **that up to 90% of product life cycle costs could be determined 'up front',** by decisions made early with the product life cycle.

The introduction of life cycle costing would ensure **that initial product proposals were far more carefully costed** and that **the tightest cost controls were at the design stage** of potential new products, the point at which the majority of costs are committed.

ANSWERS

Overall, the system would **assist in the planning and control of Telmat's products' life cycle costs** and would **monitor spending and commitments to spend during the early stages** of the products' life cycles.

(3) Life cycle costing **increases the visibility of costs** such as those associated with research, design, development and customer service, costs which traditionally are simply totalled and recorded as a period expense. Telmat's research and development costs are likely to be particularly high and must be recovered quickly.

(4) It also **enables individual product profitability to be more fully understood** as all costs are attributed to products. This would provide Telmat with **more accurate feedback information on** its success or failure in developing new products, which is vital in its operating environment, in which the ability to produce new and updated versions of its products is of vital importance to its survival.

Disadvantages of life cycle costing

If product life cycles become too short, it may not be realistic for Telmat to install a cost tracking system that **produces reports too late** for remedial action. Too much time might be spent on producing product budgets than merited by the potential benefits. If this is the case, Telmat would be advised to rely on a range of non-financial indicators to help with monitoring and control of costs.

82 Question with answer plan: SY Ltd

Text references. Look at Chapter 15 for help in answering parts (a) and (c) and Chapter 9 for part (b).

Top tips. In part (a) you obviously needed to apply the techniques to MANPAC. In (b) you were asked to evaluate strategies (plural) and provide a recommendation. Part (c) contained three requirements – explain the stages, explain the management issues and provide a diagram.

Part (c) asks for a specific lifecycle model for the MANPAC. So think about the characteristics of the MANPAC before plotting a graph as required. Look for the requirements in the question: 'discuss', 'evaluate', 'explain'.

Easy marks. Look at applying your knowledge to MANPAC. Do part (c) independently.

Answer plan

- Discuss lifecycle costing.

    Points to make: traditional approach
                     whether this is appropriate for the MANPAC
                     the lifecycle approach

- Discuss target costing

    Points to make: traditional approach
                     appropriateness to the MANPAC
                     target costing approach

- List out market-based pricing strategies: market skimming pricing
                                              market penetration pricing
                                              premium pricing
                                              price discrimination

- Recommend a strategy
- Draw a product life cycle diagram
- Discuss the five stages in the product lifecycle of the MANPAC

ANSWERS

(a) **Life cycle costing**

Life cycle costing is an **alternative** approach to that traditionally used to determine product profitability.

Traditional approach to determining product profitability

Traditional management accounting practice at SY Ltd would be to **report costs at the production stage** of the MANPAC, with **profitability assessed** on a **periodic** basis. Costs would tend to be **reported according to function**; research, design, development and customer service costs incurred on all of SY Ltd's products during a period would be **totalled** and recorded as a **period expense**.

The inappropriateness of the traditional approach for the MANPAC

Given that the MANPAC is the **first of its kind** to be introduced to the market, SY Ltd no doubt **expended** a great deal on research, development and design. And a large proportion of the MANPAC's **life cycle costs** will have been **determined** and **committed** by decisions made at these **early stages of its life cycle**. This necessitates the need for a management accounting **system** that monitors spending and commitments to spend at these **early stages**, and which recognises the **reduced life cycle** and the subsequent challenge to profitability of **high-tech** products such as MANPAC.

The life cycle approach

Life cycle costing would have offered an alternative approach more suited to the requirements of MANPAC.

(i) **Costs** would have been **traced** to the MANPAC over its **complete life cycle**, from design stage right through to when the product is removed from the market, thereby increasing their **visibility**. MANPAC's **accumulated costs** would have been **compared** with the **revenues** it had earned, so that its **total profitability** could be determined.

(ii) Traditional comparisons between MANPAC's budgeted and actual costs on a month by month basis would have been replaced by **comparing** the **actual plus projected costs and revenues with original (or revised) budgeted life cycle costs and revenues.**

(iii) Life cycle costing would have ensured that the **initial proposals** for MANPAC were very **carefully costed** and that there were **tight cost controls** at its **design stage**, the point at which the majority of its costs were committed.

(iv) Overall the system would have assisted in the planning and control of MANPAC's life cycle costs and would have **monitored spending and commitments to spend during the early stages of its life cycle.**

(v) Life cycle costing would have **increased the visibility of costs** such as those associated with research, design, development and customer service, costs which are traditionally simply totalled and recorded as a period expense. MANPAC's research and development costs would have been particularly high and would have to be recovered quickly.

Because individual product profitability is therefore more fully understood, more accurate **feedback** information is available on SY Ltd's **success or failure in developing new products.** In the market in which SY Ltd operates, where the ability to produce new and updated versions of products is of paramount importance to organisational survival, this information is vital.

Target costing

Traditional costing versus target costing for MANPAC

SY Ltd's approach to pricing the MANPAC has been to develop the product, work out its total cost (manufacturing plus selling and administration costs) and add a profit margin, thereby setting what it believes is an appropriate selling price.

The target costing approach is radically different. If it had been applied to the MANPAC, the **product** would have been **developed**, a selling **price based on capturing a target market share set** and a **profit based on**

ANSWERS

SY Ltd's required level of return established. The **balancing figure** in the price/cost/profit relationship would have been the cost of the MANPAC, a **target** that SY Ltd would have had to aim to achieve.

Applying target costing

(i) In an effort to attain the target cost, all ideas for **cost reduction** would have been examined during MANPAC's **planning, research and development processes**, the stage in MANPAC's life cycle when the largest proportion of its costs would have been committed.

(ii) As a system of control, target costing would have proved **less inflexible** than a traditional method such as **standard costing**. For example, initial production costs, determined by SY Ltd's current technology and processes, would probably have been greater than the target cost. But given the rapidly-moving nature of the technology used in the manufacture of computer games, this would probably have changed. Management would therefore have had to set **benchmarks for improvement towards the target cost**. Any **learning effect** in the manufacture of MANPAC could have been incorporated.

(iii) These benchmarks would have become increasingly more stringent as the target cost was reduced over MANPAC's life. **Cost savings** would have had to have been actively sought and **made continuously**.

(b) **Market-based pricing strategies that SY Ltd could have considered**

(i) **Market skimming pricing**

This strategy involves charging **high prices when a product is first launched** and spending heavily on advertising and sales promotion to obtain sales. As the product moves into **later stages of its life cycle**, progressively **lower prices** are charged and so the profitable 'cream' is skimmed off in stages until sales can only be sustained at lower prices.

The aim is therefore to gain high unit profits early in the product's life.

A **high price** makes it more likely that **competitors** will **enter** the market, however, and so there must be either significant barriers to entry or the product must be differentiated in some way. The 3D interactivity of MANPAC provides this differentiation.

Such a strategy would have been **appropriate** for a number of reasons.

(1) MANPAC is new and different and so high prices can be charged to take advantage of its novelty appeal.

(2) Charging high prices in the early stages of MANPAC's (expected) very short life cycle would generate the high initial cash flows needed to cover its development costs and to fund research into and development of its successor.

(3) Once the market has become saturated, MANPAC's price could be reduced to attract that part of the market that had not been exploited.

(ii) **Market penetration pricing**

This is a strategy of **low prices when a product is first launched** in order to obtain sufficient **penetration** into the market.

Although low prices would discourage new entrants into the market, it **would not be a particularly appropriate** strategy for pricing MANPAC.

Demand for MANPAC is likely to be inelastic, whereas penetration pricing is most **suited** to pricing products for which **demand** is **elastic** and so responds well to low prices.

(iii) **Premium pricing**

This strategy would involve highlighting the MANPAC's 3D interactivity as a **differentiating feature** so as to **justify a premium price**.

ANSWERS

(iv) **Price discrimination**

By adopting such a strategy, SY Ltd would charge different prices for the MANPAC to different groups of buyers. For example, the price charged in retail outlets could be different from the price charged for on-line purchase via a website.

(c) Every product goes through a **life cycle**. The following diagram illustrates the life cycle for MANPAC.

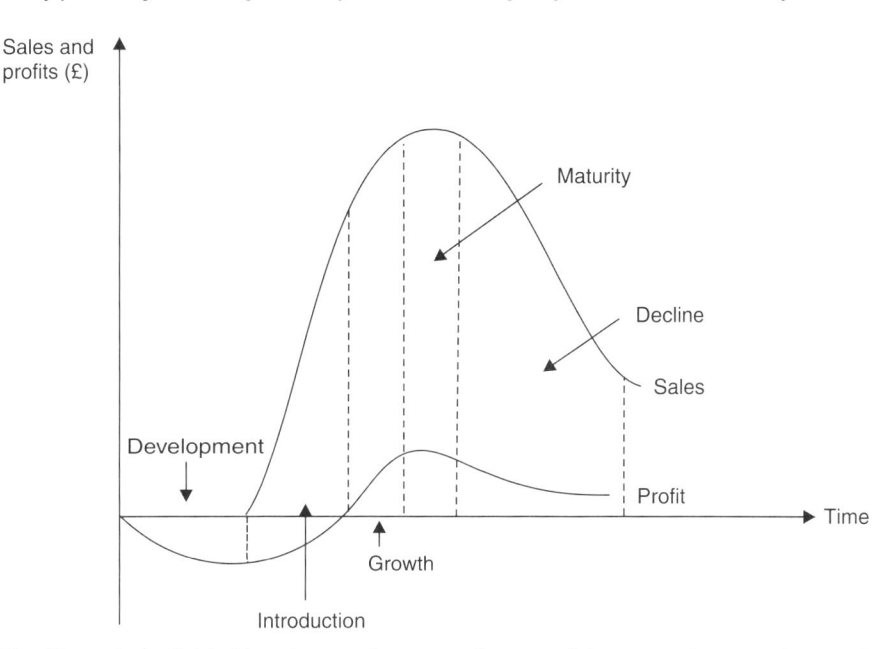

The life cycle is divided into four main stages. As you might expect for a product such as MANPAC, the growth and maturity stage are very short, as competitors in the computer game industry are quick to bring out similar games to rival the popularity of the original. The overall life cycle of such products tends to be very short as new technology results in the rapid development of more sophisticated games, making existing products obsolete.

Stages in the product life cycle of the MANPAC

(i) **Development**

During this stage the product is not earning revenue but high levels of costs are being incurred on research and product development and possibly on assets for production.

Because MANPAC is the **first game of its kind** to be introduced to the market, its development stage was probably **longer** than those of high-technology products entering as competing products in existing markets.

A very high proportion of MANPAC's costs will have been determined by decisions made early in the life cycle, at the development stage. **Life cycle costing and target costing** are particularly useful at this stage to ensure that costs will be kept to a minimum over MANPAC's life cycle.

(ii) **Introduction**

This stage represents a period of high business risk and SY Ltd should expect negative net cash flow.

Customer interest in the product should be high given the **novelty** of the product and the fact that computer games are **a buoyant market sector**. The level of initial sales achieved will very much depend on the amount of **advertising and promotion**, however, and whether or not MANPAC is launched in time for the peak selling season.

Failure to meet the required launch date could be incredibly detrimental to the overall success of the product. Getting MANPAC on the market as soon as possible will maximise its life cycle and give it as long a period as possible without a rival, which should mean increased market share in the long run. Furthermore, MANPAC's life span is unlikely to proportionally lengthen if its launch is delayed

ANSWERS

and so sales may be permanently lost. Management should therefore consider incurring extra costs to keep the launch on schedule.

And the sooner MANPAC is launched, the quicker its research and development costs will be repaid, providing SY Ltd with funds to develop further products.

At this stage in its life cycle, growth in sales is the key performance measure.

(iii) **Growth**

Growth is obviously still vital during this stage but the MANPAC should by now be making a profit, although much of the cash it generates may be being used for expansion.

Given the short product life cycles of high-technology products, management will need to ensure that the introduction and growth stages are as short as possible so that MANPAC is earning profits as quickly as possible.

By now **competitors** may be in the process of developing or even launching competing products to MANPAC, and so management should be analysing their marketing strategies.

(iv) **Maturity**

The rate of sales growth slows down during this period and MANPAC will reach a short-lived period of maturity. Cash flow should be positive and profits should be good.

Using the cash flows generated by MANPAC, SY Ltd should have **developed and be ready to launch an updated version of, or the successor to, MANPAC**. (Unless driven by competitors' actions, SY Ltd should **guard against product proliferation** (launching an updated version or a successor too quickly), however, as MANPAC's life cycle would be cut short and it may only just cover its development costs).

(v) **Decline**

Given the short lives of high-technology products, the MANPAC will go into decline relatively quickly. It will still be making a profit but management should be **determining the most appropriate time** to remove the product from the market before it becomes a loss maker.

83 Financial advisors

> **Top tips.** In part (a) you must ensure that you describe value analysis and not the value chain. This was a mistake made by many candidates according to the examiner. Also ensure that you are clear about the different focus of each technique. Value analysis has a focus on reducing cost without sacrificing the function to the customer, whereas functional analysis looks at the value to the customer of each function of a product or service.
>
> You need to read through the scenario and refer to the pertinent steps to implement the technique to answer Part (b). There were six marks for this part. Keep your answer brief, however, as you only have 18 minutes to complete the question.
>
> **Easy marks.** You could earn a few useful marks by just repeating from memory what you know of the two techniques.
>
> The question then guides you to earn easy marks from applying the steps of value analysis to the scenario. Put down the steps first (you'll get some marks for this) and then apply these to the scenario in the time allowed.
>
> **Examiner's comments.** Misreading the question so value analysis became the value chain. Most candidates ignored functional analysis. Common errors included a complete lack of understanding of the two techniques and their differences.

(a) Value analysis is a planned, scientific approach to cost reduction which reviews the material composition of a product and production design so that modifications and improvements can be made which do not reduce the value of the product to the customer or to the user.

ANSWERS

Functional analysis is concerned with improving profits by attempting to reduce costs and/or by improving products by adding new features in a cost-effective way that are so attractive to customers that profits actually increase.

Value analysis focuses on cost reduction through **a review of the processes** required to produce a product or service. **Functional analysis** focuses on the **value to the customer of each function** of the product or service and then makes decisions about whether cost reduction is needed.

(b) There are seven steps in value analysis, which need to be followed through before implementation. These are:

Step 1 **Select a product or service for study.** The service provided by the firm is high quality, personalised financial strategy advice.

Step 2 **Obtain and record information.** The questions to be asked include: What do the clients want from the service? Does it succeed? Are there alternative ways of providing it? What do these alternatives cost?

Step 3 **Analyse the information and evaluate the service.** Each aspect of the service should be analysed. Any cost reductions must be achieved without the loss of use or esteem value. (Or at least, cost savings must exceed any loss in value suffered, and customers would then have to be compensated for the loss in use or esteem value in the form of a lower selling price.) The type of questions to be asked and answered in the analysis stage is as follows.

(i) Are all the activities undertaken necessary? So does the firm need to undertake all of sponsorship, newsletters and seek new and innovative ideas, for instance. It is clear that many clients don't read the newsletter so does this still need to be produced?

(ii) Can the service be provided at a lower cost?

(iii) Can any part of the service be standardised?

(iv) Does the value provided by each aspect of the service justify its cost?

Step 4 **Consider alternatives.** From the analysis, a variety of options can be devised. This is the 'new ideas' stage of the study, and alternative options would mix ideas for eliminating unnecessary services or standardising certain features of the service.

Step 5 **Select the least cost alternative.** The costs (and other aspects of value) of each alternative should be compared.

Step 6 **Recommend.** The preferred alternative should then be recommended to the decision makers for approval.

Step 7 **Implement and follow-up.** Once a value analysis proposal is approved and accepted, its implementation must be properly planned and co-ordinated. Management should review the implementation and, where appropriate, improve the new service in the light of practical experience.

To be successful, value analysis programmes must have the full backing of senior management.

ANSWERS

84 Learning curve

> **Text reference.** Chapter 15 will help you with learning curves.
>
> **Top tips.** You should spot straight away that this question is testing your knowledge of learning curves. Part (a) asks you to apply the **expected rate of learning** to an initial **actual cost** for the first batch. Remember that the learning curve measures the **cumulative average labour cost per unit**. You will need to multiply the average time by the cumulative number of units to arrive at the costs asked for. Part (b) then gets you to calculate an **actual rate of learning** based on **actual cost** data. Part (c) is testing your understanding of how your findings in parts (a) and (b) affect management.
>
> **Easy marks.** Draw up tables as we have done to answer parts (a) and (b). Otherwise, you can use the formula for the learning curve which is given in the exam. However as the batches double, i.e. 1,2,4 and 8 you do not need to use the formula.

(a) **Revised expected cumulative direct labour costs**

Cumulative batches	Rate of learning %	Average direct labour cost per batch $'000	Cumulative direct labour cost $'000
1	–	280.00	280.00
2	80	224.00	448.00
4	80	179.20	716.80
8 (W)	–	153.10	1,224.80

Working

You will need to use the learning curve formula to work out the labour cost for batch 4 as this is when the rate of learning ends. **Remember that this is not the same as the average direct labour cost for batch 4**. Then use this to calculate the labour costs of the later batches. We know the cumulative labour cost for four batches, which is $716.80. So to work out the labour cost for the fourth batch we need to work out the cumulative direct labour cost for the first **three** batches. So here goes.

$Y_x = aX^b$

Where $a = 280$

$X^b = 3^b$

$b = \log 0.80 / \log 2 = \dfrac{-0.0969}{0.301} = -0.3219$

Therefore $3^b = 3^{-0.3219} = 0.702$ and substituting this into the main formula for the learning curve gives

$Y_x = 280 \times 0.702$
     $= \$196.60$ (rounded)

Multiply this by three batches to get $196.60 \times 3 = \$589.8$.

Deduct this from the cumulative labour cost for four batches to give the labour cost for the fourth batch.

$716.80 - \$589.80 = \$127.00$

Multiply this by four to give the total costs of batches 5–8 and then add this to the cumulative direct labour cost for batch 4 to give the cumulative direct labour cost for the eight batches. In numbers:

$127 \times 4 = \$508$
$716.80 + \$508 = \$1,224.80$

You can then divide this by eight to get the average direct labour cost for eight batches.

292

(b) **Actual learning rate**

Cumulative batches	Actual cumulative direct labour cost $'000	Average direct labour cost per batch $'000	Rate of learning %
1	280	280.00	0
2	476	238.00	85
4	809	202.25	85
8	1,376	172.00	85

(c) **Implications of the findings in parts (a) and (b)**

The actual rate of learning based on **the actual costs** recorded shows that the rate of learning is lower than expected. Costs are decreasing at a slower rate than anticipated given the budgeted direct labour cost. So the learning period is longer than anticipated.

Moreover, the **actual direct labour cost** of the first batch is $30 higher than originally planned. This is due to a longer or slower production than expected paid at a standard labour rate so slower than expected.

Management need to consider how these changes will affect the profitability of the new product as these will increase the cost above that estimated. If price is based on cost then management may have to re-consider how price is calculated. They could also look at methods of reducing costs such as target costing, and value analysis.

We have drawn up a table here that shows how these changes affect contribution.

	Estimate Batch 1 $'000	Estimate Batch 8 $'000	Actual Batch 8 $'000
Market price	500	4,000	4,000
Direct costs other than labour $300,000/batch	300	2,400	2,400
Direct labour (W)	250	1,280	1,376
Contribution	(50)	320	224

Working

Estimate. The direct labour figure for batch 8 is calculated taking the direct labour cost for the first batch and applying the expected 80% rate of learning. Therefore $250,000 × 0.8 × 0.8 × 8 batches = $1,280,000.

85 Section A answers: Activity based management

1 D **I:** This is a merit of activity based analysis, according to its proponents.

II: Activity based analysis *is* concerned with all overhead costs, including the costs of non factory-floor activities such as quality control and customer service. It therefore takes cost accounting beyond its traditional factory floor boundaries.

III: Arbitrary cost apportionment may still be required at the pooling stage for items like rent and rates.

IV: It is TQM that is based on this belief.

2 C The four correct levels are known as the manufacturing cost hierarchy.

3 Business process engineering

ANSWERS

4   Cost per movement = £75,000/30,000
                      = £2.50
    Number of movements per batch = 18
    ∴ Cost of movements per batch = £2.50 × 18
                                   = £45
    Cost of movements per chair = £45/50
                                 = £0.90

5   D   A cost driver determines the size of the costs of an activity or causes the costs of an activity. For example, the costs of the despatching activity might be determined by the number of despatches and so the number of despatches would be the cost driver.

6   A   This is the rigorous definition used by CIMA.

        Option B is a definition of activity based budgeting.

        Option C is a definition of activity driver analysis.

        Option D is a definition of activity based costing.

7   The cost per set-up is £14,280/28 = £510. The D should bear 8 × £510 = £4,080 and the E 20 × £510 = £10,200.

8   A   Long production runs (volume) reduce some costs.
        Short production runs (variety) increase some costs.

86 BPR

> **Top tips.** Don't fall into the trap of assuming that BPR can be implemented wholly by the management accountant, rather than by a team.

Having overall responsibility for the organisation's information systems, the management accountant will be the **main provider of the information** required by the BPR programme. Because BPR involves the introduction of significant changes to business processes, the organisation's information requirements are likely to change. Users will require alternative types of information in alternative formats.

At the outset there will be no way of knowing for sure the precise information requirements, however, because the chief tool of BPR is a clean sheet of paper. It is only once the programme commences that precise information requirements will become clear.

At the planning stage of a BPR programme the management accountant will therefore need to **liaise with all others on the team** and consider the changes that will be necessary to the **organisation's information systems** as a result of different ways of organising work.

Benchmarking exercises, comparing processes with those used in other organisations may need to be set up, and the management accountant is likely to be heavily involved in devising ways of collecting and analysing data from such exercises.

A **modelling approach** will help to assess the validity and consequences of alternative ways of re-engineering processes.

Costing systems may need to be reappraised: for example it might be useful to set up activity based costing systems, and the consequent changes to information collection and analysis and to accounting software need to be considered.

For reporting purposes, **alternative performance measures will need to be devised**, since information will no longer be required on a departmental/ functional basis but on a process basis.

Contribution of the management accountant to the implementation of a BPR programme

When the BPR programme is being implemented, the management accountant will need to **ensure that managers within the organisation are provided with the information they require**. It is likely that the management accounting function will need to provide a broader range of information than previously, but the emphasis must be on user friendliness and sharing. This is likely to mean the introduction of **new software and telecommunications links**, capable of handling different flows of information.

As one example, sales processes may be re-engineered so that they are geared to types of customer rather than to types of product: information will need to cut across a variety of product categories or brands. Or, re-engineered work may be devolved to lower levels in the organisation hierarchy, and the managers at these levels may have quite different information requirements to those that were catered for previously.

An important aspect of implementation will be **monitoring of progress**: are the expected benefits of BPR being realised, and if not what action is required? Indicators of success might include reduced costs, faster delivery, more satisfied customers and so on, but systems need to be in operation to measure such things.

The **management accounting function itself is likely to need to change**, as part of the BPR programme, so that it can provide the information required.

87 LM Hospital

> **Text references.** If you get stuck, look at Chapter 16 for ABC and Chapter 17 for throughput accounting.
>
> **Top tips.** You may have classified other costs as direct, for example kitchen and food costs. But use the categories of support activities as a hint to what is deemed 'direct'. Kitchen and food costs, for example, would undoubtedly be classified as a cost of 'caring for patients'.
>
> Hopefully you didn't fall into the trap of simply spreading all the costs across the two types of operation, on the (unusual) assumption that the hospital only carried out two types of operation. The resulting prices would be astronomic! Always check your answers for reasonableness (a vital check that you should carry out at the end of every calculation).
>
> Your choice of items/categories in part (b) could well have been different from ours. Ask a friend/colleague to read your answers to check their validity.
>
> **Easy marks.** This is a very time pressured question, so don't feel bad about it. Use your time now before the real exam to practise and get your timing down.

(a) (i) **Direct costs**

Consultant surgeons' fees: £5,250,000 ÷ (15 × 2,000) = £175 per hour of consultant's time
Operating theatre: £4,050,000 ÷ (4 × 9 × 300) = £375 per hour
Pre-operation costs: £1,260,000 ÷ 7,200 = £175 per operation

Indirect costs

Caring for patients	£
Nursing services/administration	9,936,000
Linen and laundry	920,000
Kitchen and food	2,256,000
Medical supplies	1,100,000
Pathology lab	920,000
	15,132,000

ANSWERS

Admissions and record keeping

	£
Updating patient records	590,000
Patient/bed scheduling	100,000
Invoicing and collections	160,000
	850,000

Facility sustaining costs

	£
Insurance of buildings/general equipment	60,000
Depreciation of buildings/general equipment	520,000
Housekeeping etc	760,000
	1,340,000

Cost drivers

(1) **The cost driver for caring for patients is patient days** as the level of the majority of these costs depends on how long patients stay in hospital. (Medical supplies and pathology lab costs are likely to be driven by another factor but insufficient information is available to consider this further).

(2) **That for admissions and record keeping is number of patients** as the level of these costs varies in line with patient numbers rather than length of stay or type of illness/treatment.

(3) **There is no cost driver for facility sustaining costs** as the ABC cost will not include these costs.

Cost per cost driver

Caring for patients: £15,132,000 ÷ 44,000 = £343.91

Admissions and record keeping: £850,000 ÷ 9,600 = £88.54

Prices for ENT operation

	Current system £	ABC system £	£
Direct costs			
Consultant/surgeon fees (£175 × 3)	525.00	525.00	
Operating theatre (£375 × 2)	750.00	750.00	
Pre-operation costs (£175 × 1)	175.00	175.00	
	1,450.00		1,450.00
Mark-up on direct costs (× 135%)	1,957.50		
Indirect costs			
Caring for patients (£343.91 × 4)		1,375.64	
Admissions and record keeping (£88.54 × 1)		88.54	
			1,464.18
			2,914.18
Mark-up on cost (15%)			437.13
Price	3407.50		3,351.31

ANSWERS

Prices for cataract operation

	Current system	ABC system	
	£	£	£
Direct costs			
Consultant/surgeon fees (£175 × 0.85)	148.75	148.75	
Operating theatre (£375 × 0.5)	187.50	187.50	
Pre-operation costs (£175 × 1)	175.00	175.00	
	511.25		511.25
Mark-up on direct costs (× 135%)	690.19		
Indirect costs			
Caring for patients (£343.91 × 1)		343.91	
Admissions and record keeping (£88.54 × 1)		88.54	
			432.45
			943.70
Mark-up on costs (× 15%)			141.56
Price	1201.44		1,085.26

(ii) (1) For both operations the **ABC approach** produces **prices lower** that those arrived at using the current system. Consideration must therefore be given to the **appropriateness of the 15% mark-up** if current profitability levels are to be maintained.

(2) An in-depth **analysis** should be carried out of the **facility sustaining costs** in order to determine an appropriate cost driver. These costs can then be **included** within the total cost for pricing purposes and the most relevant price established.

(3) The **difference** between the **two prices** for the **ENT** operation is **not significant** and use of the current system is unlikely to have a big effect on demand.

(4) There is a **marked difference** between the two **possible prices** for the **cataract** operation, principally because the **cost of caring for patients is relatively low** (as the operation only requires patients to stay in hospital for one day). The current pricing system could therefore be **overpricing** this operation, which is likely to have an effect on **demand** for it.

(b) To be of any significant value, an ABC system should **use** a **greater number of cost pools/cost drivers** than the three pools/two drivers proposed by the hospital. This would ensure that costs were allocated to products/services as **accurately** and **realistically** as possible. As mentioned above, the cost of medical supplies and the pathology laboratory are unlikely to be driven by the number of patient days but, given the information available in the question, they are most appropriately allocated by use of this cost driver.

Medical supplies

The cost of medical supplies is likely to be driven by the type and **complexity** of the operation. **Operation time** could be used as a **substitute** for operation complexity as it could be assumed that the more complex the operation, the longer the time in the operating theatre. A rate per operation hour could therefore be established and the cost of medical supplies allocated on this basis.

Pathology laboratory

The allocation of such costs on the basis of patient days is inappropriate given that **some operations will not require the services** of the laboratory and the level of demand placed on the service will **vary with the type of operation**. There are **three possible methods** of charging the cost to operations.

(i) A simple rate per test (£920,000/8,000) could be charged as necessary to each type of operation.
(ii) A charge per type of operation could be established.
(iii) An average cost per type of test could be charged as necessary to each type of operation.

ANSWERS

Nursing services and administration

Given the relative **magnitude** of these costs, they should be dealt with as **accurately** as possible. The **type** of nursing care will **vary** depending on the **type of operation** (from intensive care nursing to the provision of room service after a minor operation). **Different cost drivers** should therefore be established for different categories of nursing.

Additional **analysis** should be carried out to ascertain whether **costs other than those for nursing are being allocated** to this cost heading given the magnitude of the cost and the relatively low number of nursing hours.

(c) **What is throughput accounting (TA)?**

The **basic idea** of TA is that an organisation has a **given set of resources** available (buildings, capital equipment, labour). Using these resources, along with any necessary **purchases** (in a hospital these would include medical supplies and food), products must be manufactured/**services must be provided to generate sales revenue**. The most appropriate financial **objective** to set is therefore **maximisation of throughput** (which, in a hospital, would be of **patients**).

What relevance or value does this have for hospitals?

The requirement to generate sales revenue and the setting of financial objectives can be applied to private sector hospitals but **public sector hospitals** are more concerned with reducing costs and **treating as many patients as possible**. It is therefore the overriding objective of TA to ensure the maximisation of throughput that is of particular relevance for both private and public sector hospitals.

How can TA be applied in a hospital?

To achieve this objective TA requires the **identification** and **elimination** of any **constraints**, or **bottleneck resources**, which **limit throughput**. Such bottlenecks in hospitals are well publicised, and are frequently cited as the reasons for long waiting lists.

- Patient beds
- Intensive care beds
- Operating theatre time
- Surgeons' skills or time
- Other specialists' skills or time
- Doctors' skills or time

The management of these bottlenecks is of primary concern to the manager seeking to increase throughput.

(i) TA requires that, if a rearrangement of existing resources or buying-in of resources (such as employing additional doctors) does not alleviate the bottleneck, investment may be necessary (in equipment, buildings and so on).

(ii) Where a bottleneck cannot be eliminated, the number of patients admitted must be limited to the capacity of the bottleneck resource to ensure an even flow of patients in and out of the hospital.

(iii) The elimination of one bottleneck is likely to lead to the creation of another at a previously satisfactory point, however. For example, if a bottleneck caused by too little operating theatre time is alleviated by building additional operating theatres, a bottleneck due to the lack of appropriately skilled surgeons could then arise.

The **application of throughput accounting in a hospital** would therefore ensure that its **key and limited resources were used as effectively and efficiently as possible to ensure that the maximum number of patients were treated with the resources available.**

ANSWERS

The downside of TA

It is important to note that TA is often associated **with increasing the speed of flow through processes in order to maximise throughput**. Any measures taken in a hospital to speed up the flow of patients in and out of the **hospital** must be considered extremely carefully, however, as such action **could put patients' lives at risk and would not benefit the hospital in the long run**. Performance measures based on **maximising throughput** should not therefore be introduced or, if they are used, should be **utilised in conjunction with counter-balancing measures** such as re-admissions, deaths, recovery rates and so on.

88 ZP plc

> **Text references.** Chapter 16 covers the material needed to answer this question.
>
> **Top tips.** You might have come unstuck in part (a). However what the examiner appears to want is for you to pick out only those costs that can be identified to customers and attribute costs to them using appropriate cost drivers. Part (b) then asks for you to compare and contrast your calculations in (a) with the current costing system and make recommendations. Part (c) asks for a written answer on ABC cost classifications and how these would apply to ZP plc.
>
> In part (a) roughly equal marks could be earned for calculating travel costs, accommodation costs, and other costs, for each client profile. In part (b) once again marks were evenly spread between comparing costs recognising the similarity of costs using each system, pros and cons of using ABC, and other benefits of ABC. Part (c) awarded four marks each to ABC classifications as that could be used by ZP and examples in ZP of each.
>
> **Easy marks.** Even if you think the values you calculate in (a) are incorrect, base your comments in (b) on your results. Make sensible suggestions.
>
> **Examiner's comments.** Parts (a) and (c) were poorly answered, especially (c) where candidates failed to give examples of activities that would fit into the four activity classifications. Also, candidates often failed to read the question properly and in particular the third bullet point. Many candidates were unable to use the figures in the question to calculate the correct cost driver rates.

(a) **Attribute costs to client group using an ABC system**

	Working	D £'000	E £'000	F £'000	Total £'000
Consultants' salaries	1	40	140	60	240
Travel	2	4	7	4	15
Accommodation	3	0	8	3	11
Other costs					
Facility costs	4	31	108	46	185
		75	263	113	451

This table gives the activity-based costs of supporting each customer group based on the factors that cause the costs to be incurred as noted in the Working notes.

Workings

(1) These can be attributed as at present on the basis of chargeable hours. Effectively they are direct costs for each client group.

Total cost = £240,000

Budgeted chargeable hours = 6,000

Rate per hour = £40

Cost attributable to each group = chargeable hours per client × number of clients in group × £40

ANSWERS

(2) The travel cost is driven by the distance in miles to clients

Number of cost driver units = 50 × 3 × 10 + 70 × 8 × 5 + 100 × 3 × 5 = 5,800

Cost per cost driver (ie per mile) = £15,000/5,800 = £2.59

Cost attributable to each group = number of miles x number of visits × number of clients × £2.59

(3) The accommodation cost is driven by the number of visits to clients where the distance to the client is over 50 miles.

The cost of accommodation is therefore not attributable to client group d as the distance is not more than 50 miles.

Number of cost driver units = 8 × 5 + 3 × 5 = 55

Cost per cost driver = £11,000/55 = £200

(4) These costs have been attributed to each client group using chargeable hours as a cost driver. It could also be argued however that they would not be attributed to each client group using an activity based system, as they are facility level activities and so would not be driven by an activity which can be related to clients.

(b) **Compare and contrast the current costing system and that using ABC**

The current costing system uses chargeable hours as a basis for apportioning costs. Thus, comparing the costs attributed under activity based costing with those attributed by the current system:

	Cost rate	D £'000	E £'000	F £'000	Total £'000
Chargeable hours needed		1,000	3,500	1,500	6,000
Costs attributed using cost rate	£75/hr	75	263	113	451
Costs using ABC		75	263	113	451
Difference		0	0	0	0

Using an activity basis for allocating shows the cost of supporting individual customer groups by relating the costs incurred to the factors or 'cost drivers' that cause them to be incurred in the first place. This shows that the particular cost allocation using cost drivers results in the same allocation as using a blanket chargeable hours basis. However this is perhaps not surprising as the bulk of the costs allocated are the consultants' salaries and these are driven by chargeable hours, as they are direct costs of servicing clients.

However this would not always necessarily be the case especially where a cost driver was say, machine hours for producing tools, yet a chargeable hours basis as used here were adopted.

So in summary, the senior consultant's recommendation on using cost drivers allows a more accurate understanding of the actual costs incurred as a result of the activity for each client group.

(c) **Classifications of activities using ZP plc as an example**

The **manufacturing cost hierarchy** categorises costs and activities as unit level, batch level, product/process level and organisational/facility level.

To reflect today's more **complex business environment**, recognition must be given to the fact that **costs are created and incurred because their cost drivers occur at different levels. Cost driver analysis investigates, quantifies and explains the relationships between cost drivers and their related costs**.

Activities and their related costs fall into four different categories, known as the **manufacturing cost hierarchy**. The **categories determine the type of activity cost driver required**.

Traditionally it has been assumed that if costs did not vary with changes in production at the unit level, they were fixed rather than variable. The analysis above shows this assumption to be false, and that costs vary for reasons other than production volume or chargeable hours. To determine an accurate estimate of product or service cost, **costs should be accumulated at each successively higher level of costs.**

Unit level costs are allocated over number of units produced, batch level costs over the number of units in the batch, product level costs over the number of units produced by the product line. These costs are all related to units of product (merely at different levels) and so can be gathered together at the product level to match with revenue. Organisational level costs are not product related, however, and so should simply be deducted from net revenue.

Such an approach gives a far greater insight into product profitability.

Classification level	Cause of cost	Types of cost in ZP plc	Necessity of cost
Unit level activities and costs	Production/acquisition of a single unit of product or delivery of single unit of service	Consultants' salaries	For every hour worked for client
Batch level activities and costs	A group of things being made, handled or processed	Travel to clients, accommodation	Once for each client visit
Product/process level activities and costs	Development, production or acquisition of different items	Support staff, advertising although there is not sufficient information to say what a cost driver for this would be, ordinarily they would be process level costs.	Supports consultants and customers
Organisational/ facility level activities and costs	Some costs cannot be related to a particular product line (or client group); instead they are related to maintaining the buildings and facilities. These costs cannot be related to cost objects with any degree of accuracy and are often excluded from ABC calculations for this reason.	Office premises, telephone, comms and fax.	Supports the overall service process

89 KL

Text references. You will find data to answer this question in Chapters 1, 9 and 16 of your Study Text.

Top tips. This question is in **four parts** and looks at **three issues**. Firstly, it asks for a discussion of two methods of setting price. Secondly, it asks you to calculate full cost and then activity based cost (ABC) for three products. Finally you are asked to explain how ABC can provide useful management information.

The P2 examiner often sets a question looking at the contrast between traditional costing methods and 'modern' systems such as activity based costing.

Part (a) wants you to **compare and contrast marginal cost plus pricing and total cost plus pricing**. We start off with a definition of each. Then we discuss their advantages and disadvantages. Don't panic – we have made more points in our answer than you would need to in the real exam.

ANSWERS

> As there are six marks available, you will only need to state six advantages or disadvantages. Don't do a mind dump and write all you know, as this will not be rewarded. Make concise points and keep to short paragraphs to make it easier for the marker to read your script.
>
> Part (b) is asking for a **short calculation of full cost** per unit using absorption costing data from the question. There shouldn't be anything tricky for you to consider here.
>
> In (c) you need to calculate the **full cost using activity costing**. The best approach is to break your answer down into manageable workings as we have done and follow these through to the ultimate unit cost calculation asked for.
>
> Part (d) is discursive and wants you to **refer to the company** when making your explanation about ABC.
>
> **Easy marks**. Parts (a), (b) and (c) are self-contained so you could answer then in any order. Part (b) is very straight forward and should be able to be answered using information you have brought forward into P2 from your earlier studies.

(a) **Marginal cost pricing and total cost plus pricing**

Full cost plus pricing is a method of determining the sales price by calculating the full cost of the product and adding a percentage mark-up for profit.

Marginal cost plus pricing/mark-up pricing is a method of determining the sales price by adding a profit margin on to either marginal cost of production or marginal cost of sales.

The managing director has observed that labour costs are **fixed** over the short term. Currently KL uses full cost plus pricing based on a full cost which incorporates labour cost as a variable or marginal cost. The MD has noted that labour costs are actually fixed in the short-term, however, and hence should be included as part of overheads. This should result in a different full cost. Thus he believes that the absorption rate for overheads may be distorted as it doesn't reflect true activity. Marginal costing would exclude these overheads from costs.

Problems with and advantages of full cost-plus pricing

There are several **problems** with relying on a full cost approach to pricing.

(i) It fails to recognise that since demand may be determining price, there will be a profit-maximising combination of price and demand.

(ii) There may be a need to adjust prices to market and demand conditions.

(iii) Budgeted output volume needs to be established. Output volume is a key factor in the overhead absorption rate.

(iv) A suitable basis for overhead absorption must be selected, especially where a business produces more than one product.

However, it is a **quick, simple and cheap** method of pricing which can be delegated to junior managers (which is particularly important with jobbing work where many prices must be decided and quoted each day) and, since the size of the profit margin can be varied, a decision based on a price in excess of full cost should ensure that a company working at normal capacity will **cover all of its fixed costs and make a profit**.

The advantages and disadvantages of a marginal cost-plus approach to pricing

Here are the **advantages**.

(i) It is a **simple and easy** method to use.

(ii) The **mark-up percentage can be varied**, and so mark-up pricing can be adjusted to reflect demand conditions.

(iii) It **draws management attention to contribution**, and the effects of higher or lower sales volumes on profit. In this way, it helps to create a better awareness of the concepts and implications of marginal costing and cost-volume-profit analysis. For example, if a product costs $10 per unit and a mark-up

ANSWERS

of 150% is added to reach a price of $25 per unit, management should be clearly aware that every additional $1 of sales revenue would add 60 pence to contribution and profit.

In practice, mark-up pricing is **used** in businesses **where there is a readily identifiable basic variable cost**. Retail industries are the most obvious example, and it is quite common for the prices of goods in shops to be fixed by adding a mark-up (20% or 33.3%, say) to the purchase cost.

There are, of course, **drawbacks** to marginal cost-plus pricing.

(i) Although the size of the mark-up can be varied in accordance with demand conditions, it does not ensure that sufficient attention is paid to demand conditions, competitors' prices and profit maximisation.

(ii) It ignores fixed overheads in the pricing decision, but the sales price must be sufficiently high to ensure that a profit is made after covering fixed costs.

(b) **Calculate the full cost per unit of each product using absorption costing**

The full cost of each product will include indirect costs allocated to each product using a predetermined overhead absorption rate. In the case of KL, this is based on **direct labour hours**.

	W $	X $	Y $
Variable cost/unit			
Direct materials	35.00	45.00	30.00
Direct labour	40.00	30.00	50.00
Production overhead (W)	18.00	13.50	22.50
Full cost/unit	93.00	88.50	102.50

Working

Total overheads = $1,044,000.

	W	X	Y	Total
Total labour hours				
Hrs per unit	4	3	5	
Budgeted annual production	15,000	24,000	20,000	
Total annual direct labour hrs	60,000	72,000	100,000	232,000

Overhead absorption rate (OAR) = $1,044,000/232,000

OAR per direct labour hour = $4.50/hr per direct labour hour

	W	X	Y
Hrs per unit	4	3	5
Production overhead absorbed per unit	18.00	13.50	22.50

(c) **Calculate the full cost per unit of each product using ABC**

We have listed the steps taken to calculate the unit costs using an ABC system of costing. The references to workings are to the workings below.

Step 1 Work out the annual activity for each cost driver.

Working

Annual activity

	W	X	Y	Total
Batches				
Batch size (units)	500	400	1,000	
Annual units	15,000	24,000	20,000	
Annual number of batches	30	60	20	110

303

ANSWERS

Supplier orders				
Per batch	4	3	5	
Annual number of batches	30	60	20	
Annual supplier orders	120	180	100	400
Machine hours				
Per unit	5	8	7	
Annual units	15,000	24,000	20,000	
Annual machine hours	75,000	192,000	140,000	407,000

Step 2 Use this information to calculate the **activity cost driver rates** in **working below**. You should also be able to use information provided in the table in the question.

Working

Cost driver rates

Material ordering costs $220,000 ÷ 400 supplier orders = $ 550 per supplier order
Machine setup costs $100,000 ÷ 110 batches = $ 909 per batch
Machine running costs $400,000 ÷ 407,000 machine hours = $ 0.98 per machine hour
General facility costs $324,000 ÷ 407,000 machine hours = $ 0.80 per machine hour

Step 3 **Apply these cost driver rates** to the **supplier orders, batch sizes and machine hours** for **each product**. This will give you the **unit cost** for each product for each cost pool. See **workings 1, 2, 3 and 4.**

Workings

1

	W	X	Y
Supplier orders per batch	4	3	5
Batch size	500	400	1,000
Cost driver (supplier orders) per unit	= 4/500	= 3/400	= 5/1,000
Activity cost driver rate (per order) $	550	550	550
Unit cost $	4.40	4.125	2.75

2

	W	X	Y
Batch size in units	500	400	1,000
Activity cost driver rate (per batch) $	909	909	909
Unit cost $	1.82	2.27	0.91

3

	W	X	Y
Machine hours per unit	5	8	7
Activity cost driver rate $ (per machine hour)	0.98	0.98	0.98
Unit cost $	4.90	7.84	6.86

4

	W	X	Y
Machine hours per unit	5	8	7
Activity cost driver rate $ (W5)	0.80	0.80	0.80
Unit cost $	4.00	6.40	5.60

ANSWERS

Step 4 You should now be able to calculate the **full unit cost** using the information you have already calculated slotted into a table as below.

Using **activity based costing**, unit costs for the three products would be as follows.

	W $/unit	X $/unit	Y $/unit
Direct material	35.00	45.00	30.00
Direct labour	40.00	30.00	50.00
Material ordering costs (W1)	4.40	4.13	2.75
Machine set-up costs (W2)	1.82	2.27	0.91
Machine running costs (W3)	4.90	7.84	6.86
General facility costs (W4)	4.00	6.40	5.60
	90.12	95.64	96.12

The alternative way to approach this problem, given that we have information on all the products that the costs have to be shared between, is to use ratios rather than cost drivers.

Step 1 Work out the annual activity for each cost driver (same calculation as in Step 1 above).

Step 2 Allocate costs proportionately according to each product's activity in relation to the total.

	W	X	Y
Material ordering costs	$\frac{120}{400}$ × 220,000 = 66,000	$\frac{180}{400}$ × 220,000 = 99,000	$\frac{100}{400}$ × 220,000 = 55,000
Machine set-up costs	$\frac{30}{110}$ × 100,000 = 27,273	$\frac{60}{110}$ × 100,000 = 54,545	$\frac{20}{110}$ × 100,000 = 18,182
Machine running costs	$\frac{75}{407}$ × 400,000 = 73,710	$\frac{192}{407}$ × 400,000 = 188,698	$\frac{140}{407}$ × 400,000 = 137,592
General facility costs	$\frac{75}{407}$ × 324,000 = 59,705	$\frac{192}{407}$ × 324,000 = 152,845	$\frac{140}{407}$ × 324,000 = 111,450
Total indirect costs	$226,688	$495,088	$322,224

Step 3 Calculate indirect cost per unit and full cost per unit

	W	X	Y
Total indirect cost	226,688	495,088	322,224
Budgeted annual production (units)	15,000	24,000	20,000
Indirect cost per unit	$15.12	$20.64	$16.12
Direct costs per unit			
Material	35.00	45.00	30.00
Labour	40.00	30.00	50.00
Full cost per unit	$90.12	$95.64	$96.12

ANSWERS

(d) How ABC could provide information relevant to decisions regarding profitability

The management team of KL will need to look at **price** and **cost** when it considers profitability. ABC can be useful to business in both areas of decision making. The unit costs calculated using ABC differ to those calculated under full cost. These are summarised in the table below.

	W	X	Y
	$	$	$
Full cost per unit	93.00	88.50	102.50
ABC cost per unit	90.12	95.64	96.12
Difference	2.88	(7.14)	6.38

Costing

ABC helps with **cost reduction** because it provides an insight into causal activities and allows organisations to consider the possibility of **outsourcing particular activities**, or even of **moving to different areas in the industry value chain**, eg reduce numbers of orders and increase size of batches.

Many **costs are driven by customers** (delivery costs, discounts, after-sales service and so on), but traditional cost accounting does not account for this. Companies may be trading with certain customers at a loss but may not realise it because costs are not analysed in a way that would reveal the true situation. ABC can be **used in conjunction with customer profitability analysis (CPA)** to determine more accurately the profit earned by serving particular customers.

Pricing

The traditional costing and pricing system indicates that the firm might be wise to concentrate on its high margin, up-market products and drop its standard range. This is **absurd**, however. Much of the overhead cost incurred in such an organisation is the cost of support activities like production scheduling: the more different **varieties** of product there are, the higher the level of such activities will become. The cost of marketing and distribution also increase disproportionately to the volume of products being made.

The bulk of the overheads in such an organisation are actually the '**costs of complexity**'. Their arbitrary allocation on the basis of labour hours gives an entirely **distorted** view of production line profitability; many products that appear to be highly profitable actually make a loss if costs are allocated on the basis of what activities cause them.

The problem arises with **marginal cost-plus** approaches as well as with absorption cost based approaches, particularly in a modern manufacturing environment, where a relatively small proportion of the total cost is variable. The implication in both cases is that conventional costing should be abandoned in favour of ABC.

However, many 'purists' consider that **marginal costing** alone provides the correct information on which to **make short-term decisions including pricing.**

ABC establishes a long-run product cost and because it provides data which can be used to evaluate different business possibilities and opportunities it is particularly suited for decisions such as pricing. Pricing has long-term strategic implications and **average cost** is probably **more important** than **marginal cost** in many circumstances. **An ABC cost is an average cost**, but it is **not always a true cost** because some costs such as depreciation are usually arbitrarily allocated to products. An ABC cost is therefore **not a relevant cost for all decisions.**

Profit

The differences in unit costs between full cost, and ABC cost shown in the table show that management need to consider a few actions from the results of ABC costing. Should they increase the price of X which has a higher ABC cost than full cost?

On the other hand should management reduce the price of Y which has a lower ABC cost than full cost.

ANSWERS

90 D

Text reference. You will find most of the information to answer this question in Chapters 4, 14 and 16.

Top tips. In part(a) the examiner wants more than just a calculation of the expected number of members. So remember to multiply the expected number of members by **the annual fee**. You can answer part (b) without needing to either calculate the variations in the operating costs or multiply these by the probabilities. We show you how this is done below if you aren't sure.

Data tables are used to show the effect of changing the values of variables. In part (c) you are asked to prepare a data table that shows nine possible profit values so you need to consider what variables affect **profit**. Clearly the number of members is one variable and contribution is the other variable. In part (d), the examiner actually wants you to discuss profitability and risk using the profit values from your data table and probabilities. So work out the probability of making a profit or a loss using the values from your data table and information from the question stating the probabilities attached to the number of members and the costs. Part (e) is testing your knowledge of activity based costing. This part is also giving you an opportunity to comment on the causes of operating costs and make recommendations to management on how they might tailor their pricing according to members' circumstances.

Easy marks. You should be able to do the calculation asked for in part (a).

(a) **Expected annual fee income of D**

Number of members	Probability	Expected number of members
20,000	0.3	6,000
30,000	0.5	15,000
40,000	0.2	8,000
	Expected number of members	29,000

Expected number of members × basic fee per year gives expected annual fee income.

Therefore the annual fee is:

29,000 × $100 = $2,900,000.

(b) **Breakeven number of members**

There are two ways of calculating the costs used in the breakeven calculation here and one is longer than the other.

(i) **The quick method**

If you are confident with using probabilities, you will realise that there are **equal** probabilities for each operating cost and that the costs are **equally distributed**. So costs are plus or minus 20% around an average cost. Therefore, the operating costs will be the **average costs**. The calculation for breakeven is then as follows:

	$ per member
Annual fee	100
Operating costs	
Call-out cost (average cost)	(50)
Administration cost (average cost)	(10)
Contribution	40

Breakeven point = activity (members) at which there is neither profit nor loss

$$= \frac{\text{total fixed costs}}{\text{contribution per unit}}$$

= $1,100,000/40 = 27,500 members

307

ANSWERS

(ii) **The basic method**

Draw up a quick table setting out your calculations of the operating costs and their probabilities

Variation in cost %	Call-out cost $	Probability	Administration cost $	Probability
−20	40	1/3	8	1/3
0	50	1/3	10	1/3
+20	60	1/3	12	1/3

You can work out the **expected value** of the operating costs by multiplying out all of the probabilities. So:

$(40 + 8) \times 1/3 \times 1/3 + \$(40 + 10) \times 1/3 \times 1/3 + \$(40 +12) \times 1/3 \times 1/3 + \$(50 + 8) \times 1/3 \times 1/3 + \$(50 + 10) \times 1/3 \times 1/3 + \$(50 +12) \times 1/3 \times 1/3 + \$(60 + 8) \times 1/3 \times 1/3 + \$(60 + 10) \times 1/3 \times 1/3 + \$(60 +12) \times 1/3 \times 1/3 = \$60$.

This is the same as the average cost used in our earlier calculation. You can then follow the method used in (i) to arrive at the breakeven number of members.

(c) **Two-way data table showing possible profit values**

	Number of members		
Contribution per member	20,000	30,000	40,000
$	$	$	$
28 (W1)	(540,000) (W2)	(260,000) (W2)	20,000 (W2)
40 (W1)	(300,000) (W2)	100,000 (W2)	500,000 (W2)
52 (W1)	(60,000) (W2)	460,000 (W2)	980,000 (W2)

Workings

1 Contribution is worked out using the lowest operating costs at −20%, the average operating costs and the highest operating costs at +20%. Take these figures from the table in part(b)(ii).

$100 − \$(40+8) = \$52$
$100 − \$(50 + 10) = \$40$
$100 − \$(60+12) = \$28$

2 Take the contribution per member and multiply by the number of members. Then deduct the fixed costs of $1,100,000. So by way of example, $28 × 20,000 - $1,100,000 = $(540,000)

(d) **An explanation of the table**

The table gives a range of possible **profit or loss values** for combinations of contribution per member and number of members. However what managers need to know is the **likelihood** of losses arising, and then decide whether to carry on with the service. Managers have varying attitudes to risk so what one manager considers an acceptable level of risk or of a loss arising, another would see as too risky.

Result $	Probability(W)	
(540,000)	0.10	
(300,000)	0.10	
(60,000)	0.10	
(260,000)	0.17	0.47
100,000	0.17	
460,000	0.17	
20,000	0.06	
500,000	0.06	
980,000	0.07	0.53

Working

The probabilities are worked out combining the probabilities of the number of members and contribution from the question. So for a loss of $(540,000) the probability of 0.1 is calculated taking the probability of 20,000 members × the probability of a contribution of $28 per member.

The probabilities in the table reveal a near equal likelihood of making a profit or loss. A 47% chance of making a loss may be too high for a risk-averse manager and so they may like to reconsider their business strategy.

(e) **How data from members might improve decision-making**

The data to be requested is presumed to refer to information on members that might influence or **drive** the activities of the company. This is an activity based costing (ABC) approach. ABC looks at the factors that drive the consumption of an activity and attaches costs to these drivers. ABC acknowledges that there are many causes for costs rather than just one overall factor such as membership numbers. The absorption costing approach which uses one factor is seen as too simplistic.

The management team would use the information gathered on its members and refer to this when reviewing the costs of each activity for each type of member. They could then devise a pricing policy for members based on how they cause or **drive** costs.

Examples of how this information would be used include:

the **average annual mileage** may give the likelihood of the possibility of a breakdown occurring. The more mileage in a year, the more likely a breakdown would occur.

The **number of years a member has been a qualified driver** may have some bearing on how they look after their car.

The **age of a vehicle** is a likely indication of its reliability. The older a car is, the more likely it is to break down.

91 Section A answers: Contemporary techniques

1.   I   The use of small frequent deliveries against bulk contracts – **yes**

    II   The grouping of machines or workers by product or component instead of by type of work performed – **yes**

    III   A reduction in machine set-up time – **yes**

    IV   Production driven by demand – **yes**

    Aspect I: JIT requires close integration of suppliers with the company's manufacturing process.
    Aspect II: JIT requires the use of machine cells.
    Aspect III: JIT recognises machinery set-ups as a non-value-added activity.
    Aspect IV: Each component on a production line is produced only when needed for the next stage.

2.   D   We need to rank in terms of the throughput contribution per time on the bottleneck resource.

    (Because direct materials cost is the only unit-level manufacturing cost, conversion costs cannot be directly allocated to products and hence we do not use the TA ratio.)

ANSWERS

	J	K	L	M
Hours per product	2	1²/₃	1¹/₆	1⁵/₆
	£	£	£	£
Selling price	2,000	1,500	1,500	1,750
Direct material cost	410	200	300	400
Throughput contribution	1,590	1,300	1,200	1,350
Throughput contribution per hour	£795	£780	£1,029	£736
Ranking	2	3	1	4

3

	£
Cost of goods sold (standard charge)	100,000
Less: material costs (100 × £45)	45,000
Conversion cost allocated	55,000
Conversion cost incurred	60,000
Excess charged to cost of goods sold a/c	5,000

∴ Total charge to cost of goods sold a/c = £100,000 + £5,000
= £105,000

4 (a) The aim of TOC is to maximise **throughput contribution** while keeping **inventory** and **operational expenses** to a minimum.

(b) An assumption in TOC is that all operational expenses except direct material cost are **fixed**.

(c) An activity within an organisation which has a lower capacity than preceding or subsequent actions, thereby limiting throughput, is a **bottleneck** or **binding constraint**.

(d) Under TOC, the only inventory that a business should hold, with the exception of possibly a very small amount of finished goods inventory and raw materials that are consistent with the JIT approach, is a buffer inventory held **immediately prior to the bottleneck/binding constraint**.

5

	Standard costing	Kaizen costing
Concepts	It is used for cost control.	It is used for cost reduction.
	The cost focus is on standard costs based on static conditions.	The cost focus is on actual costs assuming dynamic conditions.
	The aim is to meet cost performance standards.	The aim is to achieve cost reduction targets.
Techniques	Standards are set every six or twelve months.	Cost reduction targets are set monthly.
	Costs are controlled using variance analysis.	Costs are reduced by implementing continuous improvement (kaizen) to attain the target profit or reduce the gap between target and estimated profit.
	Management should investigate and respond when standards are not met.	Management should investigate and respond when targets are not attained.
Employees	They are often viewed as the cause of problems.	They are viewed as the source of, and are empowered to find, the solutions.

(Adapted from Monden and Lee)

6

	RAW MATERIALS		
	£		£
B/f	500	Cost of sales *	4,090
Purchases	4,600	c/f (balance)	1,010
	5,100		5,100

* $\dfrac{10}{22} \times £8{,}998 = £4{,}090$

7 Return per hour = (sales – material cost) per hour on bottleneck resource

∴ Return per 6.5 mins = £(24.99 – 8.87)

∴ Return per hour = £(24.99 – 8.87) × $\dfrac{60}{6.5}$ = £148.80

92 Question with helping hand: Standard costing, TQM and JIT

> **Top tips.** You probably found it relatively easy to answer the first requirement of part (a) (**why** a standard costing system might need adapting). The second requirement is more difficult as it requires application rather than regurgitation.

Standard costing and JIT

In a JIT environment, standard costing could make X Ltd's managers focus on the wrong issues. Here are two examples.

(a) **Efficiency variance.** Traditionally, adverse efficiency variances should be avoided, which means that managers should try to prevent idle time and keep up production. With JIT manufacturing, however, action to eliminate idle time could result in the manufacture of unwanted electronic diaries that must be held in store and might eventually be scrapped

(b) **Materials price variance**. With JIT purchasing, the key issues should be supplier reliability, materials quality and delivery in small order quantities. X Ltd's purchasing managers should not be shopping around every month for the cheapest prices. Many JIT systems depend on long-term contractual links with suppliers, which means that material price variances are not relevant for control purposes.

X Ltd management could therefore **aim to attain standards** rather than striving for favourable variances. There should be no material price variance, for example, neither adverse nor favourable, as the price paid should be the price contracted. This approach depends, of course, on standards being set at appropriate levels (see below).

Standard costing and Total Quality Management (TQM)

Standard costing concentrates on quantity and ignores other factors contributing to effectiveness. But in X Ltd's TQM environment, the issue is no longer quantity but quality.

(a) **Predetermined standards** are **at odds** with the **philosophy of continual improvement** inherent in a TQM programme. Such continual improvements are likely to alter X Ltd's methods of working, prices, quantities of inputs and so on, whereas **standard costing** is most **appropriate** in a **stable, standardised and repetitive environment**.

Standards therefore need to be **reviewed regularly** in order to keep them up-to-date and in line with the frequent changes resulting from continual improvement.

(b) X Ltd may have set **attainable standards**, which make some allowance for wastage and inefficiencies. The use of such standards **conflicts with the elimination of waste**, a vital component of any TQM programme.

ANSWERS

Incorporating a **planned level of scrap** in material standards, for example, is **at odds with the TQM aim of zero defects** and there is **no motivation to 'get it right first time'**.

Ideal performance standards should therefore be **used**, as these are based on perfect operating conditions.

(c) The **standard costing** control system operated by X Ltd would **make individual managers responsible for the variances relating to their part of the organisation's activities**. As noted above, this could motivate managers to achieve favourable variances at the expense of X Ltd's wider aims of quality and customer care.

So instead, **standards should be set within the context of the wider aims** of X Ltd as a **TQM** programme aims to make **all personnel aware of, and responsible for**, the importance of supplying the customer with a quality product.

(d) Standard costing concentrates on quantity as a measure of effectiveness. Effectiveness in a **TQM** environment is seen in terms of high quality output, achieved as a result of high quality input and the elimination of non-value adding activities. The **cost of failing to achieve this required level of effectiveness** is measured not in variances but in terms of **internal and external failure costs**, which are not identified by traditional variance analysis.

Standard costing might **measure labour efficiency** in terms of **individual tasks** and **level of output**. In a **TQM** environment, labour is more likely to be viewed as a number of multi-task teams who are responsible for the completion of a part of the production process. The **effectiveness** of such a team is therefore more appropriately measured in terms of **re-working required**, **returns from customers**, **defects identified in subsequent stages of production** and so on.

To ensure an **effective system of control** operates within X Ltd, additional **non-financial indicators** and **costs of quality** should be reported as well as traditional variances.

Standard costing and automated manufacturing

The changes within X Ltd would have dramatically **changed product cost structures**.

(a) High levels of automation, multi-skilling and teamworking would have reduced levels of direct labour and maintained them at fairly constant levels.

(b) The rise in support activities such as setting-up, inspection and so on would have increased overhead costs, as would the huge investment in manufacturing equipment.

The **significance of variable costs would therefore have reduced**. But **standard costing** is of **most use when applied to variable costs**.

Variable costs still represent a not insignificant proportion of total costs, however. **Recent surveys** in many countries have reported very similar results: **direct costs and overheads average approximately 75% and 25% respectively** of total manufacturing costs, with average direct labour costs ranging from 10% to 15% of total manufacturing cost.

Standard costing should therefore still be viewed as a vital control tool.

(a) Given the automation of production, **variable overheads** may be **incurred** in **relation to machine time** rather than labour time, and standard costs should reflect this where appropriate.

(b) If X Ltd is now using computer aided design/computer aided manufacture (CADCAM) systems, **planning of manufacturing requirements** can be **computerised**, so that **standard costs can be more accurately constructed** by computer.

The majority of manufacturing organisations still use standard costing. If it is broadened to take into account factors such as those detailed above, its life is likely to be a lot longer.

93 Cost management techniques again

> **Top tips.** To score well on this question you must cover the traditional approaches too.

(a) **Just-in-time**

Traditional approach

The traditional manufacturing philosophy was to improve manufacturing capacity and keep production flowing (a **push production** system) so as to avoid idle labour and machinery. In such an environment, **methods of reducing costs include**:

- **Long production runs** to minimise the costs of machine downtime and resetting equipment
- Production based on **economic batch quantities** to minimise stock costs
- **A limited product range**

Such an approach led to the **build up of stocks** of raw materials, work in progress and finished goods, however, thereby **increasing both stock holding costs and the opportunity cost of funds tied up in stocks**.

JIT approach

Just-in-time (JIT) challenges such traditional views. Unlike the push system described above (in which purchasing and production are driven by stock), JIT is a **pull system, driven by demand**.

(i) **JIT production** involves the manufacture of a component only when it is needed by the next stage. Ultimately it is customer demand that drives the whole process.

(ii) **JIT purchasing** aims to match receipt and usage of material.

Stocks of raw materials, work in progress and finished goods are therefore kept at **near zero or zero levels.**

JIT and cost reduction

Such an approach allows for a wide variety of cost reduction opportunities such as:

(i) **Reduction in the costs of storing stock**

(1) Smaller stores areas should be required.
(2) Fewer staff should be needed.
(3) The costs associated with stock damaged in stores/obsolete stock should be eliminated.
(4) There should be no opportunity cost of funds tied up in large levels of stock.

(ii) **Reduction in the costs associated with scrap, defective units and reworking.** For JIT purchasing to be successful, an organisation must have confidence that suppliers will deliver on time and that the materials delivered will be of 100% quality.

(iii) **Reduction in the costs of finding and retaining customers**. Customer retention should improve because of the ability to respond to customers' product requirements as and when necessary.

(b) **Activity based management**

Traditional approach

Traditional costing systems, notably **absorption costing, assume** that all products **consume resources in proportion to their production volumes**. While this may be true for overheads such as power costs, it does not necessarily hold for all overheads, or an increasing proportion of them, especially those connected with support services. The amount of **overhead allocated** to individual products by absorption costing therefore bears **very little resemblance** to the **amount of overhead actually incurred** by the products and hence gives management **minimal understanding of the behaviour of overhead costs and**, consequently, they have a lack of **ability to control/reduce them.**

ANSWERS

ABC/ABM approach

Activity based costing (**ABC**) attempts to overcome this problem by identifying the activities or transactions (**cost drivers**) which underlie an organisation's activities and which cause the incidence of the activity, and hence the cost of the activity (overheads) to increase. Costs can then be attributed to products according to the number of cost drivers they cause/consume using cost driver rates.

Activity based management (ABM) is the term given to those **management processes that use the information provided by an activity-based cost analysis to improve organisational profitability.**

ABM and cost reduction

Because ABM analyses costs on the basis of what causes them, rather than on the basis of type of expense/cost centre, it provides management with vital information on why costs are being incurred. If management can **reduce the incidence of the cost driver, they can reduce the associated cost.**

ABM involves a variety of **cost reduction techniques**.

(i) Ensuring activities are performed as efficiently as possible

(ii) Controlling, reducing or eliminating the need to perform activities that do not add value for customers

(iii) Minimising cost drivers

(iv) Improving the design of products

In short, it aims to **ensure that customer needs are met while fewer demands are made on organisational resources**.

94 Exe plc

> **Top tips.** It was vital to note that Exe plc 'has recently invested heavily in automated processes'. In other words it is operating in a modern manufacturing environment. This should lead you to consider approaches such as TQM and JIT.

World Class Manufacturing

To survive and grow in today's global competitive market, manufacturing companies such as Exe plc need to follow a philosophy of World Class Manufacturing (WCM).

WCM is a broad term but basically it describes **the manufacture at low cost of high-quality products reaching customers quickly to provide a high level of performance and customer satisfaction.**

A WCM manufacturer will therefore have a **clear manufacturing strategy** aimed at issues such as **quality and reliability, short lead times, flexibility and customer satisfaction.**

The value chain

To compete, the world class manufacturer must appreciate that it is **not just in manufacturing that he must excel**. A clear **understanding** of the relationship between all the factors that add value to an organisation's products (the **value chain**) is vital.

Customers and suppliers are therefore important to organisations such as Exe plc because the value chain **starts externally with suppliers,** links them to the internal functions of research and development, design, production, marketing, distribution, customer service and **ends externally with customers**.

To **improve quality, reduce costs and increase innovation** (and hence improve market share), Exe plc must ensure that the **functions within the value chain are co-ordinated** within the overall organisational framework. This requires the company to develop and maintain communications with customers and suppliers.

ANSWERS

Two key elements of WCM

Element 1 – A new approach to product quality

Instead of a policy of trying to detect defects or poor quality in production as and when they occur, WCM sets out to **identify the root causes of poor quality**, eliminate them and achieve zero defects (**100% quality**).

Element 2 – Flexible approach to customer requirements

The WCM policy is to develop **close relationships** with customers in order to **know what their requirements** are, **supply them on time, with short delivery lead times and change the product mix quickly and develop new products or modify existing products** as customer needs change.

How Exe plc can achieve this

Exe plc's achievement of these elements hinges on the introduction of a system of **just-in-time (JIT)**.

JIT

The aim of a JIT system is **to produce products or obtain components as they are required by a customer or needed in production**. A JIT system is therefore a **'pull' system** in that it responds to demand (either from production or from customers) as opposed to a 'pull' system in which stock acts as buffers between the different elements of a system (purchasing, production, sales and so on).

JIT has two key elements.

Element 1 – JIT production

JIT production is driven by demand for finished products with the result that **components are only produced when needed for the next stage**.

Element 2 – JIT purchasing

JIT purchasing is based on ensuring that the **receipt and usage of materials coincide**.

JIT and communications with customers and suppliers

Communication links with customers and suppliers are therefore of vital importance to ensure that Exe plc's finished products are ready when its customers require them and that materials from Exe plc's suppliers are available only when required for Exe plc's production line. They are vital to the operation of JIT, a system that would allow Exe plc to implement WCM and improve its market position.

95 Backflush costing

> **Top tips.** This is a nice little question to take you through the key points of backflush.

Overview

Backflush costing operates by applying costs to products at a late stage in the production cycle. There is usually **no work in progress account** in a backflush system. **Actual conversion costs are recorded as incurred** just as in conventional recording systems **but they are not applied to products until later 'trigger points'**, sometimes as late as the point at which they are sold. This **avoids unnecessary work in tracking costs through the accounting system**. There are fewer accounting entries, supporting vouchers, documents and so on.

Backflush systems and stock levels

Backflush systems can prove useful for **jobbing concerns** such as PSA Ltd because such organisations do not tend to produce for stock. The **vast majority of manufacturing costs will form part of the cost of sales** and **will not be deferred in closing stock values**. The work involved under a conventional system of **tracking costs though WIP**, cost of sales and finished goods accounts for accurate stock valuation is probably **not justified**. The existence of a substantial amount of **work in progress in PSA Ltd would probably prohibit the use of backflush costing, however**.

ANSWERS

Backflush systems and efficiency and prices

Another prerequisite for the successful operation of backflush costing is **predictable levels of efficiency and fixed price and quality of materials**. This enables costs to be applied to products at the point of completion by assuming that each part of output contains the standard inputs for each cost element. In other words, there should be **insignificant cost variances**. This does **not appear to be the case with PSA Ltd**. Planning variances are identified and there are substantial inefficiencies in the use of labour and material.

Conclusion

On the basis of the available information it appears that **backflush costing is not appropriate** for PSA Ltd.

96 Question with answer plan: SWAL (Pilot paper)

> **Top tips.** The principal areas you would need to cover to score well would be:
> - Explanation of present system of stock control
> - Explanation of JIT system
> - Explanation of need for quality supplies of material
> - Explanation of need for quality during processing
>
> **Easy marks.** Using a report format would earn you at least one mark.

Answer plan

- Correct headings and addressee at beginning of report
- Explanation of JIT
- Current stock system and how this differs to a JIT system
- Implications of JIT for quality control procedures: purchasing; production.

REPORT

To: Managing director of SW
From: Management accountant
Date: 13 November 20X6
Subject: **Stock control systems**

1 Introduction

This report looks at the differences between the stock control system currently being used within SW and a just-in-time (JIT) system and then considers the extent to which the introduction of JIT would require a review of the organisation's control procedures.

2 JIT

2.1 The objective of a JIT system is to produce products or components as they are needed by the customer or by the production process, rather than for stock.

2.2 A JIT production system therefore only produces a component when needed in the next stage of production.

2.3 In a JIT purchasing system, purchases of raw materials are contracted so that, as far as possible, the receipt and usage of material coincides.

ANSWERS

3 Current stock control system versus a JIT system

3.1 A JIT stock control system for the purchase of chemicals would be fundamentally different to the one currently being used.

3.1.1 Raw materials would not be ordered when a reorder level is reached but when they were actually needed in production.

3.1.2 Stock levels would therefore be reduced to near zero levels, there would be no maximum and minimum levels.

3.1.3 Supplies would be delivered on a long-term contract basis as soon as they were needed, but in small quantities.

3.1.4 This would obviously increase ordering costs.

3.1.5 The costs of space for holding stocks of chemicals, and costs such as damage or deterioration in stores, stores administration and security would be minimal, however. In particular the interest cost and opportunity cost of tying up working capital in large inventories would be avoided.

3.1.6 The economic order quantity model would therefore not be relevant, not only because the exact quantity needed would be delivered, but because holding costs would be kept to a minimum while no direct effort would be made to minimise ordering costs.

4 JIT and the implications for quality control procedures

4.1 JIT purchasing

4.1.1 If raw material stocks were to be kept at near-zero levels, the company would have to have confidence that suppliers would deliver on time and that they would deliver chemicals of 100% quality. There could be no rejects or returns; if there were, production would be delayed because no stocks are held.

4.1.2 The reliability of the organisation's suppliers would therefore be of the utmost importance and hence we would have to build up close relationships with them. This could be achieved by doing more business with fewer suppliers and placing long-term orders so that the supplier would be assured of sales and could produce to meet the required demand.

4.1.3 A supplier quality assurance programme (such as BS EN ISO 9000) should be introduced. The quality of the chemicals delivered would be guaranteed by suppliers and the onus would be on the supplier to carry out the necessary quality checks, or face cancellation of the contract.

4.2 JIT production

4.2.1 Because stocks of components would not be held, production management within a JIT environment would seek both to eliminate scrap and defective chemicals during production and avoid the need for reworking. Defects would stop the production line, thus creating rework and possibly resulting in a failure to meet delivery dates.

4.2.2 Quality control procedures would therefore have to be in place to ensure that the correct cleaning liquid was made to the appropriate level of quality on the first pass through production.

- Products would need to be designed with quality in mind.
- Controls would have to be put in place within processes to prevent the manufacture of defective output.
- Quality awareness programmes would need to be established.
- Statistical checks on output quality both during production and for finished goods would be required.
- Continual worker training would be necessary.

5 I hope this information has proved useful but if I can be of any further assistance please do not hesitate to contact me.

Signed: Management accountant

ANSWERS

97 Question with analysis: X Group

> **Top tips.** The examiner's marking guide stated that there were two marks for introducing and explaining JIT. The remaining eight marks were awarded for stating how JIT would affect profitability in X Group.
>
> Therefore, it would be wise to concentrate effort on applying JIT specifically to the X group. The examiner is looking at your application of knowledge.
>
> **Easy marks.** It is possible to gain two marks from just memorising or paraphrasing CIMA's definitions of JIT included as Key Terms in the P2 Study Text. Look at the format requested in the question – using a report format will earn a mark or so.
>
> **Examiner's comments.** Most students made a good attempt at this question but many simply wrote all they know about JIT (simply a 'brain dump').
>
> Common errors noted by the examiner
>
> - Not discussing how JIT might affect profitability
> - Not presenting a report ('to' and 'from' is not sufficient)
> - Not relating the answer to the scenario described in the question.

REPORT

[Report format]

To: Managing Director
From: Management Accountant
Date: 11 November 20X5
Subject: How the adoption of a JIT system would affect profitability

Introduction

This report addresses how the adoption of a JIT system might affect the profitability of the X Group.

JIT definition

JIT is a customer led production system, also known as a 'pull' system. The objective is to produce products as they are required by the customer rather than build up stock to cater for demand.

Just in time production

A JIT production system is driven by demand for finished products whereby each component in a process is only made when needed for the next stage.

Just in time purchasing

A JIT purchasing system requires material to be purchased so that as far as possible it can be used straight away.

The effect on X Group's profitability

[Features picked out from first three paragraphs of the question]

The introduction of a JIT production and purchasing system would have the following impact on profitability:

- A reduction in inventory holding costs as inventories of raw materials and finished goods will disappear.

- An increase is possible for raw material costs to encourage suppliers to deliver to a JIT schedule and so additional flexibility is required.

- As demand may fluctuate, additional labour costs to cover production where no buffer stocks exist.

- Additional requirements for quality control by suppliers to ensure materials and by others to ensure finished goods are acceptable for the customer.

- Increased administration costs to plan throughput.

ANSWERS

98 MN Ltd

> **Text references.** Read Chapter 17 of your Study Text to give you some pointers for answering this question.
>
> **Top tips.** You need to begin part (a) by determining the bottleneck resource. And when calculating the cost per factory hour take care to note that labour and variable overheads are given as weekly figures, but fixed production costs are given as an annual figure.
>
> Other ratios that you might have mentioned for part (c) include days' inventory on hand, manufacturing cycle time, cost of quality, customer due date performance and process time to scheduled time. If you found this part difficult because of a lack of knowledge, make a note of the key ratios.
>
> **Easy marks.** Look at key phrases for the written section, see the bold sections in the answer. This is a time pressured question.

(a) **Key resource:**

	Machine X Output	Machine Y Output	Machine Z Output
Up to 5 hours production time lost per week ($= \frac{1}{8}$ of maximum weekly production time)	$\frac{7}{8} \times \frac{180}{4}$ = 39 TRLS		
Machine Y		52 TRLS	
Machine Z			30 TRLS

Key resource is therefore Machine Z time

	£
Selling price	2,000
Material cost	(600)
	1,400

Time on key resource   40 hours per week/30TRLS
                        = 1.3333 hours per TRL
Return per factory hour 1,400/1.3333
                        = £1,050

Cost per factory hour:

	£
Labour	5,500
Variable overhead	8,000
Fixed production costs	9,375 (450,000/48 weeks)
	22,875

Number of factory hours per week   40
Cost per factory hour   £571.88

Throughput accounting ratio $\frac{£1,050}{571.88}$

                               = 1.84

ANSWERS

(b) The following **uses** for the throughput accounting ratio have been suggested.

    (i) In a throughput environment, production priority must be given to the products best able to generate throughput, that is those products that maximise throughput per unit of key or bottleneck resource. The throughput accounting ratio can be used to **rank products**, the product with the highest value of this ratio being given the highest ranking.

    (ii) The throughput accounting ratio compares the rate at which a product earns contribution with the rate at which production costs are incurred. If the ratio is greater than one, contribution is being generated at a rate faster than that at which production costs are being incurred. The opposite is true if the ratio is less than one. The ratio can therefore be used to determine **whether or not a product should be produced**.

(c) Two other ratios which may be used by a company operating throughput accounting

    (i) **Schedule adherence**. This will highlight how well production schedules are being adhered to.

        (1) Given that products should not be made unless there is a customer waiting for them, it is vital that production is not disrupted otherwise the customer will be kept waiting.

        (2) Given that the ideal work in progress level is zero and buffer stocks are not held, it is vital that production schedules are kept to otherwise the entire production process will come to a halt.

    (ii) **First-time capability (especially of output from the bottleneck process)**. Below quality output at the bottleneck process would use up valuable resource time to transform it into saleable output, thereby reducing throughput capacity and increasing costs.

(d) **Contribution in throughput accounting and contribution in marginal costing are based on the same concept**.

    (i) They are both calculated as the difference between sales revenue and variable costs.

    (ii) They are both used to cover an organisation's fixed costs.

In both approaches, the contribution earned can be used **to assess the relative earning capabilities of different products** in order to determine an optimum production mix.

There are **differences** between the approaches, however. For example in marginal costing, material costs, labour costs and variable overheads are classified as variable costs. In throughput accounting, most factory costs, with the exception of materials costs, are classified as fixed costs.

(e) The production manager and the management accountant need to focus on **adherence to production schedules** and **maintenance of low stock levels.**

If machine Z is replaced with machine G and if machine X is overhauled, the existing bottleneck of machine Z time will be removed and the availability of machine X time increased, and so output constraints will be as follows.

Machine X 45 units per week
Machine Y 52 units per week
Machine G 45 units per week

Time on machines X and G will therefore become the **bottleneck resource** during the period from June to October, when demand is estimated to range between 40 and 48 units per week. The changeover to G and the overhaul must therefore be completed and output must be at full capacity by the beginning of June.

First time capability of output from these two machines in particular must be rigorously monitored. The **return per factory hour** given these bottleneck resources and the **throughput ratio** must also be monitored and reported as well as any other indicators that enable the maximisation of throughput.

99 SG plc

> **Text references.** Look at Chapter 17 for key data on JIT, TQM and quality costs to help in your answer.
>
> **Top tips.** This was a fairly straightforward question. In part (a) it was vital that you applied principles you had learnt from the Study Text to the scenario of the question. Part (c) in particular should have caused you very little problem – although it was important to provide examples.

(a) Total Quality Management (TQM) is the process of focusing on quality in the management of all resources and relationships within the organisation. It has two basic principles.

    (i) **Getting things right first time**, on the basis that the cost of correcting mistakes is greater than the cost of preventing them from happening in the first place.

    (ii) **Continuous improvement**, which is the belief that it is always possible to improve, no matter how high quality may be already.

TQM and SG plc

TQM is a management technique, applicable to all of an organisation's activities, not just to production. It can therefore be applied to all of SG plc's activities, not just to food production.

    (i) **In relation to design.** Products and processes should be designed with quality in mind (so that faults are not incorporated from the outset). For example, SG plc would need to ensure that specifications for food were 100% correct.

    (ii) **In relation to food production.** The quality of output depends on the quality of input materials and so TQM would require procedures for acceptance and inspection of goods inwards and measurement of rejects. Inspection of output could take place at various key stages of the production process to provide a continual check that the production process is under control. Machines should be maintained so that quality production occurs.

    (iii) **In relation to sales.** Some sub-standard output will inevitably be produced. Customer complaints should be monitored in the form of letters of complaint, returned goods, penalty discounts and so on.

    (iv) **In relation to suppliers.** Supplier quality assurance schemes could be established so that suppliers would guarantee the quality of goods supplied. The onus would then be on the supplier to carry out the necessary quality checks or face cancellation of the contract.

    (v) **In relation to employees.** Quality should be the primary concern of every employee at every stage of production. Workers must therefore be empowered and take responsibility for the quality of SG plc's products, stopping the production line if necessary. Quality circles might be set up, perhaps with responsibility for implementing improvements identified by the circle members.

    (vi) **In relation to the information system.** The information system should be designed to get the required information to the right person at the right time.

(b) **Just-in-time (JIT) systems incorporate:**

    (i) **JIT production,** which is a system driven by demand for finished products so that work in progress is only processed through a stage of production when it is needed by the next stage. The result is **minimal** (or in some cases non-existent) **stocks of work in progress and finished goods.**

    (ii) **JIT purchasing**, which seeks to match the usage of materials with the delivery of materials from external suppliers. This means that **material stocks** can be kept at **near-zero levels.**

Production management within a JIT environment therefore needs to **eliminate scrap and defective units** during production and **avoid the need for reworking of units**. Defects stop the **production line**, creating **rework** and possibly resulting in a **failure to meet delivery dates** (as **buffer stocks** of work in progress and finished goods are **not held**). **TQM** should ensure that the **correct product** is made to the **appropriate level of quality** on the **first pass through production**.

ANSWERS

For JIT purchasing to be successful, the organisation must have confidence that the **supplier will deliver on time** and will deliver **materials of 100% quality**, that there will be no rejects, returns and hence **no consequent production delays**. This confidence can be achieved by **adopting supplier quality assurance schemes** and stringent **procedures for acceptance and inspection of goods inwards**, which are integral parts of TQM.

(c) Quality costs can be classified in four ways.

(i) **Costs of internal failure** are costs arising within an organisation due to failure to achieve the quality specified. Examples relevant to the business of SG plc could include the cost of foods scrapped due to inefficiencies in goods inwards procedures, the cost of foods lost in process and the cost of foods rejected during any inspection process.

(ii) **Costs of external failure** are costs arising outside the organisation of failure to achieve specified quality after transfer of ownership to the customer. SG plc examples could include the cost of a customer complaints section and the cost of replacing and delivering returned foods.

(iii) **Costs of prevention** represent the cost of any action taken to investigate, prevent or reduce defects and failures. Examples for SG plc could include the cost of training personnel in TQM procedures and the cost of maintaining quality control/inspection equipment.

(iv) **Costs of appraisal** are the costs of assessing the level of quality achieved. Examples applicable to SG plc could be the cost of any goods inwards checks and the costs of any supplier vetting.

100 Quality costs

Top tips. You will need to make sure that you state the two main types of quality cost and their sub classifications, giving relevant examples, in your report. Four marks could be earned for this. Then make sure that you discuss them for another four marks. This may all sound obvious but the examiner often says that candidates don't answer the question set and this time he said that candidates did not give relevant examples or even use a report format. Crucially you need to bring out in your discussion the relationship between incurring costs of conformance and avoiding those of non-conformance. You also need to discuss explicitly the relationship between price and quality in your report.

Easy marks. Make sure you use the appropriate headers and so on for a report. Lay out the body of your answer in a report format and end the report appropriately, and there's two marks straight away.

Divide up your report with headings so that it is clear you have covered the points you need to discuss.

Examiner's comments. This question was well attempted although many candidates failed to use the report format. Common errors included not giving relevant examples of different quality costs and not developing the price/quality relationship.

REPORT

To: Managing Director
From: Management accountant
Date: 23 May 20X6
Subject: **Quality costs and their significance for the organisation**

1 **Introduction**

This report explains quality costs and their significance for the company.

2 **Quality costs**

There are two main types of quality cost, these being **costs of conformance** and **costs of non-conformance**. Conformance costs are further analysed into prevention costs, and appraisal costs. Costs of non-conformance can be further analysed into internal failure costs and external failure costs.

Prevention costs are the costs incurred prior or during production to prevent substandard or defective products or services being produced. Examples of these include the costs of quality engineering and design or development of quality control or inspection equipment.

Appraisal costs are the costs incurred to ensure that outputs produced meet required quality standards. Examples would include acceptance testing costs and the cost of inspection of goods inwards.

Internal failure costs are the costs arising from inadequate quality, which are identified before the transfer of ownership from supplier to purchaser. Relevant examples include re-inspection costs and losses due to lower selling prices from sub-quality goods.

External failure costs are the costs arising from inadequate quality discovered after the transfer of ownership from supplier to purchaser. Relevant examples would include product liability costs and costs of repairing products returned from customers.

3   **Significance of quality costs for the company**

To remain **successful** in the modern business environment, organisations must offer customers a **competitively priced, high-quality** product. Consideration must therefore be given to the **optimum balance between the costs of conformance and the costs of non-conformance**. There is a **trade off** between the two: the higher the expenditure on conformance (to ensure that customers receive the high quality products they demand) the lower the cost of non-conformance (as there are fewer quality failures) and vice versa.

The **problem** organisations face is **determining the level of quality customers expect** and hence the **acceptable level of external failure cost**. Some sort of research into customer preferences could be undertaken maybe with focus groups looking at our products and giving feedback on price and quality.

- A **zero defects** policy could be adopted, but this would be extremely costly and time consuming and would drive up the costs of conformance.
- A **sample testing** approach could be taken. This would keep down the costs of conformance but at the risk of increasing the costs of non-conformance.

Some **research** into customer preferences could be undertaken, possibly using focus groups to provide feedback on acceptable mixes of price and quality.

I hope this information has proved useful but if I can be of any further assistance please do not hesitate to contact me.

Signed: Management accountant

101 Section A answers: Externally-orientated techniques

1   D   **Rule I** was first suggested by the economist Pareto in the context of the distribution of wealth. It is only very approximately observed in practice.

There is no such general guidance to the effect of **rule II**.

Rule III was initially suggested by the economist Pareto on the basis of his observations of social inequality.

Rule IV is incorrect because, according to the 80/20 rule, the richest 20% of the population owns 80% of the wealth, compared to only 20% owned by the rest of the population.

2   Gain-sharing opportunities can exist in various areas of a contract and the associated supply chain.

- Changes in **technical specifications or levels of performance** may be possible, perhaps through advances in technology.
- Revised **delivery** times may lead to reduced costs and/or improved performance.
- Opportunities for the generation of an **income stream** from the use of the customer's assets by or for a **third party** could emerge or be developed.
- Opportunities may be found **within the supply chain**.

ANSWERS

3 **False**. In pain-/gain-sharing arrangements, **all cost overruns and cost savings are shared between the customer and the contractor**. A target cost is negotiated and agreed. If the actual cost is less than the target cost, the customer and contractor (and sometimes the contractor's supply chain) split any savings between them in agreed proportions. Likewise any cost overruns are shared by both parties. Sometimes the contractor's share of any cost overrun is up to a pre-arranged limit, and there may be time limits for the gain to be realised.

4

	W £'000	X £'000	Y £'000
Gross margin	1,100.0	1,750	1,200.0
Less: Customer specific costs			
Sales visits (110/100/170 × £500)	(55.0)	(50)	(85.0)
Order processing (1,000/1,000/1,500 × £100)	(100.0)	(100)	(150.0)
Despatch costs (1,000/1,000/1,500 × £100)	(100.0)	(100)	(150.0)
Billing and collections (900/1,200/1,500 × £175)	(157.5)	(210)	(262.5)
	687.5	1,290	552.5
Ranking	2	1	3

5 A Direct product costs include warehouse direct costs, transport direct costs and store direct costs.

6 Within the value chain, both primary activities and support activities are candidates for outsourcing, although many can be **eliminated** from the list immediately either **because the activity cannot be contracted out or because the organisation must control it to maintain its competitive position**.

Of the remaining activities, an organisation **should carry out only those that it can deliver on a level comparable with the best organisations in the world**. If the organisation cannot achieve benchmarked levels of performance, the activity should be outsourced so that the organisation is **only concentrating on those core activities that enhance its competitive advantage**.

7 A When reviewing stock control procedures – **yes**
  B When conducting a comparative customer profitability analysis – **yes**
  C When calculating direct product profit – **no**

A Pareto analysis of stock (**situation (A)**) might indicate that 20 per cent of stock items represent 80 per cent of the stock value. Stock control activity could then be focussed on these items.

A Pareto analysis of customers (**situation (B)**) might indicate that 20 per cent of customers generate 80 per cent of the company's profit. Resources can then be focussed on the more worthwhile customers.

A calculation of DPP (**situation (C)**) is the derivation of an absolute measure of the contribution a particular product category makes to fixed costs and profits. It can be used as the basis of a Pareto analysis, by comparing the DPP of all products, but the question does not mention that any comparison is being made.

102 AVN

> **Top tips**. The question is asking you to **explain** the components of the extended value chain and then how these might be **applied** to AVN's own circumstances. So you are being asked to show your knowledge and also use that knowledge in the scenario in the question.
>
> In part (a), do not be tempted to write all you know about value chains as that would take much longer than the six minutes you have here. Take your lead from the question where it mentions the phrase 'extended value chain'. Focus your answer on the **value added** and **linkages** between organisations in the value chain. So mention suppliers and distributors. Concentrate on the **adding of value to the end user** that underlies the idea of the value chain.

ANSWERS

> In part (b) you will need to write a few comments on how each component would apply to AVN. Think about how AVN and its products fit into the whole value chain. Look at the key terms we have put in bold. They indicate that you understand the ideas behind the value chain itself and aren't just waffling about environmental factors.
>
> **Easy marks.** In part (a) you should get a mark or so for a list of the components. In part (b) a bit of thought should allow you to apply the value chain to your components identified in (a).

(a) The **value chain** was described and popularised by Michael Porter. Its ultimate goal is to maximise **value** creation while minimising costs.

The **value chain** is the sequence of business **activities** by which, from the **perspective of the end user**, **value is added** to the products and services produced by an entity.

These activities are known as **primary** and **support** activities and are value activities.

The **primary activities** include: inbound logistics, operations (production), outbound logistics, sales and marketing, and service (maintenance). The **support activities** include: administrative infrastructure management, human resources management, R&D, and procurement.

Costs and value drivers are identified for each **value** activity.

The idea of the value chain has been **extended** beyond individual organisations. Where this occurs, the value chain is known as an **extended value chain**, and it can apply to whole supply chains and distribution networks. Individual value chains combine to deliver value to the end user.

Porter terms this larger interconnected system of **value** chains the 'value system'. A **value** system includes the value chains of an organisation's supplier (and their suppliers all the way back), the organisation itself, and its distribution channels, retailers, customers and so on to the ultimate end user. Value chains may extend to an extent that they become global.

(b) AVN should be looking at how it can **lower costs** and **enhance value** throughout the extended value chain. So AVN is looking at gaining **competitive advantage** by controlling its value chain.

The first step AVN should take is **to map the extended value chain** to determine the various activities in the chain and allocate costs and revenues to each. The elements of AVN's extended value chain would be **its suppliers, distributors and customers**.

Then AVN needs to look at controlling the **cost drivers** for the costs of each activity. These cost drivers are the executional and structural cost drivers mentioned above.

Suppliers

AVN could look at its **relationships with the suppliers of the parts** in its electronic devices. One way of doing this is through **supply chain management**. This involves AVN looking at ways of **improving its supply chain**. For instance AVN could switch to new suppliers by purchasing on-line.

AVN could require its part suppliers to be located nearby its assembly plant to minimise the cost of transportation. The company could also consider tying its suppliers into a JIT agreement so that inventory levels are kept to a minimum saving on stockholding costs. However this does need to be balanced against the risks of stock-outs and damaging relationships with customers.

AVN could try to **negotiate cheaper prices** for the components it buys in. Furthermore, the organisation could agree quality standards and inventory levels with its suppliers, thereby **building in quality without increasing cost**.

Retailers and customers

AVN should look at price and the company could consider **negotiating better margins** on its products, or consider **undertaking some market research** prior to development of new products to establish exactly what the customer sees as a quality product. This would control the research costs it incurs and direct effort

ANSWERS

to where value is added. It would also **reduce the complexity of products** being offered if some of these aren't selling. AVN should also consider the transport costs and reliability of supplying its product to customers.

Other ideas

- AVN could **share technology** with suppliers and streamline its expertise.
- AVN could consider **outsourcing** activities that aren't **core**.
- AVN could standardise components and products so it **reduces complexity** without compromising on product availability.

103 Offshoring

> **Top tips.** Real-life examples will add value to answers to questions on contemporary and externally-orientated techniques.

In an effort to cut costs, many organisations are now outsourcing activities both near shore (such as Eastern Europe) and offshore (such as the Far East and India).

There are a number of **reasons** for the **rise in offshoring**.

(a) **Infrastructure improvements**. Outsourced activities can be sustained at the appropriate level.

(b) **Improvements in, and falling costs of, technology and telecommunications**. Paper-based back office jobs can now be digitalised and telecommunicated anywhere in the world. Indian IT organisations got their big breaks as subcontractors to overloaded Western firms during the Y2K crisis and are now powerful players in the market for offshore IT services.

(c) The growth of the **Internet**

(d) **Low labour cost** (especially on lower-grade jobs)

(e) **Highly-skilled labour**. In India, for example, of the two million graduates per annum, 80% speak English.

(f) More **willingness for managers to manage people they can't see**

(g) **Time differences**. These can be used to extend the working day, which is particularly useful if the offshore organisation provides support or maintenance.

(h) **Tax incentives**

(i) **Quality certifications** such as ISO 9000

There are **disadvantages** to offshoring, however.

(a) **Cost advantages are being eroded**. Salaries in the IT sector in India, for example, have been rising in line with demand for skilled workers as US firms in particular invest heavily in training and facilities.

(b) There is often **bad press** associated with jobs leaving the home country.

(c) **Remote management** can prove **problematic**.

(d) **Environmental concerns** include inadequate infrastructure, political and market risk and cultural incompatibility.

(e) In some countries there are **problems with labour** such as language barriers, and the level of education and experience of the labour force.

104 Chains

> **Top tips.** Notice how the requirements of this question provide a ready-made framework for your answer – you need to cover the supply chain, the value chain, e-procurement and outsourcing.

The supply chain

The supply chain refers to **all the stages and activities involved in getting a finished product or service delivered to the customer**. In the case of a manufactured product, the supply chain starts with the sources of raw materials, and includes not only production activities, but also distribution (logistics) and storage and support activities such as purchasing.

Managing the supply chain involves **ensuring a smooth flow of the product to the customer**, through all the stages of the chain. It therefore involves **management of the relationship with suppliers**, and **ensuring that suppliers deliver their goods to the required specifications on time**.

The value chain

The value chain also refers to all the stages and activities involved in getting a product or service to the customer, but the **focus is on the value added at each stage of the chain**.

Managing the value chain is concerned with **identifying ways in which more value can be added at each stage** of the chain, perhaps by doing things in a different way. Activities that fail to add value should be identified and eliminated.

E-procurement and outsourcing

E-procurement and outsourcing are **ways** in which it might be **possible to add value in the supply chain**.

E-procurement involves **purchasing** items from suppliers **through the Internet** (although other methods of electronic purchasing, such as EDI or electronic data interchange, might be included in the definition). A company that buys regularly from a supplier might make an arrangement whereby the **computer systems of buyer and seller** might **exchange data** and make supply transactions. There will normally have to be pre-agreed terms and conditions of supply, product specifications and fixed prices or a formula for pricing. A company needing to buy goods from a supplier might be able to generate an automatic order within its own computer system, and despatch the order to the supplier's system. The supplier's system will respond by confirming availability and delivery arrangements. The automatic electronic processing of purchase orders, given an established buyer/supplier relationship, can result in **significant cost savings** as well as **greater purchasing efficiency**. Human intervention and paperwork are removed from this stage of the supply chain.

Outsourcing involves the **purchase of products or services externally**, rather than making the product or performing the service with the organisation's own staff. The outsourcing of production work involves having products made by an external supplier rather than making them in-house. Numerous services might also be outsourced, including IT services, facilities management and the accounting function. The term 'outsourcing' in fact usually refers to putting services out to an external provider. The organisation, having outsourced activities at which it is not particularly specialised, is then able to **focus on its core activities**, where it can **add value** more effectively. The **provider of the outsourced service** should have the **relevant expertise** which will enable it to **perform** the service **more efficiently** than the organisation's own staff. If this is the case, outsourcing can **add value** to the supply chain/value chain. The management of the organisation are responsible for managing the relationship with the service provider, but are no longer responsible for the detailed management of the service itself.

ANSWERS

105 Preferred suppliers

> **Top tips.** Note that you are writing your answer from the perspective of the supplier.

A number of matters need to be carefully considered if preferred supplier status is being sought with a customer. Many of these relate to the **maintenance of a good relationship** and **good communication**.

(a) Can the supplier **afford to make this level of commitment** to a particular customer? It may mean investing in new systems and new processes that would not otherwise be needed (for example to obtain ISO 9001:2000 certification). And this may not be a one-off expense: the supplier may be asked to invest in new equipment in the future at its own expense as a means of growing its own capabilities to match those required by the customer. The customer may also wish to influence personnel selection, how they work and what they focus on.

(b) Is the supplier in a position to **offer a competitive advantage** to a customer, and if so can it do so without compromising its own strategy or other business relationships? A good deal of existing business may be lost if other customers are always placed second in the supplier's priorities, or even if they just feel that they are placed second, despite the fact that they get the same level of service as before.

(c) Is there any danger that the customer in question will **renege on the agreement**, or **go out of business**, or be **taken over by a third party** who will not wish to continue the agreement? The supplier must beware of putting all its eggs in one basket. Too much commitment to one customer may make the supplier too inflexible, and unable to respond to changes in circumstances.

(d) **Turnover of personnel** on both sides may be a problem. If the relationship is too dependent on individuals buyers may move business from one firm to another to stay with a person who has provided good service in the past. It is important for suppliers to make sure that they meet the customer's needs via systemic approaches rather than though methods that are dependent on key persons.

(e) **Trust** is a major issue. Both the customer and supplier need to be willing to share information with each other that they might not normally share with another customer or supplier. This may be difficult for some managers and employees to accept, especially at first.

(f) Customers will often make the mistake of assuming that since they are outsourcing to an expert in the field, they can **forget about having to manage** that particular piece of their business. For day to day issues this may be true, but the effort required to understand each others expectations and objectives, together with that required to build strong relationships, can far exceed the management effort required for in-house work.

(g) The **status of work** needs to be communicated regularly and routinely. The customer should hear about problems as quickly as if it had performed the work in-house. Overspending by the supplier should not happen: if additional funds are required this should be discussed proactively with the customer. Again such methods of working may be difficult for some managers and employers to accept at first, if they are used to doing things differently.

(h) Clear definitions of **leadership** and **overall accountability** for the work will need to be established from the outset. These may conflict with existing arrangements, and once again be difficult for managers and employees to accept. On the other hand, in a preferred customer-supplier relationship, the axiom 'the customer is always right' does not hold true. The customer depends upon the expertise that the supplier brings to the table. Thus, if the supplier does not understand why the customer wants the work done in a certain manner, or the supplier thinks it has a better approach, this should be discussed. If the customer's desires prevail, there should be mutual agreement as to why this is appropriate, as well as a clear delineation of the responsibilities and liabilities of each party.

(i) Business **ethics** should not be an issue. The supplier should understand the customer's principles and behave accordingly. However, in certain circumstances this may require a change of culture, which may not be easy to achieve.

106 Partnering

> **Top tips.** Don't be afraid to add real-life examples to your answer. If relevant, they provide additional evidence that you know what you are talking about!

(a) Partnering is **particularly appropriate in the following circumstances**.

    (i) If significant input is required from specialist contractors or subcontractors (such as in the construction of a new airport terminal)

    (ii) If there is a rapid expansion of a programme of construction (say, if a supermarket chain opens lots of new branches)

    (iii) If time is a critical factor

    (iv) If projects are repetitive and based upon a set of standard designs (such as the construction of McDonalds restaurants)

    (v) If there is a particular construction problem which is best solved by a team of experts (such as the construction of oil rigs)

Partnering is less **suitable in the following circumstances**.

    (i) If it is important that costs can be predicted with certainty.

    (ii) If the project is a one-off, commissioned by a one-off customer (as the benefits of team building and supply chain management cannot be easily achieved on a single project)

    (iii) If the customer has little knowledge of the construction process (as partnering requires active involvement of a knowledgeable client)

    (iv) If the customer requires significant or complete control over the specification and delivery, so that there is little opportunity for the contractor to propose new ways of doing things.

(b) (i) **Using the wrong people.** In some situations, interpersonal skills can be more important than technical understanding.

    (ii) **Lack of cultural readiness.** All members of both the customer and contractor teams must be ready to make partnering work. Although the benefits of partnering may be obvious and achievable, an organisation may not be ready to work in the new ways required, or to be able to change in a short time.

    (iii) **Unclear objectives.** If the objectives for both customer and contractor are not clear at the outset, no amount of management effort will make the partnering relationship successful.

    (iv) **Inadequate performance measurement.** The baseline from which improvements are to be measured can be difficult to establish, even though it is crucial to the way in which the contractor's performance is assessed. And finding appropriate benchmarking measures in order to make meaningful comparisons between contractors can be difficult.

ANSWERS

107 Question with analysis: RS plc

> **Text references.** Chapter 18 has a section on DPP for answering this question.
>
> **Top tips.** An alternative approach to calculating the 'other costs' per product is to calculate the costs per m^3 for each product and then a cost per item.
>
> You may have approached the answer in 'total' terms rather than in 'per item' terms. This is perfectly valid.
>
> **Easy marks.** You can answer part (c) separately and get up to five marks before launching into the numbers.

(a) **Initial costings**

From question:

		£ per cubic metre
Warehouse costs per week:		
Refrigeration	£160,000/5,000	32.00 per week
Other	£560,000/20,000	28.00 per week
Supermarket costs per week:		
Refrigeration	15 × £24,000/5,000	72.00 per week
Other	15 × £44,000/20,000	33.00 per week
Transport costs per trip:		
Refrigerated	£4,950/90 cubic metres	55.00 per week
Standard	£3,750/90 cubic metres	41.67 per week

Direct product profit (DPP)

	Baked beans £ per item	Baked beans £ per item	Ice cream £ per item	Ice cream £ per item	White wine £ per item	White wine £ per item
Sales revenue		0.320		1.600		3.450
Direct cost		0.240		0.950		2.850
Gross profit		0.080		0.650		0.600
Warehouse costs						
Refrigeration						
£32÷24÷18 × 2 weeks			0.148			
Other						
£28÷28÷80 × 1 week	0.012					
£28÷24÷18 × 2 weeks			0.130			
£28÷42÷12 × 4 weeks					0.222	
Supermarket costs						
Refrigeration						
£72÷24÷18 × 2 weeks			0.333			
Other						
£33÷28÷80 × 1 week	0.015					
£33÷24÷18 × 2 weeks			0.153			
£33÷42÷12 × 2 weeks					0.131	
Transport						
£41.67÷28÷80	0.019					
£55÷24÷18			0.127			
£41.67÷42÷12					0.083	
		0.046		0.891		0.436
Direct product profit		0.034		(0.241)		0.164
% of sales		10.6%		(15.1%)		4.8%

330

ANSWERS

Traditional method profit

	Baked beans	Ice cream	White wine
£ per item	0.08	0.65	0.60
% of sales	25%	40.6%	17.4%

Using **DPP** the ranking of profits is as follows.

1st   Baked beans
2nd   White wine
3rd   Ice cream – loss-making

Using the **traditional method** the ranking was as follows.

1st   Ice cream
2nd   Baked beans
3rd   White wine

(b) **There are two main causes of the difference in profits between the two methods.**

Per question: Discuss differences

(i) The **traditional method focused on the gross margin** only and did not apportion overhead costs.

(ii) With **DPP, ice cream** is charged a **higher proportion of overhead** to **reflect** the fact that it **uses the high cost activities** of refrigerated transport and storage. The beans and the wine absorb only the costs of the (lower cost) resources that they use.

Ways in which profitability could be improved

Per question: suggest ways

(i) **Refrigerated transport**. At £4,950 per trip this is a high cost activity.

    (1) Care must be taken to ensure all journeys using refrigerated transport carry full loads.

    (2) Suppliers of goods requiring refrigeration should be contacted to determine whether they would be able to deliver direct to the store, thus eliminating this cost for RS.

(ii) **Adjust selling prices**. A full DPP analysis should be carried out and adjustments made to selling prices wherever possible to reflect any costs which are found not to be covered.

(iii) **Adjust the product range**. Where prices cannot be increased sufficiently and where the product does not need to be stocked in order to attract customers, consideration might be given to discontinuing that product and replacing it with a line with a higher DPP.

(c) **Ways in which DPP differs from traditional overhead absorption**

(i) Traditional absorption costing would utilise an overhead rate by department rather than by activity. Products that generate a high level of overhead spending would not be penalised as the spending would be averaged out over all products which use a department's facilities regardless of the level of cost generated by that use.

(ii) Traditional overhead absorption may have attempted to include a share of the head office costs whereas DPP would ignore this because the costs are not caused by the individual product units.

(iii) DPP is likely to provide better information for planning and control. High cost activities will be recognised and controlled more tightly. The stocking of products which utilise only the low cost activities may be encouraged. Selling prices should more accurately reflect the actual costs generated.

108 S&P Products plc

> **Text references.** You should be able to answer this from information in Chapter 18 which gives the ABC approach.
>
> **Top tips.** The requirements of part (a)(i) are not very clear. What are the different types of sales outlet? Should 'mail order' be classified as one type or should post, telephone and Internet be analysed separately? Is profitability per retail outlet required or total profit for all the department stores and total profit for all of S&P Products plc's own shops? If you had calculated profit per outlet you would probably have needed to calculate total profit as well, to be able to answer (a)(ii) sensibly.
>
> A wide range of points can be made in (b) so your answer might differ from ours.
>
> **Easy marks.** A time pressured question. Look at using key phrases in your answer – see the bold narrative below.

(a) (i) **Department stores**

	£'000
Sales revenue (£50,000 × 50)	2,500
Purchases (£2,500,000 ÷ 1.3)	1,923
Gross profit	577
Other costs	
Telephone queries/requests (£15 × 40 × 50)	30
Sales visits (£250 × 2 × 50)	25
Shop orders (£20 × 25 × 50)	25
Packaging (£100 × 28 × 50)	140
Delivery (£150 × 28 × 50)	210
Net profit	147

Own shops

	£'000
Sales revenue (£1,000,000 × 10)	10,000.0
Purchases (£10,000,000 ÷ 1.4)	7,142.9
Gross profit	2,857.1
Other costs	
Telephone queries/requests (£15 × 350 × 10)	52.5
Sales visits (£250 × 4 × 10)	10.0
Shop orders (£20 × 150 × 10)	30.0
Packaging (£100 × 150 × 10)	150.0
Delivery (£150 × 150 × 10)	225.0
Staffing, rental and service (£300,000 × 10)	3,000.0
Net profit	(610.4)

Mail order

	Post £'000	Telephone £'000	Internet £'000	Total £'000
Sales revenue				
(80,000 × 30% × £150)	3,600			
(80,000 × 60% × £300)		14,400		
(80,000 × 10% × £100)			800	
Total				18,800
Purchases				
(£3,600,000 ÷ 1.4)	2,571			
(£14,400,000 ÷ 1.4)		10,286		
(£800,000 ÷ 1.4)			571	
Total				13,428
	1,029	4,114	229	5,372

ANSWERS

	Post £'000	Telephone £'000	Internet £'000	Total £'000
Other costs				
Processing 'mail orders'				
(24,000 × £5)	120			
(48,000 × £6)		288		
(8,000 × £3)			24	
Total				432
Dealing with queries				
(24,000 × £4)	96			
(48,000 × £4)		192		
(8,000 × £1)			8	
Total				296
Packaging and delivery				
(24,000 × 2 × £10)	480			
(48,000 × 2 × £10)		960		
(8,000 × 1 × £10)			80	
Total				1,520
Maintenance of Internet link			80	80
Net profit	333	2,674	37	3,044

(ii)

> **Top tips.** If you failed to calculate a net profit for the three components of the mail order side of the business, your range of comments here will be limited.

The figures above highlight the significant differences in the profitability of the various types of sales outlet.

For example, S&P plc's own shops are budgeted to make a total loss in excess of £600,000 for the coming year. One of the main reasons for this is the £300,000 cost per shop for staffing, rental and service, which is greater than the gross profit per shop.

On the other hand, telephone 'mail order' makes a profit of over £2.5 million, principally due to the high sales revenue per order (twice that of post 'mail order' and three time that of 'mail order' via the Internet). This area represents 46% of business (in terms of revenue) but generates 104% of total profit.

The Internet mail order side of the business is not currently particularly profitable but should grow rapidly in the future. The cost of maintaining the Internet link per order should therefore fall given that the cost is likely to be semi fixed.

(b) (i)

> **Top tips.** The key points to make in part (i) are that it is dangerous to use coming year figures to make long-term decisions and that the ABC method used and its limitations need to be considered.

Help given by the information

Given that the company is carrying out a fundamental reappraisal of its business, the information shown above highlights the following.

(1) The company's own small **shops** make a significant **loss** and S&P Products plc should consider whether they should **continue** to operate. A more profitable option might be to **transfer the business to franchises in department stores,** an area of operations making a profit of nearly £150,000.

ANSWERS

(2) Overall, the **mail order** side of the business is far more **profitable** and so S&P Products plc should **concentrate** its efforts on that area in general and the **telephone** section in particular.

(3) It is vital to note that the telephone mail order business may have peaked, however, as the Internet section could be the future high growth area. The organisation should therefore **guard against setting major strategies on the basis of short-term cost and revenue information**. Long-term decisions need to consider competitors' actions, the state of the market and customers' needs and demands.

(4) In general, the identification of **cost drivers** within an ABC system can help with **cost reduction** for long-term profitability: control the incidence of the cost driver and the cost can be controlled. The ABC analysis of S&P Products plc's activities does not appear to be particularly sophisticated, however, and hence may not offer significant insight.

Possible revision/expansion of the information

The **head office and warehousing costs** need to be analysed in more detail to determine the costs attributable to each particular type of outlet given that some types of outlet may incur a greater proportion of the costs than others. Decisions regarding, say, the future operation of S&P Products plc's own shops may be affected by the degree to which these costs are directly attributable.

(ii) **Additional information needed to make a more informed judgement**

(1) Detailed analysis of head office and warehousing costs

(2) Forecast market conditions

(3) Competitors' actions

(4) New entrants in the market (especially on the Internet side of the business)

(5) Customers' purchasing patterns (for example, the extent to which customers use only one type of outlet)

(6) Customers' changing purchasing habits (such as the degree of movement between telephone and Internet purchasing)

109 FF plc

> **Text references.** Chapter 16 explains ABC and Chapter 18 applies this to customer groups.
>
> **Top tips.** Now you are near the very end of this Kit you may have noticed how many questions require you to offer criticisms/disadvantages/limitations of techniques and processes. It may be worth your while skimming through the Paper P2 Text or Passcards and seeing if you can jot down a few for each of the main techniques and processes covered.

(a) (i)

Group	W	X	Y	Z	
Individual value ('000s)	$500 – $999	$1,000 – $2,999	$3,000 – $5,999	$6,000 – $9,999	
Number of clients	1,000	1,500	2,000	1,800	
					Total
	$'000	$'000	$'000	$'000	$'000
Total contribution	500	900	1,400	2,500	5,300
Support costs					
Answering telephone enquiries (W1)	230	172	253	345	1,000
Preparing statements (W2)	31	31	63	125	250
Meeting clients (W3)	223	372	410	745	1,750
Customer profitability	16	325	674	1,285	2,300

ANSWERS

Workings

1. Cost driver rate = $1,000,000/870 enquiries

    Cost for each group

    - W   Cost driver rate × 200
    - X   Cost driver rate × 150
    - Y   Cost driver rate × 220
    - Z   Cost driver rate × 300

2. Cost driver rate = $250,000/960 statements

    Cost for each group

    - W   Cost driver rate × 120
    - X   Cost driver rate × 120
    - Y   Cost driver rate × 240
    - Z   Cost driver rate × 480

3. Cost driver rate = $1,750,000/470 meetings

    Cost for each group

    - W   Cost driver rate × 60
    - X   Cost driver rate × 100
    - Y   Cost driver rate × 110
    - Z   Cost driver rate × 200

We assume that facility level costs are incurred regardless of the client mix and so are not included within the analysis.

Commentary

The **current approach** to apportioning support costs to customer groups produces the following figures for profitability before facility costs.

W – $215,000
X – $140,000
Y – $610,000
Z – $1,335,000

Using an **activity based approach** to apportion the support costs to the four customer groups, **all four groups** make a **positive contribution** and the **relative positions of groups W and X have swapped**.

(i) Group W now appears to make very little contribution towards facility costs. Due to the relatively high proportion of support this group of clients requires, the group bears a relatively high proportion of the support costs given the number of customers in the group.

(ii) Group X, on the other hand, earns $325,000 contribution towards facility costs because the group's clients do not require as much support.

The results for **groups Y and Z** are **not significantly different**.

(ii) It is important to point out that the bank manager is **basing** his **decision making** on **misleading information**, as the analysis in part (a) has highlighted. It is apparent using an activity based analysis of support costs that **client group X** is **not loss making**, although potential levels of profit are lower than those from groups Y and Z. The performance of group W, however, should give cause for concern.

Proposal 1 v proposal 2

Proposal 1 results in the bigger increase in profit.

ANSWERS

Proposal 1

Expected facility cost = $1,000,000 × 110% = $1,100,000

Projected revised numbers of clients

Y = (2,250 × 0.30) + (2,500 × 0.40) + (2,750 × 0.30) = 2,500
Z = (2,000 × 0.20) + (2,200 × 0.50) + (2,500 × 0.30) = 2,250

We assume that the support costs can be flexed on the basis of client numbers and that facility costs are the same regardless of the number of clients in each group or the number of client groups.

	Group Y $'000	Group Z $'000	Total $'000
Flexed contribution to facility costs (W)	843	1,606	2,449
Facility cost			1,100
Revised profit			1,349
Original budgeted profit			1,300
Increase in profit			49

Working

Group Y flexed contribution to facility costs = $674,000 × 2,500/2,000 = $842,500
Group Z flexed contribution to facility costs = $1,285,000 × 2,250/1,800 = $1,606,250

Commentary. Although this proposal does lead to an increase in budgeted profit, it would be worth considering the impact of discontinuing group W only, as group X appeared profitable according to the ABC analysis in (a). The projected revised numbers of clients in groups X, Y and Z and the expected facility costs would be needed, however, before such a proposal could be evaluated.

Proposal 2

Expected facility cost = $1,000,000 × 108% = $1,080,000

Projected revised numbers of clients

Y = 2,000 + ((2,500 – 2,000) × 25%) = 2,125
Z = 1,800 + ((2,250 – 1,800) × 25%) = 1,912.5

Consider discontinuing W

	Group X $'000	Group Y $'000	Group Z $'000	Total $'000
Flexed contribution (W)	325	716	1,365	2,406
Facility cost				1,080
Revised profit				1,326
Original budgeted profit				1,300
Increase in profit				26

Consider discontinuing X

	Group W $'000	Group Y $'000	Group Z $'000	Total $'000
Flexed contribution (W)	16	716	1,365	2,097
Facility cost				1,080
Revised profit				1,017
Original budgeted profit				1,300
Fall in profit				(283)

Working

We are given no information about changing client numbers for groups W and X and so we cannot flex the contribution for these groups.

Group Y flexed contribution = $674,000 × 2,125/2,000 = $716,125
Group Z flexed contribution = $1,285,000 × 1,912.5/1,800 = $1,365,313

ANSWERS

Commentary. It is evident that the bank should not concentrate on client group W at the expense of servicing client group X as profits would fall. Discontinuing W results in a small increase in profit.

Alternative approach

You could have dealt with this part of the question by looking at just the incremental costs and revenues.

Proposal 1

	$'000
Discontinuing W and X	(341)
Facility cost increase	(100)
Extra contribution from:	
Y (500/2,000) × $674,000	169
Z (450/1,800) × £1,285,000	321
Increase in profit	49

Proposal 2

	Discontinue W $'000	Discontinue X $'000
Discontinuing W/X	(16)	(325)
Facility cost increase	(80)	(80)
Extra contribution (25% × ($(169,000 + 321,000))) (see proposal 1)	123	123
Increase/(decrease) in profit	27	(282)

(b) Difficulties of implementing ABC in the divisions of M Ltd

(i) It may prove **difficult to determine** the divisions' major **activities**.

(ii) Likewise, **identification of cost drivers** may prove **problematic**. For example, what drives the cost of visits to divisions from M Ltd's internal audit department (presuming one exists).

(iii) On the other hand, there might be **more than one possible cost driver** for all the cost items in a cost pool. If the **number of cost pools and cost drivers** becomes too **excessive**, the ABC system will be **too complex and too expensive**.

(iv) If there is a **compromise on the number of cost pools and cost drivers** used, however, the **accuracy** of the information provided by an ABC system **may not differ greatly** from that provided under the **current absorption costing system**. This should call into **question the value** of operating the new system.

(v) The **cost of collecting the information** about activities and cost drivers that is required to implement an ABC system, as well as its administration, can prove **too great in comparison with the potential benefits** of the system. For example, the company may not have sufficient spare capacity in terms of staff time and/or may need to employ additional staff with the appropriate skills.

(vi) The implementation of an ABC system may require new **computer software** to deal with its additional complexities, which M Ltd may not have the means to finance.

(vii) The **short product life cycle** of mobile phones and chips means that **activities and cost drivers will change frequently** and resources will be required to incorporate these amendments to the system.

(viii) The implementation of any change within the divisions will require the **support of divisional management**.

(ix) Some measure of **(arbitrary) cost apportionment** may still be required at the cost pooling stage for **items like rent**, rates and buildings depreciation.

ANSWERS

110 Section A answers: Mixed bank 1

1   There will be a balancing charge on the sale of the machine of £(450,000 − (1,200,000 − 950,000)) = £200,000. This will give rise to a tax payment of 30% × £200,000 = £60,000.

2

		1 year		2 years		3 years		4 years	
Year	Disc factors 12%	Cash flow £'000	PV £'000	Cash flow £'999	PV £'000	Cash flow £'000	PV £'000	Cash flow £'000	PV £'000
0	1.000	(220)	(220.000)	(220)	(220.000)	(220)	(220.000)	(220)	(220.000)
1	0.893	11	9.823	(110)	(98.230)	(110)	(98.230)	(110)	(98.230)
2	0.797			(44)	(35.068)	(132)	(105.204)	(132)	(105.204)
3	0.712					(88)	(62.656)	(154)	(109.648)
4	0.636							(110)	(69.960)
PV of cost after one replacement cycle			(210.177)		(353.298)		(486.090)		(603.042)
Cumulative PV factor		0.893		1.690		2.402		3.037	
Annualised equivalent cost		£235,000		£209,000		£202,000		£199,000	

3   C   Weighted average C/S ratio = $\frac{(2 \times 30\%) + (5 \times 20\%) + (3 \times 25\%)}{(2 + 5 + 3)}$ = 23.5%

At breakeven point, contribution = fixed costs = £100,000

∴ Breakeven revenue = £100,000/0.235 = £425,532

4   **True**

Output	Revenue per unit (W1)	Total revenue	Total variable costs		Contribution
	£	£'000	£'000		£'000
10	6,500	65.00	40.0	(W2)	25.00
11	6,350	69.85	44.4	(W3)	25.45
13	6,050	78.65	54.4	(W4)	24.25
14	5,900	82.60	60.0	(W5)	22.60
20	5,000	100.00	102.0	(W6)	(2.00)

Workings

1   8,000 − (150 × output)
2   £4,000 × 10
3   £40,000 (W2) + £4,400
4   £44,400 (W3) + £4,800 + £5,200
5   £54,400 (W4) + £5,600
6   £60,000 (W5) + £6,000 + £6,400 + £6,800 + £7,200 + £7,600 + £8,000

> **Top tips.** Did you notice how the variable costs changed? After ten units, each *additional* unit cost £400 more (not all additional units).

5   B   All other options affect cash flow.

6   B   Maximum price = costs saved by not manufacturing the 5,000 components

= (5,000 × variable cost per unit) + avoidable fixed costs
= (5,000 × $21) + $9,000 = $114,000

… ANSWERS

7   B   Let X = required number of units

X must be such that:

Sales revenue ($146 × X) = F45's own costs

F45's own costs = (variable cost per unit × X) + avoidable fixed costs

∴ X occurs when $146X = $62X + $18,000
                   $84X = $18,000
                      X = 214.29

> **Top tips.** Alternatively you could use breakeven arithmetic.
>
> Contribution per unit = $(146 − 62) = $84
>
> ∴ Breakeven point = $18,000/$84 = 214.29 units

8   C   Contribution per mix = ($(146 − 62) × 4) + ($(159 − 84) × 3)
                             = $561

Breakeven point in terms of number of mixes = fixed costs/contribution per mix

> **Top tips.** Fixed costs do not include the avoidable costs of D12 as the component is no longer being produced.

∴ Fixed costs = $36,000 + $90,000 + $200,000 = $326,000

∴ Breakeven point = $326,000/$561 = 581 mixes

Breakeven point in revenue

	$
F45 (581 × $146 × 4)	339,304
P67 (581 × $159 × 3)	277,137
	616,441

111 Section A answers: Mixed bank 2

1   Based on calculating annualised equivalents, Option 3 has the lowest cost and Option 2, the highest.

Year	Discount factors	Option 1 Cashflow £	DCF £	Option 2 Cashflow £	DCF £	Option 3 Cashflow £	DCF £
0	1.000	19,500	19,500	28,000	28,000	31,000	31,000
1	0.870	30,000	26,100	16,000	13,920	27,000	23,490
2	0.756	63,000	47,628	50,000	37,800	32,000	24,192
3	0.658	15,000	9,870			41,000	26,978
4	0.572					26,000	14,872
NPV			103,098		79,720		120,532
Cumulative discount factor			2.283		1.626		2.855
Annualised equivalent			45,159		49,028		42,218

ANSWERS

2

$Y_x = aX^b$
a = 22 minutes
b = log 0.8/log2 = −0.3219

If X = 4, $Y_4 = 22 \times 4^{-0.3219}$ = 14.08 mins
∴ Time taken for four units = 4 × 14.08 = 56.32 mins

If X = 3, $Y_3 = 22 \times 3^{-0.3219}$ = 15.45 mins

∴ Time taken for three units = 3 × 15.45 mins = 46.35 mins

∴ Time taken for fourth unit = (56.32 − 46.35) mins = 9.97 minutes

3 D

Year	Cash flow £	Discount factor 20%	PV at 20% £	Discount factor 10%	PV at 10% £
0	(75,000)	1.000	(75,000)	1.000	(75,000)
1-5	25,000	2.991	74,775	3.791	94,775
			(225)		19,775

∴ IRR = 10% + $\left(\dfrac{19,775}{19,775 + 225} \times 10\% \right)$

= 19.8875%

4

Year	Cash flow £	Discount factor 15%	PV £
0	(75,000)	1.000	(75,000)
1-5	25,000	3.352	83,800
			8,800

PV of annual labour cost savings over 5 years at 15% = £20,000 × 3.352 = £67,040

∴ PV of annual labour cost savings could fall by £8,800 before project ceased to be viable = (£8,800/£67,040) × 100% = 13.13%

5

Demand (a) Units	Probability (b)	Revenue (a) × £45 £'000	Variable cost per unit (c) £	Probability (d)	Total variable costs (a) × (c) £'000	Contribution £'000	Joint probability (b) × (d)
100,000	0.45	4,500	20	0.40	2,000	2,500	0.18
100,000	0.45	4,500	18	0.60	1,800	2,700*	0.27
120,000	0.55	5,400	20	0.40	2,400	3,000*	0.22
120,000	0.55	5,400	18	0.60	2,160	3,240*	0.33
							1.00

* Contribution higher than current level of contribution of £90,000 × £(50 − 21) = £2,610,000

∴ Probability = 0.27 + 0.22 + 0.33 = 0.82

6 **False.** EV of profit = EV of contribution − fixed costs

= £'000 ((0.18 × 2,500) + (0.27 × 2,700) + (0.22 × 3,000) + (0.33 × 3,240))

− £1,200,000 = £1,708,200

112 Section A answers: Mixed bank 3

1. (A) Planning and concept design costs – **yes**
   (B) Preliminary and detailed design costs – **yes**
   (C) Testing costs – **yes**
   (D) Production costs – **yes**
   (E) Distribution and customer service costs – **yes**

   Life cycle costs are incurred from design stage through to withdrawal from the market.

2. C   Contribution – fixed costs = target profit

   ∴ Contribution = £(34,000 + 120,000) = £154,000

   We now know contribution but need to find revenue.

   We therefore need an average C/S ratio.

   Weighted average C/S ratio = $\dfrac{(2 \times 30\%) + (3 \times 25\%) + (5 \times 40\%)}{(2 + 3 + 5)}$ = 33.5%

   ∴ Contribution/sales = 0.335

   ∴ $\dfrac{£154,000}{0.335}$ = sales revenue

   ∴ £459,701 = sales revenue

3. Time available on J = (16 – 2.5) × 60 minutes = 810 minutes
   Time available on K = (16 – 2) × 60 minutes = 840 minutes
   Time required on J = (6.5 × 40) + (9 × 60) = 800 minutes
   Time required on K = (22 × 40) + (15 × 60) = 1,780 minutes

   ∴ Process K limits throughput.

   We now need to calculate throughput contribution per minute of process K time to determine which product makes best use of the bottleneck resource.

	A £	B £
Selling price	87.50	72.50
Material cost	15.00	15.00
Throughput contribution	72.50	57.50
Throughput contribution per minute of process K time	£72.50/22 = £3.30	£57.50/15 = £3.83
Ranking	2	1

   ∴ Product B should be produced to maximum demand and any remaining time allocated to product A.

   Available process K time = 840 minutes

   Number of B produced in this time = 840/15 = 56

   ∴ The optimum production plan is to produce 56 units of B and none of A.

4. C

	W £ per unit	X £ per unit	Y £ per unit	Z £ per unit
Selling price	56	67	89	96
Variable costs	49	66	74	85
Contribution	7	1	15	11
C/S ratios	$^7/_{56}$ = 0.125	$^1/_{67}$ = 0.015	$^{15}/_{89}$ = 0.169	$^{11}/_{96}$ = 0.115
Ranking	2	4	1	3

ANSWERS

5 Contribution per mix

= (2 × £7) + (3 × £1) + (3 × £15) + (4 × £11) = £106

∴ Breakeven point in number of mixes = £15,000/£106 = 141.5

∴ Number of W sold at breakeven point = 2 × 141.5 = 283 units

6 **True**

	W	X	Y	Z
	£ per unit	£ per unit	£ per unit	£ per unit
Selling price	56	67	89	96
Material	22	31	38	46
Throughput contribution	34	36	51	50
Time on bottleneck resource	10	10	15	15
Product return per minute	£3.40	£3.60	£3.40	£3.33
Ranking	2	1	2	4

7 A

Average time per unit for first two units = 100 × 90% =	90 hours
∴ Total time for first two units = 90 × 2 =	180 hours
Less time taken for first unit	100 hours
Time taken for second unit	80 hours
Labour cost at £7 per hour	£560

If you selected **option B** you have calculated the *average* cost per unit for *both* of the first two units.

If you selected **option C** you have not made any allowance for the saving in time due to the learning effect.

Option D is the total labour cost for both units. The cost of the first unit must be deducted to derive the labour cost of the second unit.

8 420 of the units required are already in stock. There are two alternative uses for these units. They can be sold to realise 420 × £30 = £12,600, or they can be used as a substitute for material V. The saving would be 750 × £25 = £18,750. This is therefore the best alternative use for the stock of material S. The opportunity cost of using them is the saving foregone. The remaining units will have to be purchased. The relevant cost is £18,750 + (90 × £72) = £25,230.

9 A Replacement cost/market value = $6.30 per kg

Net realisable value of the 3,700 kgs in stock = $3.20 per kg

Opportunity cost of the 3,700 kgs in stock = $7.50 per kg saving on purchase of J minus $3.70 per kg modification cost = $3.80

	$
∴ Relevant cost of 3,700 kgs in stock = $3.80 × 3,700	14,060
Relevant cost of (4,200 – 3,700) kgs to purchase = $6.30 × 500	3,150
	17,210

113 Section A answers: Mixed bank 4

> **Examiner's comments.** Performance was generally good but a significant number of the students did not respond correctly to the question, for example 'to the nearest 1%' is not 11.96%.

1 C The limiting factor is cooking time in the oven (given) as

	K meal $	L meal $	M meal $
Selling price per meal	5.00	3.00	4.40
Variable costs per meal	3.60	1.80	3.15
Contribution per meal	1.40	1.20	1.25
Oven time (minutes per meal)	10	4	8
Contribution per minute of cooking time ($)	0.14	0.30	0.15625
Rank order of cooking	3	1	2

2 A

		Superior contract $	Standard contract $	Basic contract $
Step 1	Calculate contribution per contract	550	500	220

Step 2 Calculate contribution per mix = 0.20 × $550 + 0.30 × $500 + 0.50 × $220 = $370

Step 3 Calculate Breakeven point = $\frac{\text{fixed costs}}{\text{contribution per mix}} = \frac{\$1{,}000{,}000}{\$370}$ = 2,703 mixes

Step 4 Calculate Breakeven in terms of number of contracts

= 2,703 × 0.20 + 2,703 × 0.30 + 2,703 × 0.50
= 541 units Superior
   811 units of Standard
   1,352 units of Basic

Step 5 Breakeven in terms of revenue

= 541 × $1,000 + 811 × $750 + 1,352 × $400 = $1,690,050

3 C The relevant cost to be used in preparing the question is:

   (a) the bonus due to the junior consultant £5,000 or
   (b) the cost of hiring an external consultant £4,500

   As (b) is lower, then the relevant cost would be £4,500.

4 Using the IRR interpolation formula:

$$\text{IRR} = 0.10 + \left[\frac{12{,}304}{12{,}304 + 3{,}216} \times (0.15 - 0.10)\right] = 0.14 \text{ or } 14\%$$

> **Top tips.** Note the requirement to state to the nearest 1%, so there is no need to give an answer to several decimal places! See also the examiner's requirement to state to 0.01% in question 5.

ANSWERS

5 Using the relationship between the money rate and real rate of inflation.

$$(1 + 0.18) = (1 + x) \times (1 + 0.06)$$
$$1.1132 = 1 + x$$
$$0.1132 = x$$

To the nearest 0.01%, x = 11.32%

6 The formula for the learning curve is $Y_x = aX^b$

So $Y_{16} = 54 \times 16^{-0.3219}$
$= 22.12$

$Y_{16} = 54 \times 15^{-0.3219}$
$= 22.58$

Remember that these are average times for each stage and not the incremental time to produce an extra unit.

Cum units	Average time/unit hours	Total time hours
15	22.58	338.70
16	22.12	353.92
Incremental time for the 16th unit		15.22

7 This requires you to run through the different combinations of selling price and variable cost that will give a contribution exceeding $20,000/week or $20 per unit.

Clearly at a selling price of $40/unit all contributions of 1,000 units will be less than $20,000. So you should be able to eliminate a few combinations using this basic logic.

Thus the combinations of selling price and variable cost that give at least $20,000 and the probability resulting:

Sale price (unit) $	Variable cost $	Probability
50	20	0.45 × 0.55
60	30	0.25 × 0.25
60	20	0.25 × 0.55
		44.75%

8 Marginal cost = $35

Profits are maximised when marginal revenue = marginal cost, ie when 35 = a – 2bx

a = $100 + (1,000/100 × $50) = $600

b = $50/100

Therefore, 35 = $600 – x

Therefore, x = $565

P = a–bx

= $600 – $50/100 × $565

= $317.50

Top tips. The formula for a is one of the few formulae that you have to learn for the exam but the questions involving it are usually straightforward.

ANSWERS

114 Section A answers: Mixed Bank 5

Examiner's comments. Apart from 1.8, question 1 was generally quite well answered possibly because it was the first question to be tackled by most candidates.

1 A

	Service J $	Service H $	Service N $
Selling price	84	122.00	145.00
Direct materials	12	23.00	22.00
Direct labour	15	20.00	25.00
Variable overhead	12	16.00	20.00
Variable cost per unit	39	59.00	67.00
Contribution per unit	45	63.00	78.00
Direct labour cost per unit	15	20.00	25.00
Contribution per unit ($1) of limiting factor	3	3.15	3.12
Ranking	3rd	1st	2nd

2 C Because the supply of raw material s1 is unlimited, there is only one limiting factor, and so we can apply limiting factor analysis and rank the products on the basis of contribution per unit of limiting factor (ie per machine hour).

Contribution per unit is derived from the coordinates of the objective function, so the contribution per unit of x1 is $12.

Machine hours per unit are found from the machine hours constraint, so six machine hours are required per unit of x1.

Therefore, contributions per machine hour are

x1 $12/6 = $2   Rank 2nd
x2 $5/4 = $1.25   Rank 3rd
x3 $8/3 = $2.67   Rank 1st

Therefore the minimum number of x2 need to be produced (100 units using 400 hours). Product x3 should then be produced up to maximum demand (200 units using 600 hours) with the remaining hours (8,000 − 400 − 600 = 7,000) being used to produce (7,000/6) 1,166 units of x1.

3 B The material is used regularly by the organisation and so would be replaced if used on the special order. There is no shortage of supply, it being readily available at $3.24 per kg. The relevant cost of the material for the order is therefore 1,250 kgs × $3.24 = $4,050.

4

		EV $'000
Project L	(500 × 0.2 + 470 × 0.5 + 550 × 0.3)	500.0
Project M	(400 × 0.2 + 550 × 0.5 + 570 × 0.3)	526.0
Project N	(450 × 0.2 + 400 × 0.5 + 475 × 0.3)	432.5
Project O	(360 × 0.2 + 400 × 0.5 + 420 × 0.3)	398.0
Project P	(600 × 0.2 + 500 × 0.5 + 425 × 0.3)	497.5

ANSWERS

Project M has the highest EV of expected cash flows and should therefore be undertaken.

5

Market condition	Probability	Project chosen	Net cash inflow $'000	EV of net cash inflow $'000
Poor	0.2	P	600	120
Good	0.5	M	550	275
Excellent	0.3	M	570	171
EV of net cash inflows with perfect information				566
EV of net cash inflows without perfect information (from question 1.4 above)				526
Value of perfect information				40

6

	J £ per unit	K £ per unit	L £ per unit	M £ per unit
Selling price	2,000	1,500	1,500	1,750
Material cost	410	200	300	400
Throughput contribution	1,590	1,300	1,200	1,350
Minutes on bottleneck resource	120	100	70	
Throughput contribution per Minute	£1,590/120 = £13.25	£1,300/100 = £13	£1,200/70 = £17.14	£1,350/110 = £12.27
Ranking	2nd	3rd	1st	4th

7 The time to make the fourth unit is calculated by deducting (4 × cumulative average time to make four units) from (3 × cumulative average time to make three units).

$Y_x = aX^b$

a = 22 minutes
b = log 0.8/log 2 = 0.322
X = 4 and 3
Y = cumulative time to make 4 units or 3 units

$Y_4 = 22 \times 4^{-0.322} = 14.079$
Total time to make four units = 4 × 14.079 = 56.316

$Y_3 = 22 \times 3^{-0.322} = 15.445$
Total time to make three units = 3 × 15.445 = 46.335

Therefore time to make fourth unit = 56.316 – 46.335 = 9.981 minutes

8 **Impact on division A**

Loss of contribution on 2,500 units (2,500 × $(40 – 22)) = $45,000
Therefore division A's profits will fall by $45,000

Impact on XJ

Increase in variable costs on 2,500 units (2,500 × $(35 – 22)) = $32,500
Therefore KJ's profits will fall by $32,500

115 Section A answers: Mixed bank 6

1   B   Sensitivity = $\dfrac{\text{NPV of project}}{\text{PV of cashflow affected}} \times 100\%$

= ($160,000/($50,000 × 3.605*)) × 100%

= 88.77%

*discount factor over five years at 12%

2   D

Selling price £/unit	Probability	Unit var cost £	Probability	Combined probability	Monthly Contribution* £	Expected Value** £
20	0.25	8	0.20	0.050	12,000	600
	0.25	10	0.50	0.125	10,000	1,250
	0.25	12	0.30	0.075	8,000	600
25	0.40	8	0.20	0.080	17,000	1,360
	0.40	10	0.50	0.200	15,000	3,000
	0.40	12	0.30	0.120	13,000	1,560
30	0.35	8	0.20	0.070	22,000	1,540
	0.35	10	0.50	0.175	20,000	3,500
	0.35	12	0.30	0.105	18,000	1,890
				1.000		15,300

*(selling price – variable cost) × 1,000

** monthly contribution × combined probability

The **expected value** of contribution is £15,300. Note contribution excludes fixed costs.

3   C   The probability of monthly contribution > £13,500 = 0.08 + 0.2 + 0.07 + 0.175 + 0.105
= 0.63

4   $Y = aX^{-0.415}$

a = 6 hours

If the cumulative number of assignments (X) = 7, the cumulative average time per assignment (Y) = $6 \times 7^{-0.415}$

∴ Total time for seven assignments = $7 \times 6 \times 7^{-0.415}$ = 18.73 hours

If the cumulative number of assignments (X) = 6, the cumulative average time per assignment (Y) = $6 \times 6^{-0.415}$

∴ Total time for 6 assignments = $6 \times 6 \times 6^{-0.415}$ = 17.11 hours

∴ Time for seventh assignment = 18.73 – 17.11 = 1.62 hours

5

Project	Investment required $'000	Present value of cash inflows* $'000	NPV $'000	Profitability index (PI)**	Ranking as per NPV	Ranking as per PI
J	400	431	31	1.08	=2	3
K	500	543	43	1.09	1	2
L	300	331	31	1.10	=2	1

However, only $1 million is available for capital investment.

* NPV + initial investment

** PV of cash inflows/PV of total capital outlay

As projects are divisible, it is possible to invest fully in projects L and K, with the remaining balance of $200,000 being invested in J (so one half of the full investment would be made to earn one half of the NPV).

ANSWERS

Project	Priority	Outlay $'000	NPV $'000
L	1st	300	31
K	2nd	500	43
J (balance)	3rd	200	(½ of $31,000) 15
		1,000	89

6   **We know that at a discount rate of 15%, the NPV of K is $43,000. This is fairly close to zero**. It is also **positive**, which means that the **internal rate of return** is **more than 15%**. As a guess, it might be worth trying 20% next, to see what the NPV is.

Try 20%

Year	Cash flow $'000	Discount factor 20%	PV of cash flow $'000
0	(500)	1.000	(500)
1	70	0.833	58
2	90	0.694	62
3	630	0.579	365
			NPV (15)

This is fairly close to zero and negative. The internal rate of return is therefore greater than 15% but less than 20%.

Note. If the first NPV is positive, choose a higher rate for the next calculation to get a negative NPV. If the first NPV is negative, choose a lower rate for the next calculation.

So IRR = $15 + \left[\dfrac{43}{43+15} \times (20-15) \right]\% = 18.71\%$.

Note. Depending on the degree of accuracy in your calculations, there would be a range of acceptable answers to 2 decimal places.

7   The approach to derive the learning rate very much depends on the information given in the question. If you are provided with **details about cumulative production levels of 1, 2, 4, 8 or 16 (etc) units** you can use the **approach** shown below.

Let the rate of learning be r.

Cumulative production	Cumulative average time Hrs
1	3
2	$3 \times r$
4	$3 \times r^2$

$\therefore$ $3r^2 = 8.3667/4$
$r^2 = 2.092/3 = 0.697$
$r = 0.835$

$\therefore$ The rate of learning is 83.5%.

8   The decision rule in **minimax regret** considers the extent to which we might come to regret an action we had chosen.

Regret for any combination of action and circumstances	=	Payoff for **best** action in those circumstances	–	Payoff of the action **actually taken** in those circumstances

An alternative term for regret is **opportunity loss**. We may apply the rule by considering the maximum opportunity loss associated with each course of action and choosing the course which offers the smallest maximum. If we choose an action which turns out not to be the best in the actual circumstances, we have lost an opportunity to make the extra profit we could have made by choosing the best action.

Here is a payoff table for the decisions that the baker can make.

		Batches baked		
		10	11	12
Batches sold	10	500	480	460
	11	500	550	530
	12	500	550	600
Best outcome		500	550	600

		Batches baked		
		10	11	12
Batches sold	10	None	(20)*	(40)
	11	(50)**	None	(20)
	12	(100)***	(50)	None
Max regret		100	50	40

* 500−480
** 550−500
***600−500

Best outcome: choose outcome with the minimum regret

Minimum regret is 40, which means that 12 batches should be baked.

116 Section A answers: Mixed bank 7

Examiner's comments. Section A performance showed a noticeable improvement when compared to previous diets.

1   B   The relevant cost of the paper to be used in printing the brochure is the current resale value of the paper already held plus the additional cost of purchasing enough paper to fulfil the order. Therefore the relevant cost = $10 × 100 + $26 × 150 = $4,900.

2   D   The decision the farmer must make is whether to continue selling the dug potatoes in 20kg sacks or to wash and package them in 2kg cartons (effectively **a further processing decision**). As the farmer will grow the potatoes whatever the decision (the cost is incurred before the point at which the decision has to be made), this cost is not relevant to making his decision. The other cost/revenues are relevant, however, as they occur after the point at which the decision must be made, and their values affect the decision option chosen.

3   B   The existing contribution to sales (C/S) ratios for each product can be taken straight from the table.

	R	S	T	
	$	$	$	
Current C/S ratios	0.6	0.4	0.5	Average C/S ratio = 22,000/45,000 = 0.49
Revised mix				
Sales (W1)	9,000	22,500	13,500	45,000
Contribution(W2)	5,400	9,000	6,750	21,150
Average C/S ratio (W3)				0.47

Workings

1   The new sales revenue mix will affect the sales of each product. Thus for product R, the new sales figure will be 0.20 × $45,000 = $9,000 and so on for the other two products.

ANSWERS

2   Contribution is worked out by taking the current contribution to sales ratio (C/S ratio) and applying this to the new sales figure for each product. Taking product R again, the current C/S ratio is 60%, so multiply the new sales figure by 60% which gives $5,400 and so on for all three products.

3   This is worked out as $(21,150/45,000).

This is a long-hand way of doing the calculation but easier to understand if you prefer working from first principles. The examiner just multiplies through the existing C/S ratios by the new ratios thus

$(0.6 \times 0.2) + (0.4 \times 0.5) + (0.5 \times 0.3) = 0.47$

4   This question involves a **make or buy decision** (whether to make the gateaux in house or buy them in). We need to determine the number of gateaux at which the hotel is **indifferent** between making the gateaux in-house and buying them in. The relevant costs are the additional variable cost from buying in which is £2.50 per gateau and the fixed salary cost for the chef of £1,000 per month if the gateaux are made in house. The point of indifference can be stated mathematically in a breakeven calculation (when the additional cost of buying in equals the additional cost of in-house production) as follows (where x is the number of gateaux):

£2.50x = £1,000
x = 400

Therefore 400 gateaux is the minimum number of monthly sales required to make it worthwhile to prepare the gateaux in house.

5   The **payback** method looks at **how long it takes for a project's net cash inflows to equal the initial investment**. For investment A, it is clear that the project pays back sometime during year 3.

Therefore payback = 3 + ((400 – (100 + 120+140))/120)
= 3+ 40/120
= 3.33 years

6   The **discounted payback** period is the **time it takes for a project's cumulative NPV to become positive.**

With a cost of capital of 10% and the cash flows shown below, we can calculate a discounted payback period.

Year	Cash flow £'000	Discount factor 10%	Present value £'000	Cumulative NPV £'000
0	(450)	1.000	(450)	(450)
1	130	0.909	118	(332)
2	130	0.826	107	(225)
3	130	0.751	98	(127)
4	130	0.683	89	(38)
5	150	0.621	93	55

The DPP is during year 5.

DPP = 4 + (38/93)
= 4.41 years

7   The **IRR** defines the **DCF rate of return at which a project's NPV is zero**. At 10%, the project has a positive NPV of £48,000. Therefore **use a higher discount factor to calculate a negative NPV** for the project.

Choose a discount rate of say 15%.

Year	Cash flow £'000	Discount factor 15%	Present value £'000
0	(350)	1.000	(350)
1	50	0.870	44
2	110	0.756	83
3	130	0.658	86
4	150	0.572	86
5	100	0.497	50
			NPV = (1)

So IRR = $10 + \left[\dfrac{48}{48+1} \times (15-10)\right]\%$ = 14.9%, say 15%.

8   Use $Y_x = aX^b$ from your formula table:

a = 30 minutes, b = -0.2345, X = 200. All figures are given in the question.

Therefore the cumulative average time per unit (Y) = $30 \times 200^{-0.2345}$ = 8.66

∴ Total time for 200 units = 200 × 8.66 = 1,732 minutes

If the cumulative number of units (X) = 199, the cumulative average time per unit (Y) = $30 \times 199^{-0.2345}$ = 8.67

∴ Total time for 199 units = 199 × 8.67 = 1,725.33 minutes

∴ Time for 200th unit = (1,732 – 1,725.33) minutes = 6.67 minutes and this is the time per unit to be used for the quotation.

117 Section A answers: Mixed bank 8

1.1   D   The question here is asking you to consider a **further processing decision**. You need to compare the **cost of processing** the three products further (iii) with the **incremental revenue** from doing this. The **incremental revenue** is calculated by taking the unit selling price of each product after processing (iv) and subtracting the unit selling price before further processing (v). You will also need to know how many units of output there are from the common process (vii) so you can gross up the unit selling prices in (iv) and (v). Finally, you will also have to take account of any normal losses so that you can determine the actual output after further processing.

1.2   C   The relevant cost of the steel is simply **the current replacement cost** that is £4.25 per kg. Although there are 200kg in inventory, the steel is in regular use so it is likely that this inventory would be replaced if used on this contract.

1.3   C   The question is asking you to rank products when there is a scarcity of capital i.e. **capital rationing** is required. You need to use the **profitability index** to rank the projects here. Make sure that you read the entire question so you are aware that, for instance, the projects are divisible.

ANSWERS

	Investment required $'000	NPV $'000	PV of cash inflows (W1) $'000	Profitability index (PI)(W2)	Ranking from PI
Project					
J	400	125	525	1.313	3
K	350	105	455	1.300	5
L	450	140	590	1.311	4
M	500	160	660	1.320	1
N	600	190	790	1.317	2

Therefore based on the PI ranking, should choose to invest $500,000 in M with the balance of $500,000 in N.

Workings

1. The PV of cash inflows is the NPV plus the investment required.
2. The PI is simply the PV of cash inflows/the investment required.

1.4 Clearly this is a **payback** calculation. The payback period is how long it takes a **project's net cash inflows to equal the initial investment**. So set out the cumulative cash inflows in a table. These are the cash benefits of the time saved in using the new computer system.

Year	Cash benefit $'000	Cumulative benefit $'000
1	20	20
2	30	50
3	50	100
4	50	150
5	50	200

The original investment is $80,000 so the payback takes place somewhere between the second and third years of the project. The question asks for a payback period to one decimal place of one year so is 2 years +((80-50)/(100-50) x 12 months) = 2.7 years.

1.5 This question wants you to use the present value of a perpetuity to calculate the PV of the rental income. The formula for the PV of a perpetuity is $1/r where r is the discount rate. You need to learn this formula, as it is not given in the exam.

So for the rental income this is £80,000/0.08 = £1,000,000.

Therefore the NPV of the investment = £1,000,000 – £850,000 = £150,000.

1.6 The question wants you to calculate the optimum sales/production mix where there is a **limiting factor**. The limiting factor here is the **availability of fruit**.

There are **three steps** to working out the answer here.

Step 1 Confirm that the limiting factor is not sales demand.

	Small	Medium	Large	Total
Fruit per pie (kg)	0.2	0.3	0.6	
Weekly demand	200	500	300	
Fruit needed (kg)	40	150	180	370
Fruit available (kg)				300
Shortfall				70

Therefore the limiting factor is clearly the availability of fruit.

ANSWERS

Step 2 Identify the contribution earned by each pie per unit of scarce resource i.e. the fruit.

	Small	Medium	Large
Contribution per pie ($) (W)	0.50	1.60	3.00
Fruit per pie (kg)	0.20	0.30	0.60
Contribution per kg of fruit ($)	2.50	5.33	5
Ranking based on contribution	3	1	2

Working

From the data in the question. So for the small pie, for instance, the contribution is the selling price less variable costs ie $3.00 − $(1.80 + 0.40 + 0.30).

Step 3 Determine the mix of pies to be made and sold to maximise the bakery's contribution for the following week.

We know from step 2 that the priority is to manufacture the medium pies first, and then the large pies and finally the small pies.

	Demand	Fruit required (kg)	Fruit available (kg)	Pies
			300	
Pie				
Medium	500	150	150	500
Large	300	180	150 (W1)	250 (W2)
Small	200	40	0	
Total contribution				

So 500 medium pies and 250 large pies should be made and sold.

Workings

1. There are only 300 kgs of fruit in total available, so only 150 kg remain for large pies.

2. 150kg/0.60kg per pie = 250 pies

1.7 P = a−bx

When P = 25, x = 1,000
P = 35, x = 0

Using above equation

35 = a − bx0
∴ a = 35

To find b:

$$b = \frac{\text{Change in P}}{\text{Change in x}}$$

$$b = \frac{1}{100} \text{ or } 0.01$$

We can now write the equation as:

P = 35 − 0.1x
MR = 35 − 2 × 0.1x = 35 − 0.2x

ANSWERS

Optimum selling price will occur when profit is maximised – that is, when MR = MC.

We assume that MC = variable cost of $14

∴ Profit is maximised when 35 – 0.2x = 14
ie when x = 10.5

Optimal selling price = 35 – 0.1 x 105
= $24.50

1.8 You need to produce two answers here and time is limited as you would only have **seven minutes** in the real exam. Set out your workings clearly in tables so you can pick out the relevant totals. Remember that you are working out the **average C/S ratio** so you will need to calculate the **revenue per mix** and the **contribution per mix** in each case.

(i)
	Basic	Standard	Advanced	Total
Revenue per mix				
Selling price (£)	50	100	135	
Contracts sold	750	450	300	
Total (£)	37,500	45,000	40,500	123,000
Contribution per mix				
Contribution (£) (W)	20	50	70	
Contracts sold	750	450	300	
Total (£)	15,000	22,500	21,000	58,500

Average C/S ratio = 58,500/123,000 = 47.6%

(ii) Assume only one of each contract is sold:

Total contribution = 20 + 50 + 70 = 140
Total sales = 50 + 100 + 135 = 285

Average C/S ratio = $\frac{140}{285}$ = 0.491 or 49.1%.

118 Section A answers: Mixed bank 9

1.1 C The profitability index is stated as the NPV of a project/initial outlay.

Taking data from the question:

NPV = $140,500 and initial outlay = $500,000. Therefore the profitability index is

$140,500/$500,000 = 0.281 which is closest to 0.28.

1.2 C Use the standard sensitivity formula. This measures sensitivity of cash flows as:

NPV of a project/PV of the cashflow affected × 100%

Substituting data from the question.

NPV = $320,000 and PV of sales revenue = $630,000.

$320,000/$630,000 × 100% = 50.79% which is closest to 51%.

1.3 D At the breakeven point, Sales revenue = fixed costs/C/S ratio.

From the question, fixed costs = $25 per consulting hour × 100,000 hours, the C/S ratio is given and is 35%.

So sales revenue = ($25 × 100,000)/0.35
= $7,142,857 which is closest to $7,143,000.

… ANSWERS

1.4 The answer to this question can be arrived at by using a table and setting out the times and learning rate, or using the learning curve formula. Remember that the learning curve measures the **cumulative average time per unit** so far. To get the total time you need to then multiply this by the number of units produced.

Firstly, using a table to calculate the total time expected.

Number of units (a)	Rate of Learning %	Cumulative average time per unit (mins) (b)	Total time (mins) (a)× (b)
1		12.00	
2	75	9.00	
4	75	6.75	27

Secondly we can use the learning curve formula to obtain the cumulative average time per unit. So

$Y_x = aX^b$

Where $a = 12$,
         $X^b = 4^b$
         $b = \log 0.75 / \log 2 = -0.1249 / 0.301 = -0.415$

Therefore $4^b = 4^{-0.415} = 0.563$ and substituting this into the main formula for the learning curve gives

$Y_x = 12 \times 0.563$
    $= 6.75$ mins (from rounding $12 \times 0.563 = 6.76$ mins)

Multiply this by four units to get $6.75 \times 4 = 27$ mins.

1.5 The question asks you to calculate the accounting rate of return (ARR) using the **average investment value basis**. This is **(Average annual profit from investment × 100%)/Average investment**. The average annual profit is the sum of the net cash flows from the project over the life of the project, which is $170,000/5 = $34,000. The average investment is ($200,000 +$0)/2 = $100,000. Therefore the ARR will be $34,000/$100,000 × 100% = 34%.

1.6 The formula for IRR is not given in the exam so you will need to know this. You will also need to calculate the NPV for the project at a higher rate so that you can interpolate or work out the IRR between these two figures. Take a discount factor of 20%. This gives a NPV of £32,000. The workings for this are in the table below. Then substitute these NPVs and the discount factors into the formulae.

Year	Cash flow $	DF at 20%	PV $
0	(200,000)	1.000	(200,000)
1	80,000	0.833	66,640
2	90,000	0.694	62,460
3	100,000	0.579	57,900
4	60,000	0.482	28,920
5	40,000	0.402	16,080
			NPV = 32,000

So IRR = $10 + \left[\dfrac{87,980}{87,980 - 32,000} \times (20 - 10)\right]\% = 25.71\%$, say 26%

1.7 This question is asking you to calculate the optimum product mix where there is a **single limiting factor**. You can use the method in your study text to solve the problem as we have done here.

Step 1 Confirm that the limiting factor is something other than sales demand. We know this as it is stated in the question that the limiting factor is material.

So material is the limiting factor on production.

ANSWERS

Step 2 Identify the contribution earned by each product per unit of scarce resource, that is, per kg of material used.

	X	Y	Z
	$	$	$
Sales price	23	26	28
Variable cost	16	17	17
Unit contribution	7	9	11
Material (kg) per unit	0.60	0.80	0.60
Contribution per unit of limiting factor	11.67	11.25	18.33

Because material is in short supply it is most profitable to make Z, then X and finally Y.

Step 3 Determine the budgeted production and sales. Sufficient of Z will be made to meet the full sales demand, and the remaining material available will then be used to make X and finally Y.

Product	Demand	Material Required	Material Available	Priority for manufacture
	Units	kg	kg	
Z	400	240	240	1st
X	240	144	144	2nd
Y	600	480	216 (bal)	3rd
		864	600	

Product		Units
Z		400
X		240
Y (balance) (W)		270

Working

For product Y, there are 216 kg of material available and the product uses 0.80kg per unit. Therefore the company can manufacture 216/0.8 or 270 units of Y.

1.8 The question states the formulae for the demand curve and for marginal revenue. What you need to do is work out the values of 'a' and 'b' to substitute into the two formulae. You can then work out the profit-maximising price using MR = MC. Remember that 'a' is the price at which demand would be nil and 'b' is the amount by which price falls for each stepped change in demand.

Step 1 **Find the price at which demand would be nil**

Assuming demand is linear, each increase of $10 in the price would result in a fall in demand of 200 units. So if the price goes up by $60, the demand will fall by 200 units × 6 = 1,200. Therefore a = $160.

Step 2 **Extract figures from the question**

We know that P = a − bx and a = $160. We have also defined b above. So taking data from the question, and ignoring currency

b = 10/200 = 0.05

So the demand equation will be:

P = 160 − 0.05x

And the MR equation will be:

MR = 160 − 0.10x

ANSWERS

Step 3 **Calculate the selling price at which profit is maximised**

MR = MC so

160 − 0.10x = 30

x = 1,300

Substitute this value of x into the demand equation to obtain the **profit-maximising selling price**

P = 160 − 0.05 × 1,300
 = $95

ANSWERS

Mock exams

CIMA – Managerial Level

Paper P2

Management Accounting Decision Management

Mock Examination 1

Instructions to candidates:

You are allowed three hours to answer this question paper.
In the real exam, you are allowed 20 minutes reading time before the examination begins during which you should read the question paper, and if you wish, make annotations on the question paper. However, you will **not** be allowed, **under any circumstances**, to open the answer book and start writing or use your calculator during this reading time.
You are strongly advised to carefully read the question requirement before attempting the question concerned.
Answer the ONE compulsory question in Section A. This is comprised of sub-questions.
Answer ALL THREE compulsory sub-questions in Section B.
Answer TWO of the three questions in Section C.

DO NOT OPEN THIS PAPER UNTIL YOU ARE READY TO START UNDER EXAMINATION CONDITIONS

SECTION A – 20 marks

Answer ALL SEVEN sub-questions

Each of the sub-questions numbered from 1.1 to 1.7 inclusive, given below, has only ONE correct answer.

Question 1

The following data relates to questions 1.1 and 1.2.

TT Ltd has been asked to quote for a special contract. The following information is available.

Material X

| *Book value* | *Scrap value* | *Replacement cost* |
| £5.00 per kg | £0.50 per kg | £5.50 per kg |

The special contract would require 10 kgs of Material X. There are 250 kgs of this material in stock which was purchased in error over two years ago. It has just been noticed that if Material X is modified, at a cost of £2 per kg, it could then be used as a substitute for Material Y which is in regular use and currently costs £6 per kg.

Labour

The special contract would require 100 hours of labour. However, the labourers, who are each paid £15 per hour, are working at full capacity. There is a shortage of labour in the market and therefore the labour required to undertake this special contract would have to be taken from another contract, Z, which currently utilises 500 hours of labour and generates £5,000 worth of contribution. If the labour were taken from contract Z, then the whole of contract Z would have to be delayed, and such delay would invoke a penalty fee of £1,000.

1.1   Calculate the relevant cost of the materials for the special contract.   **(3 marks)**

1.2   Calculate the relevant cost of the labour for the special contract.   **(3 marks)**

1.3   Data relating to the production of the first sixteen batches of a new product are as follows.

Cumulative number of batches	*Cumulative total hours*
1	1,562.5
16	12,800

The percentage learning effect is closest to:

A   45%
B   55%
C   65%
D   85%   **(2 marks)**

1.4   A company produces two products: X and Y. The standard variable costs per unit of the products are as follows.

	X	Y
	£	£
Materials (£3 per kg)	15	12
Other variable costs	45	50
Total variable costs	60	62

MOCK EXAM 1: QUESTIONS

The management accountant determined the optimal production plan by using graphical linear programming. He noticed that the optimal plan was given at any point on the part of the feasible region that was formed by the constraint line for the availability of materials.

If the selling price of Product X is £100, the selling price of Product Y is:

(4 marks)

1.5 K plc produces three products whose contribution to sales ratios are as follows.

	Contribution/sales ratio	Selling price per unit
Product K	40%	$30
Product L	30%	$20
Product M	60%	$10

It has budgeted to sell these items in equal quantities in order to achieve its monthly sales target of $60,000.

Calculate the level of monthly fixed costs at which K plc would break even. (4 marks)

1.6 In a processing company, the information that is needed to determine the financial viability of further processing a product before resale is

(i)   the product's sale value immediately after further processing
(ii) the product's sale value before further processing
(iii) the incremental fixed costs of the further processing
(iv) the variable costs of further processing
(v)   the common fixed costs absorbed into the further process
(vi) the cost of the product prior to further processing

A   (i), (ii) and (iv) only
B   (i), (ii), (v) and (vi) only
C   (i), (ii), (iii) and (iv) only
D   All of the above

(2 marks)

1.7 A company provides three services that use the same machine, M1. The budgeted details per service are as follows.

	Service X £ per unit	Service Y £ per unit	Service Z £ per unit
Selling price	12	14	24
Variable costs	6	4	13
Fixed cost	2	5	8
Profit	4	5	3
Number of M1 machine hours	2	3	6

The fixed costs are general fixed costs that have been absorbed by the services by their direct labour content.

If M1 hours are scarce, the most and least profitable services are

	Most profitable	Least profitable
A	Y	Z
B	Z	X
C	Y	X
D	X	Z

(2 marks)

(Total for Section A = 20 marks)

SECTION B – 30 marks

Answer ALL THREE questions

Question 2

M Ltd has two divisions, X and Y. Division X is a chip manufacturer and Division Y assemble mobile phones.

The budgeted profit and loss statement for Division Y for next year shows the following results.

Mobile phone range	P	Q	R
	£'000	£'000	£'000
Sales	10,000	9,500	11,750
Less: total costs	7,200	11,700	9,250
Profit/(loss)	2,800	(2,200)	2,500
Fixed costs	2,000	5,400	5,875

Division Y uses a traditional absorption costing system based on labour hours.

The accountant of M Ltd has recently attended a course on activity based costing (ABC) and has recommended that the division should implement an ABC system rather than continue to operate the traditional absorption costing system.

A presenter at the conference stated that 'ABC provides information that is more relevant for decision making than traditional forms of costing'.

Required

Discuss this statement, using Division Y when appropriate to explain the issues you raise. **(10 marks)**

Question 3

HJK Ltd is a light engineering company which produces a range of components, machine tools and electronic devices for the motor and aircraft industry.

HJK Ltd produces two types of alarm system, one for offices and homes (X) and the other for motor vehicles (Y), on the same equipment. For financial reasons, it is important to minimise the costs of production. To match the current stock and demand position at least 100 alarm systems in total are required each week, but the quantity of one type must not exceed twice that of the other. The inputs necessary for the manufacture of one alarm system are given below, together with the availability of resources each week.

Type	Plating	Circuitry	Assembly
X	3 feet	4 units	20 minutes
Y	2 feet	8 units	8 minutes
Totals available each week	420 feet	800 units	34 hours

The management accountant estimates that the unit costs of production are £100 for X and £80 for Y. Past experience suggests that all alarms can be sold. At present, 75 of each alarm system are produced each week.

Required

State the objective function and the constraints for the production of alarm systems *and* use a graphical method of linear programming to find the optimal product mix. **(10 marks)**

Question 4

Between 20W4 and 20X6 approximately 4,000 miles of a country's railway network were closed down. The lines closed were deemed to have been rendered uneconomic by developments in road transport. An alternative view is that the lines were rendered uneconomic by inadequate investment and lack of proper commercial management.

This alternative view is now given some credence due to the fact that many of the lines closed have since been subject to partial or complete rebuilding. A case in point is the 10-mile branch line extending from town A across Isle B to the coast at town C. Isle B is a major centre for tourism and leisure pursuits. The line was closed in 20X2 but within five years various interests were calling for its reconstruction.

The old railway line passed through scenic countryside. It was felt that a reconstructed railway could itself be a tourist attraction.

Reconstruction of the line started in 20Y8 and was completed in 20Z2.

S Railway Ltd (SRL) has use of the line and offers journeys along it during summer weekends in trains pulled by steam engines, to be patronised by tourists and railway enthusiasts.

You have been engaged as a consultant by SRL to advise on its fares strategy for operations during the summer of 20Z3.

SRL is allowed to run four return train journeys per day along the line, each train having a capacity of 600 passengers. Initial market research has indicated that all trains will be filled to capacity if a fare of £2.00 per passenger for a one-way journey is charged. If this fare structure is adopted, then a significant number of passengers will have to be turned away from trains leaving at the most popular times.

Required

Explain how SRL might use 'price discrimination' (the practice of charging each customer what he is individually prepared to pay) in devising its fare structure. You should state the practical means by which price discrimination might be used and explain its benefit to SRL. **(10 marks)**

(Total for Section B = 30 marks)

SECTION C – 50 marks

Answer TWO questions

Question 5

RY Ltd, a transatlantic airline company, has recently launched a low-cost airline company providing flights within Europe. The market is highly competitive and two other low-cost airlines, B Ltd and G Ltd, together hold 98% of the market.

RY Ltd commissioned some market research to help with the pricing decision for one route, London to Paris, which it is thinking of offering. The research identified three possible market states and the likely number of passengers that would be attracted at three price levels on this route.

Ticket price		£80	£90	£100
Market	Probability	Passenger seats	Passenger seats	Passenger seats
Pessimistic	0.2	80	60	30
Most likely	0.6	100	90	80
Optimistic	0.2	150	150	120

Airport charges are incurred for each customer and these are expected to be either £5 or £6 per customer depending on the negotiations with the airports involved. The probabilities for the airport charges are 0.6 for an airport charge of £5 per passenger and 0.4 for an airport charge of £6 per passenger.

The fixed costs of a flight from London to Paris are £4,422.

Required

(a) Use decision tree analysis to advise RY Ltd on the optimum selling price to set. **(10 marks)**

(b) (i) Assuming RY Ltd knew that there would be a pessimistic market, determine the price that it should charge in order to maximise profit. **(3 marks)**

(ii) The market research company has now stated that by performing further analysis, it will be able to accurately predict the state of the market. Calculate the maximum price that RY Ltd should pay for this further analysis. **(7 marks)**

(c) Discuss the limitations of basing this decision on expected value calculations. **(5 marks)**

(Total = 25 marks)

Question 6

SS Ltd is an Internet service provider and also stores and transmits client data over the Internet via its server infrastructure. SS Ltd generates approximately £100,000 in contribution each year from these services to clients.

Because of technical advances in information technology, the existing server infrastructure will shortly become obsolete, and the company is considering what to do. The maintenance of this server infrastructure costs £24,000 per annum and is paid in advance at the beginning of each year. The service infrastructure has been fully written off but has a scrap value of £3,000. A technical consultant, hired at a cost of £5,000, prepared a report outlining that two possible replacement server infrastructures are available on the market. The details of each alternative are as follows.

MOCK EXAM 1: QUESTIONS

	Alternative 1	Alternative 2
Initial cost	£100,000	£100,000
Estimated useful life	3 year	5 years
Scrap value	£5,000	£3,000
Annual maintenance costs (in advance)	£24,000	£30,000
Annual contributions	£100,000	£105,000

SS Ltd incurs 30% tax on corporate profits. Writing down allowances are allowed at 25% each year on a reducing balance basis. At the end of the service infrastructure's life, a balancing charge or allowance will arise equal to the difference between the scrap proceeds and the tax written down value. Corporation tax is to be paid in two equal instalments: one in the year that profits are earned and the other in the following year.

SS Ltd's after tax nominal (money) discount rate is 12%.

You can assume that all cash flows occur at the end of each year unless otherwise stated.

Required

(a) Calculate for each alternative the net present value and annual equivalent cost. Advise senior management which server infrastructure to purchase, stating any assumptions you have made. **(15 marks)**

(b) Briefly explain the purpose and limitations of sensitivity analysis in relation to investment appraisal. **(4 marks)**

(c) Calculate the sensitivity of your recommendation to changes in the contribution generated by Alternative 1, and discuss its relevance to the decision. **(6 marks)**

(Total = 25 marks)

Question 7

(a) Standard costing and target costing have little in common for the following reasons.

- The former is a costing system and the latter is not.
- Target costing is proactive and standard costing is not.
- Target costs are agreed by all and are rigorously adhered to whereas standard costs are usually set without wide consultation.

Required

Discuss the comparability of standard costing and target costing by considering the validity of the statements above. **(18 marks)**

(b) A pharmaceutical company, which operates a standard costing system, is considering introducing target costing.

Required

Discuss whether the company should do this and whether the two systems would be compatible. **(7 marks)**

(Total = 25 marks)

(Total for Section C = 50 marks)

Answers

DO NOT TURN THIS PAGE UNTIL YOU HAVE COMPLETED THE MOCK EXAM

MOCK EXAM 1: ANSWERS

A PLAN OF ATTACK

What's the worst thing you could be doing right now if this was the actual exam paper? Sharpening your pencil? Wondering how to celebrate the end of the exam in 2 hours 59 minutes time? Panicking, flapping and generally getting in a right old state?

The exam allows 20 minutes reading time so read the advice on how to use this windfall.

Well, they're all pretty bad! So turn back to the paper and let's sort out a **plan of attack**.

First things first the twenty minute windfall

The 20 minutes reading time should be spent reading Section C. You have to choose two out of three questions so use 10 minutes to read the three questions thoroughly. Make sure you concentrate on all requirements. With 10 minutes taken to choose which questions you'll attempt, you can spend the remaining 10 minutes picking out the relevant data from the questions, setting up working layouts and brainstorming ideas for discussion requirements.

Leave the objective test questions until the last 40 minutes of answering time. As most of these are three or four marks, little is gained from duplicating workings which cannot go on the answer paper until the actual exams begins.

The next step

You've got **two options** now.

Option 1 (if you're thinking 'Help!')

If you're a bit **worried** about the paper, do the **questions in the order of how well you think you can answer them.**

You probably either love or hate the graphical approach to linear programming, the topic of **question 3**. But even if it's not one of your favourite topics on the Paper P2 syllabus, it's not a bad question to start with. Provided you know the six-step approach to solving graphical linear programming problems (and you need to look back to your BPP Paper P2 Study Text right now if you don't), you should be able to approach the question logically and arrive at the optimal mix.

It might be worth getting one of the longer questions out of the way next. Our choice would be **question 5**. The scenario is not too long, so you don't have an overload of information to digest, which should make the construction of the decision tree more straightforward. (A long scenario could well indicate a complicated decision tree.) And the question is divided into four parts, so even if you get stuck on one part you can move on to the next – using a 'made-up' but feasible value for any figure that you were unable to calculate in one part but need in the next. You could always do part (c) first to give yourself a bit of confidence. Although you won't be able to refer to the results of your calculations in parts (a) and (b), you can provide a few general limitations and then go back and add specifics once you have done the earlier parts of the question.

If you have a complete aversion to probability, you won't want to touch question 5 with a barge pole. In that case, you should think about doing **question 7**. You should be fairly well prepared for this type of question as there are number of quite similar ones in this Kit, it being indicative of the way in which many topics covered in Part E of the text could be examined (the suitability of a technique in a particular environment). Even if you think you can write lots for part (b), keep an eye on your time allocation as it is only worth 7 marks. You need to spend most time on part (a).

As you have to do all three 10-mark questions it is probably a good idea to do at least another one of them next. There's not a lot to choose between **questions 2 and 4**, both being single requirement discursive questions (although the provision of some numbers in the scenario to question 2 does at least give you the opportunity to do a little analysis!).

And that leaves **question 6**. It might be a good idea to start with part (b), as you should be able to pick up at least three marks for this requirement – which means you only need another ten to pass the question. Again, the scenario is not too long and complex, which means you have more chance of including all the relevant cash flows. You may think that some of the information about the timing of the cash flows is a bit ambiguous, but in such

MOCK EXAM 1: ANSWERS

circumstances you need to write down your assumptions and work through the question on the basis of those assumptions. You only need to get about half marks for part (a) (which you should easily be able to do by calculating WDAs, splitting tax payments into two portions, applying discount factors – even if you are not quite sure whether you have the flows in the correct time periods) and half of the six marks for part (c) and then you've passed the question.

What you mustn't forget is that you have to **answer question 2, question 3 and question 4 and TWO from questions 5 to 7**. Once you've decided on questions 5 and 6, for example, it might be worth putting a line through question 7 so that you are not tempted to answer it!

Option 2 (if you're thinking 'It's a doddle')

It never pays to be over confident but if you're not quaking in your shoes about the exam then **turn straight to question 2, the first of the compulsory questions**. You've got to do them so you might as well get them over and done with.

Once you've done the compulsory questions, choose two of the remaining three questions.

- If you prefer working with numbers rather than providing written answers it might be best to go for **questions 5 and 6** as **question 7** requires an entirely written answer.

- If you like writing essays, you'll obviously want to attempt **question** 7. Your reasoning for a choice between **questions 5 and 6** will probably depend on where you feel your strengths lie. If probability fills you with horror, go for question 6. If DCF and taxation leave you cold, question 5 might be the best bet.

No matter how many times we remind you....

Always, always **allocate you time** according to the marks for the question in total and for the parts of the question. Always, **always follow the requirements** exactly. And always, **always answer the entire question.** If you do the parts of the question out of order, check that you answer all of them.

You've got spare time at the end of the exam.....?

If you have allocated your time properly then you **shouldn't have time on your hands** at the end of the exam. If you find yourself with five or ten minutes spare, however, **go back to the objective test questions** that you couldn't do or **any parts of questions that you didn't finish** because you ran out of time.

Forget about it!

And don't worry if you found the paper difficult. More than likely other candidates would too. If this were the real thing you would need to **forget** the exam the minute you leave the exam hall and **think about the next one**. Or, if it's the last one, **celebrate**!

SECTION A

Question 1

1.1 The relevant cost of the 10 kg is the possible saving that would result if it were used as a substitute for material Y (replacement cost of Y less modification cost of X) = 10 kg × £(6 – 2) = £40.

1.2 The relevant cost of the 100 hours is the variable cost plus the penalty fee = (100 hrs × £15) + £1,000 = £2,500

1.3 D $Y_x = aX^b$
a = 1,562.5
Y_{16} = 12,800/16 = 800

∴ 800 = 1,562.5 × 16^b
And so 0.512 = 16^b
Taking logs, log 0.512 = b log 16
∴ b = log 0.512/log 16 = -0.2907/1.2041 = –0.2414

As b = log of learning rate/log 2, we have –0.2414 = log of learning rate/0.3010
∴ log of learning rate = -0.2414 × 0.3010 = –0.0727
So learning rate = 84.59%

1.4 Let x = output of product X
Let y = output of product Y

The objective function is maximise contribution C = £((100 – 60)x + (p – 62)y) = 40x + (p – 62)y, where p is the selling price of Y.

If the optimal solution is that part of the feasible solution that is formed by the constraint line for the availability of materials, the objective function would have the same gradient as the materials constraint if they were to be graphed.

Suppose the availability of materials is M. The materials constraint is therefore (15/3)x + (12/3)y

= 5x + 4y ≤ M, and the gradient of this constraint is –5/4.

The gradient of the objective function is –40/(p – 62)

∴ –5/4 = –40/(p – 62)
∴ p = £94

1.5 We need some additional information such as the breakeven sales quantities or values.

1.6 C Information about common fixed costs is irrelevant to any decision as they will be incurred regardless of the decision taken.

The cost of the product prior to further processing is not relevant as the cost has been incurred already, and will not be affected by the subsequent decision taken.

1.7 A

	Service X Per unit	Service Y Per unit	Service Z Per unit
Contribution	£6	£10	£11
Number of machine hours	2	3	6
Contribution per machine hour	£3	£3.33	£1.83
Ranking	2	1	3

MOCK EXAM 1: ANSWERS

SECTION B

Question 2

> **Top tips.** When answering this question it would have been all too easy to write about ABC in general rather than in the context of decision making, and it was vital to relate your answer to the scenario provided.

Product costs and absorption costing

Division Y **uses a traditional absorption costing** system based on labour hours, which means **overheads** are **absorbed** into product costs on the **basis of the number of direct labour hours** required per product.

Such an absorption basis tends to be used on the **assumption** that the **longer it takes to make a product** (in this case a particular type of mobile phone), the **more overhead is incurred** because of that product.

Such an **assumption may not be correct**, however, as not all overhead costs are incurred in proportion to time. **Product costs** derived on this basis could therefore be **inaccurate**.

ABC product costs

Activity based costing (ABC) is a form of absorption costing which attempts to assign overheads to products using bases that more accurately reflect the way in which the costs are incurred.

In the case of Division Y, for example, the cost of setting up production lines for a particular type of mobile phone is unlikely to be determined by the number of direct labour hours it takes to produce the mobile phone. Instead it is more likely that the cost is determined by the number of production runs.

The **use** of these bases, or **cost drivers**, produces, it is claimed, **more accurate product costs**.

Long-term and short-term variable costs

The **costs of non-volume related support activities** such as setting-up and production scheduling, which assist the efficient manufacture of a range of products, tend to **vary in the long term with the range and complexity of the products** manufactured rather than with some measure of volume of output.

Division Y produces a range of mobile phones. The traditional absorption costing system being used could therefore be allocating too great a proportion of overheads to high volume models (which cause relatively little diversity and hence use fewer support services) and too small a proportion of overheads to low volume models (which cause greater diversity and therefore use more support services).

Again, **an ABC system** would **overcome this problem**. By allocating overheads on the basis of models' usage of activities (by relating overheads to activities and using cost driver rates to allocate overheads to products) more realistic and accurate product costs are produced.

Decision making

Absorption costing product costs are argued as **acceptable in some instances**, such as for financial accounting purposes, stock valuation, some pricing decisions (if the mobile phones were priced at full cost plus, say) and for establishing the profitability of the various types of phone. For the vast majority of **decision-making** purposes, however, absorption costing product costs **should not be used**.

The budgeted profit and loss account for **Division Y** shows that **phone Q** is budgeted to make an **absorption costing loss of £2.2 million**, which could imply that the product should be **discontinued**. The traditional approach to absorption costing is known to be an unreliable source of decision-making information, however, because of the arbitrary nature of the way in which overheads are allocated and the resulting inaccurate and misleading product costs.

Marginal costing can help with decision making in the short term as the effects of minor volume changes are made explicit. The use of marginal costing would show that there would be a **reduction in contribution of £3,200** (sales less (total costs minus fixed costs)) **in the short term if the product were to be discontinued** (assuming all fixed costs are avoidable).

ABC is a form of absorption costing but because overheads are allocated to products on more accurate and realistic bases, the resulting product cost information is a **more valid basis for decisions**.

ABC costs are also **like marginal costs** in that they are variable costs. But they **are long-run variable costs** instead of short-run variable costs as they include all production overheads, not just short-term ones. Because the product costs include long-run as well as short-run variable costs, the **decision** reached **may differ** from that arrived at using marginal costing.

For example, if **phone Q** is particularly **complex**, say, it is likely to consume more resources and therefore **be allocated a higher proportion of (long-term and short-term) variable costs** using ABC. This would **reduce contribution**, possibly to such an extent that the phone Q should be **discontinued**.

Question 3

(a) **Define variables**

Let x = the number of X produced
Let y = the number of Y produced

Establish objective function

The **objective** is to minimise total production costs (C). The production cost of X = £100 and the production cost of Y = £80 (given in the question). The objective is to minimise C = 100x + 80y.

Establish constraints

(i) $x + y \geq 100$ (minimum production requirement)
(ii) $y \leq 2x$ (production ratio constraint)
(iii) $x \leq 2y$ (production ratio constraint)
(iv) $3x + 2y \leq 420$ (plating resources constraint)
(v) $4x + 8y \leq 800$ (circuitry resources constraint)
(vi) $x/3 + 2y/15 \leq 34$ *or*
      $20x + 8y \leq 34 \times 60$ (assembly resources constraint)

Graph the problem

For each of the constraint equations, turn the inequality sign into an equals sign, set x and then y equal to 0 and solve the resulting equations to find the points at which the constraints cross the axes. However, if when plotted on a graph the constraint goes through the origin we can only set x or y equal to 0 (as in (ii) and (iii) below) and another x or y value must be chosen. Use the coordinates determined to plot the constraints.

(i)   x = 0   ∴ 0 + y = 100
              ∴ y = 100

      y = 0   ∴ x + 0 = 100
              ∴ x = 100

      We therefore plot points at (x, y) = (0, 100) and (100, 0)

(ii) x = 0   ∴ 0 = y
      y = 100   ∴ 100 = 2x
                  ∴ 50 = x

      We therefore plot points at (x, y) = (0, 0) and (50, 100)

MOCK EXAM 1: ANSWERS

(iii) x = 0   ∴ y = 0
       y = 100 ∴ x = 200

We therefore plot points at (x, y) = (0, 0) and (200, 100)

(iv) x = 0 ∴ 2y = 420
              ∴ y = 210

      y = 0 ∴ 3x = 420
              ∴ x = 140

We therefore plot points at (x, y) = (0, 210) and (140, 0)

(v)   x = 0 ∴ 8y = 800
              ∴ y = 100

      y = 0 ∴ 4x = 800
              ∴ x = 200

We therefore plot points at (x, y) = (0, 100) and (200, 0)

(vi) x = 0 ∴ 2y/15 = 34
              ∴ y = 255

      y = 0 ∴ x/3 = 34
              ∴ x = 102

We therefore plot points at (x, y) = (0, 255) and (102, 0)

From the workings above to determine how to plot the constraints, it can be seen that we need to allow for a maximum of 200 for x and 255 for y.

Plot the points, join them up and label each line with (i) to (vi) as appropriate.

Constraints on HJK Ltd's production of alarm systems

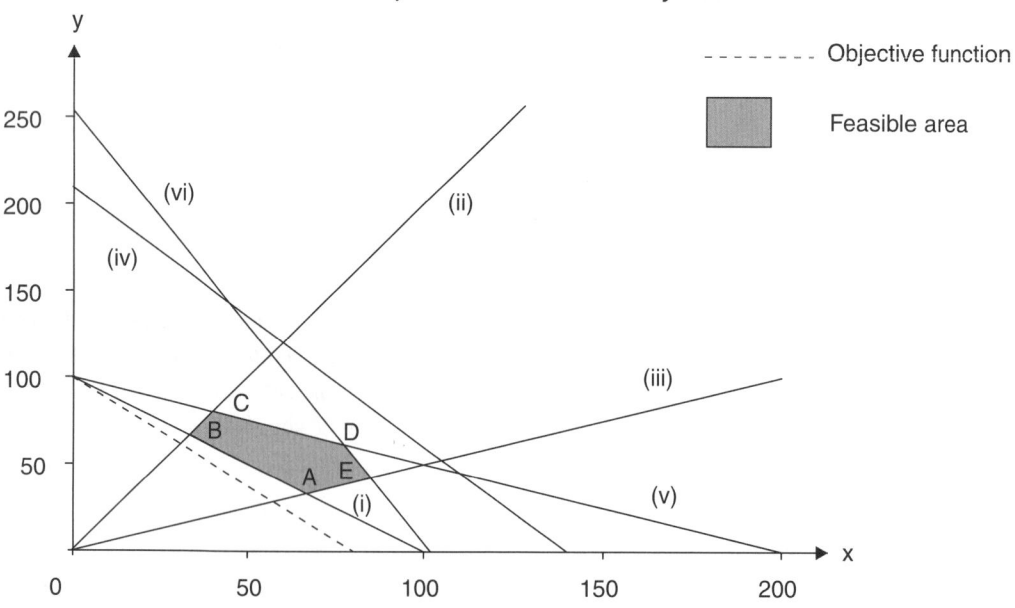

Define feasible area

Label the feasible area on the graph. You will probably make a mess if you try to shade it in, so don't do this. Our labelling gives a feasible area of ABCDE.

Determine optimal solution

We begin by establishing the slope of the objective function.

SECTION C

Question 5

> **Text reference.** You will find most of the information to answer this question in Chapter 14.
>
> **Top tips.**
>
> In (b)(i), we do not need to apply the probabilities relating to demand levels as we know that the market is pessimistic and hence we know what the demand will be at the three prices.
>
> Part (b)(ii) is tricky. It requires you to calculate the value of perfect information. In other words, you need to work out the difference between the EV as calculated in (a) when no information about the state of the market is known, and the EV the organisation could expect to earn if accurate information about the state of the market were available. The latter requires you to calculate an EV for each market state on the assumption that that market will occur and hence the price charged should be the one that maximises contribution given that market state. The probabilities of each market state occurring are then applied, the EVs summed and an overall EV determined.
>
> Bear in mind that you would not be penalised in part (b) for the use of incorrect probabilities derived in part (a).
>
> **Easy marks.** The decision tree in part (a) was not difficult to draw. Remember you need to start with a decision. Each alternative set of probabilities should sum to 1.

(a)

Price	Demand	Variable cost	Contribution	Combined probability	EV of contribution
£80	80 (0.2)	£5 (0.6)	£6,000*	0.2 × 0.6 = 0.12	£720.00**
		£6 (0.4)	£5,920	0.2 × 0.4 = 0.08	£473.60
	100 (0.6)	£5 (0.6)	£7,500	0.6 × 0.6 = 0.36	£2,700.00**
		£6 (0.4)	£7,400	0.6 × 0.4 = 0.24	£1,776.00
	150 (0.2)	£5 (0.6)	£11,250	0.2 × 0.6 = 0.12	£1,350.00
		£6 (0.4)	£11,100	0.2 × 0.4 = 0.08	£888.00
			EV of contribution from price of £80		£7,907.60
£90	60 (0.2)	£5 (0.6)	£5,100	0.2 × 0.6 = 0.12	£612.00
		£6 (0.4)	£5,040	0.2 × 0.4 = 0.08	£403.20
	90 (0.6)	£5 (0.6)	£7,650	0.6 × 0.6 = 0.36	£2,754.00
		£6 (0.4)	£7,560	0.6 × 0.4 = 0.24	£1,814.40
	150 (0.2)	£5 (0.6)	£12,750	0.2 × 0.6 = 0.12	£1,530.00
		£6 (0.4)	£12,600	0.2 × 0.4 = 0.08	£1,008.00
			EV of contribution from price of £90		£8,121.60
£100	30 (0.2)	£5 (0.6)	£2,850	0.2 × 0.6 = 0.12	£342.00
		£6 (0.4)	£2,820	0.2 × 0.4 = 0.08	£225.60
	80 (0.6)	£5 (0.6)	£7,600	0.6 × 0.6 = 0.36	£2,736.00
		£6 (0.4)	£7,520	0.6 × 0.4 = 0.24	£1,804.80
	120 (0.2)	£5 (0.6)	£11,400	0.2 × 0.6 = 0.12	£1,368.00
		£6 (0.4)	£11,280	0.2 × 0.4 = 0.08	£902.40
			EV of contribution from price of £90		£7,378.80

* £(80 − 5) × 80
** £6,000 × 0.12

The optimum selling price is £90 as this results in the highest EV of contribution.

MOCK EXAM 1: ANSWERS

(b) (i) **EVs if the market is pessimistic**

Price	Demand	EV of contribution
£80	80	(£80 – £(£5 × 0.6 + £6 × 0.4)) × 80 = £5,968
£90	60	(£90 – £(£5 × 0.6 + £6 × 0.4)) × 60 = £5,076
£100	30	(£100 – £(£5 × 0.6 + £6 × 0.4)) × 30 = £2,838

RY Ltd should choose a price of £80 as this produces the highest EV of contribution if the market is known to be pessimistic.

(ii) To work out how much RY Ltd should pay for the further analysis, we need to determine the difference in the EV of contribution with the analysis, and the EV of contribution without the analysis.

We worked out the EV without the analysis (ie selecting the highest EV of contribution) in (a) as £8,121.60. This is not necessarily the best decision in all future conditions, however.

With the analysis, we can select the best decision option as future conditions are known with certainty.

Forecast demand	Probability	Price chosen £	Contribution £	EV of contribution £
Pessimistic	0.2	80 (from (b)(i))	5,968	1,193.60
Most likely	0.6	90 (W1)	7,614	4,568.40
Optimistic	0.2	90 (W2)	12,690	2,538.00
EV of contribution with perfect information (ie the analysis)				8,300.00

The maximum price is therefore the difference between the EV without the analysis of £8,121.60 and the EV if the future state of the market is known (£8,300), which is £178.40

Workings

1 **EVs if the most likely state is known to occur**

Price	Demand	EV of contribution
£80	100	(£80 – £(£5 × 0.6 + £6 × 0.4)) × 100 = £7,460
£90	90	(£90 – £(£5 × 0.6 + £6 × 0.4)) × 90 = £7,614
£100	80	(£100 – £(£5 × 0.6 + £6 × 0.4)) × 80 = £7,568

A price of £90 would be chosen.

2 **EVs if the optimistic state is known to occur**

Price	Demand	EV of contribution
£80	150	(£80 – £(£5 × 0.6 + £6 × 0.4)) × 150 = £11,190
£90	150	(£90 – £(£5 × 0.6 + £6 × 0.4)) × 150 = £12,690
£100	120	(£100 – £(£5 × 0.6 + £6 × 0.4)) × 120 = £11,352

A price of £90 would be chosen.

(c) By basing the decision on EV calculations, a price of £90 would be charged as this results in the highest EV of contribution of £8,121.60, and hence an EV of profit after fixed costs of £(8,121.60 – 4,422) = £3,699.60.

There are a number of **disadvantages** with such an approach.

(i) Depending on the state of the market and the outcome of negotiations with the airports, if a price of £90 is charged, the contribution could vary from £5,040 to £12,750. The outcome of £8,121.60 contribution is not guaranteed. This is the average outcome that occurs only if the probabilities used in the calculation are correct and the decision is made many times over. The use of an EV therefore **ignores that range of possible values** that could occur.

MOCK EXAM 1: ANSWERS

(ii) The use of the EV approach leads to the choice of a price of £90. The **worst possible outcome** if a price of £80 is charged is £5,920 with a probability of 0.08 whereas the worst outcome if a price of £90 is charged (£5,040 also with probability of 0.08) is lower.

(iii) The **actions of competitors** can seriously undermine the accuracy of the demand data. Two other companies control a vast proportion of the market, and it is difficult to imagine that they would not retaliate were RY Ltd to offer the new route.

Question 6

> **Text reference.** You will find most of the information to answer this question in Chapters 10 to 13.
>
> **Top tips.** You may have missed that fact that the annual maintenance costs are paid in advance. The first cash flow relating to maintenance therefore occurs at time 0 but we have assumed that the tax implications are first accounted for at time 1, so that the tax cash flows occur in time 1 and time 2. You may have taken the view that the cash flow occurs at time 0, and the tax is accounted for in time 0 too and so we have set out an alternative solution to cover this option.
>
> Hopefully you noticed that because the two alternatives had different lives, they could not be compared directly and so annualised equivalents have to be calculated.
>
> If you had read through the question before starting it you might have picked up on the fact that you would need the cash flows (including those due to tax) relating to contribution in part (c) and so it would have been a good idea to show these separately in part (a) to save you time later.
>
> **Easy marks.** Part (a) required a fairly straightforward DCF analysis involving taxation. We recommend you lay out your answer in a series of tables as we have done so that both you and the marker can keep track of your workings.

(a) **Recommendation**

The figures in the table below can be found in the workings that follow.

	NPV	Years	12% disc factor for 3/5 years	Annualised equivalent
Alternative 1	£48,308	3	2.402	£20,112
Alternative 2	£102,257	5	3.605	£28,365

SS Ltd should therefore **invest in alternative 2** as this maximises the return on the investment.

Step 1 Alternative 1

WDAs and balancing charges/allowances

Year		Reducing balance £
0	Purchase	100,000
1	WDA	(25,000)
	Value at start of year 2	75,000
2	WDA	(18,750)
	Value at start of year 3	56,250
3	Sale for scrap	(5,000)
	Balancing allowance	51,250

MOCK EXAM 1: ANSWERS

Tax savings/payments due to WDA

Yr of claim	Allowance	Tax saved	Yr 1 Tax saving	Yr 2	Yr 3	Yr 4
	£	£	£	£	£	£
1	25,000	7,500	3,750	3,750		
2	18,750	5,625		2,812	2,813	
3	51,250	15,375			7,687	7,688
			3,750	6,562	10,500	7,688

Step 2 Other tax flows

Yr for tax purposes	Cash flow	Tax (due)/saved	Yr 1 Tax (payment)/saving	Yr 2	Yr 3	Yr 4
	£	£	£	£	£	£
1	(24,000)	7,200	3,600	3,600		
	100,000	(30,000)	(15,000)	(15,000)		
2	(24,000)	7,200		3,600	3,600	
	100,000	(30,000)		(15,000)	(15,000)	
3	(24,000)	7,200			3,600	3,600
	100,000	(30,000)			(15,000)	(15,000)
			(11,400)	(22,800)	(22,800)	(11,400)

Step 3 Calculate NPV

Year	Server	Other cash flows	Tax (payment)/ saving on other cash flows	Tax saved on capital allowances	Net cash flow	Discount factor 12%	PV of cash flow
	£	£	£	£	£		£
0	(100,000)	(24,000)			(124,000)	1.000	(124,000)
1		76,000*	(11,400)	3,750	68,350	0.893	61,037
2		76,000*	(22,800)	6,562	59,762	0.797	47,630
3	5,000	100,000	(22,800)	10,500	92,700	0.712	66,002
4			(11,400)	7,688	(3,712)	0.636	(2,361)
							48,308

*£((24,000) + 100,000)

MOCK EXAM 1: ANSWERS

Alternative solution

Other tax flows

Yr of claim	Cash flow	Tax (due)/saved	Tax (payment)/saving				
			Yr 0	Yr 1	Yr 2	Yr 3	Yr 4
	£	£	£	£	£	£	£
0	(24,000)	7,200	3,600	3,600			
1	(24,000)	7,200		3,600	3,600		
	100,000	(30,000)		(15,000)	(15,000)		
2	(24,000)	7,200			3,600	3,600	
	100,000	(30,000)			(15,000)	(15,000)	
3	100,000	(30,000)				(15,000)	(15,000)
			3,600	(7,800)	(22,800)	(26,400)	(15,000)

Calculate NPV

Year	Server	Other cash flows	Tax (payment)/ saving on other cash flows	Tax saved on capital allowances	Net cash flow	Discount factor 12%	PV of cash flow
	£	£	£	£	£		£
0	(100,000)	(24,000)	3,600		(120,400)	1.000	(120,400)
1		76,000*	(7,800)	3,750	71,950	0.893	64,251
2		76,000*	(22,800)	6,562	59,762	0.797	47,630
3	5,000	100,000	(26,400)	10,500	89,100	0.712	63,439
4			(15,000)	7,688	(7,312)	0.636	(4,650)
							50,270

*£((24,000) + 100,000)

Alternative 2

Step 1   WDAs and balancing charges/allowances

Year		Reducing balance £
0	Purchase	100,000
1	WDA	(25,000)
	Value at start of year 2	75,000
2	WDA	(18,750)
	Value at start of year 3	56,250
3	WDA	(14,063)
	Value at start of year 4	42,187
4	WDA	(10,547)
	Value at start of year 5	31,640
5	Sale for scrap	(3,000)
	Balancing allowance	28,640

Tax savings/payments of WDA

Yr of claim	Allowance	Tax saved	Tax saving				
			Yr 1	Yr 2	Yr 3	Yr 4	Yr 5	Yr 6
	£	£	£	£	£	£	£	£
1	25,000	7,500	3,750	3,750				
2	18,750	5,625		2,812	2,813			
3	14,063	4,219			2,109	2,110		
4	10,547	3,164				1,582	1,582	
5	28,640	8,592					4,296	4,296
			3,750	6,562	4,922	3,692	5,878	4,296

MOCK EXAM 1: ANSWERS

Step 2 Other tax flows

Yr for tax purposes	Cash flow	Tax (due) /saved	Yr 1	Yr 2	Yr 3	Yr 4	Yr 5	Yr 6
	£	£	£	£	£	£	£	£
1	75,000*	(22,500)	(11,250)	(11,250)				
2	75,000	(22,500)		(11,250)	(11,250)			
3	75,000	(22,500)			(11,250)	(11,250)		
4	75,000	(22,500)				(11,250)	(11,250)	
5	75,000	(22,500)					(11,250)	(11,250)
			(11,250)	(22,500)	(22,500)	(22,500)	(22,500)	(11,250)

*£((30,000) + 105,000) = £75,000

Step 3 Calculate NPV

Year	Server	Other cash flows	Tax (payment)/ saving on other cash flows	Tax saved on capital allowances	Net cash flow	Discount factor 12%	PV of cash flow
	£	£	£	£	£		£
0	(100,000)	(30,000)			(130,000)	1.000	(130,000)
1		75,000	(11,250)	3,750	67,500	0.893	60,278
2		75,000	(22,500)	6,562	59,062	0.797	47,072
3		75,000	(22,500)	4,922	57,422	0.712	40,884
4		75,000	(22,500)	3,692	56,192	0.636	35,738
5	3,000	105,000	(22,500)	5,878	91,378	0.567	51,811
6			(11,250)	4,296	(6,954)	0.507	(3,526)
							102,257

Alternative solution

Other tax flows

Yr of claim	Cash flow	Tax (due) /saved	Yr 0	Yr 1	Yr 2	Yr 3	Yr 4	Yr 5	Yr 6
	£	£	£	£	£	£	£		
0	(30,000)	9,000	4,500	4,500					
1	75,000*	(22,500)		(11,250)	(11,250)				
2	75,000	(22,500)			(11,250)	(11,250)			
3	75,000	(22,500)				(11,250)	(11,250)		
4	75,000	(22,500)					(11,250)	(11,250)	
5	105,000	(31,500)						(15,750)	(15,750)
			4,500	(6,750)	(22,500)	(22,500)	(22,500)	(27,000)	(15,750)

*£((30,000) + 105,000) = £75,000

Calculate NPV

Year	Server £	Other cash flows £	Tax (payment)/ saving on other cash flows £	Tax saved on capital allowances £	Net cash flow £	Discount factor 12%	PV of cash flow £
0	(100,000)	(30,000)	4,500		(125,500)	1.000	(125,500)
1		75,000	(6,750)	3,750	72,000	0.893	64,296
2		75,000	(22,500)	6,562	59,062	0.797	47,072
3		75,000	(22,500)	4,922	57,422	0.712	40,884
4		75,000	(22,500)	3,692	56,192	0.636	35,738
5	3,000	105,000	(27,000)	5,878	86,878	0.567	49,260
6			(15,750)	4,296	(11,454)	0.507	(5,807)
							105,943

(b) **Sensitivity analysis** is a term used to describe any **technique** whereby **decision options are tested for their vulnerability to changes in any variable**.

It can be used to **analyse the risk** surrounding a capital investment and enables an assessment to be made of **how responsive the investment's NPV is to changes in the variables that are used to calculate that NPV**.

The **basic approach** involves **calculating an NPV under alternative assumptions** (for example different sales volumes, different costs of capital) to **determine how sensitive it is to changing conditions**, thereby indicating those variables to which the NPV is most sensitive (most critical) and the **extent to which those variables may change** before the investment decision would change (ie a positive NPV becomes a negative NPV).

Once these **critical variables** have been identified, **management** should **review** them to assess whether or not there is a strong possibility of events occurring which will lead to a change in the investment decision. Management should also pay particular **attention to controlling** those variables to which the NPV is particularly sensitive, once the decision has been taken to proceed with the investment.

Sensitivity analysis can also be applied to an investment's accounting rate of return or its payback in much the same way.

The approach does have **limitations**, however.

(i) It requires that changes in each key variable are isolated but management is likely to be more interested in the combination of the effects of changes in two or more key variables. Looking at factors in isolation is unrealistic since they are often interdependent.

(ii) It does not examine the probability that any particular variation in costs or revenues might occur.

(c)

Year	Contribution £	Tax due £	Cash flow £	Discount factor 12%	Present value £
1	100,000	(15,000)	85,000	0.893	75,905
2	100,000	(30,000)	70,000	0.797	55,790
3	100,000	(30,000)	70,000	0.712	49,840
4		(15,000)	(15,000)	0.636	(9,540)
					171,995

The annualised equivalent of the contribution is £171,995/discount factor for 12% over 3 years = £171,995/2.402 = £71,605

The difference between the overall annualised equivalents of alternatives 1 and 2 as calculated in (a) is £(20,112 – 28,365) = £8,253.

So if the AE of contribution from alternative 1 increases by more than £8,253 to £(71,605 + 8,253) = £79,858 (an increase of (8,253/71,605) × 100% = 11.5%, alternative 1 will become the better option.

Question 7

> **Text reference.** You will find most of the information to answer this question in Chapter 15.
>
> **Top tips.** The most important thing when answering this question was to limit the time you spent on describing the two systems. In part (a), it was vital that you addressed the three statements. Indeed, this provided a ready-made structure to your answer. Discussion of each of the statements would be worth equal marks so you needed to cover all of them. You should have avoided any repetition of your answer to (a) in your answer to (b): you can't be given marks twice for the same thing so repetition would have been a complete waste of time.
>
> **Easy marks.** The requirements of the question should lead your discussion in part (a). You need to repeat knowledge rather than apply this in part (a).

(a) (i) **Standard costing is a costing system, target costing is not**

According to CIMA *Official Terminology*, costing is 'The process of determining the costs of products, services or activities' and so a **costing system** is presumably **any method of determining product/service/activity costs.**

Standard costing, by **establishing standard costs** for products and so on, is **undoubtedly a costing system** (although the *Official Terminology* definition focuses on the control aspect of the technique).

Target costing, which is not defined in the *Terminology*, involves **deducting a desired profit margin from a competitive market price to produce a target cost**. As such it can also be described as a **costing system.**

(ii) **Target costing is proactive, standard costing is not**

This issue is dependent on the relationship between cost, price and profit.

Standard costing

The traditional approach, which is dominated by standard costing, is **first to develop a product**. Then once a **detailed product design** has been produced and **production methods determined**, the **expected standard production cost** will be determined and a **selling price (probably based on cost) set**, with a **resulting profit or loss.**

Costs are controlled at monthly intervals through variance analysis. The **focus** of the **control** process is on **adverse variances** and the action required to reduce or eliminate them in the future. The standard cost, once set, is **only revised** for **changes** of a **permanent** or reasonably **long-term** nature.

As described, standard costing is **reactive.**

Target costing

The target costing approach is to **develop a product concept and the primary specification for performance and design** and **then** to **determine** the **price** that **customers** would be willing **to pay** for that concept. A **desired profit margin** is then **deducted** from the price to **leave** a figure representing the total cost. This is the **target cost.**

The target cost per unit is then split across the different functional areas and the product should be **designed so that it can be manufactured within these target costs**. If the target cost cannot be achieved for one or more areas, the **targets** for the other areas must be **reduced**, or the **product redesigned** or even **scrapped.**

Management may decide to go ahead and manufacture a product with a target cost well below the currently attainable cost determined by current technology and processes. In such circumstances, they will set **benchmarks** for **improvement** towards the target cost, by specified dates.

And once the product goes into production, the **target cost** will gradually be **reduced**, the reductions being **incorporated** into the **budgeting** process.

Target costing therefore takes a **proactive** approach to product costing, by viewing the product cost as a reducing figure rather than as one set in stone.

(iii) **Target costs are agreed by all and rigorously adhered to, whereas standard costs are set without wide consultation**

Consultation

It is probably safe to say that, **in general, more people** are involved in **establishing target costs** than in setting standard costs because a greater number of functions are involved in the process, such as **marketing and design**. Standard cost setting is principally the domain of purchasing managers and production experts.

Neither system will work properly, however, **if those striving to meet the standards/targets have not agreed to them**. Unachievable standards/targets will only **demotivate**.

Adherence

As noted in (ii) above, **target costs** are **not always immediately achievable** but are seen as ultimate aims. But given the **clarity** of the **relationship** between selling price, cost and profit, the **effect on profit of any increase in cost** over the target is more evident and may make for **rigorous adherence** to the target.

Standard costs are **not always achievable** if there has been a **change** in the basis upon which the standard was set which **is outside the control of management**. A world-wide increase in the price of a raw material, say, may cause the **standard** to be **modified** or a **planning variance** reported. And in some organisations, tight budgets are set and adverse variances expected.

(b) **Pharmaceutical companies and target costing**

The **key cost features** of a pharmaceutical company are **massive research and development costs** and **little need to control production costs until the product's patent runs out** and competitors can launch cheaper versions. In general, **research and development costs** are **covered,** usually many times over by successful products. And, because **doctors** become familiar with the product name, they **may not switch** to a cheaper version even when the patent runs out. **Target costing** would therefore appear to have **little to offer** such organisations.

In **recent years**, however, pharmaceutical companies have come under **increasing pressure** to **reduce drug prices**, particularly in poorer areas of the world. It is within this scenario that **target costing may be of value**, forcing consideration of how to reduce costs on a monthly basis, given, say, learning and experience curve effects and so on, in order to cut prices without cutting profits.

Compatibility of standard costing and target costing

The two systems were **developed in different parts of the world at different periods of time for different purposes.** Standard costing aims to control future costs by examining past costs whereas target costing aims to control future costs by examining them before they are incurred and placing limits on them. Any attempt at running them both at the same time is likely to be **problematic.**

(i) Firstly, management would need to **embrace** the **proactive approach** required for target costing, which is in sharp contrast to the reactive behaviour entrenched in a system of standard costing.

(ii) If targets are values that must be achieved, they could be used as the bases for standards. But if they are **simply 'targets' towards which the organisation should be working, their value as the bases of standards would be limited** given the negative impact of reprimanding managers for failing to achieve them.

(iii) Management are likely to be **confused** about the difference between a standard cost and a target cost and which of the two was their goal.

It is possible, however, to run a **standard costing** system so that it achieves the **same aims** as a **target costing** system, by **incorporating** any **learning** effect into the standards.

CIMA – Managerial Level

Paper P2

Management Accounting Decision Management

Mock Examination 2

Instructions to candidates:

You are allowed three hours to answer this question paper.
In the real exam, you are allowed 20 minutes reading time before the examination begins during which you should read the question paper, and if you wish, make annotations on the question paper. However, you will **not** be allowed, **under any circumstances**, to open the answer book and start writing or use your calculator during this reading time.
You are strongly advised to carefully read the question requirement before attempting the question concerned.
Answer the ONE compulsory question in Section A. This is comprised of sub-questions.
Answer ALL THREE compulsory sub-questions in Section B.
Answer TWO of the three questions in Section C.

DO NOT OPEN THIS PAPER UNTIL YOU ARE READY TO START UNDER EXAMINATION CONDITIONS

SECTION A – 20 marks

Answer all SEVEN sub-questions

Question 1

Each of the sub-questions numbered from 1.1 to 1.7 inclusive has only ONE correct answer.

1.1   PQR plc manufactures three products which have the following cost and demand data.

	Product P	Product Q	Product R
Contribution to sales ratio	20%	25%	30%
Maximum sales value (£'000)	800	1,000	1,500
Minimum sales value (£'000)	100	100	100

There are fixed costs of £700,000 per period.

The lowest breakeven sales value per period, subject to meeting the minimum sales value constraints, is nearest to

- A   £2,320,000
- B   £2,380,000
- C   £2,520,000
- D   £2,620,000

(2 marks)

1.2   GH plc has received an order to make eight units of product K. The time to product the first unit is estimated to be 100 hours and an 80% learning curve is expected. The rate of pay is £6 for each hour.

The direct material cost for each unit is £2,500 and the fixed costs associated with the order are £9,600.

Required

Calculate the average cost of each unit (to the nearest £) for this order of product K.   **(4 marks)**

1.3   A company is considering the development and marketing of a new product. Development costs will be £2m. There is a 75% probability that the development effort will be successful, and a 25% probability that it will be unsuccessful. If development *is* successful and the product *is* marketed, it is estimated that:

	Expected profit	Probability
Product very successful	£6.0m	0.4
Product moderately successful	£1.8m	0.4
Product unsuccessful	(£5.0m)	0.2

Required

Calculate the payoff/expected value of the project.   **(4 marks)**

1.4   K Ltd are considering an investment of £1,300,000. The company requires a minimum real rate of return of 10% under the present and anticipated conditions. Inflation is expected to be 3% per annum over the life of the investment and all costs and revenues are expected to increase in line with inflation. Which of the following is the most appropriate approach to take to a DCF appraisal?

- A   Increase costs and revenues at 3% per annum and discount at 10%
- B   Make no adjustment to the cash flows for inflation and discount at 10%
- C   Increase the cash flows by 3% per annum and discount at 13%
- D   Make no adjustment to the cash flows for inflation and discount at 13%

(3 marks)

MOCK EXAM 2: QUESTIONS

1.5 Which of the following are required to determine the breakeven sales value in a multi-product manufacturing environment?

    (i)   Individual product gross contribution to sales ratios
    (ii)   The general fixed cost
    (iii) The product-specific fixed cost
    (iv) The product mix ratio
    (v)   The method of apportionment of general fixed costs

    A   (i), (ii), (iii) and (iv) only
    B   (i), (iii) and (iv) only
    C   (i), (ii) and (iv) only
    D   All of them   **(2 marks)**

1.6 R Ltd is considering four projects. W has a 80% chance of resulting in a profit of £50,000 and a 20% chance of resulting in a loss of £80,000. X has a 40% chance of resulting in a profit of £20,000 and a 60% chance of resulting in a profit of £10,000. Y will result in a profit of £20,000. Z has a 95% chance of resulting in a profit of £25,000 and a 5% chance of resulting in a loss of £10,000. Which project should R Ltd select?

(3 marks)

1.7 Z plc provides a single service to its customers. An analysis of its budget for the year ending 31 December 20X2 shows that in period 4, when the budgeted activity was 5,220 service units with a sales value of £42 each, the margin of safety was 19.575%.

The budgeted contribution to sales ratio of the service is 40%.

Budgeted fixed costs in period 4 were nearest to

    A   £1,700
    B   £71,000
    C   £88,000
    D   £176,000   **(2 marks)**

(Total = 20 marks)

SECTION B – 30 marks

Answer ALL THREE questions

Question 2

A sports complex includes an ice rink and a swimming pool in its facilities. The ice rink is used for skating and for curling which became more popular after the 2020 Winter Olympics. The swimming pool is used for leisure purposes and as a venue for swimming competitions. The sports complex management is concerned at falling profit levels which are due to falling revenue and rising costs.

A proposal to change, and hence improve, the method used for heating the water in the swimming pool is currently being investigated as part of a quality improvement programme. A survey of the complex has been carried out at a cost of £30,000 to check energy usage. This has shown that the heat removed from the ice rink in keeping the ice temperature regulated to the required level for good ice conditions could be used to heat the swimming pool. At present the heat removed in the regulation of ice temperature is not utilised and is simply vented into the atmosphere outside the complex.

The following additional information is available.

(a) The expected costs for the ice rink heat extraction for the year ended 31 May 2021 are £120,000. It is estimated that due to rising prices, this cost will increase by 10% during the year to 31 May 2022. Heat extracted totalled 500,000 units of heat during the year to 31 May 2021 and this figure is expected to apply for the year to 31 May 2022.

(b) The water in the swimming pool is currently heated by a separate system which is also used for a range of other heating purposes in the sports complex. In the year ended 31 May 2021 the swimming pool share of the system had operating costs of £150,000 using 200,000 units of heat. This was made up of 70% variable avoidable cost and 30% which is a share of general fixed overhead. On average all such costs will increase by 10% through price changes in the year to 31 May 2022.

(c) In order to utilise the heat extracted from the ice rink for heating the water in the swimming pool, equipment would be hired at a cost of £75,000 per annum. This equipment would be supervised by an employee who is currently paid a salary of £15,000 for another post in the year ended 31 May 2021 and who would be retiring if not given this post. His salary for the year to 31 May 2022 would be £17,500. His previous post would not be filled on his retirement. It is anticipated that this system would help to improve the ice quality on the rink.

(d) Only part of the heat extracted from the ice rink could be recovered for use in heating the water in the swimming pool using the new equipment. The current most likely estimate of the recovery level is 25% of the heat extracted from the ice rink. If the quantity of heat available was insufficient for the heating of the swimming pool, any balance could continue to be obtained from the existing system.

Required

Prepare an analysis for the year to 31 May 2022 to show whether the sports complex should proceed with the heat recovery proposal on financial grounds where a 25% level of recovery applies. Explain any assumptions made and give reasons for the figures used in or omitted from your calculations.

(10 marks)

Question 3

Investit plc is considering which of two methods it should use to market its investment services to the public: one is direct mailing and the other is newspaper advertising. It regards these forms of marketing as mutually exclusive. It has a budget for expenditure on marketing of £200,000.

Costs of direct mailing are £0.25 for each 'shot'. Previous experience leads the company to expect a response rate of between 6% and 12% with an average of 8%. The chances of the lower, higher and average response rates actually occurring are estimated to be 15%, 20% and 65% respectively.

Newspaper advertisements have also been used in the past and these also produce a varying response. Investit's budget would allow it to run a campaign of weekly insertions (ie 52 in total) in certain suitable Sunday newspapers. Again, based on past experience, it can expect response rates varying between 700 and 2,000 per insertion, with an average of 1,400. The chances of the lower, higher and average response rates actually occurring are 20%, 25% and 55% respectively.

In either case, only 40% of the responses can be expected to produce a sale. Each sale generates a net income of £10.

Required

On the basis of expected values and standard deviations, recommend one of the marketing plans given that the management of Investit are risk averse. **(10 marks)**

Question 4

Companies operating in an advanced manufacturing environment are finding that about 90% of a product's life cycle cost is determined by decisions made early in the cycle. Management accounting systems should therefore be developed that aid the planning and control of product life-cycle costs and monitor spending at the early stages of the life cycle.

(Statement paraphrased from a well-known accounting text)

Required

Having regard to the above statement, explain activity based management and compare and contrast it with life cycle budgeting. **(10 marks)**

(Total for Section B = 30 marks)

Section C – 50 marks

Answer TWO questions

Question 5

Fuelit plc is an electricity supplier in the UK. The company has historically generated the majority of its electricity using a coal fuelled power station, but as a result of the closure of many coal mines and depleted coal resources, is now considering what type of new power station to invest in. The alternatives are a gas fuelled power station, or a new type of efficient nuclear power station.

Both types of power station are expected to generate annual revenues at current prices of £800 million. The expected operating life of both types of power station is 25 years.

Financial estimates:

	Gas £m	Nuclear £m
Building costs	600	3,300
Annual running costs (at current prices)		
Labour costs	75	20
Gas purchases	500	–
Nuclear fuel purchases	-	10
Customer relations	5	20
Sales and marketing expenses	40	40
Interest expense	51	330
Other cash outlays	5	25
Accounting depreciation	24	132

Other information:

(i) Whichever power station is selected, electricity generation is scheduled to commence in three years' time.

(ii) If gas is used most of the workers at the existing coal fired station can be transferred to the new power station. After tax redundancy costs are expected to total £4 million in year four. If nuclear power is selected fewer workers will be required and after tax redundancy costs will total £36 million, also in year four.

(iii) The real cost of capital for the Gas power station will 6% and for the Nuclear power station, 8% reflecting slightly different risk and reward requirements.

(iv) Costs of building the new power stations would be payable in two equal instalments in one and two years' time.

(v) The existing coal fired power station would need to be demolished at a cost of £10 million after tax in three years time.

(vi) Corporate tax is at the rate of 30% payable in the same year that the liability arises.

(vii) Tax depreciation is at the rate of 10% per year on a straight line basis.

(viii) At the end of twenty-five years of operations the gas plant is expected to cost £25 million (after tax) to demolish and clean up the site. Costs of decommissioning the nuclear plant are much less certain, and could be anything between £500 million and £1,000 million (after tax) depending upon what form of disposal is available for nuclear waste.

MOCK EXAM 2: QUESTIONS

Required

(a) Estimate the expected NPV of each of investment in a gas fuelled power station and investment in a nuclear fuelled power station.

State clearly any assumptions that you make.

(*Note.* It is recommended that annuity tables are used wherever possible) **(20 marks)**

(b) Discuss other information that might assist the decision process. **(5 marks)**

(Total = 25 marks)

Question 6

S plc make and sell a number of products. Products A and B are products for which market prices are available at which S plc can obtain a share of the market as detailed below. Estimated data for the forthcoming period is as follows.

(a) Product data

	Product A	Product B	Other products
Production/sales (units)	5,000	10,000	40,000
	£'000	£'000	£'000
Total direct material cost	80	300	2,020
Total direct labour cost	40	100	660

(b) Variable overhead cost is £1,500,000 of which 40% is related to the acquisition, storage and use of direct materials and 60% is related to the control and use of direct labour.

(c) It is current practice in S plc to absorb variable overhead cost into product units using overall company wide percentages on direct material cost and direct labour cost as the absorption bases.

(d) Market prices for Products A and B are £75 and £95 per unit respectively.

(e) S plc require a minimum estimated contribution: sales ratio of 40% before proceeding with the production/sale of any product.

Required

(a) Prepare estimated unit product costs for Product A and Product B where variable overhead is charged to product units as follows.

　(i)　Using the existing absorption basis as detailed above. **(5 marks)**

　(ii)　Using an activity based costing approach where cost drivers have been estimated for material and labour related overhead costs as follows.

	Product A	Product B	Other products
Direct material related overheads – cost driver is material bulk. The bulk proportions per unit are:	4	1	1.5
Direct labour related overheads – cost driver is number of labour operations (not directly time related).			
Labour operations per product unit are:	6	1	2

(10 marks)

(b) Prepare an analysis of the decision strategy which S plc may implement with regard to the production and sale of Products A and B. Use unit costs as calculated in (a)(i) and (a)(ii) together with other information given in the question in your analysis. Your answer should include relevant calculations and discussion and be prepared in a form suitable for presentation to management. **(10 marks)**

(Total = 25 marks)

Question 7

(a) EX Ltd is an established supplier of precision parts to a major aircraft manufacturer. It has been offered the choice of making either Part A or Part B for the next period, but not both.

Both parts use the same metal, a titanium alloy, of which 13,000 kilos only are available, at £12.50 per kilo. The parts are made by passing each one through two fully-automatic computer-controlled machine lines – S and T – whose capacities are limited. Target prices have been set and the following data are available for the period.

Part details

	Part A	Part B
Maximum call-off (units)	7,000	9,000
Target price	£145 per unit	£115 per unit
Alloy usage	1.6 kilos	1.6 kilos
Machine times		
Line S	0.6 hours	0.25 hours
Line T	0.5 hours	0.55 hours

Machine details

	Line S	Line T
Hours available	4,000	4,500
Variable overhead per machine hour	£80	£100

Required

(i) Calculate which part should be made during the next period to maximise contribution. **(9 marks)**

(ii) Calculate the contribution which EX Ltd will earn and whether the company will be able to meet the maximum call-off. **(2 marks)**

(iii) As an alternative to the target prices shown above, the aircraft manufacturer has offered the following alternative arrangement.

Target prices less 10% plus £60 per hour for each unused machine hour

Required

Decide whether your recommendation in (a) above will be altered and, if so, calculate the new contribution. **(9 marks)**

(b) Discuss the problems associated with joint cost apportionments in relation to the following.

  (i) Planning
  (ii) Control
  (iii) Decision making **(5 marks)**

(Total = 25 marks)

(Total for Section C = 50 marks)

Answers

DO NOT TURN THIS PAGE UNTIL YOU HAVE COMPLETED THE MOCK EXAM

A PLAN OF ATTACK

What's the worst thing you could be doing right now if this was the actual exam paper? Sharpening your pencil? Wondering how to celebrate the end of the exam in 2 hours 59 minutes time? Panicking, flapping and generally getting in a right old state?

The exam allows 20 minutes reading time so we've included advice on how to you can use this extra time.

Well, they're all pretty bad! So turn back to the paper and let's sort out a **plan of attack**.

First things first. How to use the 20 minutes reading time.

This reading time should be spent reading section C. You have to choose two out of three questions so take 10 minutes to read the questions thoroughly. Make sure you concentrate on all requirements. With the remaining 10 minutes, pick out the relevant data from the questions, setting up working layouts and brainstorming ideas for discussion points.

Leave the **objective test questions until the last 40 minutes of answering time. As most of these are three or four marks, little is to be gained from duplicating workings, which cannot go onto the answer paper until the actual exam begins.**

The next step

You've got **two options** now.

Option 1 (if you're thinking 'Help!')

If you're a bit **worried** about the paper, do the **questions in the order of how well you think you can answer them.**

We would actually suggest doing the three compulsory questions on this paper first, as they are all comparatively straightforward.

If you like discursive questions, then start with **question 4**. You've only got 18 minutes for each question and the question asks for 2 or 3 main points, so make sure you allocate your time appropriately. Ensure you **explain** and then **compare** and **contrast**.

If numbers are more your forte then you'll want to start with **question 2 or 3**. Question 3 wants more calculations than Question 2. Just set out the calculations in tables as we have done. Remember to calculate the EV for each option. Question 2 wants you to do a calculation of the proposal and then comment on this.

That then leaves a choice of two from the three questions in Section C.

Our suggestion would be to attempt **question 6** next. This question covers absorption costing and ABC and asks for a report style answer, in a 2-part question. You will have to do separate calculations in part (a) for ABC and absorption costing to answer the question in part (b) by way of illustration for any points you are making. Think about the information given in the question when answering part (b) – what decision criteria does the company have? What figures can you use to illustrate your answer in part (b)?

Section C questions on DCF (like **question 5**) will invariably require lots of calculations. You will probably be under some time pressure with question 5, unless you realised this and set your workings out in clear tables. Part (b) could be answered separately to part (a) but really needed some numbers to use as illustration and these were calculated in part (a). Remember to discuss, make recommendations and explain points as required by the question.

Question 7 is all about relevant costing within constraints so would be best attempted if you knew this area well. The calculations in part (a) should have been routine if you knew what should be brought forward knowledge combined with limiting factor analysis. Part (b) then asked for a discussion of the problems associated with joint cost appointment.

What you mustn't forget is that you have to **answer all the questions in Section B and two questions from Section C**. Once you've decided on questions 6 and 7, for example, it might be worth putting a line through question 5 so that you are not tempted to answer it!

Option 2 (if you're thinking 'It's a doddle')

It never pays to be over confident but if you're not quaking in your shoes about the exam then **turn straight to the compulsory questions** in Section B. You've got to do them so you might as well get them over and done with.

Once you've done the compulsory questions, you need to choose two of the questions in Section C.

- If you prefer working with numbers rather than providing written answers all of the questions include calculations though **question 5** would probably suit best. **The other two** include between half and three quarters of the marks for number work though as always in tandem with written commentary.

- Your reasoning for a choice between **questions 6 and 7** will probably depend on where you feel your knowledge is best. If you prefer relevant costing and limiting factor analysis then you'll choose **question 7**. If this fills you with horror, and you prefer ABC and absorption costing then go for question 6.

No matter how many times we remind you....

Always, always **allocate you time** according to the marks for the question in total and for the parts of the question. Always, **always follow the requirements** exactly. Question 6 part (b) asks for an analysis with examples so be ready to put down technical points but link these to your scenario.

If you do the parts of the question out of order, check that you answer all of them.

You've got spare time at the end of the exam.....?

If you have allocated your time properly then you **shouldn't have time on your hands** at the end of the exam. If you find yourself with five or ten minutes spare, however, **go back to the objective test questions** that you couldn't do or **any parts of questions that you didn't finish** because you ran out of time.

Forget about it!

And don't worry if you found the paper difficult. More than likely other candidates would too. If this were the real thing you would need to **forget** the exam the minute you leave the exam hall and **think about the next one**. Or, if it's the last one, **celebrate**!

MOCK EXAM 2: ANSWERS

SECTION A

Question 1

1.1 C Need to determine the lowest sales to earn contribution of £700,000.

Minimum sales must be met.

			£
P	Contribution on sales of £100,000 (× 20%)		20,000
Q	Contribution on sales of £100,000 (× 25%)		25,000
R	Contribution on sales of £100,000 (× 30%)		30,000
			75,000

Include R next as it has the **highest C/S ratio** and hence
earns the most contribution per £ of revenue

Contribution on difference between minimum and maximum sales
= 30% × £1,400,000   420,000

Q has the next **highest C/S ratio**.

Contribution on difference between minimum and maximum sales = 25%
× £900,000 = £225,000
Only require £(700,000 – 75,000 – 420,000) of contribution   205,000
∴   700,000

Revenue from this sales mix

	£'000
Minimum sales	300
R	1,400
Q (205/225 × £900,000)	820
	2,520

1.2 Formula for the learning curve is $Y = aX^b$

Here we have   Y   = cumulative average time per unit
                           a   = 100 hrs
                           X   = 8
                           b   = log 0.8/log 2 = – 0.322

∴ $Y = 100 \times 8^{-0.322}$ = 51.192 hours

∴ Total time for eight units = 51.192 × 8 = 409.536 hours

Total cost of order

	£
Labour (409.536 hrs × £6)	2,457
Material (£2,500 × 8)	20,000
Fixed costs	9,600
	32,057

∴ Average cost per unit = £32,057/8 = £4,007

403

MOCK EXAM 2: ANSWERS

1.3

		£m	£m
Development costs			(2.00)
Expected returns if development successful			
very successful	0.4 × 6m	2.40	
moderately successful	0.4 × 1.8m	0.72	
unsuccessful	0.2 × (5.0m)	(1.00)	
		2.12	
× probability of development being successful		× 0.75	
			1.59
Expected value of project			(0.41)

1.4 If the cash flows are expressed in constant price level terms, the real rate of 10% is used as the discount factor.

Option A is incorrect because the cash flows would take account of inflation but the discount rate would not.

Option C is incorrect because the money discount rate has been estimated (by addition). The correct money rate is found by

$(1 + \text{money rate}) = (1 + \text{real rate}) \times (1 + \text{inflation rate})$
$= 1.10 \times 1.03$
$= 1.133$

The money rate of 13.3% should be used to discount the inflated cash flows.

Option D is incorrect because the real cash flow, expressed in terms of constant price levels, would be discounted at an incorrect money rate.

Note. The question does not state that the cash flows are expressed in constant price level terms, but option B is the only correct answer however the cash flows are expressed.

1.5 **A** The calculation of breakeven sales value requires the average C/S ratio (from individual C/S ratios and the product mix ratio) and total fixed costs.

1.6 W has the highest EV of profit (0.8 × £50,000 – 0.2 × £80,000) and so should be chosen.

1.7 **B**

Budgeted revenue = 5,220 × £42 = £219,240

Margin of safety = 19.575%

∴ Breakeven revenue = £219,240 × (1 – 0.19575)
= £176,323.77

C/S ratio = 40%

∴ Contribution at breakeven point = £176,323.77 × 40%
= £70,529.508

At breakeven point, contribution = fixed costs

∴ Fixed costs closest to £71,000

MOCK EXAM 2: ANSWERS

SECTION B

Question 2

> **Top tips.** If you have a very disciplined mind you may have been able to do the whole calculation in four lines, but the layout below is more likely to reflect your thought processes in an exam situation – and it's kinder to your non-accounting managers, who may not be up to speed on relevant costs. Note the exam techniques of using a 'Notes' column, to fulfil the question requirements for explanations and assumptions without cluttering up the page, and of combining workings within the notes.

Heat recovery proposal

	Notes	Don't proceed £	Do proceed £	Net (saving)/cost £
Survey	1	30,000.00	30,000.00	0.00
Heat extraction	2	132,000.00	132,000.00	0.00
Pool heating	3	115,500.00	43,312.50	(72,187.50)
Equipment hire	4	0.00	75,000.00	75,000.00
Salary	5	0.00	17,500.00	17,500.00
		277,500.00	297,812.50	20,312.50

Recommendation

The **net cost** of proceeding with the proposal is £20,312.50. Unless non-financial factors are judged to be more important, the proposal **should not proceed**.

Notes

1 The cost of the **survey** is a **sunk** cost: it has already been incurred, whether or not the proposal goes ahead. (This line is strictly unnecessary in the calculation, and could be omitted, but it is included for the benefit of non-accounting managers.)

2 **Heat extraction** costs are **not incremental** costs: they will be incurred whether or not the proposal goes ahead, and so again this line is strictly unnecessary and could be omitted.

   The cost is calculated as £120,000 ×110% = £132,000.

3 **Pool heating** costs of £150,000 will rise by 10%, but only **70%** of this amount is **relevant** to the decision: the **remainder** is a **notional share of general fixed overhead**, and we must **assume** that this **percentage will not change** whatever decision is taken.

   Pool heating with the **existing** system = £150,000 × 110% × 70% = £115,500.

   If the **proposal goes ahead** the cost of **pool heating** can be calculated as follows.

Heat extracted from the ice rink (units)	500,000
Recovery level	25%
Recovered units	125,000
Heat required to heat the swimming pool (units)	200,000
Balance to be recovered from the existing system (units)	75,000

   In the absence of other information the **cost** of the balance can be **assumed** to be 75,000/200,000 × the existing heating cost of £115,500 (see above) = £43,312.50.

4 **Equipment hire** is an **incremental** cost: it will only be incurred if the proposal goes ahead.

5 The **supervisor** will retire, and will not be replaced if the proposal does not go ahead, so his **salary** is **only relevant** if he is retained to manage the **proposed** new equipment.

Question 3

> **Top tips.** It's a good idea to provide a table of results as we have done. This makes clear the information you have derived and enables you to draw the correct conclusion from it.

Option 1: direct mailing

Since each shot costs £0.25 and the total marketing budget is £200,000, the company could afford 800,000 shots.

Response rate		Units sold (40% of responses)	Net income (£10 per sale)	Probability	EV of net income
%	Units		£		£'000
6	48,000	19,200	192,000	0.15	28.8
8	64,000	25,600	256,000	0.65	166.4
12	96,000	38,400	384,000	0.20	76.8
					EV = 272.0

The standard deviation of option 1 (in £'000) is calculated as follows, where $\bar{x}$ = EV = £272,000

Net income £'000 x	Probability p	$x - \bar{x}$	$p(x - \bar{x})^2$
192	0.15	−80	960.0
256	0.65	−16	166.4
384	0.20	112	2,508.8
			Variance = 3,635.2

The standard deviation (in £'000) = $\sqrt{3,635.2}$ = 60.29, say £60,300

Option 2: advertising 52 times per year

Response rate per issue Units	per annum (× 52) Units	Units sold (40%)	Net income (£10 per sale) £	Probability	EV of net income £'000
700	36,400	14,560	145,600	0.20	29.12
1,400	72,800	29,120	291,200	0.55	160.16
2,000	104,000	41,600	416,000	0.25	104.00
					EV = 293.28

The standard deviation of option 2 (in £'000) is calculated as follows, where $\bar{x}$ = EV = £293,280

Net income £'000 x	Probability p	$x - \bar{x}$	$p(x - \bar{x})^2$
145.6	0.20	−147.68	4,361.88
291.2	0.55	−2.08	2.38
416.0	0.25	122.72	3,765.05
			Variance = 8,129.31

The standard deviation (in £'000) = $\sqrt{8,129.31}$ = 90.16, say £90,200

A solution may now be tabulated as follows.

	Low response £'000	Net income Average response £'000	High response £'000	EV of net income £'000	Standard deviation £'000
Direct mail	192	256	384	272	60.3
Newspaper advertisements	145.6	291.2	416	293.28	90.2

Recommendation

The option to advertise has a slightly higher EV but a greater 'risk', where risk is measured as a standard deviation. Investit management should therefore consider the option to use direct mail.

Question 4

> **Top tips.** 'Explain activity based management' is quite a wide requirement and so you may have had trouble producing a focused answer in the 18 minutes available. Even for short answers like this an answer plan is vital.

Activity based management (ABM)

An overview

Activity based management (ABM) is the term given to those **management processes that use the information provided by an activity-based cost analysis to improve organisational profitability**. It involves performing activities as efficiently as possible, controlling, reducing or eliminating the need to perform activities that do not add value for customers, minimising cost drivers, improving the design of products and developing better relationships with customers and suppliers. In short, it **aims to ensure that customer needs are met while fewer demands are made on organisational resources**.

ABM and TQM

ABM goes hand in hand with a commitment to the philosophy of total quality management and to a desire for continuous improvement, with the result that it **helps to deliver an improvement in product quality, an increase in customer satisfaction, lower costs and hence higher profitability**.

ABM and non-value added activities

It requires an understanding of the nature of non-value-added activities and their cost drivers, of the way in which costs are created and incurred at different levels (unit, batch, process, product and facility) in the complex modern industrial environment and of the long-term variable nature of fixed costs. But by **better understanding the underlying cost of making a product or performing a service**, new insights into product or service profitability can be obtained, with the result that product variety might be expanded or contracted, prices might be raised or lowered or a market might be entered or left.

ABM and performance

ABM **encourages and rewards employees** for developing new skills, accepting greater responsibilities and making suggestions for improvements in, for example, product design. Such improvements reduce non-value-added time and costs. Moreover, because it focuses on activities, ABM can **provide more appropriate measures of performance** than those used in traditional systems. Measures should relate to the performance that management wish to encourage or discourage and hence particularly appropriate measures relate to quality and service.

ABM versus life cycle budgeting

There are a number of similarities between ABM and life cycle budgeting. **Both attempt to increase management understanding of overhead costs** and **both look at the way in which inputs are used to produce required outputs. Both methods focus on improving and simplifying product design** but, whereas **life cycle budgeting reviews costs at the end of major stages in a product's life cycle**, ABM is a founded on an ethos of continuous improvement and hence **aims to reduce both short- and long-term costs**.

MOCK EXAM 2: ANSWERS

SECTION C

Question 5

Text references. This question asks for a lot of calculations but look at Chapters 11 and 12 if you get stuck on any aspects of NPVs.

Top tips. In (a) ensure that you answer the question and present two separate computations of NPV. Split computations into operational cash flows, which can be handled by annuities, and specific one-off cash flows, which cannot. The discount rate should be the real rate for each project, given and in each case reflecting the use of real costs and revenues, ie constant prices.

Don't be too depressed about getting aspects of the calculations wrong; instead carefully work through the answer to see why you went wrong and make sure you don't make the same mistake next time! Do also give yourself credit for the parts of the answer you got right.

Easy marks. We suggest that the easiest marks on the question are:

- Netting off the 800m revenues and costs
- The after tax demolition and redundancy costs which are given
- The t1 and t2 building costs
- The tax depreciation

The harder marks are for:

- The timings of cash flows
- The t4 – t28 operating cash in current terms
- The discount factor for the t28 demolition costs

The best answers will have correctly calculated or used:

- The real cost of capital
- The discounted cash flows

The discussion part of the question is worth five marks and you should make sure you spend enough time on this, as it should be easier to gain marks on (b) than on the more difficult calculations. The assumptions discussed in (b) range from those that only affect certain figures to those that change the whole picture (political changes or a disaster). Alternative scenarios, using different assumptions, may be helpful.

MOCK EXAM 2: ANSWERS

Discounted cash flow estimates: Gas

Annual operating cash flows	First 10 years	Last 15 years
Years	4–13	14–28
	£m	£m
Annual revenues	800.0	800
Annual costs		
Labour	75.0	75.0
Gas purchases	500.0	500.0
Sales and marketing expenses	40.0	40.0
Customer relations	5.0	5.0
Other cash outlays	5.0	5.0
	625.0	625.0
Incremental taxable	175.0	175.0
Tax at 30%	52.5	52.5
After tax cash flows	122.5	122.5
Tax depreciation	18.0	–
Incremental cash flow	140.5	122.5
Annuity factors at 6%		
Years 4–13 (8.853 – 2.673)	6.180	
Years 14–28 (13.406** – 8.853)		4.553
Present value	868.3	557.7

* Tax depreciation 600 × 10% × 30% = $18m.

** Using formula $\dfrac{1-(1+r)^{-n}}{r}$ for annuity 1-28.

Other cash flows

	Year				
	1	2	3	4	28
	£m	£m	£m	£m	£m
After tax redundancy costs				4	
Building costs (2 instalments)	300	300			
After tax demolition of coal fired station			10		
After tax demolition of gas plant					25
6% factors	0.943	0.890	0.840	0.792	0.196
Present value of costs	282.9	267.0	8.4	3.2	4.9

Total net present value = 868.3 + 557.7 – (282.9 + 267.0 + 8.4 + 3.2 + 4.9) = **£ 859.6 million**

Note: Interest is ignored from annual cost estimates because it (and the tax relief it attracts) is included in the after tax discount rate.

MOCK EXAM 2: ANSWERS

Discounted cash flow estimates: Nuclear power

	First 10 years	Last 15 years
Annual operating cash flows		
Years	4–13	14–28
	£m	£m
Annual revenues	800.0	
Annual costs		
Labour	20.0	
Nuclear fuel purchases	10.0	
Sales and marketing expenses	40.0	as for years 4–13
Customer relations	20.0	
Other cash outlays	25.0	
	115.0	
Incremental taxable cash flows	685.0	
Tax at 30%	205.5	
After tax cash flows	479.5	479.5
Tax on depreciation	99.0	
Incremental cash flow	578.5	479.5
Annuity factors at 8%		
Years 4–13 (7.904 – 2.577)	5.327	
Years 14–28 (11.051** – 7.904)		3.147
Present value	3,081.7	1,509.0

* Tax depreciation 3,300 × 10% × 30% = £99m

** Using annuity formula

Other cash flows

	Year				
	1	2	3	4	28
	£m	£m	£m	£m	£m
After tax redundancy costs				36	
Building costs (2 installments)	1,650	1,650			
After tax demolition of coal fired station			10		
After tax decommissioning of nuclear plant					1,000
8% factors	0.926	0.857	0.794	0.735	0.116
Present value of costs	1,527.9	1,414.1	7.9	26.5	116.0

Total net present value = 3,081.7 + 1,509.0 – (1,527.9 + 1,414.1 + 7.9 + 26.5 + 116.0)

= **£1,498.3 million**

Note: If the lowest estimate of nuclear plant decommissioning cost was used, the net present value would be £1,558 million.

Conclusion

On the basis of net present values applied to the estimates given, the nuclear plant should be chosen.

(b) The most significant factors to affect the decision which have not been taken into account above are:

(i) **Social and political acceptability of more nuclear powered station**

If **public opinion** is heavily **against** nuclear power, the government is unlikely to risk its political majority by deciding in favour of it. Even if a vocal minority is the only opposition, construction could be severely delayed by demonstrations and sabotaging actions. **Social and political intelligence** is therefore vital information.

MOCK EXAM 2: ANSWERS

(ii) **Risk of a rapid change in political acceptability of nuclear plants**

Future political acceptability may be influenced by a number of events. For example a number of **small leakages** could cause a nuclear plant to abandoned at any time during its life because of a fall in public acceptability. Threat of **terrorist action** may also cause political opinion to change. **Risk scenarios** need to be constructed and **contingency plans** devised.

(iii) **Risk of a large-scale nuclear accident or gas explosion**

Such risks are not easily analysed by expected values and NPV computations, but both events have actually happened in the past. Information needs to be collected to **model** these events as **scenarios**.

(iv) **Technical information**

It would be useful to evaluate the **technical information** underlying the projected construction and operation of the plants to ensure that best practice, particularly in **safety testing,** is envisaged and that costs are realistic to achieve the necessary quality. This may indicate how likely delays are during construction. **Industry information** on current developments would aid an evaluation of **how long** the stations would be **in operation**, and the consequences if technology changes. It might also enable a narrower estimate of the range of **decommissioning costs** to be made.

(v) **Fiscal changes**

Expected **future tax rates** and **capital allowances** may have a significant impact, including the possibility of 'green' taxes or constraints on polluting industries and likely treatment of gas and nuclear power under these taxes.

Question 6

Text references. Look at Chapter 16 for ABC and Chapter 1 for absorption costing.

Top tips. The calculations required in this question were very straightforward. Note that 40% of the marks available were actually for written answers. You cannot hope to pass the exam if you only practise on part (a) and ignore part (b). You may have been thrown by part (a)(i), having forgotten what you learnt about absorption costing in your earlier studies.

(a) (i) **Absorption costing approach**

	Product A	Product B
	£	£
Direct material cost per unit	16	30.00
Direct labour cost per unit	8	10.00
Variable overhead per unit (W)	13	18.75
	37	58.75

Workings

Materials-related overhead

Overhead = £1,500,000 × 40% = £600,000

Absorption base = total direct materials cost of all three products = £2,400,000

∴ Absorption rate = £(600,000 ÷ 2,400,000) × 100%
= 25% on direct material cost

MOCK EXAM 2: ANSWERS

Labour-related overhead

Overhead = £1,500,000 × 60% = £900,000

Absorption base = total direct labour cost for all three products = £800,000

∴ Absorption rate = £(900,000 ÷ 800,000) × 100%
= 112.5% on direct labour cost

Variable overhead per unit

	A £	B £
Material related 25% × £16/£30	4	7.50
Labour related 112.5% × £8/£10	9	11.25
	13	18.75

(ii) **ABC approach**

	A £	B £
Direct material cost per unit	16.00	30.00
Direct labour cost per unit	8.00	10.00
Variable overhead cost per unit (W)	71.68	14.17
	95.68	54.17

Workings

Material-related overheads

		Bulk '000
Number of cost drivers		
Product A	4 × 5,000	20
Product B	1 × 10,000	10
Product C	1.5 × 40,000	60
		90

∴ Overhead per cost driver = £600,000 ÷ 90,000
= £6.67

Labour-related overheads

		Labour operations '000
Number of cost drivers		
Product A	6 × 5,000	30
Product B	1 × 10,000	10
Product C	2 × 40,000	80
		120

∴ Overhead per cost driver = £900,000 ÷ 120,000 = £7.50

Variable overhead per unit

	A £	B £
Material related		
£6.67 × 4/1	26.68	6.67
Labour related		
£7.50 × 6/1	45.00	7.50
	71.68	14.17

(b)

REPORT

To: Management, S plc
From: Management accountant
Date: 12 December 20X6
Subject: **Production and sales strategy, Products A and B**

1 Overview

1.1 An analysis has been carried out of the variable overhead costs of production of products A and B using both our current method of calculation (absorption costing) and a more modern technique called activity based costing (ABC). The ABC approach is now widely considered to give a more accurate picture of the true costs of a product.

2 Results

2.1 The **figures** are included in Appendix 1 [ie part (a) of this answer] and may be **summarised as follows** for the two products under consideration.

	Product A		Product B	
	Absorption cost £	ABC cost £	Absorption cost £	ABC cost £
Selling price	75	75.00	95.00	95.00
Variable cost	37	95.68	58.75	54.17
Contribution	38	(20.68)	36.25	40.83
C/S ratio	51%	-	38%	43%

3 Decision

3.1 It has been stipulated that **products should have a contribution/sales ratio of at least 40%**.

3.2 Using this criterion and our existing costing method (**absorption costing**) production of **product A would continue but production of product B would cease.**

3.3 Using a 40% C/S ratio with **ABC** the opposite strategy should be adopted: **production of product B should continue but production of product A should cease.**

3.4 Note that under absorption costing, product B only narrowly fails to meet the required level of contribution, but under ABC product A fails completely (it has a negative contribution). Even with absorption costing, production of product B should not be stopped in the short term as long as it is making a positive contribution to fixed costs, unless the facilities used to produce it could be used more profitably in another way.

3.5 Given that ABC reflects the true causes of costs while absorption costing is merely an arbitrary method of allocating overheads, we should be **guided by the ABC** information and act accordingly. Unless a way can be found to reduce the costs of product A, production of it should cease but product B should continue to be produced.

4 Other factors

4.1 There are, of course, **other factors to be considered**, such as the long-term impact on business capabilities of shutting down production of a product, the reaction of customers, and the impact on staff.

Signed: Management accountant

MOCK EXAM 2: ANSWERS

Question 7

> **Text reference.** Refer to Chapter 5 to help you tackle the limiting factor parts to the question.
>
> **Top tips.** In part (a), the first step is to calculate how many units of A or B can be manufactured within the stated constraints. Then the contribution from each of these outputs can be calculated and compared.

(a) (i) **Alloy constraint**

Maximum number of either part = $\dfrac{13,000}{1.6}$ = 8,125 units

Line S constraint

Maximum number of part A = $\dfrac{4,000}{0.6}$ = 6,666 units

Maximum number of part B = $\dfrac{4,000}{0.25}$ = 16,000 units

Line T constraint

Maximum number of part A = $\dfrac{4,500}{0.5}$ = 9,000 units

Maximum number of part B = $\dfrac{4,500}{0.55}$ = 8,181 units

Taking the three constraints together, maximum possible production is as follows.

Part A	6,666 units
Part B	8,125 units

This is **below the maximum call-off for each part and so is the number of each which would be manufactured.**

Contribution achievable

Part A – 6,666 units

	£ per unit	£	£
Sales revenue	145		966,570
Alloy	20	133,320	
Line S costs	48	319,968	
Line T costs	50	333,300	
			786,588
Contribution achievable			179,982

Part B – 8,125 units

	£ per unit	£	£
Sales revenue	115		934,375
Alloy	20	162,500	
Line S costs	20	162,500	
Line T costs	55	446,875	
			771,875
Contribution achievable			162,500

Therefore **part A** should be manufactured during the next period to maximise contribution.

(ii) From (i), contribution earned will be £179,982 and the company will not be able to meet the maximum call-off. If the **constraint on line S** were **alleviated** then the **maximum call-off for part A could be met.**

(iii)   **Part A**

	£
Receipts for unused machine hours	
Line S	-
Line T [4,500 – (6,666 × 0.5)] × £60	70,020
Less reduction in sales revenue, 10% × £966,570	96,657
Reduction in contribution	26,637
Original contribution	179,982
Revised contribution	153,345

Part B

	£
Receipts for unused machine hours	
Line S [4,000 – (8,125 × 0.25)] × £60	118,125
Line T [4,500 – (8,125 × 0.55)] × £60	1,875
	120,000
Less reduction in revenue, 10% × £934,375	93,438
Increase in contribution	26,562
Original contribution	162,500
Revised contribution	189,062

Therefore the **recommendation in part** (i) **would be altered**. The company should manufacture part **B**, earning a contribution of £189,062.

(b) (i)   **Planning**

Joint cost **apportionments** are carried out on an **arbitrary basis**, often using output volume or sales value as the basis of apportionment. The resulting **unit costs** can **differ** widely **depending** on which **apportionment basis** is selected.

Managers using the resulting unit costs for **planning** purposes **may not arrive** at **correct cost projections if they assume that they are relevant for any volume of output of each product**.

(ii)   **Control**

Cost control is achieved by **comparing actual costs** with a **standard** or **budget cost**. The **budget** costs must be a **realistic target** for the actual output which was achieved. This means that budgeted costs must be **flexed** to allow for changes in output volume, and then actual costs should be compared with these flexed costs.

The **apportioned joint costs** must therefore be **separated** into their **fixed** and **variable** elements so that the total budget cost can be correctly **flexed** to allow for changes in activity.

If costs are **correctly analysed** into their fixed and variable components then **apportioned joint costs** can be used for the **control** of total costs.

No extra control information is obtained by carrying out the joint cost apportionment, however, since such an **apportionment** is purely **arbitrary**.

(iii)   **Decision making**

Apportioned joint costs are of little use for decision making and in fact they can produce information which would lead to incorrect decisions.

Simply by changing the basis of cost **apportionment** it is possible to make an unprofitable product appear profitable, and *vice versa*.

Management should be encouraged to **concentrate** attention on the **incremental costs** over which they can exercise control. They can **only control the total amount of joint costs** and they may be misled by the product 'profits' or 'losses' which result from arbitrary apportionment of joint costs.

CIMA – Managerial Level

Paper P2

Management Accounting Decision Management

Mock Examination 3

November 2007 paper

Instructions to candidates:

You are allowed three hours to answer this question paper.
In the real exam, you are allowed 20 minutes reading time before the examination begins during which you should read the question paper, and if you wish, make annotations on the question paper. However, you will **not** be allowed, **under any circumstances**, to open the answer book and start writing or use your calculator during this reading time.
You are strongly advised to carefully read the question requirement before attempting the question concerned.
Answer the ONE compulsory question in Section A. This is comprised of sub-questions.
Answer ALL THREE compulsory sub-questions in Section B.
Answer TWO of the three questions in Section C.

DO NOT OPEN THIS PAPER UNTIL YOU ARE READY TO START UNDER EXAMINATION CONDITIONS

SECTION A – 20 marks

Answer ALL EIGHT sub-questions

Question 1

1.1 (i) Penetration pricing is a strategy that is often used in the decline phase of a product's life cycle.
(ii) In the context of quality costs, Conformance Costs are always equal to Internal Failure Costs.

Which of the above statements are correct?

A (i) only
B (ii) only
C Both
D Neither (2 marks)

1.2 The following details relate to Product Z:

	$/unit
Selling price	45.00
Purchased components	14.00
Labour	10.00
Variable overhead	8.50
Fixed overhead	4.50
Time on bottleneck resource	10 minutes

Product return per minute is

A $0.80
B $1.25
C $2.10
D $3.10 (2 marks)

1.3 In the context of quality costs, customer compensation costs and test equipment running costs would be classified as:

	Customer compensation costs	Test equipment running costs
A	Internal Failure Costs	Prevention Costs
B	Internal Failure Costs	Appraisal Costs
C	External Failure Costs	Appraisal Costs
D	External Failure Costs	Prevention Costs

(2 marks)

1.4 A company has an annual money cost of capital of 20% and inflation is 8% per annum. Calculate the company's annual real percentage cost of capital to 2 decimal places (2 marks)

1.5 A project has a net present value of $683,000. The present value of the direct material cost is $825,000. Calculate the sensitivity of the project to changes in the direct material cost to 2 decimal places. (2 marks)

MOCK EXAM 3 (NOVEMBER 2007): QUESTIONS

1.6 RDE plc uses an activity based costing system to attribute overhead costs to its three products. The following budgeted data relates to the year to 31 December 2008:

Product	X	Y	Z
Production units (000)	15	25	20
Batch size (000 units)	2·5	5	4

Machine set up costs are caused by the number of batches of each product and have been estimated to be £600,000 for the year.

Calculate the machine set up costs that would be attributed to each unit of product Y. **(3 marks)**

1.7 A company is considering an investment of $400,000 in new machinery. The machinery is expected to yield incremental profits over the next five years as follows:

Year	Profit ($)
1	175,000
2	225,000
3	340,000
4	165,000
5	125,000

Thereafter, no incremental profits are expected and the machinery will be sold. It is company policy to depreciate machinery on a straight line basis over the life of the asset. The machinery is expected to have a value of $50,000 at the end of year 5.

Calculate the payback period of the investment in this machinery to the nearest 0·1 years. **(3 marks)**

1.8 A company has determined its activity level and is now predicting its costs for the quarter ended 31 March 2008. It has made the following predictions:

Variable costs	Probability	Fixed costs	Probability
$560,000	0·3	$440,000	0·15
$780,000	0·5	$640,000	0·55
$950,000	0·2	$760,000	0·30

Calculate the expected value of total cost and its standard deviation.

Note: $SD = \sqrt{\dfrac{\Sigma(x - \bar{x})^2}{n}}$

(4 marks)

(Total for Section A = 20 marks)

SECTION B – 30 MARKS

Answer ALL THREE questions

Question Two

You are the management accountant of a new small company that has developed a new product using a labour intensive production process. You have recently completed the budgets for the company for next year and, before they are approved by the Board of Directors, you have been asked to explain your calculation of the labour time required for the budgeted output. In your calculations, you anticipated that the time taken for the first unit would be 40 minutes and that a 75% learning curve would apply for the first 30 units.

Required:

(a) Explain the concept of the learning curve and why it may be relevant to the above company. **(3 marks)**

(b) Calculate the expected time for the 6th unit of output. **(3 marks)**

(c) Discuss the implications of the learning curve for a company adopting a penetration pricing policy.

(4 marks)

(Total for Question Two = 10 marks)

Note: The learning index for a 75% learning curve is −0·415

Question Three

HS manufactures components for use in computers. The business operates in a highly competitive market where there are a large number of manufacturers of similar components. HS is considering its pricing strategy for the next twelve weeks for one of its components. The Managing Director seeks your advice to determine the selling price that will maximise the profit to be made during this period.

You have been given the following data:

Market Demand

The current selling price of the component is $1,350 and at this price the average weekly demand over the last four weeks has been 8,000 components. An analysis of the market shows that for every $50 increase in selling price the demand reduces by 1,000 components per week. Equally, for every $50 reduction in selling price the demand increases by 1,000 components per week.

Costs

The direct material cost of each component is $270. This price is part of a fixed price contract with the material suppliers and the contract does not expire for another year.

Production labour and conversion costs, together with other overhead costs and the corresponding output volumes, have been collected for the last four weeks and they are as follows:

Week	Output volume (units)	$000
1	9,400	7,000
2	7,600	5,688
3	8,500	6,334
4	7,300	5,446

No significant changes in cost behaviour are expected over the next twelve weeks.

Required:

(a) Calculate the optimum (profit maximising) selling price of the component for the period.

Note: If Price = a - bq then Marginal Revenue = a - 2bq (6 marks)

(b) Identify and explain two reasons why it may be inappropriate for HS to use this theoretical pricing model in practice. (4 marks)

(Total for Question Three = 10 marks)

Question Four

The owner of a tourist hotel is facing a difficult decision. It is low season and because the weather is unpredictable at this time of the year it is difficult to predict the demand for the hotel's facilities. If the weather is poor then there will be 200 room nights demanded for the hotel's facilities. There is a 70% likelihood of the weather being poor. If the weather is good then there will be 600 room nights demanded for the hotel's facilities, but there is only a 30% chance that the weather will be good.

The owner of the hotel is considering advertising some reduced prices locally or nationally in order to improve the demand during this period.

If the reduced prices are advertised locally and if the weather is poor, then there is a 60% chance that the lower prices would affect demand and would cause there to be 300 room nights demanded, but if the weather is good, then there is a 40% chance that the lower prices would affect demand and would cause there to be 800 room nights demanded.

If these lower prices were advertised nationally there is a 50% chance that these demand levels would increase to 400 room nights and 900 room nights respectively.

The earnings expected, (before deducting the costs of any local or national advertising), at different levels of demand are as follows:

Room nights demanded	Earnings ($)
200	(35,000)
300	(15,000)
400	(5,000)
500	20,000
600	30,000
700	45,000
800	65,000
900	90,000

The costs of advertising locally and nationally are $10,000 and $25,000 respectively.

Required:

(a) Prepare a decision tree to illustrate the above problem and use this to recommend, with reasons, the best course of action for the owner of the hotel. (7 marks)

(b) Briefly discuss the limitations of using a decision tree to solve this problem. (3 marks)

(Total for Question Four = 10 marks)

(Total for Section B = 30 marks)

SECTION C – 50 MARKS

Answer TWO questions out of three

Question Five

SQ manufactures and sells a range of products. Details for one of the products, product Q, are shown below.

Existing Production Facility

The present production facility can continue to be used to produce up to 120,000 units of product Q each year. It is estimated that the facility can be used for a further five years but annual maintenance costs will rise substantially. An analysis of the latest costs is set out below:

	$ per unit
Direct materials	50
Direct labour	30
Variable production overhead	25
Fixed production overhead*	20
Variable selling and distribution overhead**	10

* The fixed production overhead costs are absorbed into product costs using an absorption rate which is 25% of prime cost. These fixed overhead costs are mainly central production facility costs that are not specific to any particular product or activity and would continue to be incurred regardless of the production method used by SQ. However they also include facility maintenance costs (see above). In addition SQ incurs annual fixed non-production costs of $24 million.

** These are selling and distribution costs that are not affected by the production method that is used for the product.

Proposed New Production Facility

The company is considering an investment of $4 million in a new production facility for product Q. The new facility is to be operational from 1 January 2008. It will have a life of five years and at the end of its life it will have a residual value of $0·4 million. It is expected that the facility will have significant benefits. Firstly it will increase SQ's production capacity for product Q by 30%, secondly it will reduce product Q's direct labour and variable production overhead costs by 20% per unit and finally the savings in annual maintenance costs will be as follows:

Year	$000
20X8	70
20X9	80
20Y0	80
20Y1	110
20Y2	130

You have also obtained the following further information:

Demand

Currently SQ produces 120,000 units of product Q each year and these sell for $150 per unit. There is significant demand for the product and SQ estimates that it could sell more units if it had the capacity to produce them. If the selling price remains unchanged, customer demand for 2008 and future years is estimated to be as shown in the following table:

Year	Customer demand (units)
20X8	130,000
20X9	140,000
20Y0	147,000
20Y1	154,000
20Y2	162,000

Cost Structure

No changes are expected to either cost structure or to cost levels other than those referred to above.

Taxation

SQ pays corporation tax at the rate of 30% of its taxable profits. Half of this tax is payable in the year in which the profit is earned and the other half is payable one year later. If the investment in the new production facility goes ahead on 1 January 2008 (the first day of SQ's accounting year) it will qualify for tax depreciation at the rate of 25% per annum on a reducing balance basis.

Cost of Capital

SQ's after tax cost of capital is 12% per annum.

Required:

(a) (i) Calculate the Net Present Value (NPV) of the investment in the new facility. **(14 marks)**

    (ii) Explain **two** other factors that SQ should consider before making its decision. **(4 marks)**

(b) A company is thinking of investing in a new project. The details are as follows:

Investment	$15,000
Time span	3 years
Annual cash inflows	$30,000
Annual cash outflows	$22,500
Cost of capital	10%
NPV @ 10%	$3,652·50

The project does not have a residual value. Ignore taxation.

(i) Calculate the Internal Rate of Return (IRR) of the investment proposal. **(3 marks)**

(ii) Calculate the sensitivity of the investment to changes in the annual cash inflows. **(4 marks)**

(Total for Question Five = 25 marks)

Question Six

DFG manufactures two products from different combinations of the same resources. Unit selling prices and unit cost details for each product are as follows:

Product	D	G
	£/unit	£/unit
Selling price	115	120
Direct material A (£5 per kg)	20	10
Direct material B (£3 per kg)	12	24
Skilled labour (£7 per hour)	28	21
Variable overhead (£2 per machine hour)	14	18
Fixed overhead*	28	36
Profit	13	11

*Fixed overhead is absorbed using an absorption rate per machine hour. It is an unavoidable central overhead cost that is not affected by the mix or volume of products produced.

The maximum weekly demand for products D and G is 400 units and 450 units respectively and this is the normal weekly production volume achieved by DFG. However, for the next four weeks the achievable production level will be reduced due to a shortage of available resources. The resources that are expected to be available are as follows:

Direct material A	1,800kg
Direct material B	3,500kg
Skilled labour	2,500 hours
Machine time	6,500 machine hours

Required:

(a) Using graphical linear programming identify the weekly production schedule for products D and G that maximises the profits of DFG during the next four weeks. **(15 marks)**

(b) The optimal solution to part *(a)* shows that the shadow prices of Skilled labour and Direct material A are as follows:

Skilled labour £Nil

Direct material A £5·82

Explain the relevance of these values to the management of DFG. **(6 marks)**

(c) Using the graph you have drawn in part *(a)* explain how you would calculate by how much the selling price of Product D could rise before the optimal solution would change.

Note: Assume that demand is not affected by the selling price. You are **not** required to perform any calculations.

(4 marks)

(Total for Question Six = 25 marks)

Question Seven

A small retail outlet sells four main groups of products: Basic Foods (milk, bread, etc); Newspapers & Magazines; Frozen Foods; and Canned Foods. A budgeted weekly profit statement is shown below:

	Basic Foods	Newspapers and Magazines	Frozen Foods	Canned Foods
	$	$	$	$
Sales revenue	800	1,000	1,500	2,400
Cost of sales	600	700	550	1,200
Gross margin	200	300	950	1,200
Power for freezers*			100	
Overheads**	100	100	200	400
Net margin	100	200	650	800

*The freezers would be emptied and switched off as necessary during redecoration.

**Overhead costs comprise general costs of heating and lighting, rent and rates, and other general overhead costs. These costs are attributed to products in proportion to the floor area occupied by each product group which is as follows:

	Basic Foods	Newspapers and Magazines	Frozen Foods	Canned Foods
Floor area (m^3)	50	50	100	200

For each product group, analysis has shown that the sales revenue achieved changes in direct proportion to the floor space allocated to the product.

The owner of the retail outlet has decided that the premises need to be redecorated but is undecided as to which of the following two options would be the most profitable.

Option 1

Close the retail outlet completely for four weeks while the redecoration takes place. The company that is to complete the redecoration would charge $2,500 under this option. It is expected that following the re-opening of the retail outlet there would be a loss of sales for the next 12 weeks because customers would have had to find alternative suppliers for their goods. The reduction in sales due to lost customers has been estimated to be 30% of the budgeted sales during the first four weeks of reopening; 20% during the next four weeks; and 10% during the third four weeks. In addition, in order to encourage customers to return to the retail outlet, there would be a 10% price reduction on all Basic Foods and Canned Foods for the entire 12 week period.

Option 2

Continue to open the retail outlet while the redecoration takes place but with a reduced amount of floor area. The useable floor area would be reduced to 40% of that originally available. After three weeks, the retail outlet would be closed for 0·5 weeks while the goods are moved to the newly redecorated area. The retail outlet would then continue to operate using 40% of its original floor area for a further three weeks before the work was fully completed. The company that is to complete the redecoration would charge $3,500 under this option, and in addition there would be product movement costs of $1,000. The owner has determined that in order to avoid losing customers there should be no reduction in the amount of floor area given to Basic Foods and Newspapers and Magazines throughout this period. The floor area to be used by Frozen Foods and Canned Foods should be determined on the basis of their profitability per unit of area. However, the Frozen Foods are presently kept in four freezers, and therefore any reductions in floor area must be determined by complete freezer units. It may be assumed that each freezer unit incurs equal amounts of power costs.

Required:

(a) Advise the owner of the retail outlet which option to choose in order to minimise the losses that will occur as a result of the decision. All workings must be shown. **(15 marks)**

(b) Explain how Activity Based Costing may be used in a retail environment to improve the decision making and profitability of the business. **(10 marks)**

(Total for Question Seven = 25 marks)

(Total for Section C = 50 marks)

Answers

DO NOT TURN THIS PAGE UNTIL YOU HAVE COMPLETED THE MOCK EXAM

////MOCK EXAM 3 (NOVEMBER 2007): ANSWERS

A PLAN OF ATTACK

What's the worst thing you could be doing right now if this was the actual exam paper? Sharpening your pencil? Wondering how to celebrate the end of the exam in 2 hours 59 minutes' time? Panicking, flapping and generally getting in a real state?

The exam allows 20 minutes' reading time so we've included advice on how you can use this extra time.

First things first – the 20 minutes' reading time

A large chunk of the 20 minutes should be spent reading Section C. These are the longest questions with the most information to digest, and you have to decide which two questions you are going to attempt. Take 10 minutes to read the questions thoroughly, making sure you read the requirements as well as the content. When you have decided which questions you are going to attempt, start picking out the relevant data from the questions, setting up working layouts and brainstorming ideas for discussion points.

Normally this would take up the entire 20 minutes, but in this exam there was a compulsory question on decision trees to consider. It is worthwhile spending a couple of minutes reading this Section B question and thinking about how to draw the decision tree. Most people know to their cost that decision trees are not easy to draw, particularly under pressure, so a bit of preparation here will be invaluable.

Don't waste time on the objective test questions. There is little to be gained from duplicating workings that cannot go into the answer book until the exam begins. Leave Question One until the last 40 minutes of the real exam time.

The next step

You have **two options** now.

Option 1 (if you're thinking 'Help!')

If you're a bit worried about the paper, do the questions in the order of how well you think you can answer them.

Question 5 on NPV is relatively straightforward therefore it may be a good idea to get one of the longer questions out of the way first. It is a very numerical question, with only 4 marks available for discussion, so if you prefer working with numbers then this is a good place to start. However, it is quite a time-pressured question so make sure you take a methodical approach to the calculations and lay them out in tabular format as much as possible.

If you prefer a more discursive questions to start with, you could try **Question 2** on learning curves. Seven out of the 10 available marks are for explanation and discussion, although part (c) is reasonably tricky as it relates learning curves to penetration pricing.

If you are familiar with the six-step approach to linear programming (as shown in the P2 Study Text) then you will probably want to attempt **Question 6**. There are 15 marks available for the graphical approach to linear programming, with the rest coming from shadow prices and sensitivity analysis.

If you really hate linear programming, you will probably want to try **Question 7** (relevant costing and ABC) next. Don't be misled by part (a) – it looks straightforward but once you get further into the question you will find quite a few complications. It might be a good idea to attempt the 10 mark narrative part (b) first as it has no connection to part (a) before getting too involved in the lengthy calculations that are required for part (a).

This leaves the remaining compulsory questions in Section B – **questions 3 and 4**. **Question 3** asks you to calculate the optimum selling price and if you are familiar with how to use the formulae then this should be quite straightforward. In part (b), remember to relate your answer to the company in the scenario, rather than giving a generic answer.

Question 4 on decision trees should be left to the end, just before you attempt **Question One**. This question is very time pressured as it only allows just over 12 minutes to draw the tree. Try answering part (b) first – at least you will have attempted 30% of the marks available before attempting part (a).

What you mustn't forget is that you have to **answer question 2, question 3 and question 4 (all questions in Section B) and TWO from questions 5, 6 and 7 (Section C).** Once you have decided on the two questions you want to answer from Section C, it might be worthwhile putting a line through the third one so that you are not tempted to answer it!

Option 2 (if you're thinking 'This is a doddle!')

It never pays to be over-confident, but if you like the look of all the questions then **turn straight to question 2, the first of the compulsory questions**. Attempt **questions 2 and 3** and then decide which two of the three Section C questions you want to answer.

If you prefer working with numbers, then you will definitely want to attempt **question 5**. **Questions 6 and 7** each have 10 marks available for explanations therefore you will have to decide where you feel your strengths lie.

If you prefer more discursive questions, you will probably want to attempt **questions 6 and 7**, particularly if investment appraisal is not one of your favourite topics!

No matter how many times we remind you...

Always, always **allocate your time** according to the marks for the question in total and for the parts of the question. Always, **always follow the requirements** exactly – and always, **always answer the entire question**. If you do the parts of the question out of order, check that you answer all of them and clearly label each part so that the marker knows which answers relate to which part of the question.

You've got spare time at the end of the exam...?

If you have allocated your time properly then you **shouldn't have time on your hands** at the end of the exam. If you find yourself with five or ten minutes to spare however **go back to the objective test questions** that you couldn't do or **any parts of questions that you didn't finish** because you ran out of time.

Forget about it!

Don't worry if you found the paper difficult. More than likely other candidates would too. If this were the real thing you would need to **forget** the exam the minute you leave the exam hall and **think about the next one**. Or, if it's the last one, **celebrate**!

MOCK EXAM 3 (NOVEMBER 2007): ANSWERS

Section A

Question 1

1.1 The correct answer is D.

Penetration pricing is a policy of low pricing used when a product is first launched in order to obtain sufficient penetration into the market.

Conformance costs are not always equal to internal failure costs (part of non-conformance costs). Conformance costs will be equal to total non-conformance costs (that is, total internal and external failure costs) at the point where total costs of quality are minimised.

1.2 The correct answer is D.

$$\text{Product return per minute} = \frac{\text{Sales price} - \text{Material Costs}}{\text{Minutes spent on bottleneck resource}}$$

$$= \frac{45.00 - 14.00}{10}$$

$$= \$3.10 \text{ per minute}$$

1.3 The correct answer is C.

Customer compensation costs are external failure costs (that is the cost resulting from inadequate quality of goods after the purchaser has taken ownership of the goods).

Test equipment running costs are appraisal costs (costs incurred to ensure that products meet required quality standards).

1.4 (1 + money rate) = (1 + real rate) × (1 + inflation rate)

$$(1 + \text{real rate}) = \frac{(1 + \text{money rate})}{(1 + \text{inflation rate})}$$

$$(1 + \text{real rate}) = \frac{(1 + 0.2)}{(1 + 0.08)}$$

(1 + real rate) = 1.1111

∴ Annual real percentage = 11.11%

1.5 The present value of the direct materials can increase by $683,000 before the project breaks even.

$$\text{Direct material costs may therefore increase by } \frac{683,000}{825,000} \times 100$$

$$= 82.79\%$$

1.6 **Step 1** **Cost driver is number of batches, therefore calculate number of batches for each product and in total.**

	X	Y	Z	Total
Number of batches $= \dfrac{\text{Production units}}{\text{Batch size}}$	$\dfrac{15}{2.5}$	$\dfrac{25}{5}$	$\dfrac{20}{4}$	
	= 6	= 5	= 5	16

433

MOCK EXAM 3 (NOVEMBER 2007): ANSWERS

Step 2 Calculate machine set-up costs attributable to product Y using number of batches as the allocation basis.

	Y
Machine set up costs	$\frac{5}{16} \times 600,000$
	= £187,500

Step 3 Calculate the machine set-up costs that would be attributable to each unit of Product Y:

Machine set up costs	=	£187,500
Production units	=	25,000
Machine set-up costs per unit	=	£7.50

1.7

Step 1 as payback is calculated using cash flows, we have to convert profits into cash flows by adding back depreciations.

$$\text{Depreciation per annum} = \frac{\text{Cost - Residual Value}}{\text{Expected useful life}}$$

$$= \frac{400,000 - 50,000}{5}$$

$$= \$70,000$$

Year	Profit ($)	Depreciation ($)	Cash flow ($)
1	175,000	70,000	245,000
2	225,000	70,000	295,000
3	340,000	70,000	410,000
4	165,000	70,000	235,000
5	125,000	70,000	195,000

Step 2 Calculate payback period using the cash flows calculated in Step 1 above.

Year	Cash flow	Cumulative Cash flow
0	(400,000)	(400,000)
1	245,000	(155,000)
2	295,000	140,000

Payback is between one and two years. Use interpolation to obtain a more accurate answer:

$$\text{Payback} = 1 + \frac{155,000}{295,000} \text{ years}$$

= 1.5 years (to nearest 0.1 years)

1.8

Expected Value of Total Costs

= Expected Value of Variable Costs + Expected Value of Fixed Costs.

Variable Costs	Probability	Expected Value	Fixed Costs	Probability	Expected Value
$560,000	0.3	$168,000	$440,000	0.15	$66,000
$780,000	0.5	$390,000	$640,000	0.55	$352,000
$950,000	0.2	$190,000	$760,000	0.30	$228,000
		$748,000			$646,000

Expected Value of Total Costs = $748,000 + 646,000

= $1,394,000

Standard Deviation:

Step 1 Produce a 2-way data table showing all possible combinations of Fixed and Variable Costs, and thus all possible outcomes for Total Costs:

Fixed Costs	Variable Costs		
	$560,000	$780,000	$950,000
$440,000	1,000,000	1,220,000	1,390,000
$640,000	1,200,000	1,420,000	1,590,000
$760,000	1,320,000	1,540,000	1,710,000

Step 2 Calculate $\sum(x-\bar{x})^2$ (where $\bar{x} = \$1,394,000$)

x ($'000)	$(x-\bar{x})^2$ ($'000)
1,000	155,236
1,200	37,636
1,220	30,276
1,320	5,476
1,390	16
1,420	676
1,540	21,316
1,590	38,416
1,710	99,856
	388,904

Step 3 Calculate standard deviation (where n=9)

$$SD = \sqrt{\frac{388,904}{9}}$$

= 207.874 or $207,874

Question 2

Text references: Chapter 15 for learning curve theory and formula; Chapter 8 for penetration pricing.

Top tips: Remember to relate your answer to part (a) to the company mentioned in the scenario – it is tempting to write all you know about learning curve theory, but this would only be answering part of the question. In part (c), avoid just defining penetration pricing – relate what you know about the circumstances in which learning curve theory may be applied to those in which penetration pricing may be used.

Easy marks: If you know the learning curve formula, part (b) provides 3 easy marks.

Section B

2 (a) The learning curve's concept is that, as complex and labour-intensive tasks are repeated, the average time taken to complete each task will decrease. In addition, learning curve theory states that the cumulative average time taken per unit or task will fall by a contest percentage every time total output doubles.

The learning curve concept is relevant to this company as its product is produced using a labour intensive production process. The company is also developing a new product, for which a learning curve effect could be expected. As the company is a small one, it may be that the product will be made in relatively small quantities, a characteristic of production for which labour time should be expected to decline as output increases.

(b) **Expected time for the 6th unit of output**:

Learning curve formula: $Y_x = aX^b$

$Y_6 = 40 \times 6^{-0.415}$

$Y_6 = 19$ minutes (to the nearest minute)

$Y_5 = 40 \times 5^{-0.415}$

$= 20.511$ or 20 minutes (to the nearest minute)

Cumulative units	Cumulative average time per unit (mins)	Total time (mins)
6	19	114
5	20	100
		14

The expected time for the 6th unit of output is therefore 14 minutes.

(c) **Implications of the learning curve where a penetration pricing policy is adopted**:

One of the circumstances in which penetration pricing may be appropriate is where significant economies of scale can be made from producing high levels of output, and companies therefore initially charge very low prices to gain a foothold in the market. Learning curve theory is more appropriate for products that are produced in small quantities, therefore a company adopting penetration pricing are less likely to be using a highly labour intensive process, given the desire to produce large volumes. Learning curve theory does not apply itself to highly mechanised processes that are generally employed to achieve high levels of output.

However, learning curve theory can be useful when quoting selling prices that are calculated on a 'cost plus' basis. Penetration pricing tends to involve setting the lowest possible price whilst still covering costs (a "cost plus zero" approach). Learning curve theory may be useful for identifying the cost of producing a product and thus identifying the lowest possible price that could be charged.

Question 3

Text references: Deriving profit – maximising selling prices is covered in Chapter 8. Target costing is in Chapter 15.

Top tips: Part (a) requires a methodical approach to ensure you have calculated all the required elements, so make sure you label all your workings. There is a temptation to use the material cost of $270 as the marginal cost, but the true marginal (variable) cost has to be calculated using the high-low method.

Easy marks: If you remember the formula for a, and the steps in calculating profit – maximising prices, you should be able to pick up the majority of the marks in part (a).

(a) **Step 1** Determine a and b for use in the Marginal Revenue equation.

b = $50

$a = \$1{,}350 + \left[\left(\dfrac{8{,}000}{1{,}000}\right) \times 50\right] = \$1{,}750$

Step 2 Calculate Marginal Revenue using the equation given in the question.

MR = $1{,}750 - (2 \times 50)q$

MR = $1{,}750 - 100q$

Step 3 Calculate Marginal Cost using the high-low method.

Highest output	9,400 units	Total Cost ($'000)	= 7,000
Lowest output	7,300 units	Total Cost ($'000)	= 5,446
Change in units	2,100	Change in cost ($'000)	= 1,554

$$\text{Variable (Marginal) Cost per unit} = \frac{\text{Change in cost}}{\text{Change in units}}$$

$$= \frac{1,554,000}{2,100}$$

$$= \$740 \text{ per unit.}$$

Step 4 Calculate optimum selling price

Profit is maximised where MR = MC

ie where $1,750 - 100q = 740 + 270$

$100q = 1,750 - 1,010$

$q = 7.40$ (profit-maximising demand)

Price = $a - bq$

$= 1,750 - (50 \times 7.4)$

$= \$1,38$

Profit maximising price is $1,380.

(b) **Why this theoretical pricing model may be inappropriate:**

It is extremely difficult to determine a demand factor with any degree of accuracy, therefore HS may end up making the wrong pricing decision. In a highly competitive environment, this could prove to be disastrous, as customers will simply switch to a different supplier.

Rather than aiming for maximum profit, most organisations will try to achieve a target profit. As HS operates in a highly competitive environment, profit maximisation is unrealistic – it would be more appropriate (and motivational) to have a target profit in mind and price accordingly.

Question 4

Text references: Decision trees are covered in Chapter 14.

Top tips: Always draw decision trees with a pencil initially, and use a ruler to make the tree as neat as possible. This is a challenging question for the marks available, so try to gain as many marks as possible through clear labelling of the tree. Remember to answer the question – it is really easy to get so involved in drawing the tree that you forget what the question actually asked.

Easy marks: There are three easy marks to be gained in part (b) if you have an appreciation of the limitations of decision trees.

MOCK EXAM 3 (NOVEMBER 2007): ANSWERS

(a)

[Decision tree diagram]

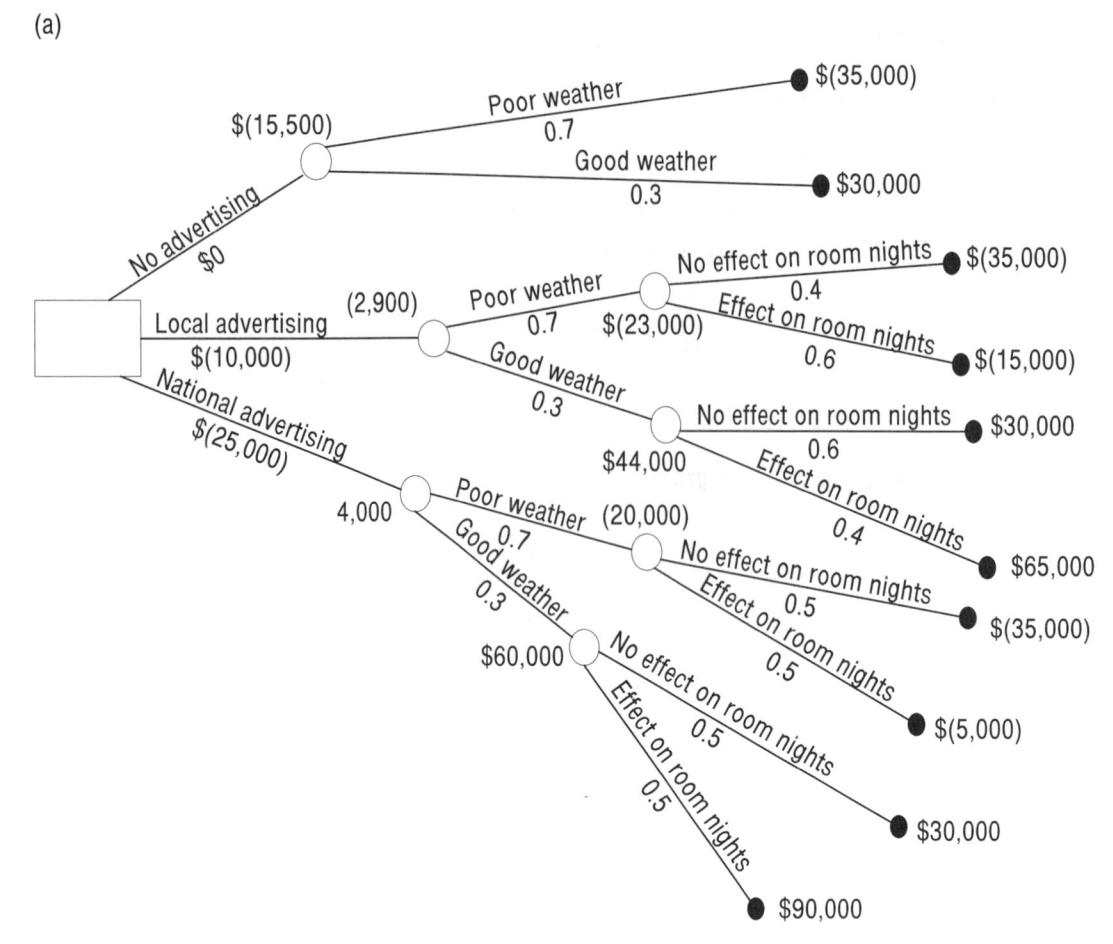

- No advertising $0 → $(15,500)
  - Poor weather 0.7 → $(35,000)
  - Good weather 0.3 → $30,000
- Local advertising $(10,000) → (2,900)
  - Poor weather 0.7 → $(23,000)
    - No effect on room nights 0.4 → $(35,000)
    - Effect on room nights 0.6 → $(15,000)
  - Good weather 0.3 → $44,000
    - No effect on room nights 0.6 → $30,000
    - Effect on room nights 0.4 → $65,000
- National advertising $(25,000) → 4,000
  - Poor weather 0.7 → (20,000)
    - No effect on room nights 0.5 → $(35,000)
    - Effect on room nights 0.5 → $(5,000)
  - Good weather 0.3 → $60,000
    - No effect on room nights 0.5 → $30,000
    - Effect on room nights 0.5 → $90,000

The expected outcomes for each level of advertising are:

No advertising: $(15,500) ie $(35,000) × 0.7 + $30,000 × 0.30

Local advertising: $(2,900) – 10,000 = $(12,900)

National advertising: $4,000 – 25,000 = $(21,000)

(Obtained by working backwards – ie rollback – through the decision tree to calculate expected values)

The best course of action for the hotel owner would be to advertise locally, as the results in the lowest expected losses. This of course assumes that the high season will generate sufficient earnings to make it worthwhile for the hotel owner to remain in business.

(b) **Limitations of decision trees in solving this problem**:

The tree starts to get very complex as more and more possible outcomes are added. This makes drawing the tree very time consuming and increases the likelihood of mistakes, which could lead to an incorrect decision being made.

Decision trees oversimplify scenarios. In reality, weather can take many forms, not just 'poor' and 'good'. Advertising might have different effects in different weeks – there will be some weeks when people will just not want to stay in hotels; others where, regardless of advertising and weather, demand will be greater. It would be dangerous to assume that the hotel industry can be simplified to this extent.

MOCK EXAM 3 (NOVEMBER 2007): ANSWERS

Question 5

Text reference: NVP and IRR are covered in Chapter 11; sensitivity analysis is covered in Chapter 13.

Top tips: There is a considerable amount of information in the question, most of it relating to part (a). A methodical approach is once again essential, with all workings labelled. An incremental approach to the NPV problem should be taken, rather than just assessing the total costs and benefits. Remember to ignore any costs that are incurred anyway (such as fixed overheads).

Easy marks: the IRR calculation is quite straightforward, as is the sensitivity analysis. If you take a methodical approach to the NPV calculation, it should be possible to pick up several marks for workings and layout.

(a) (i) **Net Present Value calculation**.

Workings:

(1) New capacity for SQ = 120,000 + 30% = 156,000 units. It is assumed (as per the question) that SQ could sell this amount.

(2) **Revised contribution per unit**

	$	
Selling price	150	
Direct Materials	(50)	
Direct Labour	(24)	($30-20%)
Variable Production Overhead	(20)	($25-20%)
Revised contribution	56	
Original contribution	45	
Incremental contribution	11	

(3) **Incremental sales units and contribution per annum**

	20X8	20X9	20Y0	20Y1	20Y2
Original sales	120,000	120,000	120,000	120,000	120,000
Revised sales	130,000	140,000	147,000	154,000	156,000*
Incremental sales	10,000	20,000	27,000	34,000	36,000
Revised contribution ($56) per unit	$560,000	1,120,000	1,512,000	1,904,000	2,016,000

*Restricted to 156,000 units due to capacity constraints

(4) **Incremental contribution on existing sales**

Existing sales = 120,000 units per annum.

Incremental contribution per unit (W2) = $11

Incremental contribution on existing sales = $1,320,000.

(5) Writing down allowances and balancing allowances/charges.

Year		Reducing balance $'000
20X7	Initial investment	4,000
20X8	WDA (25% reducing balance)	1,000
	Value at start of 2009	3,000
20X9	WDA	750
	Value at start of 2010	2,250
20Y0	WDA	562.5
	Value at start of 2011	1,687.5
20Y1	WDA	421.9
	Value at start of 2012	1,265.6
20Y2	Sale in year 5	400.0
	Balancing allowance	865.6

(6) Tax calculations and timings

Tax on incremental cash flows

	20X8 $'000	20X9 $'000	20Y0 $'000	20Y1 $'000	20Y2 $'000
Incremental contribution on new sales (W3)	560	1,120	1,512	1,904	2,016
Savings and maintenance costs	70	80	80	110	130
Incremental contributions on existing sales (W4)	1,320	1,320	1,320	1,320	1,320
Variable selling & distribution overhead*	(100)	(200)	(270)	(340)	(360)
Incremental cash flows	1,850	2,320	2,642	2,994	3,106
Capital allowances	(1,000)	(750)	(562.5)	(421.9)	(865.6)
Taxable total	850	1,570	2,079.5	2,572.1	2,240.4
Tax at 30%	255	471	623.9	771.6	672.1

*Variable selling and distribution overhead = Incremental sales units (from W3) × $10 per unit.

Timing of tax payments

	20X8 $'000	20X9 $'000	20Y0 $'000	20Y1 $'000	20Y2 $'000	20Y3 $'000
Tax charge	255	471	623.9	771.6	672.1	–
50% payable in same year	127.5	235.5	312.0	385.8	336.1	–
50% payable one year later		127.5	235.5	312.0	385.5	336.1
Tax payable	127.5	363	547.5	697.8	721.9	336.1

Net Present Value calculations

	20X7 $'000	20X8 $'000	20X9 $'000	20Y0 $'000	20Y1 $'000	20Y2 $'000	20Y3 $'000
Initial investment	(4,000)	–	–	–	–	–	–
Sale of investment		–	–	–	–	400	–
Incremental cash flows (W6)	–	1,850	2,320	2,642	2,994	3,106	–
Tax payments (W6)	–	(127.5)	(363)	(547.5)	(697.8)	(721.9)	(336.1)
	(4,000)	1,722.5	1,957	2,094.5	2,296.2	2,384.1	(336.1)
Discount factor at 12%	1.000	0.893	0.797	0.712	0.636	0.567	0.507
Present Value	(4,000)	1,538.2	1,559.7	1,491.3	1,460.4	1,351.8	(170.4)

NPV = $3,231

(ii) **Two other factors that SQ should consider**:

- Will the additional sales of Product Q have an effect on the sales figures of SQ's other products? If so, any reduction in revenue should be taken into consideration in the NPV calculation.

- Will materials still be available at their current cost throughout the five year project? If material costs are likely to rise, this will have an impact on the NPV and on the final decision.

(b) (i) **IRR calculation**

Step 1 By trial and error, find a discount factor at which NPV < 0.

Try 20% : NPV = $(15,000) + [(30,000 - 22,500) \times 2.106]$

$- (15,000) + 15,795$

$= 795$

Try 25% : NPV = $(15,000) + \left[(30,000 - 22,500) \times \dfrac{1-(1+0.25)^{-3}}{0.25} \right]$

$= (15,000) + [(30,000 - 22,500) \times 1.952]$

$= (360)$

Step 2 Calculate IRR

$IRR = 10 + \dfrac{3,652.50}{(3,652.50 + 360)} \times (25-10)$

= 23.65% (to 2 decimal places).

(ii) **Sensitivity of investment to changes in annual cash inflows**:

The present value of the cash inflows can fall by $3,652.50 before the project breaks even.

Current present value of cash inflows = $30,000 × 2.487

= $74,610

MOCK EXAM 3 (NOVEMBER 2007): ANSWERS

$$\therefore \text{The \% by which the current present value can fall} = \frac{3{,}652.50}{74{,}610} \times 100$$

$$= 4.90\% \text{ (to two decimal places)}.$$

Question 6

Text reference: Linear Programming is covered in Chapter 6.

Top tips: This was quite a straightforward linear programming question. Make sure you follow the instructions in part (c) – you are **not** required to perform any calculations! You can use the shadow prices in part (b) to check whether your graph is correct – if skilled labour is one of your binding constraints, you have done something wrong!

Easy marks: If you have read the Study Text, most of this question should be quite straightforward. There are a number of easy marks to be obtained in part (a), such as defining the objective function and constraints.

(a) **Step 1**   **Define variables**

Let D be the number of product D produced

Let G be the number of product G produced

Step 2   **Resources required by each product**

	D	G
Direct Material A	$\frac{20}{5} = 4\text{kg}$	$\frac{10}{5} = 2\text{kg}$
Direct Material B	$\frac{12}{3} = 4\text{kg}$	$\frac{24}{3} = 8\text{kg}$
Skilled Labour	$\frac{28}{7} = 4 \text{ hours}$	$\frac{21}{7} = 3 \text{ hours}$
Machine time	$\frac{14}{2} = 7 \text{ hours}$	$\frac{18}{2} = 9 \text{ hours}$

Step 3   **Establish objective function**

The objective function should be to maximise **contribution** rather than profit, as fixed overheads are not affected by the mix or volume of products produced.

	D	G
Selling price	$115	$120
Total variable costs	74	73
Contribution per unit	41	47

The objective function to be maximised is

Contribution = 41D + 47G.

MOCK EXAM 3 (NOVEMBER 2007): ANSWERS

Step 4   Establish constraints

Use the per unit resources required that were calculated in Step 2.

Direct Material A:	$4D + 2G \leq 1,800$
Direct Material B:	$4D + 8G \leq 3,500$
Skilled Labour:	$4D + 3G \leq 2,500$
Machine Time:	$7D + 9G \leq 6,500$
Product D demand:	$D \leq 400$
Product G demand:	$G \leq 450$
Non-negativity:	$D \geq 0; G \geq 0$

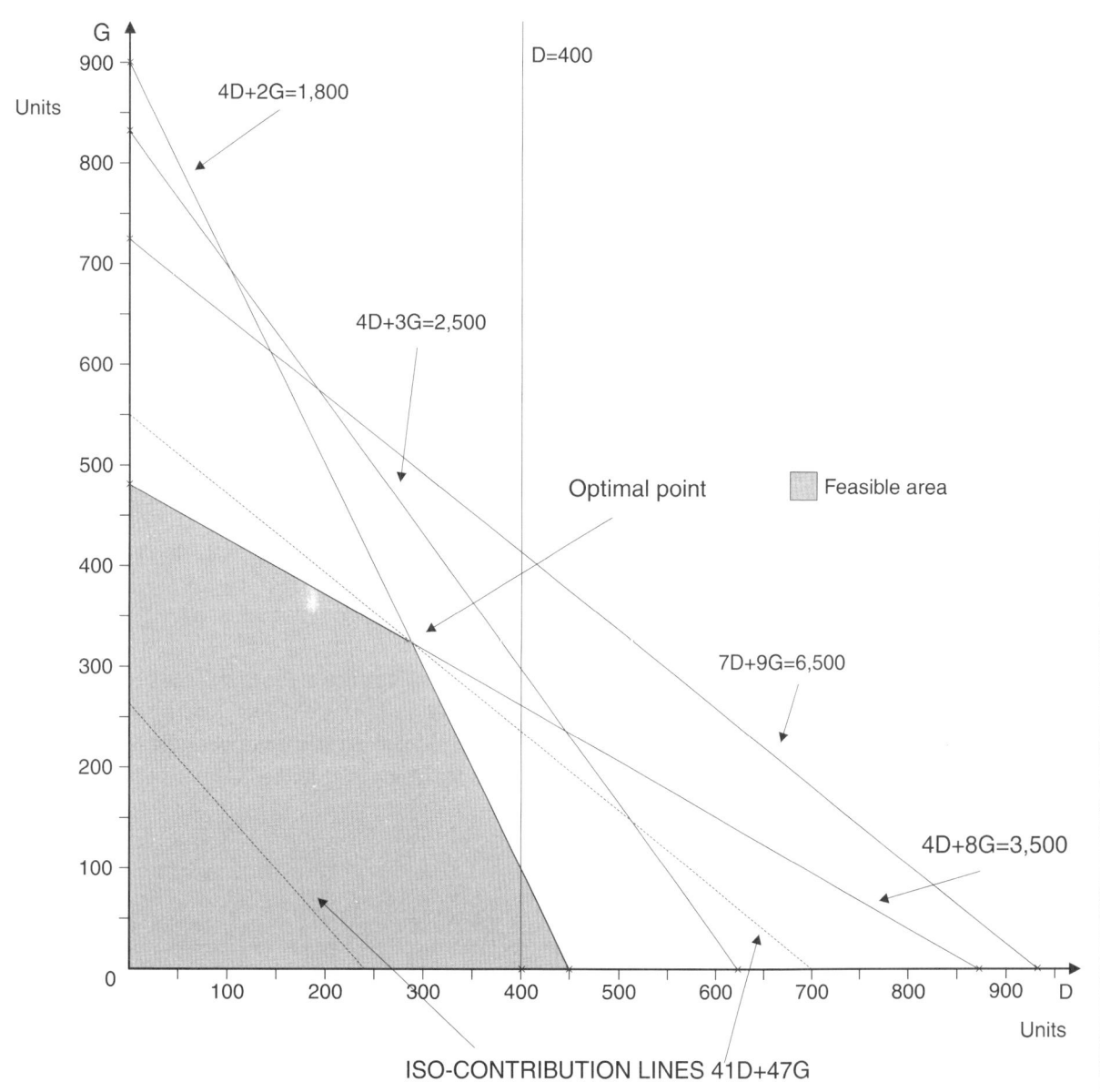

ISO-CONTRIBUTION LINES 41D+47G

The optimal point is reached at the intersection between:

$4D+2G=1,800$ (1)

$4D+8G=3,500$ (2)

Multiply equation (1) by -1

$\left.\begin{array}{r}-4D-2G= -1,800\\ 4D+8G= 3,500\end{array}\right\}$ Add

$$6G = 1,700$$

$$G = 283$$

Substitute G=283 into equation (1)

$$4D + (2 \times 283) = 1,800$$

$$4D + 566 = 1,800$$

$$4D = 1,234$$

$$D = \frac{1,234}{4}$$

$$D = 309$$

Therefore, profit is maximised when 309 units of D and 283 units of G are produced. Contribution would be $25,970.

(b) **Shadow prices**

The shadow price of a resource which is a limiting factor on production is the amount by which total contribution would fall if the organisation was deprived of one unit of that resource. Alternatively, it is the amount by which total contribution would rise if an extra unit of that resource became available.

Skilled labour: Shadow price = £0

This indicates that skilled labour, although a limiting factor, is not a **binding constraint** on production, given the current status of the other resources. Contribution would not be affected if skilled labour was increased or reduced by one hour.

Direct Material A: Shadow price = £5.82

If direct material A was increased by one kg, contribution would increase by £5.82. Similarly if supply of this material was reduced by one kg, contribution would fall by £5.82. Direct Material A is a **binding constraint** on production as the shadow price is greater than zero.

(c) **Selling price sensitivity analysis**

The sensitivity of the optimal solution to changes in the selling price of Product D can be determined by changing the slope of the iso-contribution line. As the selling price of Product D increased, the slope of the iso-contribution line would become steeper. The optimal solution will change when the slope of the iso-contribution line is such that its last point in the feasible region is no longer 309 units of Product D and 283 units of Product G.

Question 7

Text references. Short-term decisions are covered in Chapter 3; ABC is covered in Chapter 16.

Top tips. There is a lot of information in part (a) and it is thus easy to miss something out. Tackle one option at a time and label each working. Make sure you note that the financial information at the start of the question is on a weekly basis and will have to be multiplied by the appropriate number of weeks. An added complication in Option Two was that relating to the freezers which further affected the selling capacity of the frozen foods section. You have to calculate the floor area that will be allocated to this section before you can determine how many freezers can be accommodated. In part (b), make sure you relate your answer to the retail environment, rather than just stating the benefits of ABC.

Easy marks. Some of the relevant costs came straight from the question (such as redecoration costs). Calculation of the loss in sales due to the 10% price reduction in Option One is also straightforward.

MOCK EXAM 3 (NOVEMBER 2007): ANSWERS

(a) **Comparison of the two available options**

Option One

Relevant costs and savings:

(1) Redecoration costs $2,500

(2) Loss of gross profit after reopening
First four weeks	= 30% of $2,650 × 4	= $3,180
Next four weeks	= 20% of $2,650 × 4	= $2,120
Third four weeks	= 10% of $2,650 × 4	= $1,060
		6,360

(3) **Loss of gross profit during shutdown**

= 4 × $2,650 = $10,600

(4) **Savings in power for freezers**

= 4 × $100

= $400

(5) **Price reduction effects**

Basic foods: Revised revenue

First 4 weeks = 70% of $800
Next 4 weeks = 80% of $800 $1,920 × 4 = $7,680
Third 4 weeks = 90% of $800

10% lost due to price reduction = $768

Canned foods:

Revised revenue

First 4 weeks = 70% of $2,400
Next 4 weeks = 80% of $2,400 $5,760 × 4 = $23,040
Third 4 weeks = 90% of $2,400

10% lost due to price reduction = $2,304

Total price reduction effect   = $3,072

Total Relevant Costs

	$
Redecoration costs (W1)	2,500
Loss of profit due to sales reduction (W2)	6,360
Loss in sales revenue (W5)	3,072
Loss of profit during shutdown (W3)	10,600
Savings in freezer power costs (W4)	(400)
	22,132

It is assumed that general overheads will still be incurred during the shutdown.

Option Two

(1) Revised floor area

Floor area in total is reduced to 40% of 400m² = 160m²

Distribution of reduced floor area:

Basic foods	50 (unchanged)
Newspapers and Magazines	50 (unchanged)
	100

Remaining floor area to be divided between other area = 60m²

(2) Distribution of remaining floor area

Profitability per m² of floor area (using gross margin)

Frozen foods = $\dfrac{950}{100}$ = $9.50 per m²

Canned foods = $\dfrac{1,200}{200}$ = $6 per m²

Floor area allocation

Frozen foods = $\dfrac{9.50}{15.50} \times 60m^2 = 37m^2$

Canned foods = $\dfrac{6}{15.5} \times 60m^2 = 23m^2$

Floor area proportions:

	Original (%)	Revised (%)
Basic foods	$\dfrac{50}{400}$ = 12.5%	$\dfrac{50}{160}$ = 31.25%
Newspapers and Magazines	$\dfrac{50}{400}$ = 12.5%	$\dfrac{50}{160}$ = 31.25%
Frozen foods	$\dfrac{100}{400}$ = 25%	$\dfrac{37}{106}$ = 23.13%
Canned foods	$\dfrac{200}{400}$ = 50%	$\dfrac{23}{160}$ = 14.37%

Reduction in floor area%

Basic foods; Newspapers and Magazines = 0

Frozen foods = $\dfrac{100-37}{100}$ = 63%

Canned foods = $\dfrac{200-23}{200}$ = 88.5%

(3) Number of freezers

Floor space per freezer = $\dfrac{100m^2}{4}$ = 25m²

As frozen foods has a revised floor space of 37m², only one freezer can be accommodated. This represents a reduction of 75% of selling space and therefore sales revenue.

(4) Freezer cost savings

3 freezers will be non-operational for the 6 weeks of reduced operation

$$\therefore \text{Total savings for this period} = 6 \times 3 \times \frac{\$100}{4} = \$450$$

4 freezers will be non-operational for the 0.5 weeks shutdown

∴ Total savings for this period = 0.5 × $100 = $50

Total freezer cost savings = $500

(5) Reduction in gross profit (for 6 weeks of reduced operating)

Frozen foods	$950 × 6 × 75%	$4,275
Canned foods	$1,200 × 6 × 88.5%	$6,372
Total reduction		$10,647

As Basic foods and Newspapers and Magazines are not suffering reduced floor space, sales revenue and gross profit will be unaffected for these areas.

(6) Reduction in gross profit for 0.5 weeks' shutdown.

Total Gross Profit for all areas = [$200 + 300 + 950 + 1,200] × 0.5

= $2,650 × 0.5

= $1,325

Total Relevant Costs.

	$
Redecoration	3,500
Product Movement Costs	1,000
Freezer cost savings (W4)	(500)
Reduction in gross profit for 6 weeks' reduced operations (W5)	10,647
Lost profit from shutdown (W6)	1,325
	$15,972

As Option 2 results in lower losses, the retail outlet should continue to operate at reduced capacity during the redecoration period.

(b) How activity based costing can be used in a retail environment

More realistic pricing

Activity based costing (ABC) helps to address one of the main problems with traditional costing systems – that is, excessive costs are often charged to high-volume products (product-cost subsidisation). This problem could lead to the low-volume products being underpriced, probably leading to increased customer demand (and vice versa for high volume products). As ABC is based on a fairer system – with costs being allocated using cost drivers that cause the costs to occur in the first place – it helps retail organisations to determine a more realistic price for individual products. This will reduce the likelihood of lower volume products being sold at unprofitable prices, and retailers being accused of predatory pricing.

Allocation of floor space to higher demand products

Linked with the more realistic pricing aspect of ABC, retailers will be able to more accurately predict demand when 'proper' prices are set. When demand can be more accurately predicted, it will be easier to allocate floor space according to this demand, which should help to improve profitability.

Diversity of products, processes and customers

Modern retail organisations deal with numerous products and sell a wide range of products. ABC assists in identifying activities required to support each category of product, for example, and the cost drivers of these activities. By doing so, ABC can help retail organisations to determine the 'real' cost of each category of product which will again help in the pricing process.

Demands on overhead resources

Different customers place different demands on overhead resources. In a service retail environment, such as the hotel industry, a businessman staying in a hotel is more likely to place more demands on available resources (such as the Business Centre) than a leisure guest. By allocating overheads according to cost drivers, the hotel could distinguish room prices between business and leisure stays.

Mathematical tables

PRESENT VALUE TABLE

Present value of £1 ie $(1+r)^{-n}$ where r = interest rate, n = number of periods until payment or receipt.

Periods (n)	1%	2%	3%	4%	5%	6%	7%	8%	9%	10%
1	0.990	0.980	0.971	0.962	0.952	0.943	0.935	0.926	0.917	0.909
2	0.980	0.961	0.943	0.925	0.907	0.890	0.873	0.857	0.842	0.826
3	0.971	0.942	0.915	0.889	0.864	0.840	0.816	0.794	0.772	0.751
4	0.961	0.924	0.888	0.855	0.823	0.792	0.763	0.735	0.708	0.683
5	0.951	0.906	0.863	0.822	0.784	0.747	0.713	0.681	0.650	0.621
6	0.942	0.888	0.837	0.790	0.746	0.705	0.666	0.630	0.596	0.564
7	0.933	0.871	0.813	0.760	0.711	0.665	0.623	0.583	0.547	0.513
8	0.923	0.853	0.789	0.731	0.677	0.627	0.582	0.540	0.502	0.467
9	0.914	0.837	0.766	0.703	0.645	0.592	0.544	0.500	0.460	0.424
10	0.905	0.820	0.744	0.676	0.614	0.558	0.508	0.463	0.422	0.386
11	0.896	0.804	0.722	0.650	0.585	0.527	0.475	0.429	0.388	0.350
12	0.887	0.788	0.701	0.625	0.557	0.497	0.444	0.397	0.356	0.319
13	0.879	0.773	0.681	0.601	0.530	0.469	0.415	0.368	0.326	0.290
14	0.870	0.758	0.661	0.577	0.505	0.442	0.388	0.340	0.299	0.263
15	0.861	0.743	0.642	0.555	0.481	0.417	0.362	0.315	0.275	0.239
16	0.853	0.728	0.623	0.534	0.458	0.394	0.339	0.292	0.252	0.218
17	0.844	0.714	0.605	0.513	0.436	0.371	0.317	0.270	0.231	0.198
18	0.836	0.700	0.587	0.494	0.416	0.350	0.296	0.250	0.212	0.180
19	0.828	0.686	0.570	0.475	0.396	0.331	0.277	0.232	0.194	0.164
20	0.820	0.673	0.554	0.456	0.377	0.312	0.258	0.215	0.178	0.149

Periods (n)	11%	12%	13%	14%	15%	16%	17%	18%	19%	20%
1	0.901	0.893	0.885	0.877	0.870	0.862	0.855	0.847	0.840	0.833
2	0.812	0.797	0.783	0.769	0.756	0.743	0.731	0.718	0.706	0.694
3	0.731	0.712	0.693	0.675	0.658	0.641	0.624	0.609	0.593	0.579
4	0.659	0.636	0.613	0.592	0.572	0.552	0.534	0.516	0.499	0.482
5	0.593	0.567	0.543	0.519	0.497	0.476	0.456	0.437	0.419	0.402
6	0.535	0.507	0.480	0.456	0.432	0.410	0.390	0.370	0.352	0.335
7	0.482	0.452	0.425	0.400	0.376	0.354	0.333	0.314	0.296	0.279
8	0.434	0.404	0.376	0.351	0.327	0.305	0.285	0.266	0.249	0.233
9	0.391	0.361	0.333	0.308	0.284	0.263	0.243	0.225	0.209	0.194
10	0.352	0.322	0.295	0.270	0.247	0.227	0.208	0.191	0.176	0.162
11	0.317	0.287	0.261	0.237	0.215	0.195	0.178	0.162	0.148	0.135
12	0.286	0.257	0.231	0.208	0.187	0.168	0.152	0.137	0.124	0.112
13	0.258	0.229	0.204	0.182	0.163	0.145	0.130	0.116	0.104	0.093
14	0.232	0.205	0.181	0.160	0.141	0.125	0.111	0.099	0.088	0.078
15	0.209	0.183	0.160	0.140	0.123	0.108	0.095	0.084	0.074	0.065
16	0.188	0.163	0.141	0.123	0.107	0.093	0.081	0.071	0.062	0.054
17	0.170	0.146	0.125	0.108	0.093	0.080	0.069	0.060	0.052	0.045
18	0.153	0.130	0.111	0.095	0.081	0.069	0.059	0.051	0.044	0.038
19	0.138	0.116	0.098	0.083	0.070	0.060	0.051	0.043	0.037	0.031
20	0.124	0.104	0.087	0.073	0.061	0.051	0.043	0.037	0.031	0.026

MATHEMATICAL TABLES

CUMULATIVE PRESENT VALUE TABLE

This table shows the present value of £1 per annum, receivable or payable at the end of each year for n years

$$\frac{1-(1+r)^{-n}}{r}.$$

Periods (n)	1%	2%	3%	4%	5%	6%	7%	8%	9%	10%
1	0.990	0.980	0.971	0.962	0.952	0.943	0.935	0.926	0.917	0.909
2	1.970	1.942	1.913	1.886	1.859	1.833	1.808	1.783	1.759	1.736
3	2.941	2.884	2.829	2.775	2.723	2.673	2.624	2.577	2.531	2.487
4	3.902	3.808	3.717	3.630	3.546	3.465	3.387	3.312	3.240	3.170
5	4.853	4.713	4.580	4.452	4.329	4.212	4.100	3.993	3.890	3.791
6	5.795	5.601	5.417	5.242	5.076	4.917	4.767	4.623	4.486	4.355
7	6.728	6.472	6.230	6.002	5.786	5.582	5.389	5.206	5.033	4.868
8	7.652	7.325	7.020	6.733	6.463	6.210	5.971	5.747	5.535	5.335
9	8.566	8.162	7.786	7.435	7.108	6.802	6.515	6.247	5.995	5.759
10	9.471	8.983	8.530	8.111	7.722	7.360	7.024	6.710	6.418	6.145
11	10.368	9.787	9.253	8.760	8.306	7.887	7.499	7.139	6.805	6.495
12	11.255	10.575	9.954	9.385	8.863	8.384	7.943	7.536	7.161	6.814
13	12.134	11.348	10.635	9.986	9.394	8.853	8.358	7.904	7.487	7.103
14	13.004	12.106	11.296	10.563	9.899	9.295	8.745	8.244	7.786	7.367
15	13.865	12.849	11.938	11.118	10.380	9.712	9.108	8.559	8.061	7.606
16	14.718	13.578	12.561	11.652	10.838	10.106	9.447	8.851	8.313	7.824
17	15.562	14.292	13.166	12.166	11.274	10.477	9.763	9.122	8.544	8.022
18	16.398	14.992	13.754	12.659	11.690	10.828	10.059	9.372	8.756	8.201
19	17.226	15.679	14.324	13.134	12.085	11.158	10.336	9.604	8.950	8.365
20	18.046	16.351	14.878	13.590	12.462	11.470	10.594	9.818	9.129	8.514

Periods (n)	11%	12%	13%	14%	15%	16%	17%	18%	19%	20%
1	0.901	0.893	0.885	0.877	0.870	0.862	0.855	0.847	0.840	0.833
2	1.713	1.690	1.668	1.647	1.626	1.605	1.585	1.566	1.547	1.528
3	2.444	2.402	2.361	2.322	2.283	2.246	2.210	2.174	2.140	2.106
4	3.102	3.037	2.974	2.914	2.855	2.798	2.743	2.690	2.639	2.589
5	3.696	3.605	3.517	3.433	3.352	3.274	3.199	3.127	3.058	2.991
6	4.231	4.111	3.998	3.889	3.784	3.685	3.589	3.498	3.410	3.326
7	4.712	4.564	4.423	4.288	4.160	4.039	3.922	3.812	3.706	3.605
8	5.146	4.968	4.799	4.639	4.487	4.344	4.207	4.078	3.954	3.837
9	5.537	5.328	5.132	4.946	4.772	4.607	4.451	4.303	4.163	4.031
10	5.889	5.650	5.426	5.216	5.019	4.833	4.659	4.494	4.339	4.192
11	6.207	5.938	5.687	5.453	5.234	5.029	4.836	4.656	4.486	4.327
12	6.492	6.194	5.918	5.660	5.421	5.197	4.988	4.793	4.611	4.439
13	6.750	6.424	6.122	5.842	5.583	5.342	5.118	4.910	4.715	4.533
14	6.982	6.628	6.302	6.002	5.724	5.468	5.229	5.008	4.802	4.611
15	7.191	6.811	6.462	6.142	5.847	5.575	5.324	5.092	4.876	4.675
16	7.379	6.974	6.604	6.265	5.954	5.668	5.405	5.162	4.938	4.730
17	7.549	7.120	6.729	6.373	6.047	5.749	5.475	5.222	4.990	4.775
18	7.702	7.250	6.840	6.467	6.128	5.818	5.534	5.273	5.033	4.812
19	7.839	7.366	6.938	6.550	6.198	5.877	5.584	5.316	5.070	4.843
20	7.963	7.469	7.025	6.623	6.259	5.929	5.628	5.353	5.101	4.870

Learning curve

$$Y_x = aX^b$$

where Y_x = the cumulative average time per unit to produce X units

   a = the time required to produce the first unit of output

   X = the cumulative number of units

   b = the index of learning

The exponent b is defined as the log of the learning curve improvement rate divided by log 2.

Review Form & Free Prize Draw - Paper P2 Management Accounting – Decision Management (1/08)

All original review forms from the entire BPP range, completed with genuine comments, will be entered into one of two draws on 31 July 2008 and 31 January 2009. The names on the first four forms picked out on each occasion will be sent a cheque for £50.

Name: _____ Address: _____

How have you used this Kit?
(Tick one box only)
- [ ] Home study (book only)
- [ ] On a course: college _____
- [ ] With 'correspondence' package
- [ ] Other _____

Why did you decide to purchase this Kit?
(Tick one box only)
- [ ] Have used the complementary Study text
- [ ] Have used other BPP products in the past
- [ ] Recommendation by friend/colleague
- [ ] Recommendation by a lecturer at college
- [ ] Saw advertising
- [ ] Other _____

During the past six months do you recall seeing/receiving any of the following?
(Tick as many boxes as are relevant)
- [ ] Our advertisement in *Financial Management*
- [ ] Our advertisement in *Pass*
- [ ] Our advertisement in *PQ*
- [ ] Our brochure with a letter through the post
- [ ] Our website www.bpp.com

Which (if any) aspects of our advertising do you find useful?
(Tick as many boxes as are relevant)
- [ ] Prices and publication dates of new editions
- [ ] Information on product content
- [ ] Facility to order books off-the-page
- [ ] None of the above

Which BPP products have you used?

Text	[ ]	Success CD	[ ]	Learn Online	[ ]
Kit	[✓]	i-Learn	[ ]	Home Study Package	[ ]
Passcard	[ ]	i-Pass	[ ]	Home Study PLUS	[ ]

Your ratings, comments and suggestions would be appreciated on the following areas.

	Very useful	Useful	Not useful
Passing CIMA exams	[ ]	[ ]	[ ]
Passing P9	[ ]	[ ]	[ ]
Planning your question practice	[ ]	[ ]	[ ]
Questions	[ ]	[ ]	[ ]
Top Tips etc in answers	[ ]	[ ]	[ ]
Content and structure of answers	[ ]	[ ]	[ ]
'Plan of attack' in mock exams	[ ]	[ ]	[ ]
Mock exam answers	[ ]	[ ]	[ ]

Overall opinion of this Kit Excellent [ ] Good [ ] Adequate [ ] Poor [ ]

Do you intend to continue using BPP products? Yes [ ] No [ ]

The BPP author of this edition can be e-mailed at: lesleybuick@bpp.com

Please return this form to: Nick Weller, CIMA Publishing Manager, BPP Learning Media Ltd, FREEPOST, London, W12 8BR

Review Form & Free Prize Draw (continued)

TELL US WHAT YOU THINK

Please note any further comments and suggestions/errors below.

Free Prize Draw Rules

1 Closing date for 31 July 2008 draw is 30 June 2008. Closing date for 31 January 2009 draw is 31 December 2008.

2 Restricted to entries with UK and Eire addresses only. BPP employees, their families and business associates are excluded.

3 No purchase necessary. Entry forms are available upon request from BPP Learning Media Ltd. No more than one entry per title, per person. Draw restricted to persons aged 16 and over.

4 Winners will be notified by post and receive their cheques not later than 6 weeks after the relevant draw date.

5 The decision of the promoter in all matters is final and binding. No correspondence will be entered into.